D1798667

National Football League 1983 Media Information Book

Published by the National Football League.
Compiled by the NFL Public Relations Department
and the 28 NFL Public Relations Directors.
Produced by NFL Properties, Inc., Creative Services Division.
Edited by Fran Connors, AFC Director of Information.
Workman Publishing, New York

National Football League, 1983

410 Park Avenue, New York, N.Y. 10022   (212) 758-1500

Commissioner: Pete Rozelle
Executive Director: Don Weiss
Treasurer: Bill Ray
Counsel to Commissioner: Jay Moyer
Director of Operations: Jan Van Duser
Director of Administration: Joe Rhein
Director of Public Relations: Jim Heffernan
Director of Information: Joe Browne
Director of Broadcasting: Val Pinchbeck, Jr.
Director of Security: Warren Welsh
Assistant Director of Security: Charles R. Jackson
Director of Player Personnel: Joel Bussert
Supervisor of Officials: Art McNally
Assistant Supervisor of Officials: Jack Reader
Assistant Supervisor of Officials: Nick Skorich
Director of Special Events: Jim Steeg
Director of Player Relations: Buddy Young
Auditor: Tom Sullivan
Director of Personnel: Wayne Rosen
Officiating Assistant: Stu Kirkpatrick

American Football Conference
President: Lamar Hunt, Kansas City Chiefs
Assistant to President: Al Ward
Director of Information: Fran Connors

National Football Conference
President: George Halas, Chicago Bears
Assistant to President: Bill Granholm
Director of Information: Dick Maxwell

Copyright 1983 by the National Football League.
All rights reserved. No portion of this book may be reproduced—electronically, mechanically, or by any other means, including photocopying—without written permission of the publisher. Published simultaneously by Saunders of Toronto. Edited by Fran Connors, AFC Director of Information. Produced by NFL Properties, Inc., Creative Services Division.

Photography Credits
Cover: Al Messerschmidt.

Tim Alexander 124; The Allens 144; Fred Anderson 104; John Biever 112; David Boss 78, 108, 116; Jim Chaffin 100; Christine Cotter 86; Thomas J. Croke 74; Dave Cross 70; Denver Broncos 54; Malcolm Emmons 46, 148; Pete J. Groh 128; Paul Jasienski 58; Tony Kambic 82; Tak Makita 42; Al Messerschmidt 132; Russ Reed 62; John Reid, III, 66; Frank Rippon 140; Ron Ross 38, 120; Manny Rubio 96; Tony Tomsic 50; Corky Trewin 90; Herb Weitman 136.

Workman Publishing Co.,
1 West 39th Street, New York, N.Y. 10018
Manufactured in the United States of America.
First printing, July 1983.

10   9   8   7   6   5   4   3   2   1

Contents

THE NATIONAL FOOTBALL LEAGUE, 1983

American Football Conference

Eastern Division

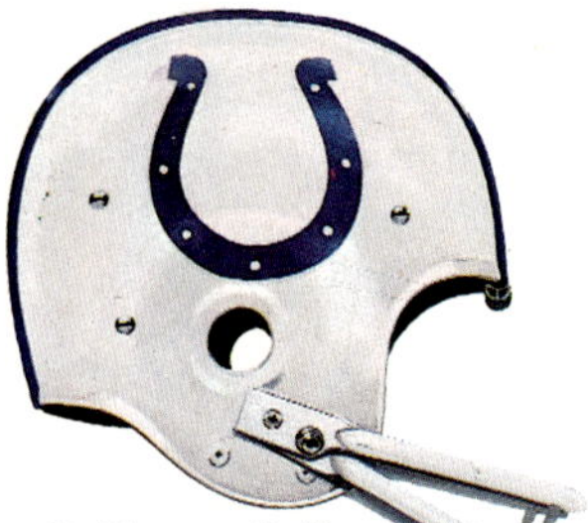

Baltimore Colts

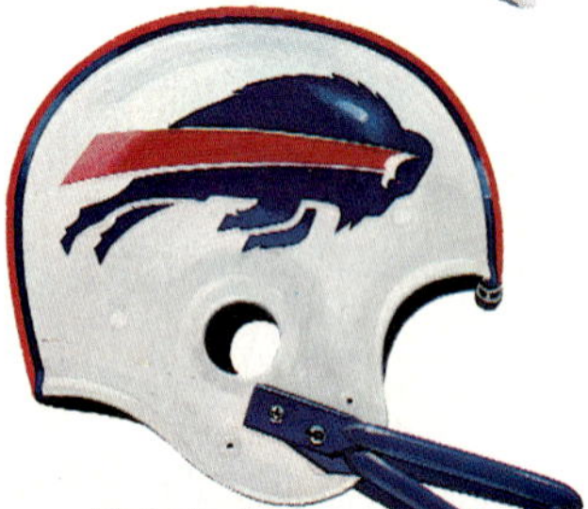

Buffalo Bills

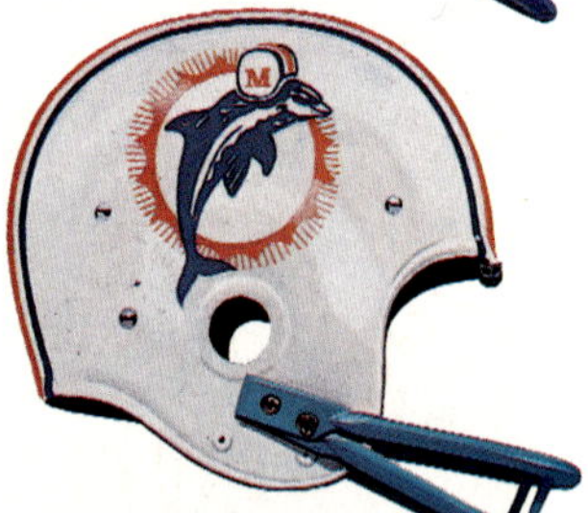

Miami Dolphins

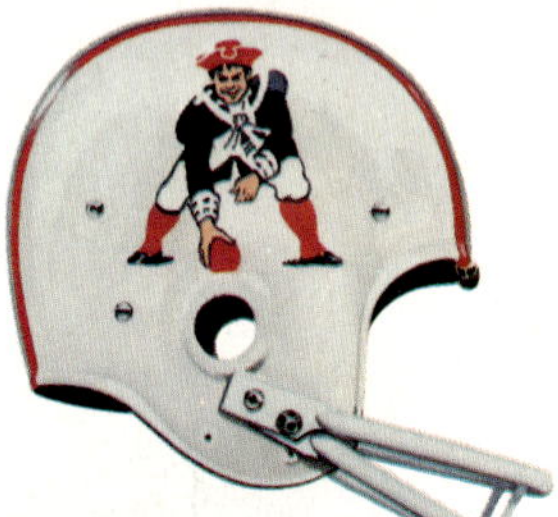

New England Patriots

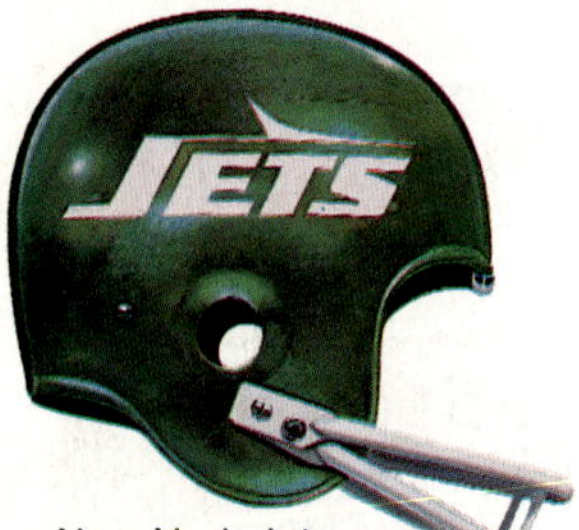

New York Jets

Central Division

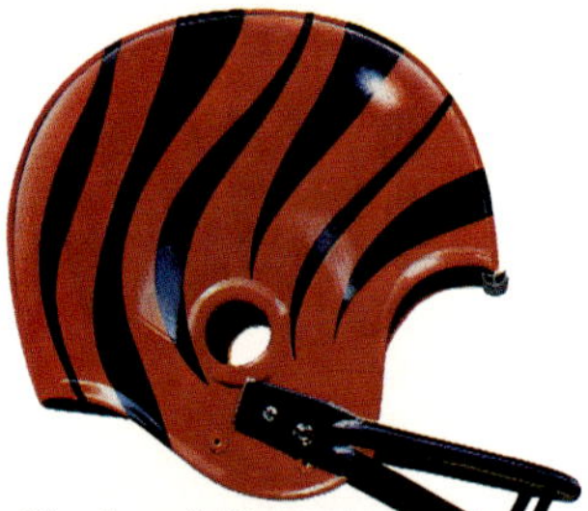

Cincinnati Bengals

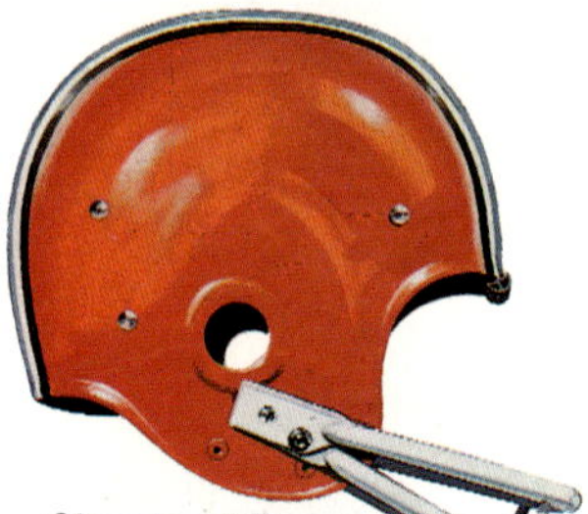

Cleveland Browns

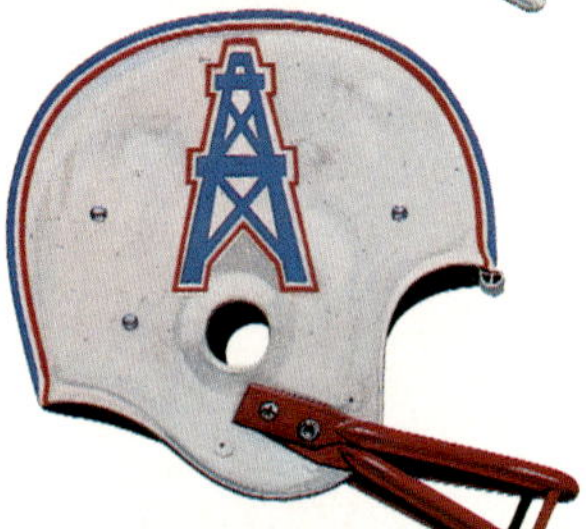

Houston Oilers

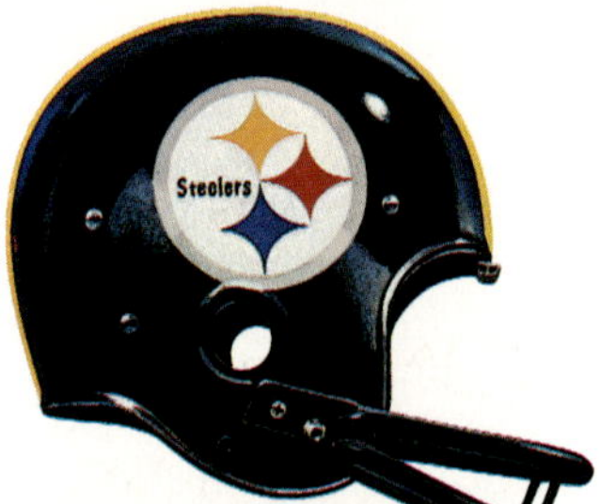

Pittsburgh Steelers

Western Division

Denver Broncos

Kansas City Chiefs

Los Angeles Raiders

San Diego Chargers

Seattle Seahawks

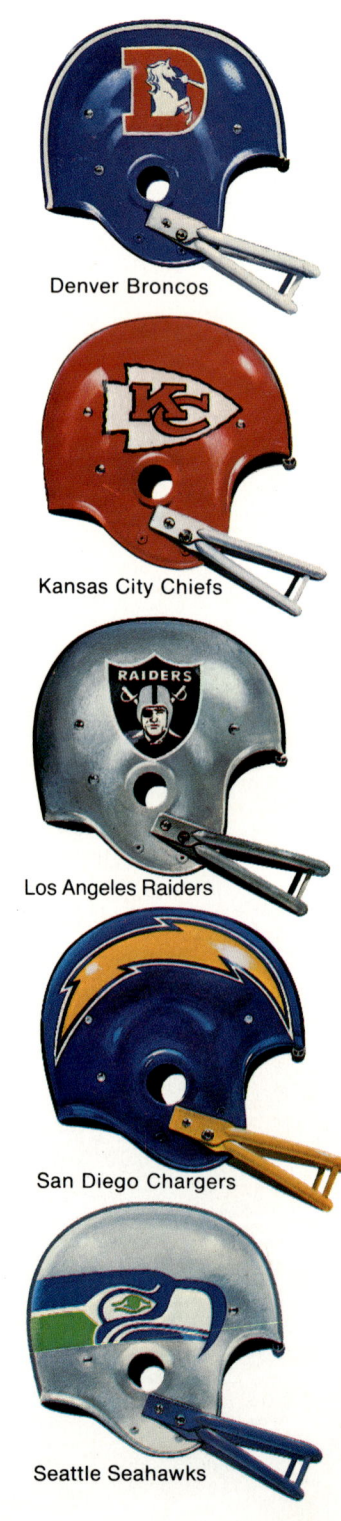

National Football Conference

Eastern Division	Central Division	Western Division

Dallas Cowboys	Chicago Bears	Atlanta Falcons
		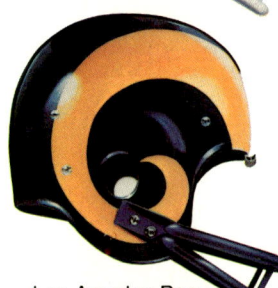
New York Giants	Detroit Lions	Los Angeles Rams

Philadelphia Eagles	Green Bay Packers	New Orleans Saints
	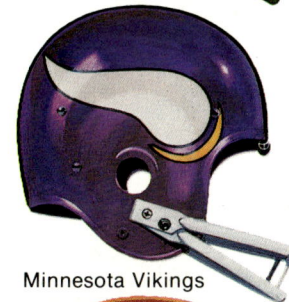	
St. Louis Cardinals	Minnesota Vikings	San Francisco 49ers

Washington Redskins	Tampa Bay Buccaneers	

Copyright © 1983 by NFL Properties, Inc.
ALL RIGHTS RESERVED. NOT TO BE USED FOR REPRODUCTION.

Waivers

The waiver system is a procedure by which player contracts or NFL rights to players are made available by a club to other clubs in the League. During the procedure the 27 other clubs either file claims to obtain the players or waive the opportunity to do so—thus the term "waiver." Claiming clubs are assigned players on a priority based on the inverse of won-and-lost standing. The claiming period normally is 10 days during the off-season and 24 hours from early July through December. In some circumstances another 24 hours is added on to allow the original club to rescind its action (known as a recall of a waiver request) and/or the claiming club to do the same (known as withdrawal of a claim). If a player passes through waivers unclaimed and is not recalled by the original club, he becomes a free agent. All waivers from July through December are no-recall and no withdrawal. Under the Collective Bargaining Agreement, from February 1 through October 11, any veteran who has acquired four years of pension credit may, if about to be assigned to another club through the waiver system, reject such assignment and become a free agent.

Active List

The Active List is the principal status for players participating for a club. It consists of all players under contract, including option, who are eligible for preseason, regular season, and postseason games. Clubs are allowed to open training camp with an unlimited number of players but thereafter must meet a series of mandatory roster reductions prior to the season opener. Teams will be permitted to dress up to 45 players for each regular season and postseason game during the 1983 season. The Active List maximums and dates for 1983 are:

August 16	60 players
August 23	50 players
August 29	45 players

Reserve List

The Reserve List is a status for players who, for reasons of injury, retirement, military service, or other circumstances, are not immediately available for participation with a club. Those players in the category of Reserve/Injured who were physically unable to play football for a minimum of four weeks from the date of going onto Reserve may be re-activated by their clubs upon clearing procedural recall waivers; in addition, each club will have three free re-activations for players meeting the four-week requirement who were placed on Reserve following the final cutdown. Clubs participating in postseason competition will be granted an additional free re-activation. Players not meeting the four-week requirement may not return in the same season to the Active List of the club which originally placed them on Reserve, but may be assigned through the waiver system to other clubs. Early in 1984 all clubs who had players on Reserve/Injured must declare a maximum of three players, from those meeting the four-week requirement, as tradeable in that year; others who were on the list cannot be traded until 1985. Players in the category of Reserve/Retired may not be reinstated during the period from 30 days before the end of the regular season on through the postseason.

Trades

Unrestricted trading between the AFC and NFC is allowed in 1983 through October 11, after which all trading will end until January 30, 1984.

Annual Player Limits

NFL

Year(s)	Limit
1982	45†–49
1978–81	45
1975–77	43
1974	47
1964–73	40
1963	37
1961–62	36
1960	38
1959	36
1957–58	35
1951–56	33
1949–50	32
1948	35
1947	35*–34
1945–46	33
1943–44	28
1940–42	33
1938–39	30
1936–37	25
1935	24
1930–34	20
1926–29	18
1925	16

†45 for first two games
*35 for first three games

AFL

Year(s)	Limit
1966–69	40
1965	38
1964	34
1962–63	33
1960–61	35

Tie-Breaking Procedures

The following procedures will be used to break standings ties for postseason playoffs and to determine regular season schedules.

To Break a Tie Within a Division

If, at the end of the regular season, two or more clubs in the same division finish with identical won-lost-tied percentages, the following steps will be taken until a champion is determined.

Two Clubs

1. Head-to-head (best won-lost-tied percentage in games between the clubs).
2. Best won-lost-tied percentage in games played within the division.
3. Best won-lost-tied percentage in games played within the conference.
4. Best won-lost-tied percentage in common games, if applicable.
5. Best net points in division games.
6. Best net points in all games.
7. Strength of schedule.
8. Best net touchdowns in all games.
9. Coin toss.

Three or More Clubs

(Note: If two clubs remain tied after a third club is eliminated during any step, tie-breaker reverts to step 1 of two-club format.)

1. Head-to-head (best won-lost-tied percentage in games among the clubs).
2. Best won-lost-tied percentage in games played within the division.
3. Best won-lost-tied percentage in games played within the conference.
4. Best won-lost-tied percentage in common games.
5. Best net points in division games.
6. Best net points in all games.
7. Strength of schedule.
8. Best net touchdowns in all games.
9. Coin toss.

To Break a Tie for the Wild Card Team

If it is necessary to break ties to determine the two Wild Card clubs from each conference, the following steps will be taken.

1. If the tied clubs are from the same division, apply division tie-breaker.
2. If the tied clubs are from different divisions, apply the following steps.

Two Clubs

1. Head-to-head, if applicable.
2. Best won-lost-tied percentage in games played within the conference.
3. Best won-lost-tied percentage in common games, minimum of four.
4. Best average net points in conference games.
5. Best net points in all games.
6. Strength of schedule.
7. Best net touchdowns in all games.
8. Coin toss.

Three or More Clubs

(Note: If two clubs remain tied after other clubs are eliminated, tie-breaker reverts to step 1 of applicable two-club format.)

1. Head-to-head sweep. (Applicable only if one club has defeated each of the others, or if one club has lost to each of the others.)
2. Best won-lost-tied percentage in games played within the conference.
3. Best won-lost-tied percentage in common games, minimum of four.
4. Best average net points in conference games.
5. Best net points in all games.
6. Strength of schedule.
7. Best net touchdowns in all games.
8. Coin toss.

Tie-Breaking Procedure for Selection Meeting

If two or more clubs are tied for selection order, the conventional strength of schedule tie-breaker will be applied, subject to the following exceptions for playoff teams.

1. The Super Bowl winner will be last and the Super Bowl loser will be next-to-last.
2. Any non-Super Bowl playoff team involved in a tie moves down in drafting priority as follows:
   A. Participation by a club in the playoffs without a victory adds one-half victory to the club's regular season won-lost-tied record.
   B. For each victory in the playoffs, one full victory will be added to the club's regular season won-lost-tied record.
3. Clubs with the best won-lost-tied records after these steps are applied will drop to their appropriate spots at the bottom of the tied segment. In no case will the above process move a club lower than the segment in which it was initially tied.

AFC Active Statistical Leaders

LEADING ACTIVE PASSERS, AMERICAN FOOTBALL CONFERENCE
1,000 or more attempts

	Yrs.	Att.	Comp.	Pct. Comp.	Yards	Avg. Gain	TD	Pct. TD	Had Int.	Pct. Int.	Rate Pts.
Ken Anderson, Cin.	12	3848	2254	58.6	28057	7.29	172	4.5	133	3.5	81.7
Dan Fouts, S.D.	10	3533	2053	58.1	27139	7.68	162	4.6	153	4.3	79.9
Brian Sipe, Clev.	9	2943	1653	56.2	20147	6.85	128	4.3	126	4.3	73.9
Terry Bradshaw, Pitt.	13	3893	2020	51.9	27912	7.17	210	5.4	210	5.4	70.7
Joe Ferguson, Buff.	10	3314	1716	51.8	22604	6.82	143	4.3	148	4.5	69.3
Jim Zorn, Sea.	7	2768	1483	53.6	18876	6.82	100	3.6	124	4.5	68.4
Richard Todd, N.Y.J.	7	2105	1125	53.4	14763	7.01	92	4.4	112	5.3	68.4
Steve Grogan, N.E.	8	2310	1189	51.5	17415	7.54	121	5.2	144	6.2	67.9
Archie Manning, Hou.	11	3460	1915	55.3	22611	6.53	121	3.5	162	4.7	67.5
Steve DeBerg, Den.	5	1532	865	56.5	9422	6.15	50	3.3	77	5.0	65.0
Jim Plunkett, Raiders	11	2769	1401	50.6	18685	6.75	121	4.4	158	5.7	63.3

TOP 10 ACTIVE RUSHERS, AFC
2,000 or more yards

	Yrs.	Att.	Yards	TD
1. Franco Harris, Pitt.	11	2602	10943	86
2. Earl Campbell, Hou.	5	1561	6995	57
3. Mark van Eeghen, N.E.	9	1557	6292	35
4. Chuck Muncie, S.D.	7	1312	5765	59
5. Greg Pruitt, Raiders	10	1162	5518	25
6. Mike Pruitt, Clev.	7	1137	4850	31
7. Pete Johnson, Cin.	6	1192	4658	50
8. Sherman Smith, Sea.	7	810	3429	28
9. Cullen Bryant, Sea.	10	801	3117	20
10. Ricky Bell, S.D.	6	822	3063	16

Other Leading Rushers

John Cappelletti, S.D.	8	823	2946	24
Joe Cribbs, Buff.	5	697	2915	17
Archie Griffin, Cin.	7	691	2808	7
Scott Dierking, N.Y.J.	6	703	2788	15
Clark Gaines, K.C.	7	582	2552	8
Ted McKnight, Buff.	6	528	2344	22
Roosevelt Leaks, Buff.	8	605	2249	27
Curtis Brown, Buff.	6	564	2171	8
Archie Manning, Hou.	11	370	2143	18

TOP 10 ACTIVE PASS RECEIVERS, AFC
200 or more receptions

	Yrs.	No.	Yards	TD
1. Charlie Joiner, S.D.	14	531	9021	47
2. Cliff Branch, Raiders	11	435	7588	62
3. Steve Largent, Sea.	7	399	6534	49
4. Riley Odoms, Den.	11	392	5693	41
5. Bob Chandler, Raiders	12	370	5243	48
6. Isaac Curtis, Cin.	10	362	6395	51
7. Frank Lewis, Buff.	12	361	6238	37
8. Dave Casper, Hou.	9	354	4936	50
9. Nat Moore, Mia.	9	339	5283	48
10. Greg Pruitt, Raiders	10	325	3051	18

Other Leading Pass Receivers

John Stallworth, Pitt.	9	299	5304	44
Jerome Barkum, N.Y.J.	11	294	4404	39
Wes Chandler, S.D.	5	283	4690	29
Franco Harris, Pitt.	11	272	2006	7
Roger Carr, Sea.	9	269	5035	31
Ozzie Newsome, Clev.	5	262	3599	23
Kellen Winslow, S.D.	4	256	3341	27
Duriel Harris, Mia.	7	251	4250	17
Rick Upchurch, Den.	8	227	3730	22
Dave Logan, Clev.	7	225	3620	22
Henry Marshall, K.C.	7	223	3621	22
Mike Pruitt, Clev.	7	220	1575	3
Chuck Muncie, S.D.	7	217	1889	2
Dan Ross, Cin.	4	215	2658	13
Stanley Morgan, N.E.	6	216	4869	35
Sherman Smith, Sea.	7	211	2342	10
Wesley Walker, N.Y.J.	6	210	4214	32

TOP 10 ACTIVE SCORERS, AFC
250 or more points

	Yrs.	TD	FG	PAT	TP
1. John Smith, N.E.	9	0	125	296	671
2. Pat Leahy, N.Y.J.	9	0	125	232	607
3. Efren Herrera, Buff.	8	0	116	256	604
4. Franco Harris, Pitt.	11	93	0	0	558
5. Chris Bahr, Raiders	7	0	105	230	545
6. Rolf Benirschke, S.D.	6	0	98	203	497
7. Cliff Branch, Raiders	11	62	0	0	372
8. Chuck Muncie, S.D.	7	61	0	0	366
9. Uwe von Schamann, Mia.	4	0	74	126	348
10. Earl Campbell, Hou.	5	57	0	0	342

Other Leading Scorers

Pete Johnson, Cin.	6	56	0	0	336
Matt Bahr, Clev.	4	0	59	140	317
Dave Casper, Hou.	9	51	0	0	306
Isaac Curtis, Cin.	10	51	0	0	306
Jim Breech, Cin.	4	0	58	126	300
Steve Largent, Sea.	7	50	0	0	300
Nat Moore, Mia.	9	49	0	0	294
Nick Lowery, K.C.	4	0	65	98	293
Bob Chandler, Raiders	12	48	0	1	289
Charlie Joiner, S.D.	14	47	0	0	282
John Stallworth, Pitt.	9	45	0	0	270
Riley Odoms, Den.	11	44	0	0	264
Greg Pruitt, Raiders	10	44	0	0	264

TOP 10 ACTIVE INTERCEPTORS, AFC
20 or more interceptions

	Yrs.	No.	Yards	TD
1. Ken Riley, Cin.	14	57	507	3
2. Mel Blount, Pitt.	13	53	704	2
3. Gary Barbaro, K.C.	7	39	771	3
4. Clarence Scott, Clev.	12	37	407	2
5. Donnie Shell, Pitt.	9	31	292	0
6. Lester Hayes, Raiders	6	30	486	3
7. Steve Nelson, N.E.	9	29	335	0
8. Steve Foley, Den.	7	28	411	0
Mike Haynes, N.E.	7	28	393	1
10. Lyle Blackwood, Mia.	10	26	469	2
Ted Hendricks, Raiders	14	26	332	1
John Harris, Sea.	5	26	311	2
Jack Lambert, Pitt.	9	26	244	0

Other Leading Interceptors

Mario Clark, Buff.	7	25	438	0
Mike Reinfeldt, Hou.	7	25	356	0
Dave Brown, Sea.	8	25	265	1
Mike Williams, S.D.	8	24	269	0
Monte Jackson, Raiders	8	23	289	3
Tim Fox, S.D.	7	21	318	0
Gregg Bingham, Hou.	10	20	275	0
J.T. Thomas, Den.	9	20	147	0

TOP 10 ACTIVE PUNT RETURNERS, AFC
40 or more punt returns

	Yrs.	No.	Yards	Avg.	TD
1. Rick Upchurch, Den.	8	244	2956	12.1	8
2. J.T. Smith, K.C.	5	155	1780	11.5	4
3. Mike Fuller, Cin.	8	252	2660	10.6	2
4. Greg Pruitt, Raiders	10	83	868	10.5	0
5. Mike Haynes, N.E.	7	111	1159	10.4	2
Stanley Morgan, N.E.	6	92	960	10.4	1
7. Tom Vigorito, Mia.	2	56	571	10.2	2
8. Cullen Bryant, Sea.	10	71	707	10.0	0
9. Bruce Harper, N.Y.J.	6	183	1784	9.7	1
Roland James, N.E.	3	40	387	9.7	1

Other Leading Punt Returners

Tony Nathan, Mia.	4	51	484	9.5	1
Dino Hall, Clev.	4	72	617	8.6	0
Wade Manning, Den.	3	51	433	8.5	0
Nesby Glasgow, Balt.	4	71	563	7.9	1
Carl Roaches, Hou.	3	105	784	7.5	0
Wes Chandler, S.D.	5	50	361	7.2	0
Cleo Montgomery, Raiders	3	48	344	7.2	0
Roland Hooks, Buff.	7	43	302	7.0	0
Bruce Laird, S.D.	11	60	405	6.8	0
Lou Piccone, Buff.	9	73	482	6.6	1
Lyle Blackwood, Mia.	10	68	319	4.7	0

TOP 10 ACTIVE KICKOFF RETURNERS, AFC
40 or more kickoff returns

	Yrs.	No.	Yards	Avg.	TD
1. Raymond Clayborn, N.E.	6	57	1538	27.0	3
2. Cullen Bryant, Sea.	10	66	1760	26.7	3
3. Greg Pruitt, Raiders	10	72	1894	26.3	1
4. Duriel Harris, Mia.	7	56	1416	25.3	0
5. Bruce Laird, S.D.	11	137	3406	24.9	0
6. Rick Upchurch, Den.	8	95	2355	24.8	0
7. Horace Ivory, Sea.	6	70	1696	24.2	1
8. Carlos Carson, K.C.	3	50	1194	23.9	0
9. Fulton Walker, Mia.	2	58	1365	23.5	1
10. James Brooks, S.D.	2	73	1698	23.3	0

Other Leading Kickoff Returners

Lou Piccone, Buff.	9	111	2559	23.1	0
Larry Anderson, Balt.	5	149	3383	22.7	1
Carl Roaches, Hou.	3	86	1956	22.7	1
Nesby Glasgow, Balt.	4	84	1904	22.7	0
David Verser, Cin.	2	45	1011	22.5	0
Tony Nathan, Mia.	4	50	1118	22.4	0
Bruce Harper, N.Y.J.	6	242	5391	22.3	0
Wes Chandler, S.D.	5	47	1021	21.7	0
Mike Fuller, Cin.	8	79	1701	21.5	0
Curtis Brown, Buff.	6	41	874	21.3	1
Dino Hall, Clev.	4	140	2948	21.1	0
Wade Manning, Den.	3	48	1005	20.9	0
Ray Griffin, Cin.	5	40	833	20.8	0
Roland Hooks, Buff.	7	48	969	20.2	0
Kurt Sohn, N.Y.J.	2	41	827	20.2	0

TOP 10 ACTIVE PUNTERS, AFC
35 or more punts

	Yrs.	No.	Avg.	LG
1. Rohn Stark, Balt.	1	46	44.4	60
2. Ray Guy, Raiders	10	701	42.9	74
3. Rich Camarillo, N.E.	2	96	42.7	76
4. Luke Prestridge, Den.	4	290	41.8	67
Pat McInally, Cin.	7	509	41.8	67
6. Craig Colquitt, Pitt.	4	279	41.2	74
7. Steve Cox, Clev.	2	116	41.0	66
8. John James, Hou.	11	916	40.8	75
9. Jeff Gossett, K.C.	2	62	40.4	56
John Goodson, Pitt.	1	49	40.4	66

Other Leading Punters

Tom Orosz, Mia.	2	118	40.2	61
Chuck Ramsey, N.Y.J.	6	398	40.1	79
Greg Cater, Buff.	3	188	39.0	71
Jeff West, Sea.	7	436	37.9	62

NFC Active Statistical Leaders

LEADING ACTIVE PASSERS, NATIONAL FOOTBALL CONFERENCE
1,000 or more attempts

	Yrs.	Att.	Comp.	Pct. Comp.	Yards	Avg. Gain	TD	Pct. TD	Had Int.	Pct. Int.	Rate Pts.
Joe Montana, S.F.	4	1130	713	63.1	8069	7.14	52	4.6	32	2.8	88.1
Danny White, Dall.	7	1177	695	59.0	9194	7.81	69	5.9	56	4.8	83.5
Ken Stabler, N.O.	13	3412	2061	60.4	25611	7.51	183	5.4	199	5.8	77.6
Joe Theismann, Wash.	9	2365	1318	55.7	16327	6.90	99	4.2	98	4.1	74.2
Ron Jaworski, Phil.	9	2440	1290	52.9	16758	6.87	115	4.7	101	4.1	73.4
Tommy Kramer, Minn.	6	2062	1147	55.6	13403	6.50	88	4.3	88	4.3	71.9
Gary Danielson, Det.	6	1161	641	55.2	8089	6.97	45	3.9	52	4.5	71.4
Steve Bartkowski, Atl.	8	2518	1347	53.5	17407	6.91	116	4.6	125	5.0	70.0
Jim Hart, St.L.	17	4978	2540	51.0	34047	6.84	205	4.1	239	4.8	66.8
Doug Williams, T.B.	5	1890	895	47.4	12648	6.69	73	3.9	73	3.9	66.2
Lynn Dickey, G.B.	10	1926	1049	54.5	13463	6.99	69	3.6	114	5.9	64.1
Dan Pastorini, Phil.	11	3050	1556	51.0	18515	6.07	103	3.4	161	5.3	59.1
Bob Avellini, Chi.	7	1057	530	50.1	6823	6.46	33	3.1	66	6.2	55.3

TOP 10 ACTIVE RUSHERS, NFC
2,000 or more yards

	Yrs.	Att.	Yards	TD
1. Walter Payton, Chi.	8	2352	10204	72
2. John Riggins, Wash.	11	2038	8089	58
3. Tony Dorsett, Dall.	6	1545	7015	45
4. Wilbert Montgomery, Phil.	6	1235	5610	43
5. Ottis Anderson, St.L.	4	1105	4920	29
6. Dexter Bussey, Det.	9	1114	4765	18
7. Robert Newhouse, Dall.	11	1151	4750	31
8. William Andrews, Atl.	4	932	4205	22
9. Wilbur Jackson, Wash.	8	971	3852	13
10. Joe Washington, Wash.	6	942	3665	10

Other Leading Rushers

Rickey Young, Minn.	8	972	3576	21
Don Calhoun, Phil.	9	860	3559	23
Billy Sims, Det.	3	781	3379	30
Wendell Tyler, S.F.	6	720	3266	33
Tony Galbreath, Minn.	7	841	3179	30
Wayne Morris, St.L.	7	819	3118	35
Roland Harper, Chi.	7	757	3044	15
Ted Brown, Minn.	4	743	3041	16
Rob Carpenter, N.Y.G.	6	690	2740	18
George Rogers, N.O.	2	500	2209	16
Horace King, Det.	8	546	2075	9
Terdell Middleton, T.B.	6	559	2044	15

TOP 10 ACTIVE PASS RECEIVERS, NFC
200 or more receptions

	Yrs.	No.	Yards	TD
1. Harold Carmichael, Phil.	12	551	8463	76
2. Drew Pearson, Dall.	10	442	7277	43
3. Rickey Young, Minn.	8	387	3092	16
4. Sammy White, Minn.	7	335	5513	45
5. Alfred Jenkins, Atl.	8	321	5771	39
Charle Young, S.F.	10	321	3889	22
7. Pat Tilley, St.L.	7	320	4780	21
8. Tony Galbreath, Minn.	7	319	2518	6
9. Joe Washington, Wash.	6	298	2557	11
10. James Lofton, G.B.	5	277	5002	26

Other Leading Pass Receivers

Freddie Solomon, S.F.	8	275	4188	33
Walter Payton, Chi.	8	275	2481	7
John Jefferson, G.B.	5	265	4515	40
Freddie Scott, Det.	9	257	4199	19
Billy Joe DuPree, Dall.	10	255	3423	40
Sam McCullum, Minn.	9	253	3703	24
Tony Hill, Dall.	6	246	4440	29
Dwight Clark, S.F.	4	245	3241	17
David Hill, Det.	7	245	3054	23
John Riggins, Wash.	11	232	2000	12
Russ Francis, S.F.	7	219	3274	30
William Andrews, Atl.	4	213	2003	7
Ted Brown, Minn.	4	207	1721	6
Tony Dorsett, Dall.	6	201	1793	6

TOP 10 ACTIVE SCORERS, NFC
250 or more points

	Yrs.	TD	FG	PAT	TP
1. Jan Stenerud, G.B.	16	0	317	457	1408
2. Mark Moseley, Wash.	12	0	209	316	943
3. Ray Wersching, S.F.	10	0	121	212	575
4. Rafael Septien, Dall.	6	0	101	245	548
5. Joe Danelo, N.Y.G.	8	0	115	190	535
6. Walter Payton, Chi.	8	79	0	0	474
7. Bob Thomas, Chi.	8	0	97	178	469
8. Harold Carmichael, Phil.	12	76	0	0	456
9. John Riggins, Wash.	11	70	0	0	420
10. Rick Danmeier, Minn.	6	0	70	154	364

Other Leading Scorers

Tony Franklin, Phil.	4	0	65	148	343
Wilbert Montgomery, Phil.	6	56	0	0	336
Neil O'Donoghue, St.L.	6	0	64	128	320
Tony Dorsett, Dall.	6	52	0	0	312
Ed Murray, Det.	3	0	63	97	286
Drew Pearson, Dall.	10	45	0	0	270
Sammy White, Minn.	7	45	0	0	270
Wendell Tyler, S.F.	6	43	0	0	258

TOP 10 ACTIVE INTERCEPTORS, NFC
20 or more interceptions

	Yrs.	No.	Yards	TD
1. Rod Perry, Rams	8	28	386	4
2. James Hunter, Det.	7	27	279	1
Herman Edwards, Phil.	6	27	90	0
4. Mike Washington, T.B.	7	26	377	3
Pat Thomas, Rams	7	26	292	1
6. Neal Colzie, T.B.	8	25	412	1
7. Cedric Brown, T.B.	7	24	501	2
8. Gary Fencik, Chi.	7	23	272	1
9. Nolan Cromwell, Rams	6	22	407	1
Randy Logan, Phil.	10	22	293	0

Other Leading Interceptors

Dwight Hicks, S.F.	4	21	374	1
Dennis Thurman, Dall.	5	20	411	2
Johnnie Gray, G.B.	8	20	327	1
Terry Schmidt, Chi.	9	20	174	2

TOP 10 ACTIVE PUNT RETURNERS, NFC
40 or more punt returns

	Yrs.	No.	Yards	Avg.	TD
1. Billy Johnson, Atl.	8	179	2313	12.9	5
2. Jeff Fisher, Chi.	2	50	562	11.2	1
3. LeRoy Irvin, Rams	3	110	1153	10.5	4
4. Neal Colzie, T.B.	8	170	1759	10.3	0
5. Mike Nelms, Wash.	3	125	1231	9.8	2
Jeff Groth, N.O.	4	59	580	9.8	0
7. Robbie Martin, Det.	2	78	725	9.3	1
8. Freddie Solomon, S.F.	8	172	1580	9.2	4
9. Butch Johnson, Dall.	7	146	1313	9.0	0
10. Stump Mitchell, St.L.	2	69	610	8.8	1

Other Leading Punt Returners

James Jones, Dall.	3	87	736	8.5	0
John Sciarra, Phil.	5	95	794	8.4	0
Theo Bell, T.B.	6	175	1453	8.3	0
Leon Bright, N.Y.G.	2	89	735	8.3	0
Rich Mauti, N.O.	5	75	610	8.1	0
Alvin Garrett, Wash.	3	43	344	8.0	0
Johnnie Gray, G.B.	8	83	647	7.8	0
Dwight Hicks, S.F.	4	54	403	7.5	0
Lenny Walterscheid, Chi.	6	57	424	7.4	0
Willard Harrell, St.L.	8	118	823	7.0	2

TOP 10 ACTIVE KICKOFF RETURNERS, NFC
40 or more kickoff returns

	Yrs.	No.	Yards	Avg.	TD
1. Mike Nelms, Wash.	3	98	2466	25.2	0
2. Billy Johnson, Atl.	8	121	2902	24.0	2
Brian Baschnagel, Chi.	7	86	2060	24.0	1
4. Roy Green, St.L.	4	81	1885	23.3	1
Stump Mitchell, St.L.	2	71	1656	23.3	0
6. Rich Mauti, N.O.	5	116	2689	23.2	0
Butch Johnson, Dall.	7	79	1832	23.2	0
Alvin Hall, Det.	2	41	951	23.2	1
9. James Owens, T.B.	4	99	2253	22.8	2
10. Jimmy Rogers, N.O.	3	70	1575	22.5	0
Wayne Wilson, N.O.	4	58	1303	22.5	0

Other Leading Kickoff Returners

Mike McCoy, G.B.	7	54	1187	22.0	0
Rick Kane, Det.	6	61	1327	21.8	0
Don Bessillieu, St.L.	4	47	1024	21.8	0
Billy Campfield, Phil.	5	65	1412	21.7	1
James Jones, Dall.	3	61	1283	21.0	0
Aundra Thompson, N.O.	6	52	1090	21.0	1
Allan Clark, G.B.	3	44	912	20.7	0
Willard Harrell, St.L.	8	81	1628	20.1	0
Alvin Garrett, Wash.	3	48	963	20.1	0
Drew Hill, Rams	4	145	2895	20.0	0

TOP 10 ACTIVE PUNTERS, NFC
35 or more punts

	Yrs.	No.	Avg.	LG
1. John Misko, Rams	1	45	43.6	59
2. Carl Birdsong, St.L.	2	123	42.7	75
3. Tom Skladany, Det.	5	268	42.4	74
4. Dave Jennings, N.Y.G.	9	757	42.0	73
5. Larry Swider, T.B.	4	284	41.3	72
6. George Roberts, Atl.	5	306	41.0	71
7. Jim Miller, S.F.	3	214	40.6	80
8. Russell Erxleben, N.O.	4	205	40.5	60
Ray Stachowicz, G.B.	2	124	40.5	72
10. Danny White, Dall.	7	489	40.4	73

Other Leading Punters

Greg Coleman, Minn.	6	429	39.9	73
Max Runager, Phil.	4	256	39.9	64
Dan Pastorini, Phil.	11	316	39.7	74
Bob Parsons, Chi.	11	805	38.8	81
Jeff Hayes, Wash.	1	51	38.0	58

Active Coaches' Career Records

Start of 1983 Season

Coach	Team(s)	Yrs.	Regular Season				Postseason				Career			
			Won	Lost	Tied	Pct.	Won	Lost	Tied	Pct.	Won	Lost	Tied	Pct.
Don Shula	Baltimore Colts, Miami Dolphins	20	201	76	6	.721	13	10	0	.565	214	86	6	.709
Joe Gibbs	Washington Redskins	2	16	9	0	.640	4	0	0	1.000	20	9	0	.690
Tom Flores	Los Angeles Raiders	4	35	22	0	.614	5	1	0	.833	40	23	0	.635
Chuck Noll	Pittsburgh Steelers	14	123	75	1	.621	14	5	0	.737	137	80	1	.631
Tom Landry	Dallas Cowboys	23	202	115	6	.635	20	14	0	.588	222	129	6	.630
Don Coryell	St. Louis Cardinals, San Diego Chargers	10	89	49	1	.644	3	6	0	.333	92	55	1	.625
Bud Grant	Minnesota Vikings	16	143	79	5	.641	10	12	0	.455	153	91	5	.624
Chuck Knox	Los Angeles Rams, Buffalo Bills, Seattle Seahawks	10	91	51	1	.640	4	7	0	.364	95	58	1	.620
O. A. (Bum) Phillips	Houston Oilers, New Orleans Saints	8	63	52	0	.548	4	3	0	.571	67	55	0	.549
Forrest Gregg	Cleveland Browns, Cincinnati Bengals	6	43	39	0	.504	2	2	0	.500	45	41	0	.523
Ron Meyer	New England Patriots	1	5	4	0	.556	0	1	0	.000	5	5	0	.500
Sam Rutigliano	Cleveland Browns	5	37	36	0	.507	0	2	0	.000	37	38	0	.493
Dan Reeves	Denver Broncos	2	12	13	0	.480	0	0	0	.000	12	13	0	.480
Bill Walsh	San Francisco 49ers	4	24	33	0	.421	3	0	0	1.000	27	33	0	.450
Monte Clark	San Francisco 49ers, Detroit Lions	6	38	49	0	.437	0	1	0	.000	38	50	0	.432
Jim Hanifan	St. Louis Cardinals	3	17	24	0	.415	0	1	0	.000	17	25	0	.405
Bart Starr	Green Bay Packers	8	44	68	3	.396	1	1	0	.500	45	69	3	.397
John McKay	Tampa Bay Buccaneers	7	36	64	1	.361	1	3	0	.250	37	67	1	.357
Mike Ditka	Chicago Bears	1	3	6	0	.333	0	0	0	.000	3	6	0	.333
Ed Biles	Houston Oilers	2	8	17	0	.320	0	0	0	.000	8	17	0	.320
Marion Campbell	Atlanta Falcons, Philadelphia Eagles	2	8	20	0	.286	0	0	0	.000	8	20	0	.286
Frank Kush	Baltimore Colts	1	0	8	1	.056	0	0	0	.000	0	8	1	.056
Dan Henning	Atlanta Falcons	0	0	0	0	.000	0	0	0	.000	0	0	0	.000
John Mackovic	Kansas City Chiefs	0	0	0	0	.000	0	0	0	.000	0	0	0	.000
Bill Parcells	New York Giants	0	0	0	0	.000	0	0	0	.000	0	0	0	.000
John Robinson	Los Angeles Rams	0	0	0	0	.000	0	0	0	.000	0	0	0	.000
Kay Stephenson	Buffalo Bills	0	0	0	0	.000	0	0	0	.000	0	0	0	.000
Joe Walton	New York Jets	0	0	0	0	.000	0	0	0	.000	0	0	0	.000

Coaches With 100 Career Victories

Start of 1983 Season

Coach	Team(s)	Yrs.	Regular Season				Postseason				Career			
			Won	Lost	Tied	Pct.	Won	Lost	Tied	Pct.	Won	Lost	Tied	Pct.
George Halas	Chicago Bears	40	319	148	31	.672	6	3	0	.667	325	151	31	.672
Earl (Curly) Lambeau	Green Bay Packers, Chicago Cardinals, Washington Redskins	33	231	133	23	.627	3	2	0	.600	234	135	23	.626
Tom Landry	Dallas Cowboys	23	202	115	6	.635	20	14	0	.588	222	129	6	.630
Don Shula	Baltimore Colts, Miami Dolphins	20	201	76	6	.721	13	10	0	.565	214	86	6	.709
Paul Brown	Cleveland Browns, Cincinnati Bengals	21	166	100	6	.621	4	8	0	.333	170	108	6	.609
Steve Owen	New York Giants	23	151	100	17	.595	3	8	0	.273	154	108	17	.582
Bud Grant	Minnesota Vikings	16	143	79	5	.641	10	12	0	.455	153	91	5	.624
Chuck Noll	Pittsburgh Steelers	14	123	75	1	.621	14	5	0	.737	137	80	1	.631
Hank Stram	Kansas City Chiefs, New Orleans Saints	17	131	97	10	.571	5	3	0	.625	136	100	10	.573
Weeb Ewbank	Baltimore Colts, New York Jets	20	130	129	7	.502	4	1	0	.800	134	130	7	.507
Sid Gillman	Los Angeles Rams, San Diego Chargers, Houston Oilers	18	122	99	7	.550	1	5	0	.167	123	104	7	.541
George Allen	Los Angeles Rams, Washington Redskins	12	116	47	5	.705	2	7	0	.222	118	54	5	.681
John Madden	Oakland Raiders	10	103	32	7	.750	9	7	0	.563	112	39	7	.731
Ray (Buddy) Parker	Chicago Cardinals, Detroit Lions, Pittsburgh Steelers	15	104	75	9	.577	3	1	0	.750	107	76	9	.581
Vince Lombardi	Green Bay Packers, Washington Redskins	10	96	34	6	.728	9	1	0	.900	105	35	6	.740

1982 Trades
1982 Interconference Trades

Linebacker **Bob Horn** from San Diego to San Francisco for a draft choice (6/9).

Defensive back **Jimmy Allen** from Detroit to Kansas City for a draft choice (7/13).

Defensive back **Pete Shaw** from San Diego to the New York Giants for a draft choice (7/13).

Running back **Kevin Long** from the New York Jets to Chicago for a draft choice (7/26).

Tackle **Angelo Fields** from Houston to Green Bay for a draft choice (7/27).

Tackle **Mark Koncar** from Green Bay to Houston for a draft choice (7/29).

Linebacker **Whitney Paul** from Kansas City to New Orleans for a draft choice (7/31).

Linebacker **Bill Matthews** from New England to the New York Giants for a draft choice (8/2).

Linebacker **Bruce Huther** from Cleveland to Chicago for a draft choice (8/5).

Wide receiver **Don Bass** from Cincinnati to New Orleans for a draft choice (8/20).

Center-tackle **Gerry Sullivan** from Cleveland to Chicago for a draft choice (8/23).

Quarterback **Tom Owen** from New England to Washington for quarterback **Tom Flick** (8/25).

Tackle **Kelvin Clark** from Denver to New Orleans for a draft choice (8/30).

Punter **Dave Smigelsky** from Baltimore to Atlanta for a draft choice (8/31).

Tackle **Jeff Williams** from San Diego to Chicago for draft choices (8/31).

Defensive end **Tony McGee** from New England to Washington for a draft choice (9/2).

Tackle **Lindsey Mason** from Los Angeles Raiders to San Francisco for a draft choice (9/6).

Quarterback **Archie Manning** from New Orleans to Houston for tackle **Leon Gray** (9/17).

1983 Interconference Trades

Defensive back **Reuben Henderson** from Chicago to San Diego for the Chargers' fourth- and eighth-round selections in 1983 (4/22). Chicago subsequently selected tight end **Pat Dunsmore** (Drake) and defensive tackle **Mark Bortz** (Iowa).

San Diego regained its 1983 first-round choice which it traded to San Francisco in 1981 by trading its second-round choice and returning to San Francisco the second-round choice the 49ers sent to the Chargers in the same 1981 trade (4/22). San Diego subsequently selected defensive back **Gill Byrd** (San Jose State). San Francisco subsequently traded its second-round choice to the Los Angeles Rams (see NFC Trades) and selected running back **Roger Craig** (Nebraska).

Houston traded its first-round choice in 1983 to the Los Angeles Rams for the Rams' first- and fourth-round choices in 1983 and the Rams' fourth-round choice in 1984 (4/23). Houston subsequently traded the Rams' first-round choice to Seattle (see AFC Trades) and selected tight end **Mike McCloskey** (Penn State). The Rams subsequently selected running back **Eric Dickerson** (Southern Methodist).

New Orleans traded Washington's fourth-round choice in 1983 to Buffalo for the Bills' third-round choice in 1984. Buffalo subsequently selected defensive end **Jimmy Payne** (Georgia) (4/26).

Los Angeles Raiders traded its sixth-round choice in 1983 to Washington for the Redskins' fifth-round choice in 1984. Washington subsequently selected tackle **Bob Winckler** (Wisconsin) (4/26).

New Orleans traded its ninth-, tenth-, eleventh-, and twelfth-round choices in 1983 to New England for the Patriots' fourth-round choice in 1984. New England subsequently selected running back **Ricky Williams** (Langston), defensive end **Toby Williams** (Nebraska), wide receiver **Steve Parker** (Abilene Christian), and running back **Waddell Kelly** (Arkansas State) (4/27).

Houston traded its eleventh and twelfth choices in 1983 to the New York Giants for the Giants' ninth-round choice in 1984. The Giants subsequently selected defensive back **Lee Jenkins** (Tennessee) and linebacker **Robbie Jones** (Alabama) (4/27).

1982 AFC Trades

Guard **Robert Pratt** from Baltimore to Seattle for a draft choice (7/13).

Defensive back **J. T. Thomas** from Pittsburgh to Denver for a draft choice (8/18).

Defensive back **Donald Dykes** from the New York Jets to San Diego for a draft choice (8/25).

Linebacker **Zack Valentine** from Pittsburgh to Baltimore for a draft choice (8/31).

Wide receiver **Roger Carr** from Baltimore to Seattle for a draft choice (9/4).

Center-guard **Glenn Hyde** from Denver to Baltimore for a draft choice (9/6).

1983 AFC Trades

Houston traded the first-round draft choice in 1983 that it obtained from the Los Angeles Rams to Seattle for the Seahawks first-, second-, and third-round choices in 1983 (4/24). Houston subsequently selected tackle **Bruce Matthews** (Southern California), defensive back **Keith Bostic** (Michigan), and tight end **Chris Dressel** (Stanford). Seattle subsequently selected running back **Curt Warner** (Penn State).

Houston traded Green Bay's third-round choice in 1983 to Miami for the Dolphins' third- and fifth-round choices in 1983. Houston subsequently selected defensive back **Steve Brown** (Oregon) and nose tackle **Jerome Foster** (Ohio State). Miami subsequently selected defensive end **Charles Benson** (Baylor) (4/26).

1982 NFC Trades

Defensive tackle **Bruce Clark** from Green Bay to New Orleans for a draft choice (6/10).

Defensive end **Elois Grooms** from New Orleans to St. Louis for a draft choice (8/3).

Nose tackle **Charlie Johnson** from Philadelphia to Minnesota for a draft choice (8/20).

Tackle **Ron Yary** from Minnesota to Los Angeles Rams for a draft choice (8/23).

Running back **James Mayberry** from Atlanta to Tampa Bay for a draft choice (8/30).

Quarterback **Chuck Fusina** from Tampa Bay to San Francisco for a draft choice (8/31).

Quarterback **Jeff Rutledge** from Los Angeles Rams to New York Giants for a draft choice (9/6).

1983 NFC Trades

Defensive end **Gary Jeter** from the New York Giants to the Los Angeles Rams for San Francisco's third-round choice and Buffalo's sixth-round choice in 1983 (4/14). The Giants subsequently selected tight end **Jamie Williams** (Nebraska) and guard **Kevin Belcher** (Texas-El Paso).

Guard **George Collins** from St. Louis to San Francisco for guard **Dan Audick** (4/21).

Running back **Wendell Tyler**, defensive end **Cody Jones,** and the Rams' 1983 third-round draft choice from the Los Angeles Rams to San Francisco for the 49ers' second-round draft choice and Cleveland's fourth-round choice in 1983 (4/25). The Rams subsequently selected linebacker **Mike Wilcher** (North Carolina) and kicker **Chuck Nelson** (Washington). San Francisco subsequently selected linebacker **Blanchard Montgomery** (UCLA).

Tackle **Jeff Williams** from Chicago to San Francisco for Cleveland's ninth-round choice and San Francisco's twelfth-round choice in 1983 (4/26). Chicago subsequently selected linebacker **Mark Zavagnin** (Notre Dame) and wide receiver **Oliver Williams** (Illinois).

Detroit traded guard **Russ Bolinger** to the Los Angeles Rams for the Rams' fifth-round choice in 1983. Detroit subsequently selected defensive back **Demetrious Johnson** (Missouri) (4/26).

Los Angeles Rams traded defensive tackle **Mike Fanning** to Detroit for a future draft choice (4/26).

San Francisco traded its sixth-round choice in 1983 to Tampa Bay for the Buccaneers' fourth-round choice in 1984. Tampa Bay subsequently selected wide receiver **Rheugene Branton** (Texas Southern) (4/26).

Monday Night Football, 1970–1982

(Home Team in capitals, games listed in chronological order.)

1982
Pittsburgh 36, DALLAS 28
Green Bay 27, NEW YORK GIANTS 19
LOS ANGELES RAIDERS 28, San Diego 24
TAMPA BAY 23, Miami 17
New York Jets 28, DETROIT 13
Dallas 37, HOUSTON 7
SAN DIEGO 50, Cincinnati 34
MIAMI 27, Buffalo 10
MINNESOTA 31, Dallas 27

1981
San Diego 44, CLEVELAND 14
Oakland 36, MINNESOTA 10
Dallas 35, NEW ENGLAND 21
Los Angeles 24, CHICAGO 7
PHILADELPHIA 16, Atlanta 13
BUFFALO 31, Miami 21
DETROIT 48, Chicago 17
PITTSBURGH 26, Houston 13
DENVER 19, Minnesota 17
DALLAS 27, Buffalo 14
SEATTLE 44, San Diego 23
ATLANTA 31, Minnesota 30
MIAMI 13, Philadelphia 10
OAKLAND 30, Pittsburgh 27
LOS ANGELES 21, Atlanta 16
SAN DIEGO 23, Oakland 10

1980
Dallas 17, WASHINGTON 3
Houston 16, CLEVELAND 7
PHILADELPHIA 35, New York Giants 3
NEW ENGLAND 23, Denver 14
CHICAGO, 23, Tampa Bay 0
DENVER 20, Washington 17
Oakland 45, PITTSBURGH 34
NEW YORK JETS 17, Miami 14
CLEVELAND 27, Chicago 21
HOUSTON 38, New England 34
Oakland 19, SEATTLE 17
Los Angeles 27, NEW ORLEANS 7
OAKLAND 9, Denver 3
MIAMI 16, New England 13 (OT)
LOS ANGELES 38, Dallas 14
SAN DIEGO 26, Pittsburgh 17

1979
Pittsburgh 16, NEW ENGLAND 13 (OT)
Atlanta 14, PHILADELPHIA 10
WASHINGTON 27, New York Giants 0
CLEVELAND 26, Dallas 7
GREEN BAY 27, New England 14
OAKLAND 13, Miami 3
NEW YORK JETS 14, Minnesota 7
PITTSBURGH 42, Denver 7
Seattle 31, ATLANTA 28
Houston 9, MIAMI 6
Philadelphia 31, DALLAS 21
LOS ANGELES 20, Atlanta 14
SEATTLE 30, New York Jets 7
Oakland 42, NEW ORLEANS 35
HOUSTON 20, Pittsburgh 17
SAN DIEGO 17, Denver 7

1978
DALLAS 38, Baltimore 0
MINNESOTA 12, Denver 9 (OT)
Baltimore 34, NEW ENGLAND 27
Minnesota 24, CHICAGO 20
WASHINGTON 9, Dallas 5
MIAMI 21, Cincinnati 0
DENVER 16, Chicago 7
Houston 24, PITTSBURGH 17
ATLANTA 15, Los Angeles 7
BALTIMORE 21, Washington 17
Oakland 34, CINCINNATI 21
HOUSTON 35, Miami 30
Pittsburgh 24, SAN FRANCISCO 7
SAN DIEGO 40, Chicago 7
Cincinnati 20, LOS ANGELES 19
MIAMI 23, New England 3

1977
PITTSBURGH 27, San Francisco 0
CLEVELAND 30, New England 27 (OT)
Oakland 37, KANSAS CITY 28
CHICAGO 24, Los Angeles 23
PITTSBURGH 20, Cincinnati 14
LOS ANGELES 35, Minnesota 3
ST. LOUIS 28, New York Giants 0
BALTIMORE 10, Washington 3
St. Louis 24, DALLAS 17
WASHINGTON 10, Green Bay 9
OAKLAND 34, Buffalo 13
MIAMI 16, Baltimore 6
Dallas 42, SAN FRANCISCO 35

1976
Miami 30, BUFFALO 21
Oakland 24, KANSAS CITY 21
Washington 20, PHILADELPHIA 17 (OT)
MINNESOTA 17, Pittsburgh 6
San Francisco 16, LOS ANGELES 0
NEW ENGLAND 41, New York Jets 7
WASHINGTON 20, St. Louis 10
BALTIMORE 38, Houston 14
CINCINNATI 20, Los Angeles 12
DALLAS 17, Buffalo 10
Baltimore 17, MIAMI 16
SAN FRANCISCO 20, Minnesota 16
OAKLAND 35, Cincinnati 20

1975
Oakland 31, MIAMI 21
DENVER 23, Green Bay 13
Dallas 36, DETROIT 10
WASHINGTON 27, St. Louis 17
New York Giants 17, BUFFALO 14
Minnesota 13, CHICAGO 9
Los Angeles 42, PHILADELPHIA 3
Kansas City 34, DALLAS 31
CINCINNATI 33, Buffalo 24
Pittsburgh 32, HOUSTON 9
MIAMI 20, New England 7
OAKLAND 17, Denver 10
SAN DIEGO 24, New York Jets 16

1974
BUFFALO 21, Oakland 20
PHILADELPHIA 13, Dallas 10
WASHINGTON 30, Denver 3
MIAMI 21, New York Jets 17
DETROIT 17, San Francisco 13
CHICAGO 10, Green Bay 9
PITTSBURGH 24, Atlanta 17
Los Angeles 15, SAN FRANCISCO 13
Minnesota 28, ST. LOUIS 24
Kansas City 42, DENVER 34
Pittsburgh 28, NEW ORLEANS 7
MIAMI 24, Cincinnati 3
Washington 23, LOS ANGELES 17

1973
GREEN BAY 23, New York Jets 7
DALLAS 40, New Orleans 3
DETROIT 31, Atlanta 6
WASHINGTON 14, Dallas 7
Miami 17, CLEVELAND 9
DENVER 23, Oakland 23
BUFFALO 23, Kansas City 14
PITTSBURGH 21, Washington 16
KANSAS CITY 19, Chicago 7
ATLANTA 20, Minnesota 14
SAN FRANCISCO 20, Green Bay 6
MIAMI 30, Pittsburgh 26
LOS ANGELES 40, New York Giants 6

1972
Washington 24, MINNESOTA 21
Kansas City 20, NEW ORLEANS 17
New York Giants 27, PHILADELPHIA 12
Oakland 34, HOUSTON 0
Green Bay 24, DETROIT 23
CHICAGO 13, Minnesota 10
DALLAS 28, Detroit 24
Baltimore 24, NEW ENGLAND 17
Cleveland 21, SAN DIEGO 17
WASHINGTON 24, Atlanta 13
MIAMI 31, St. Louis 10
Los Angeles 26, SAN FRANCISCO 16
OAKLAND 24, New York Jets 16

1971
Minnesota 16, DETROIT 13
ST. LOUIS 17, New York Jets 10
Oakland 34, CLEVELAND 20
DALLAS 20, New York Giants 13
KANSAS CITY 38, Pittsburgh 16
MINNESOTA 10, Baltimore 3
GREEN BAY 14, Detroit 14
BALTIMORE 24, Los Angeles 17
SAN DIEGO 20, St. Louis 17
ATLANTA 28, Green Bay 21
MIAMI 34, Chicago 3
Kansas City 26, SAN FRANCISCO 17
Washington 38, LOS ANGELES 24

1970
CLEVELAND 31, New York Jets 21
Kansas City 44, BALTIMORE 24
DETROIT 28, Chicago 14
Green Bay 22, SAN DIEGO 20
OAKLAND 34, Washington 20
MINNESOTA 13, Los Angeles 3
PITTSBURGH 21, Cincinnati 10
Baltimore 13, GREEN BAY 10
St. Louis 38, DALLAS 0
PHILADELPHIA 23, New York Giants 20
Miami 20, ATLANTA 7
Cleveland 21, HOUSTON 10
Detroit 28, LOS ANGELES 23

Monday Night Won-Lost Records, 1970-1982

	Total	1982	1981	1980	1979	1978	1977	1976	1975	1974	1973	1972	1971	1970
Baltimore	8-4					2-1	1-1	2-0				1-0	1-1	1-1
Buffalo	3-7	0-1	1-1				0-1	0-2	0-2	1-0	1-0			
Cincinnati	3-7	0-1				1-2	0-1	1-1	1-0	0-1				0-1
Cleveland	6-4		0-1	1-1	1-0		1-0				0-1	1-0	0-1	2-0
Denver	4-8-1		1-0	1-2	0-2	1-1			1-1	0-2	0-0-1			
Houston	6-6	0-1	0-1	2-0	2-0	2-0		0-1	0-1			0-1		0-1
Kansas City	7-3						0-1	0-1	1-0	1-0	1-1	1-0	2-0	1-0
L. A. Raiders	19-2-1	1-0	2-1	3-0	2-0	1-0	2-0	2-0	2-0	0-1	0-0-1	2-0	1-0	1-0
Miami	15-8	1-1	1-1	1-1	0-2	2-1	1-0	1-1	1-1	2-0	2-0	1-0	1-0	1-0
New England	2-10		0-1	1-2	0-2	0-2	0-1	1-0	0-1			0-1		
New York Jets	3-8	1-0		1-0	1-1			0-1	0-1	0-1	0-1	0-1	0-1	0-1
Pittsburgh	12-8	1-0	1-1	0-2	2-1	1-1	2-0	0-1	1-0	2-0	1-1		0-1	1-0
San Diego	8-4	1-1	2-1	1-0	1-0	1-0			1-0			0-1	1-0	0-1
Seattle	3-1		1-0	0-1	2-0									
Atlanta	5-8		1-2		1-2	1-0				0-1	1-1	0-1	1-0	0-1
Chicago	4-10		0-2	1-1		0-3	1-0		1-1	1-0	0-1	1-0	0-1	0-1
Dallas	11-11	1-2	2-0	1-1	0-2	1-1	1-1	1-0	1-1	0-1	1-1	1-0	0-1	0-1
Detroit	5-5-1	0-1	1-0						0-1	1-0	1-0	0-2	0-1-1	2-0
Green Bay	5-6-1	1-0			1-0		0-1		0-1	0-1	1-1	1-0	0-1-1	1-1
L. A. Rams	10-10		2-0	2-0	1-0	0-2	1-1	0-2	1-0	1-1	1-0	1-0	0-2	0-2
Minnesota	9-9	1-0	0-3		0-1	2-0	0-1	1-1	1-0	1-0	0-1	0-2	2-0	1-0
New Orleans	0-5			0-1	0-1						0-1	0-1	0-1	
New York Giants	2-7	0-1		0-1	0-1		0-1		1-0			0-1	1-0	0-1	0-1
Philadelphia	5-5		1-1	1-0	1-1			0-1	0-1	1-0		0-1		1-0
St. Louis	4-5						2-0	0-1	0-1	0-1		0-1	1-1	1-0
San Francisco	3-7					0-1	0-2	2-0		0-2	1-0	0-1	0-1	
Tampa Bay	1-1	1-0		0-1										
Washington	12-6			0-2	1-0	1-1	1-1	2-0	1-0	2-0	1-1	2-0	1-0	0-1

Monday Night Syndrome

1982

Of the 8 winning teams:
- 7 won the next week
- 1 lost the next week
- 0 tied the next week

Of the 8 losing teams:
- 5 won the next week
- 3 lost the next week
- 0 tied the next week

Of the 16 NFL teams:
- 12 won the next week
- 4 lost the next week
- 0 tied the next week

1970-82

Of the 170 winning teams:
- 97 won the next week
- 70 lost the next week
- 3 tied the next week

Of the 170 losing teams:
- 87 won the next week
- 82 lost the next week
- 1 tied the next week

Of the 4 tying teams:
- 4 won the next week
- 0 lost the next week

Of the 344 NFL teams:
- 188 won the next week
- 152 lost the next week
- 4 tied the next week

Thursday-Sunday Night Football, 1978-1982

(Home Team in capitals, games listed in chronological order.)

1982
BUFFALO 23, Minnesota 22 (Thur.)
SAN FRANCISCO 30, Los Angeles Rams 24 (Thur.)
ATLANTA 17, San Francisco 7 (Sun.)

1981
MIAMI 30, Pittsburgh 10 (Thur.)
Philadelphia 20, BUFFALO 14 (Thur.)
DALLAS 29, Los Angeles 17 (Sun.)
HOUSTON 17, Cleveland 13 (Thur.)

1980
TAMPA BAY 10, Los Angeles 9 (Thur.)
DALLAS 42, San Diego 31 (Sun.)
San Diego 27, MIAMI 24 (OT) (Thur.)
HOUSTON 6, Pittsburgh 0 (Thur.)

1979
Los Angeles 13, DENVER 9 (Thur.)
DALLAS 30, Los Angeles 6 (Sun.)
OAKLAND 45, San Diego 22 (Thur.)
MIAMI 39, New England 24 (Thur.)

1978
New England 21, OAKLAND 14 (Sun.)
Minnesota 21, DALLAS 10 (Thur.)
LOS ANGELES 10, Pittsburgh 7 (Sun.)
Denver 21, OAKLAND 6 (Sun.)

AFC vs. NFC (Regular Season), 1970-1982

	1970	1971	1972	1973	1974	1975	1976	1977	1978	1979	1980	1981	1982	Totals
Miami	2-1	3-0	3-0	3-0	2-1	3-0	0-2	2-0	3-1	4-0	4-0	3-1	1-1	33-7
L.A. Raiders	1-2	1-1-1	3-0	2-1	3-0	3-0	3-0	1-1	4-0	4-0	2-2	2-2	3-0	32-9-1
Pittsburgh	0-3	1-2	2-1	3-0	3-0	2-1	1-1	2-0	3-1	3-1	4-0	3-1	1-0	28-11
Cincinnati	1-2	1-2	2-1	2-1	2-1	3-0	2-0	2-1	2-2	2-2	2-2	2-2	1-0	24-16
Denver	2-2	1-3	1-3	0-3-1	2-2	2-1	2-0	1-1	2-2	3-1	3-1	3-1	2-1	24-21-1
Cleveland	0-3	2-1	1-2	1-2	1-2	1-3	2-0	1-1	4-0	3-1	3-1	3-1	0-2	22-19
New England	0-3	0-3	3-0	2-1	3-0	1-2	1-1	2-0	2-2	3-1	1-3	0-4	0-1	18-21
San Diego	1-2	2-1	0-3	1-2	1-2	0-3	2-0	1-1	2-2	3-1	2-2	2-2	1-0	18-21
N.Y. Jets	2-1	0-3	1-2	0-3	2-1	0-3	0-2	1-1	1-3	3-1	1-3	2-0	4-0	17-23
Buffalo	0-3	0-3	2-0-1	2-1	2-1	1-2	0-2	1-1	1-1	2-2	3-1	1-3	1-2	16-22-1
Houston	0-3	0-2-1	0-3	0-3	0-3	3-0	2-0	2-0	2-2	2-2	4-0	1-3	0-3	16-24-1
Baltimore	3-0	2-1	0-3	2-1	1-2	2-1	0-2	1-1	2-2	1-1	1-1	0-4	0-1-1	15-20-1
Kansas City	0-2-1	2-1	2-1	1-1-1	1-2	2-1	1-1	1-1	0-2	0-2	2-0	2-2	0-3	14-19-2
Seattle								1-0	3-1	3-1	1-3	0-2	1-0	9-7
Tampa Bay								0-1						0-1
TOTALS	12-27-1	15-23-2	20-19-1	19-19-2	23-17	23-17	16-12	19-9	31-21	36-16	33-19	24-28	15-14-1	286-241-7

NFC vs. AFC (Regular Season), 1970-1982

	1970	1971	1972	1973	1974	1975	1976	1977	1978	1979	1980	1981	1982	Totals
Dallas	3-0	3-0	3-0	2-1	2-1	2-1	2-0	1-1	3-1	1-3	3-1	4-0	2-1	31-10
L.A. Rams	2-1	1-2	1-2	3-0	3-1	3-0	1-1	2-0	2-2	2-2	2-2	1-3	1-2	24-18
Philadelphia	2-1	1-2	2-1	2-1	2-1	0-3	0-2	1-1	3-1	2-2	3-1	3-1	2-1	23-18
Minnesota	2-1	2-1	1-2	2-1	2-1	4-0	2-0	1-1	1-3	1-3	1-3	1-3	1-3	21-22
Detroit	3-0	4-0	2-0-1	0-3	1-2	1-2	2-0	2-0	2-2	0-4	0-2	2-2	0-1	19-18-1
Washington	2-1	1-2	1-2	2-1	2-1	1-2	1-1	1-1	2-2	2-2	1-3	2-2		18-20
San Francisco	4-0	2-1	2-1	1-2	0-3	1-2	1-1	0-2	1-3	0-4	2-2	3-1	1-3	18-25
St. Louis	2-0-1	2-1	1-2	0-2-1	2-1	2-1	1-1	0-2	0-4	1-3	1-1	3-1		15-19-2
Green Bay	2-1	2-1	2-1	1-1-1	2-1	0-3	0-2	0-3	2-2	1-3	1-3	1-1	1-1-1	15-23-2
Atlanta	1-2	3-0	2-2	2-1	0-3	1-2	0-2	0-2	1-3	1-3	2-2	1-3	1-1	15-26
N.Y. Giants	3-0	1-2	1-2	1-2	2-1	2-1	0-2	0-2	1-1	1-1	1-3	1-1	1-0	14-19
Chicago	1-2	1-2	1-2	2-2	0-3	0-3	0-2	1-1	0-4	2-2	0-4	4-0	1-1	13-28
New Orleans	0-3	0-1-2	0-3	1-2	0-3	0-3	1-2	0-2	1-3	0-4	1-3	2-2	1-0	7-31-2
Tampa Bay								0-1	2-0	2-0	1-3	0-4	2-1	7-9
Seattle							1-0							1-0
TOTALS	27-12-1	23-15-2	19-20-1	19-19-2	17-23	17-23	12-16	9-19	21-31	16-36	19-33	28-24	14-15-1	241-286-7

Regular Season Interconference Records, 1970-1982

American Football Conference

Eastern Division

	W	L	T	Pct.
Miami	33	7	0	.825
New England	18	21	0	.462
Baltimore	15	20	1	.431
New York Jets	17	23	0	.425
Buffalo	16	22	1	.423

Central Division

	W	L	T	Pct.
Pittsburgh	28	11	0	.718
Cincinnati	24	16	0	.600
Cleveland	22	19	0	.537
Houston	16	24	0	.402

Western Division

	W	L	T	Pct.
Los Angeles Raiders	32	9	1	.774
Seattle	9	7	0	.563
Denver	24	21	1	.533
San Diego	18	21	0	.462
Kansas City	14	19	2	.429

National Football Conference

Eastern Division

	W	L	T	Pct.
Dallas	31	10	0	.756
Philadelphia	23	18	0	.561
Washington	18	20	0	.474
St. Louis	15	19	2	.444
New York Giants	14	19	0	.424

Central Division

	W	L	T	Pct.
Detroit	19	18	1	.513
Minnesota	21	22	0	.488
Tampa Bay	7	9	0	.438
Green Bay	15	23	2	.400
Chicago	13	28	0	.317

Western Division

	W	L	T	Pct.
Los Angeles Rams	24	18	0	.571
San Francisco	18	25	0	.419
Atlanta	15	26	0	.366
New Orleans	7	31	2	.200

Interconference Victories, 1970-1982

Regular Season

	AFC	NFC	Tie
1970	12	27	1
1971	15	23	2
1972	20	19	1
1973	19	19	2
1974	23	17	0
1975	23	17	0
1976	16	12	0
1977	19	9	0
1978	31	21	0
1979	36	16	0
1980	33	19	0
1981	24	28	0
1982	15	14	1
Total	286	241	7

Preseason

	AFC	NFC	Tie
1970	21	28	1
1971	28	28	3
1972	27	25	4
1973	23	35	2
1974	35	25	0
1975	30	26	1
1976	30	31	0
1977	38	25	0
1978	20	19	0
1979	25	18	0
1980	22	20	1
1981	18	19	0
1982	25	16	0
Total	342	315	12

1982 Interconference Games
(Home Team in capital letters.)

AFC 15, NFC 14, 1 Tie

AFC Victories

Los Angeles Raiders 23, SAN FRANCISCO 17
Pittsburgh 36, DALLAS 28
BUFFALO 23, Minnesota 22
Los Angeles Raiders 38, ATLANTA 14
DENVER 24, San Francisco 21
Cincinnati 18, PHILADELPHIA 14
NEW YORK JETS 15, Green Bay 13
MIAMI 22, Minnesota 14
NEW YORK JETS 28, Detroit 13
San Diego 41, SAN FRANCISCO 37
SEATTLE 20, Chicago 14
Denver 27, LOS ANGELES RAMS 24
NEW YORK JETS 32, Tampa Bay 17
LOS ANGELES RAIDERS 37, Los Angeles Rams 31
NEW YORK JETS 44, Minnesota 14

NFC Victories

Philadelphia 24, CLEVELAND 21
NEW ORLEANS 27, Kansas City 17
DALLAS 31, Cleveland 14
LOS ANGELES RAMS 20, Kansas City 14
TAMPA BAY 23, Miami 17
Atlanta 34, DENVER 27
GREEN BAY 33, Buffalo 21
NEW YORK GIANTS 17, Houston 14
CHICAGO 26, New England 13
MINNESOTA 13, Baltimore 10
Dallas 37, HOUSTON 7
TAMPA BAY 24, Buffalo 23
PHILADELPHIA 35, Houston 14
San Francisco 26, KANSAS CITY 13

Ties

BALTIMORE 20, Green Bay 20

1982 Paid Attendance Breakdown

	Games	Attendance	Average
AFC Preseason	8	441,276	
NFC Preseason	8	504,193	
AFC-NFC Preseason, Interconference	41	2,182,426	
NFL Preseason Total	**57**	**3,127,895**	**54,875**
AFC Regular Season	48	2,570,522	
NFC Regular Season	48	2,940,101	
AFC-NFC Regular Season, Interconference	30	1,856,815	
NFL Regular Season Total	**126**	**7,367,438**	**58,472**
AFC First Round Playoff	4		
(New England at Miami)		70,881	
(Cleveland at Los Angeles Raiders)		55,746	
(New York Jets at Cincinnati)		58,670	
(San Diego at Pittsburgh)		52,628	
AFC Second Round Playoffs	2		
(New York Jets at Los Angeles Raiders)		88,838	
(San Diego at Miami)		73,772	
AFC Championship	1		
(New York Jets at Miami)		74,918	
NFC First Round Playoff	4		
(Detroit at Washington)		54,117	
(St. Louis at Green Bay)		54,764	
(Atlanta at Minnesota)		61,439	
(Tampa Bay at Dallas)		63,648	
NFC Second Round Playoffs	2		
(Minnesota at Washington)		54,117	
(Green Bay at Dallas)		63,702	
NFC Championship	1		
(Dallas at Washington)		55,045	
Super Bowl XVII at Pasadena, Calif.	1		
(Miami vs. Washington)		103,667	
AFC-NFC Pro Bowl at Honolulu, Hawaii	1	47,201	
NFL Postseason Total	**16**	**1,033,153**	**64,572**
NFL All Games	**199**	**11,528,486**	**57,932**

NFL's 10 Biggest Weekends

(Turnstile Count)

Weekend	Games	Attendance
October 12, 1980	14	875,466
September 6, 1981	14	865,699
September 12, 1982	14	862,954
September 19, 1982	14	850,358
September 23, 1979	14	848,777
November 2, 1980	14	844,884
November 1, 1981	14	842,978
September 27, 1981	14	841,514
October 4, 1981	14	839,776
September 21, 1980	14	839,328

NFL Paid Attendance

Year	Regular Season	Average	Post-season*	Super Bowl
1982*	7,367,438 (126 games)	58,472	1,033,153 (16)	103,667
1981	13,606,990 (224 games)	60,745	637,763 (10)	81,270
1980	13,392,230 (224 games)	59,787	624,430 (10)	75,500
1979	13,182,039 (224 games)	58,848	630,326 (10)	103,985
1978	12,771,800 (224 games)	57,017	624,388 (10)	79,641
1977	11,018,632 (196 games)	56,218	534,925 (8)	75,804
1976	11,070,543 (196 games)	56,482	492,884 (8)	103,438
1975	10,213,193 (182 games)	56,116	475,919 (8)	80,187
1974	10,236,322 (182 games)	56,244	438,664 (8)	80,997
1973	10,730,933 (182 games)	58,961	525,433 (8)	71,882
1972	10,445,827 (182 games)	57,395	483,345 (8)	90,182
1971	10,076,035 (182 games)	55,363	483,891 (8)	81,023
1970	9,533,333 (182 games)	52,381	458,493 (8)	79,204
1969	6,096,127 (127 games) NFL	54,430	162,279 (3)	80,562
	2,843,373 (70 games) AFL	40,620	167,088 (3)	
1968	5,882,313 (112 games) NFL	52,521	215,902 (3)	75,377
	2,635,004 (70 games) AFL	37,643	114,438 (2)	
1967	5,938,924 (112 games) NFL	53,026	166,208 (3)	75,546
	2,295,697 (63 games) AFL	36,439	53,330 (1)	
1966	5,337,044 (105 games) NFL	50,829	74,152 (1)	61,946**
	2,160,369 (63 games) AFL	34,291	42,080 (1)	
1965	4,634,021 (98 games) NFL	47,286	100,304 (2)	
	1,782,384 (56 games) AFL	31,828	30,361 (1)	
1964	4,563,049 (98 games) NFL	46,562	79,544 (1)	
	1,447,875 (56 games) AFL	25,855	40,242 (1)	
1963	4,163,643 (98 games) NFL	42,486	45,801 (1)	
	1,208,697 (56 games) AFL	21,584	63,171 (2)	
1962	4,003,421 (98 games) NFL	40,851	64,892 (1)	
	1,147,302 (56 games) AFL	20,487	37,981 (1)	
1961	3,986,159 (98 games) NFL	40,675	39,029 (1)	
	1,002,657 (56 games) AFL	17,904	29,556 (1)	
1960	3,128,296 (78 games) NFL	40,106	67,325 (1)	
	926,156 (56 games) AFL	16,538	32,183 (1)	
1959	3,140,000 (72 games)	43,617	57,545 (1)	
1958	3,006,124 (72 games)	41,752	123,659 (2)	
1957	2,836,318 (72 games)	39,393	119,579 (2)	
1956	2,551,263 (72 games)	35,434	56,836 (1)	
1955	2,521,836 (72 games)	35,026	85,693 (1)	
1954	2,190,571 (72 games)	30,425	43,827 (1)	
1953	2,164,585 (72 games)	30,064	54,577 (1)	
1952	2,052,126 (72 games)	28,502	97,507 (2)	
1951	1,913,019 (72 games)	26,570	57,522 (1)	
1950	1,977,753 (78 games)	25,356	136,647 (3)	
1949	1,391,735 (60 games)	23,196	27,980 (1)	
1948	1,525,243 (60 games)	25,421	36,309 (1)	
1947	1,837,437 (60 games)	30,624	66,268 (2)	
1946	1,732,135 (55 games)	31,493	58,346 (1)	
1945	1,270,401 (50 games)	25,408	32,178 (1)	
1944	1,019,649 (50 games)	20,393	46,016 (1)	
1943	969,128 (50 games)	19,383	71,315 (2)	
1942	887,920 (55 games)	16,144	36,006 (1)	
1941	1,108,615 (55 games)	20,157	55,870 (2)	
1940	1,063,025 (55 games)	19,328	36,034 (1)	
1939	1,071,200 (55 games)	19,476	32,279 (1)	
1938	937,197 (55 games)	17,040	48,120 (1)	
1937	963,039 (55 games)	17,510	15,878 (1)	
1936	816,007 (54 games)	15,111	29,545 (1)	
1935	638,178 (53 games)	12,041	15,000 (1)	
1934	492,684 (60 games)	8,211	35,059 (1)	

*Players 57-day strike reduced 224-game schedule to 126 games.
**Only Super Bowl that did not sell out.

History of Overtime Games

Preseason

Aug. 28, 1955	Los Angeles 23, New York Giants 17, at Portland, Oregon
Aug. 24, 1962	Denver 27, Dallas Texans 24, at Fort Worth, Texas
Aug. 10, 1974	San Diego 20, New York Jets 14, at San Diego
Aug. 17, 1974	Pittsburgh 33, Philadelphia 30, at Philadelphia
Aug. 17, 1974	Dallas 19, Houston 13, at Dallas
Aug. 17, 1974	Cincinnati 13, Atlanta 7, at Atlanta
Sept. 6, 1974	Buffalo 23, New York Giants 17, at Buffalo
Aug. 9, 1975	Baltimore 23, Denver 20, at Denver
Aug. 30, 1975	New England 20, Green Bay 17, at Milwaukee
Sept. 13, 1975	Minnesota 14, San Diego 14, at San Diego
Aug. 1, 1976	New England 13, New York Giants 7, at New England
Aug. 2, 1976	Kansas City 9, Houston 3, at Kansas City
Aug. 20, 1976	New Orleans 26, Baltimore 20, at Baltimore
Sept. 4, 1976	Dallas 26, Houston 20, at Dallas
Aug. 13, 1977	Seattle 23, Dallas 17, at Seattle
Aug. 28, 1977	New England 13, Pittsburgh 10, at New England
Aug. 28, 1977	New York Giants 24, Buffalo 21, at East Rutherford, N.J.
Aug. 2, 1979	Seattle 12, Minnesota 9, at Minnesota
Aug. 4, 1979	Los Angeles 20, Oakland 14, at Los Angeles
Aug. 24, 1979	Denver 20, New England 17, at Denver
Aug. 23, 1980	Tampa Bay 20, Cincinnati 14, at Tampa Bay
Aug. 5, 1981	San Francisco 27, Seattle 24, at Seattle
Aug. 29, 1981	New Orleans 20, Detroit 17, at New Orleans
Aug. 28, 1982	Miami 17, Kansas City 17, at Kansas City
Sept. 3, 1982	Miami 16, New York Giants 13, at Miami

Regular Season

Sept. 22, 1974—Pittsburgh 35, Denver 35, at Denver; Steelers win toss. Gilliam's pass intercepted and returned by Rowser to Denver's 42. Turner misses 41-yard field goal. Walden punts and Greer returns to Broncos' 39. Van Heusen punts and Edwards returns to Steelers' 16. Game ends with Steelers on own 26.

Nov. 10, 1974—New York Jets 26, New York Giants 20, at New Haven, Conn.; Giants win toss. Gogolak misses 42-yard field goal. Namath passes to Boozer for five yards and touchdown at 6:53.

Sept. 28, 1975—Dallas 37, St. Louis 31, at Dallas; Cardinals win toss. Hart's pass intercepted and returned by Jordan to Cardinals' 37. Staubach passes to DuPree for three yards and touchdown at 7:53.

Oct. 12, 1975—Los Angeles 13, San Diego 10, at San Diego; Chargers win toss. Partee punts to Rams' 14. Dempsey kicks 22-yard field goal at 9:27.

Nov. 2, 1975—Washington 30, Dallas 24, at Washington; Cowboys win toss. Staubach's pass intercepted and returned by Houston to Cowboys' 35. Kilmer runs one yard for touchdown at 6:34.

Nov. 16, 1975—St. Louis 20, Washington 17, at St. Louis; Cardinals win toss. Bakken kicks 37-yard field goal at 7:00.

Nov. 23, 1975—Kansas City 24, Detroit 21, at Kansas City; Lions win toss. Chiefs take over on downs at own 38. Stenerud kicks 26-yard field goal at 6:44.

Nov. 23, 1975—Oakland 26, Washington 23, at Washington; Redskins win toss. Bragg punts to Raiders' 42. Blanda kicks 27-yard field goal at 7:13.

Nov. 30, 1975—Denver 13, San Diego 10, at Denver; Broncos win toss. Turner kicks 25-yard field goal at 4:13.

Nov. 30, 1975—Oakland 37, Atlanta 34, at Oakland; Falcons win toss. James punts to Raiders' 16. Guy punts and Herron returns to Falcons' 41. Nick Mike-Mayer misses 45-yard field goal. Guy punts into Falcons' end zone. James punts to Raiders' 39. Blanda kicks 36-yard field goal at 15:00.

Dec. 14, 1975—Baltimore 10, Miami 7, at Baltimore; Dolphins win toss. Seiple punts to Colts' 4. Linhart kicks 31-yard field goal at 12:44.

Sept. 19, 1976—Minnesota 10, Los Angeles 10, at Minnesota; Vikings win toss. Tarkenton's pass intercepted by Monte Jackson and returned to Minnesota 16. Allen blocks Dempsey's 30-yard field goal attempt, ball rolls into end zone for touchback. Clabo punts and Scribner returns to Rams' 20. Rusty Jackson punts to Vikings' 35. Tarkenton's pass intercepted by Kay at Rams' 1, no return. Game ends with Rams on own 3.

Sept. 27, 1976—Washington 20, Philadelphia 17, at Philadelphia; Eagles win toss. Jones punts and Eddie Brown loses one yard on return to Redskins' 40. Bragg punts 51 yards into end zone for touchback. Jones punts and Eddie Brown returns to Redskins' 42. Bragg punts and Marshall returns to Eagles' 41. Boryla's pass intercepted by Dusek at Redskins' 37, no return. Bragg punts and Bradley returns, Philadelphia holding penalty moves ball back to Eagles' 8. Boryla pass intercepted by Eddie Brown and returned to Eagles' 22. Moseley kicks 29-yard field goal at 12:49.

Oct. 17, 1976—Kansas City 20, Miami 17, at Miami; Chiefs win toss. Wilson punts into end zone for touchback. Bulaich fumbles into Kansas City end zone, Collier recovers for touchback. Stenerud kicks 34-yard field goal at 14:48.

Oct. 31, 1976—St. Louis 23, San Francisco 20, at St. Louis; Cardinals win toss. Joyce punts and Leonard fumbles on return, Jones recovers at 49ers' 43. Bakken kicks 21-yard field goal at 6:42.

Dec. 5, 1976—San Diego 13, San Francisco 7, at San Diego; Chargers win toss. Morris runs 13 yards for touchdown at 5:12.

Sept. 18, 1977—Dallas 16, Minnesota 10, at Minnesota; Vikings win toss. Dallas starts on Vikings' 47 after a punt early in the overtime period. Staubach scores seven plays later on a four-yard run at 6:14.

Sept. 26, 1977—Cleveland 30, New England 27, at Cleveland; Browns win toss. Sipe throws a 22-yard pass to Logan at Patriots' 19. Cockroft kicks 35-yard field goal at 4:45.

Oct. 16, 1977—Minnesota 22, Chicago 16, at Minnesota; Bears win toss. Parsons punts 53 yards to Vikings' 18. Minnesota drives to Bears' 11. On a first-and-10, Vikings fake a field goal and holder Krause hits Voigt with a touchdown pass at 6:45.

Oct. 30, 1977—Cincinnati 13, Houston 10, at Cincinnati; Bengals win toss. Bahr kicks a 22-yard field goal at 5:51.

Nov. 13, 1977—San Francisco 10, New Orleans 7, at New Orleans; Saints win toss. Saints fail to move ball and Blanchard punts to 49ers' 41. Wersching kicks a 33-yard field goal at 6:33.

Dec. 18, 1977—Chicago 12, New York Giants 9, at East Rutherford, N.J.; Giants win toss. The ball changes hands eight times before Thomas kicks a 28-yard field goal at 14:51.

Sept. 10, 1978—Cleveland 13, Cincinnati 10, at Cleveland; Browns win toss. Collins returns kickoff 41 yards to the Browns' 47. Cockroft kicks 27-yard field goal at 4:30.

Sept. 11, 1978—Minnesota 12, Denver 9, at Minnesota; Vikings win toss. Danmeier kicks 44-yard field goal at 2:56.

Sept. 24, 1978—Pittsburgh 15, Cleveland 9, at Pittsburgh; Steelers win toss. Cunningham scores on a 37-yard "gadget" pass from Bradshaw at 3:43. Steelers start winning drive on their 21.

Sept. 24, 1978—Denver 23, Kansas City 17, at Kansas City; Denver wins toss. Dilts punts to Kansas City. Chiefs advance to Broncos' 40 where Reed fails to make first down on fourth-and-one situation. Broncos march downfield. Preston scores two-yard touchdown at 10:28.

Oct. 1, 1978—Oakland 25, Chicago 19, at Chicago; Chicago wins toss. Both teams punt on first possession. On Chicago's second offensive series, Colzie intercepts Avellini's pass and returns it to Bears' 3. Three plays later, Whittington runs two yards for a touchdown at 5:19.

Oct. 15, 1978—Dallas 24, St. Louis 21, at St. Louis; Cowboys win toss. Dallas drives from its 23 into field goal range. Septien kicks 27-yard field goal at 3:28.

Oct. 29, 1978—Denver 20, Seattle 17, at Seattle; Broncos win toss. Ball changes hands four times before Turner kicks 18-yard field goal at 12:59.

Nov. 12, 1978—San Diego 29, Kansas City 23, at San Diego; Chiefs win toss. Fouts hits Jefferson for decisive 14-yard touchdown pass on the last play (15:00) of overtime period.

Nov. 12, 1978—Washington 16, New York Giants 13, at Washington; Redskins win toss. Moseley kicks winning 45-yard field goal at 8:32 after missing first down field goal attempt of 35 yards at 4:50.

Nov. 26, 1978—Green Bay 10, Minnesota 10, at Green Bay; Packers win toss. Both teams have possession of the ball four times.

Dec. 9, 1978—Cleveland 37, New York Jets 34, at Cleveland; Browns win toss. Cockroft kicks 22-yard field goal at 3:07.

Sept. 2, 1979—Atlanta 40, New Orleans 34, at New Orleans; Falcons win toss. Bartkowski's pass intercepted by Myers and returned to Falcons' 46. Erxleben punts to Falcons' 4. James punts to Chandler on Saints' 43. Erxleben punts and Ryckman returns to Falcons' 28. James punts and Chandler returns to Saints' 36. Erxleben retrieves punt snap on Saints' 1 and attempts pass. Mayberry intercepts and returns six yards for touchdown at 8:22.

Sept. 2, 1979—Cleveland 25, New York Jets 22, at New York; Jets win toss. Leahy's 43-yard field goal attempt goes wide right at 4:41. Evans's punt blocked by Dykes is recovered by Newton. Ramsey punts into end zone for touchback. Evans punts and Harper returns to Jets' 24. Robinson's pass intercepted by Davis and returned 33 yards to Jets' 31. Cockroft kicks 27-yard field goal at 14:45.

Sept. 3, 1979—Pittsburgh 16, New England 13, at Foxboro; Patriots win toss. Hare punts to Swann at Steelers' 31. Bahr kicks 41-yard field goal at 5:10.

Sept. 9, 1979—Tampa Bay 29, Baltimore 26, at Baltimore; Colts win toss. Landry fumbles, recovered by Kollar at Colts' 14. O'Donoghue kicks 31-yard, first-down field goal at 1:41.

Sept. 15, 1979—Denver 20, Atlanta 17, at Atlanta; Broncos win toss. Broncos march 65 yards to Falcons' 7. Turner kicks 24-yard field goal at 6:15.

Sept. 23, 1979—Houston 30, Cincinnati 27, at Cincinnati; Oilers win toss. Parsley punts and Lusby returns to Bengals' 33. Bahr's 32-yard field goal attempt is wide right at 8:05. Parsley's punt downed on Bengals' 5. McInally punts and Ellender returns to Bengals' 42. Fritsch's third down, 29-yard field goal attempt hits left upright and bounces through at 14:28.

Sept. 23, 1979—Minnesota 27, Green Bay 21, at Minnesota; Vikings win toss. Kramer throws 50-yard touchdown pass to Rashad at 3:18.

Oct. 28, 1979—Houston 27, New York Jets 24, at Houston; Oilers win toss. Oilers march 58 yards to Jets' 18. Fritsch kicks 35-yard field goal at 5:10.

Nov. 18, 1979—Cleveland 30, Miami 24, at Cleveland; Browns win toss. Sipe passes 39 yards to Rucker for touchdown at 1:59.

Nov. 25, 1979—Pittsburgh 33, Cleveland 30, at Pittsburgh; Browns win toss. Sipe's pass intercepted by Blount on Steelers' 4. Bradshaw pass intercepted by Bolton on Browns' 12. Evans punts and Bell returns to Steelers' 17. Bahr kicks 37-yard field goal at 14:51.

Nov. 25, 1979—Buffalo 16, New England 13, at Foxboro; Patriots win toss. Hare's punt downed on Bills' 38. Jackson punts and Morgan returns to Patriots' 20. Grogan's pass intercepted by Haslett and returned to Bills' 42. Ferguson's 51-yard pass to Butler sets up N. Mike-Mayer's 29-yard field goal at 9:15.

Dec. 2, 1979—Los Angeles 27, Minnesota 21, at Los Angeles; Rams win toss. Clark punts and Miller returns to Vikings' 25. Kramer's pass intercepted by Brown and returned to Rams' 40. Cromwell, holding for 22-yard field goal attempt, runs around left end untouched for winning score at 6:53.

Sept. 7, 1980—Green Bay 12, Chicago 6, at Green Bay; Bears win toss. Parsons punts and Nixon returns 16 yards. Five plays later, Marcol returns own blocked field goal attempt 24 yards for touchdown at 6:00.

Sept. 14, 1980—San Diego 30, Oakland 24, at San Diego; Raiders win toss. Pastorini's first-down pass intercepted by Edwards. Millen intercepts Fouts's first-down pass and returns to San Diego 46. Bahr's 50-yard field goal attempt partially blocked by Williams and recovered on Chargers' 32. Eight plays later, Fouts throws 24-yard touchdown pass to Jefferson at 8:09.

Sept. 14, 1980—San Francisco 24, St. Louis 21, at San Francisco; Cardinals win toss. Swider punts and Robinson returns to 49ers' 32. San Francisco drives 52 yards to St. Louis 16, where Wersching kicks 33-yard field goal at 4:12.

Oct. 12, 1980—Green Bay 14, Tampa Bay 14, at Tampa Bay; Packers win toss. Teams trade punts twice. Lee returns second Tampa Bay punt to Green Bay 42. Dickey completes three passes to Buccaneers' 18, where Birney's 36-yard field goal attempt is wide right as time expires.

Nov. 9, 1980—Atlanta 33, St. Louis 27, at St. Louis; Falcons win toss. Strong runs 21 yards for touchdown at 4:20.

Nov. 20, 1980—San Diego 27, Miami 24, at Miami; Chargers win toss. Partridge punts into end zone, Dolphins take over on their own 20. Woodley's pass for Nathan intercepted by Lowe and returned 28 yards to Dolphins' 12. Benirschke kicks 28-yard field goal at 7:14.

Nov. 23, 1980—**New York Jets 31, Houston 28,** at New York; Jets win toss. Leahy kicks 38-yard field goal at 3:58.

Nov. 27, 1980—**Chicago 23, Detroit 17,** at Detroit; Bears win toss. Williams returns kickoff 95 yards for touchdown at :21.

Dec. 7, 1980—**Buffalo 10, Los Angeles 7,** at Buffalo; Rams win toss. Corral punts and Hooks returns to Bills' 34. Ferguson's 30-yard pass to Lewis sets up N. Mike-Mayer's 30-yard field goal at 5:14.

Dec. 7, 1980—**San Francisco 38, New Orleans 35,** at San Francisco; Saints win toss. Erxleben's punt downed by Hardy on 49ers' 27. Wersching kicks 36-yard field goal at 7:40.

Dec. 8, 1980—**Miami 16, New England 13,** at Miami; Dolphins win toss. Von Schamann kicks 23-yard field goal at 3:20.

Dec. 14, 1980—**Cincinnati 17, Chicago 14,** at Chicago; Bengals win toss. Breech kicks 28-yard field goal at 4:23.

Dec. 21, 1980—**Los Angeles 20, Atlanta 17,** at Los Angeles; Rams win toss. Corral's punt downed at Rams' 37. James punts into end zone for touchback. Corral's punt downed on Falcons' 17. Bartkowski fumbles when hit by Harris, recovered by Delaney. Corral kicks 23-yard field goal on first play of possession at 7:00.

Sept. 27, 1981—**Cincinnati 27, Buffalo 24,** at Cincinnati; Bills win toss. Cater punts into end zone for touchback. Bengals drive to the Bills' 10 yard line where Breech kicks 28-yard field goal at 9:33.

Sept. 27, 1981—**Pittsburgh 27, New England 21,** at Pittsburgh; Patriots win toss. Hubach punts and Smith returns five yards to midfield. Four plays later Bradshaw throws 24-yard touchdown pass to Swann at 3:19.

Oct. 4, 1981—**Miami 28, New York Jets 28,** at Miami; Jets win toss. Teams trade punts twice. Leahy's 48-yard field goal attempt is wide right as time expires.

Oct. 25, 1981—**New York Giants 27, Atlanta 24,** at Atlanta; Giants win toss. Jennings's punt goes out of bounds at New York 47. Bright returns Atlanta punt to Giants' 14. Woerner fair catches punt at own 28. Andrews fumbles on first play, recovered by Van Pelt. Danelo kicks 40-yard field goal four plays later at 9:20.

Oct. 25, 1981—**Chicago 20, San Diego 17,** at Chicago; Bears win toss. Teams trade punts. Bears' second punt returned by Brooks to Chargers' 33. Fouts pass intercepted by Fencik and returned 32 yards to San Diego 27. Roveto kicks 27-yard field goal seven plays later at 9:30.

Nov. 8, 1981—**Chicago 16, Kansas City 13,** at Kansas City; Bears win toss. Teams trade punts. Kansas City takes over on downs on their own 38. Fuller's fumble recovered by Harris on Chicago 36. Roveto's 37-yard field goal wide, but Chiefs penalized for leverage. Roveto's 22-yard field goal attempt three plays later is good at 13:07.

Nov. 8, 1981—**Denver 23, Cleveland 20,** at Denver; Browns win toss. D. Smith recovers Hill's fumble at Denver 48. Morton's 33-yard pass to Upchurch and six-yard run by Preston set up Steinfort's 30-yard field goal at 4:10.

Nov. 8, 1981—**Miami 30, New England 27,** at New England; Dolphins win toss. Orosz punts and Morgan returns six yards to New England 26. Grogan's pass intercepted by Brudzinski who returns 19 yards to Patriots' 26. Von Schamann kicks 30-yard field goal on first down at 7:09.

Nov. 15, 1981—**Washington 30, New York Giants 27,** at New York; Giants win toss. Nelms returns Giants' punt 26 yards to New York 47. Five plays later Moseley kicks 48-yard field goal at 3:44.

Dec. 20, 1981—**New York Giants 13, Dallas 10,** at New York; Cowboys win toss and kick off. Jennings punts to Dallas 40. Taylor recovers Dorsett's fumble on second down. Danelo's 33-yard field goal attempt hits right upright and bounces back. White's pass for Pearson intercepted by Hunt and returned seven yards to Dallas 24. Four plays later Danelo kicks 35-yard field goal at 6:19.

Sept. 12, 1982—**Washington 37, Philadelphia 34,** at Philadelphia; Redskins win toss. Theismann completes five passes for 63 yards to set up Moseley's 26-yard field goal at 4:47.

Sept. 19, 1982—**Pittsburgh 26, Cincinnati 20,** at Pittsburgh; Bengals win toss. Anderson's pass intended for Kreider intercepted by Woodruff and returned 30 yards to Cincinnati 2. Bradshaw completes two-yard touchdown pass to Stallworth on first down at 1:08.

Dec. 19, 1982—**Baltimore 20, Green Bay 20,** at Baltimore; Packers win toss. K. Anderson intercepts Dickey's first-down pass and returns to Packers' 42. Miller's 44-yard field goal attempt blocked by G. Lewis. Teams trade punts before Stenerud's 47-yard field goal attempt is wide right. Teams trade punts again before time expires in Colts possession.

Jan. 2, 1983—**Tampa Bay 26, Chicago 23,** at Tampa Bay; Bears win toss. Parsons punts to T. Bell at Buccaneers' 40. Capece kicks 33-yard field goal at 3:14.

Postseason

Dec. 28, 1958—**Baltimore 23, New York Giants 17,** at New York; Giants win toss. Maynard returns kickoff to Giants' 20. Chandler punts and Taseff returns one yard to Colts' 20. Colts win at 8:15 on a one-yard run by Ameche.

Dec. 23, 1962—**Dallas Texans 20, Houston Oilers 17,** at Houston; Texans win toss and kick off. Jancik returns kickoff to Oilers' 33. Norton punts and Jackson makes fair catch on Texans' 22. Wilson punts and Jancik makes fair catch on Oilers' 45. Robinson intercepts Blanda's pass and returns 13 yards to Oilers' 47. Wilson's punt rolls dead at Oilers' 12. Hull intercepts Blanda's pass and returns 23 yards to midfield. Texans win at 17:54 on a 25-yard field goal by Brooker.

Dec. 26, 1965—**Green Bay 13, Baltimore 10,** at Green Bay; Packers win toss. Moore returns kickoff to Packers' 22. Chandler punts and Haymond returns nine yards to Colts' 41. Gilburg punts and Wood makes fair catch at Packers' 21. Chandler punts and Haymond returns one yard to Colts' 41. Michaels misses 47-yard field goal. Packers win at 13:39 on a 25-yard field goal by Chandler.

Dec. 25, 1971—**Miami 27, Kansas City 24,** at Kansas City; Chiefs win toss. Podolak, after a lateral from Buchanan, returns kickoff to Chiefs' 46. Stenerud's 42-yard field goal is blocked. Seiple punts and Podolak makes fair catch at Chiefs' 17. Wilson punts and Scott returns 18 yards to Dolphins' 39. Yepremian misses 62-yard field goal. Scott intercepts Dawson's pass and returns 13 yards to Dolphins' 46. Seiple punts and Podolak loses one yard to Chiefs' 15. Wilson punts and Scott makes fair catch on Dolphins' 30. Dolphins win at 22:40 on a 37-yard field goal by Yepremian.

Dec. 24, 1977—**Oakland 37, Baltimore 31,** at Baltimore; Baltimore wins toss. Raiders start own 42 following a punt late in the first overtime. Oakland works way into a threatening position on Stabler's 19-yard pass to Branch at the Colts' 26. Four plays later, on the second play of the second overtime, Stabler hits Casper with a 10-yard touchdown pass at 15:43.

Jan. 2, 1982—**San Diego 41, Miami 38** at Miami; San Diego wins toss. San Diego drives from its 13 to Miami 8. On second-and-goal, Benirschke misses 27-yard field goal attempt wide to left at 9:15. Miami has the ball twice and San Diego twice more before the Dolphins get their third possession. Miami drives from the San Diego 46 to Chargers' 17 and on fourth-and-two, von Schamann's 34-yard field goal attempt is blocked by San Diego's Winslow after 11:27. Fouts then completes four of five passes including a 29-yarder to Joiner that puts the ball on Dolphins' 10. On first down, Benirschke kicks a 20-yard field goal at 13:52. San Diego's winning drive covered 74 yards in six plays.

Overtime Won-Lost Records, 1974–1982 (Regular Season)

	W	L	T
Atlanta	2	4	0
Baltimore	1	1	1
Buffalo	2	1	0
Chicago	4	5	0
Cincinnati	3	3	0
Cleveland	5	3	0
Dallas	3	2	0
Denver	5	1	1
Detroit	0	2	0
Green Bay	1	1	3
Houston	2	2	0
Kansas City	2	3	0
Los Angeles Raiders	3	1	0
Los Angeles Rams	3	1	1
Miami	2	4	1
Minnesota	3	2	2
New England	0	6	0
New Orleans	0	3	0
New York Giants	2	4	0
New York Jets	2	3	1
Philadelphia	0	2	0
Pittsburgh	5	0	1
St. Louis	2	4	0
San Diego	4	3	0
San Francisco	3	2	0
Seattle	0	1	0
Tampa Bay	2	0	1
Washington	5	2	0

1982 NFL Standings

American Football Conference

	W	L	T	Pct.	Pts.	OP
*L.A. Raiders	8	1	0	.889	260	200
*Miami	7	2	0	.778	198	131
*Cincinnati	7	2	0	.778	232	177
*Pittsburgh	6	3	0	.667	204	146
*San Diego	6	3	0	.667	288	221
*N.Y. Jets	6	3	0	.667	245	166
*New England	5	4	0	.556	143	157
*Cleveland	4	5	0	.444	140	182
Buffalo	4	5	0	.444	150	154
Seattle	4	5	0	.444	127	147
Kansas City	3	6	0	.333	176	184
Denver	2	7	0	.222	148	226
Houston	1	8	0	.111	136	245
Baltimore	0	8	1	.056	113	236

**Qualifier for playoffs*

National Football Conference

	W	L	T	Pct.	Pts.	OP
*Washington	8	1	0	.889	190	128
*Dallas	6	3	0	.667	226	145
*Green Bay	5	3	1	.611	226	169
*Minnesota	5	4	0	.556	187	198
*Atlanta	5	4	0	.556	183	199
*St. Louis	5	4	0	.556	135	170
*Tampa Bay	5	4	0	.556	158	178
*Detroit	4	5	0	.444	181	176
New Orleans	4	5	0	.444	129	160
N.Y. Giants	4	5	0	.444	164	160
San Francisco	3	6	0	.333	209	206
Chicago	3	6	0	.333	141	174
Philadelphia	3	6	0	.333	191	195
L.A. Rams	2	7	0	.222	200	250

**Qualifier for playoffs*

As the result of a 57-day players strike, the 1982 NFL regular season schedule was reduced from 16 weeks to nine. At the conclusion of the regular season, the NFL conducted a 16-team postseason Super Bowl Tournament. Eight teams from each conference were seeded 1-8 based on their records during the season.

Postseason Results

(Home Team in capitals)

Saturday, January 8

AFC First-Round Playoff: L.A. RAIDERS 27, Cleveland 10
AFC First-Round Playoff: MIAMI 28, New England 13
NFC First-Round Playoff: WASHINGTON 31, Detroit 7
NFC First-Round Playoff: GREEN BAY 41, St. Louis 16

Sunday, January 9

AFC First-Round Playoff: N.Y. Jets 44, CINCINNATI 17
AFC First-Round Playoff: San Diego 31, PITTSBURGH 28
NFC First-Round Playoff: DALLAS 30, Tampa Bay 17
NFC First-Round Playoff: MINNESOTA 30, Atlanta 24

Saturday, January 15

AFC Second-Round Playoff: N.Y. Jets 17, L.A. RAIDERS 14
NFC Second-Round Playoff: WASHINGTON 21, Minnesota 7

Sunday, January 16

AFC Second-Round Playoff: MIAMI 34, San Diego 13
NFC Second-Round Playoff: DALLAS 37, Green Bay 26

Saturday, January 22

NFC Championship Game: WASHINGTON 31, Dallas 17

Sunday, January 23

AFC Championship Game: MIAMI 14, N.Y. Jets 0

Sunday, January 30

Super Bowl XVII: WASHINGTON 27, Miami 17

Sunday, February 6

AFC-NFC Pro Bowl: NFC 20, AFC 19

1982 Week by Week

Attendances as they appear in the following, and in the club-by-club sections starting on page 38, are turnstile counts and not paid attendance. Paid attendance totals are on page 15.

FIRST WEEK SUMMARY

While the National Football League was kicking off its sixty-third season, the Philadelphia Eagles and Pittsburgh Steelers were celebrating golden anniversaries with mixed results. Terry Bradshaw's three touchdown passes enabled the Steelers to beat the Cowboys 36-28 on Monday night. The loss ended Dallas's NFL-record 17 straight opening day victories. The Eagles were shown little respect by division rival Washington, which rallied from a 20-point deficit to pull out a 37-34 overtime win. Comeback victories were also registered by Green Bay, Atlanta, and the Los Angeles Raiders. In what Packer coach Bart Starr described as "the greatest comeback I've ever seen," quarterback Lynn Dickey fired a pair of fourth-quarter touchdown passes just 17 seconds apart to erase a 23-0 deficit and help Green Bay defeat the Los Angeles Rams 35-23. In San Francisco, the Super Bowl XVI champion 49ers succumbed to the Raiders 23-17. Rookie running back Marcus Allen was outstanding in his NFL debut, rushing for 116 yards. Mick Luckhurst's 29-yard field goal with 58 seconds left lifted the Falcons over the Giants 16-14. Miami ended a five-year drought at the hands of the New York Jets by winning 45-28. St. Louis was victorious on opening day for the first time since 1976, defeating New Orleans 21-7. Ken Stabler opened at quarterback for the Saints—the first quarterback other than Archie Manning to start for New Orleans on opening day in the last 12 years. Minnesota christened its new home, the Metrodome, with a 17-10 win over Tampa Bay. Quarterbacks proved to be the difference in Cincinnati and Buffalo. Ken Anderson passed for 354 yards and two touchdowns in the Bengals' win over the Oilers and two scoring passes by Joe Ferguson helped the Bills defeat Kansas City 14-9. Billy Sims returned from a brief holdout to spark Detroit over Chicago. Mike Pruitt ran for 136 yards and two scores to lead Cleveland over Seattle 21-7. Three field goals by Rolf Benirschke were all San Diego needed in a 23-3 win over Denver. Ron Meyer's head coaching debut in New England was successful as the Patriots snapped a nine-game losing streak by defeating Baltimore 24-13.

SUNDAY, SEPTEMBER 12

Atlanta 16, New York Giants 14—At Giants Stadium, attendance 74,286. Mick Luckhurst booted a 29-yard field goal with 58 seconds left to catapult the Falcons over the Giants 16-14. Safety Bob Glazebrook's club-record 91-yard fumble recovery for a score had brought Atlanta within striking distance, 14-13. New York quarterback Scott Brunner threw for a personal-high 310 yards (25 of 41). He completed two touchdown passes to Earnest Gray (33 and 19 yards), which gave the Giants a 14-7 third-quarter lead. New York outgained Atlanta 378 to 272 yards total offense.

Atlanta	0	7	0	9	— 16
New York Giants	0	7	7	0	— 14

Atl — Andrews 13 run (Luckhurst kick)
NYG — Gray 33 pass from Brunner (Danelo kick)
NYG — Gray 19 pass from Brunner (Danelo kick)
Atl — Glazebrook 91 fumble recovery return (kick blocked)
Atl — FG Luckhurst 29

Detroit 17, Chicago 10—At Pontiac Silverdome, attendance 71,337. Billy Sims ran for a three-yard touchdown to spark the Lions' 17-10 win. Sims, who entered the game late in the first quarter, gained three yards on a crucial fourth and one play to set up Eric Hipple's five-yard touchdown pass to David Hill. Bob Thomas' 38-yard field goal four seconds before halftime extended Detroit's lead to 10-7. The Lions held the Bears to 154 yards total offense including just 26 yards rushing by Walter Payton.

Chicago	0	7	0	3	— 10
Detroit	7	3	0	7	— 17

Det — Hill 5 pass from Hipple (Thomas kick)
Chi — Suhey 2 run (Roveto kick)
Det — FG Thomas 38
Det — Sims 3 run (Thomas kick)
Chi — FG Roveto 42

Cleveland 21, Seattle 7—At Kingdome, attendance 55,907. Paced by a pair of Mike Pruitt touchdown runs of two and three yards, the Browns opened a 21-0 halftime lead and coasted to victory. Pruitt rushed 30 times for 136 yards and running mate Charles White added 73 yards and 66 more on five receptions. The Cleveland defense recorded a club-record eight sacks (three by rookie linebacker Chip Banks) and held Seattle to 180 total yards.

Cleveland	7	14	0	0	— 21
Seattle	0	0	7	0	— 7

Cle — Pruitt 3 run (Bahr kick)
Cle — White 18 run (Bahr kick)
Cle — Pruitt 2 run (Bahr kick)
Sea — Ivory 2 run (N. Johnson kick)

Cincinnati 27, Houston 6—At Riverfront Stadium, attendance 52,268. Ken Anderson passed for two touchdowns and ran for another as the Bengals dismantled the Oilers 27-6. Anderson, who completed 29 of 40 passes for 354 yards (to eight different receivers), opened the scoring with an 18-yard completion to tight end Dan Ross. Reggie Williams' fumble recovery set up Charles Alexander's seven-yard touchdown reception, which increased Cincinnati's lead to 24-0. Alexander's score came just 62 seconds after Anderson's two-yard scoring run.

Houston	0	0	0	6	— 6
Cincinnati	7	3	14	3	— 27

Cin — Ross 18 pass from Anderson (Breech kick)
Cin — FG Breech 43
Cin — Anderson 2 run (Breech kick)
Cin — Alexander 7 pass from Anderson (Breech kick)
Cin — FG Breech 25
Hou — Holston 38 pass from Nielsen (kick failed)

Buffalo 14, Kansas City 9—At Rich Stadium, attendance 78,746. Two first-half touchdown passes by Buffalo quarterback Joe Ferguson were all the Bills needed in their game against the Chiefs. Ferguson completed a 20-yard scoring strike to Frank Lewis 11 minutes into the game and combined with Jerry Butler on a six-yard touchdown pass in the second quarter. All the Chiefs scoring came from kicker Nick Lowery who drilled field goals of 39, 47, and 42 yards.

Kansas City	3	3	0	3	— 9
Buffalo	7	7	0	0	— 14

KC — FG Lowery 39
Buff — Lewis 20 pass from Ferguson (Mike-Mayer kick)
KC — FG Lowery 47
Buff — Butler 6 pass from Ferguson (Mike-Mayer kick)
KC — FG Lowery 42

Green Bay 35, Los Angeles Rams 23—At Milwaukee County Stadium, attendance 53,694. Two fourth-quarter touchdown passes by Lynn Dickey, just 17 seconds apart, climaxed the Packers' dramatic comeback. Trailing 23-0 at halftime, Dickey's 15-yard scoring pass to James Lofton made the score 23-21. The Packers recovered the ensuing kickoff and Dickey threw a 10-yard strike to Paul Coffman to give Green Bay the lead for good, 28-23. Running back Eddie Lee Ivery's second touchdown of the game, a 27-yard run, closed out the scoring. Ivery rushed 17 times for 109 yards in his first 100-yard effort since November 23, 1980.

L.A. Rams	10	13	0	0	— 23
Green Bay	0	0	14	21	— 35

Rams — Tyler 4 run (Lansford kick)
Rams — FG Lansford 32
Rams — Barber 8 pass from B. Jones (Lansford kick)
Rams — FG Lansford 29
Rams — FG Lansford 28
GB — Coffman 4 pass from Dickey (Stenerud kick)
GB — Ivery 3 run (Stenerud kick)
GB — Lofton 15 pass from Dickey (Stenerud kick)
GB — Coffman 10 pass from Dickey (Stenerud kick)
GB — Ivery 27 run (Stenerud kick)

Miami 45, New York Jets 28—At Shea Stadium, attendance 53,360. Tom Vigorito scored on a 59-yard punt return and defensive backs Glenn Blackwood and Don McNeal returned interceptions for touchdowns to lead the Dolphins to their first win over the Jets since 1977. Andra Franklin, who rushed for a career-high 103 yards, put the game away early with a pair of first-half touchdowns. Dolphins quarterback David Woodley became the first NFL quarterback since 1977 to be on the receiving end of a touchdown pass (15 yards from running back Tony Nathan).

Miami	14	10	21	0	— 45
New York Jets	7	7	0	14	— 28

Mia — Franklin 1 run (von Schamann kick)
NYJ — Walker 29 pass from Todd (Leahy kick)
Mia — Vigorito 59 punt return (von Schamann kick)
Mia — Franklin 1 run (von Schamann kick)
Mia — FG von Schamann 25
NYJ — Augustyniak 2 run (Leahy kick)
Mia — Woodley 15 pass from Nathan (von Schamann kick)
Mia — G. Blackwood 35 interception return (von Schamann kick)
Mia — McNeal 19 interception return (von Schamann kick)
NYJ — Barkum 7 pass from Todd (Leahy kick)
NYJ — Walker 5 pass from Todd (Leahy kick)

New England 24, Baltimore 13—At Memorial Stadium, attendance 39,055. Second-half touchdowns by Ken Toler and Robert Weathers helped make Ron Meyer's debut as an NFL head coach a successful one. Ray Clayborn's 26-yard interception in the third quarter set up Matt Cavanaugh's 30-yard scoring pass to Toler. Weather's clinching touchdown was made possible by Don Blackmon's fumble recovery early in the fourth quarter. Tony Collins rushed for 137 yards and caught four passes for 56 yards, including a 15-yard touchdown, as the Patriots snapped a nine-game losing streak.

New England	3	7	7	7	— 24
Baltimore	3	7	3	0	— 13

Balt — FG Wood 49
NE — FG Robinson 24
Balt — Pagel 1 run (Wood kick)
NE — Collins 15 pass from Cavanaugh (Robinson kick)
Balt — FG Wood 30
NE — Toler 30 pass from Cavanaugh (Robinson kick)
NE — Weathers 1 run (Robinson kick)

Los Angeles Raiders 23, San Francisco 17—At Candlestick Park, attendance 59,748. Jim Plunkett connected with Todd Christensen on a three-yard scoring pass and Chris Bahr kicked a 43-yard field goal, four minutes later, to cap the Raiders' comeback. San Francisco built a 17-13 lead on a pair of Joe Montana touchdown passes (18 and 41 yards) and Ray Wersching's 22-yard field goal. Raiders rookie Marcus Allen rushed for 116 yards on 23 carries and caught four passes for 64 yards.

L.A. Raiders	3	10	0	10	— 23
San Francisco	0	14	3	0	— 17

Raiders — FG Bahr 41
SF — Solomon 18 pass from Montana (Wersching kick)
Raiders — FG Bahr 42
SF — D. Clark 41 pass from Montana (Wersching kick)
Raiders — Allen 3 run (Bahr kick)
SF — FG Wersching 22
Raiders — Christensen 3 pass from Plunkett (Bahr kick)
Raiders — FG Bahr 43

St. Louis 21, New Orleans 7—At Louisiana Superdome, attendance 58,673. Neil Lomax threw for one touchdown and set up another to lead the Cardinals to their first opening-day victory since 1976. Lomax connected with Pat Tilley on a 12-yard scoring pass for the Cardinals final touchdown and set up Wayne Morris' one-yard scoring plunge in the first quarter with a 16-yard completion to Doug Marsh. Ken Stabler started for the Saints and completed 19 of 27 passes for 221 yards.

St. Louis	7	0	7	7	— 21
New Orleans	0	0	0	7	— 7

StL — Morris 1 run (O'Donoghue kick)
StL — Anderson 5 run (O'Donoghue kick)
StL — Tilley 12 pass from Lomax (O'Donoghue kick)
NO — Duckett 23 pass from Stabler (Erxleben kick)

San Diego 23, Denver 3—At Mile High Stadium, attendance 73,564. An alert San Diego defense recovered four fumbles and had two interceptions and Rolf Benirschke kicked three field goals (50, 24, and 40 yards) to lead the victory. Safety Andre Young's third-quarter interception set up Dan Fouts' 18-yard scoring pass to Scott Fitzkee.

San Diego	3	3	10	7	— 23
Denver	0	3	0	0	— 3

SD — FG Benirschke 50
Den — FG Karlis 40
SD — FG Benirschke 24
SD — FG Benirschke 40
SD — Fitzkee 18 pass from Fouts (Benirschke kick)
SD — Muncie 10 run (Benirschke kick)

Minnesota 17, Tampa Bay 10—At Metrodome, attendance 58,440. Touchdowns by Rickey Young and Sammy White helped the Vikings to a 14-3 third-quarter lead, and Willie Teal's interception halted the Buccaneers' final threat, to seal the win. Jim Hough's fumble recovery at the Tampa Bay 21, with less than three minutes to play, set up Rick Danmeier's 33-yard field goal. Darrin Nelson became the first rookie running back to start in a season-opener in the Vikings' 21-year history.

Tampa Bay	3	0	0	7	— 10
Minnesota	0	7	7	3	— 17

TB — FG Capece 51
Minn — Young 3 run (Danmeier kick)
Minn — S. White 22 pass from Kramer (Danmeier kick)
TB — Giles 20 pass from Williams (Capece kick)
Minn — FG Danmeier 33

Washington 37, Philadelphia 34—At Veterans Stadium, attendance 68,885. Mark Moseley's 26-yard field goal, 4:47 into overtime, capped the Redskins' comeback. Trailing 27-14, quarterback Joe Theismann, who completed 28 of 39 passes for 382 yards and three touchdowns, ignited Washington's 20-point fourth-quarter outburst with a 78-yard scoring pass to Charlie Brown. Following John Riggins' two-yard touchdown run, Moseley connected from 30 and 48 yards, the latter as regulation time expired. After winning the overtime coin toss, Theismann had completions of 28 and 27 yards to Art Monk (eight receptions, 134 yards, one touchdown), which set up Moseley's winning field goal.

Washington	0	14	0	20	3	— 37
Philadelphia	10	3	14	7	0	— 34

Phil — Montgomery 4 run (Franklin kick)
Phil — FG Franklin 44
Wash — Monk 5 pass from Theismann (Moseley kick)
Wash — Brown 8 pass from Theismann (Moseley kick)
Phil — FG Franklin 44
Phil — Montgomery 2 run (Franklin kick)
Phil — Montgomery 42 pass from Jaworski (Franklin kick)
Wash — Brown 78 pass from Theismann (Moseley kick)
Wash — Riggins 2 run (Moseley kick)
Wash — FG Moseley 30
Phil — Carmichael 4 pass from Jaworski (Franklin kick)
Wash — FG Moseley 48
Wash — FG Moseley 26

MONDAY, SEPTEMBER 13

Pittsburgh 36, Dallas 28—At Texas Stadium, attendance 63,431. Terry Bradshaw (who completed 17 of 28 passes for 246 yards) threw three touchdown passes as the Steelers ended the Cowboys' NFL record of 17 consecutive opening-day victories. Following first-half scoring passes from Bradshaw to John Stallworth and Jim Smith, Pittsburgh broke the game open in the third period capitalizing on a three-yard Dallas punt and two interceptions to score 17 straight points. Franco Harris, who rushed for 103 yards, and Stallworth, who had seven catches for 137 yards, helped balance the Steelers' attack. The win overshadowed the four-touchdown passing performance of Dallas quarterback Danny White, who suffered his first loss in Texas Stadium as Dallas' starting quarterback.

Pittsburgh	6	7	17	6	— 36
Dallas	7	7	0	14	— 28

Pitt — Stallworth 8 pass from Bradshaw (kick failed)
Dall — Pearson 4 pass from D. White (Septien kick)
Pitt — Smith 7 pass from Bradshaw (Anderson kick)
Dall — Cosbie 12 pass from D. White (Septien kick)
Pitt — Pollard 1 run (Anderson kick)
Pitt — Smith 15 pass from Bradshaw (Anderson kick)
Pitt — FG Anderson 26
Pitt — FG Anderson 43
Dall — T. Hill 45 pass from D. White (Septien kick)
Dall — DuPree 5 pass from D. White (Septien kick)
Pitt — FG Anderson 40

SECOND WEEK SUMMARY

Seven teams—four AFC and three NFC—cruised through week two with unblemished records but everyone wondered when they would be able to extend those marks as the NFL players voted to strike. The work stoppage was the first in regular-season history. Terry Bradshaw's two-yard scoring pass to John Stallworth, 1:08 into overtime, gave Pittsburgh a 26-20 win over Cincinnati. The Steelers' victory was their first over the Bengals since 1979. The Bills beat the Vikings 23-22 with 2:48 left on Joe Ferguson's 11-yard touchdown pass to Jerry Butler and Nick Mike-Mayer's extra point. The Dolphins struggled past the Colts 24-20 while the Raiders blew by the Falcons 38-14. Kickers grabbed the spotlight in two contests. In Tampa, Washington's Mark Moseley showed that not even a tropical monsoon could hinder his accuracy as he kicked three field goals in the Redskins 21-13 win over the Buccaneers. Meanwhile, the Lions' Bob Thomas connected on four field goals and got help from running back Billy Sims, who gained over 100 yards both rushing and receiving, enabling Detroit to down the Rams 19-14. At the Meadowlands, the Giants opened a 19-7 advantage over the Packers, but James Lofton's 83-yard end-around touchdown run sparked Green Bay's second-half comeback. Denver was victorious when free agent Rich Karlis hit an 18-yard field goal on the game's final play. NFC East rivals Dallas and Philadelphia rebounded from opening-day losses. The Cowboys scored 17 unanswered points in downing St. Louis 24-7 while the Eagles scored a 24-21 win on Leroy Harris' two-yard run with 22 seconds left. It was the Eagles first win in Cleveland since 1960. Powered by Earl Campbell's (142 yards rushing) 12-yard scoring run with 53 seconds remaining, the Oilers outlasted the Seahawks 23-21. The Jets dominated the Patriots in their 31-7 victory but lost Sack Exchange leader Joe Klecko with a knee injury. San Diego and Kansas City played a strange game at Arrowhead Stadium. For the second week in a row the Chargers' defense didn't allow a touchdown and the Chiefs' offense didn't score one. Kansas City was victorious anyway thanks to four Nick Lowery field goals and a blocked punt recovered in the end zone.

THURSDAY, SEPTEMBER 16

Buffalo 23, Minnesota 22—At Rich Stadium, attendance 77,753. Joe Ferguson's 11-yard touchdown pass to Jerry Butler with 2:48 remaining tied the Vikings 22-22, and Nick Mike-Mayer kicked the extra point to clinch the Bills' comeback win. Buffalo spotted Minnesota a 19-0 second-quarter lead but rebounded on scoring passes from Ferguson to Frank Lewis (six yards) and Butler (four), and on Mike-Mayer's 21-yard field goal. Butler caught seven passes for 111 yards; Lewis four for 82. Ferguson, who completed 25 of 45 passes for 330 yards, directed the 451-yard attack.

Minnesota	2	17	3	0	— 22
Buffalo	0	7	6	10	— 23

Minn — Safety, Mullaney tackled Moore in end zone
Minn — Bruer 22 pass from Kramer (Danmeier kick)
Minn — Bruer 2 pass from Kramer (Danmeier kick)
Minn — FG Danmeier 43
Buff — Lewis 6 pass from Ferguson (Mike-Mayer kick)
Buff — Butler 4 pass from Ferguson (kick failed)
Minn — FG Danmeier 42
Buff — FG Mike-Mayer 21
Buff — Butler 11 pass from Ferguson (Mike-Mayer kick)

SUNDAY, SEPTEMBER 19

Miami 24, Baltimore 20—At Orange Bowl, attendance 51,999. Tom Vigorito's 33-yard touchdown run and Uwe von Schamann's 29-yard field goal in the third quarter enabled the Dolphins to wipe out a 17-14 halftime deficit and squeak past the Colts 24-20. David Woodley ran for a touchdown and passed for another to give Miami an early 14-0 edge, but Baltimore responded with 17 unanswered points in the second quarter. The win was the Dolphins' ninth in their last 10 meetings with the Colts.

Baltimore	0	17	0	3	— 20
Miami	14	0	10	0	— 24

Mia — Woodley 1 run (von Schamann kick)
Mia — Hardy 4 pass from Woodley (von Schamann kick)
Balt — Butler 53 pass from Pagel (Wood kick)
Balt — FG Wood 51
Balt — Krauss 5 pass from Wood (Wood kick)
Mia — Vigorito 33 run (von Schamann kick)
Mia — FG von Schamann 29
Balt — FG Wood 48

Pittsburgh 26, Cincinnati 20—At Three Rivers Stadium, attendance 53,973. Terry Bradshaw fired a two-yard touchdown pass to John Stallworth with 1:08 elapsed in overtime as the Steelers halted a four-game losing streak to the Bengals. Gary Anderson's 42-yard field goal tied the game 20-20 and Tom Beasley sent the game into overtime by blocking Jim Breech's 38-yard field goal attempt on the final play of regulation time. Bradshaw was 29 of 42 for 298 yards and three touchdowns, including 11 completions to Franco Harris for 88 yards. The win kept the Steelers undefeated in overtime play (5-0-1), the only NFL team to do so since the rule was adopted in 1974.

Cincinnati	0	3	7	10	0	— 20
Pittsburgh	7	3	7	3	6	— 26

Pitt — Stallworth 15 pass from Bradshaw (Anderson kick)
Cin — FG Breech 50
Pitt — FG Anderson 25
Cin — Johnson 1 run (Breech kick)
Pitt — Cunningham 2 pass from Bradshaw (Anderson kick)
Cin — Johnson 9 run (Breech kick)
Cin — FG Breech 31
Pitt — FG Anderson 42
Pitt — Stallworth 2 pass from Bradshaw

Dallas 24, St. Louis 7—At Busch Memorial Stadium, attendance 50,705. Danny White completed 20 of 32 passes for 266 yards and two touchdowns to pace the Cowboys' eighth win over the Cardinals in their last nine meetings. White's 29-yard scoring toss to Doug Cosbie opened the scoring for the Cowboys. Dallas took the lead for good on tight end Billy Joe DuPree's six-yard touchdown run, which capped an 81-yard drive. White completed eight passes to Tony Hill for 101 yards and four to Drew Pearson for 57 yards, including a 24-yard touchdown in the fourth quarter.

Dallas	0	7	7	10	— 24
St. Louis	0	7	0	0	— 7

Dall — Cosbie 29 pass from D. White (Septien kick)
StL — Tilley 4 pass from Lomax (O'Donoghue kick)
Dall — DuPree 6 run (Septien kick)
Dall — Pearson 24 pass from D. White (Septien kick)
Dall — FG Septien 25

Detroit 19, Los Angeles Rams 14—At Anaheim Stadium, attendance 59,470. Bob Thomas kicked field goals of 45, 46, 30, and 33 yards as the Lions downed the Rams. Running back Billy Sims contributed to Detroit's winning effort by rushing for 119 yards and catching five passes for 103 more in his first start of the season. Thomas' first three field goals, plus Gary Danielson's two-yard scoring pass to tight end David Hill, gave Detroit a 16-0 third-quarter lead. Vince Ferragamo relieved quarterback Bert Jones (who left the game with a pulled muscle in the third period) and rallied Los Angeles to within 19-14, but Detroit's Doug English recovered a Ferragamo fumble on the Lions' 27 yard line to preserve the win.

Detroit	0	9	7	3	— 19
L.A. Rams	0	0	0	14	— 14

Det — FG Thomas 45
Det — FG Thomas 46
Det — FG Thomas 30
Det — Hill 2 pass from Danielson (Thomas kick)
Rams — Guman 1 run (Lansford kick)
Det — FG Thomas 33
Rams — Miller 85 pass from Ferragamo (Lansford kick)

New Orleans 10, Chicago 0—At Soldier Field, attendance 56,600. Ken Stabler fired a 10-yard touchdown pass to Larry Hardy and newcomer Toni Fritsch added a 40-yard field goal to lead the Saints to their first win. Stabler marched New Orleans 80 yards in 10 plays on the game's opening drive and Wayne Wilson, filling in for sidelined George Rogers (who was out with a hamstring injury), gained a career-high 138 yards on 33 carries. The Saints' defense, which limited the Bears to 183 total yards, was led by rookie Bruce Clark who was credited with two of New Orleans' five quarterback sacks.

New Orleans	7	0	3	0	— 10
Chicago	0	0	0	0	— 0

NO — Hardy 10 pass from Stabler (Fritsch kick)
NO — FG Fritsch 40

New York Jets 31, New England 7—At Schaefer Stadium, attendance 53,515. Freeman McNeil rushed 19 times for 106 yards and the Jets' defense held the Patriots to 57 total yards (minus four yards passing) on the way to a 31-7 win. New York capitalized on three interceptions for 17 points—Darroll Ray's 44-yard interception return set up Pat Leahy's 30-yard field goal; Lance Mehl's pickoff set up McNeil's one-yard run; and Jerry Holmes' theft led to Scott Dierking's 13-yard scoring run. New England scored their only points on rookie Ricky Smith's 98-yard kickoff return. Despite the one-sided victory, the Jets lost all-pro Joe Klecko for at least 12 weeks with a knee injury.

New York Jets	0	10	7	14	— 31
New England	0	0	7	0	— 7

NYJ — FG Leahy 30
NYJ — Todd 7 run (Leahy kick)
NYJ — Augustyniak 6 run (Leahy kick)
NE — Smith 98 kickoff return (Robinson kick)
NYJ — McNeil 1 run (Leahy kick)
NYJ — Dierking 13 pass from Todd (Leahy kick)

Los Angeles Raiders 38, Atlanta 14—At Atlanta-Fulton County Stadium, attendance 54,774. Touchdowns by Marcus Allen and Cliff Branch late in the first half helped build a 24-7 lead as the Raiders coasted to victory. Allen scored on a four-yard run and Ted Hendricks' fumble recovery set up Jim Plunkett's 30-yard touchdown pass to Branch (six catches for 138 yards) just 43 seconds later. The Raiders' defense recorded seven sacks, three interceptions, and two fumble recoveries (including Archie Reese's 75-yard touchdown return). Atlanta's Steve Bartkowski threw for 375 yards on career highs of 34 completions in 56 attempts.

L.A. Raiders	7	17	7	7	— 38
Atlanta	7	0	7	0	— 14

Raiders — Allen 14 pass from Plunkett (Bahr kick)
Atl — Andrews 1 run (Luckhurst kick)
Raiders — FG Bahr 35
Raiders — Allen 4 run (Bahr kick)
Raiders — Branch 30 pass from Plunkett (Bahr kick)
Raiders — Hawkins 1 run (Bahr kick)
Atl — Robinson 17 pass from Bartkowski (Luckhurst kick)
Raiders — Reese 75 fumble recovery return (Bahr kick)

Philadelphia 24, Cleveland 21—At Cleveland Stadium, attendance 78,830. Ron Jaworski completed 25 of 41 attempts for 334 yards and two fourth-quarter touchdowns, and Leroy Harris scored on a two-yard run (his only rush of the day) with 22 seconds left, to climax the Eagles comeback. The Browns had taken a 21-17 lead with 57 seconds remaining on Brian Sipe's 34-yard touchdown pass to Ozzie Newsome. Jaworski then drove the Philadelphia offense 65 yards in four plays for the winning score. It was the Eagles' first win in Cleveland Stadium since 1960.

Philadelphia	0	3	0	21	— 24
Cleveland	7	0	0	14	— 21

Cle — Newsome 19 pass from Sipe (Bahr kick)
Phil — FG Franklin 47
Cle — White 3 run (Bahr kick)
Phil — Smith 41 pass from Jaworski (Franklin kick)
Phil — Campfield 11 pass from Jaworski (Franklin kick)
Cle — Newsome 34 pass from Sipe (Bahr kick)
Phil — Harris 2 run (Franklin kick)

Kansas City 19, San Diego 12—At Arrowhead, attendance 60,514. Nick Lowery converted four field goal attempts (19, 27, 41, and 34 yards), including three in the second quarter, as the Chiefs defeated the Chargers for the first time since 1978. Kansas City jumped to a 7-0 lead when Gary Green blocked a punt and linebacker Dave Klug recovered in the end zone. San Diego's only touchdown came on running back Chuck Muncie's 17-yard touchdown pass to Wes Chandler.

San Diego	0	0	9	3	— 12
Kansas City	7	9	3	0	— 19

KC — Klug recovered blocked punt in end zone (Lowery kick)
KC — FG Lowery 19
KC — FG Lowery 27
KC — FG Lowery 41
SD — Chandler 17 pass from Muncie (Benirschke kick)
SD — Safety, illegal block in end zone
KC — FG Lowery 34
SD — FG Benirschke 49

Denver 24, San Francisco 21—At Mile High Stadium, attendance 73,889. Rich Karlis' 18-yard field goal with no time remaining gave the Broncos the come-from-behind win. San Francisco led 21-14 in the fourth quarter but Steve DeBerg's 37-yard touchdown pass to Rick Upchurch tied the game with 9:29 remaining. DeBerg, in relief of Craig Morton, completed 14 of 22 passes for 157 yards and two touchdowns, while Upchurch had five receptions for 77 yards and returned three punts for 94 yards (including a 67-yard touchdown). Dennis Smith's interception set up the Broncos' decisive score.

San Francisco	14	7	0	0	— 21
Denver	7	7	0	10	— 24

SF — Solomon 46 pass from Montana (Wersching kick)
Den — Upchurch 67 punt return (Karlis kick)
SF — Moore 1 run (Wersching kick)
Den — Parros 4 pass from DeBerg (Karlis kick)
SF — D. Clark 24 pass from Montana (Wersching kick)
Den — Upchurch 37 pass from DeBerg (Karlis kick)
Den — FG Karlis 18

Houston 23, Seattle 21—At Astrodome, attendance 43,117. Earl Campbell's 12-yard touchdown run with 53 seconds remaining lifted the Oilers over the Seahawks. Campbell gained 142 yards on 30 carries for his first 100-yard plus effort since the sixth game of the 1981 season. Houston grabbed a 17-7 third-quarter lead on Gifford Nielsen's 19-yard touchdown pass to Dave Casper, Florian Kempf's 24-yard field goal, and Mike Reinfeldt's fumble recovery in the end zone. Jim Zorn, after replacing starter Dave Krieg in the fourth quarter, rallied Seattle to a 21-17 lead on a three-yard run by Theotis Brown and a 29-yard pass to David Hughes, but the defense couldn't contain the Oilers as they marched 81 yards for the winning score.

Seattle	0	7	0	14	— 21
Houston	0	7	10	6	— 23

Hou — Casper 19 pass from Nielsen (Kempf kick)
Sea — Walker 40 pass from Krieg (N. Johnson kick)
Hou — FG Kempf 24
Hou — Reinfeldt fumble recovery in end zone (Kempf kick)
Sea — T. Brown 3 run (N. Johnson kick)
Sea — Hughes 29 pass from Zorn (N. Johnson kick)
Hou — Campbell 12 run (kick blocked)

Washington 21, Tampa Bay 13—At Tampa Stadium, attendance 66,187. Mark Moseley kicked field goals of 35, 21, and 19 yards, the last with 4:16 remaining, as the Redskins survived a tropical deluge to defeat the Buccaneers. Playing in a driving rain, Washington took an 18-6 halftime lead on Joe Theismann's eight-yard touchdown pass to Charlie Brown and Curtis Jordan's blocked punt which he recovered in the end zone for a score. John Riggins rushed for 136 yards on 34 carries, the eighteenth 100-yard game of his career.

Washington	9	9	0	3	— 21
Tampa Bay	0	6	0	7	— 13

Wash — Brown 8 pass from Theismann (kick failed)
Wash — FG Moseley 35
TB — House 62 pass from Williams (kick failed)
Wash — FG Moseley 21
Wash — Jordan recovered blocked punt in end zone (kick failed)
TB — Wilder 7 run (Capece kick)
Wash — FG Moseley 19

MONDAY, SEPTEMBER 20

Green Bay 27, New York Giants 19—At Giants Stadium, attendance 68,405. Second-half touchdowns by James Lofton and Eddie Lee Ivery and a pair of Jan Stenerud field goals propelled the Packers to a 27-19 win in the last game before the players' strike. Trailing 19-7, Lofton ignited Green Bay with an 83-yard touchdown on an end-around with 1:37 left in the third quarter. Ivery's 11-yard touchdown run was followed by Stenerud field goals of 37 and 22 yards, which were set up by interceptions by Rich Wingo and Maurice Harvey. The pair of kicks gave Stenerud 306 career field goals, second only to George Blanda's 335.

Green Bay	0	7	7	13	— 27
New York Giants	9	3	7	0	— 19

NYG — Morris 3 run (Danelo kick)
NYG — Safety, ball snapped out of end zone
NYG — FG Danelo 37
GB — Jensen 7 pass from Dickey (Stenerud kick)
NYG — Chatman 2 run (Danelo kick)
GB — Lofton 83 run (Stenerud kick)
GB — Ivery 11 run (Stenerud kick)
GB — FG Stenerud 37
GB — FG Stenerud 22

THIRD WEEK SUMMARY

Fifty-seven days after NFL players voted to strike, negotiators for the Players Association and the NFL Management Council reached accord on a new collective bargaining agreement on November 16, thus salvaging a nine-game regular season schedule. Play resumed Sunday, November 21. Surprisingly, many players reappeared after the eight-week hiatus in mid-season form. One of those was San Francisco quarterback Joe Montana who directed the 49ers to their first win of the season. He threw for a team-record 408 yards and three touchdowns in a 31-20 win over St. Louis. The New York Jets trounced Baltimore 37-0 as Freeman McNeil became the first Jets player to rush for over 100 yards (123) in three consecutive games. Jim Zorn's 34-yard touchdown pass to Steve Largent with 49 seconds left gave the Seahawks a 17-10 victory over the Broncos. The win was the first for interim head coach Mike McCormack. Tampa Bay outgained Dallas 382 to 185 but Robert Newhouse came off the bench to score the winning touchdown (a three-yard run) on his only carry of the day. The Bears dropped Detroit from the unbeaten ranks 20-17, giving Mike Ditka his first NFL coaching victory. Five teams maintained perfect records: the Raiders, Dolphins, and Steelers in the AFC; the Packers and Redskins in the NFC—but it wasn't easy. The Los Angeles Raiders fell behind 24-0 to San Diego but a pair of Marcus Allen touchdowns and Frank Hawkins' one-yard run increased the Raiders Monday night mark to 19-2-1 (88.6%). Miami's defense (six interceptions) and three Uwe von Schamann field goals were all the Dolphins needed in a 9-7 triumph over the Bills. Terry Bradshaw completed only 16 of 40 passes but three completions went for touchdowns in Pittsburgh's 24-10 win over Houston. Green Bay quarterbacks survived eight sacks for 62 yards in losses to guide the Packers over the Vikings 26-7. Washington opened a 21-3 lead and held off the rallying New York Giants 27-17.

SUNDAY, NOVEMBER 21

New York Jets 37, Baltimore 0—At Shea Stadium, attendance 46,970. Freeman McNeil became the first Jets player to rush for over 100 yards in three consecutive games, and Richard Todd fired two touchdown passes as the Jets beat the Colts for the second time this season. McNeil, who carried the ball 22 times for 123 yards, scored on a 34-yard run, only 1:23 into the game. Todd threw for 231 yards including scoring strikes to Lam Jones (23 yards) and McNeil (32). Pat Leahy kicked field goals of 43, 37, and 19 yards for New York.

Baltimore	0	0	0	0	— 0
New York Jets	10	17	7	3	— 37

NYJ — McNeil 34 run (Leahy kick)
NYJ — FG Leahy 43
NYJ — Augustyniak 1 run (Leahy kick)
NYJ — L. Jones 23 pass from Todd (Leahy kick)
NYJ — FG Leahy 37
NYJ — McNeil 32 pass from Todd (Leahy kick)
NYJ — FG Leahy 19

Cincinnati 18, Philadelphia 14—At Veterans Stadium, attendance 65,172. The Bengals opened an 18-0 lead and withstood the Eagles fourth-quarter rally to preserve an 18-14 win. Jim Breech's three field goals of 19, 38, and 49 yards, coupled with Ken Anderson's two-yard touchdown pass to Dan Ross and Reggie Williams' safety, staked Cincinnati to an 18-point lead. Fourth-quarter touchdowns by Perry Harrington (two yards) and Louie Giammona (one) brought Philadelphia to within four points, but Cincinnati was able to run out the final 1:22.

Cincinnati	3	8	7	0	— 18
Philadelphia	0	0	0	14	— 14

Cin — FG Breech 19
Cin — Safety, Williams tackled Jaworski in end zone
Cin — FG Breech 38
Cin — FG Breech 49
Cin — Ross 2 pass from Anderson (Breech kick)
Phil — Harrington 2 run (Franklin kick)
Phil — Giammona 1 run (Franklin kick)

Chicago 20, Detroit 17—At Soldier Field, attendance 46,783. John Roveto's 18-yard field goal with five seconds left gave the Bears a 20-17 win and Mike Ditka his first win as Chicago head coach. Rookie Jim McMahon, making his first start, completed 16 of 27 passes for 233 yards and two touchdowns to Ken Margerum (11 yards) and Emery Moorehead (28), which erased a 14-3 Detroit advantage. Roveto, who opened the scoring with a 51-yard field goal, got the chance for the winning kick on McMahon's 44-yard completion to Moorehead. The Bears' defense had seven sacks and held the Lions to 152 total yards.

Detroit	14	0	3	0	— 17
Chicago	3	7	7	3	— 20

Chi — FG Roveto 51
Det — Nichols 1 pass from Hipple (Murray kick)
Det — Oldham 35 interception return (Murray kick)
Chi — Margerum 11 pass from McMahon (Roveto kick)
Chi — Moorehead 28 pass from McMahon (Roveto kick)
Det — FG Murray 32
Chi — FG Roveto 18

New Orleans 27, Kansas City 17—At Louisiana Superdome, attendance 39,341. George Rogers ran for 123 yards on 33 carries and Ken Stabler completed 13 of 18 passes for 129 yards and one touchdown to lead the Saints past the Chiefs 27-17. Toni Fritsch booted a 19-yard field goal and backup quarterback Guido Merkens threw a 15-yard touchdown pass to Wayne Wilson on a fake field goal for a 10-0 lead. Stabler's six-yard scoring toss to Jeff Groth followed Rogers' one-yard plunge. Fritsch then added a 42-yard field goal with 24 seconds remaining to close out the scoring.

Kansas City	0	7	0	10	— 17
New Orleans	10	0	7	10	— 27

NO — FG Fritsch 19
NO — Wilson 15 pass from Merkens (Fritsch kick)
KC — Marshall 44 pass from Kenney (Lowery kick)
NO — G. Rogers 1 run (Fritsch kick)
KC — Dixon 13 pass from Fuller (Lowery kick)
NO — Groth 6 pass from Stabler (Fritsch kick)
KC — FG Lowery 35
NO — FG Fritsch 42

Atlanta 34, Los Angeles Rams 27—At Atlanta-Fulton County Stadium, attendance 39,686. Rookie Gerald Riggs ran for a pair of touchdowns and William Andrews rushed for 119 yards and a score to highlight the Falcons come-from-behind win. The Rams had a 14-0 first-quarter lead but were overtaken in the second quarter on Steve Bartkowski's 43-yard touchdown pass to Alfred Jenkins, Riggs' one-yard plunge (which was set up by Billy Johnson's 71-yard punt return), and Mick Luckhurst's 49-yard field goal. Andrews and Riggs added final period touchdowns on runs of 19 and 6 yards, respectively, while the defense held the Rams to just a field goal in the second half.

L.A. Rams	14	0	3	0	— 17
Atlanta	0	17	3	14	— 34

Rams — Tyler 5 run (Lansford kick)
Rams — Battle 51 pass from B. Jones (Lansford kick)
Atl — Jenkins 43 pass from Bartkowski (Luckhurst kick)
Atl — Riggs 1 run (Luckhurst kick)
Atl — FG Luckhurst 49
Atl — FG Luckhurst 29
Rams — FG Lansford 28
Atl — Andrews 19 run (Luckhurst kick)
Atl — Riggs 6 run (Luckhurst kick)

Miami 9, Buffalo 7—At Rich Stadium, attendance 52,945. Uwe von Schamann's third field goal of the day, a 21-yarder early in the fourth quarter, lifted Miami to a 9-7 victory and dropped Buffalo from the unbeaten ranks. The Bills led 7-6 at the half on Joe Ferguson's one-yard fumble-recovery touchdown. However, the Dolphins capitalized on seven Bills turnovers including a team record-tying six interceptions. Mike Kozlowski's fumble recovery set up von Schamann's winning kick. The loss snapped Buffalo's eight-game unbeaten streak at home.

Miami	0	6	0	3	— 9
Buffalo	0	7	0	0	— 7

Mia — FG von Schamann 42
Buff — Ferguson 1 fumble recovery (Herrera kick)
Mia — FG von Schamann 29
Mia — FG von Schamann 21

Green Bay 26, Minnesota 7—At Milwaukee County Stadium, attendance 44,681. Eddie Lee Ivery scored on a one-yard run and a five-yard pass, and Maurice Harvey returned a fumble 25 yards for a touchdown as the Packers upped their record to 3-0, their best start since 1966. Ivery's diving touchdown reception of a deflected pass with 1:37 left in the first half gave Green Bay the lead for good, 13-7. On the second-half kickoff, Harvey stole the ball from the Vikings' Sam Harrell and waltzed into the end zone untouched for a 19-7 Green Bay edge. Jan Stenerud scored his 1,366 point (two field goals, two extra points) to move into fourth place on the all-time list.

Minnesota	0	7	0	0	— 7
Green Bay	0	13	13	0	— 26

GB — FG Stenerud 18
GB — FG Stenerud 32
Minn — Kramer 4 run (Danmeier kick)
GB — Ivery 5 pass from Dickey (Stenerud kick)
GB — Harvey 25 fumble recovery return (kick failed)
GB — Ivery 1 run (Stenerud kick)

Cleveland 10, New England 7—At Cleveland Stadium, attendance 51,781. Matt Bahr kicked a 24-yard field goal as time expired to lift the Browns to a 10-7 win over the Patriots. After three scoreless quarters, Cleveland scored on Brian Sipe's 40-yard scoring strike to Ricky Feacher. New England tied the game with 3:18 remaining when Matt Cavanaugh found Preston Brown with a 38-yard reception. The Browns winning field goal was set up by Clinton Burrell's fumble recovery at the Patriots' 20 yard line with 1:24 left.

New England	0	0	0	7	— 7
Cleveland	0	0	0	10	— 10

Cle — Feacher 40 pass from Sipe (Bahr kick)
NE — Brown 38 pass from Cavanaugh (Robinson kick)
Cle — FG Bahr 24

Pittsburgh 24, Houston 10—At Astrodome, attendance 42,338. Three touchdown passes by Terry Bradshaw propelled the Steelers past the Oilers 24-10. Bradshaw followed Gary Anderson's 48-yard field goal with a 17-yard scoring pass to Greg Hawthorne to give Pittsburgh a 10-3 halftime edge. Houston evened the score early in the third quarter on a nine-yard pass from Gifford Nielsen to Dave Casper, but Jack Lambert's fumble recovery set up the winning touchdown—Bradshaw's 17-yard strike to Bennie Cunningham. Jim Smith's 27-yard catch closed out the scoring. Donnie Shell had two of the Steelers' three interceptions.

Pittsburgh	3	7	7	7	— 24
Houston	0	3	7	0	— 10

Pitt — FG Anderson 48
Pitt — Hawthorne 17 pass from Bradshaw (Anderson kick)
Hou — FG Kempf 31
Hou — Casper 9 pass from Nielsen (Kempf kick)
Pitt — Cunningham 17 pass from Bradshaw (Anderson kick)
Pitt — Smith 27 pass from Bradshaw (Anderson kick)

San Francisco 31, St. Louis 20—At Busch Memorial Stadium, attendance 38,064. Joe Montana completed three second-half touchdowns to rally the 49ers to their first win. San Francisco led 10-0 on Ray Wersching's 36-yard field goal and Jeff Moore's one-yard run before St. Louis took a 13-10 lead early in the third quarter. Montana, who completed 26 of 39 passes for a club-record 408 yards, then exploded in a 13-minute span completing scoring passes to Russ Francis (six yards), Dwight Clark (33), and Earl Cooper (17).

San Francisco	3	7	7	14	— 31
St. Louis	0	7	6	7	— 20

SF — FG Wersching 36
SF — Moore 1 run (Wersching kick)
StL — Green 17 pass from Lomax (O'Donoghue kick)
StL — FG O'Donoghue 30
StL — FG O'Donoghue 32
SF — Francis 6 pass from Montana (Wersching kick)
SF — D. Clark 33 pass from Montana (Wersching kick)
SF — Cooper 17 pass from Montana (Wersching kick)
StL — Anderson 2 run (O'Donoghue kick)

Seattle 17, Denver 10—At Mile High Stadium, attendance 73,916. Jim Zorn's 34-yard touchdown pass to Steve Largent with 49 seconds remaining rallied the Seahawks over the Broncos. Zorn, making his first start of the season, completed 22 of 41 passes for 318 yards and engineered Seattle's 80-yard winning drive in just four plays. The Seahawks fought back to tie the Broncos 7-7 in the third quarter on rookie linebacker Bruce Scholtz's 31-yard interception return and later at 10-10 on rookie Norm Johnson's 25-yard field goal with 5:36 left. Seattle's initial win of the season was also the first for interim head coach Mike McCormack.

Seattle	0	0	7	10	—	17
Denver	0	7	3	0	—	10

Den — Willhite 15 run (Karlis kick)
Sea — Scholtz 31 interception return (N. Johnson kick)
Den — FG Karlis 21
Sea — FG N. Johnson 25
Sea — Largent 34 pass from Zorn (N. Johnson kick)

Dallas 14, Tampa Bay 9—At Texas Stadium, attendance 49,578. Robert Newhouse came off the bench to score the game-winning touchdown on his only carry of the day, a three-yard run, as the Cowboys held on to win. The Buccaneers jumped to a 6-0 lead on two of Bill Capece's three field goals, but Danny White's nine-yard scoring pass to Drew Pearson gave Dallas a 7-6 halftime edge. The victory, played before the first non-sellout crowd in Texas Stadium in 45 games, brought the Cowboys' record to 4-0 against Tampa Bay.

Tampa Bay	3	3	3	0	—	9
Dallas	0	7	7	0	—	14

TB — FG Capece 26
TB — FG Capece 27
Dall — Pearson 9 pass from D. White (Septien kick)
TB — FG Capece 26
Dall — Newhouse 3 run (Septien kick)

Washington 27, New York Giants 17—At Giants Stadium, attendance 70,766. Washington jumped to a 21-3 halftime lead on Joe Theismann scoring passes to Otis Wonsley (one yard) and Charlie Brown (39), and John Riggins' two-yard run. New York closed to 24-17 on Scott Brunner's 26-yard touchdown pass to Johnny Perkins and Clifford Chatman's one-yard run, but Mark Moseley's 29-yard field goal with 1:23 left sealed the victory. Theismann completed 16 of 24 passes for 185 yards.

Washington	7	14	3	3	—	27
New York Giants	0	3	7	7	—	17

Wash — Wonsley 1 pass from Theismann (Moseley kick)
Wash — Brown 39 pass from Theismann (Moseley kick)
Wash — Riggins 2 run (Moseley kick)
NYG — FG Danelo 20
NYG — Perkins 26 pass from Brunner (Danelo kick)
Wash — FG Moseley 37
NYG — Chatman 1 run (Danelo kick)
Wash — FG Moseley 29

MONDAY, NOVEMBER 22

Los Angeles Raiders 28, San Diego 24—At Memorial Coliseum, attendance 42,162. Los Angeles overcame a 24-0 second-quarter deficit to defeat San Diego 28-24 and increase its Monday night record to 19-2-1. Jim Plunkett's one-yard touchdown pass to Todd Christensen with 36 seconds left in the first half triggered the comeback. A pair of third-quarter scores by Marcus Allen, on runs of three and six yards, brought the Raiders to within three points 24-21. Frank Hawkins' one-yard touchdown run with 5:54 remaining clinched the win. San Diego's Dan Fouts passed for more than 300 yards (25 of 42 for 357 yards) for the twenty-sixth time in his career to tie Johnny Unitas' NFL record.

San Diego	10	14	0	0	—	24
L.A. Raiders	0	7	14	7	—	28

SD — FG Benirschke 19
SD — Scales 29 pass from Fouts (Benirschke kick)
SD — Muncie 2 run (Benirschke kick)
SD — Muncie 1 run (Benirschke kick)
Raiders — Christensen 1 pass from Plunkett (Bahr kick)
Raiders — Allen 3 run (Bahr kick)
Raiders — Allen 6 run (Bahr kick)
Raiders — Hawkins 1 run (Bahr kick)

FOURTH WEEK SUMMARY

Fourth week results centered around this season's unfolding rags-to-riches story—the New Orleans Saints. After winning two of their first three games, the Saints showed just how serious they were by knocking off defending NFL champion San Francisco 23-20. New Orleans carried a 23-6 lead into the final quarter and weathered a furious rally by the 49ers. Jeff Groth's recovery of an onside kick with five seconds remaining sealed the victory. Seattle shutout Pittsburgh 16-0 to even their record at 2-2 and give interim head coach Mike McCormack his second straight victory since replacing Jack Patera on October 13. The Raiders, Dolphins, and Packers lost for the first time. The Bengals' defense bottled up the Raiders' rushing attack (33 total yards) and held rookie sensation Marcus Allen to zero net yards. Cincinnati also intercepted four Jim Plunkett passes in the 31-17 win. Meanwhile, Tampa Bay won for the first time in 1982 by holding off cross-state rival Miami 23-17. The Packers dropped a 15-12 decision to the Jets after holding a 13-6 halftime edge. Lawrence Taylor's fourth quarter 97-yard interception return for a score brought the Giants their first 1982 victory, 13-6 over the Lions on Thanksgiving Day. LeRoy Irvin's fourth punt return touchdown of his career helped the Rams to their first win, a 20-14 decision over the Chiefs. That left only one undefeated team, the Washington Redskins, who dropped Philadelphia 13-9 in the rain at RFK Stadium. Buffalo allowed only 88 yards in shutting out Baltimore 20-0 while Minnesota dominated Chicago 35-7 behind Tommy Kramer's career-high five touchdown passes. The Chargers slipped by the Broncos 30-20 as Dan Fouts threw for 337 yards to set an NFL record for most 300-yard passing games in a career (27).

THURSDAY, NOVEMBER 25

Dallas 31, Cleveland 14—At Texas Stadium, attendance 46,267. Danny White directed the Cowboys' 496-yard offensive attack, throwing for two touchdowns, and Tony Dorsett ran for 116 yards and two scores as Dallas posted its eleventh Thanksgiving Day win. Dallas opened a 17-0 halftime lead, capitalizing on interceptions by Michael Downs and Bob Breunig to set up White's four-yard touchdown pass to Billy Joe DuPree and Dorsett's one-yard plunge. Third-period scores by Dorsett and Ron Springs put the game out of reach.

Cleveland	0	0	0	14	—	14
Dallas	0	17	14	0	—	31

Dall — DuPree 4 pass from D. White (Septien kick)
Dall — Dorsett 1 run (Septien kick)
Dall — FG Septien 40
Dall — Springs 2 pass from D. White (Septien kick)
Dall — Dorsett 5 run (Septien kick)
Cle — Hall 18 pass from McDonald (Bahr kick)
Cle — Pruitt 2 run (Bahr kick)

New York Giants 13, Detroit 6—At Pontiac Silverdome, attendance 64,348. Lawrence Taylor's 97-yard interception return for a touchdown helped the Giants win their first game. Detroit led 6-0 but Brad Van Pelt's fumble recovery and Harry Carson's interception set up Joe Danelo field goals of 34 and 40 yards, respectively. The deciding score came with 11:52 left in the game when Taylor stepped in front of Lions' halfback Horace King at the Giants' 3 yard line and galloped down the sideline untouched.

New York Giants	0	0	6	7	—	13
Detroit	3	3	0	0	—	6

Det — FG Murray 46
Det — FG Murray 44
NYG — FG Danelo 34
NYG — FG Danelo 40
NYG — Taylor 97 interception return (Danelo kick)

SUNDAY, NOVEMBER 28

Buffalo 20, Baltimore 0—At Rich Stadium, attendance 33,985. Roosevelt Leaks rushed a career-high 22 times for 90 yards and two touchdowns as the Bills handed the Colts their second straight shutout defeat. Buffalo's defense limited Baltimore to 88 yards (36 rushing, 52 passing) and did not allow the Colts to cross the 50 yard line. Efren Herrera hit two field goals (47 and 41 yards), his first since joining Buffalo.

Baltimore	0	0	0	0	—	0
Buffalo	3	14	0	3	—	20

Buff — FG Herrera 47
Buff — Leaks 1 run (Herrera kick)
Buff — Leaks 1 run (Herrera kick)
Buff — FG Herrera 41

Minnesota 35, Chicago 7—At Metrodome, attendance 54,724. Tommy Kramer completed 26 of 35 passes for 342 yards and a career-high five touchdowns as the Vikings dropped the Bears 35-7. Chicago took a 7-0 lead on a 50-yard pass from rookie Jim McMahon to tight end Emery Moorehead, but Minnesota reeled off 35 straight points. Sammy White caught a career-high three touchdowns (5, 8, and 13 yards) among his 10 receptions, for a personal-best 177 yards. Kramer also threw scoring passes to Joe Senser (one yard) and Leo Lewis (31). The Vikings' defense had seven sacks, two fumble recoveries, and three interceptions by Willie Teal.

Chicago	0	7	0	0	—	7
Minnesota	0	14	7	14	—	35

Chi — Moorehead 50 pass from McMahon (Roveto kick)
Minn — S. White 5 pass from Kramer (Danmeier kick)
Minn — Senser 1 pass from Kramer (Danmeier kick)
Minn — S. White 8 pass from Kramer (Danmeier kick)
Minn — Lewis 31 pass from Kramer (Danmeier kick)
Minn — S. White 13 pass from Kramer (Danmeier kick)

San Diego 30, Denver 20—At San Diego Jack Murphy Stadium, attendance 47,629. Kellen Winslow's third touchdown catch of the day with 6:16 remaining broke a 20-20 tie and helped the Chargers even their record at 2-2. Winslow's eight catches for 107 yards included scoring receptions of 3, 28, and 2 yards. Dan Fouts (27 of 40 for 337 yards) passed for more than 300 yards for the twenty-seventh time in his 10-year career to break Johnny Unitas' NFL record. Rolf Benirschke kicked three field goals of 41, 18, and 42 yards, the last with 52 seconds left to secure the victory for San Diego.

Denver	3	7	7	3	—	20
San Diego	0	17	3	10	—	30

Den — FG Karlis 27
SD — Winslow 3 pass from Fouts (Benirschke kick)
SD — FG Benirschke 41
SD — Winslow 28 pass from Fouts (Benirschke kick)
Den — Upchurch 15 pass from DeBerg (Karlis kick)
Den — DeBerg 6 run (Karlis kick)
SD — FG Benirschke 18
Den — FG Karlis 38
SD — Winslow 2 pass from Fouts (Benirschke kick)
SD — FG Benirschke 42

New York Jets 15, Green Bay 13—At Shea Stadium, attendance 53,872. Pat Leahy's 25-yard field goal with 50 seconds left in the third quarter provided the margin of victory for the Jets and dropped the Packers from the unbeaten ranks. Green Bay built a 13-6 lead on a pair of Lynn Dickey to Phillip Epps scoring passes (24 and 23 yards) but Mike Augustyniak's four-yard touchdown run early in the third period brought New York to within one point, 13-12. Freeman McNeil, the league's leading rusher, set up Leahy's winning boot with a 36-yard run.

Green Bay	6	7	0	0	—	13
New York Jets	6	0	9	0	—	15

GB — Epps 24 pass from Dickey (kick failed)
NYJ — L. Jones 23 pass from Todd (kick failed)
GB — Epps 23 pass from Dickey (Stenerud kick)
NYJ — Augustyniak 4 run (kick blocked)
NYJ — FG Leahy 25

New England 29, Houston 21—At Schaefer Stadium, attendance 33,602. Three touchdown passes by Steve Grogan, combined with the running of Tony Collins, paced the Patriots to their second win. Grogan, making his first start since November 15, 1981, threw first-quarter scoring passes of 62 and 24 yards to Stanley Morgan (five receptions, 122 yards) and added a 14-yarder to Collins in the final period to give New England a 29-7 lead. Collins carried 32 times for 161 yards and set up field goals of 23 and 25 yards by rookie Dan Miller. Archie Manning, starting his first game for Houston, was sacked six times for 62 yards.

Houston	7	0	0	14	—	21
New England	14	6	0	9	—	29

Hou — Campbell 1 run (Kempf kick)
NE — Morgan 62 pass from Grogan (Miller kick)
NE — Morgan 24 pass from Grogan (Miller kick)
NE — FG Miller 23
NE — FG Miller 25
NE — Safety, Crump tackled Manning in end zone
NE — Collins 14 pass from Grogan (Miller kick)
Hou — Casper 14 pass from Manning (Kempf kick)
Hou — Renfro 8 pass from Manning (Kempf kick)

Los Angeles Rams 20, Kansas City 14—At Anaheim Stadium, attendance 45,793. Wendell Tyler ran for 138 yards on 25 carries and scored a pair of touchdowns to help the Rams capture their first win. Tyler's second-quarter scoring runs of one and 23 yards climaxed drives of 62 and 75 yards, respectively. LeRoy Irvin's 63-yard punt return for a touchdown, the fourth of his career, gave Los Angeles an insurmountable 20-7 lead.

Kansas City	7	0	0	7	—	14
L.A. Rams	0	14	6	0	—	20

KC — B. Jackson 1 run (Lowery kick)
Rams — Tyler 1 run (Lansford kick)
Rams — Tyler 23 run (Lansford kick)
Rams — Irvin 63 punt return (kick failed)
KC — Smith 35 pass from Fuller (Lowery kick)

New Orleans 23, San Francisco 20—At Candlestick Park, attendance 51,611. Rickey Jackson's fumble recovery and interception set up touchdown runs by Jimmy Rogers and George Rogers to lead the Saints to their third straight win. Ken Stabler's 10-yard pass to Wayne Wilson opened the scoring and capped a 99-yard drive. The 49ers were limited to a pair of field goals by Ray Wersching until the final two minutes of play when Joe Montana (27 of 42 for 334 yards) hit for two touchdown passes.

New Orleans	7	6	10	0	—	23
San Francisco	0	6	0	14	—	20

NO — Wilson 10 pass from Stabler (Fritsch kick)
SF — FG Wersching 40
NO — J. Rogers 2 run (kick failed)
SF — FG Wersching 45
NO — FG Fritsch 27
NO — G. Rogers 1 run (Fritsch kick)
SF — Moore 12 pass from Montana (Wersching kick)
SF — Francis 17 pass from Montana (Wersching kick)

Cincinnati 31, Los Angeles Raiders 17—At Riverfront Stadium, attendance 53,330. Ken Anderson passed for one touchdown and ran for another, and Pete Johnson rushed for 129 yards and a score as the Bengals dropped the Raiders from the unbeaten ranks. Cincinnati built a 14-0 lead on Anderson's three-yard pass to Rodney Holman and Ken Riley's first of three interceptions, which he returned 56 yards for a score. Los Angeles pulled to within 14-10, but Johnson's one-yard blast and Anderson's 10-yard run put the game out of reach. It was the Bengals' first victory over the Raiders since October 19, 1975.

L.A. Raiders	0	10	7	0	—	17
Cincinnati	14	7	7	3	—	31

Cin — Holman 3 pass from Anderson (Kreider run)
Cin — Riley 56 interception return (Breech kick)
Raiders — FG Bahr 31
Raiders — Branch 34 pass from Plunkett (Bahr kick)
Cin — Johnson 1 run (Breech kick)
Raiders — Branch 28 pass from Plunkett (Bahr kick)
Cin — Anderson 10 run (Breech kick)
Cin — FG Breech 35

Washington 13, Philadelphia 9—At Robert F. Kennedy Stadium, attendance 48,313. Charlie Brown caught three passes for 124 yards including the game-winning 65-yard touchdown as Washington defeated Philadelphia. Mark Moseley kicked field goals from 45 and 43 yards as the Redskins remained the NFC's only undefeated team. Down by 10 points, Philadelphia got as close as 10-9 on Ron Jaworski's 44-yard scoring bomb to Harold Carmichael and Tony Franklin's 41-yard field goal. Washington's defense had four interceptions including Mark Murphy's theft at the Redskins' 1 yard line and Tony Peters steal late in the fourth quarter, which ended late Philadelphia scoring threats.

Philadelphia	0	0	9	0	—	9
Washington	3	7	3	0	—	13

Wash — FG Moseley 45
Wash — Brown 65 pass from Theismann (Moseley kick)
Phil — FG Franklin 41
Phil — Carmichael 44 pass from Jaworski (kick failed)
Wash — FG Moseley 43

Seattle 16, Pittsburgh 0—At Kingdome, attendance 55,553. Rookie Norm Johnson kicked three field goals and Jim Zorn fired an 11-yard touchdown pass to Paul Johns to lead the Seahawks to their first shutout win ever in the Kingdome. Johnson's field goals of 35, 48, and 29 yards, the last two set up by Ken Easley and Michael Jackson interceptions, staked Seattle to a 9-0 halftime lead. Zorn then engineered the game-clinching 68-yard touchdown drive, which included a 45-yard pass to Steve Largent. The Steelers played most of the game without Terry Bradshaw who exited in the first quarter with a shoulder sprain. It was Pittsburgh's first shutout loss since December 4, 1980, against Houston.

Pittsburgh	0	0	0	0	—	0
Seattle	3	6	7	0	—	16

Sea — FG N. Johnson 35
Sea — FG N. Johnson 48

Sea — FG N. Johnson 29
Sea — Johns 11 pass from Zorn (N. Johnson kick)

St. Louis 23, Atlanta 20—At Atlanta-Fulton Country Stadium, attendance 33,411. Ottis Anderson ran for 122 yards and one touchdown to help the Cardinals edge the Falcons 23-20. St. Louis scored on their first two possessions of the game via Wayne Morris' two-yard run and Anderson's 20-yard gallop. Atlanta came within 14-13 but St. Louis built up a 10-point lead on Neil O'Donoghue's 43-yard field goal and Neil Lomax's one-yard run. Atlanta's Mick Luckhurst missed a 42-yard field goal attempt with one second left that would have sent the game into overtime.

St. Louis	7	7	3	6	—	23
Atlanta	3	3	7	7	—	20

Atl — FG Luckhurst 28
StL — Morris 2 run (O'Donoghue kick)
StL — Anderson 20 run (O'Donoghue kick)
Atl — FG Luckhurst 27
Atl — Robinson 2 pass from Bartkowski (Luckhurst kick)
StL — FG O'Donoghue 43
StL — Lomax 1 run (kick failed)
Atl — Jackson 15 pass from Bartkowski (Luckhurst kick)

MONDAY, NOVEMBER 29

Tampa Bay 23, Miami 17—At Tampa Stadium, attendance 65,854. The Buccaneers built a 23-10 lead on three Bill Capece field goals and touchdown runs by Doug Williams and James Wilder, and survived the Dolphins' late comeback bid to halt a three-game losing streak. Don Strock, who replaced David Woodley at quarterback in the second half, narrowed the margin to 23-17 with an 11-yard scoring pass to Joe Rose. Lyle Blackwood recovered the ensuing onside kickoff, but Tampa Bay's Mike Washington intercepted Strock in the end zone to preserve the victory and hand Miami its first loss. Washington and Neal Colzie each had two interceptions and Cedric Brown one, as the Buccaneers picked off five Miami passes.

Miami	0	3	0	14	—	17
Tampa Bay	3	3	10	7	—	23

TB — FG Capece 28
Mia — FG von Schamann 29
TB — FG Capece 27
TB — Williams 3 run (Capece kick)
TB — FG Capece 36
Mia — Rose 7 pass from Strock (von Schamann kick)
TB — Wilder 2 run (Capece kick)
Mia — Rose 11 pass from Strock (von Schamann kick)

FIFTH WEEK SUMMARY

The Washington Redskins, 1982's last undefeated team, joined the ranks of the once-beaten by succumbing to the Dallas Cowboys 24-10 at RFK Stadium. The determined Cowboys dominated the game, sacking Redskins quarterback Joe Theismann seven times and intercepting three of his passes. The Cowboys' victory was head coach Tom Landry's two-hundredth regular-season win.
The Dallas win created a three-way tie for first in the NFC among Dallas, Green Bay, and Washington while in the AFC five teams remained deadlocked for the top spot: Cincinnati, the Los Angeles Raiders, Miami, the New York Jets, and Pittsburgh. San Francisco's Jeff Moore and Atlanta's William Andrews each scored three touchdowns to lead their teams over the Los Angeles Rams and Denver, respectively. Marcus Allen, unproductive in the Raiders loss a week ago, bounced back with 156 yards on 24 carries and two scores to lead Los Angeles to a 28-23 victory over Seattle. San Diego's Chuck Muncie scored a pair of touchdowns before leaving the game with a bruised knee, but the Chargers weren't hurt at all as James Brooks came off the bench to add two more scores in San Diego's resounding 30-13 triumph over Cleveland. The New York Giants trailed Houston 14-3 entering the fourth quarter when rookie Butch Woolfolk scored twice within a three-minute span to give New York a 17-14 win. St. Louis' Stump Mitchell, replacing injured starter Ottis Anderson, ran for 145 yards and a touchdown to help power the Cardinals past the Eagles 23-20. Philadelphia held St. Louis' Mel Gray without a reception, thus ending his 121-game reception streak. In interconference matchups, New York Jets quarterback Richard Todd threw for 384 yards and Wesley Walker caught three scoring passes to lead the Jets over the Lions 28-13. Chicago notched their fifth consecutive win over an AFC opponent, downing New England 26-13. Miami held Minnesota to 182 total yards for a 22-14 victory, while the Packers defeated the Bills 33-21 as Jan Stenerud booted four field goals and three extra points to move into third place on the all-time scoring list with 1,382 points.

THURSDAY, DECEMBER 2

San Francisco 30, Los Angeles Rams 24—At Anaheim Stadium, attendance 58,574. Joe Montana completed 26 of 37 passes for 305 yards and two touchdowns and Jeff Moore scored three touchdowns to rally the 49ers over the Rams. Moore grabbed eight passes for 102 yards including second-quarter touchdowns of 38 and 24 yards which gave San Francisco a 20-10 lead. Los Angeles rebounded to gain a 24-23 edge but Moore's one-yard run with 4:40 left proved to be the winning margin. Ray Wersching kicked field goals of 33, 44, and 38 yards for San Francisco.

San Francisco	3	17	0	10	—	30
L.A. Rams	10	0	7	7	—	24

SF — FG Wersching 33
Rams — FG Lansford 36
Rams — Tyler 27 pass from Ferragamo (Lansford kick)
SF — FG Wersching 44
SF — Moore 38 pass from Montana (Wersching kick)
SF — Moore 24 pass from Montana (Wersching kick)
Rams — Tyler 1 run (Lansford kick)
SF — FG Wersching 38
Rams — Tyler 15 run (Lansford kick)
SF — Moore 1 run (Wersching kick)

SUNDAY, DECEMBER 5

Atlanta 34, Denver 27—At Mile High Stadium, attendance 73,984. William Andrews scored a club record-tying three touchdowns and Mick Luckhurst kicked a pair of 51-yard field goals as the Falcons outlasted the Broncos. Atlanta trailed 20-14 early in the third quarter, but Andrews' 86-yard scoring reception put the Falcons ahead to stay 21-20 with 5:50 left in the period. Following Luckhurst's field goals, Andrews converted Tom Pridemore's interception into a touchdown, scoring from two yards out with 4:18 left. Andrews rushed 16 times for 73 yards and caught three passes for 106 yards.

Atlanta	7	7	10	10	—	34
Denver	14	3	3	7	—	27

Atl — Andrews 8 run (Luckhurst kick)
Den — Winder 3 run (Karlis kick)
Den — Watson 6 pass from DeBerg (Karlis kick)
Atl — Miller 9 pass from Bartkowski (Luckhurst kick)
Den — FG Karlis 31
Den — FG Karlis 26
Atl — Andrews 86 pass from Bartkowski (Luckhurst kick)
Atl — FG Luckhurst 51
Atl — FG Luckhurst 51
Atl — Andrews 2 run (Luckhurst kick)
Den — Wright 5 pass from DeBerg (Karlis kick)

Green Bay 33, Buffalo 21—At Milwaukee County Stadium, attendance 46,655. Jan Stenerud kicked field goals of 33, 25, 31, and 42 yards to help the Packers register a 33-21 win. Green Bay's defense was superb, coming up with three fumble recoveries and two interceptions. Del Rodgers' fumble recovery in the end zone gave the Packers' a 13-7 lead. Green Bay increased its lead to 27-7 on Eddie Lee Ivery's one-yard run and Lynn Dickey's 23-yard touchdown pass to John Thompson. Stenerud's four field goals and three extra points gave him 1,382 career points, which moved him into third place on the all-time NFL scoring list.

Buffalo	0	7	0	14	—	21
Green Bay	6	7	7	13	—	33

GB — FG Stenerud 33
GB — FG Stenerud 25
Buff — Cribbs 1 run (Herrera kick)
GB — Rodgers recovered fumble in end zone (Stenerud kick)
GB — Ivery 1 run (Stenerud kick)
GB — Thompson 23 pass from Dickey (Stenerud kick)
GB — FG Stenerud 31
Buff — Brammer 8 pass from Ferguson (Herrera kick)
GB — FG Stenerud 42
Buff — Brammer 6 pass from Robinson (Herrera kick)

Cincinnati 20, Baltimore 17—At Memorial Stadium, attendance 23,598. Ken Anderson's three touchdown passes were all the Bengals needed to defeat the Colts and remain in a five-way tie for first place in the AFC. Cincinnati wiped out a 10-6 halftime deficit to take a 20-10 lead as Anderson teamed with M. L. Harris on scores of one and two yards. The Colts closed to within 20-17 on Mike Pagel's four-yard touchdown pass to Pat Beach and could have tied the game with 28 seconds remaining, but Mike Wood's 40-yard field goal attempt was wide.

Cincinnati	0	6	7	7	—	20
Baltimore	7	3	0	7	—	17

Balt — Butler 17 pass from Pagel (Wood kick)
Cin — Kreider 24 pass from Anderson (kick blocked)
Balt — FG Wood 33
Cin — M. L. Harris 1 pass from Anderson (Breech kick)
Cin — M. L. Harris 2 pass from Anderson (Breech kick)
Balt — Beach 4 pass from Pagel (Wood kick)

Dallas 24, Washington 10—At Robert F. Kennedy Stadium, attendance 54,633. The Dallas defense sacked Washington quarterback Joe Theismann seven times for 60 yards and had three interceptions to give Dallas head coach Tom Landry his 200th regular-season win. The Cowboys took a 17-0 lead into the fourth quarter on Ron Springs eight-yard scoring catch, Rafael Septien's 31-yard field goal, and Timmy Newsome's 18-yard touchdown run. The Redskins closed to 17-10 on Mark Moseley's 38-yard field goal and Theismann's 17-yard touchdown pass to Charlie Brown, but Springs' 46-yard touchdown run with 1:52 remaining handed Washington its first defeat.

Dallas	0	7	10	7	—	24
Washington	0	0	0	10	—	10

Dall — Springs 8 pass from D. White (Septien kick)
Dall — FG Septien 31
Dall — Newsome 18 run (Septien kick)
Wash — FG Moseley 38
Wash — Brown 17 pass from Theismann (Moseley kick)
Dall — Springs 46 run (Septien kick)

New York Giants 17, Houston 14—At Giants Stadium, attendance 71,184. A pair of fourth-quarter touchdowns by rookie Butch Woolfolk rallied the Giants past the Oilers 17-14. Houston led 14-3 but Woolfolk's two-yard touchdown run cut New York's deficit to 14-10 with 6:29 left. Woolfolk's 40-yard scoring reception from Scott Brunner with 3:30 left put the Giants ahead for good. Woolfolk carried 16 times for 62 yards and added 102 yards on six receptions. The Giants' defense was led by George Martin, who had three of New York's five quarterback sacks.

Houston	0	7	0	7	—	14
New York Giants	3	0	0	14	—	17

NYG — FG Danelo 26
Hou — Allen 23 pass from Nielsen (Kempf kick)
Hou — Casper 8 pass from Manning (Kempf kick)
NYG — Woolfolk 2 run (Danelo kick)
NYG — Woolfolk 40 pass from Brunner (Danelo kick)

Pittsburgh 35, Kansas City 14—At Three Rivers Stadium, attendance 52,090. Terry Bradshaw fired three touchdown passes for the fourth time this season to lead the Steelers over the Chiefs. Pittsburgh opened up a 28-7 halftime lead on Bradshaw scoring passes of three and 74 yards to John Stallworth and five yards to Greg Hawthorne, and a one-yard run by Franco Harris. Bradshaw completed 15 of 20 passes for 231 yards in three quarters of play, including four to Stallworth for 107 yards. The Steelers' defense registered eight sacks for 70 yards to increase their AFC-leading total to 23.

Kansas City	0	7	0	7	—	14
Pittsburgh	14	14	0	7	—	35

Pitt — Stallworth 3 pass from Bradshaw (Anderson kick)
Pitt — Stallworth 74 pass from Bradshaw (Anderson kick)
Pitt — Hawthorne 5 pass from Bradshaw (Anderson kick)
KC — B. Jackson 1 run (Lowery kick)
Pitt — Harris 1 run (Anderson kick)
KC — Scott 3 pass from Fuller (Lowery kick)
Pitt — Thornton 2 run (Anderson kick)

Miami 22, Minnesota 14—At Orange Bowl, attendance 45,721. Andra Franklin rushed for 129 yards and Uwe von Schamann kicked three field goals as the Dolphins prevailed 22-14. Miami took a 9-7 halftime lead on David Woodley's one-yard scoring run and von Schamann's 34-yard field goal. The Dolphins increased their advantage to 19-7 on von Schamann's 28-yard field goal and Franklin's nine-yard run. Von Schamann closed out the scoring with a 24-yard field goal with 1:46 remaining. Miami's defense held Minnesota to 182 yards, intercepting three Tommy Kramer passes and sacking Kramer five times.

Minnesota	0	7	0	7	—	14
Miami	6	3	3	10	—	22

Mia — Woodley 1 run (kick blocked)
Minn — Kramer 18 run (Danmeier kick)
Mia — FG von Schamann 34
Mia — FG von Schamann 28
Mia — Franklin 9 run (von Schamann kick)
Minn — Galbreath 1 run (Danmeier kick)
Mia — FG von Schamann 24

Chicago 26, New England 13—At Soldier Field, attendance 36,973. Jim McMahon passed for two touchdowns and ran for another as the Bears won their fifth straight over an AFC opponent. Chicago built a 23-0 lead on scoring catches of 17 yards by Ken Margerum, two yards by Emery Moorehead, a safety when Jim Osborne tackled Patriots quarterback Steve Grogan in the end zone, and a six-yard run by McMahon. Grogan's one-yard scoring plunge put the Patriots on the scoreboard 52 seconds before halftime and Rick Sanford added a touchdown with a club-record 99-yard interception return early in the third period. Terry Schmidt had two interceptions for the Bears.

New England	0	6	7	0	—	13
Chicago	14	9	0	3	—	26

Chi — Margerum 17 pass from McMahon (Roveto kick)
Chi — Moorehead 2 pass from McMahon (Roveto kick)
Chi — Safety, Osborne tackled Grogan in end zone
Chi — McMahon 6 run (Roveto kick)
NE — Grogan 1 run (kick blocked)
NE — Sanford 99 interception return (Miller kick)
NE — FG Roveto 43

St. Louis 23, Philadelphia 20—At Veterans Stadium, attendance 63,622. Stump Mitchell, replacing the injured Ottis Anderson, gained 145 yards on 25 carries to lead the Cardinals over the Eagles. Neil O'Donoghue's three field goals, coupled with scoring runs of eight yards by Wayne Morris and 32 yards by Mitchell, gave St. Louis an insurmountable 23-7 lead at the half. Mel Gray was held without a pass reception for the first time in 121 games, thus ending the second-longest pass receiving streak in NFL history.

St. Louis	10	13	0	0	—	23
Philadelphia	7	0	6	7	—	20

StL — Morris 8 run (O'Donoghue kick)
StL — FG O'Donoghue 26
Phil — Montgomery 2 run (Franklin kick)
StL — FG O'Donoghue 20
StL — Mitchell 32 run (O'Donoghue kick)
StL — FG O'Donoghue 34
Phil — Montgomery 6 pass from Jaworski (kick failed)
Phil — Spagnola 8 pass from Jaworski (Franklin kick)

San Diego 30, Cleveland 13—At Cleveland Stadium, attendance 54,064. Dan Fouts completed 13 of his first 16 passes (18 of 23 overall for 252 yards) and Chuck Muncie and James Brooks each had a pair of first-half touchdown runs as the Chargers defeated the Browns 30-13. Muncie's first of two one-yard scores was set up by Mike Williams' interception. Brooks had touchdown runs of one and 11 yards, the second set up by Tim Fox's 28-yard interception return. Brian Sipe set a Cleveland record for completions with 33 in 48 attempts (including a team-record 14 straight). His 338 yards passing also raised his career total to 20,021.

San Diego	14	13	0	3	—	30
Cleveland	3	0	10	0	—	13

SD — Muncie 1 run (Benirschke kick)
SD — Muncie 1 run (Benirschke kick)
Cle — FG Bahr 46
SD — Brooks 1 run (Benirschke kick)
SD — Brooks 11 run (kick failed)
Cle — FG Bahr 34
Cle — Newsome 4 pass from Sipe (Bahr kick)
SD — FG Benirschke 24

Los Angeles Raiders 28, Seattle 23—At Memorial Coliseum, attendance 42,170. Marcus Allen rushed for 156 yards and two touchdowns (on runs of two and three yards) as the Raiders opened a 28-0 first-half lead and withstood the Seahawks' late comeback attempt. Los Angeles scored four touchdowns within a 12-minute span of the first half. Along with Allen's two first-half scores, Kenny King scored from one yard and Rod Martin had a 39-yard interception return. Down 28-7, Seattle scored 16 unanswered fourth-quarter points but Burgess Owens' interception at the Raiders' 3 yard line ended the Seahawks' final threat.

Seattle	0	7	0	16	—	23
L.A. Raiders	7	21	0	0	—	28

Raiders — Allen 2 run (Bahr kick)
Raiders — King 1 run (Bahr kick)
Raiders — Martin 39 interception return (Bahr kick)
Raiders — Allen 3 run (Bahr kick)
Sea — Largent 10 pass from Zorn (N. Johnson kick)
Sea — T. Brown 3 run (kick failed)
Sea — Carr 23 pass from Zorn (N. Johnson kick)
Sea — FG N. Johnson 30

Tampa Bay 13, New Orleans 10—At Louisiana Superdome, attendance 61,709. Bill Capece's 50-yard field goal with 20 seconds left in the third quarter provided the winning margin and snapped the Saints three-game win streak. Ken Stabler's (29 of 43 for 333 yards) 14-yard pass to Aundra Thompson gave New Orleans a 7-0 lead. Tampa Bay came back on Capece's 29-yard field goal and Doug Williams' 34-yard scoring pass to Kevin House. The Buccaneers held the Saints to just 69 yards rushing and Neal Colzie had two fumble recoveries deep in Tampa Bay territory to thwart New Orleans scoring bids.

Tampa Bay	0	3	10	0	— 13
New Orleans	7	0	3	0	— 10

NO — Thompson 14 pass from Stabler (Fritsch kick)
TB — FG Capece 29
TB — House 34 pass from Williams (Capece kick)
NO — FG Andersen 45
TB — FG Capece 50

MONDAY, DECEMBER 6

New York Jets 28, Detroit 13—At Pontiac Silverdome, attendance 79,361. Richard Todd and Wesley Walker connected on three touchdown passes covering 56, 41, and 19 yards to lead the Jets over the Lions. Todd's 23 completions in 32 attempts for 384 yards included five to Walker for 164 yards. Bobby Jackson had two of the Jets' three interceptions and Kenny Neil two of New York's five sacks. The Jets gained 437 yards to Detroit's 274.

New York Jets	7	14	0	7	— 28
Detroit	3	0	7	3	— 13

Det — FG Murray 31
NYJ — Crutchfield 1 run (Leahy kick)
NYJ — Walker 56 pass from Todd (Leahy kick)
NYJ — Walker 41 pass from Todd (Leahy kick)
Det — Nichols 48 pass from Danielson (Murray kick)
Det — FG Murray 22
NYJ — Walker 19 pass from Todd (Leahy kick)

SIXTH WEEK SUMMARY

The east and west coasts experienced blizzards of differing natures this weekend. A scoreless game on Schaefer Stadium's frozen, snow-blanketed field was broken open when Patriots kicker John Smith kicked a 33-yard field goal with 4:45 to play to down the Dolphins 3-0. The game will be best remembered for the snow-plow assistance New England received in clearing the spot of the placement. In two inches of snow and a wind-chill factor of five degrees below zero, the New York Jets won their fifth straight, 32-17 over Tampa Bay. The Giants unveiled rookie wide receiver Floyd Eddings who caught five passes for 148 yards to lead the Giants to their third consecutive triumph, a 23-7 victory over the Eagles. In San Francisco, the 49ers and Chargers combined for 1,009 yards total offense as San Diego outlasted San Francisco 41-37. Dan Fouts threw for 444 yards and five touchdowns while counterpart Joe Montana totalled over 300 yards through the air (356) for an NFL-record fifth successive week. Buffalo blanked Pittsburgh 13-0 marking the first time since 1957 that the Steelers were shutout twice in the same season. Jim Plunkett's 35-yard touchdown pass to Calvin Muhammad with 25 seconds left lifted the Raiders over the Chiefs 21-16 and helped Los Angeles maintain a share of the lead in the AFC with the Bengals and Jets. Denver rebounded from a 21-0 deficit to defeat the Rams 27-24 as Steve DeBerg tied an NFL record by completing his last 17 passes in a row. In the NFC, Dallas and Washington became deadlocked for first place. Danny White fired three touchdown passes to lead the Cowboys over the Oilers 37-7. The win insured Dallas of an NFL-record seventeenth consecutive winning season. The Redskins relied on Mark Moseley's four field goals and an opportunistic defense to beat the Cardinals 12-7. Detroit ended a three-game losing streak by registering nine sacks and five interceptions to defeat Green Bay 30-10. The loss dropped the Packers out of first place in the NFC. Atlanta shelled New Orleans 35-0, outgaining the Saints 329 total yards to 91. Sammy White became Minnesota's career pass receiving leader with 5,513 yards by catching three passes for 78 yards in Minnesota's 13-10 victory over Baltimore.

SATURDAY, DECEMBER 11

New York Giants 23, Philadelphia 7—At Giants Stadium, attendance 66,053. Rookie wide receiver Floyd Eddings caught five passes for 148 yards in his first NFL game as the Giants captured their third straight win. Eddings catches set up Scott Brunner scoring tosses of five yards to Butch Woolfolk and 16 yards to Earnest Gray. Lawrence Taylor (three of the Giants' eight sacks) and Terry Jackson (two interceptions) led the defense which held the Eagles to 198 total yards, including just 41 rushing.

Philadelphia	7	0	0	0	— 7
New York Giants	3	14	3	3	— 23

NYG — FG Danelo 37
Phil — Carmichael 23 pass from Jaworski (Franklin kick)
NYG — Woolfolk 5 pass from Brunner (Danelo kick)
NYG — Gray 16 pass from Brunner (Danelo kick)
NYG — FG Danelo 34
NYG — FG Danelo 29

San Diego 41, San Francisco 37—At Candlestick Park, attendance 55,988. Dan Fouts completed 33 of 48 passes for a personal-high 450 yards and five touchdowns as the Chargers outlasted the 49ers. Fouts' fifth scoring pass, three yards to Chuck Muncie, gave San Francisco a 41-37 lead with 3:22 left. Wes Chandler had seven receptions for 125 yards, including touchdowns of 31, 14, and 20 yards. Kellen Winslow grabbed nine passes for 101 yards and Charlie Joiner had eight for 145. San Francisco's Joe Montana set an NFL record with his fifth straight 300-yard passing game (31 of 46 for 356 yards). The teams combined for an NFL-record 64 completions and 1,009 yards of offense (465 by San Francisco, 544 by San Diego).

San Diego	7	17	7	10	— 41
San Francisco	7	10	7	13	— 37

SD — Chandler 31 pass from Fouts (Benirschke kick)
SF — Montana 11 run (Wersching kick)
SD — FG Benirschke 25
SF — Moore 6 pass from Montana (Wersching kick)
SD — Sievers 25 pass from Fouts (Benirschke kick)
SF — FG Wersching 45
SD — Chandler 14 pass from Fouts (Benirschke kick)
SD — Chandler 20 pass from Fouts (Benirschke kick)
SF — Solomon 14 pass from Montana (Wersching kick)
SF — Ring 9 run (kick failed)
SD — FG Benirschke 41
SF — D. Clark 7 pass from Montana (Wersching kick)
SD — Muncie 3 pass from Fouts (Benirschke kick)

SUNDAY, DECEMBER 12

Minnesota 13, Baltimore 10—At Metrodome, attendance 53,981. Rick Danmeier kicked second-half field goals of 23 and 40 yards to defeat the Colts. The Vikings took a 7-3 halftime lead on Tommy Kramer's (19 of 35 for 258 yards) 24-yard touchdown pass to Sammy White. Kramer moved Minnesota within striking distance again in the third quarter but James Burroughs' 94-yard interception return gave the Colts a 10-7 edge. Danmeier's decisive field goal came with 9:09 remaining and evened the Vikings' record at 3-3. Sammy White's three receptions for 78 yards gave him a Vikings career record of 5,513 receiving yards.

Baltimore	0	3	7	0	— 10
Minnesota	7	0	3	3	— 13

Minn — S. White 24 pass from Kramer (Danmeier kick)
Balt — FG Wood 39
Balt — Burroughs 94 interception return (Wood kick)
Minn — FG Danmeier 23
Minn — FG Danmeier 40

Seattle 20, Chicago 14—At Kingdome, attendance 52,826. Jim Zorn fired a seven-yard touchdown pass and ran 15 yards for another, and Norm Johnson kicked a pair of field goals to help the Seahawks even their record at 3-3. Matt Suhey's fourth-quarter two-yard run brought Chicago to within three points, but Johnson's 34-yard field goal put the game away. The Bears were held scoreless on three final drives by the tenacious Seattle defense.

Chicago	7	0	0	7	— 14
Seattle	3	14	0	3	— 20

Sea — FG N. Johnson 30
Chi — Baschnagel 39 pass from Payton (Roveto kick)
Sea — Zorn 15 run (N. Johnson kick)
Sea — Walker 7 pass from Zorn (N. Johnson kick)
Chi — Suhey 2 run (Roveto kick)
Sea — FG N. Johnson 34

Cincinnati 23, Cleveland 10—At Riverfront Stadium, attendance 54,305. Second-quarter touchdowns by Ken Anderson and Pete Johnson were all the Bengals needed to notch their fourth straight win. Cincinnati scored on successive drives covering 58 and 75 yards, culminated by Johnson's three-yard run and Anderson's one-yard quarterback sweep. Jim Breech kicked field goals of 44, 21, and 36 yards for the Bengals.

Cleveland	0	3	7	0	— 10
Cincinnati	0	14	3	6	— 23

Cin — Johnson 3 run (Breech kick)
Cin — Anderson 1 run (Breech kick)
Cle — FG Bahr 29
Cle — Burrell 14 interception return (Bahr kick)
Cin — FG Breech 44
Cin — FG Breech 21
Cin — FG Breech 36

Denver 27, Los Angeles Rams 24—At Anaheim Stadium, attendance 48,112. Steve DeBerg tied an NFL record by completing his last 17 passes to rally the Broncos to a 27-24 victory over the Rams. Down 21-0, DeBerg hit Rick Upchurch on a 51-yard bomb and followed Aaron Kyle's interception with a seven-yard scoring pass to Rick Parros, just 64 seconds later. Denver closed the gap to 21-20 on Rich Karlis field goals of 47 and 18 yards. Parros followed with a three-yard touchdown run, set up by Louis Wright's interception, to finish the comeback. Denver's Steve Watson set career highs for receptions (10) and yards (183).

Denver	0	14	3	10	— 27
Los Angeles Rams	7	14	0	3	— 24

Rams — Guman 1 run (Lansford kick)
Rams — Tyler 1 run (Lansford kick)
Rams — Cromwell 17 run (Lansford kick)
Den — Upchurch 51 pass from DeBerg (Karlis kick)
Den — Parros 7 pass from DeBerg (Karlis kick)
Den — FG Karlis 47
Den — FG Karlis 18
Den — Parros 2 run (Karlis kick)
Rams — FG Lansford 39

Detroit 30, Green Bay 10—At Lambeau Field, attendance 51,875. Billy Sims gained 109 yards and scored one touchdown, and Detroit's defense registered nine sacks and five interceptions, as the Lions ended a three-game losing streak. Detroit opened a 23-0 halftime lead on Sims' one-yard run, Gary Danielson's 21-yard pass to Freddie Scott, and Ed Murray's three field goals from 27, 27, and 25 yards. Alvin Hall returned the second-half kickoff 96 yards for a touchdown to put the game out of reach. Doug English led the Lions' defense with four sacks.

Detroit	17	6	7	0	— 30
Green Bay	0	0	3	7	— 10

Det — FG Murray 27
Det — Sims 1 run (Murray kick)
Det — Scott 21 pass from Danielson (Murray kick)
Det — FG Murray 27
Det — FG Murray 25
Det — Hall 96 kickoff return (Murray kick)
GB — FG Stenerud 31
GB — Ellis 1 run (Stenerud kick)

New England 3, Miami 0—At Schaefer Stadium, attendance 25,716. John Smith's 33-yard field goal with 4:10 left in the game helped the Patriots even their record at 3-3. New England marched 77 yards in 11 plays to set up Smith s decisive kick. Don Blackmon's interception at the Patriots' 10 yard line with 37 seconds remaining sealed the win. Mark van Eeghen rushed for 100 yards on 22 carries for the first time since joining the Patriots. Miami's Andra Franklin gained 107 yards on 23 attempts. The game, played in 20-degree weather and three inches of snow, marked the first time Miami had failed to score in 33 games.

Miami	0	0	0	0	— 0
New England	0	0	0	3	— 3

NE — FG J. Smith 33

Atlanta 35, New Orleans 0—At Atlanta-Fulton County Stadium, attendance 39,535. Gerald Riggs and Lynn Cain each scored a pair of touchdowns as the Falcons completely dominated the Saints. Riggs scored on second-quarter runs of three and one yards and Cain added touchdowns on a 17-yard pass from Steve Bartkowski and a two-yard run in the third period. Mike Moroski replaced Bartkowski and completed a nine-yard touchdown pass to Stacey Bailey in the final minute of play. Atlanta outgained New Orleans 329 to 91 (70 rushing, 21 passing) yards while the Falcons' defense had three interceptions, three fumble recoveries, and seven sacks.

New Orleans	0	0	0	0	— 0
Atlanta	0	14	14	7	— 35

Atl — Riggs 3 run (Luckhurst kick)
Atl — Riggs 1 run (Luckhurst kick)
Atl — Cain 17 pass from Bartkowski (Luckhurst kick)
Atl — Cain 2 run (Luckhurst kick)
Atl — Bailey 9 pass from Moroski (Luckhurst kick)

Los Angeles Raiders 21, Kansas City 16—At Arrowhead, attendance 26,307. Jim Plunkett's desperation 35-yard touchdown pass to Calvin Muhammad with 25 seconds remaining defeated the Chiefs. Nick Lowery's three field goals had put the Chiefs ahead in the third quarter 9-7, but Plunkett (18 of 33 for 303 yards and three touchdowns) threw an eight-yard pass to Todd Christensen with 5:21 left to give the Raiders a 14-9 edge. Bill Kenney then took Kansas City 85 yards in seven plays, capped by Billy Jackson's one-yard scoring run with 1:55 left for a 16-14 lead. Plunkett then engineered the winning 80-yard Los Angeles drive.

L.A. Raiders	0	7	0	14	— 21
Kansas City	3	3	3	7	— 16

KC — FG Lowery 35
Raiders — Christensen 4 pass from Plunkett (Bahr kick)
KC — FG Lowery 27
KC — FG Lowery 29
Raiders — Christensen 8 pass from Plunkett (Bahr kick)
KC — B. Jackson 1 run (Lowery kick)
Raiders — Muhammad 35 pass from Plunkett (Bahr kick)

Buffalo 13, Pittsburgh 0—At Rich Stadium, attendance 58,391. The Buffalo defense held Pittsburgh to a team-record minus two yards passing (94 total yards overall) and Joe Cribbs rushed for 143 yards as the Bills recorded their second shutout in three games. Joe Ferguson engineered Buffalo's 78-yard touchdown drive, capped by Roosevelt Leaks' one-yard run, and Efren Herrera kicked field goals of 34 and 19 yards. The Bills had three interceptions, one fumble recovery, and five sacks as the Steelers suffered their second shutout in the same season for the first time since 1957.

Pittsburgh	0	0	0	0	— 0
Buffalo	0	10	3	0	— 13

Buff — Leaks 1 run (Herrera kick)
Buff — FG Herrera 34
Buff — FG Herrera 19

New York Jets 32, Tampa Bay 17—At Shea Stadium, attendance 28,147. Freeman McNeil ran for two touchdowns and Pat Leahy kicked field goals of 34 and 29 yards as the Jets won their fifth straight game. McNeil climaxed the game's opening drive with a four-yard scoring run. New York then recovered the ensuing kickoff and McNeil scored from five yards out just 64 seconds later. Tampa Bay closed to within 17-10, but Richard Todd's one-yard pass to Mickey Shuler and Scott Dierking's one-yard run put the game out of reach. Two inches of snow and a wind chill factor of minus five degrees produced the Jets' smallest home crowd in 18 seasons.

Tampa Bay	0	3	7	7	— 17
New York Jets	14	0	9	9	— 32

NYJ — McNeil 4 run (Leahy kick)
NYJ — McNeil 5 run (Leahy kick)
TB — FG Capece 32
NYJ — FG Leahy 34
TB — Wilder 1 run (Capece kick)
NYJ — Shuler 1 pass from Todd (kick failed)
NYJ — Dierking 1 run (kick blocked)
NYJ — FG Leahy 29
TB — Wilder 15 pass from Williams (Capece kick)

Washington 12, St. Louis 7—At Busch Memorial Stadium, attendance 35,308. Mark Moseley kicked field goals of 32, 30, 20, and 24 yards to lead the Redskins over the Cardinals. Washington had a 12-0 fourth-quarter lead before 17-year veteran quarterback Jim Hart came off the bench to ignite St. Louis. Hart capped the Cardinals' 63-yard drive with a five-yard pass to Greg LaFleur with 3:08 remaining. St. Louis outgained Washington 356 to 292 but the Redskins recovered three fumbles in Washington territory to halt St. Louis scoring drives.

Washington	3	3	3	3	— 12
St. Louis	0	0	0	7	— 7

Wash — FG Moseley 32
Wash — FG Moseley 30
Wash — FG Moseley 20
Wash — FG Moseley 24
StL — LaFleur 5 pass from Hart (O'Donoghue kick)

MONDAY, DECEMBER 13

Dallas 37, Houston 7—At Astrodome, attendance 51,808. Three touchdown passes by Danny White and Rafael Septien's three field goals led the Cowboys to a 37-7 win. The victory insured Dallas of an NFL-record seventeenth straight winning season. White completed 21 of 27 passes for 279 yards, including second-quarter touchdowns of 21 and 18 yards to Butch Johnson. Michael Downs' 86-yard fumble return for a score preceded White's final touchdown, a 46-yard pass to Timmy Newsome. Septien, who earlier connected on field goals of 22 and 36 yards, closed out the scoring with a career-long 53-yarder.

Dallas	0	17	10	10	— 37
Houston	7	0	0	0	— 7

Hou — Renfro 54 pass from Manning (Kempf kick)
Dall — Johnson 21 pass from D. White (Septien kick)
Dall — FG Septien 22
Dall — Johnson 18 pass from D. White (Septien kick)
Dall — FG Septien 36
Dall — Downs 86 fumble recovery return (Septien kick)
Dall — Newsome 46 pass from D. White (Septien kick)
Dall — FG Septien 53

SEVENTH WEEK SUMMARY

Four teams clinched positions in the 16-team postseason Super Bowl Tournament and a total of 25 teams remained in contention for Super Bowl XVII. In the NFC, Dallas exploded for 21 second-quarter points to defeat New Orleans and ensure their eighth consecutive playoff appearance. In Washington, Mark Moseley's NFL-record twenty-first straight field goal of 42 yards with four seconds left lifted the Redskins over the Giants 15-14 and into the playoffs for the first time since 1976. William Andrews led the Falcons into the postseason picture rushing for 108 yards in a 17-7 win over the 49ers. The Raiders were the only AFC team to clinch a spot, when they defeated the Rams 37-31 on Marcus Allen's 11-yard touchdown run with 29 seconds remaining. Dan Fouts became the first NFL quarterback to pass for more than 400 yards (435) in two straight games as San Diego downed Cincinnati 50-34. The teams combined for a league passing mark of 883 yards while the Chargers set a team record with 661 yards total offense. The Jets, Eagles, and Chiefs saw streaks come to an end. Uwe von Schamann's 47-yard field goal with three seconds left gave Miami a 20-19 win, ending New York's five-game winning streak. Led by Wilbert Montgomery's 147 yards rushing, Philadelphia snapped a four-game winless slide, downing Houston 35-14. Kansas City scored 27 second-half points to post its first win in four games, 37-16 over Denver. The Broncos' Steve DeBerg completed his first pass in that game (minus four yards to Dave Preston), for an NFL-record eighteen in a row. Each team missed a field goal in overtime as Baltimore and Green Bay played to a 20-20 tie—only the sixth time a game has ended deadlocked since 1974's overtime rule went into effect. Paul McDonald was victorious in his first NFL start, leading the Browns to a 10-9 win over the Steelers. New England remained in playoff contention recording a club-record second straight shutout, 16-0 over Seattle. The Vikings held on for a 34-31 win over the Lions, while the Cardinals took a 10-7 decision from the Bears on Neil O'Donoghue's 48-yard field goal with 25 second remaining.

SATURDAY, DECEMBER 18

Los Angeles Raiders 37, Los Angeles Rams 31—At Memorial Coliseum, attendance 56,646. Marcus Allen ran 11 yards for his third and the game's decisive touchdown with 29 seconds left to help the Raiders clinch a playoff berth. The Raiders overcame a 21-7 halftime deficit to take a 30-21 lead on Allen's pair of one-yard scoring runs, Matt Bahr's 24-yard field goal, and Jim Plunkett's (22 of 34 for 321 yards) six-yard pass to Greg Pruitt. Mike Lansford's 36-yard field goal with 1:38 to go gave the Rams a 31-30 advantage but Plunkett took the Raiders 57 yards in five plays for the winning score.

L.A. Rams	14	7	0	10	— 31
L.A. Raiders	0	7	7	23	— 37

Rams — Tyler 1 run (Lansford kick)
Rams — Tyler 18 pass from Ferragamo (Lansford kick)
Raiders — Branch 18 pass from Plunkett (Bahr kick)
Rams — Dennard 6 pass from Ferragamo (Lansford kick)
Raiders — Allen 1 run (Bahr kick)
Raiders — FG Bahr 24
Raiders — Allen 1 run (Bahr kick)
Raiders — Pruitt 6 pass from Plunkett (kick failed)
Rams — Ferragamo 1 run (Lansford kick)
Rams — FG Lansford 36
Raiders — Allen 11 run (Bahr kick)

Miami 20, New York Jets 19—At Orange Bowl, attendance 67,702. Uwe von Schamann kicked a 47-yard field goal with three seconds remaining to lift the Dolphins over the Jets. Pat Leahy's second field goal of the game, a 49-yarder with 9:06 left, gave New York a 19-17 lead. Miami backup quarterback Don Strock replaced David Woodley with 1:48 to play and maneuvered Miami from its own 17 yard line to the New York 30 in seven plays. The key play in the winning drive was a Strock to Duriel Harris pass covering 20 yards. The loss brought the Jets' five-game win streak to a halt.

New York Jets	6	10	0	3	— 19
Miami	10	7	0	3	— 20

NYJ — Walker 22 pass from Todd (kick failed)
Mia — FG von Schamann 47
Mia — Franklin 25 run (von Schamann kick)
NYJ — Gaffney 45 pass from Todd (Leahy kick)
Mia — Harris 36 pass from Woodley (von Schamann kick)
NYJ — FG Leahy 40
NYJ — FG Leahy 49
Mia — FG von Schamann 47

SUNDAY, DECEMBER 19

Atlanta 17, San Francisco 7—At Candlestick Park, attendance 53,234. One-yard touchdown runs by Steve Bartkowski and Gerald Riggs, and Mick Luckhurst's 22-yard field goal enabled the Falcons to clinch a playoff berth. William Andrews rushed for 108 yards on 24 carries and added 68 yards on four receptions to spearhead the Atlanta attack which generated 391 yards total offense. Dwight Clark caught eight passes for 101 yards including the 49ers' lone score. Atlanta's defense held Joe Montana to 177 yards passing, which halted Montana's NFL record of consecutive 300-yard passing games at five.

Atlanta	0	10	0	7	— 17
San Francisco	0	7	0	0	— 7

Atl — FG Luckhurst 22
SF — D. Clark 7 pass from Montana (Wersching kick)
Atl — Bartkowski 1 run (Luckhurst kick)
Atl — Riggs 1 run (Luckhurst kick)

Tampa Bay 24, Buffalo 23—At Tampa Stadium, attendance 62,510. Doug Williams capped scoring drives of 88 and 77 yards with a pair of two-yard touchdown passes to Melvin Carver and Gordon Jones to highlight the Buccaneers' win. Bill Capece kicked a 27-yard field goal and Carver's 13-yard scoring run gave Tampa Bay a 24-16 fourth-quarter lead. Buffalo pulled to within 24-23 on Joe Ferguson's 10-yard run and were driving to the go-ahead score when Lee Roy Selmon caused Roosevelt Leaks to fumble at the Tampa Bay 18. Cedric Brown recovered to end the Bills' threat.

Buffalo	6	3	7	7	— 23
Tampa Bay	0	10	7	7	— 24

Buff — Leaks 8 run (kick failed)
TB — Carver 2 pass from Williams (Capece kick)
Buff — FG Herrera 49
TB — FG Capece 27
Buff — Leaks 3 run (Herrera kick)
TB — Jones 2 pass from Williams (Capece kick)
TB — Carver 13 run (Capece kick)
Buff — Ferguson 10 run (Herrera kick)

Baltimore 20, Green Bay 20—At Memorial Stadium, attendance 25,920. The Colts and Packers fought to the sixth tie game since the 1974 introduction of the overtime period in regular season play. Green Bay led 20-6, but fourth-quarter touchdowns by Baltimore's Matt Bouza (12-yard pass from Mike Pagel) and Randy McMillan (one-yard run with 1:22 left) sent the game into overtime. Each team missed a field goal in the extra period. The Colts' Dan Miller had his 44-yard attempt blocked by the Packers' Gary Lewis with 11:21 to play while Green Bay's Jan Stenerud saw his 47-yard attempt sail wide with 1:56 remaining.

Green Bay	0	10	3	7	0	— 20
Baltimore	3	0	3	14	0	— 20

Balt — FG Miller 23
GB — FG Stenerud 40
GB — Thompson 1 pass from Dickey (Stenerud kick)
Balt — FG Miller 40
GB — FG Stenerud 25
GB — Ivery 1 run (Stenerud kick)
Balt — Bouza 12 pass from Pagel (Miller kick)
Balt — McMillan 1 run (Miller kick)

Philadelphia 35, Houston 14—At Veterans Stadium, attendance 44,119. Wilbert Montgomery carried 17 times for 147 yards and three touchdowns, including a club-record 90-yard run, to help the Eagles snap a four-game losing streak. Philadelphia picked off four Archie Manning passes, including Richard Blackmore's 20-yard touchdown return in the first quarter. Mike Quick's 49-yard scoring reception, the first of his career, gave the Eagles a 21-0 halftime edge. The Philadelphia defense held Houston to 43 yards rushing (218 total yards) and registered seven sacks.

Houston	0	0	7	7	— 14
Philadelphia	7	14	7	7	— 35

Phil — Blackmore 20 interception return (Franklin kick)
Phil — Montgomery 3 run (Franklin kick)
Phil — Quick 49 pass from Jaworski (Franklin kick)
Phil — Montgomery 90 run (Franklin kick)
Hou — Casper 16 pass from Manning (Kempf kick)
Hou — Craft 5 pass from Manning (Kempf kick)
Phil — Montgomery 2 run (Franklin kick)

Kansas City 37, Denver 16—At Mile High Stadium, attendance 74,192. The Chiefs exploded for 27 second-half points to overcome a 13-10 halftime deficit and win for the first time in four games. Bill Kenney threw touchdown passes to Al Dixon and Carlos Carson (with 2:06 left) to give Kansas City a 30-16 fourth-quarter advantage. Gary Barbaro's 43-yard interception return for a score 28 seconds later put the game out of reach. Denver's Steve DeBerg set an NFL record by completing his first pass of the game (to Dave Preston), his eighteenth in a row.

Kansas City	3	7	10	17	— 37
Denver	0	13	3	0	— 16

KC — FG Lowery 47
KC — Harris 56 interception return (Lowery kick)
Den — Willhite 2 run (kick failed)
Den — Upchurch 78 punt return (Karlis kick)
KC — Dixon 1 pass from Kenney (Lowery kick)
Den — FG Karlis 44
KC — FG Lowery 19
KC — FG Lowery 22
KC — Carson 33 pass from Kenney (Lowery kick)
KC — Barbaro 43 pass interception return (Lowery kick)

Minnesota 34, Detroit 31—At Pontiac Silverdome, attendance 73,058. Minnesota built a 24-7 halftime lead on the strength of three Tommy Kramer touchdown passes and then withstood a furious fourth-quarter rally by the Lions to win. Nose tackle Charlie Johnson's 44-yard fumble recovery for a touchdown proved to be the deciding score, as Detroit came on strong in the fourth quarter to outscore Minnesota 21-10. The Vikings' defense sacked Lions' quarterback Gary Danielson seven times with Doug Martin accounting for three of the sacks.

Minnesota	7	17	0	10	— 34
Detroit	7	0	3	21	— 31

Det — L. Thompson 70 pass from Danielson (Murray kick)
Minn — LeCount 15 pass from Kramer (Danmeier kick)
Minn — Lewis 5 pass from Kramer (Danmeier kick)
Minn — FG Danmeier 20
Minn — Lewis 39 pass from Kramer (Danmeier kick)
Det — FG Murray 24
Det — Sims 1 run (Murray kick)
Minn — FG Danmeier 25
Minn — C. Johnson 44 fumble recovery return (Danmeier kick)
Det — King 7 pass from Danielson (Murray kick)
Det — L. Thompson 1 pass from Danielson (Murray kick)

New England 16, Seattle 0—At Kingdome, attendance 53,457. Steve Grogan and Mark van Eeghen teamed up on a five-yard touchdown pass and John Smith kicked field goals of 21, 37, and 23 yards as the Patriots recorded a club-record second straight shutout. New England's ball-control offense generated 393 yards compared to Seattle's 171. The Patriots' defense had four interceptions (including two by Mike Haynes) and two fumble recoveries. New England became the first team to shut out two consecutive opponents since Pittsburgh did it in 1976.

New England	3	7	3	3	— 16
Seattle	0	0	0	0	— 0

NE — FG J. Smith 21
NE — van Eeghen 5 pass from Grogan (J. Smith kick)
NE — FG J. Smith 37
NE — FG J. Smith 23

Dallas 21, New Orleans 7—At Texas Stadium, attendance 64,506. The Cowboys scored 21 points in the second quarter and cruised to the win. The victory assured Dallas of its eighth straight playoff berth and sixteenth in the last 17 years. Interceptions by Anthony Dickerson and Everson Walls set up touchdowns by Tony Dorsett and Doug Cosbie. Dorsett's one-yard plunge capped Dallas' sixth straight win. New Orleans' George Rogers ran for a club-record 166 yards on 33 carries.

New Orleans	0	0	0	7	— 7
Dallas	0	21	0	0	— 21

Dall — Dorsett 2 run (Septien kick)
Dall — Cosbie 3 pass from D. White (Septien kick)
Dall — Dorsett 1 run (Septien kick)
NO — Rogers 5 run (Fritsch kick)

Washington 15, New York Giants 14—At Robert F. Kennedy Stadium, attendance 50,030. Mark Moseley's NFL-record twenty-first straight field goal from 42 yards with four seconds left guaranteed the Redskins their first postseason appearance since 1976. The Giants took a 14-3 lead into the second half but Joe Washington ran 22 yards for a score and Moseley kicked his second field goal (31 yards) to bring Washington within striking distance 14-12. John Riggins rushed 31 times for 87 yards to become the fifth player in NFL history to carry 2,000 times (2,029) and eighth player to rush for over 8,000 yards (8,062). The loss broke New York's three-game win streak.

New York Giants	7	7	0	0	— 14
Washington	0	3	6	6	— 15

NYG — Perkins 28 pass from Brunner (Danelo kick)
Wash — FG Moseley 20
NYG — Woolfolk 1 run (Danelo kick)
Wash — Washington 22 run (kick failed)
Wash — FG Moseley 31
Wash — FG Moseley 42

Cleveland 10, Pittsburgh 9—At Cleveland Stadium, attendance 67,139. Johnny Davis' decisive one-yard run in the third quarter was the only touchdown Cleveland needed to hold off the Steelers. Paul McDonald, making his first NFL start, set up Davis' winning touchdown with a 22-yard pass to Ozzie Newsome. Hanford Dixon intercepted three Terry Bradshaw passes, including two in the final 65 seconds, to preserve the victory.

Pittsburgh	0	7	0	2	— 9
Cleveland	3	0	7	0	— 10

Cle — FG Bahr 44
Pitt — Stallworth 6 pass from Bradshaw (Anderson kick)
Cle — Davis 1 run (Bahr kick)
Pitt — Safety, Cox ran ball out of end zone

St. Louis 10, Chicago 7—At Soldier Field, attendance 43,270. Neil O'Donoghue's 48-yard field goal with 25 seconds remaining lifted the Cardinals over the Bears. St. Louis jumped to a 7-0 lead on Wayne Morris' one-yard run (the 35th rushing touchdown of his career, breaking John David Crow's club mark of 34). Chicago quarterback Jim McMahon tied the game with a nine-yard pass to Emery Moorehead in the fourth quarter, but 17-year veteran quarterback Jim Hart came off the bench for the second week in a row to ignite the Cardinals' winning drive.

St. Louis	0	7	0	3	— 10
Chicago	0	0	0	7	— 7

StL — Morris 1 run (O'Donoghue kick)
Chi — Moorehead 9 pass from McMahon (Roveto kick)
StL — FG O'Donoghue 48

MONDAY, DECEMBER 20

San Diego 50, Cincinnati 34—At San Diego Jack Murphy Stadium, attendance 51,296. Dan Fouts, who completed 25 of 40 passes for 435 yards, became the first NFL quarterback to throw for over 400 yards in two consecutive games as the Chargers avenged their 1981 AFC Championship Game loss to the Bengals. The Chargers amassed a team-record 661 yards while both teams combined for 1,102 yards, second-highest total in league history. The teams also completed an NFL-high 66 passes, breaking the

NFL-record of 65 set the previous week by the Chargers and 49ers. Wide receiver Wes Chandler had 10 catches for a club-record 260 yards and two touchdowns. Reserve running back James Brooks rushed for 105 yards on only 12 carries and had three touchdowns (including a 48-yard run).

Cincinnati	10	14	10	0	— 34
San Diego	7	10	23	10	— 50

Cin — FG Breech 19
SD — Chandler 66 pass from Muncie (Benirschke kick)
Cin — Anderson 12 run (Breech kick)
Cin — B. Harris 62 interception return (Breech kick)
SD — Brooks 17 run (Benirschke kick)
Cin — Collinsworth 6 pass from Anderson (Breech kick)
SD — FG Benirschke 43
SD — Muncie 1 run (Benirschke kick)
SD — Safety, Johnson tackled Anderson in end zone
SD — Chandler 38 pass from Fouts (Benirschke kick)
Cin — FG Breech 27
SD — Brooks 48 run (Benirschke kick)
Cin — M. L. Harris 17 pass from Anderson (Breech kick)
SD — FG Benirschke 26
SD — Brooks 1 run (Benirschke kick)

EIGHTH WEEK SUMMARY

Eight more teams celebrated Super Bowl Tournament berths while 12 teams overall remained in contention for Super Bowl XVII. Added to last week's four postseason finalists were the Bengals, Dolphins, Jets, Chargers, Steelers, Packers, Cardinals, and Vikings. Cincinnati and the New York Jets both earned postseason spots with a 24-10 win over Seattle and a 42-14 win over Minnesota, respectively. The Vikings made the playoff picture anyway based on a better conference record among NFC rivals. San Diego made the playoffs for the fourth consecutive season by beating Baltimore 44-26 on the strength of Dan Fouts' five touchdown passes. Pittsburgh ended a two-year absence from the playoffs by defeating New England 37-14. Green Bay defeated Atlanta 38-7 and qualified for the playoffs for the first time since 1972 Neil Lomax's eight-yard scoring toss to Roy Green with 27 seconds left to play led the Cardinals over the Giants 27-24 and helped St. Louis into the playoffs for the first time since 1975. The Bears remained in contention for a postseason spot by outlasting the Rams 34-26. Walter Payton gained 104 yards rushing to become the fourth NFL player to rush for over 10,000 yards in a career. Not to be outdone, the Rams' Vince Ferragamo completed 30 of 46 passes for 509 yards—the second-highest passing total in NFL history. Bill Capece's last-minute 27-yard field goal gave Tampa Bay a 23-21 victory over Detroit and kept the Buccaneers in the battle for one of the two remaining NFC berths. The Raiders retained sole possession of first place in the AFC by defeating the Broncos 27-10 while the Redskins gained sole possession of the top spot in the NFC with a little help from the Eagles. Washington discarded New Orleans 27-10 and Dallas fell to Philadelphia 24-20 to end the Cowboys' six-game unbeaten streak. The AFC edged the NFC 15-14-1 in the 30-game interconference series which was reduced from 56 games by the strike.

SUNDAY, DECEMBER 26

San Diego 44, Baltimore 26—At San Diego Jack Murphy Stadium, attendance 49,711. Dan Fouts threw five touchdown passes, including three to Kellen Winslow and two to Wes Chandler, assuring the Chargers a playoff berth for the fourth straight year. San Diego opened a 23-0 lead on Fouts to Winslow touchdowns of 30 and 13 yards and a 41-yard strike to Chandler. Fouts, who completed 18 of 30 for 298 yards, added second-half touchdowns of 44 yards to Chandler (four receptions, 118 yards) and 28 yards to Winslow (seven catches, 120 yards). The Chargers gained over 500 total yards (507) for the third consecutive week in winning their fifth straight game, the team's longest winning streak in the last 18 years. Baltimore's Dan Miller kicked a 58-yard field goal, the third longest in NFL history.

Baltimore	0	3	10	13	— 26
San Diego	7	16	14	7	— 44

SD — Winslow 30 pass from Fouts (Benirschke kick)
SD — FG Benirschke 45
SD — Chandler 41 pass from Fouts (kick failed)
SD — Winslow 13 pass from Fouts (Benirschke kick)
Balt — FG Miller 46
Balt — Bouza 15 pass from Pagel (Miller kick)
Balt — FG Miller 58
SD — Brooks 8 run (Benirschke kick)
SD — Chandler 44 pass from Fouts (Benirschke kick)
Balt — Dickey 1 run (pass failed)
SD — Winslow 28 pass from Fouts (Benirschke kick)
Balt — Sherwin fumble recovery in end zone (Miller kick)

Chicago 34, Los Angeles Rams 26—At Anaheim Stadium, attendance 46,502. Walter Payton ran for 104 yards to become the fourth player in NFL history to rush for over 10,000 yards (10,095) as the Bears outlasted the Rams 34-26. The victory by the Bears overshadowed an outstanding performance by Rams quarterback Vince Ferragamo. Ferragamo completed 30 of 46 passes for 509 yards and three touchdowns, the second-highest total in NFL history. Ferragamo brought the Rams back from a 16-0 second-quarter deficit to close to within one point at 27-26 early in the fourth quarter. However, Jim McMahon (18 of 28, 280 yards, two touchdowns) fired a 10-yard scoring pass to Ken Margerum with 4:58 remaining to put the game out of reach.

Chicago	17	3	7	7	— 34
Los Angeles Rams	6	10	3	7	— 26

Chi — Moorehead 11 pass from McMahon (B. Thomas kick)
Chi — FG B. Thomas 41
Chi — Payton 2 run (B. Thomas kick)
Rams — Farmer 38 pass from Ferragamo (kick failed)
Chi — FG B. Thomas 31
Rams — Tyler 7 pass from Ferragamo (Lansford kick)
Rams — FG Lansford 29
Chi — Suhey 3 run (B. Thomas kick)
Rams — FG Lansford 37
Rams — Dennard 4 pass from Ferragamo (Lansford kick)
Chi — Margerum 10 pass from McMahon (B. Thomas kick)

Cleveland 20, Houston 14—At Astrodome, attendance 36,559. Clint Burrell's second fumble recovery of the day set up Charles White's decisive one-yard touchdown with 5:36 remaining to lead the Browns' comeback. Cleveland took a 10-7 second-quarter lead on Matt Bahr's 18-yard field goal and Paul McDonald's 56-yard touchdown pass to Dave Logan. Houston went ahead 14-10 on Donnie Craft's three-yard run early in the final quarter. The Browns fought back with Bahr's 24-yard field goal. Burrell's fumble recovery on the Oilers' 1 yard line set up the winning score.

Cleveland	0	10	0	10	— 20
Houston	7	0	7	0	— 14

Hou — Renfro 8 pass from Nielsen (Kempf kick)
Cle — FG Bahr 18
Cle — Logan 56 pass from McDonald (Bahr kick)
Hou — Craft 3 run (Kempf kick)
Cle — FG Bahr 24
Cle — White 1 run (Bahr kick)

Los Angeles Raiders 27, Denver 10—At Memorial Coliseum, attendance 44,160. Marcus Allen caught two touchdown passes as the Raiders exploded for 24 points in the second quarter to defeat the Broncos 27-10. Allen's five receptions for 91 yards included touchdowns of four and 51 yards. James Davis' 55-yard interception return, the second of Los Angeles' five interceptions, set up Kenny King's five-yard scoring run. Chris Bahr's 36-yard field goal capped the scoring. Howie Long had two of the Raiders seven quarterback sacks.

Denver	0	0	0	10	— 10
L.A. Raiders	3	24	0	0	— 27

Raiders — FG Bahr 19
Raiders — Allen 4 pass from Plunkett (Bahr kick)
Raiders — King 5 run (Bahr kick)
Raiders — Allen 51 pass from Plunkett (Bahr kick)
Raiders — FG Bahr 36
Den — FG Karlis 31
Den — Watson 18 pass from Herrmann (Karlis kick)

Tampa Bay 23, Detroit 21—At Tampa Stadium, attendance 65,997. Bill Capece's 27-yard field goal with 25 seconds remaining enabled Tampa Bay to edge the Lions 23-21. Capece also kicked second-quarter field goals of 34 and 29 yards but Gary Danielson's touchdown passes of 19 yards to Leonard Thompson and seven yards to David Hill gave Detroit a 14-6 halftime lead. Doug Williams completed 21 of 34 passes for 276 yards and rallied the Buccaneers in the second half with his three-yard scoring run and two-yard touchdown pass to James Owens. Norris Thomas' interception with three seconds left saved the win.

Detroit	7	7	7	0	— 21
Tampa Bay	0	6	7	10	— 23

Det — L. Thompson 19 pass from Danielson (Murray kick)
TB — FG Capece 34
Det — Hill 7 pass from Danielson (Murray kick)
TB — FG Capece 29
Det — Sims 3 run (Murray kick)
TB — Williams 3 run (Capece kick)
TB — Owens 2 pass from Williams (Capece kick)
TB — FG Capece 27

Green Bay 38, Atlanta 7—At Atlanta-Fulton County Stadium, attendance 50,245. Lynn Dickey threw for two touchdowns and Eddie Lee Ivery ran for two more as the Packers moved into the playoffs for the first time since 1972. Dickey completed 10 of 17 for 248 yards and had touchdown passes of 80 and 57 yards to James Lofton (three catches for 146 yards). Ivery's scores covered two and 12 yards. The loss snapped the Falcons' three-game win streak.

Green Bay	7	14	7	10	— 38
Atlanta	0	7	0	0	— 7

GB — Ivery 2 run (Stenerud kick)
GB — Ivery 12 run (Stenerud kick)
Atl — Andrews 3 pass from Bartkowski (Luckhurst kick)
GB — Lofton 80 pass from Dickey (Stenerud kick)
GB — Lofton 57 pass from Dickey (Stenerud kick)
GB — Rodgers 9 run (Stenerud kick)
GB — FG Stenerud 22

Pittsburgh 37, New England 14—At Three Rivers Stadium, attendance 51,515. Terry Bradshaw threw two touchdown passes and Gary Anderson kicked three field goals to help the Steelers end a two-year playoff drought. Pittsburgh surged to a 20-0 lead on Anderson field goals of 21 and 25 yards, Frank Pollard's one-yard run, and Bradshaw's nine-yard pass to John Stallworth. Matt Cavanaugh, the Patriots' third quarterback of the day, closed the deficit to 23-14 on touchdown passes of 23 yards to Lin Dawson and 75 yards to Stanley Morgan. Bradshaw (17 of 27 for 282 yards) rifled a 46-yard touchdown pass to Greg Hawthorne with 11:30 left to put the game out of reach.

New England	0	0	7	7	— 14
Pittsburgh	10	10	0	17	— 37

Pitt — FG Anderson 21
Pitt — Pollard 1 run (Anderson kick)
Pitt — Stallworth 9 pass from Bradshaw (Anderson kick)
Pitt — FG Anderson 25
NE — Dawson 23 pass from Cavanaugh (J. Smith kick)
Pitt — FG Anderson 44
NE — Morgan 75 pass from Cavanaugh (J. Smith kick)
Pitt — Hawthorne 46 pass from Bradshaw (Anderson kick)
Pitt — Abercrombie 1 run (Anderson kick)

St. Louis 24, New York Giants 21—At Busch Memorial Stadium, attendance 39,824. Neil Lomax fired an eight-yard touchdown pass to Roy Green with 27 seconds left to help the Cardinals clinch their first postseason berth since 1975. New York grabbed a 21-17 lead with 1:07 remaining on Scott Brunner's three-yard scoring pass to John Mistler, but Lomax brought St. Louis back 70 yards in four plays for the winning score. Roger Wehrli, who retired at the end of the season, marked his final home game with an 18-yard touchdown run on a fake field goal.

New York Giants	0	7	0	14	— 21
St. Louis	7	7	3	7	— 24

StL — Wehrli 18 run (O'Donoghue kick)
StL — Green 8 pass from Lomax (O'Donoghue kick)
NYG — Carpenter 1 run (Danelo kick)
StL — FG O'Donoghue 18
NYG — Mistler 13 pass from Brunner (Danelo kick)
NYG — Mistler 3 pass from Brunner (Danelo kick)
StL — Green 8 pass from Lomax (O'Donoghue kick)

New York Jets 42, Minnesota 14—At Metrodome, attendance 58,672. Two touchdowns each by Bobby Jackson and Freeman McNeil helped the Jets clinch their second consecutive playoff berth. Jackson scored on an 80-yard blocked field goal attempt and 77-yard interception return while McNeil scored on runs of two and one yards. Jackson's first interception set up Pat Ryan's 20-yard touchdown pass to Mickey Shuler from field goal formation. Richard Todd then threw a 39-yard scoring pass to Bruce Harper. Tommy Kramer completed 32 passes in 56 attempts for 328 yards, including 10 to Joe Senser for 115 yards.

New York Jets	7	14	7	14	— 42
Minnesota	0	7	0	7	— 14

NYJ — McNeil 2 run (Leahy kick)
NYJ — Jackson 80 blocked field goal return (Leahy kick)
NYJ — McNeil 1 run (Leahy kick)
Minn — Kramer 1 run (Danmeier kick)
NYJ — Shuler 20 pass from Ryan (Leahy kick)
Minn — Brown 16 pass from Kramer (Danmeier kick)
NYJ — Harper 39 pass from Todd (Leahy kick)
NYJ — Jackson 77 interception return (Leahy kick)

Philadelphia 24, Dallas 20—At Texas Stadium, attendance 46,199. Ron Jaworski's club-record 112th touchdown pass (10 yards to Harold Carmichael) knocked the Cowboys from first place in the NFC and snapped their six-game win streak. Greg Brown's fumble recovery in the end zone gave the Eagles an early 7-0 lead, but the Cowboys gained a 17-14 halftime edge on a pair of Danny White touchdown passes (33 yards to Butch Johnson; 11 to Doug Cosbie) and Rafael Septien's 18-yard field goal. Jaworski erased Norm Snead's record of 111 touchdown passes with 8:25 to play and Tony Franklin added a 22-yard field goal with 5:32 remaining. The victory was only Philadelphia's second in their last 12 trips to Texas Stadium.

Philadelphia	7	7	0	10	— 24
Dallas	7	10	0	3	— 20

Phil — Brown recovered fumble in end zone (Franklin kick)
Dall — Johnson 33 pass from D. White (Septien kick)
Phil — Harris 1 run (Franklin kick)
Dall — Cosbie 11 pass from D. White (Septien kick)
Dall — FG Septien 18
Dall — FG Septien 33
Phil — Carmichael 10 pass from Jaworski (Franklin kick)
Phil — FG Franklin 22

San Francisco 26, Kansas City 13—At Arrowhead, attendance 24,319. Ray Wersching kicked four field goals and Ronnie Lott returned an interception for a touchdown to lead the 49ers past the Chiefs. Wersching field goals of 32, 44, and 42 yards cut Kansas City's lead to 10-9 and Jeff Moore ran one-yard for the go-ahead score with 13:21 left. Lott's 83-yard interception return, the fourth of his career, sealed the victory with 11 seconds remaining.

San Francisco	3	0	6	17	— 26
Kansas City	3	7	0	3	— 13

KC — FG Lowery 40
SF — FG Wersching 32
KC — Hancock 41 pass from Kenney (Lowery kick)
SF — FG Wersching 44
SF — FG Wersching 42
SF — Moore 1 run (Wersching kick)
KC — FG Lowery 39
SF — FG Wersching 34
SF — Lott 83 interception return (Wersching kick)

Cincinnati 24, Seattle 10—At Riverfront Stadium, attendance 55,330. Pete Johnson ran for two touchdowns and Ken Anderson and David Verser combined for another as the Bengals clinched a playoff spot for the second straight season. Ken Riley's 56th career interception set up Johnson's one-yard scoring run. Anderson, who completed 22 of 29 passes for 265 yards, found Verser with a 56-yard bomb for a 14-3 lead. Jim Breech converted his tenth straight field goal and Mike Fuller's fumble recovery on the ensuing kickoff led to Johnson's second touchdown, a three-yard run.

Seattle	0	3	7	0	— 10
Cincinnati	0	14	0	10	— 24

Cin — Johnson 1 run (Breech kick)
Sea — FG N. Johnson 43
Cin — Verser 56 pass from Anderson (Breech kick)
Sea — Largent 2 pass from Zorn (N. Johnson kick)
Cin — FG Breech 34
Cin — Johnson 3 run (Breech kick)

Washington 27, New Orleans 10—At Louisiana Superdome, attendance 48,667. Joe Theismann and Charlie Brown hooked up on two touchdown passes as the Redskins locked up a home site in the first round of the playoffs. Theismann completed 14 of 23 passes for 264 yards including four completions to Brown for 156 yards and scoring bombs of 57 and 58 yards. Mark Moseley kicked field goals of 36 and 45 yards to extend his NFL record to 23 in a row.

Washington	7	10	0	10	— 27
New Orleans	0	7	3	0	— 10

Wash — Brown 57 pass from Theismann (Moseley kick)
NO — J. Rogers 4 run (Andersen kick)
Wash — Brown 58 pass from Theismann (Moseley kick)
Wash — FG Moseley 36
NO — FG Andersen 36

Wash — FG Moseley 45
Wash — Riggins 1 run (Moseley kick)

MONDAY, DECEMBER 27

Miami 27, Buffalo 10—At Orange Bowl, attendance 73,924. The Dolphins spotted the Bills a 10-0 lead but responded with 27 unanswered points to wrap up a playoff berth and Don Shula's 200th regular-season victory. Miami tied the score in the third quarter 10-10 on Tony Nathan's one-yard run and Uwe von Schamann's 35-yard field goal. Ron Hester recovered a muffed punt on the Bills' 2 yard line to set up Andra Franklin's two-yard touchdown run. Glenn Blackwood's fumble recovery at the Buffalo 6 yard line set up Franklin's second score, a six-yard run. Von Schamann converted Lyle Blackwood's interception into a 30-yard field goal as the Bills fell to 4-4.

Buffalo	10	0	0	0	— 10
Miami	0	7	13	7	— 27

Buff — Cribbs 62 run (Herrera kick)
Buff — FG Herrera 33
Mia — Nathan 1 run (von Schamann kick)
Mia — FG von Schamann 35
Mia — Franklin 2 run (von Schamann kick)
Mia — FG von Schamann 30
Mia — Franklin 6 run (von Schamann kick)

NINTH WEEK SUMMARY

Cleveland, Detroit, New England, and Tampa Bay rounded out the 16-team Super Bowl Tournament field in the final week of rescheduled games in the strike-shortened season. For the second week in a row, the toe of Tampa Bay's Bill Capece was the deciding factor. His 33-yard field goal, 3:14 into overtime, gave the Buccaneers a 26-23 win over Chicago and their third playoff appearance in the last four years. Steve Grogan's three touchdown passes helped the Patriots lock up a postseason berth—their first since 1978—and a 30-19 victory over the Bills. Detroit defeated NFC rival Green Bay 27-24 to round out the NFC Tournament field. Despite a 37-21 loss to Pittsburgh, Cleveland clinched the last AFC spot due to Buffalo's loss to New England. The Raiders continued their mastery over the Chargers with a 41-34 victory that assured Los Angeles the home field advantage throughout the playoffs. Joe Theismann fired three touchdown passes as the Redskins completed the season with a 28-0 shutout of the Cardinals. The victory helped the Redskins to their best record since 1942. Mark Moseley had his NFL-record streak of 23 consecutive field goals come to an end with a 40-yard miss, but his 20 of 21 this season, for 95.2 percent, set an NFL record. Cincinnati's Ken Anderson established two NFL marks in a 35-27 win over Houston. Anderson completed 27 of 31 passes, including 20 in a row, breaking Steve DeBerg's two-week old record. His season completion percentage of 70.55 was also a record. Dallas suffered their third loss of the season, 31-27 to Minnesota, but Tony Dorsett scored on an NFL-record 99-yard run from scrimmage. It was only the second loss for the Cowboys in which Dorsett had rushed for over 100 yards. The Rams staged a furious comeback to defeat the 49ers 21-20 and eliminate the defending NFL champions from the playoffs. Joe Danelo's 25-yard field goal with two seconds left gave the Giants a 26-24 win over the Eagles and a victorious sendoff to coach Ray Perkins, who was named to replace Bear Bryant as head coach at Alabama.

SUNDAY, JANUARY 2

New Orleans 35, Atlanta 6—At Louisiana Superdome, attendance 47,336. Wayne Wilson ran for three touchdowns and Ken Stabler directed a 462-yard offensive explosion as the Saints defeated the Falcons for the first time since 1979. Stabler's 24 completions for 271 yards included an 11-yard scoring pass to Kenny Duckett. Wilson's two fourth-quarter scores (17 and four-yard runs) followed punter Russell Erxleben's 39-yard touchdown pass to safety Bill Hurley from punt formation.

Atlanta	0	3	3	0	— 6
New Orleans	0	14	0	21	— 35

NO — Wilson 1 run (Anderson kick)
Atl — FG Luckhurst 40
NO — Duckett 11 pass from Stabler (Anderson kick)
Atl — FG Luckhurst 29
NO — Hurley 39 pass from Erxleben (Anderson kick)
NO — Wilson 17 run (Anderson kick)
NO — Wilson 4 run (Anderson kick)

New England 30, Buffalo 19—At Schaefer Stadium, attendance 36,218. Steve Grogan threw three touchdown passes as the Patriots gained their first playoff berth since 1978. Grogan's 11-yard scoring pass to Morris Bradshaw just before halftime cut Buffalo's lead to 13-10 and his 33-yard bomb to Ken Toler early in the third quarter put New England in front 16-13. Tony Collins' one-yard run snapped a 16-16 tie and put the Patriots out in front for good. Don Hasselbeck's two-yard touchdown reception clinched the win. Stanley Morgan led all receivers with 141 yards on seven receptions.

Buffalo	0	13	3	3	— 19
New England	3	7	6	14	— 30

NE — FG J. Smith 42
Buff — Cribbs 14 run (Herrera kick)
Buff — Butler 22 pass from Ferguson (run failed)
NE — Bradshaw 11 pass from Grogan (J. Smith kick)
NE — Toler 33 pass from Grogan (kick failed)
Buff — FG Herrera 46
NE — Collins 1 run (J. Smith kick)
Buff — FG Herrera 25
NE — Hasselbeck 2 pass from Grogan (J. Smith kick)

Tampa Bay 26, Chicago 23—At Tampa Stadium, attendance 68,112. Bill Capece's 33-yard field goal, 3:14 into overtime, catapulted the Buccaneers into the playoffs for the third time in the last four years. Capece kicked second-quarter field goals of 27 and 31 yards but Tampa Bay trailed Chicago 23-6. Doug Williams threw touchdown passes of 35 and 31 yards to Jimmie Giles to cut the deficit to three points. Capece sent the game into overtime by booting a 40-yard field goal with 26 seconds left in regulation.

Chicago	3	17	3	0	0	— 23
Tampa Bay	0	6	7	10	3	— 26

Chi — FG B. Thomas 43
Chi — FG B. Thomas 19
Chi — Wilson 39 interception return (B. Thomas kick)
TB — FG Capece 27
TB — FG Capece 31
Chi — Baschnagel 19 pass from McMahon (B. Thomas kick)
Chi — FG B. Thomas 40
TB — Giles 35 pass from Williams (Capece kick)
TB — Giles 31 pass from Williams (Capece kick)
TB — FG Capece 40
TB — FG Capece 33

Cincinnati 35, Houston 27—At Astrodome, attendance 26,522. Ken Anderson completed 27 (including an NFL-record 20 straight) of 31 passes for 323 yards and two touchdowns as the Bengals clinched the home-field advantage in the first round of the playoffs. Anderson scoring tosses to Dan Ross and Isaac Curtis, plus scoring runs by Archie Griffin and Pete Johnson, gave Cincinnati a commanding 28-13 third-quarter lead. Anderson's season completion percentage of 70.55 eclipsed Sammy Baugh's NFL mark of 70.33 set in 1945.

Cincinnati	14	7	7	7	— 35
Houston	3	10	0	14	— 27

Cin — Ross 1 pass from Anderson (Breech kick)
Hou — FG Kempf 35
Cin — A. Griffin 10 run (Breech kick)
Hou — Craft 9 run (Kempf kick)
Hou — FG Kempf 37
Cin — Johnson 1 run (Breech kick)
Cin — Curtis 44 pass from Anderson (Breech kick)
Hou — Casper 5 pass from Nielsen (Kempf kick)
Cin — Alexander 4 run (Breech kick)
Hou — Craft 3 run (Kempf kick)

Pittsburgh 37, Cleveland 21—At Three Rivers Stadium, attendance 52,312. The Steelers opened a 27-7 lead and defeated the Browns for the thirteenth consecutive time at Three Rivers Stadium. Terry Bradshaw opened the scoring, completing a three-yard pass to tackle-eligible Ray Pinney. Johnny Rodgers gave the Steelers a 13-7 lead by blocking a punt and returning it 18 yards for a touchdown. Franco Harris, who rushed for 120 yards, then capped an 81-yard drive with a six-yard run. Bradshaw followed with a 38-yard scoring pass to Jim Smith. The Browns closed to 27-21 on Ricky Feacher's 12-yard touchdown pass from Paul McDonald, but a 34-yard field goal by Gary Anderson and a one-yard run by Walter Abercrombie (his first as a pro) sealed the win.

Cleveland	0	7	0	14	— 21
Pittsburgh	7	6	7	17	— 37

Pitt — Pinney 3 pass from Bradshaw (Anderson kick)
Cle — Feacher 1 pass from McDonald (Bahr kick)
Pitt — Rodgers 18 blocked punt return (run failed)
Pitt — Harris 6 run (Anderson kick)
Pitt — Smith 38 pass from Bradshaw (Anderson kick)
Cle — Logan 8 pass from McDonald (Bahr kick)
Cle — Feacher 12 pass from McDonald (Bahr kick)
Pitt — FG Anderson 34
Pitt — Abercrombie 1 run (Anderson kick)

Seattle 13, Denver 11—At Kingdome, attendance 43,145. Dave Krieg replaced starter Jim Zorn in the second half and rallied the Seahawks to their fourth win. All Seattle could muster in three and a half quarters were two field goals by Norm Johnson but Krieg entered the game and engineered an 87-yard march climaxed by Roger Carr's 19-yard touchdown catch with 1:07 to play.

Denver	2	0	7	2	— 11
Seattle	3	0	0	10	— 13

Sea — FG N. Johnson 22
Den — Safety, Boyd tackled T. Brown in end zone
Den — Herrmann 6 run (Karlis kick)
Sea — FG N. Johnson 34
Den — Safety, Chavous tackled Krieg in end zone
Sea — Carr 19 pass from Kreig (N. Johnson kick)

Detroit 27, Green Bay 24—At Pontiac Silverdome, attendance 64,377. Reserve tight end Rob Rubick scored the deciding touchdown on a one-yard reverse with 5:47 left to put the Lions in the playoffs for the first time since 1970. The Packers led 24-20 with 10:34 to play when Eric Hipple replaced starter Gary Danielson for Detroit and directed the winning 60-yard drive. Before being replaced, Danielson had completed a nine-yard touchdown pass to David Hill and a 17-yard score to Leonard Thompson. Ed Murray kicked field goals of 49 and 28 yards and Bobby Watkins had three of Detroit's four interceptions.

Green Bay	7	7	10	0	— 24
Detroit	14	3	3	7	— 27

Det — Hill 9 pass from Danielson (Murray kick)
GB — Lofton 17 pass from Dickey (Stenerud kick)
Det — L. Thompson 25 pass from Danielson (Murray kick)
Det — FG Murray 49
GB — Ivery 11 run (Stenerud kick)
Det — FG Murray 28
GB — FG Stenerud 48
GB — Rodgers recovered fumble in end zone (Stenerud kick)
Det — Rubick 1 run (Murray kick)

Los Angeles Raiders 41, San Diego 34—At San Diego Jack Murphy Stadium, attendance 51,612. Marcus Allen scored two touchdowns in the last six minutes and James Davis returned an interception 52 yards for a touchdown with 2:41 left to give the Raiders the home-field advantage throughout the playoffs. Allen's two-yard run broke a 27-27 tie and capped an 88-yard drive with 5:24 to play. Davis' interception put the Raiders ahead 34-27 and Allen's 22-yard dash gave the Raiders a 14-point cushion with 1:37 remaining. The Chargers had staged their own comeback after trailing 20-3 in the third quarter. Touchdowns by Wes Chandler and Chuck Muncie (one- and two-yard runs) and Rolf Benirschke's 23-yard field goal gave San Diego a 27-20 lead with 10:21 to go. The Chargers gained 438 total yards to the Raiders' 354.

L.A. Raiders	0	10	10	21	— 41
San Diego	3	0	17	14	— 34

SD — FG Benirschke 27
Raiders — FG Bahr 22
Raiders — Hawkins 2 pass from Plunkett (Bahr kick)
Raiders — M. Davis 56 interception return (Bahr kick)
Raiders — FG Bahr 32
SD — Chandler 25 pass from Fouts (Benirschke kick)
SD — FG Benirschke 23
SD — Muncie 2 run (Benirschke kick)
SD — Muncie 1 run (Benirschke kick)
Raiders — Allen 2 run (Bahr kick)
Raiders — J. Davis 52 interception return (Bahr kick)
Raiders — Allen 22 run (Bahr kick)
SD — Fouts 4 run (Benirschke kick)

Los Angeles Rams 21, San Francisco 20—At Candlestick Park, attendance 54,256. Ivory Sully deflected a 24-yard field goal attempt by Ray Wersching with 1:53 remaining, knocking the 49ers out of the playoffs and snapping the Rams' four-game losing streak. San Francisco led 20-7 at halftime but the Rams came back on Wendell Tyler's one-yard run and Vince Ferragamo's 42-yard touchdown pass to George Farmer with 8:59 left for the go-ahead score. Dana McLemore set a 49ers record with a 93-yard punt return for a touchdown in the first quarter.

Los Angeles Rams	7	0	7	7	— 21
San Francisco	7	13	0	0	— 20

SF — McLemore 93 punt return (Wersching kick)
Rams — Tyler 3 pass from Ferragamo (Lansford kick)
SF — Wilson 19 pass from Montana (Wersching kick)
SF — Nehemiah 29 pass from Montana (kick failed)
Rams — Tyler 1 run (Lansford kick)
Rams — Farmer 42 pass from Ferragamo (Lansford kick)

Miami 34, Baltimore 7—At Memorial Stadium, attendance 19,073. David Woodley completed 14 of 22 passes for 239 yards and three touchdowns as the Dolphins won their third straight game and clinched the home-field advantage in the playoffs. Woodley's 11-yard touchdown pass to Nat Moore and 34-yarder to Jimmy Cefalo, plus Uwe von Schamann's 34-yard field goal, gave Miami a 17-7 lead at the half. The Dolphins added 17 second-half points, scoring on their first three possessions of the third quarter.

Miami	10	7	17	0	— 34
Baltimore	0	7	0	0	— 7

Mia — Moore 11 pass from Woodley (von Schamann kick)
Mia — FG von Schamann 34
Balt — Dixon 11 run (Miller kick)
Mia — Cefalo 34 pass from Woodley (von Schamann kick)
Mia — Franklin 1 run (von Schamann kick)
Mia — FG von Schamann 25
Mia — Hardy 4 pass from Woodley (von Schamann kick)

New York Giants 26, Philadelphia 24—At Veterans Stadium, attendance 63,917. Joe Danelo's 25-yard field goal with two seconds left to play, his fourth of the game, gave the Giants a 26-24 win in Ray Perkins' last game as head coach. New York opened a 23-14 lead on Danelo kicks of 45, 31, and 26 yards and touchdowns by Earnest Gray and Scott Brunner. Philadelphia took a 24-23 lead with 12:35 left, but Brunner drove the Giants 57 yards in eight plays to set up Danelo's winning kick.

New York Giants	3	10	10	3	— 26
Philadelphia	7	7	0	10	— 24

NYG — FG Danelo 45
Phil — Kab 2 pass from Jaworski (Franklin kick)
Phil — Montgomery 2 run (Franklin kick)
NYG — Gray 24 pass from Brunner (Danelo kick)
NYG — FG Danelo 31
NYG — FG Danelo 26
NYG — Brunner 7 run (Danelo kick)
Phil — Spagnola 18 pass from Jaworski (Franklin kick)
Phil — FG Franklin 35
NYG — FG Danelo 25

Kansas City 37, New York Jets 13—At Arrowhead, attendance 11,902. Bill Kenney threw three touchdown passes to lead the Chiefs over the Jets. Kansas City built a 27-6 halftime lead on Kenney scoring passes to Carlos Carson (28 yards) and Henry Marshall (13), Gary Green's 42-yard return of a lateral after Thomas Howard's interception, and Nick Lowery's 44- and 43-yard field goals. Kenney, who completed 11 passes in a row at one point, added a five-yard touchdown pass to Marshall in the fourth quarter.

New York Jets	6	0	0	7	— 13
Kansas City	7	20	0	10	— 37

NYJ — FG Leahy 30
NYJ — FG Leahy 20
KC — Carson 28 pass from Kenney (Lowery kick)
KC — Marshall 13 pass from Kenney (Lowery kick)
KC — Green 42 interception return after 5 lateral from Howard (Lowery kick)
KC — FG Lowery 44
KC — FG Lowery 43
KC — Marshall 5 pass from Kenney (Lowery kick)
KC — FG Lowery 44
NYJ — Shuler 10 pass from Ryan (Leahy kick)

Washington 28, St. Louis 0—At Robert F. Kennedy Stadium, attendance 52,544. Joe Theismann threw three touchdowns and the defense yielded only 196 total yards as the Redskins upped their record to 8-1, their best since 1942. Washington scored a touchdown in every quarter on Theismann's scoring passes to Rick Walker (25 yards), Clint Didier (two), and Joe Washington (eight), and Clarence Harmon's one-yard run. The defense racked up three interceptions, two fumble recoveries, and five sacks. Mark Moseley had his NFL-record streak of 23 field goals in a row end with a

40-yard miss, but his 20 of 21 this season for 95.2 percent set an NFL record.

St. Louis	0	0	0	0 —	0
Washington	7	7	7	7 —	28

Wash — Walker 25 pass from Theismann (Moseley kick)
Wash — Didier 2 pass from Theismann (Moseley kick)
Wash — Harmon 1 run (Moseley kick)
Wash — Washington 8 pass from Theismann (Moseley kick)

MONDAY, JANUARY 3

Minnesota 31, Dallas 27—At Metrodome, attendance 60,007. Rickey Young's 14-yard touchdown catch with 1:52 remaining assured the Vikings a home site in the first round of the playoffs. Dallas jumped to a 10-0 second-quarter lead, but Minnesota rebounded to tie the score at the half on Rick Danmeier's 28-yard field goal and Ted Brown's one-yard run. Brown's 13-yard touchdown reception and John Turner's 33-yard interception return for a score gave the Vikings a commanding 24-13 lead. Tony Dorsett's (16 carries, 153 yards) NFL-record 99-yard touchdown run brought the Cowboys to within four points. Ron Springs' two-yard scoring run gave Dallas a 27-24 advantage with 6:42 to play. Tommy Kramer drove Minnesota 80 yards in 10 plays on their next possession for Young's decisive score.

Dallas	3	7	3	14 —	27
Minnesota	0	10	7	14 —	31

Dall — FG Septien 42
Dall — Thurman 60 interception return (Septien kick)
Minn — FG Danmeier 28
Minn — Brown 1 run (Danmeier kick)
Minn — Brown 13 pass from Kramer (Danmeier kick)
Dall — FG Septien 22
Minn — Turner 33 interception return (Danmeier kick)
Dall — Dorsett 99 run (Septien kick)
Dall — Springs 2 run (Septien kick)
Minn — Young 14 pass from Kramer (Danmeier kick)

TENTH WEEK

SATURDAY, JANUARY 8, 1983
AFC FIRST-ROUND PLAYOFF GAME

Miami 28, New England 13—At Orange Bowl, attendance 68,842. David Woodley completed 16 of 19 passes for 246 yards to spark the number-two seed Dolphins to their first playoff victory since 1974. Miami dominated the number-seven seed Patriots throughout the game, amassing 448 yards total offense and sacking Steve Grogan four times. On offense, the Dolphins put together touchdown drives of 76, 79, 74, and 62 yards and were forced to punt only once during the game. Miami rolled up 214 rushing yards, including 112 by Andra Franklin.

New England	0	3	3	7 —	13
Miami	0	14	7	7 —	28

NE —FG J. Smith 23
Mia—Hardy 2 pass from Woodley (von Schamann kick)
Mia—Franklin 1 run (von Schamann kick)
NE —FG J. Smith 42
Mia—Bennett 2 run (von Schamann kick)
Mia—Hardy 2 pass from Woodley (von Schamann kick)
NE —Hasselbeck 22 pass from Grogan (J. Smith kick)

SATURDAY, JANUARY 8, 1983
AFC FIRST-ROUND PLAYOFF GAME

Los Angeles Raiders 27, Cleveland 10—At Memorial Coliseum, attendance 56,555. Trailing 13-10 in the third period, Cleveland was driving for a potential go-ahead touchdown when Raiders defensive end Lyle Alzado hit Cleveland running back Charles White at the Raiders' 14 yard line causing him to fumble. White's fumble was recovered at the 11 yard line by Raiders linebacker Jeff Barnes. Following that play, the Raiders marched 89 yards in 12 plays to take a 20-10 lead. Marcus Allen capped the drive with a 2-yard touchdown run. Early in the fourth period, running back Frank Hawkins climaxed an 80-yard drive with a one-yard run to increase the Raiders' lead to 27-10. Jim Plunkett sparked the Raiders' offense by completing 24 of 37 passes for a career-high 386 yards. Allen rushed 17 times for 72 yards and caught six passes for 75 yards. The Raiders achieved a club playoff record of 510 total yards on offense.

Cleveland	0	10	0	0 —	10
L.A. Raiders	3	10	7	7 —	27

Raiders—FG C. Bahr 27
Cle —FG M. Bahr 52
Raiders—Allen 2 run (C. Bahr kick)
Cle —Feacher 43 pass from McDonald (M. Bahr kick)
Raiders—FG C. Bahr 37
Raiders—Allen 3 run (C. Bahr kick)
Raiders—Hawkins 1 run (C. Bahr kick)

SATURDAY, JANUARY 8, 1983
NFC FIRST-ROUND PLAYOFF GAME

Washington 31, Detroit 7—At Robert F. Kennedy Stadium, attendance 55,045. NFC number-one seed Washington took advantage of five Detroit turnovers to topple the number-eight seed Lions. Washington recovered three Lions fumbles and cornerback Jeris White had two interceptions, including a 77-yard touchdown (third longest in playoff history). The Redskins' Joe Theismann completed 14 of 19 passes for 210 yards and threw three touchdowns to Alvin Garrett, who started in place of the injured Art Monk. Garrett had six receptions for 110 yards and touchdowns of 21, 21, and 27 yards. John Riggins rushed 25 times for 119 yards. Charlie Brown caught three passes for 69 yards. Washington compiled 366 yards (175 rush, 191 pass) and yielded 364 yards (95 rush, 269 pass). Detroit's Eric Hipple was 22 of 38 for 298 yards. Leonard Thompson caught seven passes for 150 yards to pace the Lions.

Detroit	0	0	7	0 —	7
Washington	10	14	7	0 —	31

Wash—White 77 interception return (Moseley kick)
Wash—FG Moseley 26
Wash—Garrett 21 pass from Theismann (Moseley kick)
Wash—Garrett 21 pass from Theismann (Moseley kick)
Wash—Garrett 27 pass from Theismann (Moseley kick)
Det —Hill 15 pass from Hipple (Murray kick)

SATURDAY, JANUARY 8, 1983
NFC FIRST-ROUND PLAYOFF GAME

Green Bay 41, St. Louis 16—At Lambeau Field, attendance 54,282. Green Bay, in the playoffs for first time since 1972, exploded behind Lynn Dickey's four touchdown passes to down the number-six seed Cardinals. Dickey completed 17 of 23 passes for 260 yards, including touchdown passes to John Jefferson (60 and 7 yards), James Lofton (20), and Eddie Lee Ivery (4). Ivery also rushed for 67 yards on 13 carries, including a two-yard touchdown. Jefferson caught six passes for 148 yards, and had two touchdowns. Green Bay's defense recovered two fumbles, had two interceptions, and recorded five sacks. Jan Stenerud made 46- and 34-yard field goals. St. Louis quarterback Neil Lomax was 32 of 51 for 385 yards, with two touchdowns, and two interceptions.

St. Louis	3	6	0	7 —	16
Green Bay	7	21	10	3 —	41

StL—FG O'Donoghue 18
GB—Jefferson 60 pass from Dickey (Stenerud kick)
GB—Lofton 20 pass from Dickey (Stenerud kick)
GB—Ivery 2 run (Stenerud kick)
GB—Ivery 4 pass from Dickey (Stenerud kick)
StL—Tilley 5 pass from Lomax (kick blocked)
GB—FG Stenerud 46
GB—Jefferson 7 pass from Dickey (Stenerud kick)
GB—FG Stenerud 34
StL—Shumann 18 pass from Lomax (O'Donoghue kick)

SUNDAY, JANUARY 9, 1983
AFC FIRST-ROUND PLAYOFF GAME

New York Jets 44, Cincinnati 17—At Riverfront Stadium, attendance 57,560. Freeman McNeil, a second-year player from UCLA, rushed for 202 yards on 21 carries and threw a 14-yard touchdown pass to Derrick Gaffney to help the number-six seed Jets achieve their first playoff victory since 1969. One of the key plays in the game was an interception by the Jets' Johnny Lynn that stopped a Bengals drive at the Jets' 10 yard line with 8:32 left in the second period. Following that play, the Jets drove 85 yards in 11 plays to take a 17-14 lead. McNeil's 202 yards fell four yards short of Keith Lincoln's NFL postseason record of 206. The Jets' Richard Todd enjoyed an outstanding game as he completed 20 of 28 passes for 269 yards and one touchdown. The Jets' Darrol Ray set an NFL playoff record for the longest interception return with a 98-yard touchdown, breaking the previous mark of 88 yards set by Walt Sumner of Cleveland in 1964.

New York Jets	3	17	3	21 —	44
Cincinnati	14	0	3	0 —	17

Cin —Curtis 32 pass from Anderson (Breech kick)
NYJ—FG Leahy 33
Cin —Ross 2 pass from Anderson (Breech kick)
NYJ—Gaffney 14 pass from McNeil (Leahy kick)
NYJ— Walker 4 pass from Todd (Leahy kick)
NYJ—FG Leahy 24
NYJ—FG Leahy 47
Cin —FG Breech 20
NYJ—McNeil 20 run (Leahy kick)
NYJ—Ray 98 interception return (Leahy kick)
NYJ—Crutchfield 1 run (Leahy kick)

SUNDAY, JANUARY 9, 1983
AFC FIRST-ROUND PLAYOFF GAME

San Diego 31, Pittsburgh 28—At Three Rivers Stadium, attendance 53,546. San Diego quarterback Dan Fouts hit tight end Kellen Winslow with a 12-yard touchdown pass with 1:00 remaining in the game to lift the number-five seed Chargers over the number-four seed Steelers. San Diego drove 64 yards for the winning touchdown. In that drive, Chuck Muncie gained 31 yards on five carries to help set up Winslow's decisive score. Muncie finished the game with 126 yards rushing on 25 carries to give him three consecutive 100-yard games. Fouts completed 27 of 42 passes for 333 yards and three touchdowns, two of them to Winslow. San Diego's Wes Chandler was the leading receiver in the game with nine catches for 124 yards. Winslow caught seven for 102 yards and Charlie Joiner had five for 68.

San Diego	3	14	0	14 —	31
Pittsburgh	14	0	7	7 —	28

Pitt —Ruff fumble recovery in end zone (Anderson kick)
SD —FG Benirschke 25
Pitt —Bradshaw 1 run (Anderson kick)
SD —Brooks 18 run (Benirschke kick)
SD —Sievers 10 pass from Fouts (Benirschke kick)
Pitt —Cunningham 2 pass from Bradshaw (Anderson kick)
Pitt —Stallworth 14 pass from Bradshaw (Anderson kick)
SD —Winslow 8 pass from Fouts (Benirschke kick)
SD —Winslow 12 pass from Fouts (Benirschke kick)

SUNDAY, JANUARY 9, 1983
NFC FIRST-ROUND PLAYOFF GAME

Dallas 30, Tampa Bay 17—At Texas Stadium, attendance 65,042. After trailing 17-16 to begin the fourth period, the number-two seed Cowboys scored two touchdowns to defeat number-seven seed Tampa Bay. Rookie safety Monty Hunter put the Cowboys ahead to stay with a 19-yard interception return for a touchdown with 13:21 left. Timmy Newsome's 10-yard scoring catch with 3:33 remaining put the game out of reach. Danny White, playing with a bruised right thumb, was 27 of 45 for 312 yards, with two touchdowns and two interceptions. Tony Dorsett gained 110 yards on 26 carries. Drew Pearson caught seven passes for 95 yards, Butch Johnson four for 76, and Tony Hill four for 45. Rafael Septien made three-of-three field goals (33, 33, and 19 yards). The Cowboys compiled 444 yards (179 rush, 265 pass), and yielded only 218 (105 rush, 113 pass).

Tampa Bay	0	10	7	0 —	17
Dallas	6	7	3	14 —	30

Dall—FG Septien 33
Dall—FG Septien 33
TB —Green 60 fumble recovery return (Capece kick)
TB —FG Capece 32
Dall—Springs 6 pass from D. White (Septien kick)
Dall—FG Septien 19
TB —Jones 49 pass from Williams (Capece kick)
Dall—Hunter 19 interception return (Septien kick)
Dall—Newsome 10 pass from D. White (Septien kick)

SUNDAY, JANUARY 9, 1983
NFC FIRST-ROUND PLAYOFF GAME

Minnesota 30, Atlanta 24—At Metrodome, attendance 60,560. Ted Brown's five-yard touchdown run with 1:44 remaining lifted the number-four seed Minnesota Vikings over number-five seed Atlanta. Brown rushed 23 times for 81 yards. Quarterback Tommy Kramer was 20 of 34 for 253 yards, with two touchdowns, and one interception. Sam McCullum caught four passes for 51 yards, including an 11-yard touchdown. Sammy White had a 36-yard touchdown catch. Rick Danmeier made field goals of 33, 30, and 39 yards. John Turner had two interceptions. Minnesota's defense held Atlanta to 235 yards. The Falcons scored via a recovered blocked punt in the end zone, an interception return, and a fake field goal.

Atlanta	7	0	14	3 —	24
Minnesota	3	10	3	14 —	30

Atl —Rogers recovered blocked punt in end zone (Luckhurst kick)
Minn—FG Danmeier 33
Minn—White 36 pass from Kramer (Danmeier kick)
Minn—FG Danmeier 30
Atl —Luckhurst 17 run (Luckhurst kick)
Atl —Glazebrook 35 interception return (Luckhurst kick)
Minn—FG Danmeier 39
Minn—McCullum 11 pass from Kramer (Danmeier kick)
Atl —FG Luckhurst 41
Minn—Brown 5 run (Danmeier kick)

ELEVENTH WEEK

SATURDAY, JANUARY 15, 1983
AFC SECOND-ROUND PLAYOFF GAME

New York Jets 17, Los Angeles Raiders 14—At Memorial Coliseum, attendance 90,037. Scott Dierking's one-yard run with 3:45 remaining lifted the Jets over the Raiders. The Jets drove 67 yards in six plays for the winning touchdown. Key plays in the drive were Richard Todd's passes of 11 yards to Jerome Barkum and 45 yards to Wesley Walker. New York led 10-0 at halftime on a 20-yard scoring pass from Todd to Walker and Pat Leahy's 30-yard field goal. The Raiders opened the second half by driving 77 yards in 12 plays, capped by Marcus Allen's three-yard touchdown run, which narrowed the Jets' lead to 10-7. With 1:24 left in the third period, Jim Plunkett hit Malcolm Barnwell on a 57-yard scoring pass to give the Raiders a 14-10 lead. With 2:26 remaining in the game, the Raiders drove from their own 33 to the Jets' 42, but Lance Mehl stopped the rally with an interception at the 26. It was Mehl's second interception of the game. Todd completed 15 of 24 passes for 277 yards, one touchdown, and two interceptions. Freeman McNeil rushed for 101 yards on 23 carries. Walker caught seven passes for 169 yards.

New York Jets	7	3	0	7 —	17
L.A. Raiders	0	0	14	0 —	14

NYJ —Walker 20 pass from Todd (Leahy kick)
NYJ —FG Leahy 30
Raiders—Allen 3 run (Bahr kick)
Raiders—Barnwell 57 pass from Plunkett (Bahr kick)
NYJ —Dierking 1 run (Leahy kick)

SATURDAY, JANUARY 15, 1983
NFC SECOND-ROUND PLAYOFF GAME

Washington 21, Minnesota 7—At Robert F. Kennedy Stadium, attendance 54,593. The top-seeded Redskins advanced to their first NFC Championship Game since 1972 with a 21-7 victory over number-four seed Minnesota. John Riggins rushed 37 times for a club playoff record 185 yards. Riggins had a two-yard touchdown run that capped a 71-yard scoring drive that increased the Redskins' lead to 14-0 at the end of the first period. Tight end Don Warren's three-yard touchdown catch opened Washington's scoring. With the score 14-7, Alvin Garrett scored on an 18-yard pass from Joe Theismann with 9:58 remaining in the second period. Theismann completed 17 of 23 passes for 213 yards, with two touchdowns, and one interception. Charlie Brown caught five passes for 59 yards, followed by Warren with four for 20, and Garrett with three for 75. Mark Moseley missed on 47- and 39-yard field goal attempts. For the Vikings, Tommy Kramer completed 18 of 39 passes for 252 yards and Ted Brown rushed 14 times for 65 yards, including an 18-yard touchdown, and caught seven passes for 62 yards. The Redskins had 23 first downs and held the Vikings to 15. In total net yards, Washington compiled 415 (204 rush, 211 pass), while Minnesota had 317 (79 rush, 238 pass).

Minnesota	0	7	0	0 —	7
Washington	14	7	0	0 —	21

Wash—Warren 3 pass from Theismann (Moseley kick)
Wash—Riggins 2 run (Moseley kick)

Minn—Brown 18 run (Danmeier kick)
Wash—Garrett 18 pass from Theismann (Moseley kick)

SUNDAY, JANUARY 16, 1983
AFC SECOND-ROUND PLAYOFF GAME

Miami 34, San Diego 13—At Orange Bowl, attendance 71,383. Miami, behind a sharp passing performance by David Woodley and an opportunistic defense, defeated the San Diego Chargers. Woodley completed 17 of 22 passes for 195 yards and two touchdowns (three yards to Nat Moore and six yards to Ronnie Lee). Miami's defense intercepted San Diego quarterback Dan Fouts five times and forced two fumbles. Miami opened a 24-0 lead midway through the second period. The Dolphins, who led the NFL in defense during the regular season, yielded just 247 total yards to the Chargers, who averaged 450.4 yards per game in 1982. Andra Franklin was Miami's leading rusher with 96 yards on 23 carries, while Tony Nathan contributed 83 on 19 rushes. Nathan also had eight receptions for 55 yards.

San Diego	0	13	0	0 —	13
Miami	7	20	0	7 —	34

Mia—Moore 3 pass from Woodley (von Schamann kick)
Mia—Franklin 3 run (von Schamann kick)
Mia—Lee 6 pass from Woodley (von Schamann kick)
Mia—FG von Schamann 24
SD—Joiner 28 pass from Fouts (kick failed)
Mia—FG von Schamann 23
SD—Muncie 1 run (Benirschke kick)
Mia—Woodley 7 run (von Schamann kick)

SUNDAY, JANUARY 16, 1983
NFC SECOND-ROUND PLAYOFF GAME

Dallas 37, Green Bay 26—At Texas Stadium, attendance 63,972. The number-two seed Cowboys advanced to their third straight NFC Championship Game and tenth in the last 13 years with a hard-fought 37-26 win over the number-three seed Packers. Dennis Thurman tied a Cowboys' playoff record for interceptions with three, including a 39-yard touchdown that lifted Dallas to a 20-7 halftime lead. Danny White completed 23 of 36 passes for 225 yards, had one touchdown, and one interception. Wide receiver Tony Hill caught seven passes for 142 yards, including a 49-yarder from wide receiver Drew Pearson which set up Robert Newhouse's one-yard touchdown. Running back Tony Dorsett rushed 27 times for 99 yards. Doug Cosbie caught four passes for 36 yards. Running back Timmy Newsome had seven catches for 70 yards. Rookie Rod Hill had a Cowboys playoff record 89-yard kickoff return. Dallas gained 375 yards (109 rush, 266 pass) and yielded 466 (158 rush, 308 pass). The Cowboys held the time of possession edge (38:52 to 21:08). Individually for the Packers, quarterback Lynn Dickey was 19 of 36 for 332 yards, with one touchdown, and three interceptions. Wide receiver James Lofton caught five passes for 109 yards, and also had a 71-yard end-around for a touchdown, the longest run in NFL postseason history.

Green Bay	0	7	6	13 —	26
Dallas	6	14	3	14 —	37

Dall—FG Septien 50
Dall—FG Septien 34
GB—Lofton 6 pass from Dickey (Stenerud kick)
Dall—Newsome 2 run (Septien kick)
Dall—Thurman 39 interception return (Septien kick)
GB—FG Stenerud 30
GB—FG Stenerud 33
Dall—FG Septien 24
GB—Lofton 71 run (kick failed)
Dall—Cosbie 7 pass from D. White (Septien kick)
GB—Lee 22 interception return (Stenerud kick)
Dall—Newhouse 1 run (Septien kick)

TWELFTH WEEK
SATURDAY, JANUARY 22, 1983
NFC CHAMPIONSHIP GAME

Washington 31, Dallas 17—At Robert F. Kennedy Stadium, attendance 55,045. The Washington Redskins advanced to their first Super Bowl since 1972 with a 31-17 victory over the Dallas Cowboys. Defensive tackle Darryl Grant's 10-yard interception return for a touchdown lifted Washington to a 31-17 lead with 6:55 remaining. The Redskins held a 14-3 halftime lead via Charlie Brown's 19-yard touchdown catch and fullback John Riggins' one-yard run. Mike Nelms' 76-yard third-quarter kickoff return (an NFC Championship Game record) set up Riggins' second touchdown of the day, a four-yard run. Dallas closed to a 21-17 deficit behind the passing of substitute quarterback Gary Hogeboom, who replaced an injured Danny White. Hogeboom was 14 of 29 for 162 yards, with two touchdowns, and two interceptions. Mark Moseley's 29-yard field goal with 7:12 left in the game gave Washington a 24-17 edge. The Redskins' Joe Theismann completed 12 of 20 passes for 150 yards and one touchdown. Riggins rushed 36 times for 140 yards. Brown caught three passes for 54 yards and wide receiver Alvin Garrett had four for 46 yards.

Dallas	3	0	14	0 —	17
Washington	7	7	7	10 —	31

Dall—FG Septien 27
Wash—Brown 19 pass from Theismann (Moseley kick)
Wash—Riggins 1 run (Moseley kick)
Dall—Pearson 6 pass from Hogeboom (Septien kick)
Wash—Riggins 4 run (Moseley kick)
Dall—Johnson 23 pass from Hogeboom (Septien kick)
Wash—FG Moseley 29
Wash—Grant 10 interception return (Moseley kick)

SUNDAY, JANUARY 23, 1983
AFC CHAMPIONSHIP GAME

Miami 14, New York Jets 0—At Orange Bowl, attendance 67,396. Linebacker A. J. Duhe intercepted an AFC Championship Game record three passes, returning the final one 35 yards for a touchdown early in the fourth period, to lead the Dolphins' victory. Woody Bennett ran seven yards for the first Miami touchdown on the Dolphins' initial possession of the third quarter, that followed Duhe's second interception. Early in the fourth period, Duhe batted Richard Todd's pass in the air, caught it, and raced 35 yards for the Dolphins' final touchdown. Todd was intercepted a record-tying five times by the Miami defense, which limited the Jets to an AFC title game record-low 139 yards.

New York Jets	0	0	0	0 —	0
Miami	0	0	7	7 —	14

Mia—Bennett 7 run (von Schamann kick)
Mia—Duhe 35 interception return (von Schamann kick)

THIRTEENTH WEEK
SUPER BOWL XVII
SUNDAY, JANUARY 30, 1983
PASADENA, CALIFORNIA

Washington 27, Miami 17—At Rose Bowl, attendance 103,667. Fullback John Riggins' Super Bowl record 166 yards on 38 carries sparked Washington to a 27-17 victory over AFC champion Miami. It was Riggins' fourth straight 100-yard rushing game during the playoffs, also a record. The win marked Washington's first NFL title since 1942, and was only the second time in Super Bowl history NFC teams scored consecutive wins (Green Bay did it in Super Bowls I and II and San Francisco won Super Bowl XVI). The Redskins, under second-year head coach Joe Gibbs, presented a balanced offense that accounted for 400 total yards (a Super Bowl record 276 yards rushing and 124 passing), second in Super Bowl history to the 429 yards by Oakland in Super Bowl XI. The Dolphins built a 17-10 halftime lead on a 76-yard touchdown pass from quarterback David Woodley to wide receiver Jimmy Cefalo 6:49 into the first period, a 20-yard field goal by Uwe von Schamann with 6:00 left in the half, and a Super Bowl record 98-yard kickoff return by Fulton Walker with 1:38 remaining. Washington had tied the score at 10-10 with 1:51 left before halftime on a four-yard touchdown pass from Joe Theismann to Alvin Garrett. Mark Moseley started the Redskins' scoring with a 31-yard field goal late in the first period, and added a 20-yard field goal midway through the third period to cut the Dolphins' lead to 17-14. Riggins, who was voted the game's most valuable player, gave Washington its first lead of the game with 10:01 left when he ran 43 yards off left tackle for a touchdown on a fourth-and-one play. Wide receiver Charlie Brown caught a six-yard scoring pass from Theismann with 1:55 left to complete the scoring. The Dolphins managed only 176 yards (142 in the first half). Theismann completed 15 of 23 for 143 yards, with two touchdowns, and two interceptions. For Miami, Woodley was 4 of 14 for 97 yards, with one score, and one interception.

Miami	7	10	0	0 —	17
Washington	0	10	3	14 —	27

Mia—Cefalo 76 pass from Woodley (von Schamann kick)
Wash—FG Moseley 31
Mia—FG von Schamann 20
Wash—Garrett 4 pass from Theismann (Moseley kick)
Mia—Walker 98 kickoff return (von Schamann kick)
Wash—FG Moseley 20
Wash—Riggins 43 run (Moseley kick)
Wash—Brown 6 pass from Theismann (Moseley kick)

FOURTEENTH WEEK
AFC-NFC PRO BOWL
SUNDAY, FEBRUARY 6, 1983
HONOLULU, HAWAII

NFC 20, AFC 19—At Aloha Stadium, attendance 47,201. Danny White threw an 11-yard touchdown pass to John Jefferson with 35 seconds remaining to give the NFC a 20-19 victory over the AFC. White, who completed 14 of 26 passes for 162 yards, kept the winning 65-yard drive alive with a 14-yard completion to Jefferson on a fourth-and-seven play at the AFC 25 yard line. The AFC was ahead 12-10 at halftime and increased the lead to 19-10 in the third period when Marcus Allen scored on a one-yard run. Dan Fouts, who attempted 30 passes, set Pro Bowl records for most completions (17) and yards (274). John Stallworth was the AFC's leading receiver with seven catches for 67 yards. William Andrews topped the NFC with five receptions for 48 yards. Fouts and Jefferson were voted co-players of the game.

AFC	9	3	7	0 —	19
NFC	0	10	0	10 —	20

AFC—Walker 34 pass from Fouts (Benirschke kick)
AFC—Safety, Still tackled Theismann in end zone
NFC—Andrews 3 run (Moseley kick)
NFC—FG Moseley 35
AFC—FG Benirschke 29
AFC—Allen 1 run (Benirschke kick)
NFC—FG Moseley 41
NFC—Jefferson 11 pass from D. White (Moseley kick)

Look for in 1983

Things that could happen in 1983:

• Franco Harris (Pittsburgh), with his next touchdown, will move into sole possession of fourth place in total touchdowns scored. Entering 1983, Harris shares fourth place with Jim Taylor (93 each). The top three are Jim Brown (126), Lenny Moore (113), and Don Hutson (105).

• Harris and Walter Payton (Chicago) could pass O.J. Simpson, the NFL's second-leading rusher. Simpson gained 11,236 yards in his career. Harris (10,943) needs 294 yards and Payton (10,204) needs 1,033 yards to pass Simpson. Jim Brown is the all-time leader with 12,312 yards.

• Harris already has carried the ball more times (2,602) than any player in league history. Payton (2,352), currently in fourth position, could move into second this season. He needs only eight carries to pass Brown and 53 to pass Simpson.

• Should Payton gain 1,000 yards rushing in 1983, it would mark his seventh such season and tie the NFL record shared by Brown and Harris. Also, Harris could get 1,000 yards for a record eighth time.

• Earl Campbell (Houston) needs five yards rushing to become the eleventh player to reach 7,000 yards for a career.

• Ken Anderson (Cincinnati) led the league in passing in both 1981 and 1982. No player in the history of the NFL has led in passing in three successive seasons. Anderson, in fact, is the only player who has led for two straight years on two separate occasions, having also done it in 1974 and 1975.

• Anderson (28,057 yards), Terry Bradshaw of Pittsburgh (27,912), and Dan Fouts of San Diego (27,139) are all within striking distance of 30,000 career yards passing—a plateau that has been reached previously by only seven quarterbacks.

• Fouts, who had successive 400-yard games last December, has passed for 400 yards in a game three times in his career. The league record is five such games, accomplished by Sonny Jurgensen.

• Jan Stenerud (Green Bay) needs 18 field goals to match George Blanda's career record of 335. Blanda attempted 638 field goals, while Stenerud has tried only 483. Stenerud, with 1,408 career points, needs just 32 more to pass Jim Turner and move into second position on the all-time scoring list. Blanda is at the head of that list, too, with 2,002 points.

• Rolf Benirschke (San Diego) needs two field goals to reach 100 for his career. At that point, he will likely become the all-time NFL leader in field goal percentage among players who have kicked at least 100 field goals. Entering the 1983 season, Benirschke had made 98 of 133 attempts, a percentage of 73.7. The leader going into the season is Toni Fritsch (68.0).

• Harold Carmichael (Philadelphia) needs 49 receptions to reach 600 for his career. Only three players—Charley Taylor (649), Don Maynard (633), and Raymond Berry (631)—have reached that milestone.

• Mike Fuller (Cincinnati) has 252 career punt returns, six short of Emlen Tunnell's league record of 258.

• Rick Upchurch (Denver), who already has the league record for punt return yardage (2,956), has some other accomplishments within reach. His 244 career punt returns, fourth on the all-time list, are 14 short of Tunnell's record; his total of eight touchdowns on punt returns gives him a share of the NFL record with Jack Christiansen; and he has led the league in punt return average three times, tying the record originally set by Les (Speedy) Duncan.

• Jim Hart (St. Louis), by appearing in one more game with the Cardinals, would be in his eighteenth season with one team—one short of the NFL record held by Jim Marshall, who played with the Minnesota Vikings for 19 seasons. Besides Hart, five other players have seen action for the same team for 17 seasons: John Brodie, San Francisco; Johnny Unitas, Baltimore; Lou Groza, Cleveland; Jim Bakken, St. Louis; and Mick Tingelhoff, Minnesota.

• Everson Walls (Dallas) has led the NFL in interceptions in each of his first two seasons. He is the only player in the history of the league to have accomplished that feat. If Walls leads again this season, he would also become the first player to lead the league in interceptions for three straight seasons. Only one other player, Philadelphia's Bill Bradley in 1971 and 1972, led in this category two years in a row.

1982 Professional Football Awards

	NFL	AFC	NFC
Professional Football Writers Association			
Most Valuable Player	Dan Fouts		
Rookie of the Year	Marcus Allen		
Coach of the Year		Tom Flores	Joe Gibbs
Associated Press			
Most Valuable Player	Mark Moseley		
Offensive Player-of-the-Year	Dan Fouts		
Defensive Player-of-the-Year	Lawrence Taylor		
Rookie of the Year—Offense	Marcus Allen		
Rookie of the Year—Defense	Chip Banks		
Coach of the Year	Joe Gibbs		
United Press International			
Player of the Year		Dan Fouts	Mark Moseley
Rookie of the Year		Marcus Allen	Jim McMahon
Coach of the Year		Tom Flores	Joe Gibbs
Newspaper Enterprise Association			
Jim Thorpe Trophy—MVP	Dan Fouts		
Bert Bell Trophy—Rookie of the Year	Marcus Allen		
George Halas Trophy—Defensive Player of the Year	Mark Gastineau		
The Sporting News			
Player of the Year	Mark Moseley		
Rookie of the Year	Marcus Allen		
Coach of the Year	Joe Gibbs		
Pro Football Weekly			
Offensive Most Valuable Player	Dan Fouts		
Defensive Most Valuable Player	Dan Hampton		
Offensive Rookie of the Year	Marcus Allen		
Defensive Rookie of the Year	Chip Banks		
Comeback Player of the Year	Lyle Alzado		
Coach of the Year	Joe Gibbs		
Football News			
Coach of the Year		Ron Meyer	Joe Gibbs
Man of the Year	Don Shula		
AFC-NFC Pro Bowl			
Player of the Game	Dan Fouts		
	John Jefferson		
Maxwell Club			
Player of the Year	Joe Theismann		
College and Pro Football Newsweekly			
Player of the Year	Dan Fouts		
Rookie of the Year	Marcus Allen		
Coach of the Year	Joe Gibbs		
Football Digest			
Player of the Year	Joe Theismann		
Coach of the Year	Joe Gibbs		

Past Super Bowl Most Valuable Players
(Selected by Sport Magazine)

SB I	—Bart Starr, Green Bay
SB II	—Bart Starr, Green Bay
SB III	—Joe Namath, N.Y. Jets
SB IV	—Len Dawson, Kansas City
SB V	—Chuck Howley, Dallas
SB VI	—Roger Staubach, Dallas
SB VII	—Jake Scott, Miami
SB VIII	—Larry Csonka, Miami
SB IX	—Franco Harris, Pittsburgh
SB X	—Lynn Swann, Pittsburgh
SB XI	—Fred Biletnikoff, Oakland
SB XII	—Randy White and Harvey Martin, Dallas
SB XIII	—Terry Bradshaw, Pittsburgh
SB XIV	—Terry Bradshaw, Pittsburgh
SB XV	—Jim Plunkett, Oakland
SB XVI	—Joe Montana, San Francisco
SB XVII	—John Riggins, Washington

1982 All-NFL Team
(Selected by Associated Press, Newspaper Enterprise
Association, and Professional Football Writers Association)

Offense

Wes Chandler, San Diego (AP, NEA, PFWA) . . . . Wide Receiver
Dwight Clark, San Francisco (AP, NEA, PFWA) . . . . Wide Receiver
Kellen Winslow, San Diego (AP, NEA, PFWA) . . . . Tight End
Anthony Munoz, Cincinnati (AP, NEA, PFWA) . . . . Tackle
Marvin Powell, New York Jets (AP, NEA, PFWA) . . . . Tackle
Doug Wilkerson, San Diego (AP, NEA, PFWA) . . . . Guard
John Hannah, New England (PFWA) . . . . Guard
Ed Newman, Miami (NEA) . . . . Guard
R.C. Thielemann, Atlanta (AP) . . . . Guard
Joe Fields, New York Jets (AP, NEA) . . . . Center
Mike Webster, Pittsburgh (PFWA) . . . . Center
Dan Fouts, San Diego (AP, NEA, PFWA) . . . . Quarterback
Marcus Allen, Los Angeles Raiders (AP, NEA, PFWA) . . . . Running Back
Freeman McNeil, New York Jets (AP, NEA, PFWA) . . . . . . Running Back
Mark Moseley, Washington (AP, NEA, PFWA) . . . . Kicker
Mike Nelms, Washington (PFWA) . . . . Kick Returner
Rick Upchurch, Denver (AP) . . . . Kick Returner
LeRoy Irvin, Los Angeles Rams (PFWA) . . . . Punt Returner

Defense

Mark Gastineau, New York Jets (AP, NEA, PFWA) . . . . . . Defensive End
Lee Roy Selmon, Tampa Bay (NEA, PFWA) . . . . Defensive End
Ed Jones, Dallas (AP) . . . . Defensive End
Randy White, Dallas (AP, NEA, PFWA) . . . . Defensive Tackle
Dan Hampton, Chicago (NEA, PFWA) . . . . Defensive Tackle
Doug English, Detroit (AP) . . . . Defensive Tackle
Fred Smerlas, Buffalo (AP) . . . . Nose Tackle
Jack Lambert, Pittsburgh (AP, NEA, PFWA) . . . . Middle Linebacker
Lawrence Taylor, New York Giants (AP, NEA, PFWA) . . . . . . Linebacker
Hugh Green, Tampa Bay (PFWA) . . . . Linebacker
Ted Hendricks, Los Angeles Raiders (AP) . . . . Linebacker
Rod Martin, Los Angeles Raiders (NEA) . . . . Linebacker
Louis Breeden, Cincinnati (AP, NEA) . . . . Cornerback
Mark Haynes, New York Giants (AP, PFWA) . . . . Cornerback
Mike Haynes, New England (NEA) . . . . Cornerback
Everson Walls, Dallas (PFWA) . . . . Cornerback
Nolan Cromwell, Los Angeles Rams (AP, PFWA) . . . . Safety
Donnie Shell, Pittsburgh (AP, PFWA) . . . . Safety
Gary Barbaro, Kansas City (NEA) . . . . Safety
Kenny Easley, Seattle (NEA) . . . . Safety
Dave Jennings, New York Giants (NEA, PFWA) . . . . Punter
Luke Prestridge, Denver (AP) . . . . Punter

1982 NFL All-Rookie Team
(Selected by Professional Football Writers Association)

Offense

Charlie Brown, Washington . . . . Wide Receiver
Lindsay Scott, New Orleans . . . . Wide Receiver
Pete Metzelaars, Seattle . . . . Tight End
Tootie Robbins, St. Louis . . . . Tackle
Luis Sharpe, St. Louis . . . . Tackle
Brad Edelman, New Orleans . . . . Guard
Sean Farrell, Tampa Bay . . . . Guard
Rich Umphrey, New York Giants . . . . Center
Jim McMahon, Chicago . . . . Quarterback
Marcus Allen, Los Angeles Raiders . . . . Running Back
Butch Woolfolk, New York Giants . . . . Running Back
Gary Anderson, Pittsburgh . . . . Kicker

Defense

Bruce Clark, New Orleans . . . . Defensive End
Ken Sims, New England . . . . Defensive End
Lester Williams, New England . . . . Defensive Tackle
Leo Wisniewski, Baltimore . . . . Defensive Tackle
Tom Cousineau, Cleveland . . . . Middle Linebacker
Chip Banks, Cleveland . . . . Outside Linebacker
Johnie Cooks, Baltimore . . . . Outside Linebacker
Vernon Dean, Washington . . . . Cornerback
Bobby Watkins, Detroit . . . . Cornerback
Benny Perrin, St. Louis . . . . Safety
Andre Young, San Diego . . . . Safety
Rohn Stark, Baltimore . . . . Punter

1982 All-AFC Team
(Selected by United Press International)

Offense

Wes Chandler, San Diego . . . . Wide Receiver
Wesley Walker, New York Jets . . . . Wide Receiver
Kellen Winslow, San Diego . . . . Tight End
Anthony Munoz, Cincinnati . . . . Tackle
Marvin Powell, New York Jets . . . . Tackle
Ed Newman, Miami . . . . Guard
Doug Wilkerson, San Diego . . . . Guard
Mike Webster, Pittsburgh . . . . Center
Dan Fouts, San Diego . . . . Quarterback
Marcus Allen, Los Angeles Raiders . . . . Running Back
Freeman McNeil, New York Jets . . . . Running Back
Rolf Benirschke, San Diego . . . . Kicker

Defense

Lyle Alzado, Los Angeles Raiders . . . . Defensive End
Mark Gastineau, New York Jets . . . . Defensive End
Bob Baumhower, Miami . . . . Defensive Tackle
Robert Brazile, Houston . . . . Outside Linebacker
Ted Hendricks, Los Angeles Raiders . . . . Outside Linebacker
Randy Gradishar, Denver . . . . Inside Linebacker
Jack Lambert, Pittsburgh . . . . Inside Linebacker
Lester Hayes, Los Angeles Raiders . . . . Cornerback
Mike Haynes, New England . . . . Cornerback
Kenny Easley, Seattle . . . . Safety
Gary Barbaro, Kansas City . . . . Safety
Luke Prestridge, Denver . . . . Punter

1982 All-NFC Team
(Selected by United Press International)

Offense

Dwight Clark, San Francisco . . . . Wide Receiver
James Lofton, Green Bay . . . . Wide Receiver
Jimmie Giles, Tampa Bay . . . . Tight End
Pat Donovan, Dallas . . . . Tackle
Mike Kenn, Atlanta . . . . Tackle
Kent Hill, Los Angeles Rams . . . . Guard
R.C. Thielemann, Atlanta . . . . Guard
Larry McCarren, Green Bay . . . . Center
Joe Theismann, Washington . . . . Quarterback
William Andrews, Atlanta . . . . Running Back
Tony Dorsett, Dallas . . . . Running Back
Mark Moseley, Washington . . . . Kicker

Defense

Doug Martin, Minnesota . . . . Defensive End
Lee Roy Selmon, Tampa Bay . . . . Defensive End
Randy White, Dallas . . . . Defensive Tackle
Hugh Green, Tampa Bay . . . . Outside Linebacker
Lawrence Taylor, New York Giants . . . . Outside Linebacker
Bob Breunig, Dallas . . . . Inside Linebacker
Harry Carson, New York Giants . . . . Inside Linebacker
Mark Haynes, New York Giants . . . . Cornerback
Everson Walls, Dallas . . . . Cornerback
Tony Peters, Washington . . . . Safety
Nolan Cromwell, Los Angeles Rams . . . . Safety
Dave Jennings, New York Giants . . . . Punter

Conference Leaders—1982 Individual

Rushing
AFC—Freeman McNeil
New York Jets, 786 yards
NFC—Tony Dorsett
Dallas, 745 yards

Passing
AFC—Ken Anderson
Cincinnati, 95.5 rating points
NFC—Joe Theismann
Washington, 91.3 rating points

Pass Receiving, Receptions
AFC—Kellen Winslow, San Diego, 54
NFC—Dwight Clark, San Francisco, 60

Pass Receiving, Yardage
AFC—Wes Chandler, San Diego, 1,032 yards
NFC—Dwight Clark, San Francisco, 913 yards

Interceptions
AFC—Bobby Jackson, New York Jets, 5
Ken Riley, Cincinnati, 5
Donnie Shell, Pittsburgh, 5
Dwayne Woodruff, Pittsburgh, 5
NFC—Everson Walls, Dallas, 7

Punting
AFC—Luke Prestridge, Denver, 45.0-yard average (45 punts)
NFC—Carl Birdsong, St. Louis, 43.8-yard average (54 punts)

Punt Returns
AFC—Rick Upchurch, Denver, 16.1-yard average (15 returns)
NFC—Billy Johnson, Atlanta, 11.4-yard average (24 returns)

Kickoff Returns
AFC—Mike Mosley, Buffalo, 27.1-yard average (18 returns)
NFC—Alvin Hall, Detroit, 26.6-yard average (16 returns)

Scoring, Kicker
AFC—Rolf Benirschke, San Diego,
80 points (32 PAT, 16 FG)
NFC—Mark Moseley, Washington,
76 Points (16 PAT, 20 FG)

Scoring, Non-kicker
AFC—Marcus Allen, Los Angeles Raiders,
84 points (14 touchdowns)
NFC—Wendell Tyler, Los Angeles Rams,
78 points (13 touchdowns)

Conference Leaders—1982 Team

Rushing Offense
AFC—Buffalo, 1,371 yards
NFC—Dallas, 1,313 yards

Rushing Defense
AFC—Pittsburgh, 762 yards
NFC—Detroit, 854 yards

Passing Offense
AFC—San Diego, 3,021 yards
NFC—San Francisco, 2,668 yards

Passing Defense
AFC—Miami, 1,281 yards
NFC—Tampa Bay, 1,608 yards

Interceptions By
AFC—Miami, 19
NFC—Detroit, 18

Punting
AFC—Denver, 45.0-yard average
NFC—St. Louis, 43.8-yard average

Punt Returns
AFC—Denver, 14.5-yard average (21 returns)
NFC—Atlanta, 11.4-yard average (24 returns)

Kickoff Returns
AFC—New England, 23.1-yard average (28 returns)
NFC—New Orleans, 22.2-yard average (26 returns)

Scoring
AFC—San Diego, 288 points (34 TD, 32 PAT, 16 FG, 2 Safeties)
NFC—Dallas, 226 points (28 TD, 28 PAT, 10 FG)
Green Bay, 226 points (27 TD, 25 PAT, 13 FG)

Scoring Defense
AFC—Miami, 131 points (15 TD, 14 PAT, 9 FG)
NFC—Washington, 128 points (16 TD, 14 PAT, 6 FG)

1982 Team Rankings by Yards
(Combined American and National Conferences)

	Offense			Defense		
	Total	Rush	Pass	Total	Rush	Pass
Atlanta	9	9	18	14t	17	13
Baltimore	27	14	24	26	28	15
Buffalo	11	1	20	2	16	2
Chicago	26	18	23	16	5	21
Cincinnati	2	20	3	18	3	22
Cleveland	17	23	12t	23	26	14
Dallas	5	5	9	11	13	11
Denver	15	17	15	24	7	26
Detroit	24	16	22	9	4	18
Green Bay	12	12	14	8	6	12
Houston	28	26	19	28	23	25
Kansas City	25	21	21	10	19	10
Los Angeles Raiders	10	13	10	22	2	27
Los Angeles Rams	6	15	4	27	22	24
Miami	19	3	27	1	24	1
Minnesota	14	22	5	19	14	19
New England	21	2	28	13	25	5
New Orleans	20	6	25	5	10	8
New York Giants	16	24	8	7	20	6
New York Jets	4	4	7	6	11	9
Philadelphia	18	25	11	20	15	20
Pittsburgh	8	8	17	17	1	23
St. Louis	23	7	26	14t	12	17
San Diego	1	11	1	25	9	28
San Francisco	3	28	2	21	21	16
Seattle	22	27	16	12	27	3
Tampa Bay	13	19	6	3	18	4
Washington	7	10	12t	4	8	7

Ten Best Rushing Performances, 1982

	Attempts	Yards	TD
1. George Rogers New Orleans vs. Dallas, December 19	33	166	1
2. Tony Collins New England vs. Houston, November 28	32	161	1
3. Marcus Allen L.A. Raiders vs. Seattle, December 5	24	156	2
4. Tony Dorsett Dallas vs. Minnesota, January 3	16	153	1
5. Wilbert Montgomery Philadelphia vs. Houston, December 19	17	147	3
6. Stump Mitchell St. Louis vs. Philadelphia, December 5	22	145	1
7. Joe Cribbs Buffalo vs. Pittsburgh, December 12	30	143	0
8. Earl Campbell Houston vs. Seattle, September 19	30	142	1
9. Wayne Wilson New Orleans vs. Chicago, September 19	33	138	0
Wendell Tyler L.A. Rams vs. Kansas City, November 28	25	138	2

100-Yard Rushing Performances, 1982

First Week

Tony Collins, New England	137 yards vs. Baltimore
Mike Pruitt, Cleveland	136 yards vs. Seattle
Marcus Allen, L.A. Raiders	116 yards vs. San Francisco
Freeman McNeil, N.Y. Jets	116 yards vs. Miami
Eddie Lee Ivery, Green Bay	109 yards vs. L.A. Rams
Andra Franklin, Miami	103 yards vs. N.Y. Jets
Franco Harris, Pittsburgh	103 yards vs. Dallas

Second Week

Earl Campbell, Houston	142 yards vs. Seattle
Wayne Wilson, New Orleans	138 yards vs. Chicago
John Riggins, Washington	136 yards vs. Tampa Bay
Billy Sims, Detroit	119 yards vs. L.A. Rams
Freeman McNeil, N.Y. Jets	106 yards vs. New England

Third Week

Freeman McNeil, N.Y. Jets	123 yards vs. Baltimore
George Rogers, New Orleans	123 yards vs. Kansas City
William Andrews, Atlanta	119 yards vs. L.A. Rams

Fourth Week

Tony Collins, New England	161 yards vs. Houston
Wendell Tyler, L.A. Rams	138 yards vs. Kansas City
Pete Johnson, Cincinnati	129 yards vs. L.A. Raiders
Ottis Anderson, St. Louis	122 yards vs. Atlanta
Tony Dorsett, Dallas	116 yards vs. Cleveland
Billy Sims, Detroit	114 yards vs. N.Y. Giants

Fifth Week

Marcus Allen, L.A. Raiders	156 yards vs. Seattle
Stump Mitchell, St. Louis	145 yards vs. Philadelphia
Andra Franklin, Miami	129 yards vs. Minnesota

Sixth Week

Joe Cribbs, Buffalo	143 yards vs. Pittsburgh
Ottis Anderson, St. Louis	109 yards vs. Washington
Billy Sims, Detroit	109 yards vs. Green Bay
Andra Franklin, Miami	107 yards vs. New England
Mark van Eeghen, New England	100 yards vs. Miami

Seventh Week

George Rogers, New Orleans	166 yards vs. Dallas
Wilbert Montgomery, Philadelphia	147 yards vs. Houston
William Andrews, Atlanta	108 yards vs. San Francisco
James Brooks, San Diego	105 yards vs. Cincinnati
Tony Dorsett, Dallas	105 yards vs. New Orleans
Tony Collins, New England	103 yards vs. Seattle

Eighth Week

Chuck Muncie, San Diego	126 yards vs. Baltimore
Ottis Anderson, St. Louis	110 yards vs. N.Y. Giants
Joe Cribbs, Buffalo	108 yards vs. Miami
Walter Payton, Chicago	104 yards vs. L.A. Rams
Franco Harris, Pittsburgh	101 yards vs. New England

Ninth Week

Tony Dorsett, Dallas	153 yards vs. Minnesota
Chuck Muncie, San Diego	129 yards vs. L.A. Raiders
Marcus Allen, L.A. Raiders	126 yards vs. San Diego
Franco Harris, Pittsburgh	120 yards vs. Cleveland
Walter Payton, Chicago	109 yards vs. Tampa Bay
Joe Cribbs, Buffalo	104 yards vs. New England
Ted Brown, Minnesota	100 yards vs. Dallas

Times 100 or More

Allen, Anderson, Collins, Cribbs, Dorsett, Franklin, Harris, McNeil, Sims 3; Andrews, Muncie, Payton, Rogers 2.

Ten Best Passing Yardage Performances, 1982

	Att.	Comp.	Yards	TD
1. Vince Ferragamo L.A. Rams vs. Chicago, December 26	46	30	509	3
2. Dan Fouts San Diego vs. San Francisco, December 11	48	33	444	5
3. Dan Fouts San Diego vs. Cincinnati, December 20	40	25	435	1
4. Ken Anderson Cincinnati vs. San Diego, December 20	56	40	416	2
5. Joe Montana San Francisco vs. St. Louis, November 21	39	26	408	3
6. Richard Todd N.Y. Jets vs. Detroit, December 6	32	23	384	3
7. Joe Theismann Washington vs. Philadelphia, September 12	39	28	382	3
8. Steve Bartkowski Atlanta vs. L.A. Raiders, September 19	56	34	375	1
9. Ron Jaworski Philadelphia vs. Washington, September 12	38	27	371	2
10. Doug Williams Tampa Bay vs. Chicago, January 2	49	25	367	2

300-Yard Passing Performances, 1982

First Week
Joe Theismann, Washington	382 yards vs. Philadelphia
Ron Jaworski, Philadelphia	371 yards vs. Washington
Ken Anderson, Cincinnati	354 yards vs. Houston
Danny White, Dallas	347 yards vs. Pittsburgh
Scott Brunner, N.Y. Giants	310 yards vs. Atlanta

Second Week
Steve Bartkowski, Atlanta	375 yards vs. L.A. Raiders
Joe Montana, San Francisco	336 yards vs. Denver
Ron Jaworski, Philadelphia	334 yards vs. Cleveland
Joe Ferguson, Buffalo	330 yards vs. Minnesota
Ken Anderson, Cincinnati	323 yards vs. Pittsburgh

Third Week
Joe Montana, San Francisco	408 yards vs. St. Louis
Dan Fouts, San Diego	357 yards vs. L.A. Raiders
Jim Zorn, Seattle	318 yards vs. Denver

Fourth Week
Tommy Kramer, Minnesota	342 yards vs. Chicago
Dan Fouts, San Diego	337 yards vs. Denver
Joe Montana, San Francisco	334 yards vs. New Orleans
Jim Plunkett, L.A. Raiders	318 yards vs. Cincinnati

Fifth Week
Richard Todd, N.Y. Jets	384 yards vs. Detroit
Brian Sipe, Cleveland	338 yards vs. San Diego
Ken Stabler, New Orleans	333 yards vs. Tampa Bay
Joe Montana, San Francisco	305 yards vs. L.A. Rams

Sixth Week
Dan Fouts, San Diego	444 yards vs. San Francisco
Joe Montana, San Francisco	356 yards vs. San Diego
Steve DeBerg, Denver	307 yards vs. L.A. Rams
Jim Plunkett, L.A. Raiders	303 yards vs. Kansas City

Seventh Week
Dan Fouts, San Diego	435 yards vs. Cincinnati
Ken Anderson, Cincinnati	416 yards vs. San Diego
Gary Danielson, Detroit	347 yards vs. Minnesota
Jim Plunkett, L.A. Raiders	321 yards vs. L.A. Rams

Eighth Week
Vince Ferragamo, L.A. Rams	509 yards vs. Chicago
Tommy Kramer, Minnesota	328 yards vs. N.Y. Jets
Scott Brunner, N.Y. Giants	326 yards vs. St. Louis

Ninth Week
Doug Williams, Tampa Bay	367 yards vs. Chicago
Ken Anderson, Cincinnati	323 yards vs. Houston
Paul McDonald, Cleveland	313 yards vs. Pittsburgh
Dan Fouts, San Diego	303 yards vs. L.A. Raiders

> **Times 300 or more**
> Fouts, Montana 5; Anderson 4; Brunner, Jaworski, Kramer 2.

Ten Best Receiving Yardage Performances, 1982

	Yards	No.	TD
1. Wes Chandler San Diego vs. Cincinnati, December 20	260	10	2
2. Steve Watson Denver vs. L.A. Rams, December 12	183	10	0
George Farmer L.A. Rams vs. Chicago, December 26	183	9	1
4. Sammy White Minnesota vs. Chicago, November 28	177	10	0
5. Roy Green St. Louis vs. Dallas, September 19	170	10	0
6. Wesley Walker N.Y. Jets vs. Detroit, December 6	164	5	3
7. Leonard Thompson Detroit vs. Minnesota, December 19	161	5	2
8. Cris Collinsworth Cincinnati vs. San Diego, December 20	156	9	1
Charlie Brown Washington vs. New Orleans, December 26	156	4	2
10. Floyd Eddings N.Y. Giants vs. Philadelphia, December 11	148	5	0

100-Yard Receiving Performances, 1982
(Number in parentheses is receptions.)

First Week
John Stallworth, Pittsburgh	137 yards (7) vs. Dallas
Art Monk, Washington	134 yards (8) vs. Philadelphia
Tony Hill, Dallas	130 yards (6) vs. Pittsburgh
Wes Chandler, San Diego	120 yards (4) vs. Denver
John Jefferson, Green Bay	116 yards (6) vs. L.A. Rams
Dwight Clark, San Francisco	106 yards (6) vs. L.A. Raiders
Lindsay Scott, New Orleans	103 yards (6) vs. St. Louis
Doug Cosbie, Dallas	102 yards (5) vs. Pittsburgh
Jimmie Giles, Tampa Bay	100 yards (5) vs. Minnesota

Second Week
Roy Green, St. Louis	170 yards (10) vs. Dallas
Cris Collinsworth, Cincinnati	144 yards (9) vs. Pittsburgh
Sammy White, Minnesota	142 yards (9) vs. Buffalo
Cliff Branch, L.A. Raiders	138 yards (6) vs. Atlanta
Willie Miller, L.A. Rams	131 yards (3) vs. Detroit
Dwight Clark, San Francisco	127 yards (9) vs. Denver
Ozzie Newsome, Cleveland	122 yards (8) vs. Philadelphia
Jerry Butler, Buffalo	111 yards (7) vs. Minnesota
Freddie Solomon, San Francisco	109 yards (4) vs. Denver
Kevin House, Tampa Bay	105 yards (4) vs. Washington
Billy Sims, Detroit	103 yards (5) vs. L.A. Rams
Tony Hill, Dallas	101 yards (8) vs. St. Louis
James Lofton, Green Bay	101 yards (4) vs. N.Y. Giants
Harold Carmichael, Philadelphia	100 yards (6) vs. Cleveland

Third Week
Wes Chandler, San Diego	118 yards (7) vs. L.A. Raiders
Kellen Winslow, San Diego	105 yards (8) vs. L.A. Raiders
Paul Johns, Seattle	103 yards (5) vs. Denver
J.T. Smith, Kansas City	101 yards (6) vs. New Orleans

Fourth Week
Sammy White, Minnesota	177 yards (10) vs. Chicago
Charlie Brown, Washington	124 yards (3) vs. Philadelphia
Stanley Morgan, New England	122 yards (5) vs. Houston
Charlie Joiner, San Diego	121 yards (7) vs. Denver
Harold Carmichael, Philadelphia	109 yards (6) vs. Washington
Steve Largent, Seattle	109 yards (5) vs. Pittsburgh
Kellen Winslow, San Diego	107 yards (8) vs. Denver
Dave Casper, Houston	100 yards (6) vs. New England

Fifth Week
Wesley Walker, N.Y. Jets	164 yards (5) vs. Detroit
Ozzie Newsome, Cleveland	140 yards (10) vs. San Diego
Stanley Morgan, New England	130 yards (7) vs. Chicago
John Stallworth, Pittsburgh	107 yards (4) vs. Kansas City
William Andrews, Atlanta	106 yards (3) vs. Denver
Jeff Moore, San Francisco	102 yards (8) vs. L.A. Rams
Butch Woolfolk, N.Y. Giants	102 yards (6) vs. Houston
Steve Watson, Denver	101 yards (5) vs. Atlanta
Art Monk, Washington	100 yards (7) vs. Dallas

Sixth Week

Steve Watson, Denver	183 yards (10) vs. L.A. Rams
Floyd Eddings, N.Y. Giants	148 yards (5) vs. Philadelphia
Charlie Joiner, San Diego	145 yards (8) vs. San Francisco
Dwight Clark, San Francisco	135 yards (12) vs. San Diego
Wes Chandler, San Diego	125 yards (7) vs. San Francisco
James Wilder, Tampa Bay	116 yards (11) vs. N.Y. Jets
Cliff Branch, L.A. Raiders	111 yards (5) vs. Kansas City
Steve Largent, Seattle	111 yards (8) vs. Chicago
Al Dixon, Kansas City	102 yards (6) vs. L.A. Raiders
Kellen Winslow, San Diego	101 yards (9) vs. San Francisco

Seventh Week

Wes Chandler, San Diego	260 yards (10) vs. Cincinnati
Leonard Thompson, Detroit	161 yards (5) vs. Minnesota
Cris Collinsworth, Cincinnati	156 yards (9) vs. San Diego
Cliff Branch, L.A. Raiders	128 yards (5) vs. L.A. Rams
Kellen Winslow, San Diego	116 yards (6) vs. Cincinnati
Carlos Carson, Kansas City	110 yards (3) vs. Denver
Dave Casper, Houston	102 yards (5) vs. Philadelphia
Dwight Clark, San Francisco	101 yards (8) vs. Atlanta
John Jefferson, Green Bay	101 yards (5) vs. Baltimore

Eighth Week

George Farmer, L.A. Rams	183 yards (9) vs. Chicago
Charlie Brown, Washington	156 yards (4) vs. New Orleans
James Lofton, Green Bay	146 yards (3) vs. Atlanta
Stanley Morgan, New England	127 yards (4) vs. Pittsburgh
Preston Dennard, L.A. Rams	122 yards (5) vs. Chicago
Kellen Winslow, San Diego	120 yards (7) vs. Baltimore
Wes Chandler, San Diego	118 yards (4) vs. Baltimore
Joe Senser, Minnesota	115 yards (10) vs. N.Y. Jets
Dwight Clark, San Francisco	104 yards (4) vs. Kansas City
Walter Payton, Chicago	102 yards (5) vs. L.A. Rams
Wendell Tyler, L.A. Rams	102 yards (8) vs. Chicago

Ninth Week

Stanley Morgan, New England	141 yards (7) vs. Buffalo
Wes Chandler, San Diego	138 yards (6) vs. L.A. Raiders
James Lofton, Green Bay	128 yards (7) vs. Detroit
Ozzie Newsome, Cleveland	123 yards (9) vs. Pittsburgh
Lynn Swann, Pittsburgh	114 yards (5) vs. Cleveland
Frank Lewis, Buffalo	113 yards (7) vs. New England
Ricky Feacher, Cleveland	109 yards (9) vs. Pittsburgh
Dan Ross, Cincinnati	101 yards (9) vs. Houston

Times 100 or More
Chandler 6; Clark, Winslow 5; Morgan 4; Branch, Lofton, Newsome 3; Brown, Carmichael, Casper, Collinsworth, Hill, Jefferson, Joiner, Largent, Monk, Stallworth, White 2.

1983 American Football Conference

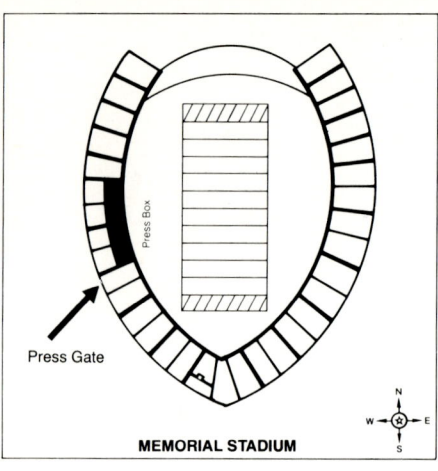

MEMORIAL STADIUM

Baltimore Colts

**American Football Conference
Eastern Division**

Team Colors: Royal Blue, White,
and Silver

**P.O. Box 2000
Owings Mills, Maryland 21117
Telephone: (301) 356-9600**

Club Officials
President-Treasurer: Robert Irsay
Vice President: Harriet Irsay
Vice President-General Counsel: Michael G. Chernoff
General Manager: Ernie Accorsi
Controller: Elizabeth H. Moses
Director of Player Personnel: Jack Bushofsky
Pro Personnel Director: Bob Terpening
Public Relations Director: Walt Gutowski
Assistant Director of Public Relations: Marge Blatt
Administrative Assistant: Pete Ward
Assistant Business Manager: James Irsay
Ticket Manager: Carol Martin
Director of Sales: Bob Leffler
Head Trainer: John Lopez
Equipment Manager: Jon Scott

Stadium: Memorial Stadium • **Capacity:** 60,586
33rd and Ellerslie Streets
Baltimore, Maryland 21218
Playing Surface: Grass
Training Camp: Goucher College
Towson, Maryland 21204

1983 SCHEDULE
Preseason
Aug. 4	at Houston	7:00
Aug. 13	at Minnesota	7:30
Aug. 20	at New York Giants	8:00
Aug. 26	at Atlanta	8:00

Regular Season
Sept. 4	at New England	1:00
Sept. 11	**Denver**	4:00
Sept. 18	at Buffalo	1:00
Sept. 25	**Chicago**	2:00
Oct. 2	at Cincinnati	1:00
Oct. 9	**New England**	2:00
Oct. 16	**Buffalo**	2:00
Oct. 23	**Miami**	2:00
Oct. 30	at Philadelphia	1:00
Nov. 6	at New York Jets	4:00
Nov. 13	**Pittsburgh**	2:00
Nov. 20	at Miami	1:00
Nov. 27	at Cleveland	1:00
Dec. 4	**New York Jets**	4:00
Dec. 11	at Denver	2:00
Dec. 18	**Houston**	2:00

1982 TEAM STATISTICS

	Baltimore	Opp.
Total First Downs	152	197
Rushing	62	87
Passing	80	89
Penalty	10	21
Third Down Efficiency	51/135	52/119
Third Down Percentage	37.8	43.7
Total Net Yards	2483	3296
Total Offensive Plays	596	605
Avg. Gain per Play	4.2	5.4
Avg. Gain per Game	275.9	366.2
Net Yards Rushing	1044	1473
Total Rushing Plays	293	348
Avg. Gain per Rush	3.6	4.2
Avg. Gain Rushing per Game	116.0	163.7
Net Yards Passing	1439	1823
Lost Attempting to Pass	20/174	11/97
Gross Yards Passing	1613	1920
Attempts/Completions	283/142	246/138
Percent Completed	50.2	56.1
Had Intercepted	10	5
Avg. Net Passing per Game	159.9	202.6
Punts/Avg.	46/44.4	41/39.9
Punt Returns/Avg.	14/5.6	26/8.7
Kickoff Returns/Avg.	42/17.9	25/21.5
Interceptions/Avg. Ret.	5/30.0	10/12.9
Penalties/Yards	52/433	59/466
Fumbles/Ball Lost	24/11	11/6
Total Points	113	236
Avg. Points per Game	12.6	26.2
Touchdowns	12	28
Rushing	4	10
Passing	6	18
Returns and Recoveries	2	0
Field Goals	10/18	14/19
Conversions	11/11	26/28
Safeties	0	0
Avg. Time of Possession	27:52	32:08

1982 TEAM RECORD

Preseason (3-2)

Baltimore		Opponents
14	Minnesota	30
19	*New York Giants	14
34	Atlanta	3
15	Pittsburgh	37
26	Chicago	17
108		101

Regular Season (0-8-1)

Baltimore		Opponents	Att.
13	*New England	24	39,055
20	Miami	24	51,999
0	New York Jets	37	46,970
0	Buffalo	20	33,985
17	*Cincinnati	20	23,598
10	Minnesota	13	53,981
20	*Green Bay (OT)	20	25,920
26	San Diego	44	49,711
7	*Miami	34	19,073
113		236	344,292

*Home Game   (OT) Overtime

Score by Periods

Baltimore	13	40	23	37	0	— 113
Opponents	54	77	68	37	0	— 236

Attendance

Home 107,646   Away 236,646   Total 344,292
Single game home record, 60,763 (12-14-77)
Single season home record, 418,292 (1968)

1982 INDIVIDUAL STATISTICS

Rushing

	Att	Yds	Avg	LG	TD
McMillan	101	305	3.0	13	1
Dixon	58	249	4.3	32	1
Dickey	66	232	3.5	25	1
Franklin	43	152	3.5	19	0
Pagel	19	82	4.3	32	1
Butler	3	10	3.3	10	0
Stark	1	8	8.0	8	0
Schlichter	1	3	3.0	3	0
Wright	1	3	3.0	3	0
Baltimore	293	1044	3.6	32	4
Opponents	348	1473	4.2	54	10

Field Goal Success

Distance	1-19	20-29	30-39	40-49	50 Over
Made-Att.	0-0	1-2	3-8	4-6	2-2

Passing

	Att	Comp	Pct	Yds	TD	Int	Tkld	Rate
Pagel	221	111	50.2	1281	5	7	16/129	62.4
Humm	23	13	56.5	130	0	1	1/10	54.8
Schlichter	37	17	45.9	197	0	2	3/35	40.0
Wood	1	1	100.0	5	1	0	0/0	
Stark	1	0	0	0	0	0	0/0	
Baltimore	283	142	50.2	1613	6	10	20/174	
Opponents	246	138	56.1	1920	18	5	11/97	

Receiving

	No	Yds	Avg	LG	TD
Bouza	22	287	13.0	34	2
Sherwin	21	280	13.3	33	0
Dickey	21	228	10.9	34	0
Dixon	20	185	9.3	24	0
Butler	17	268	15.8	53t	2
McMillan	15	90	6.0	17	0
Franklin	9	61	6.8	15	0
Henry	7	110	15.7	23	0
Beach	4	45	11.3	17	1
Smith	2	36	18.0	23	0
McCall	2	6	3.0	4	0
Wright	1	12	12.0	12	0
Krauss	1	5	5.0	5t	1
Baltimore	142	1613	11.4	53t	6
Opponents	138	1920	13.9	55	18

Interceptions

	No	Yds	Avg	LG	TD
K. Anderson	2	25	12.5	25	0
Burroughs	1	94	94.0	94t	1
Bracelin	1	31	31.0	31	0
Hatchett	1	0	0.0	0	0
Baltimore	5	150	30.0	94t	1
Opponents	10	129	12.9	26	0

Punting

	No	Yds	Avg	In 20	LG
Stark	46	2044	44.4	8	60
Baltimore	46	2044	44.4	8	60
Opponents	41	1634	39.9	13	67

Punt Returns

	No	FC	Yds	Avg	LG	TD
L. Anderson	8	3	54	6.8	28	0
Glasgow	4	5	24	6.0	8	0
Bouza	2	5	0	0.0	0	0
Baltimore	14	13	78	5.6	28	0
Opponents	26	4	226	8.7	29	0

Kickoff Returns

	No	Yds	Avg	LG	TD
L. Anderson	27	517	19.1	33	0
Dixon	11	197	17.9	27	0
Bouza	3	31	10.3	12	0
Franklin	1	8	8.0	8	0
Baltimore	42	753	17.9	33	0
Opponents	25	538	21.5	30	0

Scoring

	TD	TD R	TD P	TD Rt	PAT	FG	TP
Wood					6/6	6/10	24
Miller					5/5	4/8	17
Bouza	2	0	2	0			12
Butler	2	0	2	0			12
Beach	1	0	1	0			6
Burroughs	1	0	0	1			6
Dickey	1	1	0	0			6
Dixon	1	1	0	0			6
Krauss	1	0	1	0			6
McMillan	1	1	0	0			6
Pagel	1	1	0	0			6
Sherwin	1	0	1	0			6
Baltimore	12	4	6	2	11/11	10/18	113
Opponents	28	10	18	0	26/28	14/19	236

Sacks

Bracelin 2, Cooks 1½, Delaney 1, Hunter 1, Krauss 2, D. Thompson 1, Wisniewski 2½.

FIRST PLAYERS SELECTED

Year	Player, College, Position
1953	Billy Vessels, Oklahoma, B
1954	Cotton Davidson, Baylor, B
1955	George Shaw, Oregon, B
1956	Lenny Moore, Penn State, B
1957	Jim Parker, Ohio State, G
1958	Lenny Lyles, Louisville, B
1959	Jackie Burkett, Auburn, C
1960	Ron Mix, Southern California, T
1961	Tom Matte, Ohio State, RB
1962	Wendell Harris, Louisiana State, S
1963	Bob Vogel, Ohio State, T
1964	Marv Woodson, Indiana, CB
1965	Mike Curtis, Duke, LB
1966	Sam Ball, Kentucky, T
1967	Bubba Smith, Michigan, DT
1968	John Williams, Minnesota, G
1969	Eddie Hinton, Oklahoma, WR
1970	Norman Bulaich, Texas Christian, RB
1971	Leonard Dunlap, North Texas State, DB
1972	Tom Drougas, Oregon, T
1973	Bert Jones, Louisiana State, QB
1974	John Dutton, Nebraska, DE
1975	Ken Huff, North Carolina, G
1976	Ken Novak, Purdue, DT
1977	Randy Burke, Kentucky, WR
1978	Reese McCall, Auburn, TE
1979	Barry Krauss, Alabama, LB
1980	Curtis Dickey, Texas A&M, RB
1981	Randy McMillan, Pittsburgh, RB
1982	Johnie Cooks, Mississippi State, LB
1983	John Elway, Stanford, QB

COLTS COACHING HISTORY

(222-192-7)

1953	Keith Molesworth	3-9-0
1954-62	Weeb Ewbank	60-53-1
1963-69	Don Shula	73-25-4
1970-72	Don McCafferty*	26-11-1
1972	John Sandusky	4-5-0
1973-74	Howard Schnellenberger**	4-13-0
1974	Joe Thomas	2-9-0
1975-79	Ted Marchibroda	41-36-0
1980-81	Mike McCormack	9-23-0
1982	Frank Kush	0-8-1

*Released after five games in 1972
**Released after three games in 1974

BALTIMORE COLTS 1983 VETERAN ROSTER

No.	Name	Pos.	Ht.	Wt.	Birth-date	NFL Exp.	College	Birthplace	Residence	Games in '82
26	Anderson, Kim	CB	5-10	182	7/19/57	4	Arizona State	Pasadena, Calif.	Los Angeles, Calif.	9
30	†Anderson, Larry	S	5-11	188	9/25/56	6	Louisiana Tech	Monroe, La.	Shreveport, La.	9
87	Bailey, Elmer	WR	6-0	195	12/13/57	4	Minnesota	Evanston, Ill.	Miami, Fla.	1
81	Beach, Pat	TE	6-4	243	12/28/59	2	Washington State	Grant's Pass, Ore.	Pullman, Wash.	9
85	Bouza, Matt	WR	6-3	211	4/8/59	2	California	San Jose, Calif.	Walnut Creek, Calif.	9
52	†Bracelin, Greg	LB	6-1	210	4/16/57	4	California	Lawrence, Kan.	Aurora, Colo.	9
45	Burroughs, James	CB	6-1	192	1/21/58	2	Michigan State	Pahokee, Fla.	Pahokee, Fla.	8
80	Butler, Ray	WR	6-2	195	6/28/56	4	Southern California	Sweeny, Tex.	Lake Jackson, Tex.	9
98	Cooks, Johnie	LB	6-4	243	11/23/58	2	Mississippi State	Leland, Miss.	Leland, Miss.	9
73	Crosby, Cleveland	DE	6-5	250	4/3/56	2	Arizona	Westpoint, Miss.	East St. Louis, Ill.	9
75	Crouch, Terry	G	6-2	278	7/6/59	2	Oklahoma	Dallas, Tex.	Owings Mills, Md.	9
34	†Delaney, Jeff	S	6-1	197	12/28/56	4	Pittsburgh	Pittsburgh, Pa.	Pittsburgh, Pa.	8
33	Dickey, Curtis	RB	6-0	209	11/27/56	4	Texas A&M	Madisonville, Tex.	Bryan, Tex.	8
31	Dixon, Zachary	RB	6-1	204	3/5/56	5	Temple	Dorchester, Mass.	Owings Mills, Md.	9
53	Donaldson, Ray	C	6-4	260	5/18/58	4	Georgia	Rome, Ga.	Rome, Ga.	9
72	Durham, Steve	DE	6-5	256	10/11/58	2	Clemson	Greer, S.C.	Greer, S.C.	8
78	Foley, Tim	T	6-6	275	5/30/58	2	Notre Dame	Cincinnati, Ohio	St. Bernard, Ohio	0*
28	Franklin, Cleveland	RB	6-2	216	4/24/55	6	Baylor	Brenham, Tex.	Columbia, Md.	9
25	Glasgow, Nesby	S	5-10	180	4/15/57	5	Washington	Los Angeles, Calif.	Redmond, Wash.	9
	Griffin, Wade	T	6-5	278	8/7/54	6	Mississippi	Winona, Miss.	Bartlett, Tenn.	0*
68	†Hart, Jeff	T	6-5	272	9/10/53	7	Oregon State	Portland, Ore.	Beaverton, Ore.	9
42	Hatchett, Derrick	CB	5-11	183	8/14/58	4	Texas	Bryan, Tex.	Baltimore, Md.	9
27	Hemphill, Darryl	S	6-0	195	3/29/60	2	West Texas State	San Antonio, Tex.	San Antonio, Tex.	3
88	Henry, Bernard	WR	6-0	185	4/9/60	2	Arizona State	Los Angeles, Calif.	Los Angeles, Calif.	6
	t-Herrmann, Mark	QB	6-4	184	1/8/59	3	Purdue	Cincinnati, Ohio	Englewood, Colo.	2
63	Hudson, Nat	G	6-3	265	10/11/57	3	Georgia	Rome, Ga.	Rome, Ga.	2
62	†Huff, Ken	G	6-4	259	2/21/53	9	North Carolina	Hutchinson, Kan.	Glen Arm, Md.	9
57	†Humiston, Mike	LB	6-3	238	8/8/59	3	Weber State	Oceanside, Calif.	Tumwater, Wash.	7
92	Hunter, James	NT	6-5	251	9/13/57	2	Southern California	Haskell, Okla.	Los Angeles, Calif.	9
94	Jenkins, Fletcher	DE	6-2	258	11/4/59	2	Washington	Tacoma, Wash.	Baltimore, Md.	9
51	Jones, Ricky	LB	6-2	222	3/9/59	7	Tuskegee	Birmingham, Ala.	Birmingham, Ala.	9
55	Krauss, Barry	LB	6-3	232	3/17/57	5	Alabama	Pompano Beach, Fla.	Baltimore, Md.	9
86	McCall, Reese	TE	6-6	238	6/16/56	6	Auburn	Bessemer, Ala.	Randallstown, Md.	7
32	McMillan, Randy	RB	6-0	220	12/17/58	3	Pittsburgh	Havre de Grace, Md.	Timonium, Md.	9
1	Miller, Dan	K	5-10	172	12/30/60	2	Miami	West Palm Beach, Fla.	Clewiston, Fla.	5*
49	Odom, Cliff	LB	6-2	225	9/15/58	3	Texas-Arlington	Beaumont, Tex.	Arlington, Tex.	9
60	Padjen, Gary	LB	6-2	246	7/2/58	2	Arizona State	Salt Lake City, Utah	Owings Mills, Md.	8
18	Pagel, Mike	QB	6-2	201	9/13/60	2	Arizona State	Douglas, Ariz.	Phoenix, Ariz.	9
83	Sherwin, Tim	TE	6-6	237	5/4/58	3	Boston College	Watervliet, N.Y.	Cockeysville, Md.	9
54	Shiver, Sanders	LB	6-2	227	2/14/55	8	Carson-Newman	Glasden, S.C.	Baltimore, Md.	8
96	Simmons, Dave	LB	6-5	219	1/19/57	3	North Carolina	Wayne Co., N.C.	Goldsboro, N.C.	6
79	Sinnott, John	T	6-4	275	4/15/58	3	Brown	Wexford, Ireland	Derham, Mass.	9
84	Smith, Holden	WR	6-1	191	11/5/58	2	California	San Jose, Calif.	Los Gatos, Calif.	3
3	Stark, Rohn	P	6-3	195	6/4/59	2	Florida State	Minneapolis, Minn.	Tallahassee, Fla.	9
90	Taylor, Hosea	DE	6-5	260	12/3/58	2	Houston	Longview, Tex.	Longview, Tex.	0*
99	Thompson, Donnell	DE	6-4	254	10/27/58	3	North Carolina	Lumberton, N.C.	Timonium, Md.	9
64	Utt, Ben	G	6-4	255	6/13/59	2	Georgia Tech	Richmond, Calif.	Austin, Tex.	9
69	Wisniewski, Leo	NT	6-2	263	11/6/59	2	Penn State	Hancock, Mich.	Pittsburgh, Pa.	7
38	Wright, Johnnie	RB	6-2	210	9/13/58	2	South Carolina-Columbus	Fort Myers, Fla.	Fort Myers, Fla.	7

* Foley, Griffin, and Taylor missed '82 season due to injuries; Miller played 2 games with New England, 3 with Baltimore in '82.

†Option playout; subject to developments.

t-Colts traded for Herrmann (Denver).

Also played with Colts in '82—LB Joe Harris (9 games), C Glenn Hyde (5), QB David Humm (2), CB Sid Justin (5), T Greg Murtha (5), CB Dwayne O'Steen (3), DE Harry Stanback (2), QB Art Schlichter (3), G Arland Thompson (3), K Mike Wood (6).

COACHING STAFF

Head Coach, Frank Kush

Pro Career: Became Colts tenth head coach on December 21, 1981. Baltimore finished 0-8-1 last season. Entered pro coaching ranks for first time in 1981 when he was named head coach of Hamilton Tiger-Cats of the Canadian Football League. Guided Hamilton to an 11-4-1 mark and a first-place finish in the Eastern Conference before being tabbed by the Colts. No pro playing experience.

Background: In 1958, succeeded Dan Devine as head coach at Arizona State where he compiled 176-54-1 record in 22 seasons, including 6-1 mark in bowl competition. His 1975 team was 12-0 and ranked number two in both wire service polls. Kush began coaching career at Arizona State as defensive line coach in 1955. He played defensive guard at Michigan State from 1950-52 and was a consensus All-America in his senior year, helping the Spartans achieve a 9-0 record and capture the national championship.

Personal: Born January 20, 1929, Windber, Pa. Frank and his wife, Fran, have three sons—Dan, David, and Damian. They live in Baltimore.

ASSISTANT COACHES

Zeke Bratkowski, offensive coordinator-quarterbacks; born October 20, 1931, Danville, Ill., lives in Baltimore. Quarterback Georgia 1951-53. Pro quarterback Chicago Bears 1954, 1957-60, Los Angeles Rams 1961-63, Green Bay Packers 1963-68, 1971. Pro coach: Green Bay Packers 1969-70, 1975-81, Chicago Bears 1972-74, Colts since 1982.

Gunther Cunningham, defensive line; born June 19, 1946, Munich, Germany, lives in Reisterstown, Md. Linebacker Oregon 1965-67. No pro playing experience. College coach: Oregon 1969-71, Arkansas 1972, Stanford 1973-76, California 1977-80. Pro coach: Hamilton Tiger-Cats (CFL) 1981, Colts since 1982.

Hal Hunter, offensive line; born June 3, 1934, Canonsburg, Pa., lives in Pikesville, Md. Linebacker-guard Pittsburgh 1953-55. Pro guard Pittsburgh Steelers 1956. College coach: Richmond 1958-61, West Virginia 1962-63, Maryland 1964-65, Duke 1966-70, Kentucky 1971-72, Indiana 1973-76, California (Pa.) State 1977-80 (head coach). Pro coach: Hamilton Tiger-Cats (CFL) 1981, Colts since 1982.

Richard Mann, wide receivers; born April 20, 1947, Aliquippa, Pa., lives in Baltimore. Wide receiver Arizona State 1966-68. No pro playing experience. College coach: Arizona State 1974-79, Louisville 1980-81. Pro coach: Joined Colts in 1982.

Roger Theder, running backs; born September 22, 1939, Watertown, Wis., lives in Baltimore. Quarterback Western Michigan 1960-62. No pro playing experience. College coach: Bowling Green 1963, Northern Illinois 1964-67, Stanford 1968-71, California 1972-81 (head coach 1978-81). Pro coach: Joined Colts in 1982.

Bob Valesente, defensive backs; born July 19, 1940, Seneca Falls, N.Y., lives in Baltimore. Running back-defensive back Ithaca College 1959-62. No pro playing experience. College coach: Cornell 1964-73, Cincinnati 1976-77, Arizona 1978-79, Mississippi State 1980-81. Pro coach: Joined Colts in 1982.

Rick Venturi, linebackers; born February 23, 1946, Taylorville, Ill., lives in Reisterstown, Md. Quarterback Northwestern 1965-67. No pro playing experience. College coach: Northwestern 1968-72, 1978-80 (head coach), Purdue 1973-76, Illinois 1977. Pro coach: Joined Colts in 1982.

Mike Westhoff, tight ends-special teams-weight training; born January 10, 1948, Pittsburgh, Pa., lives in Baltimore. Tight end Wichita State. No pro playing experience. College coach: Indiana 1974-75, Dayton 1976, Indiana State 1977, Northwestern 1978-80, Texas Christian 1981. Pro coach: Joined Colts in 1982.

BALTIMORE COLTS 1983 FIRST-YEAR ROSTER

Name	Pos.	Ht.	Wt.	Birth-date	College	Birthplace	Residence	How Acq.
Abramowitz, Sid	T	6-5	280	5/21/60	Tulsa	Culver City, Calif.	Ft. Riley, Kan.	D5
Ballard, Quinton	NT	6-3	260	11/18/60	Elon College	Ahoskie, N.C.	Gates, N.C.	FA
Budness, James	LB	6-2	230	2/24/60	Boston College	Springfield, Mass.	Chicopee, Mass.	FA
Cook, Arthur (1)	LB	6-3	220	8/24/58	Morgan State	Richmond, Va.	Richmond, Va.	FA
Cummings, Mack	WR	6-0	195	3/3/59	E. Tennessee State	Gainesville, Fla.	Gainesville, Fla.	FA
Feasel, Grant	C	6-7	255	6/28/60	Abilene Christian	Barstow, Calif.	Barstow, Calif.	D6
Finister, Carlton (1)	RB	5-11	198	1/20/59	Northwestern	Monroe, La.	Natchitoches, La.	FA
Gaines, Robert (1)	WR	6-3	195	4/14/57	Washington	Pittsburg, Calif.	Richmond, Calif.	FA
Giles, Jamie (1)	NT	6-1	265	5/13/59	Texas Tech	Corpus Christi, Tex.	Corpus Christi, Tex.	FA
Happel, Brian (1)	K	6-1	190	11/27/60	Texas-Arlington	E. Stroudsburg, Pa.	Arlington, Tex.	FA
t-Hinton, Chris	T	6-4	265	7/31/61	Northwestern	Chicago, Ill.	Robbins, Ill.	D1
Lindstrom, Chris (1)	NT	6-7	245	4/3/60	Boston University	Weymouth, Mass.	Perry Hall, Md.	FA
Maxwell, Vernon	LB	6-2	225	10/25/61	Arizona State	Birmingham, Ala.	Carson, Calif.	D2
McCarroll, John (1)	CB	6-2	192	9/12/59	Kansas	Greer, S.C.	Lyman, S.C.	FA
McClelland, Leo (1)	RB	6-2	205	8/8/59	Temple	Philadelphia, Pa.	Philadelphia, Pa.	FA
Mills, Jim	T	6-8	270	9/23/61	Hawaii	Vancouver, B.C., Can.	Vancouver, B.C., Can.	D9
Milner, Hobson (1)	RB	6-2	225	8/13/59	Cincinnati	Columbus, Ohio	Columbus, Ohio	FA
Moore, Alvin	CB-S	6-0	197	5/3/59	Arizona State	Randolph, Ariz.	Casa Grande, Ariz.	D7
Porter, Gregory (1)	K	5-9	155	7/28/60	Texas Christian	Little Rock, Ark.	Dallas, Tex.	FA
Rose, Chris	T	6-5	260	1/29/61	Stanford	Red Bank, N.J.	Devon, Pa.	D9a
Smith, Phil	WR	6-3	190	4/28/60	San Diego State	Los Angeles, Calif.	Compton, Calif.	D4
Stanback, Harry (1)	DE	6-5	255	8/17/58	North Carolina	Rome, Ga.	Rome, Ga.	FA
Taylor, Jim Bob	QB	6-2	205	9/9/59	Georgia Tech	San Antonio, Tex.	Somerset, Tex.	D11
Turner, Joseph (1)	CB-S	6-2	200	12/31/59	Southern California	Brooklyn, N.Y.	Oxnard, Calif.	FA
Vernon, Larry (1)	K	5-10	175	10/12/56	New Mexico State	Inglewood, Calif.	Albuquerque, N.M.	FA
Williams, Brian (1)	TE	6-5	240	10/14/57	Southern	New Orleans, La.	Des Allemands, La.	FA
Williams, Carl	WR	5-10	180	2/3/60	Texas Southern	Freeport, Tex.	Brazoria, Tex.	D12

Players who report to an NFL team for the first time are designated on rosters as rookies (R). If a player reported to an NFL training camp in a previous year but was not on the active squad for three or more regular season or postseason games, he is listed on the first-year roster and designated by a (1). Thereafter, a player who is on the active squad for three or more regular season or postseason games is credited with an additional year of playing experience.

t-Colts traded for Hinton (Denver).

NOTES

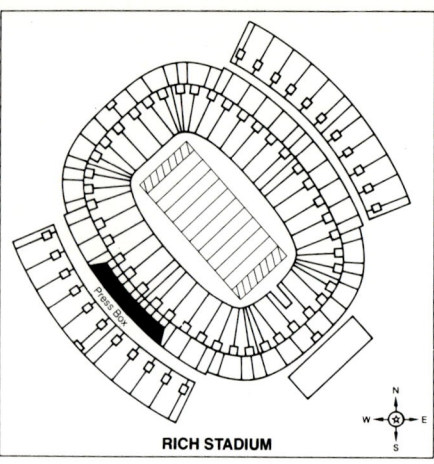

RICH STADIUM

Buffalo Bills

**American Football Conference
Eastern Division**

Team Colors: Royal Blue, Scarlet Red, and White

**One Bills Drive
Orchard Park, New York 14127
Telephone: (716) 648-1800**

Club Officials
President: Ralph C. Wilson, Jr.
Executive-Vice President: Patrick J. McGroder, Jr.
Vice President and Head Coach: Kay Stephenson
Vice President-Player Personnel: Norm Pollom
Vice President-Public Relations: L. Budd Thalman
Ticket Director: Jim Cipriano
Assistant Public Relations Director: Dave Senko
Trainers: Ed Abramoski, Bud Tice
Equipment Manager: Dave Hojnowski

Stadium: Rich Stadium • **Capacity:** 80,020
One Bills Drive
Orchard Park, New York 14127

Playing Surface: AstroTurf

Training Camp: Fredonia State University College
Fredonia, New York 14063

1983 SCHEDULE
Preseason
Aug. 6	at Chicago	6:00
Aug. 13	**Cleveland**	6:00
Aug. 20	at Detroit	7:00
Aug. 27	**Washington**	6:00

Regular Season
Sept. 4	**Miami**	1:00
Sept. 11	at Cincinnati	1:00
Sept. 18	**Baltimore**	1:00
Sept. 25	**Houston**	1:00
Oct. 3	**New York Jets** (Monday)	9:00
Oct. 9	at Miami	1:00
Oct. 16	at Baltimore	2:00
Oct. 23	**New England**	1:00
Oct. 30	**New Orleans**	1:00
Nov. 6	at New England	1:00
Nov. 13	at New York Jets	1:00
Nov. 20	**Los Angeles Raiders**	1:00
Nov. 27	at Los Angeles Rams	1:00
Dec. 4	at Kansas City	12:00
Dec. 11	**San Francisco**	1:00
Dec. 18	at Atlanta	1:00

1982 TEAM STATISTICS

	Buffalo	Opp.
Total First Downs	180	151
Rushing	83	64
Passing	84	72
Penalty	13	15
Third Down Efficiency	57/129	34/112
Third Down Percentage	44.2	30.4
Total Net Yards	2927	2334
Total Offensive Plays	604	536
Avg. Gain per Play	4.8	4.4
Avg. Gain per Game	325.2	259.3
Net Yards Rushing	1371	1034
Total Rushing Plays	319	268
Avg. Gain per Rush	4.3	3.9
Avg. Gain Rushing per Game	152.3	114.9
Net Yards Passing	1556	1300
Lost Attempting to Pass	12/115	12/82
Gross Yards Passing	1671	1382
Attempts/Completions	273/149	256/114
Percent Completed	54.6	44.5
Had Intercepted	17	13
Avg. Net Passing per Game	172.9	144.4
Punts/Avg.	35/37.9	44/39.3
Punt Returns/Avg.	26/4.6	10/3.0
Kickoff Returns/Avg.	36/22.0	34/17.8
Interceptions/Avg. Ret.	13/9.4	17/15.8
Penalties/Yards	69/582	49/395
Fumbles/Ball Lost	23/9	14/8
Total Points	150	154
Avg. Points per Game	16.7	17.1
Touchdowns	18	15
Rushing	9	6
Passing	8	8
Returns and Recoveries	1	1
Field Goals	9/18	16/20
Conversions	15/18	14/15
Safeties	0	1
Avg. Time of Possession	32:46	27:14

1982 TEAM RECORD

Preseason (3-1)

Buffalo		Opponents
14	Dallas	10
14	*Chicago	21
20	Washington	14
13	*Detroit	10
61		55

Regular Season (4-5)

Buffalo		Opponents	Att.
14	*Kansas City	9	79,306
23	*Minnesota	22	77,733
7	*Miami	9	52,945
20	*Baltimore	0	33,985
21	Green Bay (Mil.)	33	46,655
13	*Pittsburgh	0	58,391
23	Tampa Bay	24	62,510
10	Miami	27	73,924
19	New England	30	36,218
150		154	521,667

*Home Game

Score by Periods

Buffalo	26	68	19	37	—	150
Opponents	14	57	36	47	—	154

Attendance

Home 302,360   Away 219,307   Total 521,667
Single game home record, 79,791 (9-16-74)
Single season home record, 601,138 (1981)

1982 INDIVIDUAL STATISTICS

Rushing

	Att	Yds	Avg	LG	TD
Cribbs	134	633	4.7	62t	3
Leaks	97	405	4.2	17	5
Brown	41	187	4.6	19	0
Ferguson	16	46	2.9	13	1
Moore	16	38	2.4	9	0
Hooks	5	23	4.6	9	0
Kofler	2	21	10.5	12	0
Whittington	7	15	2.1	4	0
Holt	1	3	3.0	3	0
Buffalo	319	1371	4.3	62t	9
Opponents	268	1034	3.9	30	6

Field Goal Success

Distance	1-19	20-29	30-39	40-49	50 Over
Made-Att.	1-1	2-4	2-4	4-9	0-0

Passing

	Att	Comp	Pct	Yds	TD	Int	Tkld	Rate
Ferguson	264	144	54.5	1597	7	16	11/105	56.3
Robinson	8	5	62.5	74	1	0	1/10	—
Cribbs	1	0	0.0	0	0	1	0/0	—
Buffalo	273	149	54.6	1671	8	17	12/115	
Opponents	256	114	44.5	1382	8	13	12/82	

Receiving

	No	Yds	Avg	LG	TD
Lewis	28	443	15.8	39	2
Butler	26	336	12.9	47	4
Brammer	25	225	9.0	22	2
Cribbs	13	99	7.6	31	0
Leaks	13	91	7.0	11	0
Piccone	12	140	11.7	29	0
Mosley	9	96	10.7	31	0
Tuttle	7	107	15.3	26	0
Brown	6	38	6.3	28	0
Holt	4	45	11.3	23	0
Barnett	4	39	9.8	22	0
Moore	1	8	8.0	8	0
Haslett	1	4	4.0	4	0
Buffalo	149	1671	11.2	47	8
Opponents	114	1382	12.1	45	8

Interceptions

	No	Yds	Avg	LG	TD
Simpson	4	45	11.3	24	0
Freeman	3	27	9.0	14	0
B. Williams	1	20	20.0	20	0
Keating	1	14	14.0	14	0
Parrish	1	8	8.0	8	0
Romes	1	8	8.0	8	0
Marve	1	0	0.0	0	0
Robertson	1	0	0.0	0	0
Buffalo	13	122	9.4	24	0
Opponents	17	268	15.8	40	0

Punting

	No	Yds	Avg	In 20	LG
Cater	35	1328	37.9	13	61
Buffalo	35	1328	37.9	13	61
Opponents	44	1730	39.3	11	61

Punt Returns

	No	FC	Yds	Avg	LG	TD
Mosley	11	6	61	5.5	16	0
Holt	10	0	45	4.5	21	0
Hooks	4	0	13	3.3	8	0
Simpson	1	0	0	0.0	0	0
Tuttle	0	1	0		0	0
Buffalo	26	7	119	4.6	21	0
Opponents	10	13	30	3.0	10	0

Kickoff Returns

	No	Yds	Avg	LG	TD
Mosley	18	487	27.1	66	0
Holt	7	156	22.3	37	0
Piccone	3	50	16.7	23	0
McKnight	3	34	11.3	17	0
Whittington	2	39	19.5	21	0
Brown	1	17	17.0	17	0
Keating	1	9	9.0	9	0
Roopenian	1	0	0.0	0	0
Buffalo	36	792	22.0	66	0
Opponents	34	604	17.8	32	0

Scoring

	TD	TD R	TD P	TD Rt	PAT	FG	TP
Herrera					11/12	8/14	35
Leaks	5	5	0	0			30
Butler	4	0	4	0			24
Cribbs	3	3	0	0			18
Brammer	2	0	2	0			12
Ferguson	2	1	0	1			12
Lewis	2	0	2	0			12
Mike-Mayer					4/5	1/4	7
Buffalo	18	9	8	1	15/18	9/18	150
Opponents	15	6	8	1	14/15	16/20	154

Sacks

Freeman 1, Simpson 1, Smerlas 2, White 4, B. Williams 4.

FIRST PLAYERS SELECTED

Year	Player, College, Position
1960	Richie Lucas, Penn State, QB
1961	Ken Rice, Auburn, T
1962	Ernie Davis, Syracuse, RB
1963	Dave Behrman, Michigan State, C
1964	Carl Eller, Minnesota, DE
1965	Jim Davidson, Ohio State, T
1966	Mike Dennis, Mississippi, RB
1967	John Pitts, Arizona State, S
1968	Haven Moses, San Diego State, WR
1969	O.J. Simpson, Southern California, RB
1970	Al Cowlings, Southern California, DE
1971	J. D. Hill, Arizona State, WR
1972	Walt Patulski, Notre Dame, DE
1973	Paul Seymour, Michigan, TE
1974	Reuben Gant, Oklahoma State, TE
1975	Tom Ruud, Nebraska, LB
1976	Mario Clark, Oregon, DB
1977	Phil Dokes, Oklahoma State, DT (2)
1978	Terry Miller, Oklahoma State, RB
1979	Tom Cousineau, Ohio State, LB
1980	Jim Ritcher, North Carolina State, C
1981	Booker Moore, Penn State, RB
1982	Perry Tuttle, Clemson, WR
1983	Tony Hunter, Notre Dame, TE

BILLS COACHING HISTORY

(144-181-8)

1960-61	Buster Ramsey	11-16-1
1962-65	Lou Saban	38-19-4
1966-68	Joe Collier*	13-17-1
1968	Harvey Johnson	1-10-1
1969-70	John Rauch	7-20-1
1971	Harvey Johnson	1-13-0
1972-76	Lou Saban**	32-28-1
1976-77	Jim Ringo	3-20-0
1978-82	Chuck Knox	38-38-0

*Released after two games in 1968
**Resigned after five games in 1976

BUFFALO BILLS 1983 VETERAN ROSTER

No.	Name	Pos.	Ht.	Wt.	Birth-date	NFL Exp.	College	Birthplace	Residence	Games in '82
84	Barnett, Buster	TE	6-5	225	11/24/58	3	Jackson State	Brooksville, Miss.	Jackson, Miss.	9
73	Borchardt, Jon	T	6-5	255	8/13/57	5	Montana State	Minneapolis, Minn.	Orchard Park, N.Y.	9
86	Brammer, Mark	TE	6-3	235	5/3/58	4	Michigan State	Traverse City, Mich.	Orchard Park, N.Y.	9
47	Brown, Curtis	RB	5-10	203	12/7/54	7	Missouri	St. Louis, Mo.	West Seneca, N.Y.	9
80	Butler, Jerry	WR	6-0	178	10/12/57	5	Clemson	Greenwood, S.C.	East Amherst, N.Y.	7
7	Cater, Greg	P	6-0	191	4/17/57	4	Tennessee-Chattanooga	LaGrange, La.	Etowah, Tenn.	9
29	Clark, Mario	CB	6-2	195	3/29/54	8	Oregon	Pasadena, Calif.	Pasadena, Calif.	9
20	Cribbs, Joe	RB	5-11	190	1/5/58	4	Auburn	Sulligent, Ala.	Amherst, N.Y.	7
78	Cross, Justin	T	6-6	257	4/29/59	2	Western State, Colo.	Montreal, Canada	West Falls, N.Y.	9
70	Devlin, Joe	T	6-5	250	2/23/54	8	Iowa	Phoenixville, Pa.	Eden, N.Y.	9
12	Ferguson, Joe	QB	6-1	195	4/23/50	11	Arkansas	Alvin, Tex.	Shreveport, La.	9
85	Franklin, Byron	WR	6-1	179	9/4/58	2	Auburn	Florence, Ala.	East Aurora, N.Y.	0*
22	†Freeman, Steve	S	5-11	185	5/8/53	9	Mississippi State	Lamesa, Tex.	Lamesa, Tex.	9
53	Grant, Will	C	6-4	248	3/7/54	6	Kentucky	Milton, Mass.	Orchard Park, N.Y.	9
55	Haslett, Jim	LB	6-3	232	12/9/55	5	Indiana, Pa.	Pittsburgh, Pa.	Orchard Park, N.Y.	6
1	†Herrera, Efren	K	5-9	190	7/30/51	9	UCLA	Guadalajara, Mex.	Bellevue, Wash.	7
87	Holt, Robert	WR	6-1	182	10/4/59	2	Baylor	Dennison, Tex.	Grand Prairie, Tex.	7
25	Hooks, Roland	RB	6-0	195	1/2/53	8	North Carolina State	Brooklyn, N.Y.	Westminster, Colo.	6
97	Irvin, Darrell	DE	6-4	255	1/21/58	4	Oklahoma	Pawhuska, Okla.	Tulsa, Okla.	9
91	†Johnson, Ken	DE	6-5	253	3/25/55	5	Knoxville	Nashville, Tenn.	Nashville, Tenn.	6
72	Jones, Ken	T	6-5	250	12/1/52	8	Arkansas State	St. Louis, Mo.	Niagara Falls, N.Y.	9
52	Keating, Chris	LB	6-2	223	10/12/57	5	Maine	Boston, Mass.	Orchard Park, N.Y.	9
10	Kofler, Matt	QB	6-3	192	8/30/59	2	San Diego State	Kelso, Wash.	El Cajon, Calif.	4
42	Kush, Rod	S	6-0	188	12/29/56	4	Nebraska-Omaha	Omaha, Neb.	Gretna, Neb.	9
48	Leaks, Roosevelt	RB	5-10	225	1/31/53	9	Texas	Brenham, Tex.	Austin, Tex.	9
82	†Lewis, Frank	WR	6-1	196	7/7/47	13	Grambling	New Orleans, La.	Houma, La.	8
60	Lumpkin, Joey	LB	6-2	230	2/19/60	2	Arizona State	Ardmore, Okla.	Scottsdale, Ariz.	6
61	Lynch, Tom	G	6-5	250	5/24/55	7	Boston College	Chicago, Ill.	Windham, N.H.	8
54	Marve, Eugene	LB	6-2	230	8/14/60	2	Saginaw Valley State	Flint, Mich.	Otisville, Mich.	9
33	†McKnight, Ted	RB	6-1	212	2/26/54	7	Minnesota-Duluth	Duluth, Minn.	Lenexa, Kan.	3
34	Moore, Booker	RB	5-11	224	6/23/59	2	Penn State	Flint, Mich.	East Aurora, N.Y.	5
88	Mosley, Mike	WR-KR	6-2	192	6/30/58	2	Texas A&M	Hillsboro, Tex.	Humble, Tex.	9
59	Nelson, Shane	LB	6-1	225	5/25/55	6	Baylor	Mathis, Tex.	Lancaster, N.Y.	1
38	Nixon, Jeff	S	6-3	190	10/13/56	5	Richmond	Furstein Feldbruch, Ger.	Blasdell, N.Y.	7
62	Parker, Ervin	LB	6-5	240	8/19/58	4	South Carolina State	Georgetown, S.C.	Georgetown, S.C.	9
89	†Piccone, Lou	WR	5-9	175	1/17/49	10	West Liberty State	Vineland, N.J.	Holland, N.Y.	8
40	Riddick, Robb	RB	6-0	195	4/26/57	2	Millersville State	Quakertown, Pa.	Orchard Park, N.Y.	0*
51	Ritcher, Jim	C-G	6-3	251	5/21/58	4	North Carolina State	Berea, Ohio	Orchard Park, N.Y.	9
26	Romes, Charles	CB	6-1	190	12/16/54	7	North Carolina Central	Durham, N.C.	Buffalo, N.Y.	9
99	Roopenian, Mark	NT	6-5	254	7/10/58	2	Boston College	Medford, Mass.	Watertown, Mass.	9
57	Sanford, Lucius	LB	6-2	216	2/14/56	6	Georgia Tech	Atlanta, Ga.	Buffalo, N.Y.	9
76	Smerlas, Fred	NT	6-3	270	4/8/57	5	Boston College	Waltham, Mass.	Waltham, Mass.	9
81	Tuttle, Perry	WR	6-0	178	8/2/59	2	Clemson	Lexington, N.C.	Lexington, N.C.	7
41	†Villapiano, Phil	LB	6-2	225	2/26/49	12	Bowling Green	Long Branch, N.J.	Middleton, N.J.	9
65	†Vogler, Tim	C	6-3	245	10/20/56	5	Ohio State	Covington, Ohio	Hamburg, N.Y.	6
83	†White, Sherman	DE	6-5	250	10/6/48	12	California	Manchester, N.H.	Oakland, Calif.	9
77	†Williams, Ben	DE	6-3	245	9/1/54	8	Mississippi	Yazoo City, Miss.	Jackson, Miss.	9
27	Williams, Chris	CB	6-0	197	1/12/59	3	Louisiana State	Alexander, La.	Tioga, La.	5

* Franklin and Riddick missed '82 season due to injuries.

†Option playout; subject to developments.

Traded—Guard Reggie McKenzie to Seattle.

Retired—Isiah Robertson, 12-year linebacker, 9 games in '82; Bill Simpson, 8-year safety, 9 in '82.

Also played with Bills in '82—RB Allan Clark (1 game), K Nick Mike-Mayer (2), CB Lemar Parrish (7); QB Matt Robinson (5), RB Arthur Whittington (2).

COACHING STAFF

Head Coach, Kay Stephenson

Pro Career: Became the youngest head coach in the National Football League when he was promoted to lead the Bills on February 1, 1983. Served as the Bills' quarterback coach from 1978-82. Signed as a free agent with the San Diego Chargers in 1967 before being traded to the Bills in 1968. Injury riddled in 1968 and 1969 and was with Oakland and Atlanta briefly before retiring in 1970. Played one year with the Jacksonville Sharks of the WFL in 1974. Joined Jacksonville coaching staff as offensive coordinator and director of player personnel in 1975. Quarterback coach with the Los Angeles Rams in 1977 before joining the Bills in 1978.

Background: Attended Pensacola, Fla., High School and the University of Florida where he was backup quarterback to Steve Spurrier 1963-66. Assistant football coach at Rice University in 1971. Head coach and Athletic Director at Baker County, Fla., High School in 1973.

Personal: Born December 17, 1944, DeFuniak Springs, Fla. Kay and wife, Mary Jac, live in Orchard Park, New York.

ASSISTANT COACHES

Jerry Glanville, defensive backfield; born October 14, 1941, Detroit, lives in Orchard Park, N.Y. Guard-linebacker Northern Michigan 1961-63. No pro playing experience. College coach: Northern Michigan 1966, Western Kentucky 1967, Georgia Tech 1968-73. Pro coach: Detroit Lions 1974-76, Atlanta Falcons 1977-82, first year with Bills.

Milt Jackson, receivers; born October 16, 1943, Groesbeck, Tex., lives in Orchard Park, N.Y. Defensive back Tulsa 1966-67. Pro defensive back San Francisco 49ers 1967-68. College coach: Oregon State 1973, Rice 1974, California 1975-76, Oregon 1977-78, UCLA 1979. Pro coach: San Francisco 49ers 1980-82, first year with Bills.

Don Lawrence, defensive line; born June 4, 1937, Cleveland, Ohio, lives in Orchard Park, N.Y. Tackle Notre Dame 1953-55. Pro tackle Washington Redskins 1956-61. College coach: Notre Dame 1963-67, Kansas State 1968-69, Cincinnati 1970, Virginia 1971-73 (head coach), Texas Christian 1974-75, Missouri 1976-77. Pro coach: British Columbia Lions (CFL) 1978-79, Kansas City Chiefs 1980-82, first year with Bills.

Andy MacDonald, running backs; born January 2, 1930, Flint, Mich., lives in Orchard Park, N.Y. Quarterback Central Michigan 1950-51. No pro playing experience. College coach: Iowa 1961-64, Northern Arizona 1965-68, Tulsa 1969, Colorado State 1970-71, Michigan State 1973-75. Pro coach: Seattle Seahawks 1976-82, first year with Bills.

Miller McCalmon, defensive assistant-special teams; born January 9, 1947, Denver, Colo., lives in Orchard Park, N.Y. Defensive back Tulsa 1968-69. No pro playing experience. College coach: Tulsa 1970, Colorado State 1971-72. Pro coach: Baltimore Colts 1978-79, Bills since 1980.

Perry Moss, offensive assistant; born August 4, 1926, Tulsa, Okla., lives in Orchard Park, N.Y. Quarterback Tulsa 1944, Illinois 1946-47. Pro quarterback Green Bay Packers 1948. College coach: Illinois 1949, Washington 1950-51, Louisiana State 1952-53, Miami 1954-56, Wisconsin 1957-58, Florida State 1959, Marshall 1969. Pro coach: Ottawa Roughriders (CFL) head coach 1960-63, Chicago Bears 1970-73, Green Bay Packers 1974, San Antonio (WFL) head coach 1975, first year with Bills.

Jim Niblack, offensive line; born August 29, 1930, Americus, Ga., lives in Orchard Park, N.Y. Tackle Florida 1952-55. No pro playing experience. College coach: Florida 1976, Kentucky 1977-78. Pro coach: Jacksonville (WFL) 1974-75, first year with Bills.

Al Sandahl, offensive assistant; born July 5, 1939, Wetaskiwin, Alberta, Canada, lives in Orchard Park, N.Y. Tight end Lutheran College 1960-63. No pro playing experience. College coach: Mississippi State 1973-74, Oklahoma State 1975-77, Washington State 1978, UCLA 1979, Colorado State 1980-81, Iowa State 1982. Pro coach: First year with Bills.

BUFFALO BILLS 1983 FIRST-YEAR ROSTER

Name	Pos.	Ht.	Wt.	Birth-date	College	Birthplace	Residence	How Acq.
Brown, Gurnest	NT	6-3	265	12/15/59	Maryland	Wilson, N.C.	Wilson, N.C.	D7
Caldwell, Darryl	G	6-5	245	2/2/60	Tennessee State	Birmingham, Ala.	Birmingham, Ala.	FA
Campbell, Grant	P	6-1	190	2/17/59	Nebraska-Lincoln	Provo, Utah	Lincoln, Neb.	FA
Chivers, DeWayne	TE	6-4	226	6/26/59	South Carolina	Camden, S.C.	Camden, S.C.	D6 ('82)
Dawkins, Julius	WR	6-1	196	1/4/61	Pittsburgh	Monessen, Pa.	Monessen, Pa.	D12
Durham, James	CB	6-0	193	11/12/59	Houston	Lufkin, Tex.	Lufkin, Tex.	D8
Ehde, Mark	T	6-3	280	7/5/61	Syracuse	Buffalo, N.Y.	Grand Island, N.Y.	FA
Fischer, Mark	C	6-4	253	9/28/60	Notre Dame	Massillon, Ohio	Massillon, Ohio	FA
Grate, Zack	LB	6-4	230	4/6/59	South Carolina State	Georgetown, S.C.	Georgetown, S.C.	FA
Hambrick, Darral	WR	6-4	208	12/20/60	Nevada-Las Vegas	Los Angeles, Calif.	Los Angeles, Calif.	FA
Hunter, Tony	TE	6-4	237	5/22/60	Notre Dame	Cincinnati, Ohio	Cincinnati, Ohio	D1
Jackson, Greg (1)	S	6-1	200	6/6/59	Puget Sound	Seattle, Wash.	Seattle, Wash.	FA
Jones, Max (1)	LB	6-3	230	10/22/60	Massachusetts	Jamaica, West Indies	Montclair, N.J.	FA
Junkin, Trey	LB	6-2	221	1/23/61	Louisiana Tech	Conway, Ark.	Belvidere, Ill.	D4
Kennedy, Michael (1)	S	6-0	195	2/26/60	Toledo	Toledo, Ohio	Toledo, Ohio	FA
Kilson, David	CB-S	6-1	200	8/11/61	Nevada-Reno	San Francisco, Calif.	Sacramento, Calif.	FA
LaFond, Scott	G	6-2	260	4/20/59	Massachusetts	Laconia, N.H.	Laconia, N.Y.	FA
McCullough, Ken (1)	K-P	6-2	210	5/8/55	Arkansas	Beebe, Ark.	Searcy, Ark.	FA
Nett, Joseph	G	6-2	270	9/8/60	Syracuse	Syracuse, N.Y.	Prospect, Conn.	FA
Niece, Robert	T	6-5	280	4/12/59	Louisville	Columbus, Ohio	Columbus, Ohio	FA
Parker, George	RB	5-9	188	8/13/58	Norfolk State	Norfolk, Va.	Norfolk, Va.	D9
Payne, Jimmy	DE	6-3	264	2/9/60	Georgia	Athens, Ga.	Athens, Ga.	D4a
Robinson, Walter	RB	5-10	200	3/1/60	Canisius	Lockport, N.Y.	Lockport, N.Y.	FA
Ross, Joseph	K-P	6-5	218	10/27/59	Syracuse	Pittsburgh, Pa.	Pittsburgh, Pa.	FA
Talley, Darryl	LB	6-3	231	11/12/60	West Virginia	Cleveland, Ohio	East Cleveland, Ohio	D2
Tharpe, Richard	NT	6-3	237	10/31/60	Louisville	Central Islip, N.Y.	Central Islip, N.Y.	D10
Vandenboom, Matt	S	6-3	201	4/18/60	Wisconsin	Appleton, Wis.	Kimberly, Wis.	D5
Virkus, Scott	TE	6-5	248	9/7/59	San Francisco C.C.	Palo Alto, Calif.	Rochester, N.Y.	FA
Ware, Amero	RB	5-11	205	9/28/59	Drake	St. Louis, Mo.	St. Louis, Mo.	FA
Washington, Riley	CB	6-0	175	5/5/56	Buffalo	Ormond Beach, Fla.	Buffalo, N.Y.	FA
Watson, Allan	WR	6-3	208	4/1/61	Kentucky	Miami, Fla.	Miami, Fla.	FA
Wells, Ron	LB	6-1	232	10/2/61	Fort Lewis	Rantoul, Ill.	Littleton, Colo.	FA
White, Larry	DE	6-2	251	10/11/61	Jackson State	Tuscaloosa, Ala.	Tuscaloosa, Ala.	D11
Williams, Van (1)	RB	6-0	208	3/15/59	Carson-Newman	Johnson City, Tenn.	Johnson City, Tenn	D4 ('82)
Wilson, Brian	G	6-2	275	2/23/60	Buffalo	Buffalo, N.Y.	Orchard Park, N.Y.	FA
Wilson, Jeffrey	P	6-2	195	3/15/60	Bethel	Minneapolis, Minn.	Robbinsdale, Minn.	FA

Players who report to an NFL team for the first time are designated on rosters as rookies (R). If a player reported to an NFL training camp in a previous year but was not on the active squad for three or more regular season or postseason games, he is listed on the first-year roster and designated by a (1). Thereafter, a player who is on the active squad for three or more regular season or postseason games is credited with an additional year of playing experience.

NOTES

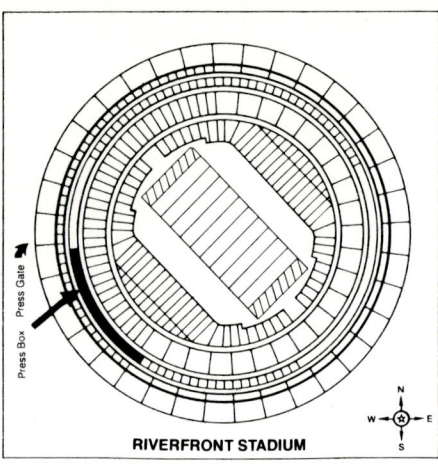

RIVERFRONT STADIUM

Cincinnati Bengals

American Football Conference
Central Division

Team Colors: Black, Orange, and White

200 Riverfront Stadium
Cincinnati, Ohio 45202
Telephone: (513) 621-3550

Club Officials
President: John Sawyer
General Manager: Paul E. Brown
Assistant General Manager: Michael Brown
Business Manager: John Murdough
Director of Public Relations: Allan Heim
Director of Player Personnel: Pete Brown
Ticket Manager: Paul Kelly
Trainer: Marv Pollins
Equipment Manager: Tom Gray

Stadium: Riverfront Stadium • **Capacity:** 59,754
200 Riverfront Stadium
Cincinnati, Ohio 45202

Playing Surface: AstroTurf

Training Camp: Wilmington College
Wilmington, Ohio 45177

1983 SCHEDULE

Preseason
Aug. 6	**Kansas City**	7:00
Aug. 12	at Washington	7:30
Aug. 18	**New York Jets**	9:00
Aug. 27	at Detroit	7:00

Regular Season
Sept. 4	**Los Angeles Raiders**	1:00
Sept. 11	**Buffalo**	1:00
Sept. 15	at Cleveland (Thursday)	8:30
Sept. 25	at Tampa Bay	1:00
Oct. 2	**Baltimore**	1:00
Oct. 10	**Pittsburgh** (Monday)	9:00
Oct. 16	at Denver	2:00
Oct. 23	**Cleveland**	1:00
Oct. 30	**Green Bay**	4:00
Nov. 6	at Houston	12:00
Nov. 13	at Kansas City	12:00
Nov. 20	**Houston**	1:00
Nov. 28	at Miami (Monday)	9:00
Dec. 4	at Pittsburgh	1:00
Dec. 11	**Detroit**	1:00
Dec. 17	at Minnesota (Saturday)	3:00

1982 TEAM STATISTICS

	Cincinnati	Opp.
Total First Downs	207	170
Rushing	63	61
Passing	123	102
Penalty	21	7
Third Down Efficiency	66/122	35/104
Third Down Percentage	54.1	33.7
Total Net Yards	3288	2893
Total Offensive Plays	606	551
Avg. Gain per Play	5.4	5.3
Avg. Gain per Game	365.3	321.4
Net Yards Rushing	949	850
Total Rushing Plays	269	223
Avg. Gain per Rush	3.5	3.8
Avg. Gain Rushing per Game	105.4	94.4
Net Yards Passing	2339	2043
Lost Attempting to Pass	27/162	22/207
Gross Yards Passing	2501	2250
Attempts/Completions	310/219	306/187
Percent Completed	70.6	61.1
Had Intercepted	9	14
Avg. Net Passing per Game	259.9	227.0
Punts/Avg.	31/38.7	37/40.1
Punt Returns/Avg.	17/5.6	17/4.0
Kickoff Returns/Avg.	31/20.7	45/18.9
Interceptions/Avg. Ret.	14/17.1	9/10.3
Penalties/Yards	56/475	64/551
Fumbles/Ball Lost	12/7	19/6
Total Points	232	177
Avg. Points per Game	25.8	19.7
Touchdowns	27	21
Rushing	13	8
Passing	12	12
Returns and Recoveries	2	1
Field Goals	14/18	10/12
Conversions	26/27	19/20
Safeties	1	1
Avg. Time of Possession	33:26	26:34

1982 TEAM RECORD

Preseason (1-3)

Cincinnati		Opponents
20	Kansas City	26
27	Green Bay	41
23	*Detroit	27
28	*Washington	21
98		115

Regular Season (7-2)

Cincinnati		Opponents	Att.
27	*Houston	6	53,268
20	Pittsburgh (OT)	26	53,973
18	Philadelphia	14	65,172
31	*Los Angeles Raiders	17	53,330
20	Baltimore	17	23,598
23	*Cleveland	10	54,305
34	San Diego	50	51,296
24	*Seattle	10	55,330
35	Houston	27	26,522
232		177	436,794

*Home Game   (OT) Overtime

Score by Periods

Cincinnati	48	76	62	46	0	—	232
Opponents	24	42	51	54	6	—	177

Attendance

Home 216,233   Away 220,561   Total 436,794

Single game home record, 60,284 (10-17-71)
Single season home record, 422,430 (1981)

1982 INDIVIDUAL STATISTICS

Rushing

	Att	Yds	Avg	LG	TD
Johnson	156	622	4.0	21	7
Alexander	64	207	3.2	18	1
Anderson	25	85	3.4	12t	4
A. Griffin	12	39	3.3	10t	1
Curtis	3	15	5.0	8	0
Tate	2	2	1.0	2	0
Verser	1	1	1.0	1	0
M. L. Harris	2	−3	−1.5	5	0
Schonert	3	−8	−2.7	−3	0
Collinsworth	1	−11	−11.0	−11	0
Cincinnati	269	949	3.5	21	13
Opponents	223	850	3.8	48t	8

Field Goal Success

Distance	1-19	20-29	30-39	40-49	50 Over
Made-Att.	2-2	3-3	5-6	3-5	1-2

Passing

	Att	Comp	Pct	Yds	TD	Int	Tkld	Rate
Anderson	309	218	70.6	2495	12	9	26/154	95.5
Schonert	1	1	100.0	6	0	0	1/8	—
Cincinnati	310	219	70.6	2501	12	9	27/162	
Opponents	306	187	61.1	2250	12	14	22/207	

Receiving

	No	Yds	Avg	LG	TD
Collinsworth	49	700	14.3	50	1
Ross	47	508	10.8	28	3
Johnson	31	267	8.6	25	0
Curtis	23	320	13.9	45	1
A. Griffin	22	172	7.8	22	0
Kreider	16	230	14.4	28	1
Alexander	14	85	6.1	14	1
M. L. Harris	10	103	10.3	17t	3
Verser	4	98	24.5	56t	1
Holman	3	18	6.0	10	1
Cincinnati	219	2501	11.4	56t	12
Opponents	187	2250	12.0	66t	12

Interceptions

	No	Yds	Avg	LG	TD
Riley	5	88	17.6	56t	1
Breeden	2	9	4.5	9	0
B. Harris	1	62	62.0	62t	1
Browner	1	29	29.0	29	0
R. Griffin	1	21	21.0	21	0
Williams	1	20	20.0	20	0
LeClair	1	11	11.0	11	0
Fuller	1	0	0.0	0	0
Kemp	1	0	0.0	0	0
Cincinnati	14	240	17.1	62t	2
Opponents	9	93	10.3	35	1

Punting

	No	Yds	Avg	In 20	LG
McInally	31	1201	38.7	7	53
Cincinnati	31	1201	38.7	7	53
Opponents	37	1484	40.1	8	52

Punt Returns

	No	FC	Yds	Avg	LG	TD
Fuller	17	8	95	5.6	13	0
Cincinnati	17	8	95	5.6	13	0
Opponents	17	5	68	4.0	28	0

Kickoff Returns

	No	Yds	Avg	LG	TD
Tate	14	314	22.4	55	0
Verser	16	320	20.0	33	0
Fuller	1	9	9.0	9	0
Cincinnati	31	643	20.7	55	0
Opponents	45	851	18.9	57	0

Scoring

	TD	TD R	TD P	TD Rt	PAT	FG	TP
Breech					25/26	14/18	67
Johnson	7	7	0	0			42
Anderson	4	4	0	0			24
M. L. Harris	3	0	3	0			18
Ross	3	0	3	0			18
Alexander	2	1	1	0			12
Kreider	1	0	1	0	1-run		7
Collinsworth	1	0	1	0			6
Curtis	1	0	1	0			6
A. Griffin	1	1	0	0			6
B. Harris	1	0	0	1			6
Holman	1	0	1	0			6
Riley	1	0	0	1			6
Verser	1	0	1	0			6
Williams		(Safety)					2
Cincinnati	27	13	12	2	26/27	14/18	232
Opponents	21	8	12	1	19/20	10/12	177

Sacks

Breeden 1, Browner 3, Collins 1, Edwards 6, B. Harris 2, Kemp 1, LeClair 2½, Whitley 1, Williams 4½.

FIRST PLAYERS SELECTED

Year	Player, College, Position
1968	Bob Johnson, Tennessee, C
1969	Greg Cook, Cincinnati, QB
1970	Mike Reid, Penn State, DT
1971	Vernon Holland, Tennessee State, T
1972	Sherman White, California, DE
1973	Isaac Curtis, San Diego State, WR
1974	Bill Kollar, Montana State, DT
1975	Glenn Cameron, Florida, LB
1976	Billy Brooks, Oklahoma, WR
1977	Eddie Edwards, Miami, DT
1978	Ross Browner, Notre Dame, DT
1979	Jack Thompson, Washington State, QB
1980	Anthony Munoz, Southern California, T
1981	David Verser, Kansas, WR
1982	Glen Collins, Mississippi State, DE
1983	Dave Rimington, Nebraska, C

BENGALS COACHING HISTORY
(108-111-1)

1968-75	Paul Brown	55-59-1
1976-78	Bill Johnson*	18-15-0
1978-79	Homer Rice	8-19-0
1980-82	Forrest Gregg	27-18-0

*Resigned after five games in 1978

CINCINNATI BENGALS 1983 VETERAN ROSTER

No.	Name	Pos.	Ht.	Wt.	Birth-date	NFL Exp.	College	Birthplace	Residence	Games in '82
40	Alexander, Charles	RB	6-1	221	7/28/57	5	Louisiana State	Galveston, Tex.	Baton Rouge, La.	9
14	Anderson, Ken	QB	6-3	212	2/15/49	13	Augustana, Ill.	Batavia, Ill.	Ft. Mitchell, Ky.	9
61	Boyarsky, Jerry	NT	6-3	290	5/15/59	3	Pittsburgh	Scranton, Pa.	Olyphant, Pa.	2
10	Breech, Jim	K	5-6	161	4/11/56	5	California	Sacramento, Calif.	Cincinnati, Ohio	9
34	Breeden, Louis	CB	5-11	185	10/26/53	6	North Carolina Central	Hamlet, N.C.	Mason, Ohio	6
79	Browner, Ross	DE	6-3	261	3/22/54	6	Notre Dame	Warren, Ohio	Atlanta, Ga.	9
74	Bujnoch, Glenn	G	6-6	265	12/20/53	8	Texas A&M	Houston, Tex.	Cincinnati, Ohio	9
67	Burley, Gary	DE	6-3	274	12/8/52	8	Pittsburgh	Urbancrest, Ohio	Cincinnati, Ohio	4
50	Cameron, Glenn	LB	6-2	228	2/21/53	9	Florida	Coral Gables, Fla.	Cincinnati, Ohio	9
76	Collins, Glen	DE	6-6	260	7/10/59	2	Mississippi State	Jackson, Miss.	Jackson, Miss.	7
80	Collinsworth, Cris	WR	6-5	192	1/27/59	2	Florida	Dayton, Ohio	Titusville, Fla.	9
85	Curtis, Isaac	WR	6-1	192	10/20/50	11	San Diego State	Santa Ana, Calif.	Cincinnati, Ohio	9
52	†Dinkel, Tom	LB	6-3	237	7/25/56	6	Kansas	Topeka, Kan.	Topeka, Kan.	9
73	Edwards, Eddie	DE	6-5	256	4/25/54	7	Miami	Sumter, S.C.	Marietta, Ga.	9
49	Frazier, Guy	LB	6-2	215	7/20/59	3	Wyoming	Detroit, Mich.	Cincinnati, Ohio	9
42	Fuller, Mike	KR-S	5-10	182	4/7/53	9	Auburn	Jackson, Miss.	Carlsbad, Calif.	9
45	Griffin, Archie	RB	5-9	184	8/21/54	8	Ohio State	Columbus, Ohio	Columbus, Ohio	9
44	Griffin, Ray	CB	5-10	186	6/29/56	6	Ohio State	Columbus, Ohio	Columbus, Ohio	9
53	Harris, Bo	LB	6-3	226	1/16/53	9	Louisiana State	Shreveport, La.	Shreveport, La.	9
83	Harris, M. L.	TE	6-5	238	1/16/54	4	Kansas State	Columbus, Ohio	Cincinnati, Ohio	9
27	Hicks, Bryan	S	6-0	192	1/24/57	4	McNeese State	Lake Charles, La.	Lake Charles, La.	7
82	Holman, Rodney	TE	6-3	230	4/20/60	2	Tulane	Ypsilanti, Mich.	Ypsilanti, Mich.	9
37	Jackson, Robert	S	5-10	184	10/10/58	2	Central Michigan	Grand Rapids, Mich.	Cincinnati, Ohio	9
46	Johnson, Pete	RB	6-0	249	3/2/54	7	Ohio State	Peach County, Ga.	Westerville, Ohio	9
26	Kemp, Bobby	S	6-0	186	5/29/59	3	Cal State-Fullerton	Oakland, Calif.	Upland, Calif.	9
86	Kreider, Steve	WR	6-3	192	5/12/58	5	Lehigh	Reading, Pa.	Cincinnati, Ohio	9
62	Lapham, Dave	G	6-4	262	6/24/52	10	Syracuse	Wakefield, Mass.	Cincinnati, Ohio	9
55	LeClair, Jim	LB	6-3	234	10/30/50	12	North Dakota	St. Paul, Minn.	Milford, Ohio	8
87	McInally, Pat	P	6-6	212	5/7/53	8	Harvard	Villa Park, Calif.	Villa Park, Calif.	9
65	Montoya, Max	G	6-5	275	5/12/56	5	UCLA	Alexander, Ala.	Covina, Calif.	9
60	Moore, Blake	C	6-5	267	5/8/58	4	Wooster	Durham, N.C.	Cincinnati, Ohio	4
78	Munoz, Anthony	T	6-6	278	8/19/58	4	Southern California	Ontario, Calif.	Cincinnati, Ohio	9
68	Obrovac, Mike	T	6-6	275	10/11/55	3	Bowling Green	Canton, Ohio	Cincinnati, Ohio	9
51	Razzano, Rick	LB	5-11	227	11/15/55	4	Virginia Tech	New Castle, Pa.	Mason, Ohio	9
13	†Riley, Ken	CB	6-0	183	8/6/47	15	Florida A&M	Bartow, Fla.	Bartow, Fla.	9
89	Ross, Dan	TE	6-4	235	2/9/57	5	Northeastern	Malden, Mass.	West Boxford, Mass.	9
72	St. Clair, Mike	DE	6-5	254	9/2/53	8	Grambling	Cleveland, Ohio	Cincinnati, Ohio	8
15	Schonert, Turk	QB	6-1	185	1/15/57	4	Stanford	Placentia, Calif.	Placentia, Calif.	2
59	Schuh, Jeff	LB	6-2	228	5/22/58	3	Minnesota	Crystal, Minn.	Crystal, Minn.	9
25	Simmons, John	CB	5-11	192	12/1/58	3	Southern Methodist	Little Rock, Ark.	Little Rock, Ark.	2
56	Simpkins, Ron	LB	6-1	235	4/2/58	3	Michigan	Detroit, Mich.	Detroit, Mich.	5
23	Tate, Rodney	RB-KR	5-11	190	2/14/59	2	Texas	Okanulgee, Okla.	Beggs, Okla.	9
81	†Verser, David	WR-KR	6-1	200	3/1/58	3	Kansas	Kansas City, Kan.	Culver City, Calif.	9
63	Wagner, Ray	T	6-3	290	11/15/57	2	Kent State	Altoona, Pa.	Kent, Ohio	4
70	Weaver, Emanuel	NT	6-4	260	6/28/60	2	South Carolina	New Orleans, La.	Columbia, S.C.	5
75	Whitley, Wilson	NT	6-3	265	4/28/55	7	Houston	Brenham, Tex.	Houston, Tex.	9
57	Williams, Reggie	LB	6-0	228	9/19/54	8	Dartmouth	Flint, Mich.	Cincinnati, Ohio	9
77	Wilson, Mike	T	6-5	271	5/28/55	6	Georgia	Norfolk, Va.	Gainesville, Ga.	9

†Option playout; subject to developments.

Traded—Center Blair Bush to Seattle, quarterback Jack Thompson to Tampa Bay.

Also played with Bengals in '82—S Oliver Davis (9 games).

COACHING STAFF

Head Coach, Forrest Gregg

Pro Career: Named Bengals head coach on December 28, 1979. After posting a 6-10 record in 1980, Gregg led Bengals to a 12-4 mark in 1981 and an appearance in Super Bowl XVI, losing to 49ers 26-21. Last season Cincinnati finished 7-2 and made its second straight playoff appearance. Was previously head coach of Cleveland Browns, where he compiled an 18-23 record from 1975-77, including 9-5 record in 1976. Also was head coach of Toronto Argonauts (CFL) in 1979 before signing to take over Bengals. Served as an NFL assistant coach from 1972-74. He was offensive line coach with San Diego Chargers in 1972-73 before joining Browns in same capacity in 1974. Had outstanding 15-year playing career in NFL as a guard-tackle with Green Bay Packers 1956-70 (he played in the Packers' two Super Bowl wins) and as a player-coach with Dallas Cowboys in Super Bowl championship season of 1971. Inducted into the Pro Football Hall of Fame in 1977. Career record: 45-40.

Background: Tackle at Southern Methodist 1953-55. Twice named to the All-Southwest Conference team. Captain of the SMU team his senior year. Spent 1957 in military service.

Personal: Born October 18, 1933 in Birthright, Tex. Attended Sulphur Springs (Tex.) High School. He and his wife, Barbara, live in Cincinnati and have two children — Forrest Jr. and Karen.

ASSISTANT COACHES

Hank Bullough, defensive coordinator-linebackers; born January 24, 1934, Scranton, Pa., lives in Cincinnati. Lineman Michigan State 1951-54. Pro lineman Green Bay Packers 1955, 1958. College coach: Michigan State 1959-69. Pro coach: Baltimore Colts 1970-72, New England Patriots 1973-79, Bengals since 1980.

Bruce Coslet, special teams-tight ends; born August 5, 1946, Oakdale, Calif., lives in Cincinnati. Tight end Pacific 1967-69. Pro tight end Cincinnati Bengals 1969-76. Pro coach: San Francisco 49ers 1980, Bengals since 1981.

Dick LeBeau, defensive backfield; born September 9, 1937, London, Ohio, lives in Cincinnati. Halfback Ohio State 1957-59. Pro defensive back Detroit Lions 1959-72. Pro coach: Philadelphia Eagles 1973-75, Green Bay Packers 1976-79, Bengals since 1980.

Jim McNally, offensive line; born December 13, 1943, Buffalo, N.Y., lives in Cincinnati. Guard University of Buffalo 1961-65. No pro playing experience. College coach: Buffalo 1966-69, Marshall 1973-75, Boston College 1976-78, Wake Forest 1979. Pro coach: Joined Bengals in 1980.

Dick Modzelewski, defensive line; born January 16, 1931, West Natrona, Pa., lives in Cincinnati. Tackle Maryland 1950-52. Pro defensive tackle Washington Redskins 1953-54, Pittsburgh Steelers 1955, New York Giants 1956-63, Cleveland Browns 1964-66. Pro coach: Cleveland Browns 1968-77, New York Giants 1978, Bengals since 1979.

George Sefcik, offensive backfield; born December 27, 1939, Cleveland, Ohio, lives in Cincinnati. Halfback Notre Dame 1959-61. No pro playing experience. College coach: Notre Dame 1963-68, Kentucky 1969-72. Pro coach: Baltimore Colts 1973-74, Cleveland Browns 1975-77, Bengals since 1978.

Kim Wood, strength; born July 12, 1945, Barrington, Ill., lives in Cincinnati. Running back Wisconsin 1965-68. No pro playing experience. Pro coach: Joined Bengals in 1975.

CINCINNATI BENGALS 1983 FIRST-YEAR ROSTER

Name	Pos.	Ht.	Wt.	Birth-date	College	Birthplace	Residence	How Acq.
Cali, Gary	WR	5-11	190	5/10/58	Newberry College	Brooklyn, N.Y.	St. Matthews, S.C.	FA
Christensen, Jeff	QB	6-3	202	1/8/60	Eastern Illinois	Gibson City, Ill.	Saybrook, Ill.	D5
Christopher, John	P	6-2	192	12/10/60	Morehead State	Sandusky, Ohio	Norwalk, Ohio	FA
DeAyala, Kiki	LB	6-0	230	10/23/61	Texas	Miami, Fla.	Houston, Tex.	D6
Drake, Darryl (1)	WR	6-2	172	12/11/56	Western Kentucky	Louisville, Ky.	Bowling Green, Ky.	FA
Fuller, Dan	LB	6-2	233	9/20/61	Ashland College	Honolulu, Hawaii	Broadview Hts., Ohio	FA
Gannon, Chuck	T	6-5	274	3/7/61	Indiana	Detroit, Mich.	Ypsilanti, Mich.	FA
Griffin, James	S	6-2	197	9/7/61	Middle Tennessee	Camilla, Ga.	Pelham, Ga.	D7
Gustafson, Jim	WR	6-1	176	3/16/61	St. Thomas College	Minneapolis, Minn.	St. Paul, Minn.	FA
Haffey, Mike	WR	5-9	178	6/26/60	Miami, Ohio	Fairfax County, Va.	Birmingham, Mich.	FA
Hannula, Jim (1)	T	6-6	251	7/2/59	Northern Illinois	Elgin, Ill.	Villa Hills, Ky.	D9 ('81)
Horton, Ray	CB	5-10	189	4/12/60	Washington	Tacoma, Wash.	Seattle, Wash.	D2
King, Arthur (1)	NT	6-4	260	6/20/60	Grambling	Birmingham, Ala.	Birmingham, Ala.	D6 ('82)
Kinnebrew, Larry	RB	6-1	266	6/11/59	Tennessee State	Rome, Ga.	Rome, Ga.	D6a
Krumrie, Tim	NT	6-2	247	5/20/60	Wisconsin-Madison	Eau Claire, Wis.	Madison, Wis.	D10
Maidlow, Steve	LB	6-2	234	6/6/60	Michigan State	Lansing, Mich.	East Lansing, Mich.	D4
Martin, Mike	WR	5-10	186	11/18/60	Illinois	Washington, D.C.	Washington, D.C.	D8
Polenz, Mark	T	6-4	240	6/3/61	Central Michigan	Lansing, Mich.	New Boston, Mich.	FA
Poole, Greg	S	6-1	197	2/6/61	North Carolina	Concord, N.C.	China Grove, N.C.	FA
Richard, Donald Ray	G	6-1	256	3/8/60	Texas Christian	Austin, Tex.	Austin, Tex.	FA
Rimington, Dave	C	6-3	292	8/13/62	Nebraska	Omaha, Neb.	Omaha, Neb.	D1
Roberts, Jeff (1)	LB	6-2	235	12/23/60	Tulane	Miami, Fla.	Carol City, Fla.	FA
Smith, Gilbert (1)	WR	5-10	175	1/3/60	Texas-Arlington	Carlsbad, N.M.	Arlington, Tex.	FA
Sullivan, Steve	WR	5-10	158	3/8/58	Austin College	Oklahoma City, Okla.	Richardson, Tex.	FA
Turner, Jimmy	CB	6-0	187	6/15/59	UCLA	Sherman, Tex.	Los Angeles, Calif.	D3
Williams, Gary	WR	6-2	215	9/4/59	Ohio State	Wilmington, Ohio	Columbus, Ohio	D11
Wilson, Stanley	RB	5-10	209	8/23/61	Oklahoma	Los Angeles, Calif.	Norman, Okla.	D9
Young, Andre	LB	6-1	212	4/16/60	Bowling Green	Akron, Ohio	Akron, Ohio	D12

Players who report to an NFL team for the first time are designated on rosters as rookies (R). If a player reported to an NFL training camp in a previous year but was not on the active squad for three or more regular season or postseason games, he is listed on the first-year roster and designated by a (1). Thereafter, a player who is on the active squad for three or more regular season or postseason games is credited with an additional year of playing experience.

NOTES

49

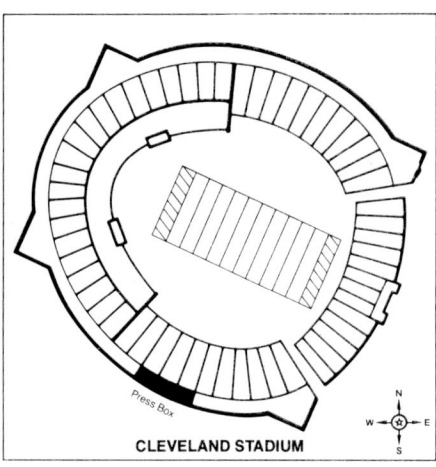

CLEVELAND STADIUM

Cleveland Browns

American Football Conference
Central Division

Team Colors: Seal Brown,
Orange, and White

Tower B
Cleveland Stadium
Cleveland, Ohio 44114
Telephone: (216) 696-5555

Club Officials

President: Arthur B. Modell
Assistant to the President: Paul Warfield
Vice President and General Counsel: James N. Bailey
Vice President and Consultant: Nate Wallack
Vice President, Finance: Mike Poplar
Director of Operations: Denny Lynch
Director of Public Relations: Kevin Byrne
Director of Programs and Promotions: John Minco
Director of Player Personnel: Bill Davis
Special Scouts: Dave Beckman, Tom Heckert,
   Tim Miner, Mike Nixon
Film Coordinator: Ed Ulinski
Ticket Director: Bill Breit
Trainer: Leo Murphy
Equipment Manager: Charles Cusick

Stadium: Cleveland Stadium ▪ **Capacity:** 80,322
         West 3rd Street
         Cleveland, Ohio 44114
Playing Surface: Grass
Training Camp: Lakeland Community College
         Mentor, Ohio 44094

1983 SCHEDULE

Preseason

Aug. 6	at Green Bay	7:00
Aug. 13	at Buffalo	6:00
Aug. 20	at Denver	7:00
Aug. 26	**Los Angeles Raiders**	8:00

Regular Season

Sept. 4	**Minnesota**	1:00
Sept. 11	at Detroit	1:00
Sept. 15	**Cincinnati** (Thursday)	8:30
Sept. 25	at San Diego	1:00
Oct. 2	**Seattle**	1:00
Oct. 9	**New York Jets**	1:00
Oct. 16	at Pittsburgh	1:00
Oct. 23	at Cincinnati	1:00
Oct. 30	**Houston**	1:00
Nov. 6	vs. Green Bay at Milwaukee	12:00
Nov. 13	**Tampa Bay**	1:00
Nov. 20	at New England	1:00
Nov. 27	**Baltimore**	1:00
Dec. 4	at Denver	2:00
Dec. 11	at Houston	12:00
Dec. 18	**Pittsburgh**	1:00

1982 TEAM STATISTICS

	Cleveland	Opp.
Total First Downs..................	176	189
Rushing.........................	64	82
Passing.........................	96	94
Penalty.........................	16	13
Third Down Efficiency............	43/127	52/116
Third Down Percentage..........	33.9	44.8
Total Net Yards..................	2718	3114
Total Offensive Plays...........	616	594
Avg. Gain per Play..............	4.4	5.2
Avg. Gain per Game.............	302.0	346.0
Net Yards Rushing..............	873	1292
Total Rushing Plays.............	256	306
Avg. Gain per Rush..............	3.4	4.2
Avg. Gain Rushing per Game.....	97.0	143.6
Net Yards Passing..............	1845	1822
Lost Attempting to Pass........	26/212	22/145
Gross Yards Passing............	2057	1967
Attempts/Completions...........	334/174	266/144
Percent Completed.............	52.1	54.1
Had Intercepted................	16	17
Avg. Net Passing per Game......	205.0	202.4
Punts/Avg......................	49/38.3	40/38.8
Punt Returns/Avg...............	23/5.8	30/7.2
Kickoff Returns/Avg.............	38/19.8	23/18.4
Interceptions/Avg. Ret.........	17/6.0	16/10.3
Penalties/Yards.................	59/461	57/436
Fumbles/Ball Lost..............	15/8	20/11
Total Points....................	140	182
Avg. Points per Game..........	15.6	20.2
Touchdowns....................	17	23
Rushing.......................	7	13
Passing.......................	9	9
Returns and Recoveries	1	1
Field Goals....................	7/16	7/11
Conversions...................	17/17	21/23
Safeties......................	0	1
Avg. Time of Possession	30:00	30:00

1982 TEAM RECORD

Preseason (4-0)

Cleveland		Opponents
17	Detroit	16
26	*Los Angeles Rams	23
20	New Orleans	17
27	Los Angeles Raiders	10
90		66

Regular Season (4-5)

Cleveland		Opponents	Att.
21	Seattle	7	55,907
21	*Philadelphia	24	78,830
10	*New England	7	47,281
14	Dallas	31	46,267
13	*San Diego	30	54,064
10	Cincinnati	23	54,305
10	*Pittsburgh	9	67,139
20	Houston	14	36,559
21	Pittsburgh	37	52,312
140		182	492,664

*Home Game

Score by Periods

Cleveland	20	34	24	62	—	140
Opponents	28	60	38	56	—	182

Attendance

Home 247,314   Away 245,350   Total 492,664
Single game home record, 85,703 (9-21-70)
Single season home record, 619,683 (1980)

1982 INDIVIDUAL STATISTICS

Rushing

	Att	Yds	Avg	LG	TD
Pruitt	143	516	3.6	17	3
White	69	259	3.8	18t	3
C. Miller	16	61	3.8	17	0
Sipe	13	44	3.4	12	0
Hall	2	14	7.0	13	0
Davis	4	3	0.8	2	1
Cox	2	−11	−5.5	0	0
McDonald	7	−13	−1.9	10	0
Cleveland	256	873	3.4	18t	7
Opponents	306	1292	4.2	34	13

Field Goal Success

Distance	1-19	20-29	30-39	40-49	50 Over
Made-Att.	1-1	3-4	1-3	2-7	0-1

Passing

	Att	Comp	Pct	Yds	TD	Int	Tkld	Rate
Sipe	185	101	54.6	1064	4	8	13/117	61.0
McDonald	149	73	49.0	993	5	8	13/95	59.5
Cleveland	334	174	52.1	2057	9	16	26/212	
Opponents	266	144	54.1	1967	9	17	22/145	

Receiving

	No	Yds	Avg	LG	TD
Newsome	49	633	12.9	54	3
White	34	283	8.3	36	0
Feacher	28	408	14.6	46	3
Logan	23	346	15.0	56t	2
Pruitt	22	140	6.4	13	0
Walker	8	136	17.0	46	0
Hall	5	78	15.6	31	1
C. Miller	3	20	6.7	11	0
Fulton	1	9	9.0	9	0
Oden	1	4	4.0	4	0
Cleveland	174	2057	11.8	56t	9
Opponents	144	1967	13.7	60	9

Interceptions

	No	Yds	Avg	LG	TD
Dixon	4	22	5.5	22	0
L. Johnson	4	17	4.3	17	0
Scott	3	29	9.7	24	0
Banks	1	14	14.0	14	0
Burrell	1	14	14.0	14t	1
Cousineau	1	6	6.0	6	0
Ambrose	1	0	0.0	0	0
Bolton	1	0	0.0	0	0
Flint	1	0	0.0	0	0
Cleveland	17	102	6.0	24	1
Opponents	16	164	10.3	37	0

Punting

	No	Yds	Avg	In 20	LG
Cox	48	1877	39.1	11	52
Cleveland	49	1877	38.3	11	52
Opponents	40	1552	38.8	9	54

Punt Returns

	No	FC	Yds	Avg	LG	TD
Walker	19	6	101	5.3	14	0
Hall	4	0	33	8.3	10	0
Cleveland	23	6	134	5.8	14	0
Opponents	30	2	216	7.2	24	0

Kickoff Returns

	No	Yds	Avg	LG	TD
Walker	13	295	22.7	36	0
Hall	22	430	19.5	32	0
Nicolas	2	16	8.0	10	0
Green	1	13	13.0	13	0
Cleveland	38	754	19.8	36	0
Opponents	23	424	18.4	30	0

Scoring

	TD	TD R	TD P	TD Rt	PAT	FG	TP
Bahr					17/17	7/15	38
Feacher	3	0	3	0			18
Newsome	3	0	3	0			18
Pruitt	3	3	0	0			18
White	3	3	0	0			18
Logan	2	0	2	0			12
Burrell	1	0	0	1			6
Davis	1	1	0	0			6
Hall	1	0	1	0			6
Cox						0/1	0
Cleveland	17	7	9	1	17/17	7/16	140
Opponents	23	13	9	1	21/23	7/11	182

Sacks

Baldwin 1, Banks 5½, Burrell 2, Cousineau 1, Dixon 1, Franks 2, Golic 4, Harris 1½, Robinson 3, Weathers 1.

FIRST PLAYERS SELECTED

Year	Player, College, Position
1950	Ken Carpenter, Oregon State, B
1951	Ken Konz, Louisiana State, B
1952	Bert Rechichar, Tennessee, DB
1953	Doug Atkins, Tennessee, DE
1954	Bobby Garrett, Stanford, QB
1955	Kurt Burris, Oklahoma, C
1956	Preston Carpenter, Arkansas, B
1957	Jim Brown, Syracuse, B
1958	Jim Shofner, Texas Christian, DB
1959	Rick Kreitling, Illinois, DE
1960	Jim Houston, Ohio State, DE
1961	Edward Nutting, Georgia Tech, T (2)
1962	Gary Collins, Maryland, WR
1963	Tom Hutchinson, Kentucky, WR
1964	Paul Warfield, Ohio State, WR
1965	James Garcia, Purdue, T (2)
1966	Milt Morin, Massachusetts, TE
1967	Bob Matheson, Duke, LB
1968	Marvin Upshaw, Trinity, Texas, DT-DE
1969	Ron Johnson, Michigan, RB
1970	Mike Phipps, Purdue, QB
1971	Clarence Scott, Kansas State, CB
1972	Thom Darden, Michigan, DB
1973	Steve Holden, Arizona State, WR
1974	Billy Corbett, Johnson C. Smith, T (2)
1975	Mack Mitchell, Houston, DE
1976	Mike Pruitt, Purdue, RB
1977	Robert Jackson, Texas A&M, LB
1978	Clay Matthews, Southern California, LB
1979	Willis Adams, Houston, WR
1980	Charles White, Southern California, RB
1981	Hanford Dixon, Southern Mississippi, DB
1982	Chip Banks, Southern California, LB
1983	Ron Brown, Arizona State, WR (2)

BROWNS COACHING HISTORY
(279-175-9)

1950-62	Paul Brown	115-49-5
1963-70	Blanton Collier	79-38-2
1971-74	Nick Skorich	30-26-2
1975-77	Forrest Gregg*	18-23-0
1977	Dick Modzelewski	0-1-0
1978-82	Sam Rutigliano	37-38-0

*Released after 13 games in 1977

CLEVELAND BROWNS 1983 VETERAN ROSTER

No.	Name	Pos.	Ht.	Wt.	Birth-date	NFL Exp.	College	Birthplace	Residence	Games in '82
80	Adams, Willis	WR	6-2	194	8/22/56	4	Houston	Weimer, Tex.	Shaker Heights, Ohio	1
52	Ambrose, Dick	LB	6-0	228	1/17/53	9	Virginia	New Rochelle, N.Y.	North Ridgeville, Ohio	9
61	Baab, Mike	C	6-4	270	12/6/59	2	Texas	Fort Worth, Tex.	Euless, Tex.	7
9	Bahr, Matt	K	5-10	165	7/6/56	5	Penn State	Philadelphia, Pa.	Pittsburgh, Pa.	9
99	Baldwin, Keith	DE	6-4	245	10/13/60	2	Texas A&M	Houston, Tex.	Cleveland, Ohio	9
56	Banks, Chip	LB	6-4	233	9/18/59	2	Southern California	Fort Lawton, Okla.	Augusta, Ga.	9
91	Bradley, Henry	NT	6-2	260	9/4/53	5	Alcorn State	St. Joseph, La.	San Diego, Calif.	6
47	†Braziel, Larry	CB	6-0	184	9/25/54	5	Southern California	Fort Worth, Tex.	Randallstown, Md.	6
49	Burrell, Clinton	S	6-1	192	9/4/56	4	Louisiana State	Franklin, La.	Middleburg Heights, Ohio	9
50	Cousineau, Tom	LB	6-3	225	5/6/57	2	Ohio State	Bloomington, Ind.	Lakewood, Ohio	9
53	Cowher, Bill	LB	6-3	225	5/8/57	3	North Carolina State	Pittsburgh, Pa.	Olmsted Falls, Ohio	9
15	Cox, Steve	P-K	6-4	195	5/11/58	3	Arkansas	Shreveport, La.	Charleston, Ark.	9
38	Davis, Johnny	RB	6-1	235	7/17/56	6	Alabama	Montgomery, Ala.	Warrensville Heights, Ohio	2
64	DeLamielleure, Joe	G	6-3	245	3/16/51	11	Michigan State	Detroit, Mich.	Charlotte, N.C.	9
54	DeLeone, Tom	C	6-2	248	8/13/50	12	Ohio State	Kent, Ohio	Medina, Ohio	9
73	Dieken, Doug	T	6-5	252	2/12/49	13	Illinois	Streator, Ill.	Bay Village, Ohio	9
29	Dixon, Hanford	CB	5-11	182	12/25/58	3	Southern Mississippi	Mobile, Ala.	Lakewood, Ohio	9
83	Feacher, Ricky	WR	5-10	174	2/11/54	8	Mississippi Valley	Crystal River, Fla.	Warrensville Heights, Ohio	9
20	Flint, Judson	S	6-0	201	1/26/57	4	Memphis State	Farrell, Pa.	Cleveland Heights, Ohio	9
94	Franks, Elvis	DE	6-4	238	7/9/57	4	Morgan State	Doucette, Tex.	North Olmsted, Ohio	9
86	Fulton, Dan	WR	6-2	186	9/2/56	4	Nebraska-Omaha	Memphis, Tenn.	Warrensville Heights, Ohio	9
79	Golic, Bob	NT	6-2	248	10/26/57	4	Notre Dame	Cleveland, Ohio	Willowick, Ohio	6
26	†Hall, Dino	RB-KR	5-7	165	12/6/55	4	Glassboro State	Atlantic City, N.J.	Pleasantville, N.J.	9
90	Harris, Marshall	DE	6-6	261	12/6/55	4	Texas Christian	San Antonio, Tex.	Berea, Ohio	9
36	Jackson, Bill	S	6-1	202	7/1/60	2	North Carolina	Winston-Salem, N.C.	Middleburg Heights, Ohio	9
68	Jackson, Robert	G	6-5	260	4/1/53	9	Duke	Charlotte, N.C.	Bay Village, Ohio	9
51	Johnson, Eddie	LB	6-1	210	2/3/59	3	Louisville	Albany, Ga.	Strongsville, Ohio	9
48	†Johnson, Lawrence	CB	5-11	204	9/11/57	4	Wisconsin	Gary, Ind.	Shaker Heights, Ohio	8
23	Kafentzis, Mark	S	5-10	185	6/30/58	2	Hawaii	Richland, Wash.	Honolulu, Hawaii	9
85	Logan, Dave	WR	6-4	216	2/2/54	8	Colorado	Fargo, N.D.	Strongsville, Ohio	9
57	Matthews, Clay	LB	6-2	230	3/15/56	6	Southern California	Palo Alto, Calif.	Los Angeles, Calif.	2
16	McDonald, Paul	QB	6-2	185	2/23/58	4	Southern California	Montebello, Calif.	Strongsville, Ohio	9
71	Miller, Matt	T	6-6	270	7/30/56	4	Colorado	Durango, Colo.	Medina, Ohio	9
82	Newsome, Ozzie	TE	6-2	232	3/15/56	6	Alabama	Muscle Shoals, Ala.	Cleveland, Ohio	9
58	Nicolas, Scott	LB	6-3	226	8/7/60	2	Miami	Wichita Falls, Tex.	Olmsted Falls, Ohio	9
43	Pruitt, Mike	RB	6-0	225	4/3/54	8	Purdue	Chicago, Ill.	Westlake, Ohio	9
63	Risien, Cody	T	6-7	255	3/22/54	3	Texas A&M	Bryan, Tex.	Houston, Tex.	9
92	Robinson, Mike	DE	6-4	270	8/19/56	3	Arizona	Cleveland, Ohio	Cleveland, Ohio	8
22	Scott, Clarence	S	6-0	190	4/9/49	13	Kansas State	Atlanta, Ga.	Decatur, Ga.	9
17	Sipe, Brian	QB	6-1	195	8/8/49	10	San Diego State	San Diego, Calif.	Encinitas, Calif.	6
12	Trocano, Rick	QB-S	6-0	188	4/4/59	3	Pittsburgh	Cleveland, Ohio	Brooklyn, Ohio	2
59	Turner, Kevin	LB	6-2	223	2/5/58	4	Pacific	Fremont, Calif.	North Olmsted, Ohio	8
42	Walker, Dwight	RB-WR	5-10	185	1/10/59	2	Nicholls State	Metairie, La.	Parma, Ohio	9
55	Weathers, Curtis	LB	6-5	220	9/16/56	5	Mississippi	Memphis, Tenn.	Middleburg Heights, Ohio	7
25	White, Charles	RB	5-10	183	1/22/58	4	Southern California	Los Angeles, Calif.	Strongsville, Ohio	9
81	Whitwell, Mike	WR	6-0	175	11/14/58	2	Texas A&M	Kenedy, Tex.	North Olmsted, Ohio	9

†Option playout; subject to developments.

Traded—Tackle Andy Frederick to Chicago.

Also played with Browns in '82—CB Ron Bolton (4 games), NT Mark Buben (3), RB David Green (9), RB Cleo Miller (5), TE McDonald Oden (9).

COACHING STAFF

Head Coach, Sam Rutigliano

Pro Career: Starts his sixth season as an NFL head coach. His teams have produced records of 8-8 (1978), 9-7 (1979), 11-5 (1980), 5-11 (1981), and 4-5 (1982). The 1980 Browns won first AFC Central title since 1971. Pro assistant for 11 years before taking over at Cleveland. Was receivers coach with the Denver Broncos 1967-70, offensive coordinator with the New England Patriots 1971-72 and receivers coach in 1973, defensive backfield coach with the New York Jets 1974-75, and receivers coach for the New Orleans Saints for two years prior to his present assignment with the Browns. Career record: 37-38. No pro playing experience.

Background: Played end at Tulsa from 1954-56. Earned master's degree at Columbia University. Coached on the college level at Connecticut 1964-65 and Maryland 1966.

Personal: Born July 1, 1932, Brooklyn, N.Y. Sam and his wife, Barbara, live in Cleveland and have three children — Paul, Alison, and Kerry.

ASSISTANT COACHES

Dave Adolph, linebackers; born June 6, 1937, Akron, Ohio, lives in Akron. Guard-linebacker Akron University 1955-58. No pro playing experience. College coach: Akron 1963-64, Connecticut 1965-68, Kentucky 1969-72, Illinois 1973-76, Ohio State 1977-78. Pro coach: Joined Browns in 1979.

Joe Daniels, receivers; born November 15, 1942, Bethel Park, Pa., lives in Cleveland. No pro playing experience. College coach: East Stroudsburg 1966, New Hampshire 1967-68, Boston College 1969-76, West Virginia 1977-79, Pittsburgh 1980-82. Pro coach: First year with Browns.

Jim Garrett, director of research and development; born June 19, 1930, Rutherford, N.J., lives in Cleveland Heights. Running back Utah State, 1949-52. Pro running back Philadelphia Eagles 1954, British Columbia Lions (CFL) 1955, New York Giants 1956, Ottawa Rough Riders (CFL) 1957. College coach: Coast Guard 1957-58, Lehigh 1959, Susquehanna 1960-66 (head coach). Pro coach: New York Giants 1970-73, Houston Texans (WFL) 1974 (head coach), New Orleans Saints 1976-77, Browns since 1978.

Howard Mudd, offensive line; born February 10, 1942, Midland, Mich., lives in Cleveland. Guard Hillsdale 1961-64. Pro guard San Francisco 49ers 1964-69, Chicago Bears 1970-71. College coach: California 1972-73. Pro coach: San Diego Chargers 1974-76, San Francisco 49ers 1977, Seattle Seahawks 1978-82, first year with Browns.

John Petercuskie, special teams; born January 31, 1925, Old Forge, Pa., lives in Strongsville, Ohio. Guard East Stroudsburg State 1947-49. No pro playing experience. College coach: Dartmouth 1966-68, Boston College 1969-72, Princeton 1973-77. Pro coach: Joined Browns in 1978.

Tom Pratt, defensive line; born June 21, 1935, Edgerton, Wis., lives in Medina, Ohio. Linebacker Miami 1954-56. No pro playing experience. College coach: Miami 1957-59, Southern Mississippi 1960-62. Pro coach: Kansas City Chiefs 1963-77, New Orleans Saints 1978-80, Browns since 1981.

Dave Redding, strength and conditioning; born June 14, 1952, North Platte, Neb., lives in Medina, Ohio. Defensive end Nebraska 1972-75. No pro playing experience. College coach: Nebraska 1976, Washington State 1977, Missouri 1978-81. Pro coach: Joined Browns in 1982.

Joe Scannella, running backs; born May 2, 1931, Passaic, N.J., lives in Strongsville, Ohio. Quarterback Lehigh 1947-50. Pro safety Saskatchewan Roughriders (CFL) 1951-52. College coach: Cornell 1960, C.W. Post 1963-68 (head coach 1964-68), Vermont 1970-71. Pro coach: Montreal Alouettes (CFL) 1969, Oakland Raiders 1972-77, Montreal Alouettes (CFL) 1978-81 (head coach), Browns since 1982.

Marty Schottenheimer, defensive coordinator-defensive backs; born September 23, 1943, Canonsburg, Pa., lives in Strongsville, Ohio. Linebacker Pittsburgh 1962-65. Pro linebacker Buffalo Bills 1965-68, Boston Patriots 1969-70. Pro coach: Portland Storm (WFL) 1974, New York Giants 1975-77, Detroit Lions 1978-79, Browns since 1980.

CLEVELAND BROWNS 1983 FIRST-YEAR ROSTER

Name	Pos.	Ht.	Wt.	Birth-date	College	Birthplace	Residence	How Acq.
Belk, Rocky	WR	6-0	187	6/20/60	Miami	Alexandria, Va.	Alexandria, Va.	D7
Bittner, Jamie	LB	6-3	230	11/6/58	Delaware	Bridgeport, Conn.	Teaneck, N.J.	FA
Brown, John	TE	6-4	220	8/24/59	Pittsburgh	Ridgway, Pa.	Lower Burrell, Pa.	FA
Brown, Ron	WR	5-11	185	3/31/61	Arizona State	Los Angeles, Calif.	Tempe, Ariz.	D2
Brown, Sam	S	6-2	190	1/31/59	Georgia Tech	Fort Valley, Ga.	Warner Robins, Ga.	FA
Camp, Reggie	DE	6-4	264	2/28/61	California	San Francisco, Calif.	Richmond, Calif.	D3
Campbell, Todd	NT	6-2	260	1/28/61	West Virginia	New Kensington, Pa.	New Kensington, Pa.	FA
Collins, David (1)	P	6-5	220	4/11/57	Fort Lewis	Wichita Falls, Tex.	Iowa Park, Tex.	FA
Contz, Bill	T	6-5	260	12/5/61	Penn State	Belle Vernon, Pa.	Belle Vernon, Pa.	D5
Dyett, Marvin	DE	6-4	240	11/23/60	Georgia Tech	W. Palm Beach, Fla.	W. Palm Beach, Fla.	FA
Farren, Paul	C	6-5	251	12/24/60	Boston University	Cohasset, Mass.	Cohasset, Mass.	D12
Forsythe, Steve	WR	6-0	185	2/24/61	Frostburg State	Williamsport, Md.	Williamsport, Md.	FA
Forts, Will	LB	6-0	215	4/4/60	Georgia	Fulton County, Ga.	Fayetteville, Ga.	FA
Gayle, Jimmy	RB	5-10	192	1/22/60	Ohio State	Hampton, Va.	Hampton, Va.	FA
Gibler, James	TE	6-4	235	4/30/60	Missouri	Independence, Mo.	Columbia, Mo.	FA
Green, Boyce	RB	5-11	215	6/24/60	Carson-Newman	Beaufort, S.C.	Port Royal, S.C.	D11
Harrison, Victor	WR	5-9	183	2/9/61	North Carolina	Henderson, N.C.	Henderson, N.C.	FA
Hessen, Fred	QB	6-1	205	4/14/60	Lamar	Torrance, Calif.	Wilmington, Calif.	FA
Hill, Bill	CB	5-10	175	4/21/59	Rutgers	Neptune, N.J.	Farmingdale, N.J.	FA
Hinton, Marvin	WR	5-10	167	2/7/60	Southern Illinois	Memphis, Tenn.	Memphis, Tenn.	FA
Holman, Walt	RB	5-10	208	4/6/59	West Virginia State	Vaiden, Miss.	Vaiden, Miss.	FA
Holt, Harry	TE	6-4	230	12/29/57	Arizona	Harlingen, Tex.	Tucson, Ariz.	FA
Hopkins, Thomas	T	6-6	260	1/13/60	Alabama A&M	Butler, Ala.	Butler, Ala.	D10
Jones, Chuck	WR	6-0	192	8/27/61	Georgia	Hahira, Ga.	Valdosta, Ga.	FA
Martin, John	LB	6-2	223	9/26/60	Mt. Union	Fort Hood, Tex.	Willowick, Ohio	FA
Mather, Mark	C-G	6-4	250	1/12/61	Miami, Ohio	Cincinnati, Ohio	Cincinnati, Ohio	FA
McAdoo, Howard	LB	6-2	234	1/14/62	Michigan State	Harbor City, Calif.	Palos Verdes, Calif.	D11a
McClearn, Mike	G-T	6-4	280	1/7/61	Temple	Newburgh, N.Y.	Newburgh, N.Y.	D8
McLaughlin, David	RB	6-0	195	8/16/60	Mt. Union	Salem, Ohio	Lisbon, Ohio	FA
Miller, William (1)	RB	5-9	190	1/3/57	Ouachita Baptist	Rison, Ark.	Cleveland, Ohio	FA
Murray, Thomas	RB	6-1	212	2/15/60	Massachusetts	Winchester, Mass.	Winchester, Mass.	FA
Norris, Carnie	RB	5-9	195	1/1/61	Georgia	Spartanburg, S.C.	Spartanburg, S.C.	FA
Nowaske, Jim	DE	6-4	255	4/14/61	Adrian	Detroit, Mich.	Lincoln Park, Mich.	FA
Passerotti, Rich	G	6-2	260	6/30/60	Mercyhurst, Pa.	Erie, Pa.	Harbor Creek, Pa.	FA
Potts, Vincent	WR	5-10	168	9/6/60	Bowling Green	Kalamazoo, Mich.	Kalamazoo, Mich.	FA
Prather, Rich	RB	6-0	210	6/14/61	Frostburg State	Silver Spring, Md.	Rockville, Md.	FA
Puzzuoli, Dave	NT	6-3	260	1/12/61	Pittsburgh	Stamford, Conn.	Stamford, Conn.	D6a
Reed, David	DE	6-5	255	4/6/61	Muskingum	Zanesville, Ohio	Caldwell, Ohio	FA
Ruzek, Roger	K	6-1	190	12/17/60	Weber State	San Francisco, Calif.	San Francisco, Calif.	FA
Schafer, Steve	TE	6-3	248	6/22/61	Toledo	Berea, Ohio	Avon, Ohio	FA
Smith, Blane	S	5-10	188	12/22/59	Southern Methodist	Houston, Tex.	Houston, Tex.	FA
Stearns, Michael	T	6-4	307	3/14/59	Mississippi	Southbridge, Mass.	Charlton City, Mass.	FA
Straka, Tim	TE	6-3	220	9/27/59	Wisconsin	Madison, Wis.	Madison, Wis.	D6
Sullivan, Ray	DE	6-4	240	8/20/61	Maine	Boston, Mass.	Foxboro, Mass.	FA
Van Pelt, Chris	CB	6-3	190	12/15/60	Michigan State	Fort Wayne, Ind.	Fort Wayne, Ind.	FA
Voltapetti, Barry (1)	T	6-7	260	8/30/59	Florida State	Hollywood, Fla.	Hollywood, Fla.	FA

Players who report to an NFL team for the first time are designated on rosters as rookies (R). If a player reported to an NFL training camp in a previous year but was not on the active squad for three or more regular season or postseason games, he is listed on the first-year roster and designated by a (1). Thereafter, a player who is on the active squad for three or more regular season or postseason games is credited with an additional year of playing experience.

NOTES

Larrye Weaver, offensive coordinator-quarterbacks; born November 17, 1931, Monte Vista, Colo., lives in Cleveland. Running back-defensive back Fullerton J.C. 1958-59, Adams State 1960-61. Pro defensive back New York Giants 1955. College coach: North Dakota State 1964-66, Arizona 1967-68, UCLA 1969-70. Pro coach: Los Angeles Rams 1971-72, New England Patriots 1973-76, San Diego Chargers 1977-82, first year with Browns.

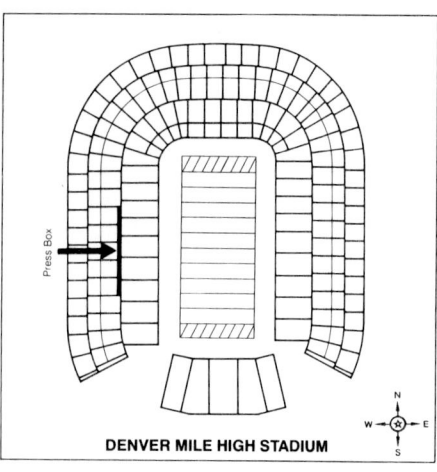

DENVER MILE HIGH STADIUM

Denver Broncos

American Football Conference
Western Division

Team Colors: Orange, Royal Blue, and White

5700 Logan Street
Denver, Colorado 80216
Telephone: (303) 296-1982

Club Officials

Chairman of the Board: Edgar F. Kaiser, Jr.
General Manager: Hein Poulus
Director of Football Operations: John Beake
Director of Administration: Sandy Waters
Coordinator of College Scouting: Reed Johnson
Coordinator of Combine Scouting: Carroll Hardy
Director of Public Relations: Charlie Lee
Publicity Director: Jim Saccomano
Treasurer: Robert M. Hurley
Ticket Manager: Gail Stuckey
Equipment Manager: Bill Harpole
Trainer: Steve Antonopulos

Stadium: Denver Mile High Stadium • **Capacity:** 75,103
1900 West Eliot
Denver, Colorado 80204
Playing Surface: Grass (PAT)
Training Camp: University of Northern Colorado
Greeley, Colorado 80521

1983 SCHEDULE

Preseason

Aug. 5	**Seattle**	7:00
Aug. 13	**Atlanta**	7:00
Aug. 20	**Cleveland**	7:00
Aug. 26	at Minnesota	7:30

Regular Season

Sept. 4	at Pittsburgh	1:00
Sept. 11	at Baltimore	4:00
Sept. 18	**Philadelphia**	2:00
Sept. 25	**Los Angeles Raiders**	2:00
Oct. 2	at Chicago	12:00
Oct. 9	at Houston	12:00
Oct. 16	**Cincinnati**	2:00
Oct. 23	**San Diego**	2:00
Oct. 30	**Kansas City**	2:00
Nov. 6	at Seattle	1:00
Nov. 13	at Los Angeles Raiders	1:00
Nov. 20	**Seattle**	2:00
Nov. 27	at San Diego	1:00
Dec. 4	**Cleveland**	2:00
Dec. 11	**Baltimore**	2:00
Dec. 18	at Kansas City	12:00

1982 TEAM STATISTICS

	Denver	Opp.
Total First Downs...................	170	176
Rushing........................	52	53
Passing........................	103	104
Penalty.......................	15	19
Third Down Efficiency...........	43/121	48/132
Third Down Percentage.........	35.5	36.4
Total Net Yards..................	2837	3169
Total Offensive Plays...........	592	616
Avg. Gain per Play.............	4.8	5.1
Avg. Gain per Game............	315.2	352.1
Net Yards Rushing..............	1018	935
Total Rushing Plays.............	257	293
Avg. Gain per Rush............	4.0	3.2
Avg. Gain Rushing per Game.....	113.1	103.9
Net Yards Passing..............	1819	2234
Lost Attempting to Pass.........	24/200	16/116
Gross Yards Passing............	2019	2350
Attempts/Completions..........	311/181	307/172
Percent Completed.............	58.2	56.0
Had Intercepted..............	19	12
Avg. Net Passing per Game.....	202.1	248.2
Punts/Avg.......................	45/45.0	42/39.4
Punt Returns/Avg..............	21/14.5	25/9.1
Kickoff Returns/Avg............	40/20.5	26/20.8
Interceptions/Avg. Ret.	12/8.8	19/22.7
Penalties/Yards...............	54/516	63/571
Fumbles/Ball Lost.............	24/17	17/7
Total Points...................	148	226
Avg. Points per Game	16.4	25.1
Touchdowns...................	16	25
Rushing.....................	6	8
Passing.....................	8	14
Returns and Recoveries	2	3
Field Goals.................	11/13	17/24
Conversions................	15/16	25/25
Safeties....................	2	0
Avg. Time of Possession	29:46	30:14

1982 TEAM RECORD

Preseason (4-0)

Denver		Opponents
33	Los Angeles Rams	20
17	*Miami	14
27	*Minnesota	17
20	New York Jets	13
97		64

Regular Season (2-7)

Denver		Opponents	Att.
3	*San Diego	23	73,564
24	*San Francisco	21	73,899
10	*Seattle	17	73,916
20	San Diego	30	47,629
27	*Atlanta	34	73,984
27	Los Angeles Rams	24	48,112
16	*Kansas City	37	74,192
10	Los Angeles Raiders	27	44,160
11	Seattle	13	43,145
148		226	552,601

*Home Game

Score by Periods

Denver	26	54	26	42	—	148
Opponents	40	79	40	67	—	226

Attendance

Home 369,555   Away 183,046   Total 552,601

Single game home record, 74,997 (10-7-79)
Single season home record, 598,402 (1981)

1982 INDIVIDUAL STATISTICS

Rushing

	Att	Yds	Avg	LG	TD
Willhite	70	347	5.0	23	2
Parros	77	277	3.6	14	1
Winder	67	259	3.9	18	1
Preston	19	81	4.3	13	0
Poole	7	36	5.1	20	0
DeBerg	8	27	3.4	6t	1
Herrmann	3	7	2.3	6t	1
Lytle	2	2	1.0	2	0
Watson	1	−4	−4.0	−4	0
J. Wright	1	−4	−4.0	−4	0
Upchurch	2	−10	−5.0	−3	0
Denver	257	1018	4.0	23	6
Opponents	293	935	3.2	46	8

Field Goal Success

Distance	1-19	20-29	30-39	40-49	50 Over
Made-Att.	2-2	3-3	3-4	3-4	0-0

Passing

	Att	Comp	Pct	Yds	TD	Int	Tkld	Rate
DeBerg	223	131	58.7	1405	7	11	16/130	67.2
Herrmann	60	32	53.3	421	1	4	4/48	53.5
Morton	26	18	69.2	193	0	3	3/19	51.1
Willhite	2	0	0.0	0	0	1	0/0	—
Upchurch	0	0	—	0	0	0	1/3	—
Denver	311	181	58.2	2019	8	19	24/200	
Opponents	307	172	56.0	2350	14	12	16/116	

Receiving

	No	Yds	Avg	LG	TD
Parros	37	259	7.0	24	2
Watson	36	555	15.4	41	2
Upchurch	26	407	15.7	51t	3
Willhite	26	227	8.7	27	0
Preston	14	134	9.6	20	0
Winder	11	83	7.5	22	0
Egloff	10	96	9.6	17	0
J. Wright	9	120	13.3	39	1
Odoms	8	82	10.3	18	0
Manning	3	46	15.3	30	0
Lytle	1	10	10.0	10	0
Denver	181	2019	11.2	51t	8
Opponents	172	2350	13.7	86t	14

Interceptions

	No	Yds	Avg	LG	TD
Kyle	3	26	8.7	14	0
Wilson	2	22	11.0	16	0
L. Wright	2	18	9.0	18	0
Harden	2	3	1.5	3	0
Smith	1	29	29.0	29	0
T. Jackson	1	8	8.0	8	0
Thomas	1	0	0.0	0	0
Denver	12	106	8.8	29	0
Opponents	19	431	22.7	60	3

Punting

	No	Yds	Avg	In 20	LG
Prestridge	45	2026	45.0	14	65
Denver	45	2026	45.0	14	65
Opponents	42	1653	39.4	9	80

Punt Returns

	No	FC	Yds	Avg	LG	TD
Upchurch	15	3	242	16.1	78t	2
Willhite	6	4	63	10.5	23	0
Denver	21	7	305	14.5	78t	2
Opponents	25	3	227	9.1	25	0

Kickoff Returns

	No	Yds	Avg	LG	TD
Manning	15	346	23.1	34	0
Willhite	17	337	19.8	26	0
Wilson	6	123	20.5	30	0
Uecker	1	12	12.0	12	0
Poole	1	0	0.0	0	0
Denver	40	818	20.5	34	0
Opponents	26	541	20.8	68	0

Scoring

	TD	TD R	TD P	TD Rt	PAT	FG	TP
Karlis					15/16	11/13	48
Upchurch	5	0	3	2			30
Parros	3	1	2	0			18
Watson	2	0	2	0			12
Willhite	2	2	0	0			12
DeBerg	1	1	0	0			6
Herrmann	1	1	0	0			6
Winder	1	1	0	0			6
J. Wright	1	0	1	0			6
Boyd	(Safety)						2
Chavous	(Safety)						2
Denver	16	6	8	2	15/16	11/13	148
Opponents	25	8	14	3	25/25	17/24	226

Sacks

Chavous 5, Gradishar 2, T. Jackson 1, Jones 2, Latimer 1, Manor 2, Smith 2, L. Wright 1.

FIRST PLAYERS SELECTED

Year	Player, College, Position
1960	Roger LeClerc, Trinity, Connecticut, C
1961	Bob Gaiters, New Mexico State, RB
1962	Merlin Olsen, Utah State, DT
1963	Kermit Alexander, UCLA, CB
1964	Bob Brown, Nebraska, T
1965	Dick Butkus, Illinois, LB (2)
1966	Jerry Shay, Purdue, DT
1967	Floyd Little, Syracuse, RB
1968	Curley Culp, Arizona State, DE (2)
1969	Grady Cavness, Texas-El Paso, DB (2)
1970	Bob Anderson, Colorado, RB
1971	Marv Montgomery, Southern California, T
1972	Riley Odoms, Houston, TE
1973	Otis Armstrong, Purdue, RB
1974	Randy Gradishar, Ohio State, LB
1975	Louis Wright, San Jose State, DB
1976	Tom Glassic, Virginia, G
1977	Steve Schindler, Boston College, G
1978	Don Latimer, Miami, DT
1979	Kelvin Clark, Nebraska, T
1980	Rulon Jones, Utah State, DE (2)
1981	Dennis Smith, Southern California, DB
1982	Gerald Willhite, San Jose State, RB
1983	Chris Hinton, Northwestern, G

BRONCOS COACHING HISTORY

(136-185-9)

1960-61	Frank Filchock	7-20-1
1962-64	Jack Faulkner*	9-22-1
1964-66	Mac Speedie**	6-19-1
1966	Ray Malavasi	4-8-0
1967-71	Lou Saban***	20-42-3
1971	Jerry Smith	2-3-0
1972-76	John Ralston	34-33-3
1977-80	Robert (Red) Miller	42-25-0
1981-82	Dan Reeves	12-13-0

*Released after four games in 1964
**Resigned after two games in 1966
***Resigned after nine games in 1971

DENVER BRONCOS 1983 VETERAN ROSTER

No.	Name	Pos.	Ht.	Wt.	Birth-date	NFL Exp.	College	Birthplace	Residence	Games in '82
54	Bishop, Keith	C-G	6-3	260	3/10/57	3	Baylor	San Diego, Calif.	Englewood, Colo.	9
77	Boyd, Greg	DE	6-6	280	9/15/53	6	San Diego State	Merced, Calif.	Englewood, Colo.	9
64	Bryan, Bill	C	6-2	258	6/21/55	6	Duke	Burlington, N.C.	Burlington, N.C.	9
58	Busick, Steve	LB	6-4	227	12/10/58	3	Southern California	Los Angeles, Calif.	Aurora, Colo.	9
68	†Carter, Rubin	NT	6-0	256	12/12/52	9	Miami	Pompano Beach, Fla.	Aurora, Colo.	9
79	Chavous, Barney	DE	6-3	258	3/22/51	11	South Carolina State	Aiken, S.C.	Aurora, Colo.	9
78	Clark, Brian	T	6-6	260	9/22/60	2	Clemson	Anderson, S.C.	St. Petersburg, Fla.	0*
59	Comeaux, Darren	LB	6-1	227	4/15/60	2	Arizona State	Shawnee, Okla.	San Diego, Calif.	3
17	DeBerg, Steve	QB	6-3	205	1/19/54	7	San Jose State	Oakland, Calif.	Denver, Colo.	9
55	Dennison, Rick	LB	6-2	215	6/22/58	2	Colorado State	Kalispel, Mont.	Ft. Collins, Colo.	9
85	†Egloff, Ron	TE	6-5	227	10/3/55	7	Wisconsin	Plymouth, Mich.	Englewood, Colo.	9
56	†Evans, Larry	LB	6-2	220	7/11/53	8	Mississippi College	Mountrose, Miss.	Denver, Colo.	9
43	Foley, Steve	S	6-2	190	11/11/53	7	Tulane	New Orleans, La.	New Orleans, La.	1
62	Glassic, Tom	G	6-3	260	4/17/54	8	Virginia	Elizabeth, N.J.	Littleton, Colo.	9
53	Gradishar, Randy	LB	6-2	231	3/3/52	10	Ohio State	Warren, Ohio	Littleton, Colo.	9
31	Harden, Mike	S	6-1	192	2/16/58	4	Michigan	Memphis, Tenn.	Aurora, Colo.	5
60	Howard, Paul	G	6-3	260	9/12/50	10	Brigham Young	San Jose, Calif.	Redding, Calif.	9
28	Jackson, Roger	CB-S	6-0	186	2/28/59	2	Bethune-Cookman	Macon, Ga.	Denver, Colo.	9
57	Jackson, Tom	LB	5-11	220	4/4/51	11	Louisville	Cleveland, Ohio	Denver, Colo.	9
75	Jones, Rulon	DE	6-6	260	3/25/58	4	Utah State	Salt Lake City, Utah	Thornton, Colo.	9
3	Karlis, Rich	K	6-0	180	5/23/59	2	Cincinnati	Salem, Ohio	Denver, Colo.	9
76	Lanier, Ken	T	6-3	269	7/8/59	3	Florida State	Columbus, Ohio	Denver, Colo.	9
41	Lytle, Rob	RB	5-11	195	11/12/54	7	Michigan	Fremont, Ohio	Fremont, Ohio	9
83	Manning, Wade	WR	5-11	190	7/25/55	4	Ohio State	Meadville, Pa.	Denver, Colo.	9
66	Manor, Brison	DE	6-4	248	8/10/52	7	Arkansas	Bridgeton, N.J.	North Little Rock, Ark.	9
82	McDaniel, Orlando	WR	6-0	180	12/1/60	2	Louisiana State	Lake Charles, La.	Baton Rouge, La.	3
71	Minor, Claudie	T	6-4	278	4/21/51	10	San Diego State	Pomona, Calif.	Englewood, Colo.	9
88	Odoms, Riley	TE	6-4	235	3/1/50	12	Houston	Corpus Christi, Tex.	Houston, Tex.	8
24	Parros, Rick	RB	5-11	200	6/14/58	3	Utah State	Brooklyn, N.Y.	Denver, Colo.	9
34	Poole, Nathan	RB	5-9	212	12/17/56	4	Louisville	Alexander City, Ala.	Aurora, Colo.	9
46	Preston, Dave	RB	5-11	195	5/29/55	6	Bowling Green	Dayton, Ohio	Englewood, Colo.	8
11	†Prestridge, Luke	P	6-4	235	9/17/56	5	Baylor	Houston, Tex.	Englewood, Colo.	9
50	Ryan, Jim	LB	6-1	215	5/18/57	3	William & Mary	Bellmawr, N.J.	Denver, Colo.	9
49	Smith, Dennis	S	6-3	200	2/3/59	3	Southern California	Santa Monica, Calif.	Santa Monica, Calif.	8
70	Studdard, Dave	T	6-4	260	11/22/55	5	Texas	San Antonio, Tex.	Westminster, Colo.	9
51	Swenson, Bob	LB	6-3	225	7/1/53	8	California	Stockton, Calif.	Longmont, Colo.	4
26	Thomas, J. T.	S	6-2	196	4/22/51	10	Florida State	Macon, Ga.	Monroeville, Pa.	9
37	Trimble, Steve	CB	5-10	181	5/11/58	3	Maryland	Cumberland, Md.	Aurora, Colo.	6
67	Uecker, Keith	T	6-5	260	6/20/60	2	Auburn	Auburn, Ala.	Hollywood, Fla.	5
80	Upchurch, Rick	WR-KR	5-10	180	5/20/52	9	Minnesota	Toledo, Ohio	Englewood, Colo.	9
81	Watson, Steve	WR	6-4	195	5/28/57	5	Temple	Baltimore, Md.	Arvada, Colo.	9
47	Willhite, Gerald	RB	5-10	200	5/30/59	2	San Jose State	Sacramento, Calif.	Rancho Cordova, Calif.	9
45	Wilson, Steve	CB	5-10	195	8/9/60	2	Howard	Jacksonville, Fla.	Richardson, Tex.	8
23	Winder, Sammy	RB	5-11	203	7/15/59	2	Southern Mississippi	Madison, Miss.	Jackson, Miss.	8
52	Woodard, Ken	LB	6-1	218	1/22/60	2	Tuskegee Institute	Detroit, Mich.	Detroit, Mich.	9
87	Wright, Jim	TE	6-3	240	9/1/56	4	Texas Christian	Fort Hood, Tex.	Houston, Tex.	9
20	†Wright, Louis	CB	6-2	200	1/31/53	9	San Jose State	Gilmer, Tex.	Bakersfield, Calif.	9

* Clark active for 7 games in '82, but did not play.

†Option playout; subject to developments.

Retired—Aaron Kyle, 7-year cornerback, 9 games in '82; Craig Morton, 18-year quarterback, 3 in '82.

Traded—Quarterback Mark Herrmann to Baltimore.

Also played with Broncos in '82—NT Don Latimer (9 games), LB Mark Merrill (2).

COACHING STAFF

Head Coach, Dan Reeves

Pro Career: Became ninth head coach in Broncos history on February 28, 1981, after spending entire pro career as both player and coach with Dallas Cowboys. Guided Broncos to 10-6 mark in 1981 and 2-7 record last year. He joined the Cowboys as a free agent running back in 1965 and became a member of the coaching staff in 1970 when he undertook the dual role of player-coach for two seasons. Was Cowboys offensive backfield coach from 1972-76 and became offensive coordinator in 1977. Was an all-purpose running back during his eight seasons as a player, rushing for 1,990 yards and catching 129 passes for 1,693. Career record: 12-13.

Background: Quarterback at South Carolina from 1962-64 and was inducted into the school's Hall of Fame in 1978.

Personal: Born January 19, 1944, Rome, Ga. Dan and his wife, Pam, live in Denver and have three children—Dana, Laura, and Lee.

ASSISTANT COACHES

Marvin Bass, special assistant; born August 28, 1919, Norfolk, Va., lives in Denver. Tackle William & Mary 1940-42. No pro playing experience. College coach: William & Mary 1944-48, 1950-51 (head coach), North Carolina 1949, 1953-55, South Carolina 1956-59, 1961-65, Georgia Tech 1960, Richmond 1973. Pro coach: Washington Redskins 1952, Montreal Beavers (Continental League) 1966-67, Montreal Alouettes (CFL) 1968, Buffalo Bills 1969-71, Birmingham Americans (WFL) 1974-75, Broncos since 1982.

Joe Collier, assistant head coach, defense; born June 7, 1932, Rock Island, Ill., lives in Denver. End Northwestern 1950-53. No pro playing experience. College coach: Western Illinois 1957-59. Pro coach: Boston Patriots 1960-62, Buffalo Bills 1963-68 (head coach 1966-68), Broncos since 1969.

John Hadl, offensive coordinator; born February 15, 1940, Lawrence, Kan., lives in Denver. Quarterback-halfback Kansas 1959-61. Pro quarterback San Diego Chargers 1962-72, Los Angeles Rams 1973-74, Green Bay Packers 1974-75, Houston Oilers 1976-77. College coach: Kansas 1978-81. Pro coach: Los Angeles Rams 1982, first year with Broncos.

Stan Jones, defensive line; born November 24, 1931, Altoona, Pa., lives in Denver. Tackle Maryland 1950-53. Pro lineman Chicago Bears 1954-65, Washington Redskins 1966. Pro coach: Denver Broncos 1967-71, Buffalo Bills 1972-75, rejoined Broncos in 1976.

Myrel Moore, linebackers-special teams; born March 9, 1934, Sebastopol, Calif., lives in Denver. Receiver California-Davis 1955-57. Pro defensive back Washington Redskins 1958. College coach: Santa Ana J.C. 1959-62, California 1963-71. Pro coach: Denver Broncos 1972-77, Oakland Raiders 1978-79, rejoined Broncos in 1983.

Nick Nicolau, running backs; born May 5, 1933, New York, N.Y., lives in Denver. Running back Southern Connecticut 1957-59. No pro playing experience. College coach: Southern Connecticut 1960, Springfield 1961, Bridgeport 1962-69 (head coach 1965-69), Massachusetts 1970, Connecticut 1971-72, Kentucky 1973-75, Kent State 1976. Pro coach: Hamilton Tiger-Cats (CFL) 1977, Montreal Alouettes 1978-79, New Orleans Saints 1980, Broncos since 1981.

Fran Polsfoot, tight ends; born April 19, 1927, Montesano, Wash., lives in Denver. End Washington State 1946-49. Pro end Chicago Cardinals 1950-52, Washington Redskins 1953. College coach: Wisconsin State 1954-61. Pro coach: St. Louis Cardinals 1962-67, Houston Oilers 1968-71, 1975-76, Cleveland Browns 1972-74, Broncos since 1977.

Dan Radakovich, offensive line; born November 27, 1935, Duquesne, Pa., lives in Denver. Center-linebacker Penn State 1954-56. No pro playing experience. College coach: Penn State 1960-69, Cincinnati 1970, Colorado 1972-73, North Carolina State 1982. Pro coach: Pittsburgh Steelers 1971, 1974, San Francisco 49ers 1978, Los Angeles Rams 1979-81, first year with Broncos.

DENVER BRONCOS 1983 FIRST-YEAR ROSTER

Name	Pos.	Ht.	Wt.	Birth-date	College	Birthplace	Residence	How Acq.
Bailey, Don	C	6-3	250	3/24/61	Miami	Miami, Fla.	Miami, Fla.	D11
Baldwin, Bruce	CB-S	6-1	200	9/5/59	Harding College	Jacksonville, Ill.	Jacksonville, Ill.	D5a
Bowyer, Walt	DE	6-4	245	9/8/60	Arizona State	Pittsburgh, Pa.	Tempe, Ariz.	D10
Clarkson, Steve	QB	6-0	205	10/31/61	San Jose State	Los Angeles, Calif.	Los Angeles, Calif.	FA
Cone, Ray	LB	6-2	220	4/3/61	Colorado	Wiesbaden, Germany	Boulder, Colo.	FA
Cooper, Mark	T	6-5	267	2/14/60	Miami	Miami, Fla.	Miami, Fla.	D2
Dupree, Myron	CB-S	5-11	180	10/15/61	N. Carolina Central	New York, N.Y.	Rocky Mount, N.C.	D7
t-Elway, John	QB	6-3	205	6/28/60	Stanford	Port Angeles, Wash.	San Jose, Calif.	D1
Gross, Lynn	G	6-2	278	8/1/60	Delaware State	Philadelphia, Pa.	Philadelphia, Pa.	FA
Harris, George	LB	6-2	223	12/2/60	Houston	Waco, Tex.	Waco, Tex.	D5
Hawkins, Brian	S	6-1	190	7/26/59	San Jose State	Clinton, Okla.	San Jose, Calif.	D9
Heflin, Victor	CB	6-0	184	7/7/60	Delaware State	Springfield, Mass.	Dayton, Ohio	D6
Kubiak, Gary	QB	6-0	192	8/15/61	Texas A&M	Houston, Tex.	Houston, Tex.	D8
Lewis, Bobby	WR	5-10	173	2/19/62	Northeast Louisiana	New Orleans, La.	New Orleans, La.	FA
Mecklenburg, Karl	NT-DE	6-3	250	9/1/60	Minnesota	Seattle, Wash.	Minneapolis, Minn.	D12
Sampson, Clinton	WR	5-11	183	1/4/61	San Diego State	Los Angeles, Calif.	Los Angeles, Calif.	D3
Simon, Kenny	RB	5-11	205	11/22/60	Alabama	Montgomery, Ala.	Montgomery, Ala.	FA
Taylor, Dwight	CB	6-0	184	1/2/60	Elizabeth City State	Wilson, N.C.	Wilson, N.C.	FA
White, Tim	WR	5-9	173	3/7/60	Southern California	Neptune, N.J.	South Belmar, N.J.	FA
Young, Reggie	RB	6-0	191	3/10/59	Hawaii	Springfield, Mass.	Sacramento, Calif.	FA

Players who report to an NFL team for the first time are designated on rosters as rookies (R). If a player reported to an NFL training camp in a previous year but was not on the active squad for three or more regular season or postseason games, he is listed on the first-year roster and designated by a (1). Thereafter, a player who is on the active squad for three or more regular season or postseason games is credited with an additional year of playing experience.

t-Broncos traded for Elway (Baltimore)

NOTES

_____
_____
_____
_____
_____
_____
_____
_____
_____
_____
_____
_____
_____
_____
_____
_____
_____
_____
_____
_____

Charlie West, defensive backs; born August 31, 1946, Big Spring, Tex., lives in Denver. Defensive back Texas El-Paso 1963-67. Pro defensive back Minnesota Vikings 1968-73, Detroit Lions 1974-78, Denver Broncos 1978-79. College coach: MacAlister 1981, California 1982. Pro coach: First year with Broncos.

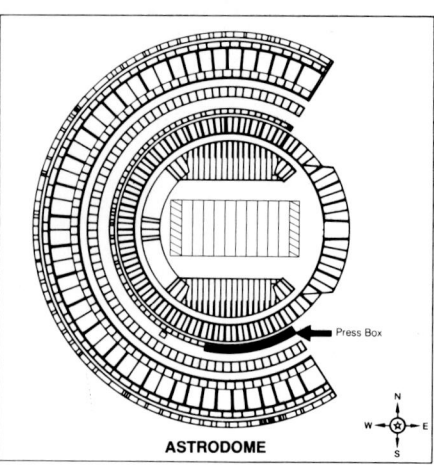

ASTRODOME

Houston Oilers

**American Football Conference
Central Division**

Team Colors: Columbia Blue, Scarlet,
and White

**Box 1516
Houston, Texas 77001
Telephone: (713) 797-9111**

Club Officials
President: K. S. (Bud) Adams, Jr.
Executive Vice President-General Manager:
  Ladd K. Herzeg
Vice President-Player Personnel: Mike Holovak
Media Relations Director: Bob Hyde
Business Manager: Lewis Mangum
Marketing Director: Rick Nichols
Ticket Coordinator: David Fuqua
Head Trainer: Jerry Meins
Assistant Trainer: Joel Krekelberg
Equipment Manager: Gordon Batty

Stadium: Astrodome • **Capacity:** 50,496
  Loop 610, Kirby and Fannin Streets
  Houston, Texas 77202

Playing Surface: AstroTurf

Training Camp: Angelo State University
  San Angelo, Texas 76901

1983 SCHEDULE

Preseason
Aug. 4	**Baltimore**	7:00
Aug. 13	**Tampa Bay**	8:00
Aug. 20	at New Orleans	7:00
Aug. 27	at Dallas	8:00

Regular Season
Sept. 4	**Green Bay**	12:00
Sept. 11	at Los Angeles Raiders	1:00
Sept. 18	**Pittsburgh**	12:00
Sept. 25	at Buffalo	1:00
Oct. 2	at Pittsburgh	1:00
Oct. 9	**Denver**	12:00
Oct. 16	at Minnesota	12:00
Oct. 23	**Kansas City**	12:00
Oct. 30	at Cleveland	1:00
Nov. 6	**Cincinnati**	12:00
Nov. 13	**Detroit**	12:00
Nov. 20	at Cincinnati	1:00
Nov. 27	at Tampa Bay	1:00
Dec. 4	**Miami**	12:00
Dec. 11	**Cleveland**	12:00
Dec. 18	at Baltimore	2:00

1982 TEAM STATISTICS

	Houston	Opp.
Total First Downs	138	187
Rushing	52	67
Passing	81	106
Penalty	5	14
Third Down Efficiency	43/123	60/130
Third Down Percentage	35.0	46.2
Total Net Yards	2373	3438
Total Offensive Plays	551	613
Avg. Gain per Play	4.3	5.6
Avg. Gain per Game	263.7	382.0
Net Yards Rushing	799	1225
Total Rushing Plays	225	298
Avg. Gain per Rush	3.6	4.1
Avg. Gain Rushing per Game	88.8	136.1
Net Yards Passing	1574	2213
Lost Attempting to Pass	39/308	31/240
Gross Yards Passing	1882	2453
Attempts/Completions	287/153	284/179
Percent Completed	53.3	63.0
Had Intercepted	15	3
Avg. Net Passing per Game	174.9	245.9
Punts/Avg.	55/39.7	38/43.0
Punt Returns/Avg.	19/5.5	35/8.4
Kickoff Returns/Avg.	45/20.1	26/21.7
Interceptions/Avg. Ret.	3/15.7	15/3.1
Penalties/Yards	52/424	59/454
Fumbles/Ball Lost	14/11	20/14
Total Points	136	245
Avg. Points per Game	15.1	27.2
Touchdowns	18	30
Rushing	5	10
Passing	12	18
Returns and Recoveries	1	2
Field Goals	4/6	11/18
Conversions	16/18	30/30
Safeties	0	1
Avg. Time of Possession	27:40	32:20

1982 TEAM RECORD

Preseason (2-2)

Houston		Opponents
22	*New Orleans	20
16	*New York Jets	33
21	*Tampa Bay	6
14	Dallas	20
73		79

Regular Season (1-8)

Houston		Opponents	Att.
6	Cincinnati	27	53,268
23	*Seattle	21	43,117
10	*Pittsburgh	24	42,338
21	New England	29	33,602
14	New York Giants	17	71,184
7	*Dallas	37	51,808
14	Philadelphia	35	44,119
14	*Cleveland	20	36,559
27	*Cincinnati	35	26,522
136		245	402,517

*Home Game

Score by Periods

Houston	24	27	31	54	—	136
Opponents	48	71	45	81	—	245

Attendance

Home 200,344   Away 202,173   Total 402,517
Single game home record, 55,293 (12-10-79)
Single season home record, 400,156 (1980)

1982 INDIVIDUAL STATISTICS

Rushing

	Att	Yds	Avg	LG	TD
Campbell	157	538	3.4	22	2
Manning	13	85	6.5	24	0
Edwards	15	58	3.9	8	0
Craft	18	42	2.3	10	3
Nielsen	9	37	4.1	9	0
Armstrong	8	15	1.9	5	0
Bailey	1	13	13.0	13	0
Casper	2	9	4.5	8	0
Allen	2	2	1.0	9	0
Houston	225	799	3.6	24	5
Opponents	298	1225	4.1	90t	10

Field Goal Success

Distance	1-19	20-29	30-39	40-49	50 Over
Made-Att.	0-0	1-1	3-3	0-1	0-1

Passing

	Att	Comp	Pct	Yds	TD	Int	Tkld	Rate
Manning	125	66	52.8	877	6	6	27/216	71.3
Nielsen	161	87	54.0	1005	6	8	12/92	64.6
Campbell	1	0	0.0	0	0	1	0/0	—
Houston	287	153	53.3	1882	12	15	39/308	
Opponents	284	179	63.0	2453	18	3	31/240	

Receiving

	No	Yds	Avg	LG	TD
Casper	36	573	15.9	38	6
Bailey	26	367	14.1	27	0
Craft	23	230	10.0	49	1
Renfro	21	295	14.0	54t	3
Campbell	18	130	7.2	46	0
Armstrong	12	75	6.3	14	0
Edwards	9	53	5.9	21	0
Holston	5	116	23.2	38t	1
Allen	2	35	17.5	23t	1
Thomaselli	1	8	8.0	8	0
Houston	153	1882	12.3	54t	12
Opponents	179	2453	13.7	62t	18

Interceptions

	No	Yds	Avg	LG	TD
Brazile	1	31	31.0	31	0
Bingham	1	8	8.0	8	0
Perry	1	8	8.0	8	0
Houston	3	47	15.7	31	0
Opponents	15	47	3.1	22	1

Punting

	No	Yds	Avg	In 20	LG
James	31	1260	40.6	4	56
Parsley	24	926	38.6	3	51
Houston	55	2186	39.7	7	56
Opponents	38	1634	43.0	11	73

Punt Returns

	No	FC	Yds	Avg	LG	TD
Roaches	19	4	104	5.5	25	0
Houston	19	4	104	5.5	25	0
Opponents	35	11	293	8.4	24	0

Kickoff Returns

	No	Yds	Avg	LG	TD
Roaches	21	441	21.0	45	0
Allen	15	292	19.5	38	0
Tullis	5	91	18.2	28	0
T. Wilson	2	40	20.0	26	0
Riley	1	27	27.0	27	0
Thomaselli	1	7	7.0	7	0
Smith	0	7	—	7L	0
Houston	45	905	20.1	45	0
Opponents	26	564	21.7	55	0

Scoring

	TD	TD R	TD P	TD Rt	PAT	FG	TP
Casper	6	0	6	0			36
Kempf					16/18	4/6	28
Craft	4	3	1	0			24
Renfro	3	0	3	0			18
Campbell	2	2	0	0			12
Allen	1	0	1	0			6
Holston	1	0	1	0			6
Reinfeldt	1	0	0	1			6
Houston	18	5	12	1	16/18	4/6	136
Opponents	30	10	18	2	30/30	11/18	245

Sacks

Baker 7½, Bethea 1, Bingham 3, Brazile 6½, Corker 1, Hunt 1, Kennard 3, Riley 1½, Skaugstad 3, Stensrud 1½, Washington 1.

FIRST PLAYERS SELECTED

Year	Player, College, Position
1960	Billy Cannon, Louisiana State, RB
1961	Mike Ditka, Pittsburgh, E
1962	Ray Jacobs, Howard Payne, DT
1963	Danny Brabham, Arkansas, LB
1964	Scott Appleton, Texas, DT
1965	Lawrence Elkins, Baylor, WR
1966	Tommy Nobis, Texas, LB
1967	George Webster, Michigan State, LB
1968	Mac Haik, Mississippi, WR (2)
1969	Ron Pritchard, Arizona State, LB
1970	Doug Wilkerson, N. Carolina Central, G
1971	Dan Pastorini, Santa Clara, QB
1972	Greg Sampson, Stanford, DE
1973	John Matuszak, Tampa, DE
1974	Steve Manstedt, Nebraska, LB (4)
1975	Robert Brazile, Jackson State, LB
1976	Mike Barber, Louisiana Tech, TE (2)
1977	Morris Towns, Missouri, T
1978	Earl Campbell, Texas, RB
1979	Mike Stensrud, Iowa State, DE (2)
1980	Angelo Fields, Michigan State, T (2)
1981	Michael Holston, Morgan State, WR (3)
1982	Mike Munchak, Penn State, G
1983	Bruce Matthews, Southern California, T

OILERS COACHING HISTORY

(155-176-6)

1960-61	Lou Rymkus*	12-7-1
1961	Wally Lemm	10-2-0
1962-63	Frank (Pop) Ivy	17-12-0
1964	Sammy Baugh	4-10-0
1965	Hugh Taylor	4-10-0
1966-70	Wally Lemm	28-38-4
1971	Ed Hughes	4-9-1
1972-73	Bill Peterson**	1-18-0
1973-74	Sid Gillman	8-15-0
1975-80	O.A. (Bum) Phillips	59-38-0
1981-82	Ed Biles	8-17-0

*Released after five games in 1961
**Released after five games in 1973

HOUSTON OILERS 1983 VETERAN ROSTER

No.	Name	Pos.	Ht.	Wt.	Birth-date	NFL Exp.	College	Birthplace	Residence	Games in '82
56	Abraham, Robert	LB	6-1	217	7/13/60	2	North Carolina State	Myrtle Beach, S.C.	Myrtle Beach, S.C.	9
31	Allen, Gary	RB	5-10	183	4/23/60	2	Hawaii	Baldwin Park, Calif.	Baldwin Park, Calif.	7
39	†Armstrong, Adger	RB	6-0	225	6/21/57	4	Texas A&M	Houston, Tex.	Houston, Tex.	6
86	Arnold, Walt	TE	6-3	234	8/31/58	4	New Mexico	Galveston, Tex.	Albuquerque, N.M.	9
80	†Bailey, Harold	WR	6-2	193	4/12/57	3	Oklahoma State	Houston, Tex.	Houston, Tex.	9
75	†Baker, Jesse	DE	6-5	272	7/10/57	5	Jacksonville State	Conyers, Ga.	Stafford, Tex.	9
65	Bethea, Elvin	DE	6-2	252	3/1/46	16	North Carolina A&T	Trenton, N.J.	Houston, Tex.	9
54	Bingham, Gregg	LB	6-1	225	3/13/51	11	Purdue	Chicago, Ill.	Missouri City, Tex.	7
52	Brazile, Robert	LB	6-4	245	2/7/53	9	Jackson State	Pineland, Ala.	Houston, Tex.	9
81	Bryant, Steve	WR	6-2	194	10/10/59	2	Purdue	Los Angeles, Calif.	Los Angeles, Calif.	7
00	†Burrough, Ken	WR	6-3	220	7/14/48	12	Texas Southern	Jacksonville, Fla.	Houston, Tex.	0*
34	Campbell, Earl	RB	5-11	240	3/29/55	6	Texas	Tyler, Tex.	Houston, Tex.	9
58	†Carter, David	C	6-2	262	11/27/53	7	Western Kentucky	Vincennes, Ind.	Sugarland, Tex.	9
87	Casper, Dave	TE	6-4	241	2/2/52	10	Notre Dame	Chilton, Wis.	Houston, Tex.	9
40	Craft, Donnie	RB	6-0	209	11/19/59	2	Louisville	Panama City, Fla.	Houston, Tex.	9
66	Davidson, Greg	C	6-2	254	4/24/58	4	North Texas State	Independence, Iowa	Houston, Tex.	9
35	Edwards, Stan	RB	6-0	215	5/20/60	2	Michigan	Detroit, Mich.	Detroit, Mich.	7
60	Fisher, Ed	G	6-3	259	5/31/49	10	Arizona State	Stockton, Calif.	Houston, Tex.	9
36	Hartwig, Carter	CB-S	6-0	205	2/2/56	5	Southern California	Culver City, Calif.	Houston, Tex.	9
84	Holston, Mike	WR	6-3	192	1/8/58	3	Morgan State	Washington, D.C.	Seat Pleasant, Md.	9
50	†Hunt, Daryl	LB	6-3	239	11/3/56	5	Oklahoma	Odessa, Tex.	Missouri City, Tex.	9
6	†James, John	P	6-3	196	1/21/49	12	Florida	Panama City, Fla.	Gainesville, Fla.	5*
22	Kay, Bill	CB	6-1	190	1/10/60	3	Purdue	Detroit, Mich.	Houston, Tex.	9
4	Kempf, Florian	K	5-9	170	5/25/56	2	Pennsylvania	Philadelphia, Pa.	Philadelphia, Pa.	9
71	Kennard, Ken	DE	6-2	258	10/4/54	7	Angelo State	Fort Worth, Tex.	Houston, Tex.	9
72	†Koncar, Mark	T	6-5	270	5/5/53	7	Colorado	Murray, Utah	Sandy, Utah	5
10	Luck, Oliver	QB	6-2	198	4/5/60	2	West Virginia	Cleveland, Ohio	Cleveland, Ohio	0*
8	Manning, Archie	QB	6-3	211	5/19/49	13	Mississippi	Drew, Miss.	New Orleans, La.	7*
63	Munchak, Mike	G	6-3	263	5/3/60	2	Penn State	Scranton, Pa.	Houston, Tex.	4
14	Nielsen, Gifford	QB	6-4	210	10/25/54	6	Brigham Young	Provo, Utah	Sugarland, Tex.	9
32	Perry, Vernon	S	6-2	210	9/22/53	5	Jackson State	Jackson, Miss.	Jackson, Miss.	7
21	Randle, Tate	CB	6-0	202	8/15/59	2	Texas Tech	Fredricksburg, Tex.	Fort Stockton, Tex.	7
37	Reinfeldt, Mike	S	6-2	196	5/6/53	8	Wisconsin-Milwaukee	Baraboo, Wis.	Missouri City, Tex.	9
64	†Reihner, George	G	6-4	260	4/27/55	4	Penn State	Pittsburgh, Pa.	Carlisle, Pa.	3
82	Renfro, Mike	WR	6-0	184	6/19/55	6	Texas Christian	Fort Worth, Tex.	Missouri City, Tex.	9
53	†Riley, Avon	LB	6-3	219	2/10/59	3	UCLA	Savannah, Ga.	Savannah, Ga.	9
85	Roaches, Carl	KR-WR	5-8	170	10/2/53	4	Texas A&M	Houston, Tex.	Houston, Tex.	9
62	Schuhmacher, John	T	6-3	269	9/23/55	4	Southern California	Salem, Ore.	Missouri City, Tex.	9
90	Skaugstad, Daryle	DE	6-5	268	4/8/57	3	California	Des Moines, Wash.	Missouri City, Tex.	9
83	Smith, Tim	WR	6-2	202	3/20/57	4	Nebraska	Tucson, Ariz.	Stafford, Tex.	9
67	Stensrud, Mike	NT	6-5	290	2/19/56	5	Iowa State	Lake Mills, Iowa	Lake Mills, Iowa	9
70	Taylor, Malcolm	DE	6-6	288	6/20/60	2	Tennessee State	Crystal Springs, Md.	Columbia, Tenn.	9
28	Thomaselli, Rich	RB	6-1	196	2/26/57	3	West Virginia Wesleyan	Fallansbee, W. Va.	Houston, Tex.	9
51	Thompson, Ted	LB	6-1	229	1/17/53	9	Southern Methodist	Atlanta, Tex.	Missouri City, Tex.	9
76	Towns, Morris	T	6-4	261	1/10/54	7	Missouri	St. Louis, Mo.	Houston, Tex.	9
20	Tullis, Willie	CB-KR	6-0	190	4/5/58	3	Troy State	Newville, Ala.	Houston, Tex.	9
68	†Williams, Ralph	T	6-3	276	3/27/58	2	Southern	Monroe, La.	West Monroe, La.	7
33	Wilson, J.C.	CB	6-0	178	3/11/56	6	Pittsburgh	Cleveland, Ohio	Houston, Tex.	7

* Burrough missed '82 season due to injury; James played 2 games with Detroit, 5 with Houston in '82; Luck active for 9 games, but did not play; Manning played 1 game with New Orleans, 6 with Houston in '82.

†Option playout; subject to developments.

Traded—Tight end Tim Wilson to Los Angeles Raiders.

Also played with Oilers in '82—LB John Corker (3 games), P Cliff Parsley (4), CB Greg Stemrick (8), LB Ted Washington (9).

COACHING STAFF

Head Coach, Ed Biles

Pro Career: Named head coach on January 2, 1981. Starting third year as head coach of the Oilers. Posted 7-9 record in 1981 and 1-8 record in 1982. Joined Oilers in 1974 as defensive backfield coach under Sid Gillman. Helped transform NFL's twenty-sixth ranked defense in terms of points allowed in 1973 to fifth place ranking in 1975 (226). Became Oilers defensive coordinator in 1975. Broke into professional coaching ranks as an assistant coach with New Orleans in 1969 before joining the New York Jets in 1971. No pro playing experience.

Background: Quarterback at Miami, Ohio 1949-52. College assistant coach at Xavier, Ohio 1957-60. Head coach at Xavier 1961-68.

Personal: Born October 18, 1931, Cincinnati, Ohio. Ed and wife, Jackie, live in Missouri City, Texas, and have four children—Jim, Jay, Mike, and Sharon.

ASSISTANT COACHES

Bill Allerheiligen, strength and conditioning; born February 10, 1951 Concordia, Kan., lives in Houston. College coach: Nebraska 1977-78, Kansas State 1979-80, Notre Dame 1981. Pro coach: Oilers since 1982.

Andy Bourgeois, receivers; born March 29, 1938 New Orleans, lives in Missouri City, Tex. Defensive back Louisiana State 1958-60. No pro playing experience. College coach: Tulane 1970, Texas Christian 1971-72. Pro coach: Oilers since 1973.

Kay Dalton, offensive coordinator; born May 4, 1938 Moab, Utah, lives in Houston. Tight end Colorado State 1950-54. No pro playing experience. College coach: Trinidad State 1958-60, Western State, Colo. 1961-65, Colorado 1971-72. Pro coach: Montreal Alouettes (CFL) 1966-69 (head coach 1967-69), British Columbia Lions (CFL) 1970, Denver Broncos 1973-76, Buffalo Bills 1977, Kansas City Chiefs 1978-82, first year with Oilers.

Ken Houston, defensive backfield, born November 12, 1944 Lufton, Tex., lives in Kingwood, Tex. Linebacker Prairie View A&M 1962-66. Pro defensive back Houston Oilers 1967-72, Washington Redskins 1973-80. Pro Coach: Joined Oilers in 1982.

Elijah Pitts, running backs; born February 3, 1938 Mayflower, Ark., lives in Stafford, Tex. Running back Philander Smith 1957-60. Pro running back Green Bay Packers 1961-69, 1971, Los Angeles Rams 1970, New Orleans Saints 1970. Pro coach: Los Angeles Rams 1974-77, Buffalo Bills 1978-80, Oilers since 1981.

Dick Selcer, linebackers; born August 22, 1937 Cincinnati, Ohio, lives in Missouri City, Tex. Running back Notre Dame 1955-58. No pro playing experience. College coach: Xavier, Ohio 1962-64, 1970-71 (head coach), Cincinnati 1965-66, Brown 1967-69, Wisconsin 1972-74, Kansas State 1975-77, Southwestern Louisiana 1978-80. Pro coach: Joined Oilers in 1981.

Ralph Staub, defensive line; born April 11, 1928 Cincinnati, Ohio, lives in Missouri City, Tex. Offensive-defensive end Cincinnati. No pro playing experience. College coach: Cincinnati 1967-69, Northwestern 1969-70, Ohio State 1970-76, Cincinnati (head coach) 1977-80. Pro coach: Joined Oilers in 1982.

Chuck Studley, defensive coordinator; born January 17, 1929 Maywood, Ill., lives in Houston. Guard Illinois 1949-51. No pro playing experience. College coach: Massachusetts 1960, Cincinnati 1961-66. Pro coach: Cincinnati Bengals 1969-78, San Francisco 49ers 1979-82, first year with Oilers.

Bill Walsh, offensive line; born September 8, 1927 Phillipsburg, N.J., lives in Houston, Tex. Center Notre Dame 1945-48. Pro center: Pittsburgh Steelers 1949-54. College coach: Notre Dame 1955-58, Kansas State 1959. Pro coach: Kansas City Chiefs 1960-74, Atlanta Falcons 1975-82, first year with Oilers.

HOUSTON OILERS 1983 FIRST-YEAR ROSTER

Name	Pos.	Ht.	Wt.	Birth-date	College	Birthplace	Residence	How Acq.
Baxter, Joel	K	5-10	170	1/17/61	Rice	Miami, Fla.	Miami, Fla.	FA
Blair, Darren	CB	6-1	175	7/8/61	Northeast Missouri	Warren, Ohio	Kansas City, Mo.	FA
Boles, Anthony	LB	6-1	220	12/14/60	Louisiana Tech	Houston, Tex.	Ruston, La.	FA
Bostic, Keith	S	6-1	209	1/17/61	Michigan	Ann Arbor, Mich.	Detroit, Mich.	D2a
Boucher, Scott	G	6-2	250	9/15/58	Northeast Louisiana	Houston, Tex.	Houston, Tex.	FA
Brown, Steve	CB	5-11	178	5/20/60	Oregon	Sacramento, Calif.	Sacramento, Calif.	D3b
Cook, Donald	S	6-0	200	1/28/61	E. Tennessee State	Florence, Ala.	Florence, Ala.	FA
Davis, James	WR	5-9	165	1/8/61	Ft. Hays State	Liberty, Tex.	Cleveland, Tex.	FA
Dressel, Chris	TE	6-4	230	2/7/61	Stanford	Placentia, Calif.	Stanford, Calif.	D3a
Engel, Dennis	G	6-2	260	5/16/61	Stanford	Augusta, Ga.	Stanford, Calif.	FA
Foster, Jerome	NT	6-2	268	7/25/60	Ohio State	Detroit, Mich.	Detroit, Mich.	D5a
Frye, Philip	RB	5-11	195	12/20/58	Cal Lutheran	Washington, D.C.	Thousand Oaks, Calif.	FA
Grimes, Bobby	G	6-3	255	11/9/59	Houston	Colorado City, Tex.	Houston, Tex.	FA
Hasselberg, Sven	LB	6-1	235	4/21/58	Cal Poly-SLO	Los Angeles, Calif.	Redondo Beach, Calif.	FA
Haworth, Steve	S	5-11	189	9/16/61	Oklahoma	Manila, Philippines	Durant, Okla.	D6
Hill, Greg	CB	6-1	194	2/12/61	Oklahoma State	Orange, Tex.	Orange, Tex.	D4
Jackson, Victor	CB	5-9	180	8/26/61	Angelo State	Dallas, Tex.	Dallas, Tex.	FA
Joiner, Tim	LB	6-4	230	1/7/61	Louisiana State	Los Angeles, Calif.	Baton Rouge, La.	D3
Kader, Joe	LB	6-4	225	11/10/59	Louisville	Cleveland, Ohio	Seven Hills, Ohio	FA
Kidd, Billy	C	6-3	255	11/28/59	Houston	Dallas, Tex.	Keller, Tex.	FA
Kjergaard, David	DE	6-4	238	2/24/61	Concordia	Enid, Okla.	Covington, Okla.	FA
Martin, Donald	G	6-2	275	4/5/61	Rice	Brownsville, Tex.	Houston, Tex.	FA
Matthews, Bruce	T	6-4	276	8/8/61	Southern California	Arcadia, Calif.	Los Angeles, Calif.	D1
McCloskey, Mike	TE	6-5	244	2/2/61	Penn State	Philadelphia, Pa.	Philadelphia, Pa.	D4a
Meadows, Darryl	S	6-1	202	2/15/61	Toledo	Cincinnati, Ohio	Cincinnati, Ohio	FA
Mitchell, Michael	CB	5-10	175	10/18/61	Howard Payne	Waco, Tex.	Waco, Tex.	FA
Mitchell, Osby	T	6-5	270	7/13/60	Rice	Houston, Tex.	Houston, Tex.	FA
Moriarty, Larry	RB	6-1	228	4/24/58	Notre Dame	Santa Barbara, Calif.	Goleta, Calif.	D5
Olding, Joseph	NT	6-1	238	12/26/60	Cincinnati	Cincinnati, Ohio	Cincinnati, Ohio	FA
Potter, Kevin	S	5-10	188	12/19/59	Missouri	St. Louis, Mo.	Columbia, Mo.	D9
Salem, Harvey	T	6-6	274	1/15/61	California	Berkeley, Calif.	Oakland, Calif.	D2
Simon, Victor	LB	6-1	219	10/9/59	Southern Methodist	Houston, Tex.	Houston, Tex.	FA
Sochia, Brian	DE	6-3	252	7/21/61	Northwest Oklahoma	Massena, N.Y.	Alva, Okla.	FA
Stiger, Ronnie	WR	6-1	195	11/5/60	Lamar	Queen City, Tex.	Raywood, Tex.	FA
Taylor, Michael	P	6-2	200	12/22/59	Southwest Texas St.	Pasadena, Tex.	Galena Park, Tex.	FA
Thompson, Robert	LB	6-3	221	2/4/60	Michigan	Chicago, Ill.	Blue Island, Ill.	D8
Walls, Herkie	WR-KR	5-8	160	7/18/61	Texas	Garland, Tex.	Dallas, Tex.	D7
Williams, George	S	6-1	193	1/2/59	San Diego State	San Diego, Calif.	San Diego, Calif.	FA
Winship, Rob	DE	6-3	253	5/29/61	Sam Houston State	Houston, Tex.	Houston, Tex.	FA
Wright, Michael	RB	5-9	198	10/4/58	Texas Christian	Ennis, Tex.	Dallas, Tex.	FA

Players who report to an NFL team for the first time are designated on rosters as rookies (R). If a player reported to an NFL training camp in a previous year but was not on the active squad for three or more regular season or postseason games, he is listed on the first-year roster and designated by a (1). Thereafter, a player who is on the active squad for three or more regular season or postseason games is credited with an additional year of playing experience.

NOTES

_____
_____
_____
_____
_____
_____
_____
_____
_____
_____
_____
_____
_____

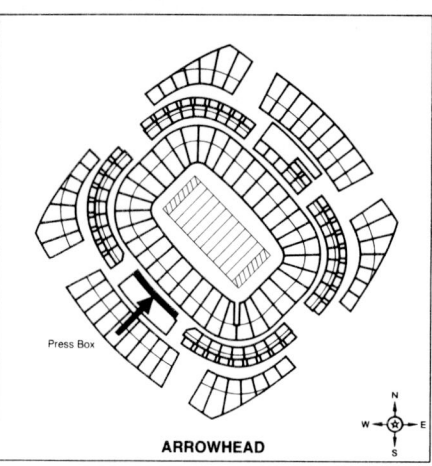

Press Box

ARROWHEAD

N
W—E
S

Kansas City Chiefs

American Football Conference
Western Division

Team Colors: Red, Gold, and White

One Arrowhead Drive
Kansas City, Missouri 64129
Telephone: (816) 924-9300

Club Officials
Owner: Lamar Hunt
President: Jack Steadman
Vice President and General Manager: Jim Schaaf
Director of Player Personnel: Les Miller
Manager of Administration: Don Steadman
Treasurer: Randy Cooper
Secretary: Jim Seigfried
Stadium Manager: Bob Wachter
Ticket Manager: Joe Mazza
Public Relations Director: Bob Sprenger
Assistant Director of Public Relations: Gary Heise
Promotions Director: Russ Cline
Promotions Manager: Mitch Wheeler
Director of Sales: David Smith
Trainer: Wayne Rudy
Assistant Trainer: Dave Kendall
Equipment Coordinator: Jon Phillips

Stadium: Arrowhead Stadium • **Capacity:** 78,067
One Arrowhead Drive
Kansas City, Missouri 64129

Playing Surface: Tartan Turf

Training Camp: William Jewell College
Liberty, Missouri 64068

1983 SCHEDULE

Preseason
Aug. 6	at Cincinnati	7:00
Aug. 13	**Detroit**	7:30
Aug. 20	**St. Louis**	7:30
Aug. 27	at Chicago	6:00

Regular Season
Sept. 4	**Seattle**	3:00
Sept. 12	**San Diego** (Monday)	8:00
Sept. 18	at Washington	1:00
Sept. 25	at Miami	1:00
Oct. 2	**St. Louis**	3:00
Oct. 9	at Los Angeles Raiders	1:00
Oct. 16	**New York Giants**	3:00
Oct. 23	at Houston	12:00
Oct. 30	at Denver	2:00
Nov. 6	**Los Angeles Raiders**	12:00
Nov. 13	**Cincinnati**	12:00
Nov. 20	at Dallas	3:00
Nov. 27	at Seattle	1:00
Dec. 4	**Buffalo**	12:00
Dec. 11	at San Diego	1:00
Dec. 18	**Denver**	12:00

1982 TEAM STATISTICS

	Kansas City	Opp.
Total First Downs	163	170
Rushing	71	69
Passing	79	92
Penalty	13	9
Third Down Efficiency	48/126	65/123
Third Down Percentage	38.1	52.8
Total Net Yards	2498	2732
Total Offensive Plays	573	557
Avg. Gain per Play	4.4	4.9
Avg. Gain per Game	277.6	303.6
Net Yards Rushing	943	1065
Total Rushing Plays	269	280
Avg. Gain per Rush	3.5	3.8
Avg. Gain Rushing per Game	104.8	118.3
Net Yards Passing	1555	1667
Lost Attempting to Pass	40/309	15/120
Gross Yards Passing	1864	1787
Attempts/Completions	264/145	262/155
Percent Completed	54.9	59.2
Had Intercepted	8	12
Avg. Net Passing per Game	172.8	185.2
Punts/Avg.	38/40.5	37/39.7
Punt Returns/Avg.	15/8.6	22/15.4
Kickoff Returns/Avg.	34/21.3	42/18.9
Interceptions/Avg. Ret.	12/17.3	8/22.8
Penalties/Yards	43/372	60/486
Fumbles/Ball Lost	13/4	23/10
Total Points	176	184
Avg. Points per Game	19.6	20.4
Touchdowns	17	22
Rushing	3	7
Passing	10	12
Returns and Recoveries	4	3
Field Goals	19/24	10/14
Conversions	17/17	20/22
Safeties	0	1
Avg. Time of Possession	30:11	29:49

1982 TEAM RECORD

Preseason (2-1-1)

Kansas City		Opponents
26	*Cincinnati	20
3	New Orleans	6
17	*Miami (OT)	17
10	St. Louis	6
56		49

Regular Season (3-6)

Kansas City		Opponents	Att.
9	Buffalo	14	79,306
19	*San Diego	12	60,514
17	New Orleans	27	39,341
14	Los Angeles Rams	20	45,793
14	Pittsburgh	35	52,090
16	*Los Angeles Raiders	21	26,307
37	Denver	16	74,192
13	*San Francisco	26	24,319
37	*New York Jets	13	11,902
176		184	413,764

*Home Game   (OT) Overtime

Score by Periods

Kansas City	33	63	16	64	—	176
Opponents	40	55	31	58	—	184

Attendance

Home 123,042   Away 290,722   Total 413,764
Single game home record, 82,094 (11-5-72)
Single season home record, 509,291 (1972)

1982 INDIVIDUAL STATISTICS

Rushing

	Att	Yds	Avg	LG	TD
Delaney	95	380	4.0	36	0
B. Jackson	86	243	2.8	18	3
Hadnot	46	172	3.7	25	0
Fuller	10	56	5.6	12	0
Kenney	13	40	3.1	12	0
Marshall	3	25	8.3	16	0
Bledsoe	10	20	2.0	5	0
Thompson	4	7	1.8	4	0
Gaines	1	0	0.0	0	0
Studdard	1	0	0.0	0	0
Kansas City	269	943	3.5	36	3
Opponents	280	1065	3.8	24	7

Field Goal Success

Distance	1-19	20-29	30-39	40-49	50 Over
Made-Att.	2-2	4-4	5-5	8-10	0-3

Passing

	Att	Comp	Pct	Yds	TD	Int	Tkld	Rate
Kenney	169	95	56.2	1192	7	6	23/166	77.0
Fuller	93	49	52.7	665	3	2	17/143	77.3
Gagliano	1	1	100.0	7	0	0	0/0	—
Marshall	1	0	0.0	0	0	0	0/0	—
Kansas City	264	145	54.9	1864	10	8	40/309	
Opponents	262	155	59.2	1787	12	12	15/120	

Receiving

	No	Yds	Avg	LG	TD
Marshall	40	549	13.7	44t	3
Carson	27	494	18.3	51	2
Dixon	18	251	13.9	37	2
Hadnot	14	96	6.9	28	0
Delaney	11	53	4.8	13	0
Smith	10	168	16.8	51	1
Scott	8	49	6.1	13	1
Hancock	7	116	16.6	41t	1
B. Jackson	5	41	8.2	13	0
Rome	2	25	12.5	16	0
Gaines	2	17	8.5	10	0
Bledsoe	1	5	5.0	5	0
Kansas City	145	1864	12.9	51	10
Opponents	155	1787	11.5	74t	12

Interceptions

	No	Yds	Avg	LG	TD
Harris	3	66	22.0	56t	1
Barbaro	3	48	16.0	43t	1
Green	2	42	21.0	42t	1
Howard	2	10	5.0	5	0
Burruss	1	25	25.0	25	0
Roquemore	1	17	17.0	17	0
Kansas City	12	208	17.3	56t	3
Opponents	8	182	22.8	83t	1

Punting

	No	Yds	Avg	In 20	LG
Gossett	33	1366	41.4	6	56
deBruijn	5	174	34.8	1	56
Kansas City	38	1540	40.5	7	56
Opponents	37	1468	39.7	6	66

Punt Returns

	No	FC	Yds	Avg	LG	TD
Hancock	12	5	103	8.6	30	0
Smith	3	1	26	8.7	16	0
Kansas City	15	6	129	8.6	30	0
Opponents	22	3	338	15.4	78t	2

Kickoff Returns

	No	Yds	Avg	LG	TD
Hancock	27	609	22.6	68	0
Thompson	2	41	20.5	23	0
Roquemore	2	25	12.5	18	0
Cherry	1	39	39.0	39	0
Mangiero	1	8	8.0	8	0
Lindstrom	1	1	1.0	1	0
Kansas City	34	723	21.3	68	0
Opponents	42	794	18.9	75	0

Scoring

	TD	TD R	TD P	TD Rt	PAT	FG	TP
Lowery					17/17	19/24	74
B. Jackson	3	3	0	0			18
Marshall	3	0	3	0			18
Carson	2	0	2	0			12
Dixon	2	0	2	0			12
Barbaro	1	0	0	1			6
Green	1	0	0	1			6
Hancock	1	0	1	0			6
Harris	1	0	0	1			6
Klug	1	0	0	1			6
Scott	1	0	1	0			6
Smith	1	0	1	0			6
Kansas City	17	3	10	4	17/17	19/24	176
Opponents	22	7	12	3	20/22	10/14	184

Sacks

Blanton 1, Howard 3, C. Jackson 1, Kremer, Lindstrom 3, Mangiero 1, Parrish 1, Still 4.

FIRST PLAYERS SELECTED

Year	Player, College, Position
1960	Don Meredith, Southern Methodist, QB
1961	E.J. Holub, Texas Tech, C
1962	Ronnie Bull, Baylor, RB
1963	Buck Buchanan, Grambling, DT
1964	Pete Beathard, Southern California, QB
1965	Gale Sayers, Kansas, RB
1966	Aaron Brown, Minnesota, DE
1967	Gene Trosch, Miami, DE-DT
1968	Mo Moorman, Texas A&M, G
1969	Jim Marsalis, Tennessee State, CB
1970	Sid Smith, Southern California, T
1971	Elmo Wright, Houston, WR
1972	Jeff Kinney, Nebraska, RB
1973	Gary Butler, Rice, TE (2)
1974	Woody Green, Arizona State, RB
1975	Elmore Stephens, Kentucky, TE (2)
1976	Rod Walters, Iowa, G
1977	Gary Green, Baylor, DB
1978	Art Still, Kentucky, DE
1979	Mike Bell, Colorado State, DE
1980	Brad Budde, Southern California, G
1981	Willie Scott, South Carolina, TE
1982	Anthony Hancock, Tennessee, WR
1983	Todd Blackledge, Penn State, QB

CHIEFS COACHING HISTORY

Dallas Texans 1960-62
(172-151-10)

1960-74	Hank Stram	129-79-10
1975-77	Paul Wiggin*	11-24-0
1977	Tom Bettis	1-6-0
1978-82	Marv Levy	31-42-0

*Released after seven games in 1977

KANSAS CITY CHIEFS 1983 VETERAN ROSTER

No.	Name	Pos.	Ht.	Wt.	Birth-date	NFL Exp.	College	Birthplace	Residence	Games in '82
76	Acker, Bill	NT-DE	6-3	255	11/7/56	4	Texas	Freer, Tex.	Freer, Tex.	3
26	†Barbaro, Gary	S	6-4	210	2/11/54	8	Nicholls State	New Orleans, La.	Metairie, La.	9
85	Beckman, Ed	TE	6-4	239	1/2/55	7	Florida State	Key West, Fla.	Kansas City, Mo.	9
99	Bell, Mike	DE	6-4	260	8/30/57	4	Colorado State	Wichita, Kan.	Overland Park, Kan.	6
57	Blanton, Jerry	LB	6-1	236	12/20/56	5	Kentucky	Toledo, Ohio	Toledo, Ohio	9
45	Bryant, Trent	CB	5-10	178	8/14/57	3	Arkansas	Arkadelphia, Ark.	Arkadelphia, Ark.	9
66	Budde, Brad	G	6-4	260	5/9/58	4	Southern California	Detroit, Mich.	Laguna Beach, Calif.	9
34	Burruss, Lloyd	S	6-0	202	10/31/57	3	Maryland	Charlottesville, Va.	Charlottesville, Va.	9
88	Carson, Carlos	WR-KR	5-11	174	12/28/58	4	Louisiana State	Lake Worth, Fla.	Grandview, Mo.	9
20	†Cherry, Deron	S	5-11	190	9/12/59	3	Rutgers	Riverside, N.J.	Palmyra, N.J.	7
41	Christopher, Herb	S	5-10	198	4/7/54	5	Morris Brown	Thomasville, Ga.	College Park, Ga.	9
65	Condon, Tom	G	6-3	275	10/26/52	10	Boston College	Derby, Conn.	Kansas City, Mo.	7
50	Daniels, Calvin	LB	6-3	236	12/26/58	2	North Carolina	Morehead City, N.C.	Kansas City, Mo.	9
84	†Dixon, Al	TE	6-5	238	4/5/54	7	Iowa State	Drew, Miss.	Plainfield, N.J.	8
4	Fuller, Steve	QB	6-4	198	1/5/57	5	Clemson	Enid, Okla.	Spartanburg, S.C.	9
11	Gagliano, Bob	QB	6-3	195	9/5/58	3	Utah State	Los Angeles, Calif.	Glendale, Calif.	1
21	Gaines, Clark	RB	6-1	214	2/1/54	7	Wake Forest	Elberton, Ga.	Freeport, N.Y.	9
77	Getty, Charlie	T	6-4	270	7/24/52	10	Penn State	Paterson, N.J.	Kansas City, Mo.	9
7	Gossett, Jeff	P	6-2	197	1/25/57	3	Eastern Illinois	Charleston, Ill.	Charleston, Ill.	8
24	Green, Gary	CB	5-11	191	10/2/55	7	Baylor	San Antonio, Tex.	San Antonio, Tex.	9
48	Hadnot, James	RB	6-2	245	7/11/57	4	Texas Tech	Jasper, Tex.	Lubbock, Tex.	9
82	Hancock, Anthony	WR-KR	6-0	187	6/10/60	2	Tennessee	Cleveland, Ohio	Kansas City, Mo.	9
44	Harris, Eric	CB	6-3	202	8/11/55	4	Memphis State	Memphis, Tenn.	Memphis, Tenn.	8
56	Haynes, Louis	LB	6-0	227	1/17/60	2	North Texas State	New Orleans, La.	New Orleans, La.	6
60	Herkenhoff, Matt	T	6-4	272	4/2/51	8	Minnesota	Melrose, Minn.	Kansas City, Mo.	9
52	Howard, Thomas	LB	6-2	215	8/18/54	7	Texas Tech	Lubbock, Tex.	Lubbock, Tex.	9
43	Jackson, Billy	RB	5-10	215	9/13/59	3	Alabama	Phenix City, Ala.	Phenix City, Ala.	9
51	Jackson, Charles	LB	6-2	222	3/22/55	6	Washington	Berkeley, Calif.	Fairway, Kan.	9
9	Kenney, Bill	QB	6-4	211	1/20/55	5	Northern Colorado	San Francisco, Calif.	Lee's Summit, Mo.	7
55	Klug, Dave	LB	6-4	230	5/17/58	3	Concordia, Minn.	Litchfield, Minn.	Litchfield, Minn.	9
91	Kremer, Ken	NT	6-4	252	7/16/57	5	Ball State	Hammond, Ind.	Parkville, Mo.	9
71	†Lindstrom, Dave	DE	6-6	255	11/16/54	6	Boston University	Cambridge, Mass.	Overland Park, Kan.	9
8	Lowery, Nick	K	6-4	189	5/27/56	4	Dartmouth	Munich, Germany	McLean, Va.	9
74	Mangiero, Dino	NT-DE	6-2	264	12/19/58	4	Rutgers	New York, N.Y.	Staten Island, N.Y.	6
89	†Marshall, Henry	WR	6-2	220	8/9/54	8	Missouri	Broxton, Ga.	Kansas City, Mo.	9
53	Olenchalk, John	C-LB	6-0	225	11/27/55	2	Stanford	Stockton, Calif.	Danville, Calif.	9
61	Parrish, Don	NT-DE	6-2	255	4/6/55	6	Pittsburgh	Tallahassee, Fla.	Tallahassee, Fla.	8
38	Roquemore, Durwood	S	6-1	180	1/19/60	2	Texas A&I	Dallas, Tex.	Dallas, Tex.	9
70	Rourke, Jim	T-G	6-5	263	2/10/57	4	Boston College	Weymouth, Mass.	Abington, Mass.	9
81	Scott, Willie	TE	6-4	245	2/13/59	3	South Carolina	Newberry, S.C.	Newberry, S.C.	9
73	Simmons, Bob	G	6-4	255	7/7/54	7	Texas	Temple, Tex.	Kansas City, Mo.	8
86	Smith, J.T.	WR-KR	6-2	185	10/29/55	6	North Texas State	Leonard, Tex.	Kansas City, Mo.	5
59	Spani, Gary	LB	6-2	228	1/9/56	6	Kansas State	Satanta, Kan.	Lee's Summit, Mo.	8
69	Steinfeld, Al	C-T	6-4	256	10/28/58	2	C.W. Post	Brooklyn, N.Y.	Brooklyn, N.Y.	7
67	Still, Art	DE	6-7	252	12/5/55	6	Kentucky	Camden, N.J.	Kansas City, Mo.	9
64	Studdard, Les	C	6-4	260	12/14/58	2	Texas	El Paso, Tex.	Austin, Tex.	9
39	Thompson, Del	RB	6-0	203	2/21/58	2	Texas-El Paso	Kermit, Tex.	Hamilton, Tex.	6

†Option playout; subject to developments.

Retired—Jack Rudney, 14-year center, 7 games in '82.

Also played with Chiefs in '82—RB Curtis Bledsoe (3 games), P Case deBruijn (1), RB Joe Delaney (8), WR Stan Rome (7).

COACHING STAFF

Head Coach,
John Mackovic

Pro Career: Begins first season as Chiefs head coach. Comes to the Chiefs after serving as quarterback coach with the Dallas Cowboys in 1981-82. No pro playing experience.

Background: Played quarterback for Wake Forest 1961-64. Was freshman coach at Army in 1967-68 before coaching at San Jose State as offensive coordinator 1969-70. Returned to Army as an assistant 1971-72, then to Arizona 1973-76, and Purdue 1977. Became head coach at Wake Forest 1978-80 before going to the Cowboys.

Personal: Born October 1, 1943, Barberton, Ohio. John and his wife, Arlene, live in Kansas City, and have two children—Aimee and John III.

ASSISTANT COACHES

Bud Carson, defensive coordinator-defensive backs; born April 28, 1931, Brackenridge, Pa., lives in Kansas City. Defensive back North Carolina 1948-52. No pro playing experience. College coach: North Carolina 1957-64, South Carolina 1965, Georgia Tech 1966-71 (head coach). Pro coach: Pittsburgh Steelers 1972-77, Los Angeles Rams 1978-81, Baltimore Colts 1982, first year with Chiefs.

Walt Corey, defensive line; born May 9, 1938, Latrobe, Pa., lives in Kansas City. Defensive end Miami, Fla. 1957-59. Pro linebacker Kansas City Chiefs 1960-66. College coach: Utah State 1967-69, Miami 1970-71. Pro coach: Kansas City Chiefs 1971-74, Cleveland Browns 1975-77, rejoined Chiefs in 1978.

Dan Daniel, inside linebackers; born April 10, 1933, Huron, S.D., lives in Kansas City. Quarterback-defensive back Huron College 1958-62. No pro playing experience. College coach: MacAlister College 1965, Colorado State 1966-69, Navy 1970, Wyoming 1971, Houston 1972-77. Pro coach: Edmonton Eskimoes (CFL) 1978-81, Calgary Stampeders (CFL) 1982, first year with Chiefs.

Doug Graber, defensive backs and defensive quality control; born September 26, 1944, Detroit, Mich., lives in Kansas City. Defensive back Wayne State 1963-66. No pro playing experience. College coach: Michigan Tech 1969-71, Eastern Michigan 1972-75, Ball State 1976-77, Wisconsin 1978-81, Montana State 1982 (head coach). Pro coach: First year with the Chiefs.

J.D. Helm, offensive assistant and quality control; born December 27, 1940, El Dorado Springs, Mo., lives in Overland Park, Kan. Running back Kansas 1959-60. No pro playing experience. College coach: Brigham Young 1969-75. Pro coach: Joined Chiefs in 1976.

C.T. Hewgley, offensive and defensive lines-coordinator of strength and conditioning program; born August 22, 1925, Nashville, Tenn., lives in Kansas City. Tackle Wyoming 1947-50. No pro playing experience. College coach: Miami 1968-70, Wyoming 1971-73, Nebraska-Omaha 1974 (head coach), Michigan State 1976-79, Arizona State 1980-82. Pro coach: First year with the Chiefs.

Rod Humenuik, offensive line-running game; born June 17, 1938, Detroit, Mich., lives in Kansas City. Guard Southern California 1956-58. Pro guard Winnipeg Blue Bombers (CFL) 1960-62. College coach: Fullerton, Calif., J.C. 1964-65, Southern California 1966-70, Cal State-Northridge 1971-72 (head coach). Pro coach: Toronto Argonauts (CFL) 1973-74, Cleveland Browns 1975-82, first year with Chiefs.

Pete McCulley, quarterbacks; born November 29, 1931, Franklin, Miss., lives in Kansas City. Quarterback Louisiana Tech 1954-56. No pro playing experience. College coach: Stephen F. Austin 1959, Houston 1960-61, Baylor 1963-69, Navy 1970-72. Pro coach: Baltimore Colts 1973-75, Washington Redskins 1976-77, San Francisco 49ers 1978 (head coach nine games), New York Jets 1979-82, first year with Chiefs.

Willie Peete, offensive backs; born September 14, 1937, Mesa, Ariz., lives in Kansas City. Wide receiver Arizona 1956-59. No pro playing experience. College coach: Arizona 1970-82. Pro coach: First year with the Chiefs.

Jim Vechiarella, outside linebackers-special teams; born February 20, 1937, Youngstown, Ohio, lives in Kansas City. Linebacker Youngstown State 1955-57. No pro playing experience. College coach: Youngstown State 1964-74, Southern Illinois 1976-77, Tulane 1978-80. Pro coach: Charlotte Hornets (WFL) 1975, Los Angeles Rams 1980-82, first year with Chiefs.

Richard Williamson, receivers; born April 13, 1941, Fort Deposit, Ala., lives in Kansas City. Wide receiver Alabama 1959-62. No pro playing experience. College coach: Arkansas 1968-69, 1972-74, Alabama 1963-67, 1970-71, Memphis State 1975-80. Pro coach: First year with the Chiefs.

KANSAS CITY CHIEFS 1983 FIRST-YEAR ROSTER

Name	Pos.	Ht.	Wt.	Birth-date	College	Birthplace	Residence	How Acq.
Abrams, Willie	RB	5-10	201	6/29/58	Bethune-Cookman	Columbia, S.C.	Columbia, S.C.	FA
Arnold, Jim	P	6-2	212	1/31/61	Vanderbilt	Dalton, Ga.	Dalton, Ga.	D5
Blackledge, Todd	QB	6-3	225	2/25/61	Penn State	Canton, Ohio	Lee-Summit, Mo.	D1
Blakely, Robert (1)	WR	6-0	195	9/20/59	North Dakota State	St. Paul, Minn.	St. Paul, Minn.	FA
Fisher, Marcus (1)	CB	5-9	183	3/8/59	Montana	Detroit, Mich.	Detroit, Mich.	FA
Gardner, Ellis	T	6-4	263	9/16/61	Georgia Tech	Chattanooga, Tenn.	Signal Mtn., Tenn.	D6
Jackson, Dwayne	DE	6-3	247	6/27/60	South Carolina State	Atlanta, Ga.	Atlanta, Ga.	D11
Jones, Kenny	T	6-4	251	9/12/60	Tennessee	Nashville, Tenn.	Knoxville, Tenn.	D12
Lewis, Albert	CB	6-2	190	10/6/60	Grambling	Mansfield, La.	Mansfield, La.	D3
Lingner, Adam	C	6-4	240	11/2/60	Illinois	Indianapolis, Ind.	Rock Island, Ill.	D9
Lutz, David	T	6-5	280	12/30/59	Georgia Tech	Monroe, N.C.	Atlanta, Ga.	D2
McNorton, Kyle (1)	LB	6-1	220	5/20/60	Kansas	Topeka, Kan.	Topeka, Kan.	FA
Posey, Daryl	RB	6-0	209	5/13/60	Mississippi College	Biloxi, Miss.	Biloxi, Miss.	D7a
Shumate, Mark	NT	6-4	260	3/30/60	Wisconsin	Madison, Wis.	Madison, Wis.	D10
Smith, Greg (1)	NT	6-2	275	10/22/59	Kansas	Chicago, Ill.	Lena, Miss.	FA
Thomas, Ken	RB	5-9	211	2/11/60	San Jose State	Hanford, Calif.	San Jose, Calif.	D7
Walker, James (1)	LB	6-1	250	12/9/58	Kansas State	Wichita, Kan.	Wichita, Kan.	FA
Washington, Ron (1)	WR	5-11	195	1/6/58	Arizona State	Phoenix, Ariz.	Mesa, Ariz.	FA
Washington, Tim (1)	CB	5-9	184	11/7/59	Fresno State	Fresno, Calif.	Fresno, Calif.	FA
Wetzel, Ron	TE	6-5	242	11/10/60	Arizona State	Pittsburgh, Pa.	Pittsburgh, Pa.	D4

Players who report to an NFL team for the first time are designated on rosters as rookies (R). If a player reported to an NFL training camp in a previous year but was not on the active squad for three or more regular season or postseason games, he is listed on the first-year roster and designated by a (1). Thereafter, a player who is on the active squad for three or more regular season or postseason games is credited with an additional year of playing experience.

NOTES

_____

_____

_____

_____

_____

_____

_____

_____

_____

_____

_____

_____

_____

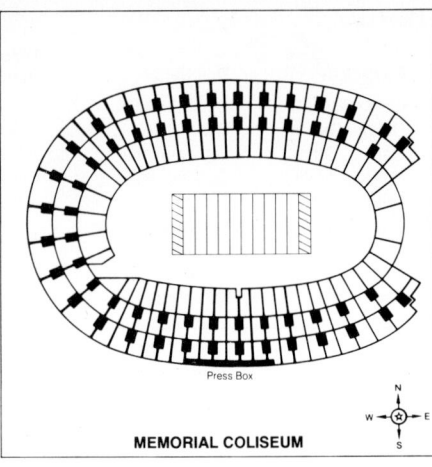

Press Box

MEMORIAL COLISEUM

Los Angeles Raiders

**American Football Conference
Western Division**

Team Colors: Silver and Black

**332 Center Street
El Segundo, California 90245
Telephone: (213) 322-3451**

Club Officials
General Partners: Al Davis, E. W. McGah
Managing General Partner: Al Davis
Executive Assistant: Al LoCasale
Player Personnel: Ron Wolf
Business Manager: Ken LaRue
Senior Administrators: Tom Grimes, Irv Kaze
Publications Director: Bill Glazier
Marketing/Promotions: Gil Hernandez, Mike Ornstein
Ticket Operations: Peter Eiges
Comptroller: Dee Rutledge
Trainers: George Anderson, H. Rod Martin
Equipment Manager: Richard Romanski

Stadium: Los Angeles Memorial Coliseum •
  Capacity: 92,498
  3911 South Figueroa Street
  Los Angeles, California 90037

Playing Surface: Grass

Training Camp: El Rancho Tropicana
  Santa Rosa, California 95401

1983 SCHEDULE

Preseason
Aug. 6	**San Francisco**	6:00
Aug. 13	at New York Jets (Giants Stadium)	8:00
Aug. 20	**Chicago**	8:00
Aug. 26	at Cleveland	8:00

Regular Season
Sept. 4	at Cincinnati	1:00
Sept. 11	**Houston**	1:00
Sept. 19	**Miami** (Monday)	6:00
Sept. 25	at Denver	2:00
Oct. 2	at Washington	1:00
Oct. 9	**Kansas City**	1:00
Oct. 16	at Seattle	1:00
Oct. 23	at Dallas	8:00
Oct. 30	**Seattle**	1:00
Nov. 6	at Kansas City	12:00
Nov. 13	**Denver**	1:00
Nov. 20	at Buffalo	1:00
Nov. 27	**New York Giants**	1:00
Dec. 1	at San Diego (Thursday)	6:00
Dec. 11	**St. Louis**	1:00
Dec. 18	**San Diego**	1:00

1982 TEAM STATISTICS

	L.A. Raiders	Opp.
Total First Downs	175	206
Rushing	65	53
Passing	95	121
Penalty	15	32
Third Down Efficiency	38/115	44/129
Third Down Percentage	33.0	34.1
Total Net Yards	2955	3066
Total Offensive Plays	582	647
Avg. Gain per Play	5.1	4.7
Avg. Gain per Game	328.3	340.7
Net Yards Rushing	1080	778
Total Rushing Plays	292	234
Avg. Gain per Rush	3.7	3.3
Avg. Gain Rushing per Game	120.0	86.4
Net Yards Passing	1875	2288
Lost Attempting to Pass	23/211	38/329
Gross Yards Passing	2086	2617
Attempts/Completions	267/154	375/193
Percent Completed	57.7	51.5
Had Intercepted	15	18
Avg. Net Passing per Game	208.3	254.2
Punts/Avg.	47/39.1	49/38.3
Punt Returns/Avg.	27/7.7	17/4.2
Kickoff Returns/Avg.	36/20.9	43/19.8
Interceptions/Avg. Ret.	18/19.8	15/12.0
Penalties/Yards	86/840	53/588
Fumbles/Ball Lost	22/9	18/11
Total Points	260	200
Avg. Points per Game	28.9	22.2
Touchdowns	33	24
Rushing	15	12
Passing	14	11
Returns and Recoveries	4	1
Field Goals	10/16	11/14
Conversions	32/33	23/24
Safeties	0	0
Avg. Time of Possession	29:52	30:08

1982 TEAM RECORD

Preseason (2-2)

Los Angeles Raiders		Opponents
17	San Francisco	14
16	Detroit	30
24	*Green Bay	3
10	*Cleveland	27
67		74

Regular Season (8-1)

Los Angeles Raiders		Opponents	Att.
23	San Francisco	17	59,748
38	Atlanta	14	54,774
28	*San Diego	24	42,162
17	Cincinnati	31	53,330
28	*Seattle	23	42,170
21	Kansas City	16	26,307
37	*Los Angeles Rams	31	56,646
27	*Denver	10	44,160
41	San Diego	34	51,612
260		200	430,909

*Home Game

Score by Periods

L.A. Raiders	20	113	45	82	—	260
Opponents	51	52	37	60	—	200

Attendance

Home 185,138   Away 245,771   Total 430,909
Single game home record, 74,121 (9-12-73 at Berkeley), 58,843 (12-11-72 at Oakland), 56,646 (12-18-82 at L.A. Coliseum)
Single season home record, 423,838 (1979)

1982 INDIVIDUAL STATISTICS

Rushing

	Att	Yds	Avg	LG	TD
Allen	160	697	4.4	53	11
King	69	264	3.8	21	2
F. Hawkins	27	54	2.0	11	2
Pruitt	4	22	5.5	13	0
Barnwell	2	18	9.0	14	0
Willis	6	15	2.5	5	0
Branch	2	10	5.0	7	0
Plunkett	15	6	0.4	10	0
Taylor	4	3	0.8	2	0
Guy	2	−3	−1.5	7	0
Christensen	1	−6	−6.0	−6	0
L.A. Raiders	292	1080	3.7	53	15
Opponents	234	778	3.3	55	12

Field Goal Success

Distance	1-19	20-29	30-39	40-49	50 Over
Made-Att.	1-1	2-3	4-5	3-5	0-2

Passing

	Att	Comp	Pct	Yds	TD	Int	Tkld	Rate
Plunkett	261	152	58.2	2035	14	15	23/211	77.3
Allen	4	1	25.0	47	0	0	0/0	—
Wilson	2	1	50.0	4	0	0	0/0	—
L.A. Raiders	267	154	57.7	2086	14	15	23/211	
Opponents	375	193	51.5	2617	11	18	38/329	

Receiving

	No	Yds	Avg	LG	TD
Christensen	42	510	12.1	50	4
Allen	38	401	10.6	51t	3
Branch	30	575	19.2	51	4
Barnwell	23	387	16.8	52	0
King	9	57	6.3	20	0
F. Hawkins	7	35	5.0	9	1
Muhammad	3	92	30.7	43	1
Pruitt	2	29	14.5	23	1
L.A. Raiders	154	2086	13.5	52	14
Opponents	193	2617	13.6	50	11

Interceptions

	No	Yds	Avg	LG	TD
Owens	4	56	14.0	35	0
Millen	3	77	25.7	60	0
Martin	3	60	20.0	39t	1
J. Davis	2	107	53.5	55	1
Hayes	2	0	0.0	0	0
M. Davis	1	56	56.0	56t	1
Jackson	1	0	0.0	0	0
McElroy	1	0	0.0	0	0
Watts	1	0	0.0	0	0
L.A. Raiders	18	356	19.8	60	3
Opponents	15	180	12.0	56t	1

Punting

	No	Yds	Avg	In 20	LG
Guy	47	1839	39.1	12	57
L.A. Raiders	47	1839	39.1	12	57
Opponents	49	1878	38.3	9	52

Punt Returns

	No	FC	Yds	Avg	LG	TD
Pruitt	27	7	209	7.7	25	0
L.A. Raiders	27	7	209	7.7	25	0
Opponents	17	13	71	4.2	13	0

Kickoff Returns

	No	Yds	Avg	LG	TD
Pruitt	14	371	26.5	55	0
Montgomery	17	312	18.4	39	0
Hill	2	20	10.0	17	0
Jensen	1	27	27.0	27	0
Millen	1	13	13.0	13	0
Willis	1	11	11.0	11	0
L.A. Raiders	36	754	20.9	55	0
Opponents	43	851	19.8	85	0

Scoring

	TD	TD R	TD P	TD Rt	PAT	FG	TP
Allen	14	11	3	0			84
Bahr					32/33	10/16	62
Branch	4	0	4	0			24
Christensen	4	0	4	0			24
F. Hawkins	3	2	1	0			18
King	2	2	0	0			12
J. Davis	1	0	0	1			6
M. Davis	1	0	0	1			6
Martin	1	0	0	1			6
Muhammad	1	0	1	0			6
Pruitt	1	0	1	0			6
Reese	1	0	0	1			6
L.A. Raiders	33	15	14	4	32/33	10/16	260
Opponents	24	12	11	1	23/24	11/14	200

Sacks

Alzado 7, Barnes 1½, Browning 1, J. Davis 1, M. Davis 2½, Hendricks 7, Kinlaw 1, Long 5½, Martin 1, McKinney 1, Millen 2½, Nelson 1, Reese 1, Vaughan 4, Watts 1.

FIRST PLAYERS SELECTED

Year	Player, College, Position
1960	Dale Hackbart, Wisconsin, CB
1961	Joe Rutgens, Illinois, DT
1962	Roman Gabriel, North Carolina State, QB
1963	George Wilson, Alabama, RB (6)
1964	Tony Lorick, Arizona State, RB
1965	Harry Schuh, Memphis State, T
1966	Rodger Bird, Kentucky, S
1967	Gene Upshaw, Texas A&I, G
1968	Eldridge Dickey, Tennessee State, QB
1969	Art Thoms, Syracuse, DT
1970	Raymond Chester, Morgan State, TE
1971	Jack Tatum, Ohio State, S
1972	Mike Siani, Villanova, WR
1973	Ray Guy, Southern Mississippi, K-P
1974	Henry Lawrence, Florida A&M, T
1975	Neal Colzie, Ohio State, DB
1976	Charles Philyaw, Texas Southern, DT (2)
1977	Mike Davis, Colorado, DB (2)
1978	Dave Browning, Washington, DE (2)
1979	Willie Jones, Florida State, DE (2)
1980	Marc Wilson, Brigham Young, QB
1981	Ted Watts, Texas Tech, DB
1982	Marcus Allen, Southern California, RB
1983	Don Mosebar, Southern California, T

RAIDERS COACHING HISTORY

Oakland 1960-81
(219-121-11)

1960-61	Eddie Erdelatz*	6-10-0
1961-62	Marty Feldman**	2-15-0
1962	Red Conkright	1-8-0
1963-65	Al Davis	23-16-3
1966-68	John Rauch	35-10-1
1969-78	John Madden	112-39-7
1979-82	Tom Flores	40-23-0

*Released after two games in 1961
**Released after five games in 1962

LOS ANGELES RAIDERS 1983 VETERAN ROSTER

No.	Name	Pos.	Ht.	Wt.	Birth-date	NFL Exp.	College	Birthplace	Residence	Games in '82
32	Allen, Marcus	RB	6-2	205	3/22/60	2	Southern California	San Diego, Calif.	San Diego, Calif.	9
77	Alzado, Lyle	DE	6-3	250	4/3/49	13	Yankton	Brooklyn, N.Y.	Brentwood, Calif.	9
10	Bahr, Chris	K	5-10	175	2/3/53	8	Penn State	State College, Pa.	Cincinnati, Ohio	9
56	Barnes, Jeff	LB	6-2	225	3/1/55	7	California	Philadelphia, Pa.	San Leandro, Calif.	9
80	Barnwell, Malcolm	WR	5-11	185	6/28/58	3	Virginia Union	Charleston, S.C.	Charleston, S.C.	9
40	Berns, Rick	RB	6-2	205	2/5/56	4	Nebraska	Okinawa, Japan	Tampa, Fla.	9
21	†Branch, Cliff	WR	5-11	170	8/1/48	12	Colorado	Houston, Tex.	Oakland, Calif.	9
73	Browning, Dave	DE	6-5	245	8/18/56	6	Washington	Spokane, Wash.	Alameda, Calif.	5
81	Burke, Randy	WR	6-2	195	5/26/55	5	Kentucky	Miami, Fla.	Sparks, Md.	0*
85	Chandler, Bob	WR	6-1	180	4/24/49	12	Southern California	Long Beach, Calif.	Whittier, Calif.	2
46	Christensen, Todd	TE-RB	6-3	230	8/3/56	5	Brigham Young	Bellefonte, Pa.	Alameda, Calif.	9
50	Dalby, Dave	C	6-3	250	8/19/50	12	UCLA	Alexandria, Minn.	Castro Valley, Calif.	9
79	Davis, Bruce	T	6-6	280	6/21/56	5	UCLA	Rutherford, N.C.	Daly City, Calif.	9
45	Davis, James	CB	6-0	190	6/12/57	2	Southern	Los Angeles, Calif.	Los Angeles, Calif.	9
36	Davis, Mike	S	6-2	205	4/15/56	6	Colorado	Los Angeles, Calif.	Oakland, Calif.	9
8	†Guy, Ray	P	6-3	195	12/22/49	11	Southern Mississippi	Swainsboro, Ga.	Hattiesburg, Miss.	9
86	Harvey, Marvin	TE	6-3	220	10/17/59	2	Southern Mississippi	Donnasonville, Ga.	Marianna, Fla.	0*
27	Hawkins, Frank	RB	5-9	210	7/3/59	3	Nevada-Reno	Las Vegas, Nev.	Las Vegas, Nev.	9
61	Hawkins, Mike	LB	6-3	245	11/29/55	6	Texas A&I	Bay City, Tex.	Bay City, Tex.	3
37	Hayes, Lester	CB	6-0	200	1/22/55	7	Texas A&M	Houston, Tex.	Alameda, Calif.	9
83	Hendricks, Ted	LB	6-7	230	11/1/47	15	Miami	Guatemala City, Guat.	Orinda, Calif.	9
48	Hill, Kenny	S	6-0	195	7/25/58	3	Yale	Oak Grove, La.	Daly City, Calif.	9
42	Jackson, Monte	CB	5-11	195	7/14/53	9	San Diego State	Sherman, Tex.	San Diego, Calif.	9
31	Jensen, Derrick	RB	6-1	220	4/27/56	5	Texas-Arlington	Waukegan, Ill.	Arlington, Tex.	9
90	Jones, Willie	DE	6-4	250	11/22/57	4	Florida State	Dublin, Ga.	Alameda, Calif.	0*
33	King, Kenny	RB	5-11	205	3/7/57	5	Oklahoma	Clarendon, Tex.	Alameda, Calif.	9
62	Kinlaw, Reggie	NT	6-2	245	1/9/57	4	Oklahoma	Miami, Fla.	Oakland, Calif.	9
70	Lawrence, Henry	T	6-4	270	9/26/51	10	Florida A&M	Danville, Pa.	Palmetto, Fla.	9
75	Long, Howie	DE	6-5	265	1/12/60	3	Villanova	Sommerville, Mass.	Charleston, Mass.	9
60	Marsh, Curt	G	6-5	270	8/25/59	3	Washington	Tacoma, Wash.	Snohomish, Wash.	9
53	Martin, Rod	LB	6-2	215	4/7/54	7	Southern California	Welch, W. Va.	Alameda, Calif.	9
65	Marvin, Mickey	G	6-4	210	10/5/55	7	Tennessee	Hendersonville, N.C.	Etowah, N.C.	9
26	McElroy, Vann	S	6-2	190	1/13/60	2	Baylor	Birmingham, Ala.	Uvalde, Tex.	7
23	McKinney, Odis	S	6-2	190	5/19/57	6	Colorado	Detroit, Mich.	Woodland Hills, Calif.	9
55	Millen, Matt	LB	6-2	255	3/12/58	3	Penn State	Hokendauqua, Pa.	Alameda, Calif.	9
28	Montgomery, Cleotha	RB	5-8	185	7/1/56	3	Abilene Christian	Greenville, Miss.	Greenville, Miss.	9
82	Muhammad, Calvin	WR	5-11	190	12/10/58	2	Texas Southern	Jacksonville, Fla.	San Leandro, Calif.	7
76	Muransky, Ed	T	6-7	280	1/20/60	2	Michigan	Youngstown, Ohio	Youngstown, Ohio	5
51	Nelson, Bob	LB	6-4	235	6/30/53	7	Nebraska	Stillwater, Minn.	Wayzata, Minn.	9
54	Peterson, Cal	LB	6-3	225	10/6/52	8	UCLA	Los Angeles, Calif.	Canoga Park, Calif.	4
16	Plunkett, Jim	QB	6-2	215	12/5/47	13	Stanford	San Jose, Calif.	Atherton, Calif.	9
34	Pruitt, Greg	RB-KR	5-10	190	8/18/51	11	Oklahoma	Houston, Tex.	Shaker Heights, Ohio	9
84	Ramsey, Derrick	TE	6-5	235	12/23/56	6	Kentucky	Hastings, Fla.	San Leandro, Calif.	9
29	Reed, Tony	RB	5-10	190	3/30/55	6	Colorado	San Francisco, Calif.	Lafayette, Colo.	0*
74	Reese, Archie	NT	6-3	275	2/4/56	6	Clemson	Mayesville, S.C.	Mt. View, Calif.	9
68	Robinson, Johnny	NT	6-2	260	2/14/58	3	Louisiana Tech	Jonesboro, La.	Ruston, La.	7
52	Romano, Jim	C	6-3	260	3/4/53	2	Penn State	Glen Cove, N.Y.	Glen Head, N.Y.	5
58	Squirek, Jack	LB	6-4	225	2/16/59	2	Illinois	Cleveland, Ohio	Valley View, Ohio	9
66	†Sylvester, Steve	C-G	6-4	260	4/3/53	9	Notre Dame	Cincinnati, Ohio	Cincinnati, Ohio	5
67	Van Divier, Randy	G	6-5	265	6/5/58	3	Washington	Anaheim, Calif.	Reistertown, Md.	1
99	Vaughan, Ruben	NT	6-2	240	8/5/56	3	Colorado	Los Angeles, Calif.	Foster City, Calif.	9
41	Watts, Ted	CB	6-0	190	5/29/59	3	Texas Tech	Tarpon Springs, Fla.	Tarpon Springs, Fla.	9
38	Willis, Chester	RB	5-11	195	5/2/58	3	Auburn	Elerberton, Ga.	Oakland, Calif.	8
6	Wilson, Marc	QB	6-6	205	2/15/57	4	Brigham Young	Bremerton, Wash.	Orinda Calif.	8
	t-Wilson, Tim	TE	6-3	235	1/14/55	7	Maryland	New Castle, Del.	Houston, Tex.	9

* Burke last active with Baltimore in '81; Harvey last active with Kansas City in '81; Jones missed '82 season due to injury; Reed last active with Kansas City in '81.

†Option playout; subject to developments.

Retired—John Matuszak, 10-year defensive end, on injured reserve in '82; Burgess Owens, 11-year safety, 8 games in '82; Art Shell, 16-year tackle, 8 in '82, Gene Upshaw, 15-year guard, on injured reserve in '82.

t-Raiders traded for T. Wilson (Houston).

COACHING STAFF

Head Coach, Tom Flores

Pro Career: Begins fifth year as head coach. Guided Raiders to 27-10 Super Bowl XV victory over Philadelphia. Has been with Raiders organization as either a player or coach for 16 years. Played six years at quarterback for Raiders from 1960-66. After spending two years (1967-68) with the Buffalo Bills and two seasons (1969-70) with the Kansas City Chiefs, Flores returned to Oakland as receivers coach in February, 1972. Ranks as Raiders number-three all-time passer with 11,635 yards and 92 touchdowns. He also passed for a club record six touchdowns in one game in 1963. Career record: 40-23.

Background: Quarterback at Fresno J.C. 1954-55 and College of Pacific 1956-57. Coached at his alma mater in 1959 before joining Raiders as a quarterback in 1960.

Personal: Born March 21, 1937 in Fresno, Calif. Tom and his wife, Barbara, live in Los Angeles, Calif. They have twin sons, Mark and Scott, and a daughter, Kimberly.

ASSISTANT COACHES

Sam Boghosian, offensive line; born December 22, 1931, Fresno, Calif., lives in Los Angeles. Guard UCLA 1951-54. No pro playing experience. College coach: UCLA 1955-64, Oregon State 1965-73. Pro coach: Houston Oilers 1974-75, Seattle Seahawks 1976-77, Raiders since 1979.

Willie Brown, assistant; born December 2, 1940, Yazu City, Miss., lives in Los Angeles. Defensive back Grambling 1959-62. Pro cornerback Denver 1963-66, Oakland Raiders 1967-78. Pro coach: Joined Raiders in 1979.

Chet Franklin, defensive backfield; born March 19, 1935, Ontario, Ore., lives in Los Angeles. Guard Utah 1954-56. No pro playing experience. College coach: Stanford 1959, Oklahoma 1960-62, Colorado 1963-70. Pro coach: San Francisco 49ers 1971-74, Kansas City Chiefs 1975-77, New Orleans Saints 1978-79, Raiders since 1980.

Earl Leggett, defensive line; born May 5, 1933, Jacksonville, Fla., lives in Los Angeles. Tackle Hinds J.C. 1953-54, Louisiana State 1955-56. Pro defensive tackle Chicago Bears 1957-65, Los Angeles Rams 1966, New Orleans Saints 1967-68. College coach: Nicholls State 1971, Texas Christian 1972-73. Pro coach: Southern California Sun (WFL) 1974-75, Seattle Seahawks 1976-77, San Francisco 49ers 1978, Raiders since 1980.

Joe Madro, assistant; born March 21, 1913, Cleveland, lives in Los Angeles. Guard Ohio State 1937-39. No pro playing experience. College coach: Ohio State 1940, Denison 1941, Miami, Ohio 1947-48, Cincinnati 1949-54. Pro coach: Los Angeles Rams 1955-59, San Diego Chargers 1960-71, Houston Oilers 1972-74, Raiders since 1977.

Bob Mischak, assistant; born October 25, 1932, Newark, N.J., lives in Los Angeles, Calif. Guard Army 1951-53. Pro guard New York Titans 1960-62, Oakland Raiders 1963-65. College coach: Army 1966-73. Pro coach: Joined Raiders in 1973.

Steve Ortmayer, special teams; born February 13, 1944, Painesville, Ohio, lives in Los Angeles. La Verne College 1966. No pro playing experience. College coach: Colorado 1967-73, Georgia Tech 1974. Pro coach: Kansas City Chiefs 1975-77, Raiders since 1978.

Charlie Sumner, linebackers; born October 19, 1930, Radford, Va., lives in Los Angeles. Back William & Mary 1952-54. Pro defensive back Chicago Bears 1955-60, Minnesota Vikings 1961-62. Pro coach: Oakland Raiders 1963-68, Pittsburgh Steelers 1969-72, New England Patriots 1973-78, rejoined Raiders in 1979.

Ray Willsey, offensive backfield; born September 30, 1929, Regina, Saskatchewan, lives in Los Angeles. Quarterback-defensive back California 1951-52. Pro back Edmonton Eskimos (CFL) 1953. College coach: California 1954-55, 1964-71 (head coach), Washington 1956, Texas 1957-59. Pro coach: St. Louis Cardinals 1960-61, 1973-77, Washington Redskins 1962-63, Raiders since 1978.

LOS ANGELES RAIDERS 1983 FIRST-YEAR ROSTER

Name	Pos.	Ht.	Wt.	Birth-date	College	Birthplace	Residence	How Acq.
Adams, Stanley (1)	LB	6-2	220	5/22/60	Memphis State	Marion, Ark.	Memphis, Tenn.	FA
Benefield, Greg (1)	C	6-3	260	2/10/60	Mississippi State	Tupelo, Miss.	Memphis, Tenn.	FA
Bonner, Mark	G	6-5	250	10/19/59	Oregon State	Sacramento, Calif.	Sacramento, Calif.	FA
Burton, Maurice	CB	5-10	175	3/9/58	Morgan State	Benton Harbor, Mich.	Benton Harbor, Mich.	FA
Byrd, Darryl	LB	6-1	220	9/3/60	Illinois	San Diego, Calif.	Champaign, Ill.	FA
Caldwell, Tony	LB	6-1	225	4/1/61	Washington	Los Angeles, Calif.	Seattle, Wash.	D3
Carver, Dale	LB	6-2	225	3/5/61	Georgia	Melbourne, Fla.	Athens, Ga.	FA
Casey, Derrick	LB	6-1	230	11/2/60	San Francisco State	San Francisco, Calif.	San Leandro, Calif.	FA
Cole, Robert	NT	6-2	265	3/20/61	Alcorn State	Olive Branch, Miss.	Memphis, Tenn.	FA
Conque, Clint	LB	6-1	225	11/2/60	Nicholls State	Baton Rouge, La.	Thibodaux, La.	FA
Courville, Vince	WR	5-10	160	12/5/59	Texas Southern	Galveston, Tex.	Galveston, Tex.	FA
DeBose, Ronnie (1)	TE	6-6	235	10/13/58	UCLA	Los Angeles, Calif.	Carson, Calif.	FA
Dillon, Robert	S	5-11	195	10/10/59	Grambling	McComb, Miss.	Oakland, Calif.	FA
DiLulo, Paul	RB	6-0	225	5/12/59	Boise State	Billings, Mont.	Boise, Idaho	FA
Dorn, David	WR	6-1	195	7/25/59	Rutgers	Elmer, N.J.	Glassboro, N.J.	FA
Dotterer, Mike	RB	5-11	185	12/14/60	Stanford	Saskatoon, Sask.	Palo Alto, Calif.	D8
Fifer, Maceo	T	6-5	265	3/11/59	Houston	Kerrville, Tex.	Kerrville, Tex.	FA
Fishback, Ricky	S	5-11	210	3/26/60	Arkansas State	Rutherford Cty., Tenn.	Murfreesboro, Tenn.	FA
Fitzpatrick, Greg (1)	LB	6-2	225	3/29/57	Youngstown State	Stamford, Conn.	Los Angeles, Calif.	FA
Hailey, Ken	CB	5-10	170	7/12/61	San Francisco State	Oceanside, Calif.	Oceanside, Calif.	FA
Henderson, Curtis (1)	WR	5-10	195	8/4/58	Morgan State	Woonsocket, R.I.	Woonsocket, R.I.	FA
Hurst, Hubert	G	6-3	270	5/3/61	Livingston	Thomasville, Ala.	Southgate, Calif.	FA
Jordan, Kent	TE	6-7	245	10/29/59	St. Mary's, Calif.	Berkeley, Calif.	Piedmont, Calif.	D9
Lindquist, Scott	QB	6-3	195	7/2/61	Northern Arizona	Kingsburg, Calif.	Flagstaff, Ariz.	D12
Lomeli, Dan	K	5-10	215	4/5/59	Boise State	San Jose, Calif.	Santa Clara, Calif.	FA
McCall, Jeff	RB	6-2	230	7/4/60	Clemson	Fayetteville, N.C.	Fayetteville, N.C.	D7
McClanahan, Derek	CB	5-10	185	12/14/59	Jackson State	Birmingham, Ala.	Birmingham, Ala.	FA
Middleton, Kevin	S	5-11	185	9/8/61	Wichita State	Macon, Ga.	Macon, Ga.	FA
Miller, Deron	TE	6-4	235	7/11/61	Rice	Flemington, N.J.	Doylestown, Pa.	FA
Mosebar, Don	T	6-6	270	9/11/61	Southern California	Yakima, Wash.	Los Angeles, Calif.	D1
Murray, Joe	G	6-4	260	11/7/60	Southern California	Los Angeles, Calif.	Los Angeles, Calif.	FA
Nobles, Gary	WR	5-8	165	11/27/58	San Diego State	Los Angeles, Calif.	Altadena, Calif.	FA
Pickel, Bill	NT	6-5	260	11/5/59	Rutgers	Queens, N.Y.	Highland Park, N.J.	D2
Prater, Sam (1)	LB	6-2	235	8/24/59	North Alabama	Memphis, Tenn.	Florence, Ala.	FA
Prudhomme, Dwight	QB	6-3	200	1/11/61	S.W. Louisiana	Opelousas, La.	Lafayette, La.	FA
Ranson, W.C.	T	6-4	250	10/13/59	Houston	Lynchburg, Va.	Streetman, Tex.	FA
Rogers, Grayson (1)	QB	6-3	215	11/7/58	Pacific	Chico, Calif.	Bakersfield, Calif.	FA
Simmons, Victor (1)	WR	6-1	190	11/5/60	Oregon State	Joliet, Ill.	Corvallis, Ore.	FA
Sperbeck, Marshall	QB	6-2	205	5/19/60	Nevada-Reno	Sacramento, Calif.	Sacramento, Calif.	FA
Thompson, Frank	DE	6-6	255	12/23/58	Jackson State	Madison, Miss.	Jackson, Miss.	FA
Townsend, Greg	DE	6-3	240	11/3/61	Texas Christian	Los Angeles, Calif.	Compton, Calif.	D4
Vela, David	WR	6-1	185	6/17/60	Southwest Texas	San Antonio, Tex.	San Antonio, Tex.	FA
Williams, Dokie	WR	5-11	180	8/25/60	UCLA	Oceanside, Calif.	Inglewood, Calif.	D5
Williams, Robert	RB	6-1	215	2/18/61	Washington State	Los Angeles, Calif.	Compton, Calif.	FA

Players who report to an NFL team for the first time are designated on rosters as rookies (R). If a player reported to an NFL training camp in a previous year but was not on the active squad for three or more regular season or postseason games, he is listed on the first-year roster and designated by a (1). Thereafter, a player who is on the active squad for three or more regular season or postseason games is credited with an additional year of playing experience.

NOTES

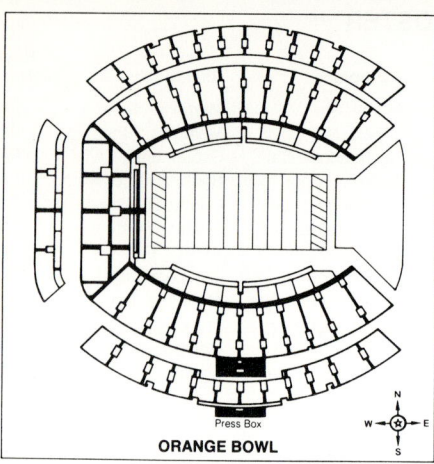

ORANGE BOWL

Miami Dolphins

**American Football Conference
Eastern Division**

Team Colors: Aqua, Coral, and White

**3550 Biscayne Boulevard
Miami, Florida 33137
Telephone:** (305) 576-1000

Club Officials
President: Joseph Robbie
Vice President-General Manager: J. Michael Robbie
Vice President-Head Coach: Don Shula
Vice President: Don Poss
Director of Pro Personnel: Charley Winner
Director of Player Personnel: Chuck Connor
Director of Public Relations: Dick Horning
Ticket Director: Ross Paul
Controller: Howard Rieman
Trainer: Bob Lundy
Equipment Manager: Danny Dowe

Stadium: Orange Bowl • **Capacity:** 75,459
1501 N.W. Third Street
Miami, Florida 33125
Playing Surface: Grass (PAT)
Training Camp: 16400-D NW 32nd Avenue
Miami, Florida 33054

1983 SCHEDULE

Preseason
Aug. 6	at Dallas	8:00
Aug. 13	**New Orleans**	8:00
Aug. 19	at Washington	8:00
Aug. 26	at New York Giants	8:00

Regular Season
Sept. 4	at Buffalo	1:00
Sept. 11	**New England**	4:00
Sept. 19	at Los Angeles Raiders (Monday)	6:00
Sept. 25	**Kansas City**	1:00
Oct. 2	at New Orleans	3:00
Oct. 9	**Buffalo**	1:00
Oct. 16	at New York Jets	1:00
Oct. 23	at Baltimore	2:00
Oct. 30	**Los Angeles Rams**	1:00
Nov. 6	at San Francisco	1:00
Nov. 13	at New England	1:00
Nov. 20	**Baltimore**	1:00
Nov. 28	**Cincinnati** (Monday)	9:00
Dec. 4	at Houston	12:00
Dec. 10	**Atlanta** (Saturday)	4:00
Dec. 16	**New York Jets** (Friday)	9:00

1982 TEAM STATISTICS

	Miami	Opp.
Total First Downs	165	147
Rushing	84	77
Passing	66	65
Penalty	15	5
Third Down Efficiency	52/125	46/117
Third Down Percentage	41.6	39.3
Total Net Yards	2658	2312
Total Offensive Plays	582	548
Avg. Gain per Play	4.6	4.2
Avg. Gain per Game	295.3	256.9
Net Yards Rushing	1344	1285
Total Rushing Plays	333	293
Avg. Gain per Rush	4.0	4.4
Avg. Gain Rushing per Game	149.3	142.8
Net Yards Passing	1314	1027
Lost Attempting to Pass	11/87	29/254
Gross Yards Passing	1401	1281
Attempts/Completions	238/129	226/119
Percent Completed	54.2	52.7
Had Intercepted	13	19
Avg. Net Passing per Game	146.0	114.1
Punts/Avg.	35/38.7	40/40.1
Punt Returns/Avg.	22/8.8	14/5.5
Kickoff Returns/Avg.	24/21.1	33/21.3
Interceptions/Avg. Ret.	19/14.8	13/7.4
Penalties/Yards	34/240	57/461
Fumbles/Ball Lost	15/10	17/8
Total Points	198	131
Avg. Points per Game	22.0	14.6
Touchdowns	22	15
Rushing	11	7
Passing	8	7
Returns and Recoveries	3	1
Field Goals	15/20	9/15
Conversions	21/22	14/15
Safeties	0	0
Avg. Time of Possession	31:18	28:42

1982 TEAM RECORD

Preseason (2-1-1)

Miami		Opponents
24	*Washington	7
14	Denver	17
17	Kansas City (OT)	17
16	*New York Giants (OT)	13
71		54

Regular Season (7-2)

Miami		Opponents	Att.
45	New York Jets	28	53,360
24	*Baltimore	20	51,999
9	Buffalo	7	52,945
17	Tampa Bay	23	65,854
22	*Minnesota	14	45,721
0	New England	3	25,716
20	*New York Jets	19	67,307
27	*Buffalo	10	73,924
34	Baltimore	7	19,073
198		131	455,899

*Home Game   (OT) Overtime

Score by Periods

Miami	54	43	64	37	—	198
Opponents	26	58	10	37	—	131

Attendance

Home 238,951   Away 216,948   Total 455,899
Single game home record, 78,939 (1-2-72)
Single season home record, 557,881 (1972)

1982 INDIVIDUAL STATISTICS

Rushing

	Att	Yds	Avg	LG	TD
Franklin	177	701	4.0	25t	7
Nathan	66	233	3.5	15	1
Woodley	36	207	5.8	29	2
Vigorito	19	99	5.2	33t	1
Hill	13	51	3.9	13	0
Diana	8	31	3.9	7	0
Bennett	9	15	1.7	5	0
Harris	1	13	13.0	13	0
Cowan	1	3	3.0	3	0
Strock	3	−9	−3.0	0	0
Miami	333	1344	4.0	33t	11
Opponents	293	1285	4.4	62t	7

Field Goal Success

Distance	1-19	20-29	30-39	40-49	50 Over
Made-Att.	0-0	8-9	4-5	3-5	0-1

Passing

	Att	Comp	Pct	Yds	TD	Int	Tkld	Rate
Woodley	179	98	54.7	1080	5	8	10/82	63.4
Strock	55	30	54.5	306	2	5	1/5	44.8
Hill	1	0	0.0	0	0	0	0/0	—
Jensen	1	0	0.0	0	0	0	0/0	—
Nathan	2	1	50.0	15	1	0	0/0	—
Miami	238	129	54.2	1401	8	13	11/87	
Opponents	226	119	52.7	1281	7	19	29/254	

Receiving

	No	Yds	Avg	LG	TD
Vigorito	24	186	7.8	26	0
Harris	22	331	15.0	45	1
Cefalo	17	356	20.9	46	1
Rose	16	182	11.4	44	2
Nathan	16	114	7.1	16	0
Hardy	12	66	5.5	19	2
Moore	8	82	10.3	23	1
Hill	6	33	5.5	10	0
Franklin	3	9	3.0	6	0
Diana	2	21	10.5	13	0
Lee	2	6	3.0	5	0
Woodley	1	15	15.0	15t	1
Miami	129	1401	10.9	46	8
Opponents	119	1281	10.8	53t	7

Interceptions

	No	Yds	Avg	LG	TD
McNeal	4	42	10.5	23	1
Walker	3	54	18.0	30	0
G. Blackwood	2	42	21.0	35t	1
L. Blackwood	2	41	20.5	21	0
Small	2	41	20.5	21	0
Kozlowski	1	36	36.0	36	0
Gordon	1	15	15.0	15	0
Brudzinski	1	5	5.0	5	0
Rhone	1	4	4.0	4	0
Bokamper	1	1	1.0	1	0
Duhe	1	0	0.0	0	0
Miami	19	281	14.8	36	2
Opponents	13	96	7.4	51	0

Punting

	No	Yds	Avg	In 20	LG
Orosz	35	1353	38.7	11	61
Miami	35	1353	38.7	11	61
Opponents	40	1605	40.1	5	61

Punt Returns

	No	FC	Yds	Avg	LG	TD
Vigorito	20	5	192	9.6	59t	1
G. Blackwood	2	0	2	1.0	2	0
Kozlowski	0	1	0	—	0	0
Miami	22	6	194	8.8	59t	1
Opponents	14	7	77	5.5	22	0

Kickoff Returns

	No	Yds	Avg	LG	TD
Walker	20	433	21.7	32	0
Heflin	2	49	24.5	31	0
Diana	1	15	15.0	15	0
Kozlowski	1	10	10.0	10	0
Miami	24	507	21.1	32	0
Opponents	33	704	21.3	66	0

Scoring

	TD	TD R	TD P	TD Rt	PAT	FG	TP
v. Schamann					21/22	15/20	66
Franklin	7	7	0	0			42
Woodley	3	2	1	0			18
Hardy	2	0	2	0			12
Rose	2	0	2	0			12
Vigorito	2	1	0	1			12
G. Blackwood	1	0	0	1			6
Cefalo	1	0	1	0			6
Harris	1	0	1	0			6
McNeal	1	0	0	1			6
Moore	1	0	1	0			6
Nathan	1	1	0	0			6
Miami	22	11	8	3	21/22	15/20	198
Opponents	15	7	7	1	14/15	9/15	131

Sacks

Barnett ½, Baumhower 3½, Betters 4, G. Blackwood 2, L. Blackwood 1, Bokamper 3½, Bowser 2, Brudzinski 4½, Duhe 2, Gordon 3, Hester 1, Kozlowski 1, Rhone 1.

FIRST PLAYERS SELECTED

Year	Player, College, Position
1966	Rick Norton, Kentucky, QB
1967	Bob Griese, Purdue, QB
1968	Larry Csonka, Syracuse, RB
1969	Bill Stanfill, Georgia, DE
1970	Jim Mandich, Michigan, TE (2)
1971	Otto Stowe, Iowa State, WR (2)
1972	Mike Kadish, Notre Dame, DT
1973	Chuck Bradley, Oregon, C (2)
1974	Donald Reese, Jackson State, DE
1975	Darryl Carlton, Tampa, T
1976	Larry Gordon, Arizona State, LB
1977	A.J. Duhe, Louisiana State, DT
1978	Guy Benjamin, Stanford, QB (2)
1979	Jon Giesler, Michigan, T
1980	Don McNeal, Alabama, DB
1981	David Overstreet, Oklahoma, RB
1982	Roy Foster, Southern California, G
1983	Dan Marino, Pittsburgh, QB

DOLPHINS COACHING HISTORY

(156-100-4)

1966-69	George Wilson	15-39-2
1970-82	Don Shula	141-61-2

MIAMI DOLPHINS 1983 VETERAN ROSTER

No.	Name	Pos.	Ht.	Wt.	Birth-date	NFL Exp.	College	Birthplace	Residence	Games in '82
70	Barnett, Bill	DE	6-4	260	5/10/56	4	Nebraska	St. Paul, Minn.	Lincoln, Neb.	5
73	Baumhower, Bob	NT	6-5	260	8/4/55	7	Alabama	Portsmouth, Va.	Fort Lauderdale, Fla.	9
34	Bennett, Woody	RB	6-2	222	3/24/55	5	Miami	York, Pa.	York, Pa.	1
75	Betters, Doug	DE	6-7	260	6/11/56	6	Nevada-Reno	Lincoln, Neb.	Pembroke Pines, Fla.	9
72	Bishop, Richard	NT	6-1	265	3/23/50	8	Louisville	Macon, Ga.	Macon, Ga.	2
47	Blackwood, Glenn	S	6-0	186	2/23/57	5	Texas	San Antonio, Tex.	Pembroke Pines, Fla.	9
42	Blackwood, Lyle	S	6-1	188	5/2/51	11	Texas Christian	San Antonio, Tex.	Austin, Tex.	9
58	Bokamper, Kim	DE	6-6	250	9/25/54	7	San Jose State	San Diego, Calif.	Plantation, Fla.	9
56	Bowser, Charles	LB	6-3	222	10/2/59	2	Duke	Plymouth, N.C.	Plymouth, N.C.	9
59	Brudzinski, Bob	LB	6-4	230	1/1/55	7	Ohio State	Fremont, Ohio	Long Beach, Calif.	9
81	Cefalo, Jimmy	WR	5-11	188	10/5/56	6	Penn State	Pittston, Pa.	North Miami, Fla.	9
76	Clark, Steve	NT	6-4	255	8/2/60	2	Utah	Salt Lake City, Utah	Salt Lake City, Utah	2
63	Dennard, Mark	C	6-1	252	11/2/55	5	Texas A&M	Bay City, Tex.	Bryan, Tex.	8
33	Diana, Rich	RB	5-9	220	9/6/60	2	Yale	New Haven, Conn.	Hamden, Conn.	9
77	Duhe, A.J.	LB	6-4	248	11/27/55	7	Louisiana State	New Orleans, La.	Miami Shores, Fla.	9
85	Duper, Mark	WR	5-9	185	1/25/59	2	Northwestern Louisiana	Pineville, La.	Monroeville, La.	2
61	Foster, Roy	G-T	6-4	275	5/24/60	2	Southern California	Los Angeles, Calif.	Los Angeles, Calif.	9
37	Franklin, Andra	RB	5-10	225	8/22/59	3	Nebraska	Anniston, Ala.	Hialeah, Fla.	9
79	Giesler, Jon	T	6-4	260	12/23/56	5	Michigan	Toledo, Ohio	Pembroke Pines, Fla.	9
74	Green, Cleveland	T	6-3	262	9/11/57	5	Southern	Bolton, Miss.	Miami, Fla.	3
84	Hardy, Bruce	TE	6-4	230	6/1/56	6	Arizona State	Murray, Utah	West Jordan, Utah	9
82	Harris, Duriel	WR	5-11	176	11/27/54	8	New Mexico State	Port Arthur, Tex.	North Miami, Fla.	9
88	Heflin, Vince	WR	6-0	185	7/7/59	2	Central State, Ohio	Dayton, Ohio	Miami, Fla.	6
53	Hester, Ron	LB	6-1	218	5/26/59	2	Florida State	Atlanta, Ga.	Umatilla, Ga.	9
31	Hill, Eddie	RB	6-2	210	5/13/57	5	Memphis State	Nashville, Tenn.	Nashville, Tenn.	9
11	Jensen, Jim	QB	6-4	212	11/14/58	3	Boston University	Abington, Pa.	Warrington, Pa.	6
49	Judson, William	CB	6-1	181	3/26/59	2	South Carolina State	Detroit, Mich.	Miami, Fla.	9
40	Kozlowski, Mike	S	6-0	198	2/24/56	4	Colorado	Newark, N.J.	Pembroke Pines, Fla.	9
67	Kuechenberg, Bob	G	6-2	255	10/14/47	14	Notre Dame	Gary, Ind.	Miami Beach, Fla.	9
68	Laakso, Eric	T	6-4	265	11/29/56	6	Tulane	New York, N.Y.	Pembroke Pines, Fla.	9
44	Lankford, Paul	CB	6-1	178	6/15/58	2	Penn State	New York, N.Y.	Farmingdale, N.Y.	7
86	Lee, Ronnie	TE	6-3	236	12/24/56	5	Baylor	Pine Bluff, Ark.	Miami Lakes, Fla.	9
28	McNeal, Don	CB	5-11	192	5/6/58	4	Alabama	Atmore, Ala.	Miami, Fla.	9
89	Moore, Nat	WR	5-9	188	9/19/51	10	Florida	Tallahassee, Fla.	Miami, Fla.	9
22	Nathan, Tony	RB	6-0	206	12/14/56	5	Alabama	Birmingham, Ala.	Miami, Fla.	8
64	Newman, Ed	G	6-2	255	6/4/51	11	Duke	Woodbury, N.Y.	Miami, Fla.	8
3	Orosz, Tom	P	6-1	204	9/26/59	3	Ohio State	Painesville, Ohio	Columbus, Ohio	9
78	Poole, Ken	DE	6-3	251	10/20/58	2	Northeast Louisiana	Hermitage, Ark.	Hermitage, Ark.	0*
54	Potter, Steve	LB	6-3	235	11/6/57	3	Virginia	Bradford, Pa.	Erie, Pa.	9
55	Rhone, Earnie	LB	6-2	224	8/20/53	8	Henderson, Ark.	Ogden, Ark.	Miami Lakes, Fla.	9
80	Rose, Joe	TE	6-3	230	6/24/57	4	California	Marysville, Calif.	Williams, Calif.	9
52	Shull, Steve	LB	6-1	220	3/27/58	4	William & Mary	Philadelphia, Pa.	Pembroke Pines, Fla.	9
48	Small, Gerald	CB	5-11	192	8/10/56	6	San Jose State	Washington, N.C.	North Miami, Fla.	9
57	Stephenson, Dwight	C	6-2	255	11/20/57	4	Alabama	Murfreesboro, N.C.	Hampton, Va.	9
10	Strock, Don	QB	6-5	220	11/27/50	10	Virginia Tech	Pottstown, Pa.	Miami Springs, Fla.	9
60	Toews, Jeff	G	6-3	255	11/4/57	5	Washington	San Jose, Calif.	Pembroke Pines, Fla.	9
32	Vigorito, Tom	RB-KR	5-10	197	10/23/59	3	Virginia	Passaic, N.J.	Wayne, N.J.	9
5	von Schamann, Uwe	K	6-0	188	4/23/56	5	Oklahoma	West Berlin, Germany	Memphis, Tenn.	9
41	Walker, Fulton	CB-KR	5-10	193	4/30/58	3	West Virginia	Martinsburg, W. Va.	Martinsburg, W. Va.	9
16	Woodley, David	QB	6-2	204	10/25/58	4	Louisiana State	Shreveport, La.	Davie, Fla.	9

* Poole missed '82 season due to injury.

Retired—Vern Den Herder, 12-year defensive end, 7 games in '82.

Also played with Dolphins in '82—RB Larry Cowan (2 games), LB Larry Gordon (9).

COACHING STAFF

Head Coach, Don Shula

Pro Career: Starts twenty-first season as NFL head coach, fourteenth at Miami where he has guided Dolphins to playoffs nine times including 17-0 season and Super Bowl VII win in 1972. Has highest winning percentage (.709) among active NFL coaches. Captured back-to-back NFL championships, defeating Washington 14-7 in Super Bowl VII and Minnesota 24-7 in Super Bowl VIII. Lost to Dallas 24-3 in Super Bowl VI and 27-17 to Washington in Super Bowl XVII. Is a part-owner and vice president of the Dolphins. Started his pro playing career with Cleveland Browns as defensive back in 1951. After two seasons with Browns, spent 1953-56 with Baltimore Colts and 1957 with Washington Redskins. Joined Detroit Lions as defensive coach in 1960 and was named head coach of the Colts in 1963. Baltimore had a 13-1 record in 1968 and captured NFL championship before losing to New York Jets in Super Bowl III. Career record: 214-86-6.

Background: Outstanding offensive player at John Carroll University in Cleveland before becoming defensive specialist as a pro. His alma mater gave him doctorate in humanities, May, 1973. Served as assistant coach at Virginia in 1958 and at Kentucky in 1959.

Personal: Born January 4, 1930, in Painesville, Ohio. Don and his wife, Dorothy, live in Miami Lakes and have five children—David, Donna, Sharon, Annie, and Mike.

ASSISTANT COACHES

Bill Arnsparger, assistant head coach-defense; born December 16, 1926, Paris, Ky., lives in Miami. Tackle Miami, Ohio 1946-49. No pro playing experience. College coach: Miami, Ohio 1950, Ohio State 1951-53, Kentucky 1954-61, Tulane 1962-63. Pro coach: Baltimore Colts 1964-69, Miami Dolphins 1970-73, New York Giants 1974-76 (head coach), rejoined Dolphins in 1976.

Tom Keane, defensive backfield-punters; born September 7, 1926, Bellaire, Ohio, lives in Miami. Back Ohio State 1944, West Virginia 1946-47. Pro back Los Angeles Rams 1948-51, Dallas Texans 1952, Baltimore Colts 1953-54, Chicago Cardinals 1957. Pro coach: Calgary Stampeders (CFL) 1960, Wheeling (UFL) 1961-64, Pittsburgh Steelers 1965, Dolphins since 1966.

Bob Matheson, special teams; born November 25, 1944, Boone, N.C., lives in Miami. Linebacker Duke 1964-66. Pro linebacker Cleveland Browns 1967-70, Miami Dolphins 1971-80. College coach: Duke 1981-82. Pro coach: First year with Dolphins.

John Sandusky, offensive line-running game; born December 28, 1925, Philadelphia, lives in Miami. Tackle Villanova 1946-49. Pro tackle Cleveland Browns 1950-55, Green Bay Packers 1956. College coach: Villanova 1956-58. Pro coach: Baltimore Colts 1959-72 (head coach 1972), Philadelphia Eagles 1973-75, Dolphins since 1976.

Mike Scarry, defensive line-run defense; born February 1, 1920, Duquesne, Pa., lives in Miami. Center Waynesburg 1939-41. Pro center Cleveland Rams 1944-45, Cleveland Browns (AAFC) 1946-47. College coach: Western Reserve 1948-49, Santa Clara 1950-52, Loras 1953, Washington State 1954-55, Cincinnati 1956-62, Waynesburg 1963-65. Pro coach: Washington Redskins 1966-68, Dolphins since 1970.

David Shula, assistant receivers coach; born March 12, 1959, Lexington, Ky. Wide receiver Dartmouth 1977-80. Pro receiver Baltimore Colts 1981. Pro coach: Joined Dolphins in 1982.

Carl Taseff, offensive backfield-special teams; born September 28, 1928, Cleveland, lives in Key Biscayne, Fla. Back John Carroll 1947-50. Pro defensive back Cleveland Browns 1951, Baltimore Colts 1953-61, Philadelphia Eagles 1961, Buffalo Bills 1962. Pro coach: Boston Patriots 1964, Detroit Lions 1965-68, Dolphins since 1970.

Junior Wade, strength-flexibility; born February 2, 1947, Bath, S.C., lives in Hialeah, Fla. South Carolina State 1969. No college or pro playing experience. Pro coach: First year with Dolphins.

MIAMI DOLPHINS 1983 FIRST-YEAR ROSTER

Name	Pos.	Ht.	Wt.	Birth-date	College	Birthplace	Residence	How Acq.
Atha, Bob	WR-P	5-11	180	9/22/60	Ohio State	Marietta, Ohio	Worthington, Ohio	FA
Benson, Charles	DE	6-3	267	11/21/60	Baylor	Houston, Tex.	Waco, Tex.	D3
Bergdale, John	WR	6-0	188	10/27/59	Augustana	Hawarden, Ind.	Hawarden, Ind.	FA
Brown, Mark	LB	6-2	226	7/18/61	Purdue	New Brunswick, N.J.	Los Angeles, Calif.	D9
Charles, Mike	NT	6-4	283	11/21/60	Syracuse	Newark, N.J.	East Orange, N.J.	D2
Clayton, Mark	WR	5-9	172	4/8/61	Louisville	Indianapolis, Ind.	Indianapolis, Ind.	D8
Dumas, Harold	LB	6-0	218	7/6/61	Ft. Hays State	Beaumont, Tex.	Crosby, Tex.	FA
Jenkins, Joe (1)	TE	6-5	233	11/5/57	Alcorn State	Gulfport, Miss.	Gulfport, Miss.	FA
Keuchler, Lamar	CB-S	5-10	190	12/15/60	Ohio State	Marion, Ohio	Columbus, Ohio	FA
Locklin, Ray (1)	RB	6-2	239	9/12/57	New Mexico State	Rockdale, Tex.	Euless, Tex.	FA
Lukens, Joe	G	6-4	262	9/2/61	Ohio State	Cincinnati, Ohio	Cincinnati, Ohio	D11
Marino, Dan	QB	6-3	214	9/15/61	Pittsburgh	Pittsburgh, Pa.	Pittsburgh, Pa.	D1
Mason, Larry	RB	5-10	195	3/21/61	Troy State	McAlla, Ala.	Bessemer, Ala.	FA
McCune, Ken	DE	6-6	260	2/12/59	Texas	Freeport, Tex.	Austin, Tex.	FA
McKenney, James	S	5-9	165	10/21/57	E. Tennessee State	Harrisonburg, Va.	Pompano Beach, Fla.	FA
Overstreet, David	RB	5-11	208	9/20/58	Oklahoma	Rusky, Tex.	Dallas, Tex.	D1 ('81)
Pierce, Kurt (1)	G	6-7	260	1/24/59	Virginia	Washington, D.C.	Rockville, Md.	FA
Reed, Anthony	RB	6-0	200	7/23/61	South Carolina State	Orangeburg, S.C.	Orangeburg, S.C.	D10
Roby, Reggie	P	6-2	243	7/30/61	Iowa	Waterloo, Iowa	Waterloo, Iowa	D6
Ryan, Eric	G-T	6-3	272	12/30/60	Florida State	Petersburg, Va.	Ft. Myers, Fla.	FA
Sekerak, Brian	LB	6-2	220	3/28/61	Lockhaven State	Colver, Pa.	Nanty Glo, Pa.	FA
Shaver, Don (1)	RB	5-11	230	5/6/59	Kutztown State	Glen Cove, N.Y.	Sea Cliff, N.Y.	FA
Smith, Johnny (1)	WR	5-11	183	8/1/58	Florida	Columbus, Ohio	Venice, Fla.	FA
Smith, Joseph	WR	5-11	185	6/10/59	Clemson	Hampton, Va.	Newport News, Va.	FA
Stenslokken, Jeffrey (1)	DE	6-5	247	8/20/60	Kearney State	Bismark, N.D.	Omaha, Neb.	FA
Sturdivant, John (1)	DE	6-3	265	5/25/59	Ohio State	Newport News, Va.	Hampton, Va.	FA
Tilley, Emmett	LB	5-11	240	2/13/61	Duke	Durham, N.C.	Durham, N.C.	FA
Udinski, Mack	C	6-0	260	8/16/60	Virginia Tech	New York, N.Y.	Blacksburg, Va.	FA
Woetzel, Keith	LB	6-2	225	11/15/60	Rutgers	Ridgewood, N.J.	Waldwick, N.J.	D7
Yole, Everett	CB-S	5-11	180	1/11/60	Shepherd College	Ft. Hood, Tex.	Shepherdstown, W. VA.	FA

Players who report to an NFL team for the first time are designated on rosters as rookies (R). If a player reported to an NFL training camp in a previous year but was not on the active squad for three or more regular season or postseason games, he is listed on the first-year roster and designated by a (1). Thereafter, a player who is on the active squad for three or more regular season or postseason games is credited with an additional year of playing experience.

NOTES

_____
_____
_____
_____
_____
_____
_____
_____
_____
_____
_____
_____
_____
_____
_____
_____
_____

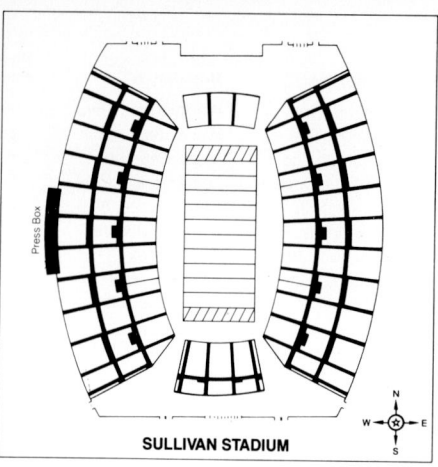

SULLIVAN STADIUM

New England Patriots

**American Football Conference
Eastern Division**

Team Colors: Red, White, and Blue

**Sullivan Stadium
Route 1
Foxboro, Massachusetts 02035
Telephone: (617) 543-7911, 262-1776**

Club Officials
President: William H. Sullivan, Jr.
Executive Vice President: Charles W. Sullivan
Vice President: Francis J. (Bucko) Kilroy
General Manager: Patrick J. Sullivan
Director of Player Development: Dick Steinberg
Executive Director of Player Personnel:
  Darryl Stingley
Director, Marketing: Miceal Chamberlain
Director of Media Relations: Tom Hoffman
Director, Pro Scouting: Bill McPeak
Director, Public Affairs: Claudia Smith
Personnel Scouts: George Blackburn, Bobby Grier,
  Joe Mendes, Pat Naughton, Bob Teahan
Stadium Manager: Billy Sullivan III
Film Manager: Ken Deininger
Ticket Manager: Kevin Fitzgerald
Assistant Director, Media Relations: Dave Wintergrass
Trainer: Tom Healion
Equipment Manager: George Luongo

Stadium: Sullivan Stadium • **Capacity:** 61,297
  Route 1
  Foxboro, Massachusetts 02035
Playing Surface: Super Turf
Training Camp: Bryant College
  Smithfield, Rhode Island 02917

1983 SCHEDULE

Preseason
Aug. 6	vs. Pittsburgh at Knoxville, Tenn.	7:30
Aug. 14	at San Francisco	1:00
Aug. 20	at Los Angeles Rams	7:00
Aug. 26	at Tampa Bay	8:00

Regular Season
Sept. 4	**Baltimore**	1:00
Sept. 11	at Miami	4:00
Sept. 18	**New York Jets**	1:00
Sept. 25	at Pittsburgh	1:00
Oct. 2	**San Francisco**	1:00
Oct. 9	at Baltimore	2:00
Oct. 16	**San Diego**	1:00
Oct. 23	at Buffalo	1:00
Oct. 30	at Atlanta	1:00
Nov. 6	**Buffalo**	1:00
Nov. 13	**Miami**	1:00
Nov. 20	**Cleveland**	1:00
Nov. 27	at New York Jets	1:00
Dec. 4	**New Orleans**	1:00
Dec. 11	at Los Angeles Rams	1:00
Dec. 18	at Seattle	1:00

1982 TEAM STATISTICS

	New England	Opp.
Total First Downs	146	185
Rushing	74	87
Passing	63	88
Penalty	9	10
Third Down Efficiency	37/110	47/122
Third Down Percentage	33.6	38.5
Total Net Yards	2633	2808
Total Offensive Plays	526	602
Avg. Gain per Play	5.0	4.7
Avg. Gain per Game	292.6	312.0
Net Yards Rushing	1347	1289
Total Rushing Plays	324	315
Avg. Gain per Rush	4.2	4.1
Avg. Gain Rushing per Game	149.7	143.2
Net Yards Passing	1286	1519
Lost Attempting to Pass	15/134	20/172
Gross Yards Passing	1420	1691
Attempts/Completions	187/93	267/142
Percent Completed	49.7	53.2
Had Intercepted	9	12
Avg. Net Passing per Game	142.9	168.8
Punts/Avg.	49/43.7	43/39.7
Punt Returns/Avg.	16/8.7	26/7.3
Kickoff Returns/Avg.	28/23.1	32/19.2
Interceptions/Avg. Ret.	12/14.7	9/11.1
Penalties/Yards	52/412	39/290
Fumbles/Ball Lost	16/8	19/11
Total Points	143	157
Avg. Points per Game	15.9	17.4
Touchdowns	17	18
Rushing	3	9
Passing	12	9
Returns and Recoveries	2	0
Field Goals	8/13	10/15
Conversions	15/17	17/18
Safeties	1	1
Avg. Time of Possession	28:20	31:40

1982 TEAM RECORD

Preseason (1-3)

New England		Opponents
20	Pittsburgh	24
7	Philadelphia	14
21	Dallas	36
41	*Green Bay	27
89		101

Regular Season (5-4)

New England		Opponents	Att.
24	Baltimore	13	39,055
7	*New York Jets	31	53,515
7	Cleveland	10	47,281
29	*Houston	21	33,602
13	Chicago	26	36,973
3	*Miami	0	25,716
16	Seattle	0	53,457
14	Pittsburgh	37	51,515
30	*Buffalo	19	36,218
143		157	377,332

*Home Game

Score by Periods

New England	23	33	37	50	—	143
Opponents	34	49	13	61	—	157

Attendance

Home 149,051   Away 228,281   Total 377,332
Single game home record, 61,457 (12-5-71)
Single season home record, 475,081 (1978)

1982 INDIVIDUAL STATISTICS

Rushing

	Att	Yds	Avg	LG	TD
Collins	164	632	3.9	54	1
van Eeghen	82	386	4.7	17	0
Tatupu	30	168	5.6	26	0
Weathers	24	83	3.5	18	1
Grogan	9	42	4.7	19	1
Cunningham	9	21	2.3	4	0
Ferguson	1	5	5.0	5	0
Toler	1	4	4.0	4	0
Cavanaugh	2	3	1.5	3	0
Morgan	2	3	1.5	3	0
New England	324	1347	4.2	54	3
Opponents	315	1289	4.1	48	9

Field Goal Success

Distance	1-19	20-29	30-39	40-49	50 Over
Made-Att.	0-1	5-5	2-4	1-3	0-0

Passing

	Att	Comp	Pct	Yds	TD	Int	Tkld	Rate
Grogan	122	66	54.1	930	7	4	8/48	84.2
Cavanaugh	60	27	45.0	490	5	5	7/86	66.7
Flick	5	0	0.0	0	0	0	0/0	—
New Eng.	187	93	49.7	1420	12	9	15/134	
Opponents	267	142	53.2	1691	9	12	20/172	

Receiving

	No	Yds	Avg	LG	TD
Morgan	28	584	20.9	75t	3
Collins	19	187	9.8	33	2
Hasselbeck	15	158	10.5	41	1
Dawson	13	160	12.3	26	1
Bradshaw	6	111	18.5	48	1
Brown	4	114	28.5	41	1
Weathers	3	24	8.0	22	0
Toler	2	63	31.5	33t	2
van Eeghen	2	14	7.0	9	1
Jones	1	5	5.0	5	0
New England	93	1420	15.3	75t	12
Opponents	142	1691	11.9	46t	9

Interceptions

	No	Yds	Avg	LG	TD
Haynes	4	26	6.5	26	0
James	3	12	4.0	12	0
Sanford	2	105	52.5	99t	1
Blackmon	2	7	3.5	7	0
Clayborn	1	26	26.0	26	0
New England	12	176	14.7	99t	1
Opponents	9	100	11.1	44	0

Punting

	No	Yds	Avg	In 20	LG
Camarillo	49	2140	43.7	10	76
New England	49	2140	43.7	10	76
Opponents	43	1709	39.7	12	81

Punt Returns

	No	FC	Yds	Avg	LG	TD
R. Smith	16	8	139	8.7	19	0
New England	16	8	139	8.7	19	0
Opponents	26	9	191	7.3	21	0

Kickoff Returns

	No	Yds	Avg	LG	TD
R. Smith	24	567	23.6	98t	1
Taylor	2	46	23.0	27	0
Dombroski	1	19	19.0	19	0
Lee	1	14	14.0	14	0
New England	28	646	23.1	98t	1
Opponents	32	614	19.2	58	0

Scoring

	TD	TD R	TD P	TD Rt	PAT	FG	TP
J. Smith					6/7	5/8	21
Collins	3	1	2	0			18
Morgan	3	0	3	0			18
Toler	2	0	2	0			12
Miller					4/5	2/3	10
Robinson					5/5	1/2	8
Bradshaw	1	0	1	0			6
Brown	1	0	1	0			6
Dawson	1	0	1	0			6
Grogan	1	1	0	0			6
Hasselbeck	1	0	1	0			6
Sanford	1	0	0	1			6
R. Smith	1	0	0	1			6
Weathers	1	1	0	0			6
van Eeghen	1	0	1	0			6
Crump	(Safety)						2
New England	17	3	12	2	15/17	8/13	143
Opponents	18	9	9	0	17/18	10/15	157

Sacks

Adams 2, Blackmon 4½, Crump 1, Henson 1, James 2, McGrew 1½, Sims 3, Weishuhn 2, L. Williams 2, Zamberlin 1.

FIRST PLAYERS SELECTED

Year	Player, College, Position
1960	Ron Burton, Northwestern, RB
1961	Tommy Mason, Tulane, RB
1962	Gary Collins, Maryland, WR
1963	Art Graham, Boston College, WR
1964	Jack Concannon, Boston College, QB
1965	Jerry Rush, Michigan State, DE
1966	Karl Singer, Purdue, T
1967	John Charles, Purdue, S
1968	Dennis Byrd, North Carolina State, DE
1969	Ron Sellers, Florida State, WR
1970	Phil Olsen, Utah State, DE
1971	Jim Plunkett, Stanford, QB
1972	Tom Reynolds, San Diego State, WR (2)
1973	John Hannah, Alabama, G
1974	Steve Corbett, Boston College, G (2)
1975	Russ Francis, Oregon, TE
1976	Mike Haynes, Arizona State, DB
1977	Raymond Clayborn, Texas, DB
1978	Bob Cryder, Alabama, T
1979	Rick Sanford, South Carolina, DB
1980	Roland James, Tennessee, DB
1981	Brian Holloway, Stanford, T
1982	Kenneth Sims, Texas, DT
1983	Tony Eason, Illinois, QB

PATRIOTS COACHING HISTORY

Boston 1960-70
(147-174-9)

1960-61	Lou Saban*	7-12-0
1961-68	Mike Holovak	53-47-9
1969-70	Clive Rush**	5-18-0
1970-72	John Mazur***	9-19-0
1972	Phil Bengtson	1-4-0
1973-78	Chuck Fairbanks	46-42-0
1979-81	Ron Erhardt	21-27-0
1982	Ron Meyer	5-5-0

*Released after five games in 1961
**Released after nine games in 1970
***Released after nine games in 1972

NEW ENGLAND PATRIOTS 1983 VETERAN ROSTER

No.	Name	Pos.	Ht.	Wt.	Birth-date	NFL Exp.	College	Birthplace	Residence	Games in '82
85	Adams, Julius	DE	6-3	270	4/26/48	12	Texas Southern	Macon, Ga.	Roberta, Ga.	9
55	Blackmon, Don	LB	6-3	245	3/14/58	3	Tulsa	Pompano Beach, Fla.	Ft. Lauderdale, Fla.	9
88	Bradshaw, Morris	WR	6-1	195	10/19/52	10	Ohio State	Highland, Ill.	Alameda, Calif.	8
58	Brock, Pete	C	6-5	275	7/14/54	8	Colorado	Portland, Ore.	Norfolk, Mass.	9
81	Brown, Preston	WR	5-11	187	3/2/58	3	Vanderbilt	Nashville, Tenn.	Huntsville, Ala.	9
3	Camarillo, Rich	P	5-11	191	11/29/59	3	Washington	Whittier, Calif.	Pico Rivera, Calif.	9
12	Cavanaugh, Matt	QB	6-2	212	10/27/56	6	Pittsburgh	Youngstown, Ohio	Foxboro, Mass.	7
65	Clark, Steve	T	6-5	270	10/29/59	2	Kansas State	Chattanooga, Tenn.	Manhattan, Kan.	0*
26	Clayborn, Ray	CB	6-0	186	1/2/55	7	Texas	Ft. Worth, Tex.	Austin, Tex.	9
33	Collins, Tony	RB	5-11	203	5/27/59	3	East Carolina	Sanford, Fla.	Stoughton, Mass.	9
44	Cowan, Larry	RB	5-11	194	7/11/60	2	Jackson State	Mobile, Ala.	Prichard, Ala.	9*
91	Crump, George	DE	6-4	260	7/22/59	2	East Carolina	Portsmouth, Va.	Chesapeake, Va.	9
75	Cryder, Bob	G	6-4	293	9/7/56	6	Alabama	East St. Louis, Ill.	Stoughton, Mass.	9
87	Dawson, Lin	TE	6-3	240	6/24/59	3	North Carolina State	Norfolk, Va.	Kinston, N.C.	8
47	Dombroski, Paul	CB-S	6-0	185	8/8/56	4	Linfield	Sumter, S.C.	Stoughton, Mass.	9
43	Ferguson, Vagas	RB	6-0	213	3/6/57	3	Notre Dame	Richmond, Ind.	Stoughton, Mass.	2
10	Flick, Tom	QB	6-1	190	8/30/58	3	Washington	Patuxent River, Md.	Kirkland, Wash.	3
59	Golden, Tim	LB	6-2	220	11/15/59	2	Florida	Pahokee, Fla.	Ft. Lauderdale, Fla.	9
14	Grogan, Steve	QB	6-4	210	7/24/53	9	Kansas State	San Antonio, Tex.	Foxboro, Mass.	6
68	Haley, Darryl	T	6-4	279	2/16/61	2	Utah	Gardena, Calif.	Los Angeles, Calif.	9
80	†Hasselbeck, Don	TE	6-7	245	4/1/55	7	Colorado	Cincinnati, Ohio	Norfolk, Mass.	9
40	†Haynes, Mike	CB	6-2	202	7/1/53	8	Arizona State	Denison, Tex.	Norfolk, Mass.	9
70	Henson, Luther	NT	6-0	275	3/25/59	2	Ohio State	Sandusky, Ohio	Columbus, Ohio	8
76	Holloway, Brian	T	6-7	288	7/25/59	3	Stanford	Omaha, Neb.	Stephentown, N.Y.	9
51	Ingram, Brian	LB	6-4	230	10/31/59	2	Tennessee	Memphis, Tenn.	Salinas, Calif.	8
38	James, Roland	S	6-2	191	2/18/58	4	Tennessee	Jamestown, Ohio	Attleboro, Mass.	7
83	Jones, Cedric	WR	5-11	184	6/1/60	2	Duke	Norfolk, Va.	Garysburgh, N.C.	2
74	Jordan, Shelby	T	6-7	280	1/23/52	8	Washington, Mo.	St. Louis, Mo.	Smithfield, R.I.	9
22	Lee, Keith	CB-S	5-11	193	12/22/57	3	Colorado State	San Antonio, Tex.	Westminster, Colo.	9
31	Marion, Fred	CB-S	6-2	196	1/2/59	2	Miami, Fla.	Gainesville, Fla.	Miami, Fla.	9
50	McGrew, Larry	LB	6-5	233	7/23/57	3	Southern California	Berkeley, Calif.	Richmond, Calif.	8
86	Morgan, Stanley	WR	5-11	181	2/17/55	7	Tennessee	Easley, S.C.	Memphis, Tenn.	9
57	Nelson, Steve	LB	6-2	230	4/26/51	10	North Dakota State	Farmington, Minn.	Norfolk, Mass.	9
98	Owens, Dennis	NT	6-1	252	2/24/60	2	North Carolina State	Clinton, N.C.	Hampton, Va.	9
25	Sanford, Rick	S	6-1	192	1/9/57	5	South Carolina	Rock Hill, S.C.	Foxboro, Mass.	9
77	Sims, Kenneth	DE	6-5	279	10/31/59	2	Texas	Kosse, Tex.	Austin, Tex.	9
1	Smith, John	K	6-0	185	12/30/48	10	Southampton, Eng.	Leafield, England	Norfolk, Mass.	4
27	Smith, Ricky	CB-S-KR	6-0	174	7/20/60	2	Alabama State	Quincy, Fla.	Pensacola, Fla.	9
78	Spears, Ron	DE	6-6	255	11/23/59	2	San Diego State	Los Angeles, Calif.	Los Angeles, Calif.	7
30	Tatupu, Mosi	RB	6-0	227	4/26/55	6	Southern California	Pago Pago, Amer. Samoa	San Diego, Calif.	9
56	Tippett, Andre	LB	6-3	231	12/27/59	2	Iowa	Birmingham, Ala.	Stoughton, Mass.	9
82	Toler, Ken	WR	6-2	191	5/9/59	3	Mississippi	Greenville, Miss.	Jackson, Miss.	9
34	van Eeghen, Mark	RB	6-2	220	4/19/52	10	Colgate	Cambridge, Mass.	Cranston, R.I.	9
24	Weathers, Robert	RB	6-2	217	9/13/60	2	Arizona State	Westfield, N.Y.	Stoughton, Mass.	6
53	Weishuhn, Clayton	LB	6-2	220	10/9/59	2	Angelo State	San Angelo, Tex.	San Angelo, Tex.	9
62	Wheeler, Dwight	C	6-3	269	1/13/55	5	Tennessee State	Memphis, Tenn.	Nashville, Tenn.	9
72	Williams, Lester	NT	6-2	272	1/19/59	2	Miami	Miami, Fla.	Plantation, Fla.	9
61	Wooten, Ron	G	6-4	280	6/28/59	2	North Carolina	Cape Cod, Mass.	Foxboro, Mass.	9
54	Zamberlin, John	LB	6-2	226	2/13/56	5	Pacific Lutheran	Tacoma, Wash.	Tacoma, Wash.	8

* Clark missed '82 season due to injury. Cowan played 3 games with Miami, 6 with New England in '82.

†Option playout; subject to developments.

Retired—John Hannah, 10-year guard, 8 games in '82.

Also played with New England in '82—K Dan Miller (2 games), K Rex Robinson (3), RB Greg Taylor (1), TE Brian Williams (1).

COACHING STAFF

Head Coach, Ron Meyer

Pro Career: Begins second year in pro coaching ranks as head coach of the Patriots. Led New England to 5-4 record last season and first postseason playoff berth since 1978. Made his first appearance in NFL as a personnel assistant with Dallas from 1971-72. Named New England head coach January 15, 1982. No pro playing experience.

Background: Walk-on defensive back at Purdue 1959-62. Selected to the All-Big 10 Academic Team and recipient of Nobel Kizer Award for athletic and academic achievement in 1963. Assistant coach at Purdue 1965-70. Became head coach at Nevada-Las Vegas in 1973 and directed Rebels to a three-year record of 27-8, including an undefeated (11-0) regular season in 1974 before losing in the National Semifinals in NCAA Division II. Head coach at Southern Methodist 1976-81, where he led Mustangs to 1981 Southwest Conference title.

Personal: Born February 17, 1941, in Westerville, Ohio. He and his wife, Cindy, live in Westwood, Mass. with their four children—Ron, Jr., Ralph, Katryn, and Elizabeth.

ASSISTANT COACHES

Tommy Brasher, defensive line; born December 30, 1940, El Dorado, Ark., lives in Dover, Mass. Linebacker Arkansas 1961-63. No pro playing experience. College coach: Arkansas 1970, Virginia Tech 1971-73, Northeast Louisiana 1974, 1976, Southern Methodist 1977-81. Pro coach: Shreveport (WFL) 1975, Patriots since 1982.

Cleve Bryant, offensive backs; born March 27, 1947, Marrianna, Fla., lives in Norfolk, Mass. Quarterback Ohio University 1967-69. No pro playing experience. College coach: Miami, Ohio 1977, North Carolina 1978-81. Pro coach: Joined Patriots in 1982.

LeBaron Caruthers, strength and conditioning; born April 20, 1954, Nashville, Tenn., lives in Mansfield, Mass. Tackle East Carolina 1972-73. No pro playing experience. College coach: Auburn 1978-79, Southern Methodist 1980-81. Pro coach: Joined Patriots in 1982.

Steve Endicott, receivers; born December 27, 1950, Grants Pass, Ore., lives in Weymouth, Mass. Quarterback Oregon State 1969-71. No pro playing experience. College coach: Oregon State 1972, Miami 1973-75, Southern Methodist 1976-81. Pro coach: Winnipeg Blue Bombers (CFL) 1977, Toronto Argonauts (CFL) 1978, Patriots since 1982.

Lew Erber, offensive coordinator-quarterbacks; born May 27, 1934, Clifton, N.J., lives in Foxboro. Running back Montclair State 1954-55. No pro playing experience. College coach: Iowa State 1967-68, California Western 1969-72, San Diego State 1973, California 1974. Pro coach: San Francisco 49ers 1975, Oakland Raiders 1976-81, Patriots since 1982.

Bill Muir, offensive line; born October 26, 1942, Pittsburgh, Pa., lives in Plainville, Mass. Tackle Susquehanna 1963-65. No pro playing experience. College coach: Susquehanna 1965, Delaware Valley 1966-67, Rhode Island 1970-71, Idaho State 1972-73, Southern Methodist 1976-77. Pro coach: Orlando (Continental Football League) 1968-69, Houston-Shreveport (WFL) 1974-75, Patriots since 1982.

Rod Rust, defensive coordinator; born August 2, 1928, Webster City, Iowa, lives in Foxboro. Center-linebacker Iowa State 1947-50. No pro playing experience. College coach: New Mexico 1960-62, Stanford 1963-66, North Texas State 1967-72 (head coach). Pro coach: Montreal Alouettes (CFL) 1973-75, Philadelphia Eagles 1976-77, Kansas City Chiefs 1978-82, first year with Patriots.

Dante Scarnecchia, special teams-tight ends; born February 15, 1948, Los Angeles, Calif., lives in Wrentham, Mass. Center California Western 1966-69. No pro playing experience. College coach: California Western 1970-72, Iowa State 1973-74, Southern Methodist 1975-76, 1980-81, Pacific 1977-78. Pro coach: Joined Patriots in 1982.

NEW ENGLAND PATRIOTS 1983 FIRST-YEAR ROSTER

Name	Pos.	Ht.	Wt.	Birth-date	College	Birthplace	Residence	How Acq.
Addazio, Steve	G	6-1	265	6/1/59	Central Connecticut	Waterbury, Conn.	Farmington, Conn.	FA
Bass, Mike	K	5-11	218	6/1/60	Illinois	San Jose, Calif.	Champaign, Ill.	D6
Brown, Dennis	RB	5-11	195	9/10/59	Washington	Los Angeles, Calif.	Edmonds, Wash.	FA
Burnett, Harris (1)	C	6-3	260	11/10/59	Cal State-Fullerton	Downey, Calif.	Rowland Heights, Calif.	FA
Collins, Ken (1)	NT	6-3	260	7/27/60	Washington State	Wenatchee, Wash.	Pullman, Wash.	D8('82)
Craver, Jon	LB	6-3	240	3/24/61	James Madison	York, Pa.	Hagerstown, Md.	FA
Creswell, Smiley	DE	6-4	251	12/11/59	Michigan State	Everett, Wash.	Monroe, Wash.	D5
Eason, Calvin	CB-S	5-11	192	9/18/59	Houston	Houston, Tex.	Houston, Tex.	D11a
Eason, Tony	QB	6-4	212	10/8/59	Illinois	Walnut Grove, Calif.	Walnut Grove, Calif.	D1
Edwards, Dow	WR	5-10	172	10/18/61	Panhandle State	New Orleans, La.	New Orleans, La	FA
Ekern, Andy	T	6-6	263	7/26/61	Missouri	Columbia, Mo.	Columbia, Mo.	D12a
Gordon, Eddy	TE	6-5	212	2/21/61	San Diego State	Dallas, Tex.	La Mesa, Calif.	FA
Graham, Keith (1)	CB-S	5-10	170	2/12/57	Idaho	Tucson, Ariz.	Yuma, Ariz.	FA
Guyer, Doug	LB	6-4	230	12/7/61	Boston College	Philadelphia, Pa.	Wayne, Pa.	FA
Higgins, John (1)	CB	6-1	200	1/26/59	Nevada-Las Vegas	Lynwood, Calif.	Lynwood, Calif	FA
Howard, Doug	G-T	6-6	265	6/14/59	North Carolina State	Washington, D.C.	Raleigh, N.C.	FA
Jezulin, Michael	P	6-0	182	1/8/60	San Diego State	Torrance, Calif.	Redondo Beach, Calif.	FA
Kelly, Waddell	RB	6-2	208	2/2/59	Arkansas State	Gould, Ark.	Gould, Ark.	D12
Kerrigan, Mike (1)	QB	6-3	190	4/27/60	Northwestern	Chicago, Ill.	Chicago, Ill.	FA
Land, Doug (1)	RB	6-1	225	10/14/59	Long Beach State	Los Angeles, Calif.	Lynwood, Calif.	FA
Lee, Keith A.	LB	6-4	230	5/11/60	Virginia	Frederick, Md.	Charlottesville, Va.	FA
Lewis, Darryl	TE	6-6	226	4/16/61	Texas-Arlington	Mt. Pleasant, Tex.	Mt. Pleasant, Tex.	D5a
Lippett, Ronnie	CB	5-11	180	12/10/60	Miami	Melborne, Fla.	Sebring, Fla.	D8
Moore, Steve	T	6-4	285	10/1/60	Tennessee State	Memphis, Tenn.	Memphis, Tenn.	D3a
Mut, Tom	WR	6-2	187	7/8/60	Rhode Island	New Haven, Conn.	West Haven, Conn.	FA
Newby, Jonathan	WR	6-0	185	6/12/60	Western Kentucky	McKeesport, Pa.	Clairton, Pa.	FA
Parker, Steve	WR-KR	5-9	167	5/19/59	Abilene Christian	Limestone Cnty., Tex.	Abilene, Tex.	D11
Pierce, Jeff (1)	P	6-2	195	2/19/60	Georgia Tech	Piedmont, Ala.	Atlanta, Ga.	FA
Rembert, Johnny	LB	6-3	234	1/19/61	Clemson	Hollandale, Miss.	Arcadia, Fla.	D4
Reynolds, Ed	LB	6-5	230	9/23/61	Virginia	Stuttgart, Germany	Ridgeway, Va.	FA
Skoruppa, Tom	G	6-0	195	7/8/55	Texas-Arlington	Corpus Christi, Tex.	Corpus Christi, Tex.	FA
Smallwood, Reggie (1)	CB-S	6-3	205	1/17/59	Norfolk State	Portsmouth, Va.	Newport News, Va	FA
Smith, Terry (1)	CB-S	5-11	192	1/29/59	Furman	Miami, Fla.	Linville, N.C.	FA
Starring, Stephen	WR	5-10	172	7/30/61	McNeese State	Baton Rouge, La.	Vinton, La	D3
Verria, Joe (1)	NT	6-2	252	11/4/57	Bridgewater State	Providence, R.I.	Providence, R.I.	FA
Wicks, Paris	RB	5-8	175	2/26/61	Youngstown State	Summit County, Ohio	Youngstown, Ohio	FA
Williams, James	TE	6-1	227	4/18/61	Wyoming	Tuscaloosa, Ala.	Syracuse, N.Y.	D10
Williams, Ricky	RB	6-0	195	4/27/60	Langston	Santa Monica, Calif.	Santa Monica, Calif.	D9
Williams, Toby	DE	6-3	254	11/19/59	Nebraska	Washington, D.C.	Lincoln, Neb.	D10a
Wilson, Darryal	WR	6-0	182	9/19/60	Tennessee	Florence, Ala.	Bristol, Va.	D2

Players who report to an NFL team for the first time are designated on rosters as rookies (R). If a player reported to an NFL training camp in a previous year but was not on the active squad for three or more regular season or postseason games, he is listed on the first-year roster and designated by a (1). Thereafter, a player who is on the active squad for three or more regular season or postseason games is credited with an additional year of playing experience.

NOTES

Steve Sidwell, linebackers; born August 30, 1944, Winfield, Kan., lives in Wrentham, Mass. Center-linebacker Colorado 1963-66. No pro playing experience. College coach: Colorado 1968-73, Nevada-Las Vegas 1974, Southern Methodist 1976-81. Pro coach: Joined Patriots in 1982.

Steve Walters, defensive backs; born June 16, 1948, Jonesboro, Ark., lives in Wrentham, Mass. Defensive back Arkansas 1969-70. No pro playing experience. College coach: Tampa 1973, Northeast Louisiana 1974-75, Morehead State 1976, Tulsa 1977-78, Memphis State 1979, Southern Methodist 1980-81. Pro coach: Joined Patriots in 1982.

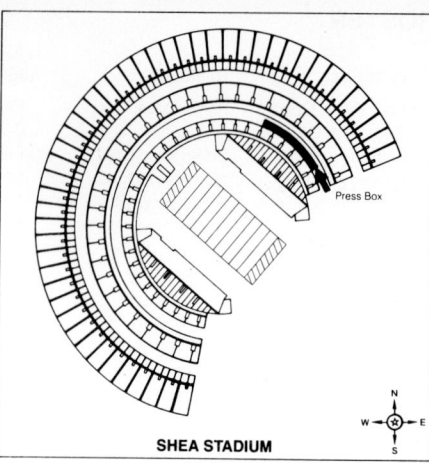

SHEA STADIUM

New York Jets

**American Football Conference
Eastern Division**

Team Colors: Kelly Green and White

**598 Madison Avenue
New York, New York 10022
Telephone: (212) 421-6600**

Club Officials

Chairman of the Board: Leon Hess
President-Chief Operating Officer: Jim Kensil
Secretary and Administrative Manager: Steve Gutman
Director of Player Personnel: Mike Hickey
Pro Personnel Director: Jim Royer
Talent Scouts: Joe Collins, Don Grammer, Sid Hall,
  Marv Sunderland
Director of Public Relations: Frank Ramos
Assistant Director of Public Relations: Ron Cohen
Director of Operations: Tim Davey
Traveling Secretary: Mike Kensil
Ticket Manager: Bob Parente
Film Director: Jim Pons
Trainer: Bob Reese
Assistant Trainer: Pepper Burruss
Equipment Manager: Bill Hampton

Stadium: Shea Stadium • **Capacity:** 60,372
  Flushing, New York 11368

Playing Surface: Grass

Training Center: 1000 Fulton Avenue
  Hempstead, New York 11550
  516-538-6600

1983 SCHEDULE

Preseason

Aug. 7	at New York Giants	8:00
Aug. 13	**Los Angeles Raiders** (Giants Stadium)	8:00
Aug. 18	at Cincinnati	9:00
Aug. 27	at New Orleans	7:00

Regular Season

Sept. 4	at San Diego	1:00
Sept. 11	**Seattle**	4:00
Sept. 18	at New England	1:00
Sept. 25	**Los Angeles Rams**	4:00
Oct. 3	at Buffalo (Monday)	9:00
Oct. 9	at Cleveland	1:00
Oct. 16	**Miami**	1:00
Oct. 23	**Atlanta**	1:00
Oct. 30	at San Francisco	1:00
Nov. 6	**Baltimore**	4:00
Nov. 13	**Buffalo**	1:00
Nov. 21	at New Orleans (Monday)	8:00
Nov. 27	**New England**	1:00
Dec. 4	at Baltimore	4:00
Dec. 10	**Pittsburgh** (Saturday)	12:30
Dec. 16	at Miami (Friday)	9:00

1982 TEAM STATISTICS

	New York Jets	Opp.
Total First Downs..................	193	160
Rushing.........................	87	54
Passing.........................	95	88
Penalty	11	18
Third Down Efficiency...........	51/118	62/135
Third Down Percentage	43.2	45.9
Total Net Yards.................	3218	2629
Total Offensive Plays	606	587
Avg. Gain per Play.............	5.3	4.5
Avg. Gain per Game	357.6	292.1
Net Yards Rushing..............	1317	983
Total Rushing Plays	304	269
Avg. Gain per Rush...........	4.3	3.7
Avg. Gain Rushing per Game	146.3	109.2
Net Yards Passing..............	1901	1646
Lost Attempting to Pass........	23/206	20/171
Gross Yards Passing	2107	1817
Attempts/Completions	279/165	298/159
Percent Completed	59.1	53.4
Had Intercepted	9	17
Avg. Net Passing per Game	211.2	182.9
Punts/Avg......................	36/37.4	42/42.1
Punt Returns/Avg...............	23/8.0	17/9.0
Kickoff Returns/Avg............	33/20.2	35/21.2
Interceptions/Avg. Ret.........	17/15.4	9/16.9
Penalties/Yards................	63/533	43/345
Fumbles/Ball Lost..............	18/9	20/9
Total Points...................	245	166
Avg. Points per Game	27.2	18.4
Touchdowns....................	31	20
Rushing.......................	13	5
Passing.......................	16	10
Returns and Recoveries	2	5
Field Goals	11/17	9/15
Conversions	26/31	19/20
Safeties......................	0	0
Avg. Time of Possession	30:41	29:19

1982 TEAM RECORD

Preseason (1-3)

New York Jets		Opponents
19	Green Bay	21
33	Houston	16
10	New York Giants	22
13	*Denver	20
75		79

Regular Season (6-3)

New York Jets		Opponents	Att.
28	*Miami	45	53,360
31	New England	7	53,515
37	*Baltimore	0	46,970
15	*Green Bay	13	53,872
28	Detroit	13	79,361
32	*Tampa Bay	17	28,147
19	Miami	20	67,307
42	Minnesota	14	58,672
13	Kansas City	37	11,902
245		166	453,106

*Home Game

Score by Periods

New York Jets	63	72	39	71	—	245
Opponents	40	54	42	30	—	166

Attendance

Home 182,349   Away 270,757   Total 453,106
Single game home record, 63,962 (11-5-72)
Single season home record, 441,099 (1971)

1982 INDIVIDUAL STATISTICS

Rushing

	Att	Yds	Avg	LG	TD
McNeil	151	786	5.2	48	6
Augustyniak	50	178	3.6	16	4
Dierking	38	130	3.4	11	1
Harper	20	125	6.3	40	0
Crutchfield	22	78	3.5	8	1
Barber	8	24	3.0	4	0
J. Jones	1	2	2.0	2	0
Ryan	1	−1	−1.0	−1	0
Todd	13	−5	−0.4	7t	1
N.Y. Jets	304	1317	4.3	48	13
Opponents	269	983	3.7	25t	5

Field Goal Success

Distance	1-19	20-29	30-39	40-49	50 Over
Made-Att.	1-1	3-5	4-5	3-6	0-0

Passing

	Att	Comp	Pct	Yds	TD	Int	Tkld	Rate
Todd	261	153	58.6	1961	14	8	23/206	87.3
Ryan	18	12	66.7	146	2	1	0/0	105.1
N.Y. Jets	279	165	59.1	2107	16	9	23/206	
Opponents	298	159	53.4	1817	10	17	20/171	

Receiving

	No	Yds	Avg	LG	TD
Walker	39	620	15.9	56t	6
Augustyniak	24	189	7.9	15	0
Barkum	19	182	9.6	29	1
J. Jones	18	294	16.3	51	2
McNeil	16	187	11.7	32t	1
Harper	14	177	12.6	39t	1
Dierking	12	80	6.7	13t	1
Gaffney	11	207	18.8	45t	1
Shuler	8	132	16.5	51	3
B. Jones	3	32	10.7	17	0
Newton	1	7	7.0	7	0
N.Y. Jets	165	2107	12.8	56t	16
Opponents	159	1817	11.4	48t	10

Interceptions

	No	Yds	Avg	LG	TD
Jackson	5	84	16.8	77t	1
Ray	3	91	30.3	44	0
Holmes	3	2	0.7	2	0
Mehl	2	38	19.0	38	0
Schroy	1	34	34.0	34	0
Buttle	1	9	9.0	9	0
Lynn	1	3	3.0	3	0
Springs	1	0	0.0	0	0
N.Y. Jets	17	261	15.4	77t	1
Opponents	9	152	16.9	47t	3

Punting

	No	Yds	Avg	In 20	LG
Ramsey	35	1348	38.5	8	54
N.Y. Jets	36	1348	37.4	8	54
Opponents	42	1770	42.1	5	76

Punt Returns

	No	FC	Yds	Avg	LG	TD
Harper	23	5	184	8.0	24	0
N.Y. Jets	23	5	184	8.0	24	0
Opponents	17	9	153	9.0	59t	1

Kickoff Returns

	No	Yds	Avg	LG	TD
Harper	18	368	20.4	37	0
Sohn	15	299	19.9	32	0
N.Y. Jets	33	667	20.2	37	0
Opponents	35	743	21.2	98t	1

Scoring

	TD	TD R	TD P	TD Rt	PAT	FG	TP
Leahy					26/31	11/17	59
McNeil	7	6	1	0			42
Walker	6	0	6	0			36
Augustyniak	4	4	0	0			24
Shuler	3	0	3	0			18
Dierking	2	1	1	0			12
Jackson	2	0	0	2			12
J. Jones	2	0	2	0			12
Barkum	1	0	1	0			6
Crutchfield	1	1	0	0			6
Gaffney	1	0	1	0			6
Harper	1	0	1	0			6
Todd	1	1	0	0			6
N.Y. Jets	31	13	16	2	26/31	11/17	245
Opponents	20	5	10	5	19/20	9/15	166

Sacks

Bennett 1, Crable 1, Gastineau 6, Klecko 2, Lyons 1½, Neil 4, Rudolph 2, Salaam 2½.

FIRST PLAYERS SELECTED

Year	Player, College, Position
1960	George Izo, Notre Dame, QB
1961	Tom Brown, Minnesota, G
1962	Sandy Stephens, Minnesota, QB
1963	Jerry Stovall, Louisiana State, S
1964	Matt Snell, Ohio State, RB
1965	Joe Namath, Alabama, QB
1966	Bill Yearby, Michigan, DT
1967	Paul Seiler, Notre Dame, T
1968	Lee White, Weber State, RB
1969	Dave Foley, Ohio State, T
1970	Steve Tannen, Florida, CB
1971	John Riggins, Kansas, RB
1972	Jerome Barkum, Jackson State, WR
1973	Burgess Owens, Miami, DB
1974	Carl Barzilauskas, Indiana, DT
1975	Anthony Davis, Southern California, RB (2)
1976	Richard Todd, Alabama, QB
1977	Marvin Powell, Southern California, T
1978	Chris Ward, Ohio State, T
1979	Marty Lyons, Alabama, DE
1980	Johnny (Lam) Jones, Texas, WR
1981	Freeman McNeil, UCLA, RB
1982	Bob Crable, Notre Dame, LB
1983	Ken O'Brien, Cal-Davis, QB

JETS COACHING HISTORY

New York Titans 1960-62 (147-178-7)

1960-61	Sammy Baugh	14-14-0
1962	Clyde (Bulldog) Turner	5-9-0
1963-73	Weeb Ewbank	74-77-6
1974-75	Charley Winner*	9-14-0
1975	Ken Shipp	1-4-0
1976	Lou Holtz**	3-10-0
1976	Mike Holovak	0-1-0
1977-82	Walt Michaels	41-49-1

*Released after nine games in 1975
**Resigned after 13 games in 1976

NEW YORK JETS 1983 VETERAN ROSTER

No.	Name	Pos.	Ht.	Wt.	Birth-date	NFL Exp.	College	Birthplace	Residence	Games in '82
60	Alexander, Dan	G	6-4	260	6/17/55	7	Louisiana State	Houston, Tex.	Houston, Tex.	9
35	Augustyniak, Mike	RB	5-11	226	7/17/56	3	Purdue	Fort Wayne, Ind.	Point Lookout, N.Y.	9
31	Barber, Marion	RB	6-3	224	12/6/59	2	Minnesota	Ft. Lauderdale, Fla.	Minneapolis, Minn.	6
83	Barkum, Jerome	TE	6-4	227	7/18/50	12	Jackson State	Gulfport, Miss.	Gulfport, Miss.	9
78	Bennett, Barry	DT-DE	6-4	257	12/10/55	6	Concordia	Long Prairie, Minn.	Buffalo, Minn.	7
64	Bingham, Guy	C-G-T	6-3	255	2/25/58	4	Montana	Koizumi Gumma Ken, Jap.	Aberdeen, Wash.	7
54	Blinka, Stan	LB	6-2	230	4/29/58	5	Sam Houston State	Columbus, Ohio	Huntsville, Tex.	8
51	Buttle, Greg	LB	6-3	232	6/20/54	8	Penn State	Atlantic City, N.J.	Point Lookout, N.Y.	7
88	Coombs, Tom	TE	6-3	236	5/31/59	2	Idaho	Eureka, Calif.	Olympia, Wash.	3
50	Crable, Bob	LB	6-3	228	9/22/59	2	Notre Dame	Cincinnati, Ohio	Cincinnati, Ohio	9
55	Crosby, Ron	LB	6-3	227	3/2/55	6	Penn State	McKeesport, Pa.	Venetia, Pa.	9
45	Crutchfield, Dwayne	RB	6-0	235	9/30/59	2	Iowa State	Cincinnati, Ohio	Cincinnati, Ohio	6
25	Dierking, Scott	RB	5-10	220	5/24/55	7	Purdue	Great Lakes, Ill.	West Chicago, Ill.	9
65	Fields, Joe	C	6-2	253	11/14/53	9	Widener	Woodbury, N.J.	Woodbury Heights, N.J.	9
38	Floyd, George	CB-S	5-11	190	12/21/60	2	Eastern Kentucky	Tampa, Fla.	Walton, Ky.	7
81	Gaffney, Derrick	WR	6-1	182	5/24/55	6	Florida	Jacksonville, Fla.	Jacksonville, Fla.	9
99	Gastineau, Mark	DE	6-5	269	11/20/56	5	East Central Oklahoma	Ardmore, Okla.	Atlantic Beach, N.Y.	9
94	Guilbeau, Rusty	DE	6-4	250	11/20/58	2	McNeese State	Sunset, La.	Sunset, La.	4
42	Harper, Bruce	RB-KR	5-8	177	6/20/55	7	Kutztown State	Englewood, N.J.	Englewood, N.J.	9
47	Holmes, Jerry	CB-S	6-2	175	12/22/57	4	West Virginia	Newport News, Va.	Hampton, Va.	9
40	Jackson, Bobby	CB	5-10	180	12/23/56	6	Florida State	Albany, Ga.	Westbury, N.Y.	9
27	Johnson, Jesse	S-CB	6-3	188	8/23/57	4	Colorado	Fort Collins, Colo.	Boulder, Colo.	9
89	Jones, Bobby	WR	5-11	185	7/12/55	6	No College	Sharon, Pa.	Brookfield, Ohio	9
80	Jones, Johnny (Lam)	WR	5-11	180	4/4/58	4	Texas	Lawton, Okla.	Austin, Tex.	8
73	Klecko, Joe	DE	6-3	269	10/15/53	7	Temple	Chester, Pa.	West Chester, Pa.	2
5	Leahy, Pat	K	6-0	189	3/19/51	10	St. Louis	St. Louis, Mo.	St. Louis, Mo.	9
71	Luscinski, Jim	T-G	6-5	275	12/16/58	2	Norwich	Arlington, Mass.	Hanover, Mass.	6
29	Lynn, Johnny	CB	6-0	198	12/19/56	4	UCLA	Los Angeles, Calif.	Altadena, Calif.	8
93	Lyons, Marty	DT	6-5	269	1/5/57	5	Alabama	Tokoma Park, Md.	Freeport, N.Y.	7
24	McNeil, Freeman	RB	5-11	216	4/22/59	3	UCLA	Jackson, Miss.	Dix Hills, N.Y.	9
56	Mehl, Lance	LB	6-3	235	2/14/58	4	Penn State	Bellaire, Ohio	Shadyside, Ohio	9
77	Neil, Kenny	DE-DT	6-4	244	1/8/59	3	Iowa State	Cincinnati, Ohio	Ames, Iowa	9
62	Pellegrini, Joe	C-G	6-4	252	4/8/57	2	Harvard	Boston, Mass.	Point Lookout, N.Y.	9
79	Powell, Marvin	T	6-5	271	8/30/55	7	Southern California	Fort Bragg, N.C.	Long Beach, N.Y.	8
15	Ramsey, Chuck	P	6-2	189	2/24/52	7	Wake Forest	Rock Hill, S.C.	Knoxville, Tenn.	9
28	Ray, Darrol	S	6-1	206	6/25/58	4	Oklahoma	San Francisco, Calif.	Norman, Okla.	9
61	Roman, John	T	6-4	265	8/31/52	8	Idaho State	Ventnor, N.J.	New York, N.Y.	9
76	Rudolph, Ben	DT-DE	6-5	270	8/29/57	3	Long Beach State	Evergreen, Ala.	Daphne, Ala.	9
10	Ryan, Pat	QB	6-3	210	9/16/55	6	Tennessee	Hutchinson, Kan.	Knoxville, Tenn.	9
74	Salaam, Abdul	DT	6-3	269	2/12/53	8	Kent State	New Brockton, Ala.	Cincinnati, Ohio	9
48	Schroy, Ken	S	6-2	198	9/22/52	7	Maryland	Valley Forge, Pa.	Hicksville, N.Y.	9
82	Schuler, Mickey	TE	6-3	236	8/21/56	6	Penn State	Harrisburg, Pa.	Enola, Pa.	9
87	Sohn, Kurt	WR-KR	5-11	176	6/26/57	3	Fordham	Ithaca, N.Y.	Levittown, N.Y.	9
45	Springs, Kirk	S-CB	6-0	192	8/10/58	3	Miami, Ohio	Cincinnati, Ohio	Cincinnati, Ohio	9
14	Todd, Richard	QB	6-2	206	11/19/53	8	Alabama	Birmingham, Ala.	Jericho, N.Y.	9
70	Waldemore, Stan	G-C-T	6-4	269	2/20/55	6	Nebraska	Newark, N.J.	Nutley, N.J.	9
85	Walker, Wesley	WR	6-0	179	5/26/55	7	California	San Bernardino, Calif.	Dix Hills, N.Y.	9
72	Ward, Chris	T	6-3	267	12/16/55	6	Ohio State	Cleveland, Ohio	Dix Hills, N.Y.	9
57	Woodring, John	LB	6-2	232	4/4/59	3	Brown	Philadelphia, Pa.	Port Washington, N.Y.	9

Also played with Jets in '82—TE-C Steve Alvers (3 games), RB Tom Newton (9).

COACHING STAFF

Head Coach, Joe Walton

Pro Career: Begins first year as head coach of the Jets. Entered pro coaching ranks as an assistant with the New York Giants in 1969-73. Joined the Washington Redskins' staff in 1974 and became the Redskins' offensive coordinator in 1978. Originally came to the Jets as the offensive coordinator in 1981.

Background: Played tight end for the University of Pittsburgh 1953-56, before playing professionally for the Washington Redskins 1957-60 and the New York Giants 1961-63. Walton did some radio work before joining the Giants staff as a scout in 1967-68.

Personal: Born December 15, 1935, Beaver Falls, Pa. Joe and his wife, Ginger, have three children, Jodi 19, Stacy 17, and Joseph, Jr. 11. They live in Long Island.

ASSISTANT COACHES

Bill Baird, defensive backs; born March 1, 1939, Lindsay, Calif., lives in New York City. Defensive back San Francisco State 1959-61. Pro defensive back New York Jets 1963-69. College coach: Stanford 1970, Fresno State 1973-75, 1979, Pacific 1980. Pro coach: Joined Jets in 1981.

Ralph Baker, linebackers; born August 25, 1942, Lewiston, Pa., lives in New York. Linebacker Penn State 1961-63. Pro linebacker New York Jets 1964-74. Pro coach: Joined Jets in 1980.

Ray Callahan, defensive line; born April 28, 1933, Lebanon, Ky., lives in Long Island. Guard-linebacker Kentucky 1952-56. No pro playing experience. College coach: Kentucky 1963-67, Cincinnati 1967-72 (head coach 1969-72). Pro coach: Baltimore Colts 1973, Florida Blazers (WFL) 1974, Chicago Bears 1975-77, Houston Oilers 1981-82, first year with Jets.

Mike Faulkiner, special assistant to the head coach; born March 27, 1947, Cameron, W. Va., lives in Long Island. Quarterback-defensive back at West Virginia Tech 1967-70. No pro playing experience. College coach: Eastern Illinois 1971. Pro coach: Toronto Argonauts (CFL) 1979, New York Giants 1980, Montreal Alouettes (CFL) 1982, first year with the Jets.

Joe Gardi, assistant head coach-defensive coordinator; born March 2, 1929, Newark, N.J., lives in Sayville, N.Y. Offensive-defensive tackle Maryland 1956-59. No pro playing experience. College coach: Maryland 1970-74. Pro coach: Philadelphia Bell (WFL) 1974-75 (interim head coach one game in 1975), Portland Thunder (WFL) 1975 (head coach), Jets since 1976.

Bobby Hammond, running backs; born February 20, 1952, Orangeburg, S.C., lives in New York. Running back Morgan State 1973-75. Pro running back New York Giants 1976-79, Washington Redskins 1979-80. Pro coach: First year with Jets.

Rich Kotite, receivers; born October 13, 1942, Brooklyn, N.Y., lives in Long Island. End Wagner 1963-65. Pro tight end New York Giants 1967, 1969-72, Pittsburgh Steelers 1968. College coach: Tennessee-Chattanooga 1973-76. Pro coach: New Orleans Saints 1977, Cleveland Browns 1978-82, first year with Jets.

Larry Pasquale, special teams; born April 21, 1941, New York, N.Y., lives in New York. Quarterback Bridgeport 1961-63. No pro playing experience. College coach: Slippery Rock State 1967, Boston University 1968, Navy 1969-70, Massachusetts 1971-75, Idaho State 1976. Pro coach: Montreal Alouettes (CFL) 1977-78, Detroit Lions 1979, Jets since 1980.

Jim Ringo, offensive line; born November 21, 1932, Orange, N.J. lives in Long Island. Center Syracuse 1950-52. Pro center Green Bay Packers 1953-63, Philadelphia Eagles 1964-66. Pro coach: Chicago Bears 1969-71, Buffalo Bills 1972-77 (1976-77 head coach), New England Patriots 1978-81, Los Angeles Rams 1982, first year with Jets.

NEW YORK JETS 1983 FIRST-YEAR ROSTER

Name	Pos.	Ht.	Wt.	Birth-date	College	Birthplace	Residence	How Acq.
Askew, Mike (1)	WR-KR	5-9	175	4/4/59	Kean College	Paterson, N.J.	Spring Valley, N.Y.	FA
Bradley, Ramiro	DT	6-7	295	9/17/58	Kansas State	Trenton, N.J.	Manhattan, Kan.	FA
Brewer, Robert	TE	6-4	230	1/27/60	Indiana Central	Kendallville, Ind.	Indianapolis, Ind.	FA
Brockington, Fred (1)	WR	6-3	200	6/1/59	Michigan	Detroit, Mich.	Detroit, Mich.	FA
Bruckner, Nicholas	WR	5-11	185	5/19/61	Syracuse	Astoria, N.Y.	Seldon, N.Y.	FA
Cabrera, Rafael	WR	6-4	195	1/8/60	Iona	Brooklyn, N.Y.	Brooklyn, N.Y.	FA
Caldwell, Rodney	G	6-4	275	5/12/58	Maryland	Philadelphia, Pa.	Paramus, N.J.	FA
Coleman, Gary	S	6-1	204	1/12/61	Kansas	Lawrence, Kan.	Lawrence, Kan.	FA
Cook, Charles (1)	DT	6-3	255	5/13/59	Miami	Miami, Fla.	Gainesville, Fla.	FA
Crum, Stu	K	5-7	165	11/4/59	Tulsa	San Jose, Calif.	Tulsa, Okla.	D12
Emmett, Marcene(1)	CB-S	6-0	195	3/11/58	North Alabama	Mobile, Ala.	Florence, Ala.	FA
Fike, Danny	T	6-6	270	6/16/61	Florida	Mobile, Ala.	Pensacola, Fla.	D10
Harmon, Mike	WR-KR	6-0	210	7/24/61	Mississippi	Kosciusko, Miss.	University, Miss.	D11
Harrington, Patrick	G	6-4	250	12/25/57	Towson State	Pennsauken, N.J.	Cherry Hill, N.J.	FA
Hector, Johnny	RB	5-11	200	11/26/60	Texas A&M	Lafayette, La.	College Station, Tex.	D2
Howell, Wes	TE	6-3	220	3/8/60	California	Castro Valley, Calif.	Castro Valley, Calif.	D4
Huber, Randall	S	6-0	197	10/8/58	Millikin	Clinton, Ill.	Ocean City, Md.	FA
Humphrey, Bobby	WR	5-10	170	8/23/61	New Mexico State	Lubbock, Tex.	Las Cruces, N.M.	D9
Hunter, Jimmy	LB	6-2	217	4/10/60	Indiana	Birmingham, Ala.	Bloomington, Ind.	FA
Iorio, Anthony	G	6-4	258	1/26/61	Hillsdale College	Brooklyn, N.Y.	West Sayville, N.Y.	FA
Jerue, Mark (1)	LB	6-3	229	1/15/60	Washington	Seattle, Wash.	Seattle, Wash.	D5 ('82)
Johnson, James	DE	6-4	245	9/29/61	Western Illinois	Chicago, Ill.	Chicago, Ill.	FA
Klever, Rocky (1)	RB	6-2	225	7/10/59	Montana	Portland, Ore.	Seaside, Ore.	D9 ('82)
Kyger, Jeff (1)	P	6-0	208	3/27/59	Slippery Rock	Columbia, Mo.	Bellevue, Wash.	FA
McElroy, Reggie (1)	T	6-6	270	3/4/60	West Texas State	Beaumont, Tex.	Amarillo, Tex.	D2 ('82)
Mullen, Davlin	CB-KR	6-1	175	2/17/60	Western Kentucky	McKeesport, Pa.	Clairton, Pa.	D8
Newbold, Darrin	LB	6-2	225	11/14/59	Southwest Missouri	Aurora, Mo.	Aurora, Mo.	D7
Northup, Kevin	QB	6-2	208	12/20/58	Central Michigan	Bay City, Mich.	Midland, Mich.	FA
O'Brien, Ken	QB	6-4	210	11/27/60	Cal-Davis	Rockville Center, N.Y.	Davis, Calif.	D1
Patterson, Samuel (1)	CB-S	5-9	172	6/13/59	Ferris State	Owensboro, Ky.	Cincinnati, Ohio	FA
Purdham, Robert	LB	6-2	220	9/24/59	Virginia Tech	Winchester, Va.	Manassas, Va.	FA
Ramsey, Hans	G	6-3	255	7/25/60	Morgan State	Bronx, N.Y.	Bronx, N.Y.	FA
Robinson, Ricky	DE	6-6	252	8/5/58	Tennessee State	Covington, Ga.	Nashville, Tenn.	FA
Rucks, Timothy	T	6-5	265	12/21/60	Carthage	Waukegan, Ill.	Waukegan, Ill.	FA
Walker, John	DT	6-6	270	9/12/61	Nebraska-Omaha	Omaha, Neb.	Omaha, Neb.	D5
Wallace, Julius	DT	6-2	283	10/13/60	West Liberty State	Wheeling, W. Va.	Wheeling, W. Va.	FA
Wright, Darin	DT	6-3	250	8/10/61	Toledo	Toledo, Ohio	Toledo, Ohio	FA

Players who report to an NFL team for the first time are designated on rosters as rookies (R). If a player reported to an NFL training camp in a previous year but was not on the active squad for three or more regular season or postseason games, he is listed on the first-year roster and designated by a (1). Thereafter, a player who is on the active squad for three or more regular season or postseason games is credited with an additional year of playing experience.

NOTES

_____
_____
_____
_____
_____
_____
_____
_____
_____
_____
_____
_____

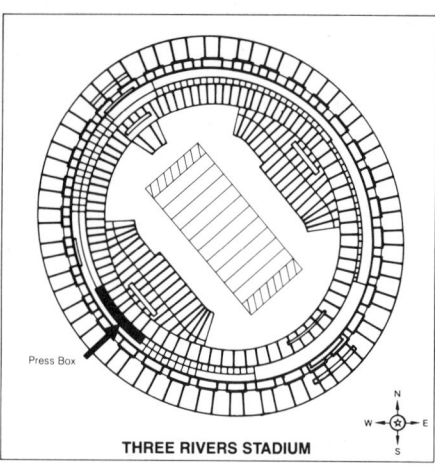

THREE RIVERS STADIUM

Pittsburgh Steelers

**American Football Conference
Central Division**

Team Colors: Black and Gold

**Three Rivers Stadium
300 Stadium Circle
Pittsburgh, Pennsylvania 15212
Telephone: (412) 323-1200**

Club Officials
Chairman of the Board: Arthur J. Rooney, Sr.
President: Daniel M. Rooney
Vice President: John R. McGinley
Vice President: Arthur J. Rooney, Jr.
Traveling Secretary: Jim Boston
Controller: Dennis P. Thimons
Publicity Director: Joe Gordon
Assistant Publicity Director: John Evenson
Director of Player Personnel: Dick Haley
Director of Public Relations: Ed Kiely
Assistant Director of Player Personnel:
    William Nunn, Jr.
Pro Talent Scout: Tom Modrak
Talent Scout-West Coast: Bob Schmitz
College Talent Scout: Joe Krupa
Director of Ticket Sales: Geraldine R. Glenn
Trainer: Ralph Berlin
Equipment Manager: Anthony Parisi

Stadium: Three Rivers Stadium • **Capacity:** 59,000
    300 Stadium Circle
    Pittsburgh, Pennsylvania 15212
Playing Surface: AstroTurf
Training Camp: St. Vincent College
    Latrobe, Pennsylvania 15650

1983 SCHEDULE
Preseason
July 30	vs. New Orleans at Canton, Ohio (HOF)	2:00
Aug. 6	vs. New England at Knoxville, Tenn.	7:30
Aug. 12	**New York Giants**	8:00
Aug. 20	at Dallas	8:00
Aug. 25	at Philadelphia	7:30

Regular Season
Sept. 4	**Denver**	1:00
Sept. 11	at Green Bay	12:00
Sept. 18	at Houston	12:00
Sept. 25	**New England**	1:00
Oct. 2	**Houston**	1:00
Oct. 10	at Cincinnati (Monday)	9:00
Oct. 16	**Cleveland**	1:00
Oct. 23	at Seattle	1:00
Oct. 30	**Tampa Bay**	1:00
Nov. 6	**San Diego**	1:00
Nov. 13	at Baltimore	2:00
Nov. 20	**Minnesota**	1:00
Nov. 24	at Detroit (Thanksgiving)	12:30
Dec. 4	**Cincinnati**	1:00
Dec. 10	at New York Jets (Saturday)	12:30
Dec. 18	at Cleveland	1:00

1982 TEAM STATISTICS

	Pittsburgh	Opp.
Total First Downs	171	174
Rushing	69	49
Passing	91	111
Penalty	11	14
Third Down Efficiency	47/121	45/127
Third Down Percentage	38.8	35.4
Total Net Yards	2970	2874
Total Offensive Plays	583	599
Avg. Gain per Play	5.1	4.8
Avg. Gain per Game	330.0	319.3
Net Yards Rushing	1187	762
Total Rushing Plays	289	236
Avg. Gain per Rush	4.1	3.2
Avg. Gain Rushing per Game	131.9	84.7
Net Yards Passing	1783	2112
Lost Attempting to Pass	19/139	34/273
Gross Yards Passing	1922	2385
Attempts/Completions	275/141	329/176
Percent Completed	51.3	53.5
Had Intercepted	16	17
Avg. Net Passing per Game	198.1	234.7
Punts/Avg.	49/40.4	53/38.1
Punt Returns/Avg.	36/8.8	28/6.5
Kickoff Returns/Avg.	28/20.3	36/22.8
Interceptions/Avg. Ret.	17/7.5	16/10.5
Penalties/Yards	59/459	45/355
Fumbles/Ball Lost	18/9	17/8
Total Points	204	146
Avg. Points per Game	22.7	16.2
Touchdowns	25	17
Rushing	7	5
Passing	17	12
Returns and Recoveries	1	0
Field Goals	10/12	9/14
Conversions	22/24	17/17
Safeties	1	0
Avg. Time of Possession	30:20	29:40

1982 TEAM RECORD

Preseason (4-0)

Pittsburgh		Opponents
24	New England	20
13	New York Giants	10
37	*Baltimore	15
27	*Philadelphia	24
101		69

Regular Season (6-3)

Pittsburgh		Opponents	Att.
36	Dallas	28	63,431
26	*Cincinnati (OT)	20	53,973
24	Houston	10	42,338
0	Seattle	16	55,553
35	*Kansas City	14	52,090
0	Buffalo	13	58,391
9	Cleveland	10	67,139
37	*New England	14	51,515
37	*Cleveland	21	52,312
204		146	496,742

*Home Game   (OT) Overtime

Score by Periods

Pittsburgh	47	54	38	59	6	—	204
Opponents	13	43	38	52	0	—	146

Attendance

Home 209,890   Away 286,852   Total 496,742
Single game home record, 54,563 (11-16-80)
Single season home record, 424,106 (1980)

1982 INDIVIDUAL STATISTICS

Rushing

	Att	Yds	Avg	LG	TD
Harris	140	604	4.3	21	2
Pollard	62	238	3.8	18	2
Abercrombie	21	100	4.8	34	2
Davis	24	72	3.0	9	0
Hawthorne	15	68	4.5	11	0
Thornton	6	33	5.5	13	1
Stoudt	11	28	2.5	8	0
Swann	1	25	25.0	25	0
Bradshaw	8	10	1.3	6	0
Stallworth	1	9	9.0	9	0
Pittsburgh	289	1187	4.1	34	7
Opponents	236	762	3.2	33	5

Field Goal Success

Distance	1-19	20-29	30-39	40-49	50 Over
Made-Att.	0-0	4-4	1-2	5-5	0-1

Passing

	Att	Comp	Pct	Yds	TD	Int	Tkld	Rate
Bradshaw	240	127	52.9	1768	17	11	18/131	81.4
Stoudt	35	14	40.0	154	0	5	1/8	14.2
Pittsburgh	275	141	51.3	1922	17	16	19/139	
Opponents	329	176	53.5	2385	12	17	34/273	

Receiving

	No	Yds	Avg	LG	TD
Harris	31	249	8.0	20	0
Stallworth	27	441	16.3	74t	7
Cunningham	21	277	13.2	31	2
Swann	18	265	14.7	60	0
Smith	17	387	22.8	51	4
Hawthorne	12	182	15.2	46t	3
Pollard	6	39	6.5	11	0
Sweeney	5	50	10.0	17	0
Abercrombie	1	14	14.0	14	0
Davis	1	11	11.0	11	0
Thornton	1	4	4.0	4	0
Pinney	1	3	3.0	3t	1
Pittsburgh	141	1922	13.6	74t	17
Opponents	176	2385	13.6	75t	12

Interceptions

	No	Yds	Avg	LG	TD
Woodruff	5	53	10.6	30	0
Shell	5	27	5.4	18	0
Johnson	2	5	2.5	5	0
Toews	1	20	20.0	20	0
Woods	1	12	12.0	12	0
Lambert	1	6	6.0	6	0
Blount	1	2	2.0	2	0
Ham	1	2	2.0	2	0
Pittsburgh	17	127	7.5	30	0
Opponents	16	168	10.5	28	0

Punting

	No	Yds	Avg	In 20	LG
Goodson	49	1981	40.4	11	66
Pittsburgh	49	1981	40.4	11	66
Opponents	53	2019	38.1	9	54

Punt Returns

	No	FC	Yds	Avg	LG	TD
Woods	13	2	142	10.9	20	0
Sydnor	22	3	172	7.8	21	0
Merriweather	1	0	3	3.0	3	0
Pittsburgh	36	5	317	8.8	21	0
Opponents	28	5	182	6.5	17	0

Kickoff Returns

	No	Yds	Avg	LG	TD
Bohannon	14	329	23.5	57	0
Abercrombie	7	139	19.9	46	0
French	2	38	19.0	26	0
Sydnor	2	37	18.5	20	0
Moser	1	18	18.0	18	0
Donnalley	1	8	8.0	8	0
Swann	1	0	0.0	0	0
Pittsburgh	28	569	20.3	57	0
Opponents	36	821	22.8	39	0

Scoring

	TD	TD R	TD P	TD Rt	PAT	FG	TP
Anderson					22/22	10/12	52
Stallworth	7	0	7	0			42
Smith	4	0	4	0			24
Hawthorne	3	0	3	0			18
Abercrombie	2	2	0	0			12
Cunningham	2	0	2	0			12
Harris	2	2	0	0			12
Pollard	2	2	0	0			12
Pinney	1	0	1	0			6
Rodgers	1	0	0	1			6
Thornton	1	1	0	0			6
Team		(Safety)					2
Pittsburgh	25	7	17	1	22/24	10/12	204
Opponents	17	5	12	0	17/17	9/14	146

Sacks

Beasley 6, Cole 5, Dunn 6, Goodman 1½, Ham 3, Hinkle 1, Kohrs 2, Lambert 4, Shell 1, Toews 2½, Willis 1, Woodruff 1.

FIRST PLAYERS SELECTED

(Since 1943)

Year	Player, College, Position
1943	Bill Daley, Minnesota, B
1944	Johnny Podesto, St. Mary's, California, B
1945	Paul Duhart, Florida, B
1946	Felix (Doc) Blanchard, Army, B
1947	Hub Bechtol, Texas, E
1948	Dan Edwards, Georgia, E
1949	Bobby Gage, Clemson, B
1950	Lynn Chandnois, Michigan State, B
1951	Butch Avinger, Alabama, B
1952	Ed Modzelewski, Maryland, B
1953	Ted Marchibroda, St. Bonaventure, B
1954	Johnny Lattner, Notre Dame, B
1955	Frank Varrichione, Notre Dame, T
1956	Gary Glick, Colorado A&M, B
1957	Len Dawson, Purdue, B
1958	Larry Krutko, West Virginia, B (2)
1959	Tom Barnett, Purdue, B (8)
1960	Jack Spikes, Texas Christian, RB
1961	Myron Pottios, Notre Dame, LB (2)
1962	Bob Ferguson, Ohio State, RB
1963	Frank Atkinson, Stanford, T (8)
1964	Paul Martha, Pittsburgh, S
1965	Roy Jefferson, Utah, WR (2)
1966	Dick Leftridge, West Virginia, RB
1967	Don Shy, San Diego State, RB (2)
1968	Mike Taylor, Southern California, T
1969	Joe Greene, North Texas State, DT
1970	Terry Bradshaw, Louisiana Tech, QB
1971	Frank Lewis, Grambling, WR
1972	Franco Harris, Penn State, RB
1973	J. T. Thomas, Florida State, DB
1974	Lynn Swann, Southern California, WR
1975	Dave Brown, Michigan, DB
1976	Bennie Cunningham, Clemson, TE
1977	Robin Cole, New Mexico, LB
1978	Ron Johnson, Eastern Michigan, DB
1979	Greg Hawthorne, Baylor, RB
1980	Mark Malone, Arizona State, QB
1981	Keith Gary, Oklahoma, DE
1982	Walter Abercrombie, Baylor, RB
1983	Gabriel Rivera, Texas Tech, DT

STEELERS COACHING HISTORY

(298-335-20)

1933	Forrest (Jap) Douds	3-6-2
1934	Luby DiMelio	2-10-0
1935-36	Joe Bach	10-14-0
1937-39	Johnny Blood (McNally)	6-19-0
1939-40	Walter Kiesling	3-13-3
1941	Bert Bell	0-2-0
	Aldo (Bluff) Donelli	0-5-0
1941-44	Walter Kiesling*	13-20-2
1945	Jim Leonard	2-8-0
1946-47	Jock Sutherland	13-10-1
1948-51	Johnny Michelosen	20-26-2
1952-53	Joe Bach	11-13-0
1954-56	Walter Kiesling	14-22-0
1957-64	Raymond (Buddy) Parker	51-47-6
1965	Mike Nixon	2-12-0
1966-68	Bill Austin	11-28-3
1969-82	Chuck Noll	137-80-1

*Co-Coach in Philadelphia-Pittsburgh merger in 1943 and in Chicago Cardinal-Pittsburgh merger in 1944.

PITTSBURGH STEELERS 1983 VETERAN ROSTER

No.	Name	Pos.	Ht.	Wt.	Birth-date	NFL Exp.	College	Birthplace	Residence	Games in '82
34	Abercrombie, Walter	RB	5-11	201	9/26/59	2	Baylor	Waco, Tex.	Waco, Tex.	6
1	Anderson, Gary	K	5-11	156	7/16/59	2	Syracuse	Parys, Orange Free State, South Africa	Downington, Pa.	9
65	Beasley, Tom	DE-NT	6-5	248	8/11/54	6	Virginia Tech	Bluefield, W. Va.	Prosperity, Pa.	7
54	Bingham, Craig	LB	6-2	211	9/29/59	2	Syracuse	Kingston, Jamaica	Stamford, Conn.	7
47	Blount, Mel	CB	6-3	205	4/10/48	14	Southern	Vidalia, Ga.	Pittsburgh, Pa.	9
23	Bohannon, Fred	S-CB	6-0	201	5/31/58	2	Mississippi Valley State	Birmingham, Ala.	Birmingham, Ala.	7
71	Boures, Emil	C-G	6-1	252	1/29/60	2	Pittsburgh	Bridgeport, Pa.	Pittsburgh, Pa.	4
12	Bradshaw, Terry	QB	6-3	210	9/2/48	14	Louisiana Tech	Shreveport, La.	Grand Cane, La.	9
79	†Brown, Larry	T	6-4	270	6/16/49	13	Kansas	Jacksonville, Fla.	Pittsburgh, Pa.	8
56	Cole, Robin	LB	6-2	220	9/11/55	7	New Mexico	Los Angeles, Calif.	Washington, Pa.	9
5	Colquitt, Craig	P	6-1	182	6/9/54	5	Tennessee	Knoxville, Tenn.	Knoxville, Tenn.	0*
77	Courson, Steve	G	6-1	260	10/1/55	6	South Carolina	Philadelphia, Pa.	Pittsburgh, Pa.	8
89	Cunningham, Bennie	TE	6-5	260	12/23/54	8	Clemson	Laurens, S.C.	Piedmont, S.C.	9
45	Davis, Russell	RB	6-1	231	9/15/56	4	Michigan	Millen, Ga.	Pittsburgh, Pa.	7
55	Donnalley, Rick	C-G	6-2	257	12/11/58	2	North Carolina	Wilmington, Del.	Pittsburgh, Pa.	5
67	†Dunn, Gary	NT	6-3	260	8/24/53	7	Miami	Coral Gables, Fla.	Miami, Fla.	9
20	French, Ernest	S	5-11	195	9/5/59	2	Alabama A&M	Tensaw, Ala.	Pittsburgh, Pa.	3
95	Goodman, John	DE	6-6	250	11/21/58	3	Oklahoma	Oklahoma City, Okla.	Garland, Tex.	9
17	Goodson, John	P	6-3	204	3/18/60	2	Texas	Houston, Tex.	Houston, Tex.	9
32	Harris, Franco	RB	6-2	225	3/7/50	12	Penn State	Fort Dix, N.J.	Pittsburgh, Pa.	9
27	Hawthorne, Greg	RB-WR	6-2	225	9/5/56	5	Baylor	Fort Worth, Tex.	Fort Worth, Tex.	9
53	Hinkle, Bryan	LB	6-1	214	6/4/59	2	Oregon	Long Beach, Calif.	Silverdale, Wash.	9
62	Ilkin, Tunch	T	6-3	253	9/23/57	4	Indiana State	Istanbul, Turkey	Pittsburgh, Pa.	8
29	†Johnson, Ron	S	5-10	200	6/8/56	6	Eastern Michigan	Detroit, Mich.	Pittsburgh, Pa.	9
90	Kohrs, Bob	LB-DE	6-3	245	11/8/58	3	Arizona State	Phoenix, Ariz.	Pittsburgh, Pa.	9
58	Lambert, Jack	LB	6-4	220	7/8/52	10	Kent State	Mantua, Ohio	Pittsburgh, Pa.	8
50	Little, David	LB	6-1	220	1/3/59	3	Florida	Miami, Fla.	Miami, Fla.	9
16	Malone, Mark	QB	6-4	223	11/22/58	4	Arizona State	El Cajon, Calif.	Pittsburgh, Pa.	0*
57	Merriweather, Mike	LB	6-2	215	11/26/60	2	Pacific	Albans, N.Y.	Vallejo, Calif.	9
64	Nelson, Edmund	NT-DE	6-3	263	4/30/60	2	Auburn	Live Oak, Fla.	Tampa, Fla.	7
66	Petersen, Ted	T	6-5	256	2/7/55	6	Eastern Illinois	Kankakee, Ill.	Pittsburgh, Pa.	7
44	Pollard, Frank	RB	5-10	210	6/15/57	4	Baylor	Meridian, Tex.	Meridian, Tex.	9
87	Rodgers, John	TE	6-2	220	2/7/60	2	Louisiana Tech	Omaha, Tex.	Daingerfield, Tex.	7
36	Ruff, Guy	LB	6-1	215	8/18/60	2	Syracuse	Ravenna, Ohio	Windham, Ohio	2
31	†Shell, Donnie	S	5-11	190	8/26/52	10	South Carolina State	Whitmire, S.C.	Columbia, S.C.	9
82	†Stallworth, John	WR	6-2	191	7/15/52	10	Alabama A&M	Tuscaloosa, Ala.	Huntsville, Ala.	9
18	Stoudt, Cliff	QB	6-4	218	3/27/55	7	Youngstown State	Oberlin, Ohio	Pittsburgh, Pa.	6
85	Sweeney, Calvin	WR	6-2	190	1/12/55	4	Southern California	Riverside, Calif.	Santa Monica, Calif.	7
83	Sydnor, Willie	WR-KR	5-11	170	3/21/59	2	Syracuse	Bryn Mawr, Pa.	Rosemont, Pa.	7
51	Toews, Loren	LB	6-3	220	11/3/51	11	California	Dinuba, Calif.	Pittsburgh, Pa.	9
42	Washington, Anthony	CB	6-1	204	2/4/58	3	Fresno State	San Francisco, Calif.	Fresno, Calif.	9
41	Washington, Sam	S	5-8	180	3/7/60	2	Mississippi Valley State	Tampa, Fla.	Tampa, Fla.	4
52	Webster, Mike	C	6-1	255	3/18/52	10	Wisconsin	Tomahawk, Wis.	Pittsburgh, Pa.	9
93	Willis, Keith	DE	6-1	251	7/29/59	2	Northeastern	Newark, N.J.	Newark, N.J.	9
73	Wolfley, Craig	G	6-1	265	5/19/58	4	Syracuse	Buffalo, N.Y.	Pittsburgh, Pa.	9
49	Woodruff, Dwayne	CB	5-11	198	2/18/57	5	Louisville	Bowling Green, Ky.	Louisville, Ky.	9
22	Woods, Rick	S-KR	6-0	196	1/16/59	2	Boise State	Boise, Idaho	Boise, Idaho	5

* Colquitt missed '82 season due to injury; Malone active for 3 games in '82, but did not play.

†Option playout; subject to developments.

Retired—Jack Ham, 12-year linebacker, 8 games in '82; Lynn Swann, 9-year wide receiver, 9 in '82.

Also played with Steelers in '82—C Tyrone McGriff (8 games), RB Rick Moser (6), T Ray Pinney (9), WR Jim Smith (8), RB Sidney Thornton (4).

COACHING STAFF

Head Coach, Chuck Noll

Pro Career: Became first NFL coach to win four Super Bowls when Steelers defeated Los Angeles 31-19 in Super Bowl XIV. Has guided Steelers into postseason play nine of last eleven years. Led Steelers to consecutive NFL championships twice (1974-75, 1978-79). Has fourth highest won-lost percentage among active coaches (.631) and ranks eighth among the NFL's all-time winningest coaches with a career record of 137-80-1. Played pro ball as guard-linebacker for Cleveland Browns from 1953-59. At age 28, he started coaching career as defensive coach with Los Angeles (San Diego) Chargers in 1960. Left after 1965 season to become Don Shula's defensive backfield assistant in Baltimore. Remained with Colts until taking over Pittsburgh reins as head coach in 1969.

Background: Was an all-state star at Benedictine High in Cleveland. Captained the University of Dayton team, playing both tackle and linebacker. He was drafted by the Browns in 1953.

Personal: Born in Cleveland on January 5, 1932. He and wife, Marianne, live in Pittsburgh and have one son—Chris.

ASSISTANT COACHES

Ron Blackledge, offensive line; born April 15, 1938, Canton, Ohio, lives in Pittsburgh. Tight end and defensive end Bowling Green 1957-59. No pro playing experience. College coach: Ashland 1968-69, Cincinnati 1970-72, Kentucky 1973-75, Princeton 1976, Kent State 1977-81 (head coach 1979-81). Pro coach: Joined Steelers in 1982.

Tony Dungy, defensive backfield; born October 6, 1955, Jackson, Mich., lives in Pittsburgh. Quarterback Minnesota 1973-76. Pro safety Pittsburgh Steelers 1977-78, San Francisco 49ers 1979. College coach: Minnesota 1980. Pro coach: Joined Steelers in 1981.

Dennis Fitzgerald, linebackers; born March 13, 1936, Ann Arbor, Mich., lives in Pittsburgh. Running back Michigan 1958-60. No pro playing experience. College coach: Michigan 1961-68, Kentucky 1969-70, Kent State 1971-77 (head coach 1975-77), Syracuse 1978-80, Tulane 1981. Pro coach: Joined Steelers in 1982.

Dick Hoak, offensive backfield; born December 8, 1939, Jeannette, Pa., lives in Greenburg, Pa. Halfback-quarterback Penn State 1958-60. Pro running back Pittsburgh Steelers 1961-70. Pro coach: Steelers since 1972.

Jon Kolb, conditioning; born August 30, 1947, Ponca City, Okla., lives in Pittsburgh. Center-linebacker Oklahoma State 1966-68. Pro tackle Pittsburgh Steelers 1969-81. Pro coach: Joined Steelers in 1982.

Tom Moore, receivers; born November 7, 1938, Owatonna, Minn., lives in Pittsburgh. Quarterback Iowa 1957-60. No pro playing experience. College coach: Iowa 1961-62, Dayton 1965-68, Wake Forest 1969, Georgia Tech 1970-71, Minnesota 1972-73, 1975-76. Pro coach: New York Stars (WFL) 1974, Steelers since 1977.

Woody Widenhofer, defensive coordinator; born January 20, 1943, Butler, Pa., lives in Pittsburgh. Linebacker Missouri 1961-64. No pro playing experience. College coach: Michigan State 1969-70, Eastern Michigan 1971, Minnesota 1972. Pro coach: Joined Steelers in 1973.

PITTSBURGH STEELERS 1983 FIRST-YEAR ROSTER

Name	Pos.	Ht.	Wt.	Birth-date	College	Birthplace	Residence	How Acq.
Best, Greg	S	5-10	185	1/14/60	Kansas State	New Brighton, Pa.	New Brighton, Pa.	FA
Bowen, Pat	S	6-0	190	4/9/60	South Carolina	Mechanicsburg, Pa.	Mechanicsburg, Pa.	FA
Capers, Wayne	WR	6-2	193	5/17/61	Kansas	Miami, Fla.	Miami, Fla.	D2
Clayton, Harvey	CB	5-9	170	4/4/61	Florida State	Kendall, Fla.	Florida City, Fla.	FA
Coye, Conrad	DE	6-4	235	9/1/61	Northeastern	Kingston, Jamaica	Allston, Mass.	FA
Crane, Darryl	WR	5-11	194	10/24/60	Florida A&M	Jacksonville, Fla.	Jacksonville, Fla.	FA
Dallafior, Ken (1)	T	6-3	268	8/26/59	Minnesota	Royal Oak, Mich.	Madison Hgts., Mich.	D5 ('82)
DeGruttola, Gary	S	5-10	192	11/26/61	Westminster	New Castle, Pa.	Ellwood City, Pa.	FA
Dunaway, Craig	TE	6-2	233	3/27/61	Michigan	Lake Charles, La.	Corpus Christi, Tex.	D8a
Fowlkes, Dennis	LB	6-2	230	3/11/61	West Virginia	Columbus, Ohio	Columbus, Ohio	FA
Garrity, Gregg	WR	5-10	171	11/24/60	Penn State	Pittsburgh, Pa.	Pittsburgh, Pa.	D5a
Gary, Keith	DE	6-3	255	9/14/59	Oklahoma	Bethesda, Md.	Chester, Va.	D1 ('81)
Gissendanner, D. (1)	WR	6-3	180	12/31/58	Pittsburgh	McKeesport, Pa.	Pittsburgh, Pa.	FA
Goff, Ricky	LB	6-2	233	9/6/60	Tulane	Baton Rouge, La.	Baton Rouge, La.	FA
Graham, Russ (1)	T	6-4	265	5/5/61	Oklahoma State	Borger, Tex.	Borger, Tex.	FA
Harris, Ananias	QB	6-2	190	6/17/61	Alabama A&M	Pensacola, Fla.	Pensacola, Fla.	FA
Harris, Tim	RB	5-9	206	6/15/61	Washington State	Compton, Calif.	Compton, Calif.	FA
Hull, Jay	G	6-2	240	8/25/60	Wichita State	Kansas City, Mo.	Wichita, Kan.	FA
Joyner, Russ	LB	6-3	242	9/7/60	Boston College	New York, N.Y.	New York, N.Y.	FA
Kennell, Lonnie	NT	6-2	248	2/8/61	Wichita State	Crescent City, Fla.	Crescent City, Fla.	FA
Kinney, Alfred	WR	5-8	160	1/31/61	Northeast Louisiana	Fort Worth, Tex.	Fort Worth, Tex.	FA
Kirchner, Mark	T	6-3	261	10/19/59	Baylor	Pasadena, Tex.	Houston, Tex.	D7
LaCroix, Lawrence	CB	5-11	183	1/9/61	Houston	Tyler, Tex.	Tyler, Tex.	FA
Langan, Bill	G	6-1	245	1/16/60	Westminster	Pittsburgh, Pa.	Pittsburgh, Pa.	FA
Metcalf, Isaac	CB-S	6-2	193	4/18/61	Baylor	Waco, Tex.	Richfield, Tex.	D4
Meyer, John (1)	T	6-6	257	5/28/59	Arizona State	Phoenix, Ariz.	Phoenix, Ariz.	D2 ('82)
Muller, Jack	T	6-4	250	6/23/60	Slippery Rock	Pittsburgh, Pa.	Zelienople, Pa.	FA
Odum, Henry	RB	5-10	200	2/12/59	South Carolina State	Bamburg, S.C.	Denmark, S.C.	D8
Peters, Guy (1)	DE	6-3	260	5/4/60	Temple	Pittsburgh, Pa.	Freedom, Pa.	FA
Rash, Lou	CB	5-9	170	6/5/60	Mississippi Valley St.	Cleveland, Miss.	Cleveland, Miss.	FA
Raugh, Mark	TE	6-2	208	5/4/60	West Virginia	Roaring Spring, Pa.	Roaring Spring, Pa.	D11
Rivera, Gabriel	NT-DT	6-2	293	4/7/61	Texas Tech	Crystal City, Tex.	Crystal City, Tex.	D1
Rostosky, Pete	G	6-4	235	7/29/61	Connecticut	Monongahela, Pa.	Monongahela, Pa.	FA
Schoen, Jon	WR	6-1	200	12/26/60	Boston College	Washington, D.C.	Rockville, Md.	FA
Seabaugh, Todd	LB	6-4	220	3/16/61	San Diego State	Santa Paula, Calif.	Santa Paula, Calif.	D3
Skansi, Paul	WR	5-11	190	1/11/60	Washington	Tacoma, Wash.	Gig Harbor, Wash.	D5
Smith, Gary (1)	G	6-1	265	1/27/60	Virginia Tech	Bitburg, Germany	Hampton, Va.	FA
Smith, Ken	G	6-2	260	10/16/60	Miami, Ohio	Indianapolis, Ind.	Indianapolis, Ind.	FA
Smith, Randy	WR	6-3	193	3/30/61	Heidelberg	Bellefontaine, Ohio	Huntsville, Ohio	FA
Stancil, Hercules	WR	6-2	186	5/7/61	Ottawa, Kansas	Bartow, Fla.	Bradley, Fla.	FA
Straughter, Roosevelt	S	5-9	184	1/26/61	Northeast Louisiana	Mangham, La.	Mangham, La.	D10
Sunseri, Sal (1)	LB	6-0	225	8/1/59	Pittsburgh	Pittsburgh, Pa.	Pittsburgh, Pa.	D10 ('82)
Warman, Gary	LB	6-0	225	5/14/60	Geneva	Natrona Heights, Pa.	Valencia, Pa.	FA
Wiley, Roger	RB	5-10	210	9/17/59	Sam Houston State	Houston, Tex.	Houston, Tex.	D12
Williams, Eric	S	5-11	183	2/21/60	North Carolina State	Garner, N.C.	Garner, N.C.	D6
Williams, Keith	WR	5-11	175	9/19/60	Pittsburgh	Syracuse, N.Y.	Syracuse, N.Y.	FA
Williams, Ken	LB	6-1	204	7/3/61	Louisiana Tech	Bank, Ark.	Bank, Ark.	FA
Wilson, Frank	TE-RB	6-2	233	10/11/58	Rice	Austin, Tex.	Austin, Tex.	D8 ('81)
Wingle, Blake	G	6-2	267	4/17/60	UCLA	Pottsville, Calif.	Ontario, Calif.	D9
Winters, Chet	RB	6-0	205	10/22/60	Oklahoma	Chicago, Ill.	Jacksonville, Ark.	FA

Players who report to an NFL team for the first time are designated on rosters as rookies (R). If a player reported to an NFL training camp in a previous year but was not on the active squad for three or more regular season or postseason games, he is listed on the first-year roster and designated by a (1). Thereafter, a player who is on the active squad for three or more regular season or postseason games is credited with an additional year of playing experience.

NOTES

_____

_____

_____

_____

_____

_____

_____

_____

_____

_____

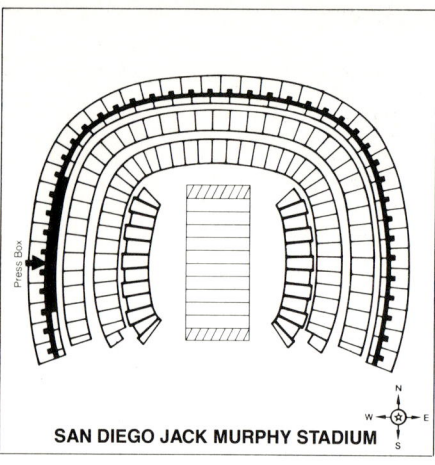

SAN DIEGO JACK MURPHY STADIUM

San Diego Chargers

**American Football Conference
Western Division**

Team Colors: Royal Blue, Gold, and White

**San Diego Jack Murphy Stadium
P.O. Box 20666
San Diego, California 92120
Telephone: (619) 280-2111**

Club Officials
President: Eugene V. Klein
General Manager: John R. Sanders
Assistant General Manager: Paul (Tank) Younger
Assistant to the President: Jack Teele
Administrative Assistant, Player Personnel:
   John Trump
Chief Scout: Aubrey (Red) Phillips
Director of Public Relations: Rick Smith
Business Manager: Pat Curran
Director of Advertising-Promotions: Rich Israel
Director of Ticket Operations: John McConaha
Assistant Public Relations Director: Rodney Knox
Public Relations Assistant: Bill Johnston
Controller: Frances Beede
Trainer: Ric McDonald
Equipment Manager: Sid Brooks

Stadium: San Diego Jack Murphy Stadium •
   Capacity: 52,675
   9449 Friars Road
   San Diego, California 92108

Playing Surface: Grass

Training Camp: University of California-San Diego
   La Jolla, California 92037

1983 SCHEDULE
Preseason
Aug. 6	at Los Angeles Rams	7:00
Aug. 13	**Philadelphia**	6:00
Aug. 20	**San Francisco**	6:00
Aug. 26	**Los Angeles Rams**	7:00

Regular Season
Sept. 4	**New York Jets**	1:00
Sept. 12	at Kansas City (Monday)	8:00
Sept. 18	at Seattle	1:00
Sept. 25	**Cleveland**	1:00
Oct. 2	at New York Giants	4:00
Oct. 9	**Seattle**	1:00
Oct. 16	at New England	1:00
Oct. 23	at Denver	2:00
Oct. 31	**Washington** (Monday)	6:00
Nov. 6	at Pittsburgh	1:00
Nov. 13	**Dallas**	1:00
Nov. 20	at St. Louis	12:00
Nov. 27	**Denver**	1:00
Dec. 1	**Los Angeles Raiders** (Thursday)	6:00
Dec. 11	**Kansas City**	1:00
Dec. 18	at Los Angeles Raiders	1:00

1982 TEAM STATISTICS

	San Diego	Opp.
Total First Downs	233	196
Rushing	72	65
Passing	145	119
Penalty	16	12
Third Down Efficiency	53/102	39/103
Third Down Percentage	52.0	37.9
Total Net Yards	4048	3253
Total Offensive Plays	617	591
Avg. Gain per Play	6.6	5.5
Avg. Gain per Game	449.8	361.4
Net Yards Rushing	1121	961
Total Rushing Plays	267	230
Avg. Gain per Rush	4.2	4.2
Avg. Gain Rushing per Game	124.6	106.8
Net Yards Passing	2927	2292
Lost Attempting to Pass	12/94	19/145
Gross Yards Passing	3021	2437
Attempts/Completions	338/208	342/233
Percent Completed	61.5	68.1
Had Intercepted	12	13
Avg. Net Passing per Game	325.2	254.7
Punts/Avg.	23/37.7	27/44.9
Punt Returns/Avg.	12/11.5	7/12.3
Kickoff Returns/Avg.	45/19.8	51/19.4
Interceptions/Avg. Ret.	13/11.4	12/21.8
Penalties/Yards	64/530	70/612
Fumbles/Ball Lost	17/8	19/12
Total Points	288	221
Avg. Points per Game	32.0	24.6
Touchdowns	34	25
Rushing	15	10
Passing	19	10
Returns and Recoveries	0	5
Field Goals	16/22	16/19
Conversions	32/34	23/24
Safeties	2	0
Avg. Time of Possession	29:18	30:42

1982 TEAM RECORD

Preseason (2-2)

San Diego		Opponents
28	*Chicago	27
16	*Dallas	26
23	*San Francisco	9
14	Los Angeles Rams	20
81		82

Regular Season (6-3)

San Diego		Opponents	Att.
23	Denver	3	73,564
12	Kansas City	19	60,514
24	Los Angeles Raiders	28	42,162
30	*Denver	20	47,629
30	Cleveland	13	54,064
41	San Francisco	37	55,988
50	*Cincinnati	34	51,296
44	*Baltimore	26	49,711
34	*Los Angeles Raiders	41	51,612
288		221	486,540

*Home Game

Score by Periods

San Diego	51	90	83	64	—	288
Opponents	30	63	71	57	—	221

Attendance

Home 200,248   Away 286,292   Total 486,540

Single game home record, 54,611 (12-31-72)
Single season home record, 411,661 (1981)

1982 INDIVIDUAL STATISTICS

Rushing

	Att	Yds	Avg	LG	TD
Muncie	138	569	4.1	27	8
Brooks	87	430	4.9	48t	6
Cappelletti	22	82	3.7	17	0
Chandler	5	32	6.4	21	0
Fouts	9	8	0.9	9	1
Jodat	3	7	2.3	3	0
Bell	2	6	3.0	4	0
Luther	1	−13	−13.0	−13	0
San Diego	267	1121	4.2	48t	15
Opponents	230	961	4.2	30	10

Field Goal Success

Distance	1-19	20-29	30-39	40-49	50 Over
Made-Att.	2-2	6-7	0-1	7-7	1-5

Passing

	Att	Comp	Pct	Yds	TD	Int	Tkld	Rate
Fouts	330	204	61.8	2883	17	11	12/94	93.6
Luther	4	2	50.0	55	0	1	0/0	—
Muncie	3	2	66.7	83	2	0	0/0	—
Winslow	1	0	0	0	0	0	0/0	—
San Diego	338	208	61.5	3021	19	12	12/94	
Opponents	342	233	68.1	2437	10	13	19/145	

Receiving

	No	Yds	Avg	LG	TD
Winslow	54	721	13.4	40	6
Chandler	49	1032	21.1	66t	9
Joiner	36	545	15.1	43	0
Muncie	25	207	8.5	39	1
Brooks	13	66	5.1	12	0
Sievers	12	173	14.4	26	1
Cappelletti	7	48	6.9	22	0
Scales	6	105	17.5	29t	1
Fitzkee	3	47	15.7	18t	1
Duckworth	2	77	38.5	55	0
Jodat	1	0	0.0	0	0
San Diego	208	3021	14.5	66t	19
Opponents	233	2437	10.5	49	10

Interceptions

	No	Yds	Avg	LG	TD
Fox	4	103	25.8	35	0
Thrift	2	16	8.0	9	0
Williams	2	12	6.0	6	0
A. Young	2	9	4.5	9	0
Gregor	1	6	6.0	6	0
Lowe	1	2	2.0	2	0
Allen	1	0	0.0	0	0
San Diego	13	148	11.4	35	0
Opponents	12	262	21.8	62t	3

Punting

	No	Yds	Avg	In 20	LG
Buford	21	868	41.3	5	71
San Diego	23	868	37.7	5	71
Opponents	27	1213	44.9	3	60

Punt Returns

	No	FC	Yds	Avg	LG	TD
Brooks	12	4	138	11.5	29	0
Chandler	0	1	0	—	0	0
San Diego	12	5	138	11.5	29	0
Opponents	7	2	86	12.3	30	0

Kickoff Returns

	No	Yds	Avg	LG	TD
Brooks	33	749	22.7	47	0
A. Young	4	45	11.3	16	0
Jodat	3	45	15.0	16	0
Bauer	2	24	12.0	15	0
Sievers	1	17	17.0	17	0
Bell	1	10	10.0	10	0
Gissinger	1	0	0.0	0	0
San Diego	45	890	19.8	47	0
Opponents	51	991	19.4	36	0

Scoring

	TD	TD R	TD P	TD Rt	PAT	FG	TP
Benirschke					32/34	16/22	80
Chandler	9	0	9	0			54
Muncie	9	8	1	0			54
Brooks	6	6	0	0			36
Winslow	6	0	6	0			36
Fitzkee	1	0	1	0			6
Fouts	1	1	0	0			6
Scales	1	0	1	0			6
Sievers	1	0	1	0			6
Johnson		(Safety)					2
Team		(Safety)					2
San Diego	34	15	19	0	32/34	16/22	288
Opponents	25	10	10	5	23/24	16/19	221

Sacks

Ackerman 3, Ferguson 4½, Johnson 4, Jones 1½, Kelcher 2, King 1, Lowe 2, W. Young 1.

FIRST PLAYERS SELECTED

Year	Player, College, Position
1960	Monty Stickles, Notre Dame, E
1961	Earl Faison, Indiana, DE
1962	Bob Ferguson, Ohio State, RB
1963	Walt Sweeney, Syracuse, G
1964	Ted Davis, Georgia Tech, LB
1965	Steve DeLong, Tennessee, DE
1966	Don Davis, Cal State-Los Angeles, DT
1967	Ron Billingsley, Wyoming, DE
1968	Russ Washington, Missouri, DT
1969	Marty Domres, Columbia, QB
1970	Walker Gillette, Richmond, WR
1971	Leon Burns, Long Beach State, RB
1972	Pete Lazetich, Stanford, DE (2)
1973	Johnny Rodgers, Nebraska, WR
1974	Bo Matthews, Colorado, RB
1975	Gary Johnson, Grambling, DT
1976	Joe Washington, Oklahoma, RB
1977	Bob Rush, Memphis State, C
1978	John Jefferson, Arizona State, WR
1979	Kellen Winslow, Missouri, TE
1980	Ed Luther, San Jose State, QB (4)
1981	James Brooks, Auburn, RB
1982	Hollis Hall, Clemson, DB (7)
1983	Billy Ray Smith, Arkansas, LB

CHARGERS COACHING HISTORY

Los Angeles 1960
(175-151-11)

1960-69	Sid Gillman*	83-51-6
1969-70	Charlie Waller	9-7-3
1971	Sid Gillman**	4-6-0
1971-73	Harland Svare***	7-17-2
1973	Ron Waller	1-5-0
1974-78	Tommy Prothro****	21-39-0
1978-82	Don Coryell	50-26-0

*Retired after nine games in 1969
**Released after 10 games in 1971
***Resigned after eight games in 1973
****Resigned after four games in 1978

SAN DIEGO CHARGERS 1983 VETERAN ROSTER

No.	Name	Pos.	Ht.	Wt.	Birth-date	NFL Exp.	College	Birthplace	Residence	Games in '82
91	Ackerman, Richard	DT	6-4	254	6/16/59	2	Memphis State	La Grange, Ill.	Bloomingdale, Ill.	9
27	Allen, Jeff	CB	5-11	194	7/18/58	3	Cal-Davis	Richmond, Va.	San Diego, Calif.	9
37	Bauer, Hank	RB	5-10	200	7/15/54	7	California Lutheran	Scottsbluff, Neb.	San Diego, Calif.	9
42	Bell, Ricky	RB	6-1	216	4/8/55	7	Southern California	Houston, Tex.	San Diego, Calif.	4
6	Benirschke, Rolf	K	6-1	179	2/7/55	7	Cal-Davis	Boston, Mass.	San Diego, Calif.	9
50	Bradley, Carlos	LB	6-0	226	4/27/60	3	Wake Forest	Philadelphia, Pa.	San Diego, Calif.	9
21	Brooks, James	RB-KR	5-9	177	2/28/58	3	Auburn	Warner Robins, Ga.	Warner Robins, Ga.	9
7	Buford, Maury	P	6-0	185	2/18/60	2	Texas Tech	Mt. Pleasant, Tex.	Mt. Pleasant, Tex.	9
25	Cappelletti, John	RB	6-1	215	6/9/52	9	Penn State	Philadelphia, Pa.	Westminster, Calif.	9
89	Chandler, Wes	WR	6-0	183	8/22/56	6	Florida	New Smyrna Beach, Fla.	New Orleans, La.	8
77	Claphan, Sam	T	6-6	267	10/10/56	3	Oklahoma	Tahlequah, Okla.	Norman, Okla.	2
82	Duckworth, Bobby	WR	6-3	197	11/27/58	2	Arkansas	Crossett, Ark.	San Diego, Calif.	5
76	Ferguson, Keith	DE	6-5	241	4/3/59	3	Ohio State	Miami, Fla.	San Diego, Calif.	9
14	Fouts, Dan	QB	6-3	205	6/10/51	11	Oregon	San Francisco, Calif.	Sisters, Ore.	9
48	Fox, Tim	S	5-11	186	11/1/53	8	Ohio State	Canton, Ohio	Foxboro, Mass.	7
75	Gissinger, Andrew	T	6-5	279	7/4/59	2	Syracuse	Barberton, Ohio	San Diego, Calif.	9
	Goode, Don	LB	6-2	231	6/21/51	9	Kansas	Houston, Tex.	Houston, Tex.	0*
	t-Greene, Ken	S	6-3	205	5/8/56	6	Washington State	Lewiston, Idaho	Vancouver, Wash.	8
43	Gregor, Bob	S	6-2	190	2/10/57	3	Washington State	Riverside, Calif.	San Diego, Calif.	4
	t-Henderson, Reuben	CB	6-1	200	10/3/58	3	San Diego State	Santa Monica, Calif.	Oakland, Calif.	5
88	Holohan, Pete	TE	6-4	240	7/25/59	3	Notre Dame	Albany, N.Y.	Liverpool, N.Y.	9
40	Jodat, Jim	RB	5-11	208	3/3/54	7	Carthage	Milwaukee, Wis.	Huntington Beach, Calif.	7
79	Johnson, Gary	DT	6-2	251	8/31/53	9	Grambling	Shreveport, La.	San Diego, Calif.	9
18	Joiner, Charlie	WR	5-11	180	10/14/47	15	Grambling	Many, La.	Houston, Tex.	9
68	†Jones, Leroy	DE	6-8	270	9/29/50	8	Norfolk State	Greenwood, Miss.	San Diego, Calif.	8
74	Kelcher, Louie	DT	6-5	310	8/23/53	9	Southern Methodist	Beaumont, Tex.	Olivenhain, Calif.	8
57	King, Linden	LB	6-5	245	6/28/55	6	Colorado State	Memphis, Tenn.	El Cajon, Calif.	9
30	†Laird, Bruce	S	6-1	195	5/23/50	12	American International	Lowell, Mass.	Towson, Md.	9
53	Lewis, David	LB	6-4	245	10/15/54	7	Southern California	Houston, Tex.	San Diego, Calif.	9
64	Loewen, Chuck	G-T	6-4	264	1/23/57	4	South Dakota	Mountain Lake, Minn.	Tempe, Ariz.	9
51	Lowe, Woodrow	LB	6-0	226	6/9/54	8	Alabama	Columbus, Ga.	San Diego, Calif.	9
11	Luther, Ed	QB	6-3	202	1/2/57	4	San Jose State	Gardena, Calif.	Carlsbad, Calif.	9
62	Macek, Don	C-G	6-2	260	7/2/54	8	Boston College	Manchester, N.H.	San Diego, Calif.	9
60	McKnight, Dennis	C-G	6-3	253	9/12/59	2	Drake	Dallas, Tex.	San Diego, Calif.	7
24	McPherson, Miles	S	6-0	175	3/30/60	2	New Haven	Brooklyn, N.Y.	Anaheim, Calif.	6
	Moore, Jeff	WR	6-1	188	3/2/57	3	Tennessee	Memphis, Tenn.	Orange, Calif.	0*
46	Muncie, Chuck	RB	6-2	228	3/17/53	8	California	Uniontown, Pa.	San Diego, Calif.	9
52	Preston, Ray	LB	6-0	220	1/25/54	8	Syracuse	Lawrence, Mass.	San Diego, Calif.	9
56	Rush, Bob	C-T	6-5	270	2/27/55	6	Memphis State	Santa Monica, Calif.	Germantown, Tenn.	9
87	Scales, Dwight	WR	6-2	182	5/30/53	7	Grambling	Little Rock, Ark.	San Diego, Calif.	9
66	Shields, Billy	T	6-8	284	8/23/53	9	Georgia	Vicksburg, Miss.	San Diego, Calif.	9
85	Sievers, Eric	TE	6-4	235	11/9/57	3	Maryland	Urbana, Ill.	San Diego, Calif.	9
59	†Thrift, Cliff	LB	6-1	230	5/3/56	5	East Central Oklahoma	Dallas, Tex.	San Diego, Calif.	9
70	Washington, Russ	T	6-7	295	12/17/46	16	Missouri	Kansas City, Mo.	San Diego, Calif.	9
67	White, Ed	G	6-2	279	4/4/47	15	California	San Diego, Calif.	La Costa, Calif.	9
63	Wilkerson, Doug	G	6-3	258	3/27/47	14	North Carolina Central	Fayetteville, N.C.	Spring Valley, Calif.	9
29	Williams, Mike	CB	5-10	186	11/22/53	9	Louisiana State	Covington, La.	San Diego, Calif.	9
80	Winslow, Kellen	TE	6-5	251	11/5/57	5	Missouri	St. Louis, Mo.	San Diego, Calif.	9
90	†Woodcock, John	DE	6-3	257	3/19/54	7	Hawaii	Eureka, Calif.	Fremont, Calif.	6
49	Young, Andre	S	6-0	203	11/22/60	2	Louisiana Tech	West Monroe, La.	West Monroe, La.	8
90	Young, Wilbur	DT	6-6	285	4/20/49	13	William Penn, Iowa	New York, N.Y.	Kansas City, Mo.	9

* Goode last active with Cleveland in '81; Moore last active with Los Angeles Rams in '81.

†Option playout; subject to developments.

t-Chargers traded for Greene (St. Louis); Henderson (Chicago).

Retired—Willie Buchanon, 11-year cornerback, 9 games in '82; Dewey Selmon, 7-year linebacker, 8 in '82.

Also played with Chargers in '82—CB Donald Dykes (1), WR Scott Fitzkee (9).

COACHING STAFF

Head Coach, Don Coryell

Pro Career: Guided Chargers to a 6-3 mark and fourth straight playoff berth in 1982. Became head coach of the Chargers after fourth game of 1978 season and led them to eight wins in final 12 games. Before coming to Chargers was St. Louis Cardinals head coach for five seasons, compiling a 42-29-1 record and leading Cardinals to the NFC East titles in 1974-75. Career record: 92-55-1.

Background: Played defensive back for University of Washington 1947-49. Assistant coach Punahou Academy, Honolulu, 1951. Head coach Farrington High School, Honolulu, 1952. Head coach University of British Columbia 1953-54. Head coach, Fort Ord, California, army team 1956. Head coach Whittier College 1957-59 (23-5-1). Offensive backfield coach at Southern California 1960. Head coach at San Diego State from 1961-72 where he compiled a 104-19-2 record.

Personal: Born October 17, 1924 in Seattle, Washington. Graduated from Lincoln High School, Seattle, in 1943. Served in United States Army 1943-46, released as first lieutenant. Don and his wife, Aliisa, live in San Diego and have two children —Mike and Mindy.

ASSISTANT COACHES

Tom Bass, defensive coordinator; born August 2, 1936, Riverside, Calif., lives in San Diego. Linebacker San Jose State 1955-57. No pro playing experience. College coach: San Jose State 1958-59, San Diego State 1960-62. Pro coach: San Diego Chargers 1964-67, Cincinnati Bengals 1968-69, Tampa Bay Buccaneers 1977-81, rejoined Chargers in 1982.

Marv Braden, special assistant; born January 25, 1938, Kansas City, Mo., lives in San Diego. Linebacker Southwest Missouri State 1956-59. No pro playing experience. College coach: Northeast Missouri State 1967-68 (head coach), U. S. International 1969-72, Iowa State 1973, Southern Methodist 1974-75, Michigan State 1976. Pro coach: Denver Broncos 1977-80, Chargers since 1981.

Earnel Durden, offensive backs; born January 24, 1937, Los Angeles, lives in La Mesa, Calif. Halfback Oregon State 1956-58. No pro playing experience. College coach: Compton, Calif., J.C., 1966-67, Long Beach State 1968, UCLA 1969-70. Pro coach: Los Angeles Rams 1971-72, Houston Oilers 1973, Chargers since 1974.

Dave Levy, offensive coordinator; born October 25, 1932, Carrollton, Mo., lives in Solana Beach, Calif. Guard UCLA 1953-54. No pro playing experience. College coach: UCLA 1954, Long Beach City College 1955, Southern California 1960-75. Pro coach: Joined Chargers in 1980.

Al Saunders, receivers; born February 1, 1947, London, Eng., lives in San Diego. Defensive back San Jose State 1966-68. No pro playing experience. College coach: Southern California 1970-71, Missouri 1972, Utah State 1973-75, California 1976-81, Tennessee 1982. Pro coach: First year with Chargers.

Jerry Smith, defensive line; born September 9, 1930, Dayton, Ohio, lives in San Diego. Linebacker Wisconsin 1948-51. Pro linebacker San Francisco 49ers 1952-53, Green Bay Packers 1956. College coach: Dayton 1959. Pro coach: Boston Patriots 1960-61, Buffalo Bills 1962-68, New Orleans Saints 1969-70, Denver Broncos 1971, Houston Oilers 1972, Cleveland Browns 1973, Baltimore Colts 1974-76, Chargers since 1977.

Jim Wagstaff, defensive backfield; born June 12, 1936, American Falls, Idaho, lives in San Diego. Back Idaho State 1954-58. Pro defensive back Chicago Cardinals 1959, Buffalo Bills 1960-61. College coach: Boise State 1969-72. Pro coach: Los Angeles Rams 1973-77, Buffalo Bills 1978-80, Chargers since 1981.

SAN DIEGO CHARGERS 1983 FIRST-YEAR ROSTER

Name	Pos.	Ht.	Wt.	Birth-date	College	Birthplace	Residence	How Acq.
Blaylock, Billy	S	5-10	185	4/19/61	Tennessee Tech	Marietta, Ga.	Marietta, Ga.	D12
Brown, Don (1)	T	6-6	262	4/2/59	Santa Clara	San Jose, Calif.	San Jose, Calif.	FA
Byrd, Gill	CB	5-11	191	2/20/61	San Jose State	San Francisco, Calif.	San Francisco, Calif.	D1b
Doolittle, Steve (1)	LB	6-3	225	6/5/59	Colorado	Kansas City, Kan.	Tucson, Ariz.	FA
Ehin, Chuck	DE	6-4	255	7/1/61	Brigham Young	Marysville, Calif.	Layton, Utah	D12a
Elko, Bill	NT	6-5	278	12/28/59	Louisiana State	New York, N.Y.	Windber, Pa.	D7
Fortune, Hosea (1)	WR	6-0	174	3/4/59	Rice	New Orleans, La.	Los Angeles, Calif.	D9
Green, Mike	LB	6-0	226	6/29/61	Oklahoma State	Port Arthur, Tex.	Port Arthur, Tex.	D8
Jackson, Earnest	RB	5-10	208	12/18/59	Texas A&M	Needville, Tex.	Lamar, Tex.	D9
James, Jimmy	LB	6-1	218	10/25/60	Minnesota	Cleveland, Ohio	Garfield Heights, Ohio	FA
Kearse, Tim	WR	5-11	173	10/24/59	San Jose State	York, Pa.	York, Pa.	D11
Krainock, Steve (1)	QB	6-0	208	12/21/59	Richmond	Riverside, Calif.	Poway, Calif.	FA
Lyles, Warren (1)	NT	6-1	265	7/2/59	Alabama	Birmingham, Ala.	Birmingham, Ala.	D9 ('82)
Mathison, Bruce	QB	6-3	210	4/25/59	Nebraska	Superior, Wis.	Superior, Wis.	D10
Nelson, Derrie (1)	LB	6-1	236	2/8/58	Nebraska	York, Neb.	York, Neb.	FA
Pleasant, Mike (1)	RB	6-1	195	8/16/58	Oklahoma	Muskogee, Okla.	Muskogee, Okla.	FA
Smith, Billy Ray	LB	6-3	242	8/10/61	Arkansas	Fayetteville, Ark.	Plano, Tex.	D1
Walters, Danny	CB	6-1	186	11/4/60	Arkansas	Prescott, Ark.	Chicago, Ill.	D4
Williams, George	CB	6-1	190	1/2/59	San Diego State	San Diego, Calif.	San Diego, Calif.	FA

Players who report to an NFL team for the first time are designated on rosters as rookies (R). If a player reported to an NFL training camp in a previous year but was not on the active squad for three or more regular season or postseason games, he is listed on the first-year roster and designated by a (1). Thereafter, a player who is on the active squad for three or more regular season or postseason games is credited with an additional year of playing experience.

NOTES

Chuck Weber, linebackers; born March 26, 1930, Philadelphia, lives in San Diego. Linebacker West Chester State 1949-53. Pro linebacker Cleveland Browns 1955-56, Chicago Cardinals 1956-58, Philadelphia Eagles 1959-61. Pro coach: Boston Patriots 1964-67, San Diego Chargers 1968-69, Cincinnati Bengals 1970-75, St. Louis Cardinals 1976-77, Cleveland Browns 1978-79, Baltimore Colts 1980-81, rejoined Chargers in 1982.

Ernie Zampese, quarterbacks-passing game; born March 12, 1936, Santa Barbara, Calif., lives in San Diego. Halfback Southern California 1956-58. No pro playing experience. College coach: Hancock J.C. 1962-65, Cal Poly-SLO 1966, San Diego State 1967-75. Pro coach: San Diego Chargers 1976, rejoined Chargers in 1978.

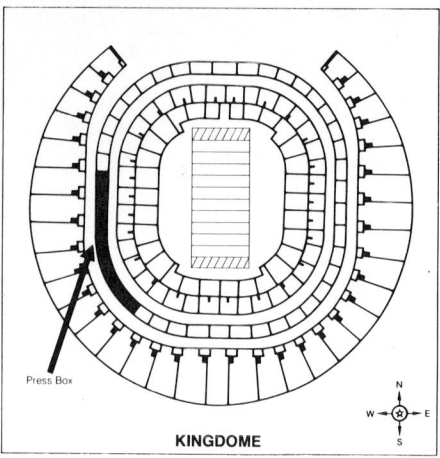

KINGDOME

Press Box

N
W   E
S

Seattle Seahawks

American Football Conference
Western Division

Team Colors: Blue, Green, and Silver

5305 Lake Washington Boulevard
Kirkland, Washington 98033
Telephone: (206) 827-9777

Club Officials
President-General Manager: Mike McCormack
Assistant General Manager: Chuck Allen
Public Relations Director: Gary Wright
Assistant Public Relations Director: Dave Neubert
Director of Player Personnel: Dick Mansperger
Business Manager: Bob Anderson
Ticket Manager: James Nagaoka
Trainer: Jim Whitesel
Equipment Manager: Walt Loeffler

Stadium: Kingdome • **Capacity:** 64,757
    201 South King Street
    Seattle, Washington 98104

Playing Surface: AstroTurf

Training Camp: Eastern Washington University
     Cheney, Washington 99004

1983 SCHEDULE
Preseason
Aug. 5	at Denver	7:00
Aug. 12	**Green Bay**	7:30
Aug. 19	**Minnesota**	7:30
Aug. 27	at San Francisco	2:00

Regular Season
Sept. 4	at Kansas City	3:00
Sept. 11	at New York Jets	4:00
Sept. 18	**San Diego**	1:00
Sept. 25	**Washington**	1:00
Oct. 2	at Cleveland	1:00
Oct. 9	at San Diego	1:00
Oct. 16	**Los Angeles Raiders**	1:00
Oct. 23	**Pittsburgh**	1:00
Oct. 30	at Los Angeles Raiders	1:00
Nov. 6	**Denver**	1:00
Nov. 13	at St. Louis	12:00
Nov. 20	at Denver	2:00
Nov. 27	**Kansas City**	1:00
Dec. 4	**Dallas**	1:00
Dec. 11	at New York Giants	1:00
Dec. 18	**New England**	1:00

1982 TEAM STATISTICS

	Seattle	Opp.
Total First Downs	159	167
Rushing	51	86
Passing	89	68
Penalty	19	13
Third Down Efficiency	43/130	50/126
Third Down Percentage	33.1	39.7
Total Net Yards	2594	2794
Total Offensive Plays	589	600
Avg. Gain per Play	4.4	4.7
Avg. Gain per Game	288.2	310.4
Net Yards Rushing	795	1461
Total Rushing Plays	227	337
Avg. Gain per Rush	3.5	4.3
Avg. Gain Rushing per Game	88.3	162.3
Net Yards Passing	1799	1333
Lost Attempting to Pass	36/269	17/135
Gross Yards Passing	2068	1468
Attempts/Completions	326/176	246/138
Percent Completed	54.0	56.1
Had Intercepted	13	13
Avg. Net Passing per Game	199.9	148.1
Punts/Avg.	49/38.6	50/40.6
Punt Returns/Avg.	21/10.9	19/3.6
Kickoff Returns/Avg.	29/18.8	24/15.0
Interceptions/Avg. Ret.	13/12.3	13/6.8
Penalties/Yards	59/523	44/406
Fumbles/Ball Lost	21/11	18/9
Total Points	127	147
Avg. Points per Game	14.1	16.3
Touchdowns	14	18
Rushing	4	12
Passing	9	4
Returns and Recoveries	1	2
Field Goals	10/14	6/15
Conversions	13/14	17/18
Safeties	0	2
Avg. Time of Possession	28:04	31:56

1982 TEAM RECORD

Preseason (1-3)

Seattle		Opponents
14	*St. Louis	0
3	Minnesota	7
13	Los Angeles Rams	23
13	San Francisco	17
43		47

Regular Season (4-5)

Seattle		Opponents	Att.
7	*Cleveland	21	55,907
21	Houston	23	43,117
17	Denver	10	73,916
16	*Pittsburgh	0	55,553
23	Los Angeles Raiders	28	42,170
20	*Chicago	14	52,826
0	*New England	16	53,457
10	Cincinnati	24	55,330
13	*Denver	11	43,145
127		147	475,421

*Home Game

Score by Periods

Seattle	9	37	28	53	—	127
Opponents	26	70	23	28	—	147

Attendance

Home 260,888   Away 214,533   Total 475,421
Single game home record, 62,948 (10-29-78)
Single season home record, 487,881 (1979)

1982 INDIVIDUAL STATISTICS

Rushing

	Att	Yds	Avg	LG	TD
Smith	63	202	3.2	19	0
Doornink	45	178	4.0	46	0
T. Brown	53	141	2.7	17	2
Zorn	15	113	7.5	35	1
Hughes	30	106	3.5	13	0
Ivory	13	51	3.9	27	1
Largent	1	8	8.0	8	0
Johns	1	−1	−1.0	−1	0
Krieg	6	−3	−0.5	4	0
Seattle	227	795	3.5	46	4
Opponents	337	1461	4.3	53	12

Field Goal Success

Distance	1-19	20-29	30-39	40-49	50 Over
Made-Att.	0-0	3-4	5-6	2-3	0-1

Passing

	Att	Comp	Pct	Yds	TD	Int	Tkld	Rate
Zorn	245	126	51.4	1540	7	11	20/152	62.1
Krieg	78	49	62.8	501	2	2	16/117	79.0
N. Johnson	1	1	100.0	27	0	0	0/0	—
Lane	1	0	0.0	0	0	0	0/0	—
Smith	1	0	0.0	0	0	0	0/0	—
Seattle	326	176	54.0	2068	9	13	36/269	
Opponents	246	138	56.1	1468	4	13	17/135	

Receiving

	No	Yds	Avg	LG	TD
Largent	34	493	14.5	45	3
Doornink	22	176	8.0	44	0
Smith	19	196	10.3	39	0
Carr	15	265	17.7	50	2
Johns	15	234	15.6	35	1
Metzelaars	15	152	10.1	26	0
T. Brown	12	95	7.9	18	0
Hughes	11	98	8.9	29t	1
Walker	10	156	15.6	40t	2
Tice	9	46	5.1	12	0
Sawyer	8	92	11.5	17	0
Ivory	5	38	7.6	12	0
Zorn	1	27	27.0	27	0
Seattle	176	2068	11.8	50	9
Opponents	138	1468	10.6	56t	4

Interceptions

	No	Yds	Avg	LG	TD
Easley	4	48	12.0	44	0
Harris	4	33	8.3	18	0
Jackson	2	29	14.5	28	0
Scholtz	1	31	31.0	31t	1
Dufek	1	16	16.0	16	0
D. Brown	1	3	3.0	3	0
Seattle	13	160	12.3	44	1
Opponents	13	88	6.8	39t	1

Punting

	No	Yds	Avg	In 20	LG
West	48	1835	38.2	8	52
Doornink	1	54	54.0	1	54
Seattle	49	1889	38.6	9	54
Opponents	50	2032	40.6	10	59

Punt Returns

	No	FC	Yds	Avg	LG	TD
Johns	19	10	210	11.1	37	0
Easley	1	2	15	15.0	15	0
G. Johnson	1	2	3	3.0	3	0
Seattle	21	14	228	10.9	37	0
Opponents	19	23	69	3.6	18	0

Kickoff Returns

	No	Yds	Avg	LG	TD
Ivory	10	224	22.4	30	0
Lane	11	172	15.6	32	0
Johns	3	57	19.0	23	0
McAlister	2	41	20.5	21	0
T. Brown	2	33	16.5	19	0
Hughes	1	17	17.0	17	0
Seattle	29	544	18.8	32	0
Opponents	24	361	15.0	34	0

Scoring

	TD	TD R	TD P	TD Rt	PAT	FG	TP
N. Johnson					13/14	10/14	43
Largent	3	0	3	0			18
T. Brown	2	2	0	0			12
Carr	2	0	2	0			12
Walker	2	0	2	0			12
Hughes	1	0	1	0			6
Ivory	1	1	0	0			6
Johns	1	0	1	0			6
Scholtz	1	0	0	1			6
Zorn	1	1	0	0			6
Seattle	14	4	9	1	13/14	10/14	127
Opponents	18	12	4	2	17/18	6/15	147

Sacks

Bell 1, Bryant 3, Butler 2, Easley 2, Green 3, Hardy 2, Nash 1, Scholtz 1, Tuiasosopo 2.

FIRST PLAYERS SELECTED

Year	Player, College, Position
1976	Steve Niehaus, Notre Dame, DT
1977	Steve August, Tulsa, G
1978	Keith Simpson, Memphis State, DB
1979	Manu Tuiasosopo, UCLA, DT
1980	Jacob Green, Texas A&M, DE
1981	Ken Easley, UCLA, DB
1982	Jeff Bryant, Clemson, DE
1983	Curt Warner, Penn State, RB

SEAHAWKS COACHING HISTORY
(39-62-0)

1976-82	Jack Patera*	35-59-0
1982	Mike McCormack	4-3-0

*Released after 2 games in 1982

SEATTLE SEAHAWKS 1983 VETERAN ROSTER

No.	Name	Pos.	Ht.	Wt.	Birth-date	NFL Exp.	College	Birthplace	Residence	Games in '82
12	Adkins, Sam	QB	6-2	214	5/21/55	7	Wichita State	Van Nuys, Calif.	Woodinville, Wash.	0*
63	†Anderson, Fredell	DE	6-4	245	10/30/54	4	Prairie View	Toppenish, Wash.	Bellevue, Wash.	1
76	August, Steve	T	6-5	254	9/4/54	7	Tulsa	Jeanette, Pa.	Redmond, Wash.	8
65	Bailey, Edwin	G	6-4	265	5/15/59	3	South Carolina State	Savannah, Ga.	Bellevue, Wash.	9
82	Bell, Mark	DE	6-4	240	8/30/57	4	Colorado State	Wichita, Kan.	Wichita, Kan.	9
68	Boyd, Dennis	T	6-6	255	11/5/55	6	Oregon State	Washington, D.C.	Kirkland, Wash.	2
22	Brown, Dave	CB	6-2	190	1/16/53	9	Michigan	Akron, Ohio	Woodinville, Wash.	9
30	Brown, Theotis	RB	6-2	225	4/20/57	5	UCLA	Chicago, Ill.	Redmond, Wash.	9
31	Bryant, Cullen	RB	6-1	235	5/20/51	11	Colorado	Fort Sill, Okla.	Broomfield, Colo.	1*
77	Bryant, Jeff	DE	6-5	260	5/22/60	2	Clemson	Atlanta, Ga.	Decatur, Ga.	9
53	Butler, Keith	LB	6-4	225	5/16/56	6	Memphis State	Anniston, Ala.	Bothell, Wash.	8
	t-Bush, Blair	C	6-3	252	11/25/56	6	Washington	Fort Hood, Tex.	Seattle, Wash.	8
71	Campbell, Jack	T	6-5	277	12/16/58	2	Utah	Los Angeles, Calif.	Kirkland, Wash.	1
87	Carr, Roger	WR	6-2	195	7/1/52	10	Louisiana Tech	Seminole, Okla.	Cotton Valley, La.	9
33	Doornink, Dan	RB	6-3	210	2/1/56	6	Washington State	Wapato, Wash.	Kirkland, Wash.	8
25	Dufek, Dan	S	6-0	195	4/28/54	7	Michigan	Ann Arbor, Mich.	Kirkland, Wash.	9
66	Dugan, Bill	G	6-4	271	6/5/59	3	Penn State	Hornell, N.Y.	Hornell, N.Y.	9
45	Easley, Kenny	S	6-3	206	1/15/59	3	UCLA	Chesapeake, Va.	Bellevue, Wash.	8
64	Essink, Ron	T	6-6	254	7/30/58	4	Grand Valley State	Zeeland, Mich.	Seattle, Wash.	7
50	Flones, Brian	LB	6-1	228	9/1/59	3	Washington State	Mt. Vernon, Wash.	Sedro Woolley, Wash.	9
56	Gaines, Greg	LB	6-3	220	10/16/58	2	Tennessee	Martinsville, Va.	Old Hickory, Tenn.	0*
78	Graham, David	DE	6-6	250	4/6/59	2	Morehouse	Chicago, Ill.	Tallahassee, Fla.	3
79	Green, Jacob	DE	6-3	247	1/21/57	4	Texas A&M	Pasadena, Tex.	Houston, Tex.	9
75	Hardy, Robert	DT	6-2	250	7/3/56	5	Jackson State	Tulsa, Okla.	Issaquah, Wash.	8
44	†Harris, John	S	6-2	200	6/13/56	6	Arizona State	Fort Benning, Ga.	Woodinville, Wash.	9
46	Hughes, David	RB	6-0	220	6/1/59	3	Boise State	Honolulu, Hawaii	Kirkland, Wash.	9
32	†Ivory, Horace	RB-KR	6-0	198	8/8/54	7	Oklahoma	Fort Worth, Tex.	Fort Worth, Tex.	6
55	Jackson, Michael	LB	6-1	220	7/15/57	5	Washington	Pasco, Wash.	Bellevue, Wash.	8
85	Johns, Paul	WR	5-11	170	11/14/58	3	Tulsa	Waco, Tex.	Bellevue, Wash.	9
27	Johnson, Greggory	S	6-1	188	10/20/58	3	Oklahoma State	Houston, Tex.	Bellevue, Wash.	9
9	Johnson, Norm	K	6-2	193	5/31/60	2	UCLA	Inglewood, Calif.	Garden Grove, Calif.	9
26	†Justin, Kerry	CB	5-11	175	5/3/55	6	Oregon State	New Orleans, La.	Kirkland, Wash.	9
62	Kauahi, Kani	C	6-2	260	9/6/59	2	Hawaii	Kehaka, Hawaii	DeSoto, Tex.	2
17	Krieg, Dave	QB	6-1	185	10/20/58	4	Milton	Iola, Wis.	Rothschild, Wis.	3
60	Kuehn, Art	C	6-3	255	2/12/53	8	UCLA	Victoria, B.C.	Woodinville, Wash.	6
37	Lane, Eric	RB	6-0	195	1/6/59	3	Brigham Young	Oakland, Calif.	Bellevue, Wash.	9
80	Largent, Steve	WR	5-11	184	9/28/54	8	Tulsa	Tulsa, Okla.	Tulsa, Okla.	8
48	McAlister, Ken	S	6-5	210	4/15/60	2	San Francisco	Oakland, Calif.	Oakland, Calif.	9
	t-McKenzie, Reggie	G	6-5	242	7/27/50	12	Michigan	Detroit, Mich.	East Amherst, N.Y.	9
88	Metzelaars, Pete	TE	6-7	240	5/24/60	2	Wabash	Three Rivers, Mich.	Bellevue, Wash.	9
72	Nash, Joe	DT	6-3	250	10/11/60	2	Boston College	Boston, Mass.	West Roxbury, Mass.	7
52	Norman, Joe	LB	6-1	220	10/15/56	4	Indiana	Millersburg, Ohio	Bellevue, Wash.	0*
61	†Pratt, Robert	G	6-4	250	5/25/51	10	North Carolina	Richmond, Va.	Richmond, Va.	9
57	Robinson, Shelton	LB	6-2	233	9/14/60	2	North Carolina	Goldsboro, N.C.	Goldsboro, N.C.	9
81	Sawyer, John	TE	6-2	230	7/26/53	8	Southern Mississippi	Baker, La.	Baton Rouge, La.	7
58	Scholtz, Bruce	LB	6-6	240	9/26/58	2	Texas	LaGrange, Tex.	Bellevue, Wash.	9
42	Simpson, Keith	CB	6-1	195	3/9/56	6	Memphis State	Memphis, Tenn.	Kirkland, Wash.	8
47	Smith, Sherman	RB	6-4	225	11/1/54	8	Miami, Ohio	Youngstown, Ohio	Woodinville, Wash.	9
59	Thomas, Rodell	LB	6-2	225	8/2/58	3	Alabama State	Quincy, Fla.	Quincy, Fla.	8
86	Tice, Mike	TE	6-7	250	2/2/59	3	Maryland	Bayshore, N.Y.	Bellevue, Wash.	9
74	Tuiasosopo, Manu	DT	6-3	252	8/30/57	5	UCLA	Los Angeles, Calif.	Woodinville, Wash.	9
89	Walker, Byron	WR	6-4	190	7/28/60	2	Citadel	Scott Base, Ill.	Warner Robins, Ga.	9
8	†West, Jeff	P	6-2	220	4/6/53	8	Cincinnati	Ravenna, Ohio	Bellevue, Wash.	9
70	White, Mike	DT	6-5	266	8/11/57	5	Albany State	Augusta, Ga.	Bellevue, Wash.	5
54	Williams, Eugene	LB	6-1	220	6/15/60	2	Tulsa	Longview, Tex.	Longview, Tex.	9
51	Yarno, John	C	6-5	251	12/17/54	7	Idaho	Spokane, Wash.	Redmond, Wash.	9
10	Zorn, Jim	QB	6-2	200	5/10/53	8	Cal Poly-Pomona	Whittier, Calif.	Mercer Island, Wash.	9

* Adkins active for 7 games in '82, but did not play; Bryant played 1 game with Los Angeles Rams in '82; Gaines and Norman missed '82 season due to injuries.

†Option playout; subject to developments.

t-Seahawks traded for Bush (Cincinnati), McKenzie (Buffalo).

COACHING STAFF

Head Coach, Chuck Knox

Pro Career: Named head coach of Seahawks on January 26, 1983 after five seasons as head coach of Buffalo where he led Bills to AFC East title in 1980. Led Los Angeles Rams to five straight NFC West titles before taking over Bills in 1978. Pro assistant with New York Jets 1963-66, coaching offensive line, before moving to Detroit in 1967. Served Lions in same capacity until named head coach of Rams in 1973. No pro playing experience. Career record: 95-58-1.

Background: Played tackle for Juniata College in Huntington, Pa., 1950-53. Was assistant coach at his alma mater in 1954, then spent 1955 season as line coach at Ellwood City high in Pennsylvania. Moved to Wake Forest as an assistant coach for 1959-60, then Kentucky in 1961-62.

Personal: Born April 27, 1932 in Sewickley, Pa., Chuck and his wife, Shirley, live in Seattle and have four children—Chris, Kathy, Colleen, and Chuck.

ASSISTANT COACHES

Tom Catlin, assistant head coach-defensive coordinator-linebackers; born September 8, 1931, Ponca City, Okla., lives in Seattle. Center-linebacker Oklahoma 1950-52. Pro linebacker Cleveland Browns 1953-54, 1957-58, Philadelphia Eagles 1959. College coach: Army 1956. Pro coach: Dallas Texans-Kansas City Chiefs 1960-65, Los Angeles Rams 1966-77, Buffalo Bills 1978-82, first year with Seahawks.

George Dyer, defensive line; born May 4, 1940, Alhambra, Calif., lives in Seattle. Center-linebacker U.C. Santa Barbara 1961-63. No pro playing experience. College coach: Humboldt State 1964-66, Coalinga, Calif., J.C. 1967 (head coach), Portland State 1968-71, Idaho 1972, San Jose State 1973, Michigan State 1977-79, Arizona State 1980-81. Pro coach: Winnipeg Blue Bombers (CFL) 1974-76 (head coach), Buffalo Bills 1982, first year with Seahawks.

Chick Harris, offensive backfield; born September 21, 1945, Durham, N.C., lives in Seattle. Running back Northern Arizona 1966-69. No pro playing experience. College coach: Colorado State 1970-72, Long Beach State 1973-74, Washington 1975-80. Pro coach: Buffalo Bills 1981-82, first year with Seahawks.

Ralph Hawkins, defensive backfield; born May 4, 1935, Washington, D.C., lives in Seattle. Quarterback-defensive back Maryland 1953-55. Pro defensive back New York Titans (AFL) 1960. College coach: Maryland 1959-60, Southern Methodist 1961, Kentucky 1962-65, Army 1966, Maryland 1967, Cincinnati 1968. Pro coach: Buffalo Bills 1969-72, Washington Redskins 1973-77, Baltimore Colts 1978, New York Giants 1979-80, Buffalo Bills 1981-82, first year with Seahawks.

Ken Meyer, quarterbacks; born July 14, 1926, Erie, Pa., lives in Seattle. Quarterback Denison 1947-50. No pro playing experience. College coach: Denison 1952-57, Wake Forest 1958-59, Florida State 1960-62, Alabama 1963-67, Tulane 1981-82. Pro coach: San Francisco 49ers 1968, 1977 (head coach), New York Jets 1969-72, Los Angeles Rams 1973-76, Chicago Bears 1978-80, first year with Seahawks.

Steve Moore, receivers; born August 19, 1947, Los Angeles, Calif., lives in Seattle. Running back U.C. Santa Barbara 1968-69. No pro playing experience. College coach: U.C. Santa Barbara 1970-71, Army 1975, Rice 1976-77. Pro coach: Buffalo Bills 1978-82, first year with Seahawks.

Ray Prochaska, offensive coordinator-offensive line; born August 9, 1919, Ulysses, Neb., lives in Seattle. End Nebraska 1939-40. Pro end Cleveland Rams 1941. College coach: Nebraska 1946-54. Pro coach: Edmonton (CFL) 1955-57, Chicago-St. Louis Cardinals 1958-65, Los Angeles Rams 1966-70, 1973-77, Cleveland Browns 1971-72, Buffalo Bills 1978-82, first year with Seahawks.

Rusty Tillman, tight ends-special teams; born February 27, 1948, Beloit, Wis., lives in Seattle. Linebacker Northern Arizona 1967-69. Pro linebacker Washington Redskins 1970-77. Pro coach: Joined Seahawks in 1979.

SEATTLE SEAHAWKS 1983 FIRST-YEAR ROSTER

Name	Pos.	Ht.	Wt.	Birth-date	College	Birthplace	Residence	How Acq.
Ball, John	RB	6-1	215	2/13/61	Texas Southern	Tampa, Fla.	Houston, Tex.	FA
Bazel, Reggie	RB	6-0	205	6/21/61	Tennessee Tech	Harriman, Tex.	Harriman, Tex.	FA
Beautrow, Jim	TE	6-3	225	1/6/60	San Diego State	Santa Barbara, Calif.	Santa Barbara, Calif.	FA
Beck, Curlin	RB	6-0	200	8/24/60	West Virginia	Cleveland, Ohio	Bedford Heights, Ohio	FA
Boyd, Jerome	LB	6-2	225	9/18/61	Oregon State	Los Angeles, Calif.	Corvallis, Ore.	FA
Brown, Freddie	WR	5-9	162	1/29/60	Louisiana Tech	Monroe, La.	Ruston, La.	FA
Butts, Reggie	WR	5-8	175	10/23/61	Tulane	Jacksonville, Fla.	New Orleans, La.	FA
Canady, Willie	CB	6-0	180	5/19/61	Fort Valley State	Montezuma, Ga.	Montezuma, Ga.	FA
Castor, Chris	WR	6-0	170	8/13/60	Duke	Burlington, N.C.	Cary, N.C.	D5
Cella, Tony	T	6-6	245	1/8/61	Rutgers	Chester, Pa.	Claymont, Del.	FA
Childress, Jack	LB	6-2	210	5/4/60	Southern Oregon	Roseburg, Ore.	Myrtle Creek, Ore.	FA
Clancy, Sam (1)	TE	6-7	250	5/5/58	Pittsburgh	Pittsburgh, Pa.	Bellevue, Wash.	D11('82)
Clasby, Bob	T	6-5	259	9/28/60	Notre Dame	Detroit, Mich.	Milton, Mich.	D9
Clivio, Andy	RB	6-2	200	3/10/61	Holy Cross	Boston, Mass.	Woburn, Mass.	FA
Crum, Joe	G	6-4	265	10/8/60	Utah State	Rawlins, Wyo.	Rawlins, Wyo.	FA
Dickey, Darrell	QB	6-2	195	12/6/59	Kansas State	Galveston, Tex.	Manhattan, Kan.	FA
Dillon, William	S	6-1	180	4/20/59	Virginia Tech	Chicago, Ill.	Oak Park, Ill.	FA
Doubiago, Dan	T	6-4	245	9/25/60	Utah	Escondido, Calif.	Manhattan Beach, Calif.	FA
Dow, Don	T	6-6	280	8/15/60	Washington	Seattle, Wash.	Kirkland, Wash.	D12
Dufek, Joe	QB	6-4	215	8/23/61	Yale	Ann Arbor, Mich.	Ann Arbor, Mich.	FA
Foster, Greg	G	6-4	270	11/24/60	San Diego State	Taft, Calif.	Taft, Calif.	FA
Gaynor, Ron	QB	6-2	195	12/15/59	West Chester State	Akron, Ohio	Jacobus, Pa.	FA
Gipson, Reginald	RB	6-2	200	7/27/60	Alabama A&M	Birmingham, Ala.	Brighton, Ala.	D6
Gresham, Tony	RB	6-0	220	2/25/61	S.E. Oklahoma	Greenville, S.C.	Byars, Okla.	FA
Gunn, Jeff	WR	6-2	185	8/11/61	Norfolk State	Richmond, Va.	Norfolk, Va.	FA
Hardy, David	K	5-7	180	7/7/59	Texas A&M	Fort Worth, Tex.	Huntsville, Tex.	FA
Hernandez, Matt	T	6-6	260	10/16/61	Purdue	Detroit, Mich.	East Detroit, Mich.	D8
Ingalls, Steve	T	6-5	265	1/16/61	Northern Iowa	Lancaster, Wis.	Pepin, Wis.	FA
Jones, T.J.	WR	6-1	198	5/11/60	Washington State	Maldone, Mo.	Columbia, Mo.	FA
Krenk, Mitch	TE	6-4	225	11/19/59	Nebraska	Crete, Neb.	Lincoln, Neb.	FA
Lively, Steve	G	6-4	276	9/30/59	Boston College	Boston, Mass.	Mansfield, Mass.	FA
Mayberry, Bob	G	6-5	245	9/10/60	Clemson	New Castle, Pa.	Sharon, Pa.	D11
McCondichie, Derrick	G	6-4	260	4/26/59	Central State, Ohio	Chicago, Ill.	Detroit, Mich.	FA
Merriman, Sam	LB	6-3	225	5/5/61	Idaho	Tucson, Ariz.	Tucson, Ariz.	D7
Michalewicz, Steve	DE	6-4	233	4/9/59	Connecticut	Hartford, Conn.	Windsor Locks, Conn.	FA
Middleton, Frank	RB	6-0	208	10/28/60	Florida A&M	Savannah, Ga.	Savannah, Ga.	FA
Mosley, Sam	TE	6-7	225	3/14/59	Nevada-Reno	East Orange, N.J.	Fort Dodge, Iowa	FA
Moyer, Paul	S	6-1	201	7/26/61	Arizona State	Anaheim, Calif.	Villa Park, Calif.	FA
Ninneman, Steve	G	6-4	255	1/9/61	North Dakota	St. Paul, Minn.	South St. Paul, Minn.	FA
Pearson, Garry	RB	5-11	185	3/4/61	Massachusetts	New York, N.Y.	Springfield, Mass.	FA
Pellum, Forrest	S	5-11	180	10/5/59	Oregon State	Palm Springs, Calif.	Banning, Calif.	FA
Peoples, Carlton	CB	6-0	178	11/9/60	Tennessee	Memphis, Tenn.	Memphis, Tenn.	FA
Phillips, Padro	DE	6-4	259	12/5/59	Virginia Tech	Newport News, Va.	Hampton, Va.	FA
Poles, Junior	DE	6-4	275	2/24/61	Boston College	Fort Dixon, N.C.	Caledonia, N.Y.	FA
Pyles, Dave	T	6-5	270	9/3/60	Miami, Ohio	Portsmouth, Ohio	Wheelersburg, Ohio	FA
Riccio, Kevin	T	6-5	223	5/26/61	Virginia	West Islip, N.Y.	West Islip, N.Y.	FA
Robertson, Dwight	RB	6-1	195	7/20/60	Oregon	Covington, La.	Covington, La.	FA
Speros, Pete	G	6-2	255	8/15/61	Penn State	Washington, D.C.	Potomac, Va.	D10
Spitzer, Rich	G	6-2	250	2/6/61	Rutgers	Montclair, N.J.	Flanders, N.J.	FA
Stephens, Wayde	P	6-2	215	9/8/60	Puget Sound	Raymond, Wash.	Raymond, Wash.	FA
Thomas, Charles (1)	RB	6-1	200	11/19/60	Auburn	Atlanta, Ga.	Opelika, Fla.	FA
Thompson, Bruce	P	5-10	168	11/24/60	Southern Mississippi	Denver, Colo.	Huntsville, Ala.	FA
Warner, Curt	RB	5-11	205	3/18/61	Penn State	Wyoming, W. Va.	Wyoming, W. Va.	D1

Players who report to an NFL team for the first time are designated on rosters as rookies (R). If a player reported to an NFL training camp in a previous year but was not on the active squad for three or more regular season or postseason games, he is listed on the first-year roster and designated by a (1). Thereafter, a player who is on the active squad for three or more regular season or postseason games is credited with an additional year of playing experience.

NOTES

_____

_____

_____

_____

_____

Joe Vitt, special assignments; born August 23, 1954, Camden, N.J., lives in Seattle. Linebacker Towson State 1973-75. No pro playing experience. Pro coach: Baltimore Colts 1979-81, Seahawks since 1982.

1983 National Football Conference

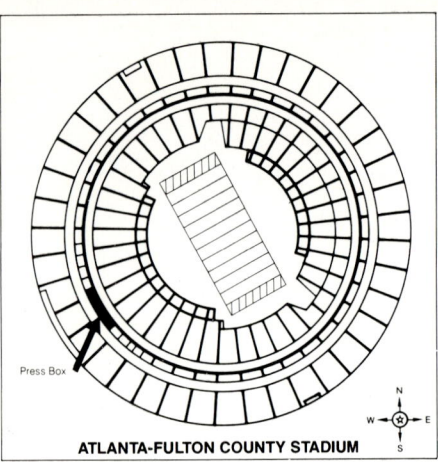

ATLANTA-FULTON COUNTY STADIUM

Atlanta Falcons

**National Football Conference
Western Division**

Team Colors: Red, Black, White,
and Silver

**Suwanee Road at I-85
Suwanee, Georgia 30174
Telephone: (404) 588-1111**

Club Officials
Chairman of the Board: Rankin M. Smith, Sr.
President: Rankin Smith, Jr.
Executive Vice President: Eddie LeBaron
General Manager: Tom Braatz
Corporate Secretary: Taylor Smith
Chief Financial Officer: Jim Hay
Director of Pro Personnel: Bill Jobko
Scouts: Bob Cegelski, John Jelacic, Bob Riggle,
 Bill Striegel, Dick Szymanski
Ticket Manager: Ken Grantham
Assistant Ticket Manager: Joan Nave
Public Relations Director: Charlie Dayton
Assistant Director of Public Relations: Bob Dickinson
Assistant Director of Community Affairs:
 Carol Henderson
Head Trainer: Jerry Rhea
Assistant Trainer: Billy Brooks
Equipment Manager: Whitey Zimmerman
Assistant Equipment Manager: Horace Daniel

Stadium: Atlanta-Fulton County Stadium •
 Capacity: 60,748
 521 Capitol Avenue, S.W.
 Atlanta, Georgia 30312
Playing Surface: Grass
Training Camp: Suwanee Road at I-85
 Suwanee, Georgia 30174

1983 SCHEDULE

Preseason
Aug. 6	**Washington**	8:00
Aug. 13	at Denver	7:00
Aug. 20	at Tampa Bay	8:00
Aug. 26	**Baltimore**	8:00

Regular Season
Sept. 4	at Chicago	12:00
Sept. 11	**New York Giants**	1:00
Sept. 18	at Detroit	1:00
Sept. 25	at San Francisco	1:00
Oct. 2	**Philadelphia**	1:00
Oct. 9	**New Orleans**	1:00
Oct. 16	at Los Angeles Rams	1:00
Oct. 23	at New York Jets	1:00
Oct. 30	**New England**	1:00
Nov. 6	at New Orleans	12:00
Nov. 14	**Los Angeles Rams** (Monday)	9:00
Nov. 20	**San Francisco**	4:00
Nov. 27	**Green Bay**	4:00
Dec. 4	at Washington	1:00
Dec. 10	at Miami (Saturday)	4:00
Dec. 18	**Buffalo**	1:00

1982 TEAM STATISTICS

	Atlanta	Opp.
Total First Downs	190	170
Rushing	79	66
Passing	92	84
Penalty	19	20
Third Down Efficiency	49/118	38/109
Third Down Percentage	41.5	34.9
Total Net Yards	2963	2848
Total Offensive Plays	610	551
Avg. Gain per Play	4.9	5.2
Avg. Gain per Game	329.2	316.4
Net Yards Rushing	1181	1044
Total Rushing Plays	310	253
Avg. Gain per Rush	3.8	4.1
Avg. Gain Rushing per Game	131.2	116.0
Net Yards Passing	1782	1804
Lost Attempting to Pass	25/210	18/141
Gross Yards Passing	1992	1945
Attempts/Completions	275/176	280/157
Percent Completed	64.0	56.1
Had Intercepted	11	10
Avg. Net Passing per Game	198.0	200.4
Punts/Avg.	43/39.3	38/41.7
Punt Returns/Avg.	24/11.4	24/8.2
Kickoff Returns/Avg.	29/17.7	30/22.6
Interceptions/Avg. Ret.	10/9.0	11/5.3
Penalties/Yards	77/655	60/549
Fumbles/Ball Lost	14/10	24/15
Total Points	183	199
Avg. Points per Game	20.3	22.1
Touchdowns	22	26
Rushing	12	13
Passing	9	12
Returns and Recoveries	1	1
Field Goals	10/14	6/12
Conversions	21/22	25/26
Safeties	0	0
Avg. Time of Possession	32:51	27:09

1982 TEAM RECORD

Preseason (2-2)

Atlanta		Opponents
20	*Minnesota	17
3	Baltimore	34
24	*Philadelphia	21
0	Tampa Bay	34
47		106

Regular Season (5-4)

Atlanta		Opponents	Att.
16	New York Giants	14	74,286
14	*Los Angeles Raiders	38	54,774
34	*Los Angeles Rams	17	39,686
20	*St. Louis	23	33,411
34	Denver	27	73,984
35	*New Orleans	0	39,535
17	San Francisco	7	53,234
7	*Green Bay	38	50,245
6	New Orleans	35	47,336
183		199	446,491

*Home Game

Score by Periods

Atlanta	17	68	44	54	—	183
Opponents	49	69	30	51	—	199

Attendance

Home 217,651   Away 248,840   Total 466,491
Single game home record, 59,257 (10-30-77)
Single season home record, 442,457 (1980)

1982 INDIVIDUAL STATISTICS

Rushing

	Att	Yds	Avg	LG	TD
Andrews	139	573	4.1	19t	5
Riggs	78	299	3.8	37	5
Cain	54	173	3.2	8	1
Robinson	19	108	5.7	16	0
Hodge	2	11	5.5	11	0
Strong	4	9	2.3	4	0
Bartkowski	13	4	0.3	10	1
A. Jackson	1	4	4.0	4	0
Atlanta	310	1181	3.8	37	12
Opponents	253	1044	4.1	41	13

Field Goal Success

Distance	1-19	20-29	30-39	40-49	50 Over
Made-Att.	0-0	6-6	0-3	2-3	2-2

Passing

	Att	Comp	Pct	Yds	TD	Int	Tkld	Rate
Bartkowski	262	166	63.4	1905	8	11	20/177	78.1
Moroski	13	10	76.9	87	1	0	4/31	119.7
Andrews	0	0	0.0	0	0	0	1/2	—
Atlanta	275	176	64.0	1992	9	11	25/210	
Opponents	280	157	56.1	1945	12	10	18/141	

Receiving

	No	Yds	Avg	LG	TD
Andrews	42	503	12.0	86t	2
A. Jackson	26	361	13.9	40	1
Jenkins	24	347	14.5	43t	1
Riggs	23	185	8.0	15	0
Miller	20	221	11.1	39	1
Hodge	14	160	11.4	23	0
Cain	13	101	7.8	17t	1
Robinson	7	55	7.9	29	2
Bailey	2	24	12.0	15	1
Mikeska	2	19	9.5	12	0
B. Johnson	2	11	5.5	6	0
Krepfle	1	5	5.0	5	0
Atlanta	176	1992	11.3	86t	9
Opponents	157	1945	12.4	80t	12

Interceptions

	No	Yds	Avg	LG	TD
K. Johnson	2	30	15.0	30	0
Kuykendall	2	22	11.0	22	0
Butler	2	0	0.0	0	0
Pridemore	1	28	28.0	28	0
Glazebrook	1	10	10.0	10	0
Curry	1	0	0.0	0	0
Gaison	1	0	0.0	0	0
Atlanta	10	90	9.0	30	0
Opponents	11	58	5.3	19	0

Punting

	No	Yds	Avg	In 20	LG
Smigelsky	26	1000	38.5	6	54
Roberts	17	690	40.6	3	54
Atlanta	43	1690	39.3	9	54
Opponents	38	1585	41.7	6	64

Punt Returns

	No	FC	Yds	Avg	LG	TD
B. Johnson	24	4	273	11.4	71	0
Atlanta	24	4	273	11.4	71	0
Opponents	24	3	197	8.2	35	0

Kickoff Returns

	No	Yds	Avg	LG	TD
R. Brown	24	466	19.4	33	0
Gaison	2	14	7.0	14	0
Hodge	1	23	23.0	23	0
Laughlin	1	10	10.0	10	0
Scully	1	0	0.0	0	0
Atlanta	29	513	17.7	33	0
Opponents	30	678	22.6	76	0

Scoring

	TD	TD R	TD P	TD Rt	PAT	FG	TP
Luckhurst					21/22	10/14	51
Andrews	7	5	2	0			42
Riggs	5	5	0	0			30
Cain	2	1	1	0			12
Robinson	2	0	2	0			12
Bailey	1	0	1	0			6
Bartkowski	1	1	0	0			6
Glazebrook	1	0	0	1			6
A. Jackson	1	0	1	0			6
Jenkins	1	0	1	0			6
Miller	1	0	1	0			6
Atlanta	22	12	9	1	21/22	10/14	183
Opponents	26	13	12	1	25/26	6/12	199

Sacks

Curry 1, K. Johnson 1, Merrow 2½, Perko 1, Richardson 2, Rogers 2, Smith 3½, Williams 3, Yeates 1, Zele 1.

FIRST PLAYERS SELECTED

Year	Player, College, Position
1966	Tommy Nobis, Texas, LB
1967	Leo Carroll, San Diego State, DE (2)
1968	Claude Humphrey, Tennessee State, DE
1969	George Kunz, Notre Dame, T
1970	John Small, Citadel, DE
1971	Joe Profit, Northeast Louisiana, RB
1972	Clarence Ellis, Notre Dame, DB
1973	Greg Marx, Notre Dame, DT (2)
1974	Gerald Tinker, Kent State, WR (2)
1975	Steve Bartkowski, California, QB
1976	Bubba Bean, Texas A&M, RB
1977	Warren Bryant, Kentucky, T
1978	Mike Kenn, Michigan, T
1979	Don Smith, Miami, DE
1980	Junior Miller, Nebraska, TE
1981	Bobby Butler, Florida State, DB
1982	Gerald Riggs, Arizona State, RB
1983	Mike Pitts, Alabama, DE

FALCONS COACHING HISTORY

(97-144-4)

1966-68	Norb Hecker*	4-26-1
1968-74	Norm Van Brocklin**	37-49-3
1974-76	Marion Campbell***	6-19-0
1976	Pat Peppler	3-6-0
1977-82	Leeman Bennett	47-44-0

*Released after three games in 1968
**Released after eight games in 1974
***Released after five games in 1976

ATLANTA FALCONS 1983 VETERAN ROSTER

No.	Name	Pos.	Ht.	Wt.	Birth-date	NFL Exp.	College	Birthplace	Residence	Games in '82
31	Andrews, William	RB	6-0	200	12/25/55	5	Auburn	Thomasville, Ga.	Duluth, Ga.	9
82	Bailey, Stacey	WR	6-0	162	2/10/60	2	San Jose State	San Rafael, Calif.	San Rafael, Calif.	5
10	Bartkowski, Steve	QB	6-4	213	11/12/52	9	California	Des Moines, Iowa	Cumming, Ga.	9
99	Brown, Clay	TE	6-2	225	9/20/58	2	Brigham Young	Los Angeles, Calif.	Englewood, Colo.	1
46	Brown, Reggie	RB	5-11	211	3/12/60	2	Oregon	Denoran, N.J.	Newark, N.J.	8
66	Bryant, Warren	T	6-6	270	11/11/55	7	Kentucky	Miami, Fla.	Roswell, Ga.	9
23	Butler, Bobby	CB	5-11	170	5/28/59	3	Florida State	Boynton Beach, Fla.	Norcross, Ga.	9
21	Cain, Lynn	RB	6-1	205	10/16/55	5	Southern California	Los Angeles, Calif.	Dunwoody, Ga.	9
89	Curran, Willie	WR	5-10	175	12/30/59	2	UCLA	Inglewood, Calif.	Oxnard, Calif.	7
50	Curry, Buddy	LB	6-3	221	6/4/58	4	North Carolina	Danville, Va.	Norcross, Ga.	9
59	Davis, Paul	LB	6-1	215	7/10/58	3	North Carolina	Appalachia, Va.	Norcross, Ga.	9
34	Gaison, Blane	S	6-0	185	5/13/58	3	Hawaii	Kanehoe, Hawaii	Kanehoe, Hawaii	9
36	Glazebrook, Bob	S	6-1	200	3/7/56	6	Fresno State	Fresno, Calif.	Lawrenceville, Ga.	9
83	Hodge, Floyd	WR	6-0	195	7/18/59	2	Utah	Compton, Calif.	Duluth, Ga.	9
64	Howell, Pat	G	6-5	253	3/12/57	5	Southern California	Fresno, Calif.	Clovis, Calif.	9
85	Jackson, Alfred	WR	5-11	176	8/3/55	6	Texas	Cameron, Tex.	Austin, Tex.	9
84	Jenkins, Alfred	WR	5-9	155	1/25/52	8	Morris Brown	Hogansville, Ga.	College Park, Ga.	9
81	Johnson, Billy	WR-KR	5-9	170	1/21/52	8	Widener	Bouthwyn, Pa.	Doraville, Ga.	9
37	Johnson, Kenny	CB	5-10	176	1/7/58	4	Mississippi State	Moss Point, Miss.	Moss Point, Miss.	9
20	Jones, Earl	CB	6-0	178	7/19/57	4	Norfolk State	Tuscaloosa, Ala.	Virginia Beach, Va.	9
78	Kenn, Mike	T	6-6	257	2/9/56	6	Michigan	Evanston, Ill.	Roswell, Ga.	9
14	Komlo, Jeff	QB	6-2	200	7/30/56	5	Delaware	Cleverly, Md.	Radnor, Pa.	0*
54	Kuykendall, Fulton	LB	6-5	225	6/10/53	9	UCLA	Coronado, Calif.	Roswell, Ga.	9
51	Laughlin, Jim	LB	6-0	212	7/5/58	4	Ohio State	Lyndhurst, Ohio	Lyndhurst, Ohio	9
18	Luckhurst, Mick	K	6-0	180	3/31/58	3	California	Redbourn, England	Norcross, Ga.	9
75	Merrow, Jeff	DE	6-4	255	7/11/53	8	West Virginia	Akron, Ohio	Buford, Ga.	8
87	Mikeska, Russ	TE	6-3	225	9/10/55	5	Texas A&M	Temple, Tex.	Norcross, Ga.	5
80	Miller, Junior	TE	6-4	235	11/26/57	4	Nebraska	Midland, Tex.	Lincoln, Neb.	9
15	Moroski, Mike	QB	6-4	200	9/4/57	5	Cal-Davis	Novato, Calif.	Cumming, Ga.	9
53	Musser, Neal	LB	6-2	218	3/20/57	3	North Carolina State	Elon, N.C.	Elon, N.C.	8
71	Perko, Mike	NT	6-4	235	3/30/57	2	Utah State	Seattle, Wash.	Buford, Ga.	9
27	Pridemore, Tom	S	5-10	186	4/29/56	6	West Virginia	Ansted, W. Va.	Lawrenceville, Ga.	9
56	Richardson, Al	LB	6-2	206	9/23/57	4	Georgia Tech	Miami, Fla.	Decatur, Ga.	8
42	Riggs, Gerald	RB	6-1	230	11/6/60	2	Arizona State	Tulluha, La.	Alpharetta, Ga.	9
12	Roberts, George	P	6-0	186	6/10/54	6	Virginia Tech	Lynchburg, Va.	Miami Springs, Fla.	3
33	Robinson, Bo	RB	6-2	225	5/27/56	5	West Texas State	LaMesa, Tex.	Doraville, Ga.	9
77	Rogers, Doug	DE	6-5	255	6/23/60	2	Stanford	Bakersfield, Calif.	Buford, Ga.	9
67	Sanders, Eric	T	6-6	255	10/22/58	3	Nevada-Reno	Reno, Nev.	Roswell, Ga.	9
70	Scott, Dave	G	6-4	265	12/26/53	8	Kansas	Paterson, N.J.	Lawrence, Kan.	9
61	Scully, John	C	6-5	255	8/2/58	3	Notre Dame	Long Island, N.Y.	Roswell, Ga.	9
65	Smith, Don	NT	6-5	248	5/9/57	5	Miami	Oakland, Calif.	Tarpon Springs, Fla.	9
47	Spivey, Mike	CB	6-0	198	3/10/54	7	Colorado	Houston, Tex.	Denver, Colo.	8
25	Strong, Ray	RB	5-9	184	5/7/56	6	Nevada-Las Vegas	Berkeley, Calif.	Duluth, Ga.	9
68	Thielemann, R.C.	G	6-4	247	8/12/55	7	Arkansas	Houston, Tex.	Norcross, Ga.	9
57	Van Note, Jeff	C	6-2	247	2/7/46	15	Kentucky	South Orange, N.J.	Roswell, Ga.	9
52	White, Lyman	LB	6-0	217	1/3/59	2	Louisiana State	Franklin, La.	Baton Rouge, La.	2
58	Williams, Joel	LB	6-0	215	12/13/56	5	Wisconsin-LaCrosse	Miami, Fla.	Norcross, Ga.	9
79	Yeates, Jeff	DE	6-3	248	8/3/51	10	Boston College	Buffalo, N.Y.	Atlanta, Ga.	9
63	Zele, Mike	NT	6-3	236	7/3/56	5	Kent State	Euclid, Ohio	Euclid, Ohio	9

* Komlo active for 7 games in 1982, but did not play.

Also played with Falcons in '82—LB Robert Jackson (4 games), TE Keith Krepfle (4), P Dave Smigelsky (6).

COACHING STAFF

Head Coach, Dan Henning

Pro Career: Begins first season as Falcons head coach. Came from the Washington Redskins where he was assistant head coach under Joe Gibbs, helping the Redskins to a 20-9 record over the past two seasons and a Super Bowl victory in 1982. Also was an assistant with Houston 1972, New York Jets 1976-78, and Miami Dolphins 1979-80. Played quarterback for the San Diego Chargers 1964-67.

Background: Played quarterback for William and Mary 1960-63. Began college coaching career with Florida State 1968-70, 1974, Virginia Tech 1971, 1973.

Personal: Born June 21, 1942, Bronx, N.Y. Dan and his wife, Sandy, have five children—Mary K 20, Patty 19, Danny 17, Terry 14, and Mike 9. They reside in Atlanta.

ASSISTANT COACHES

Jack Christiansen, defensive backfield; born December 20, 1928, Sublett, Kan., lives in Atlanta. Defensive halfback Colorado State 1948-50. Pro defensive back Detroit Lions 1951-58. College coach: Stanford 1968-76 (head coach 1972-76). Pro coach: San Francisco 49ers 1959-67 (head coach 1963-67), Kansas City Chiefs 1977, Seattle Seahawks 1978-82, first year with Falcons.

Steve Crosby, running backs; born July 3, 1950, Pawnee Rock, Kan., lives in Atlanta. Running back Fort Hays (Kan.) College 1971-73. Pro running back New York Giants 1974-76. Pro coach: Miami Dolphins 1977-82, first year with Falcons.

George Dostal, strength and conditioning; born October 25, 1934, Cleveland, Ohio, lives in Lawrenceville, Ga. Fullback-linebacker Kent State 1964-67. No pro playing experience. College coach: Clemson 1977-82. Pro coach: First year with Falcons.

Sam Elliott, administrative assistant; born August 3, 1946, Huntington, W. Va., lives in Atlanta. Quarterback-defensive back Ohio State 1965-67. No pro playing experience. College coach: Ohio State 1968, Florida State 1969-70, 1974, Kent State 1971-73. Pro coach: First year with Falcons.

Ted Fritsch, special teams; born August 26, 1950, Green Bay, Wis., lives in Atlanta. Center St. Norbert 1969-71. Pro center Atlanta Falcons 1972-75, Washington Redskins 1976-79. Pro coach: First year with Falcons.

Bob Fry, offensive coordinator-offensive line; born November 11, 1930, Cincinnati, Ohio, lives in Atlanta. Tackle Kentucky 1949-52. Pro tackle Los Angeles Rams 1953-59, Dallas Cowboys 1960-64. Pro coach: Atlanta Falcons 1966-68, Pittsburgh Steelers 1969-73, New York Jets 1974-82, rejoined Falcons in 1983.

Bob Harrison, receivers; born September 9, 1941, Cleveland, Ohio, lives in Atlanta. End Kent State 1961-64. No pro playing experience. College coach: Kent State 1969-70, Iowa 1971-73, Cornell 1974, North Carolina State 1975-76, Tennessee 1977-82. Pro coach: First year with Falcons.

Bobby Jackson, linebackers; born February 16, 1940, Forsyth, Ga., lives in Atlanta. Linebacker-running back Samford 1959-62. No pro playing experience. College coach: Florida State 1965-69, Kansas State 1970-74, Louisville 1975-76, Tennessee 1977-82. Pro coach: First year with Falcons.

John Marshall, defensive coordinator; born October 2, 1945, Arroyo Grande, Calif., lives in Atlanta. Oregon 1960. No pro playing experience. College coach: Oregon 1970-76, Southern California 1977-79. Pro coach: Green Bay Packers 1980-82, first year with Falcons.

Gary Puetz, assistant offensive line; born March 14, 1952, Chicago, Ill., lives in Atlanta. Offensive line Valpariso 1969-72. Pro offensive lineman New York Jets 1973-78, Tampa Bay Buccaneers 1978, Philadelphia Eagles 1979, New England Patriots 1979-81, Washington Redskins 1982. Pro coach: First year with Falcons.

ATLANTA FALCONS 1983 FIRST-YEAR ROSTER

Name	Pos.	Ht.	Wt.	Birth-date	College	Birthplace	Residence	How Acq.
Benish, Dan	DE	6-5	259	11/21/61	Clemson	Youngstown, Ohio	Hubbard, Ohio	FA
Britt, James	CB-S	6-0	185	9/12/60	Louisiana State	Minden, La.	Minden, La.	D2
Brown, Greg	LB	6-2	228	12/27/61	Miami	Monterey, Calif.	Dale City, Va.	FA
Butler, Earnest	G	6-3	254	10/29/60	North Carolina State	New Bern, N.C.	New Bern, N.C.	FA
Clark, Brian (1)	K	6-2	198	6/28/58	Florida	Canton, Ohio	Sarasota, Fla.	FA
Cochran, Mickey	G	6-4	273	1/10/60	Cameron	Chattanooga, Tenn.	Owenton, Ky.	FA
Collins, Earl	RB	6-1	220	11/25/60	Alabama	Tallapoosa, Ga.	Mobile, Ala.	FA
Cox, Arthur	TE	6-3	245	2/5/61	Texas Southern	Plant City, Fla.	Plant City, Fla.	FA
deBruijn, Case (1)	P	6-1	174	4/11/60	Idaho State	Denhaague, Neth.	Manassas, Va.	FA
Dixon, Rich	LB	6-2	225	8/6/59	California	Roswell, N.M.	Berkeley, Calif.	FA
Dufour, Dan	G	6-5	287	10/18/60	UCLA	Lynn, Mass.	Wakefield, Mass.	FA
Erb, James	LB	6-2	214	8/2/60	Iowa	Iowa City, Iowa	Wellman, Iowa	FA
Floyd, Stanley	WR	5-9	180	6/23/61	Houston	Albany, Ga.	Knoxville, Tenn.	FA
Ford, Mariet	WR	5-8	156	8/28/61	California	San Francisco, Calif.	Walnut Creek, Calif.	FA
Foster, Kevin	CB-S	6-3	188	11/13/59	Kearney State	Ord, Neb.	Kearney, Neb.	FA
Frye, David	LB	6-2	200	6/21/61	Purdue	Cincinnati, Ohio	Cincinnati, Ohio	FA
Gentry, Bob	CB-S	6-2	200	3/20/60	Kansas	Hot Springs, Ark.	Hot Springs, Ark.	FA
Gerleman, Loren	G	6-3	245	3/6/61	Iowa	Decorah, Iowa	Decorah, Iowa	FA
Giacomarro, Ralph	P	6-0	190	1/17/61	Penn State	Passaic, N.J.	Saddlebrook, N.J.	D10
Harper, John	LB	6-3	234	6/12/60	Southern Illinois	Memphis, Tenn.	Memphis, Tenn.	D4
Hendley, Richard	P	5-9	182	1/13/61	Clemson	Greenville, S.C.	Greenville, S.C.	FA
Lowery, Greg	P	6-0	185	11/17/59	Jacksonville State	Grosse Point, Mich.	Huntsville, Ala.	FA
Mashburn, Rick	P	5-11	195	3/20/60	Lenoir-Rhyne	Franklin, N.C.	Franklin, N.C.	FA
Matthews, Allama	TE	6-3	230	8/24/61	Vanderbilt	Jacksonville, Fla.	Miami, Fla.	D12
Miller, Brett	T	6-7	290	10/2/58	Iowa	Lynwood, Calif.	Glendale, Calif.	D5
North, Lee (1)	C	6-1	257	2/27/60	Tennessee	Atlanta, Ga.	Decatur, Ga.	FA
Pitts, Mike	DE	6-5	260	9/25/60	Alabama	Pell City, Ala.	Baltimore, Md.	D1
Price, Jerry	TE	6-3	246	4/12/61	Mississippi State	Meridian, Miss.	Enterprise, Miss.	FA
Provence, Andrew	NT	6-3	265	3/8/61	South Carolina	Savannah, Ga.	Savannah, Ga.	D3
Rade, John	LB	6-1	214	8/31/60	Boise State	Ceres, Calif.	Modesto, Calif.	D8
Robinson, Carl	RB	6-1	216	12/9/60	Texas	Temple, Tex.	Temple, Tex.	FA
Salley, John	CB-S	6-1	190	5/18/60	Wyoming	Lake Charles, La.	Laramie, Wyo.	D11
Simeta, Mike	NT	6-4	267	3/29/59	Kansas State	Los Angeles, Calif.	Manhattan, Kan.	FA
Turk, Jeff	CB-S	6-0	164	1/11/61	Boise State	San Diego, Calif.	San Diego, Calif.	D7
Van Norman, Kris	CB-S	6-1	193	6/30/60	Nebraska	Minden, Neb.	Minden, Neb.	FA
Vernoy, Scott (1)	P	6-5	205	5/12/60	Cal State-Fullerton	Lynwood, Calif.	Downey, Calif.	FA
Young, Ben	TE	6-4	235	1/13/60	Texas-Arlington	Toledo, Ohio	Grapevine, Tex.	FA
Zappala, Greg	LB	6-2	214	5/1/61	Miami	Pittsburgh, Pa.	Pittsburgh, Pa.	FA

Players who report to an NFL team for the first time are designated on rosters as rookies (R). If a player reported to an NFL training camp in a previous year but was not on the active squad for three or more regular season or postseason games, he is listed on the first-year roster and designated by a (1). Thereafter, a player who is on the active squad for three or more regular season or postseason games is credited with an additional year of playing experience.

NOTES

_____
_____
_____
_____
_____
_____
_____
_____

Dan Sekanovich, assistant head coach-defensive line; born July 27, 1933, Hazleton, Pa., lives in Atlanta. Defensive end Tennessee 1951-53. Pro defensive end Montreal Alouettes (CFL) 1955. College coach: Susquehanna 1961-63, Connecticut 1964-67, Pittsburgh 1968, Navy 1969-70, Kentucky 1971-72. Pro coach: Montreal Alouettes (CFL) 1973-76, New York Jets 1977-82, first year with Falcons.

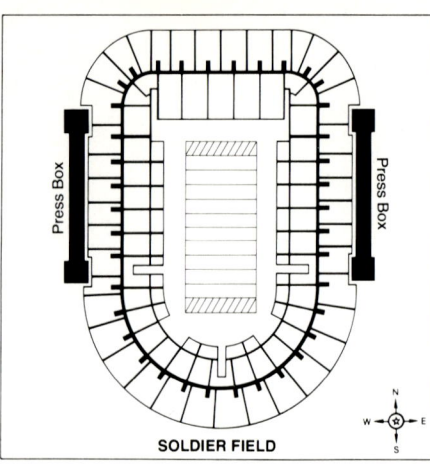

SOLDIER FIELD

Chicago Bears

National Football Conference
Central Division

Team Colors: Navy Blue, Orange, and White

Corporate Headquarters and Ticket Offices:
55 E. Jackson Blvd., Chicago, Illinois 60604
Telephone: (312) 663-5100 (Administrative),
　　　　　　(312) 663-5408 (Tickets),
Halas Hall (Coaching Staff, Personnel, Public Relations):
250 North Washington, Lake Forest, Illinois 60045
Telephone: (312) 295-6600 (Halas Hall)

Club Officials
Chairman of the Board, President, CEO:
　George S. Halas
Executive Vice President-General Manager: Jim Finks
Vice President: Ed McCaskey
Assistant to General Manager: Bill McGrane
Director, Pro Scouting: Bill Tobin
Director, College Scouting: Jim Parmer
Stadium Operations-Admissions Director:
　George Arneson
Business Manager: Rudy Custer
Treasurer: Jerry Vainisi
Public Relations Director: Patrick McCaskey
Film Director: Mitch Friedman
Trainer: Fred Caito
Physical Coordinator: Clyde Emrich
Equipment Manager: Ray Earley

Stadium: Soldier Field • **Capacity:** 65,793
　　　　　 425 McFetridge Place
　　　　　 Chicago, Illinois 60605

Playing Surface: AstroTurf

Training Camp: Halas Hall, 250 N. Washington,
　　　　　　　 Lake Forest, Illinois 60045

1983 SCHEDULE

Preseason
Aug. 6	**Buffalo**	6:00
Aug. 13	at St. Louis	6:00
Aug. 20	at Los Angeles Raiders	8:00
Aug. 27	**Kansas City**	6:00

Regular Season
Sept. 4	**Atlanta**	12:00
Sept. 11	**Tampa Bay**	12:00
Sept. 18	at New Orleans	12:00
Sept. 25	at Baltimore	2:00
Oct. 2	**Denver**	12:00
Oct. 9	**Minnesota**	12:00
Oct. 16	at Detroit	1:00
Oct. 23	at Philadelphia	1:00
Oct. 30	**Detroit**	12:00
Nov. 6	at Los Angeles Rams	1:00
Nov. 13	**Philadelphia**	12:00
Nov. 20	at Tampa Bay	1:00
Nov. 27	**San Francisco**	12:00
Dec. 4	at Green Bay	12:00
Dec. 11	at Minnesota	12:00
Dec. 18	**Green Bay**	12:00

1982 TEAM STATISTICS

	Chicago	Opp.
Total First Downs	153	166
Rushing	56	53
Passing	83	102
Penalty	14	11
Third Down Efficiency	47/128	36/119
Third Down Percentage	36.7	30.3
Total Net Yards	2493	2851
Total Offensive Plays	571	585
Avg. Gain per Play	4.4	4.9
Avg. Gain per Game	277.0	316.8
Net Yards Rushing	988	902
Total Rushing Plays	276	261
Avg. Gain per Rush	3.6	3.5
Avg. Gain Rushing per Game	109.8	100.2
Net Yards Passing	1505	1949
Lost Attempting to Pass	33/244	30/240
Gross Yards Passing	1749	2189
Attempts/Completions	262/141	294/164
Percent Completed	53.8	55.8
Had Intercepted	11	13
Avg. Net Passing per Game	167.2	216.6
Punts/Avg.	59/41.6	49/41.6
Punt Returns/Avg.	24/5.9	34/9.2
Kickoff Returns/Avg.	34/18.3	30/17.9
Interceptions/Avg. Ret.	13/7.6	11/17.7
Penalties/Yards	58/422	52/451
Fumbles/Ball Lost	16/8	20/7
Total Points	141	174
Avg. Points per Game	15.7	19.3
Touchdowns	16	20
Rushing	5	4
Passing	10	14
Returns and Recoveries	1	2
Field Goals	9/20	12/17
Conversions	16/16	18/20
Safeties	1	0
Avg. Time of Possession	29:28	30:32

1982 TEAM RECORD

Preseason (1-3)

Chicago		Opponents
27	San Diego	28
21	Buffalo	14
3	*St. Louis	10
17	*Baltimore	26
68		78

Regular Season (3-6)

Chicago		Opponents	Att.
10	Detroit	17	71,337
0	*New Orleans	10	56,600
20	*Detroit	17	46,783
7	Minnesota	35	54,724
26	*New England	13	36,973
14	Seattle	20	52,826
7	*St. Louis	10	43,270
34	Los Angeles Rams	26	46,502
23	Tampa Bay (OT)	26	68,112
141		174	477,127

*Home Game   (OT) Overtime

Score by Periods

Chicago	44	50	17	30	0	—	141
Opponents	37	60	30	44	3	—	174

Attendance

Home 183,626   Away 293,501   Total 477,127
Single game home record, 80,259 (11-24-66)
Single season home record, 511,541 (1981)

1982 INDIVIDUAL STATISTICS

Rushing

	Att	Yds	Avg	LG	TD
Payton	148	596	4.0	26	1
Suhey	70	206	2.9	15	3
McMahon	24	105	4.4	11	1
McClendon	17	47	2.8	13	0
Gentry	4	21	5.3	9	0
Harper	3	7	2.3	8	0
C. Thomas	5	4	0.8	3	0
Moorehead	2	3	1.5	6	0
Evans	2	0	0.0	6	0
Watts	1	−1	−1.0	−1	0
Chicago	276	988	3.6	26	5
Opponents	261	902	3.5	47	4

Field Goal Success

Distance	1-19	20-29	30-39	40-49	50 Over
Made-Att.	2-2	0-0	1-6	5-7	1-5

Passing

	Att	Comp	Pct	Yds	TD	Int	Tkld	Rate
McMahon	210	120	57.1	1501	9	7	27/196	80.1
Avellini	20	8	40.0	84	0	0	4/31	52.9
Evans	28	12	42.9	125	0	4	2/17	16.8
Payton	3	1	33.3	39	1	0	0/0	—
Baschnagel	1	0	0.0	0	0	0	0/0	—
Chicago	262	141	53.8	1749	10	11	33/244	
Opponents	294	164	55.8	2189	14	13	30/240	

Receiving

	No	Yds	Avg	LG	TD
Suhey	36	333	9.3	45	0
Payton	32	311	9.7	40	0
Moorehead	30	363	12.1	50t	5
Margerum	14	207	14.8	28	3
Baschnagel	12	194	16.2	39t	2
Watts	8	217	27.1	40	0
Earl	4	56	14.0	18	0
Scott	2	44	22.0	27	0
Gentry	1	9	9.9	9	0
Harper	1	8	8.0	8	0
McClendon	1	7	7.0	7	0
Chicago	141	1749	12.4	50t	10
Opponents	164	2189	13.3	65	14

Interceptions

	No	Yds	Avg	LG	TD
Schmidt	4	39	9.8	29	0
Fisher	3	19	6.3	19	0
Wilson	2	39	19.5	39t	1
Fencik	2	2	1.0	2	0
Frazier	2	0	0.0	0	0
Chicago	13	99	7.6	39t	1
Opponents	11	195	17.7	99t	2

Punting

	No	Yds	Avg	In 20	LG
Parsons	58	2394	41.3	10	81
McMahon	1	59	59.0	0	59
Chicago	59	2453	41.6	10	81
Opponents	49	2038	41.6	8	65

Punt Returns

	No	FC	Yds	Avg	LG	TD
Gentry	17	5	89	5.2	16	0
Fisher	7	6	53	7.6	17	0
Chicago	24	11	142	5.9	17	0
Opponents	34	7	314	9.2	37	0

Kickoff Returns

	No	Yds	Avg	LG	TD
Watts	14	330	23.6	36	0
Gentry	9	161	17.9	23	0
Fisher	7	102	14.6	20	0
Harper	2	10	5.0	10	0
Bell	1	14	14.0	14	0
Muckensturm	1	5	5.0	5	0
Chicago	34	622	18.3	36	0
Opponents	30	537	17.9	32	0

Scoring

	TD	TD R	TD P	TD Rt	PAT	FG	TP
Moorehead	5	0	5	0			30
Roveto					10/10	4/13	22
B. Thomas					6/6	5/7	21
Margerum	3	0	3	0			18
Suhey	3	3	0	0			18
Baschnagel	2	0	2	0			12
McMahon	1	1	0	0			6
Payton	1	1	0	0			6
Wilson	1	0	0	1			6
Osborne	(Safety)						2
Chicago	16	5	10	1	16/16	9/20	141
Opponents	20	4	14	2	18/20	12/17	174

Sacks

Bell 1, Campbell 1, Frazier 1, Hampton 9, Harris 3½, Hartenstine 3, Herron 1, McMichael 2½, Osborne 4½, Singletary 1, Wilson 2½.

FIRST PLAYERS SELECTED

Since 1939

Year	Player, College, Position
1939	Sid Luckman, Columbia, B
1940	C. (Bulldog) Turner, Hardin-Simmons, C
1941	Tom Harmon, Michigan, B
1942	Frankie Albert, Stanford, B
1943	Bob Steuber, Missouri, B
1944	Ray Evans, Kansas, B
1945	Don Lund, Michigan, B
1946	Johnny Lujack, Notre Dame, B
1947	Bob Fenimore, Oklahoma A&M, B
1948	Bobby Layne, Texas, B
1949	Dick Harris, Texas, C
1950	Chuck Hunsinger, Florida, B
1951	Bob Williams, Notre Dame, B
1952	Jim Dooley, Miami, B
1953	Billy Anderson, Compton (Calif.) JC, B
1954	Stan Wallace, Illinois, B
1955	Ron Drzewiecki, Marquette, B
1956	Menan (Tex) Schriewer, Texas, E
1957	Earl Leggett, Louisiana State, T
1958	Chuck Howley, West Virginia, G
1959	Don Clark, Ohio State, B
1960	Roger Davis, Syracuse, G
1961	Mike Ditka, Pittsburgh, E
1962	Ronnie Bull, Baylor, RB
1963	Dave Behrman, Michigan State, C
1964	Dick Evey, Tennessee, DT
1965	Dick Butkus, Illinois, LB
1966	George Rice, Louisiana State, DT
1967	Loyd Phillips, Arkansas, DE
1968	Mike Hull, Southern California, RB
1969	Rufus Mayes, Ohio State, T
1970	George Farmer, UCLA, WR (3)
1971	Joe Moore, Missouri, RB
1972	Lionel Antoine, Southern Illinois, T
1973	Wally Chambers, Eastern Kentucky, DE
1974	Waymond Bryant, Tennessee State, LB
1975	Walter Payton, Jackson State, RB
1976	Dennis Lick, Wisconsin, T
1977	Ted Albrecht, California, T
1978	Brad Shearer, Texas, DT (3)
1979	Dan Hampton, Arkansas, DT
1980	Otis Wilson, Louisville, LB
1981	Keith Van Horne, Southern California, T
1982	Jim McMahon, Brigham Young, QB
1983	Jimbo Covert, Pittsburgh, T

BEARS COACHING HISTORY

Chicago Staleys 1921
(471-313-42)

1920-29	George Halas	85-31-19
1930-32	Ralph Jones	24-10-7
1933-42	George Halas*	88-25-4
1942-45	Hunk Anderson-Luke Johnsos**	24-12-2
1946-55	George Halas	77-42-2
1956-57	John (Paddy) Driscoll	14-10-1
1958-67	George Halas	75-53-6
1968-71	Jim Dooley	20-36-0
1972-74	Abe Gibron	11-30-1
1975-77	Jack Pardee	20-23-0
1978-81	Neill Armstrong	30-35-0
1982	Mike Ditka	3-6-0

*Retired November 1 to re-enter Navy
**Co-coaches

CHICAGO BEARS 1983 VETERAN ROSTER

No.	Name	Pos.	Ht.	Wt.	Birth-date	NFL Exp.	College	Birthplace	Residence	Games in '82
64	Albrecht, Ted	T-G	6-4	250	10/8/54	6	California	Harvey, Ill.	Deerfield, Ill.	0*
7	†Avellini, Bob	QB	6-2	210	8/28/53	9	Maryland	Queens, N.Y.	Chicago, Ill.	2
84	Baschnagel, Brian	WR	6-0	184	1/8/54	8	Ohio State	Kingston, N.Y.	Chicago, Ill.	9
79	Becker, Kurt	G	6-5	251	12/22/58	2	Michigan	Aurora, Ill.	Libertyville, Ill.	5
25	Bell, Todd	S	6-0	207	11/28/58	3	Ohio State	Middletown, Ohio	Middletown, Ohio	9
54	Cabral, Brian	LB	6-1	224	6/23/56	5	Colorado	Ft. Benning, Ga.	Vernon Hills, Ill.	8
59	Campbell, Gary	LB	6-1	220	3/4/52	7	Colorado	Honolulu, Hawaii	Schaumberg, Ill.	9
57	Chesley, Al	LB	6-3	240	8/23/57	5	Pittsburgh	Washington, D.C.	Philadelphia, Pa.	8*
72	Doerger, Jerry	T	6-5	270	7/18/60	2	Wisconsin	Cincinnati, Ohio	Cincinnati, Ohio	1
81	Earl, Robin	TE	6-5	240	3/18/55	7	Washington	Boise, Idaho	Hoffman Estates, Ill.	9
8	Evans, Vince	QB	6-2	212	6/14/55	7	Southern California	Greensboro, N.C.	Chicago, Ill.	4
45	†Fencik, Gary	S	6-1	197	6/11/54	8	Yale	Chicago, Ill.	Chicago, Ill.	9
24	Fisher, Jeff	S	5-10	188	2/25/58	3	Southern California	Culver City, Calif.	Woodland Hills, Calif.	9
21	Frazier, Leslie	CB	6-0	189	4/3/59	3	Alcorn State	Columbus, Miss.	Vernon Hills, Ill.	9
	t-Frederick, Andy	T	6-6	265	7/25/54	7	New Mexico	Oak Park, Ill.	Dallas, Tex.	7
29	Gentry, Dennis	RB	5-8	173	2/10/59	2	Baylor	Lubbock, Tex.	Temple, Tex.	9
99	†Hampton, Dan	DT	6-5	255	9/19/57	5	Arkansas	Oklahoma City, Okla.	Lake Bluff, Ill.	9
35	†Harper, Roland	RB	5-11	210	2/28/53	8	Louisiana Tech	Seguin, Tex.	Gurnee, Ill.	8
90	Harris, Al	DE	6-5	250	12/31/56	5	Arizona State	Bangor, Maine	Aurora, Colo.	8
73	Hartenstine, Mike	DE	6-3	243	7/27/53	9	Penn State	Allentown, Pa.	Lake Bluff, Ill.	9
71	Hartnett, Perry	G	6-5	275	4/28/60	2	Southern Methodist	Galveston, Tex.	Dallas, Tex.	9
51	†Herron, Bruce	LB	6-2	220	4/14/54	6	New Mexico	Victoria, Tex.	Chicago, Ill.	9
63	Hilgenberg, Jay	C	6-3	250	3/21/59	3	Iowa	Iowa City, Iowa	Iowa City, Iowa	9
65	Jackson, Noah	G	6-2	265	4/14/54	9	Tampa	Jacksonville Beach, Fla.	Lake Forest, Ill.	9
62	†Jiggetts, Dan	T	6-5	270	3/10/54	8	Harvard	Brooklyn, N.Y.	Long Grove, Ill.	9
70	Lick, Dennis	T	6-3	265	4/26/54	8	Wisconsin	Chicago, Ill.	Northbrook, Ill.	0*
82	†Margerum, Ken	WR	5-10	170	10/5/58	3	Stanford	Fountain Valley, Calif.	Stanford, Calif.	9
37	McClendon, Willie	RB	6-1	205	9/13/57	5	Georgia	Brunswick, Ga.	Hoffman Estates, Ill.	9
67	†McKinnely, Phil	T	6-4	250	7/8/54	8	UCLA	Oakland, Calif.	Norcross, Ga.	8
9	McMahon, Jim	QB	6-1	187	8/21/59	2	Brigham Young	Jersey City, N.J.	Northbrook, Ill.	8
76	McMichael, Steve	DT	6-1	245	10/17/57	4	Texas	Houston, Tex.	Highland Park, Ill.	9
87	Moorehead, Emery	TE	6-2	220	3/22/54	7	Colorado	Evanston, Ill.	Evanston, Ill.	9
58	†Muckensturm, Jerry	LB	6-4	220	10/13/53	7	Arkansas State	Belleville, Ill.	Jonesboro, Ark.	6
52	Neal, Dan	C	6-4	255	8/30/49	11	Kentucky	Corbin, Ky.	Deerfield, Ill.	9
68	Osborne, Jim	DT	6-3	245	9/7/49	12	Southern	Sylvania, Ga.	Olympia Fields, Ill.	9
86	†Parsons, Bob	P	6-5	225	6/29/50	12	Penn State	Bethlehem, Pa.	Des Plaines, Ill.	9
34	Payton, Walter	RB	5-10	202	7/25/54	9	Jackson State	Columbus, Miss.	Arlington Heights, Ill.	9
	t-Saldi, Jay	TE	6-3	230	10/8/54	8	South Carolina	White Plains, N.Y.	Dallas, Tex.	5
44	†Schmidt, Terry	CB	6-0	177	5/28/52	10	Ball State	Columbus, Ind.	Lake Forest, Ill.	9
89	Scott, James	WR	6-1	190	3/28/52	7	Henderson J.C.	Longview, Tex.	Dallas, Tex.	5
50	Singletary, Mike	LB	5-11	230	10/9/58	3	Baylor	Houston, Tex.	Houston, Tex.	9
69	Sorey, Revie	G	6-2	260	9/10/53	8	Illinois	Brooklyn, N.Y.	Chicago, Ill.	0*
26	†Suhey, Matt	RB	5-11	217	7/7/58	4	Penn State	Bellefonte, Pa.	Highland Park, Ill.	9
16	†Thomas, Bob	K	5-10	175	8/7/52	8	Notre Dame	Rochester, N.Y.	Lisle, Ill.	4*
33	Thomas, Calvin	RB	5-11	220	1/7/60	2	Illinois	St. Louis, Mo.	Chicago, Ill.	6
78	Van Horne, Keith	T	6-6	265	11/6/57	3	Southern California	Lebanon, Pa.	Clarendon Hills, Ill.	9
75	Waechter, Henry	DE	6-5	270	2/13/59	2	Nebraska	Dubuque, Iowa	Walton, Neb.	9
23	†Walterscheid, Lenny	S	5-11	190	9/13/54	7	Southern Utah State	Gainesville, Tex.	Libertyville, Ill.	9
80	Watts, Rickey	WR	6-1	203	5/16/57	5	Tulsa	Longview, Tex.	Highwood, Ill.	9
88	†Williams, Brooks	TE	6-4	226	12/7/54	6	North Carolina	Baltimore, Md.	Virginia Beach, Va.	9
74	Williams, Jeff	G	6-4	260	4/15/55	6	Rhode Island	Gloucester, Mass.	San Diego, Calif.	5
43	†Williams, Walt	CB	6-1	185	7/10/56	7	New Mexico State	Port Arthur, Tex.	Midland, Tex.	5*
55	Wilson, Otis	LB	6-2	222	9/15/57	4	Louisville	New York, N.Y.	Libertyville, Ill.	9

* Albrecht and Sorey missed '82 season due to injuries; Chesley played 4 games with Philadelphia, 4 with Chicago in '82; Lick active for 4 games in '82, but did not play; B. Thomas played 2 games with Detroit, 2 games with Chicago in '82; W. Williams played 1 game with Minnesota, 4 with Chicago in '82.

†Option playout; subject to developments.

t-Bears traded for Frederick (Cleveland), Saldi (Dallas).

Traded—Cornerback Reuben Henderson to San Diego.

Retired—Doug Plank, 8-year safety, 1 game in '82.

Also played with Bears in '82—LB Bruce Huther (4 games), K John Roveto (7).

COACHING STAFF

Head Coach, Mike Ditka

Pro Career: Became tenth head coach in Bears 62-year history on January 20, 1982 after serving nine years as an offensive assistant with Dallas Cowboys. Bears finished 3-5 last year. Ditka is a 21-year veteran of the NFL as both a player and coach. Had 12-year playing career as a tight end with the Chicago Bears (1961-66), Philadelphia Eagles (1967-68), and Dallas Cowboys (1969-72). A first-round draft choice by Chicago in 1961, Ditka was NFL rookie of the year, all-NFL (1961-64), and played in five Pro Bowls (1962-66). He joined the Cowboys' coaching staff in 1973. In addition to working with the Dallas special teams, he coached the Cowboys' receivers.

Background: Played at Pittsburgh from 1958-60 and was a unanimous All-America his senior year. A two-way performer, he played both defensive end and linebacker. He also was one of the nation's leading punters with a 40-plus yard average over three years.

Personal: Born October 18, 1939, Carnegie, Pa. Mike and his wife, Diana, live in Chicago and have four chidren—Michael, Mark, Megan, and Matt.

ASSISTANT COACHES

Jim Dooley, research and quality control; born February 8, 1930, Stoutsville, Mo., lives in Chicago. End Miami 1949-51. Pro receiver Chicago Bears 1952-61. Pro coach: Chicago Bears 1962-71 (head coach 1968-71), Buffalo Bills 1972, rejoined Bears in 1981.

Dale Haupt, defensive line; born April 12, 1929, Manitowic, Wis., lives in Chicago. Guard Wyoming 1951-53. Pro guard Green Bay Packers 1954. College coach: Tennessee 1960-63, Iowa State 1964-65, Richmond 1966-71, North Carolina State 1972-76, Duke 1977. Pro coach: Joined Bears in 1978.

Ed Hughes, offensive coordinator; born October 23, 1927, Buffalo, N.Y., lives in Chicago. Halfback Tulsa 1952-53. Pro defensive back Los Angeles Rams 1954-55, New York Giants 1956-58. Pro coach: Dallas Texans 1960-62, Denver Broncos 1963, Washington Redskins 1964-67, San Francisco 49ers 1968-70, Houston Oilers 1971 (head coach), St. Louis Cardinals 1972, Dallas Cowboys 1973-76, Detroit Lions 1977, New Orleans Saints 1978-80, Philadelphia Eagles 1981, Bears since 1982.

Jim LaRue, defensive backfield; born August 11, 1925, Clinton, Okla., lives in Chicago. Halfback Carson-Newman 1943, Duke 1944-45, Maryland 1947-49. No pro playing experience. College coach: Maryland 1950, Kansas State 1951-54, Houston 1955-56, Southern Methodist 1957-58, Arizona 1959-66 (head coach), Utah 1967-73, Wake Forest 1974-75. Pro coach: Buffalo Bills 1976-77, Bears since 1978.

Ted Plumb, receivers; born August 20, 1939, Reno, Nev., lives in Chicago. End Baylor 1959-61. No pro playing experience. College coach: Cerritos, Calif., J.C. 1966-67, Texas Christian 1968-70, Tulsa 1971, Kansas 1972-73. Pro coach: New York Giants 1974-76, Atlanta Falcons 1977-79, Bears since 1980.

Johnny Roland, offensive backs; born May 21, 1943, Corpus Christi, Tex., lives in Chicago. Running back Missouri 1963-65. Pro running back St. Louis Cardinals 1966-72, New York Giants 1973. College coach: Notre Dame 1975. Pro coach: Green Bay Packers 1974, Philadelphia Eagles 1976-78, first year with Bears.

Buddy Ryan, defensive coordinator; born February 16, 1934, Frederick, Okla., lives in Chicago. Guard Oklahoma State 1952-55. No pro playing experience. College coach: Buffalo 1961-65, Vanderbilt 1966, University of Pacific 1967. Pro coach: New York Jets 1968-75, Minnesota Vikings 1976-77, Bears since 1978.

Dick Stanfel, offensive line; born July 20, 1927, San Francisco, Calif., lives in Chicago. Guard San Francisco 1948-51. Pro guard Detroit Lions 1952-55, Washington Redskins 1956-58. College coach: Notre Dame 1959-62, California 1963. Pro coach: Philadelphia Eagles 1964-70, San Francisco 49ers 1971-75, New Orleans Saints 1976-80 (head coach, 4 games in 1980), Bears since 1981.

CHICAGO BEARS 1983 FIRST-YEAR ROSTER

Name	Pos.	Ht.	Wt.	Birth-date	College	Birthplace	Residence	How Acq.
Bortz, Mark	DT	6-5	267	2/12/61	Iowa	Pardeeville, Wis.	Pardeeville, Wis.	D8a
Covert, Jimbo	T	6-4	271	3/22/60	Pittsburgh	Conway, Pa.	Conway, Pa.	D1
Delwiche, Larry (1)	P	5-11	198	2/3/60	Salem, W. Va.	Oshkosh, Wis.	Troy, Ohio	FA
Dent, Richard	DE	6-2	240	12/13/60	Tennessee State	Atlanta, Ga.	Atlanta, Ga.	D8
Drain, Sel	S	5-11	179	9/23/61	Ball State	East St. Louis, Ill.	Muncie, Ind.	FA
Duerson, Dave	CB	6-0	202	11/28/60	Notre Dame	Muncie, Ind.	Muncie, Ind.	D3
Dunsmore, Pat	TE	6-2	230	10/2/57	Drake	Duluth, Minn.	Ankeny, Iowa	D4a
Fada, Rob	G	6-2	258	5/7/51	Pittsburgh	Fairborn, Ohio	Fairborn, Ohio	D9a
Finzer, Dave (1)	P-K	6-0	195	2/3/59	DePauw	Chicago, Ill.	Wilmette, Ill.	FA
Gault, Willie	WR	6-0	178	9/5/60	Tennessee	Griffin, Ga.	Knoxville, Tenn.	D1a
Glasgow, Brian	TE	6-4	230	6/9/61	Northern Illinois	Burlington, Iowa	DeKalb, Ill.	FA
Hansen, Rick	QB	6-1	205	2/10/60	San Diego State	Seattle, Wash.	Escondido, Calif.	FA
Hutchison, Anthony	RB	5-10	180	2/4/61	Texas Tech	Houston, Tex.	San Antonio, Tex.	D10
Janata, John	T	6-7	255	4/10/61	Illinois	Chicago, Ill.	Berwyn, Ill.	FA
Johnson, Ron	WR	5-11	180	7/19/59	Winston-Salem	Charlotte, N.C.	Philadelphia, Pa.	FA
Jones, Jerry	WR	6-1	198	6/29/61	Texas-El Paso	Laurel, Miss.	Laurel, Miss.	FA
Kimble, Don	LB	6-2	227	10/31/60	Texas-El Paso	Houston, Tex.	Houston, Tex.	FA
Lundy, Nate (1)	WR	6-1	170	10/15/58	Indiana	Great Lakes, Ill.	Chicago, Ill.	FA
McCarrell, Dave	QB	6-3	205	8/31/61	Wheaton, Ill.	Chicago, Ill.	Morton Grove, Ill.	FA
McKinnon, Dennis	WR	6-2	185	8/22/61	Florida State	Quitman, Miss.	Hollywood, Fla.	FA
Plater, Dan (1)	WR	6-1	187	7/22/60	Brigham Young	Reno, Nev.	Provo, Utah	FA
Richardson, Mike	CB	5-11	197	5/23/61	Arizona State	Compton, Calif.	Tempe, Ariz.	D2
Ruzich, Dan	LB	6-2	220	8/25/61	Kansas State	Evergreen Park, Ill.	Hometown, Ill.	FA
Stump, Don (1)	P-K	6-1	213	2/11/60	McNeese State	Carbondale, Ill.	Port Arthur, Tex.	FA
Sutton, Ted	RB	5-9	210	1/21/58	East Carolina	Kingston, N.C.	Kingston, N.C.	FA
Williams, Oliver	WR	6-3	195	10/17/60	Illinois	Los Angeles, Calif.	Champaign, Ill.	D12
Worthy, Gary	RB	6-0	195	4/12/60	Wilmington, Ohio	Dayton, Ohio	Dayton, Ohio	D11

Players who report to an NFL team for the first time are designated on rosters as rookies (R). If a player reported to an NFL training camp in a previous year but was not on the active squad for three or more regular season or postseason games, he is listed on the first-year roster and designated by a (1). Thereafter, a player who is on the active squad for three or more regular season or postseason games is credited with an additional year of playing experience.

NOTES

_____
_____
_____
_____
_____
_____
_____
_____
_____
_____
_____
_____
_____
_____
_____
_____
_____

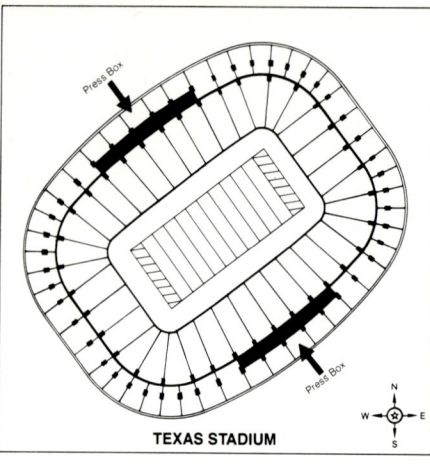

TEXAS STADIUM

Dallas Cowboys

**National Football Conference
Eastern Division**

Team Colors: Royal Blue, Metallic Silver
Blue, and White

**6116 North Central Expressway
Dallas, Texas 75206
Telephone: (214) 369-8000**

Club Officials

Chairman of the Board: Clint W. Murchison, Jr.
President-General Manager: Texas E. Schramm
Vice President-Personnel Development: Gil Brandt
Vice President-Treasurer: Don Wilson
Vice President-Administration: Joe Bailey
Public Relations Director: Doug Todd
Business Manager: Dan Werner
Assistant Public Relations Director: Greg Aiello
Ticket Manager: Kay Lang
Trainers: Don Cochren, Ken Locker
Equipment Manager: William T. (Buck) Buchanan
Cheerleaders Director: Suzanne Mitchell

Stadium: Texas Stadium • **Capacity:** 65,101
Irving, Texas 75062

Playing Surface: Texas Turf

Training Camp: California Lutheran College
Thousand Oaks, California 91360

1983 SCHEDULE

Preseason
Aug. 6	**Miami**	8:00
Aug. 15	at Los Angeles Rams	7:00
Aug. 20	**Pittsburgh**	8:00
Aug. 27	**Houston**	8:00

Regular Season
Sept. 5	at Washington (Monday)	9:00
Sept. 11	at St. Louis	12:00
Sept. 18	**New York Giants**	3:00
Sept. 25	**New Orleans**	12:00
Oct. 2	at Minnesota	12:00
Oct. 9	**Tampa Bay**	3:00
Oct. 16	at Philadelphia	4:00
Oct. 23	**Los Angeles Raiders**	8:00
Oct. 30	at New York Giants	1:00
Nov. 6	**Philadelphia**	12:00
Nov. 13	at San Diego	1:00
Nov. 20	**Kansas City**	3:00
Nov. 24	**St. Louis** (Thanksgiving)	3:00
Dec. 4	at Seattle	1:00
Dec. 11	**Washington**	3:00
Dec. 19	at San Francisco (Monday)	6:00

1982 TEAM STATISTICS

	Dallas	Opp.
Total First Downs	180	162
Rushing	70	56
Passing	99	95
Penalty	11	11
Third Down Efficiency	44/111	42/125
Third Down Percentage	39.6	33.6
Total Net Yards	3199	2753
Total Offensive Plays	579	581
Avg. Gain per Play	5.5	4.7
Avg. Gain per Game	355.4	305.9
Net Yards Rushing	1313	1011
Total Rushing Plays	296	260
Avg. Gain per Rush	4.4	3.9
Avg. Gain Rushing per Game	145.9	112.3
Net Yards Passing	1886	1742
Lost Attempting to Pass	25/264	32/260
Gross Yards Passing	2150	2002
Attempts/Completions	258/160	289/152
Percent Completed	62.0	52.6
Had Intercepted	14	15
Avg. Net Passing per Game	209.6	193.6
Punts/Avg.	37/41.7	49/42.5
Punt Returns/Avg.	30/8.1	21/5.6
Kickoff Returns/Avg.	33/19.7	41/22.8
Interceptions/Avg. Ret.	15/10.9	14/8.9
Penalties/Yards	42/304	52/431
Fumbles/Ball Lost	29/12	20/10
Total Points	226	145
Avg. Points per Game	25.1	16.1
Touchdowns	28	17
Rushing	10	5
Passing	16	10
Returns and Recoveries	2	2
Field Goals	10/14	9/15
Conversions	28/28	16/17
Safeties	0	0
Avg. Time of Possession	30:48	29:12

1982 TEAM RECORD

Preseason (3-1)

Dallas		Opponents
10	*Buffalo	14
26	San Diego	16
36	*New England	21
20	*Houston	14
92		65

Regular Season (6-3)

Dallas		Opponents	Att.
28	*Pittsburgh	36	63,431
24	St. Louis	7	50,705
14	*Tampa Bay	9	49,578
31	*Cleveland	14	46,267
24	Washington	10	54,633
37	Houston	7	51,808
21	*New Orleans	7	64,506
20	*Philadelphia	24	46,199
27	Minnesota	31	60,007
226		145	487,134

*Home Game

Score by Periods

Dallas	17	100	51	58	—	226
Opponents	23	34	27	61	—	145

Attendance

Home 269,981   Away 217,153   Total 487,134
Single game home record, 80,259 (11-24-66)
Single season home record, 511,541 (1981)

1982 INDIVIDUAL STATISTICS

Rushing

	Att	Yds	Avg	LG	TD
Dorsett	177	745	4.2	99t	5
Springs	59	243	4.1	46t	2
Newsome	15	98	6.5	25	1
D. White	17	91	5.4	21	0
Newhouse	14	79	5.6	27	1
T. Hill	1	22	22.0	22	0
Peoples	7	22	3.1	7	0
Johnson	1	9	9.0	9	0
DuPree	1	6	6.0	6t	1
Hogeboom	3	0	0.0	0	0
Cosbie	1	-2	-2.0	-2	0
Dallas	296	1313	4.4	99t	10
Opponents	260	1011	3.9	32	5

Field Goal Success

Distance	1-19	20-29	30-39	40-49	50 Over
Made-Att.	1-1	3-3	3-4	2-4	1-2

Passing

	Att	Comp	Pct	Yds	TD	Int	Tkld	Rate
D. White	247	156	63.2	2079	16	12	25/264	91.1
Hogeboom	8	3	37.5	45	0	1	0/0	—
Pearson	2	1	50.0	26	0	1	0/0	—
Dorsett	1	0	0.0	0	0	0	0/0	—
Dallas	258	160	62.0	2150	16	14	25/264	
Opponents	289	152	52.6	2002	10	15	32/260	

Receiving

	No	Yds	Avg	LG	TD
T. Hill	35	526	15.0	47	1
Cosbie	30	441	14.7	45	4
Pearson	26	382	14.7	48	3
Dorsett	24	179	7.5	18	0
Springs	17	163	9.6	34	2
Johnson	12	269	22.4	49	3
DuPree	7	41	5.9	12	2
Newsome	6	118	19.7	46t	1
Donley	2	23	11.5	12	0
Saldi	1	8	8.0	8	0
Dallas	160	2150	13.4	49	16
Opponents	152	2002	13.2	54t	10

Interceptions

	No	Yds	Avg	LG	TD
Walls	7	61	8.7	37	0
Thurman	3	75	25.0	60t	1
Downs	1	22	22.0	22	0
Dickerson	1	4	4.0	4	0
Breunig	1	1	1.0	1	0
Clinkscale	1	0	0.0	0	0
E. Jones	1	0	0.0	0	0
Dallas	15	163	10.9	60t	1
Opponents	14	125	8.9	33t	1

Punting

	No	Yds	Avg	In 20	LG
D. White	37	1542	41.7	6	56
Dallas	37	1542	41.7	6	56
Opponents	49	2083	42.5	10	60

Punt Returns

	No	FC	Yds	Avg	LG	TD
Fellows	25	0	189	7.6	17	0
R. Hill	4	0	39	9.8	26	0
Donley	1	0	14	14.0	14	0
Dallas	30	0	242	8.1	26	0
Opponents	21	3	118	5.6	14	0

Kickoff Returns

	No	Yds	Avg	LG	TD
Fellows	16	359	22.4	35	0
Donley	8	151	18.9	33	0
Newsome	5	74	14.8	26	0
J. Jones	2	46	23.0	27	0
Thurman	1	17	17.0	17	0
Cosbie	1	4	4.0	4	0
Dallas	33	651	19.7	35	0
Opponents	41	936	22.8	40	0

Scoring

	TD	TD R	TD P	TD Rt	PAT	FG	TP
Septien					28/28	10/14	58
Dorsett	5	5	0	0			30
Cosbie	4	0	4	0			24
Springs	4	2	2	0			24
DuPree	3	1	2	0			18
Johnson	3	0	3	0			18
Pearson	3	0	3	0			18
Newsome	2	1	1	0			12
Downs	1	0	0	1			6
T. Hill	1	0	1	0			6
Newhouse	1	1	0	0			6
Thurman	1	0	0	1			6
Dallas	28	10	16	2	28/28	10/14	226
Opponents	17	5	10	2	16/17	9/15	145

Sacks

Barnes 1, Bethea 2, Breunig 1½, Clinkscale 2, Dickerson 2½, Downs 1, Dutton 2, Hegman 1½, Hunter 1, E. Jones 6, Martin 8, Smerek 1, R. White 2½.

FIRST PLAYERS SELECTED

Year	Player, College, Position
1960	None
1961	Bob Lilly, Texas Christian, DT
1962	Sonny Gibbs, Texas Christian, QB (2)
1963	Lee Roy Jordan, Alabama, LB
1964	Scott Appleton, Texas, DT
1965	Craig Morton, California, QB
1966	John Niland, Iowa, G
1967	Phil Clark, Northwestern, DB (3)
1968	Dennis Homan, Alabama, WR
1969	Calvin Hill, Yale, RB
1970	Duane Thomas, West Texas State, RB
1971	Tody Smith, Southern California, DE
1972	Bill Thomas, Boston College, RB
1973	Billy Joe DuPree, Michigan State, TE
1974	Ed (Too Tall) Jones, Tennessee State, DE
1975	Randy White, Maryland, LB
1976	Aaron Kyle, Wyoming, DB
1977	Tony Dorsett, Pittsburgh, RB
1978	Larry Bethea, Michigan State, DE
1979	Robert Shaw, Tennessee, C
1980	Bill Roe, Colorado, LB (3)
1981	Howard Richards, Missouri, T
1982	Rod Hill, Kentucky State, DB
1983	Jim Jeffcoat, Arizona State, DE

COWBOYS COACHING HISTORY
(222-129-6)

1960-82	Tom Landry	222-129-6

DALLAS COWBOYS 1983 VETERAN ROSTER

No.	Name	Pos.	Ht.	Wt.	Birth-date	NFL Exp.	College	Birthplace	Residence	Games in '82
62	Baldinger, Brian	C-G	6-4	253	1/7/59	2	Duke	Massapequa, N.Y.	Massapequa, N.Y.	4
31	Barnes, Benny	S	6-1	204	3/3/51	12	Stanford	Lufkin, Tex.	Dallas, Tex.	9
76	Bethea, Larry	DT	6-5	244	7/21/56	6	Michigan State	Florence, S.C.	Richardson, Tex.	8
53	Breunig, Bob	LB	6-2	225	7/4/53	9	Arizona State	Inglewood, Calif.	Dallas, Tex.	9
59	Brown, Guy	LB	6-4	227	6/1/55	7	Houston	Palestine, Tex.	Richardson, Tex.	9
18	Carano, Glenn	QB	6-3	204	11/18/55	7	Nevada-Las Vegas	San Pedro, Calif.	Dallas, Tex.	7
47	Clinkscale, Dextor	S	5-11	190	4/13/58	3	South Carolina State	Greenville, S.C.	Dallas, Tex.	9
61	Cooper, Jim	T	6-5	263	9/28/55	7	Temple	Philadelphia, Pa.	Richardson, Tex.	9
84	Cosbie, Doug	TE	6-6	232	2/27/56	5	Santa Clara	Mountain View, Calif.	Plano, Tex.	9
51	Dickerson, Anthony	LB	6-2	222	6/9/57	4	Southern Methodist	Texas City, Tex.	Garland, Tex.	9
83	Donley, Doug	WR	6-0	173	2/6/59	3	Ohio State	Cambridge, Ohio	Garland, Tex.	6
67	Donovan, Pat	T	6-5	257	7/1/53	9	Stanford	Helena, Mont.	Dallas, Tex.	9
33	Dorsett, Tony	RB	5-11	192	4/7/54	7	Pittsburgh	Aliquippa, Pa.	Dallas, Tex.	9
26	Downs, Michael	S	6-3	203	6/9/59	3	Rice	Dallas, Tex.	Dallas, Tex.	9
89	DuPree, Billy Joe	TE	6-4	223	3/7/50	11	Michigan State	West Monroe, La.	Dallas, Tex.	9
78	Dutton, John	DT	6-7	275	2/6/51	10	Nebraska	Evansville, Ind.	Dallas, Tex.	9
27	Fellows, Ron	CB	6-0	174	11/7/58	3	Missouri	South Bend, Ind.	Dallas, Tex.	9
58	Hegman, Mike	LB	6-1	228	1/17/53	8	Tennessee State	Memphis, Tenn.	Dallas, Tex.	9
25	Hill, Rod	CB	6-0	182	3/14/59	2	Kentucky State	Detroit, Mich.	Dallas, Tex.	9
80	Hill, Tony	WR	6-2	198	6/23/56	7	Stanford	San Diego, Calif.	Dallas, Tex.	9
14	Hogeboom, Gary	QB	6-4	199	8/21/58	4	Central Michigan	Grand Rapids, Mich.	Dallas, Tex.	4
34	Hunter, Monty	S	6-0	202	1/21/59	2	Salem, W. Va.	Dover, Ohio	Dallas, Tex.	9
86	Johnson, Butch	WR	6-1	187	5/28/54	8	Cal-Riverside	Los Angeles, Calif.	Carrollton, Tex.	9
72	Jones, Ed	DE	6-9	272	2/23/51	9	Tennessee State	Jackson, Tenn.	Dallas, Tex.	9
23	Jones, James	RB	5-10	202	12/6/58	4	Mississippi State	Vicksburg, Miss.	Dallas, Tex.	5
57	King, Angelo	LB	6-1	230	2/10/58	3	South Carolina State	Columbia, S.C.	Dallas, Tex.	9
79	Martin, Harvey	DE	6-5	260	11/16/50	11	East Texas State	Dallas, Tex.	Carrollton, Tex.	9
44	†Newhouse, Robert	RB	5-10	219	1/9/50	12	Houston	Longview, Tex.	Dallas, Tex.	9
30	Newsome, Timmy	RB	6-1	231	5/17/58	4	Winston-Salem State	Ahoskie, N.C.	Dallas, Tex.	9
88	Pearson, Drew	WR	6-0	193	1/12/51	11	Tulsa	South River, N.J.	Dallas, Tex.	9
22	Peoples, George	RB	6-0	211	8/25/60	2	Auburn	Tampa, Fla.	Seffner, Fla.	8
65	Petersen, Kurt	G	6-4	268	6/17/57	4	Missouri	St. Louis, Mo.	Carrollton, Tex.	9
75	Pozderac, Phil	T	6-9	270	12/19/59	2	Notre Dame	Cleveland, Ohio	Dallas, Tex.	7
64	Rafferty, Tom	C-G	6-3	259	8/2/54	8	Penn State	Syracuse, N.Y.	Dallas, Tex.	9
70	Richards, Howard	G-T	6-6	258	8/7/59	3	Missouri	St. Louis, Mo.	Richardson, Tex.	8
50	Rohrer, Jeff	LB	6-3	232	12/25/58	2	Yale	Manhattan Beach, Calif.	Dallas, Tex.	8
68	Scott, Herbert	G	6-2	260	1/18/53	9	Virginia Union	Virginia Beach, Va.	Lucas, Tex.	6
1	Septien, Rafael	K	5-10	180	12/12/53	7	Southwest Louisiana	Mexico City, Mex.	Dallas, Tex.	9
60	Smerek, Don	DT	6-7	257	12/20/57	3	Nevada-Reno	Waterford, Mich.	Dallas, Tex.	7
55	Spradlin, Danny	LB	6-1	241	3/3/59	3	Tennessee	Maryville, Tenn.	Maryville, Tenn.	9
20	Springs, Ron	RB	6-1	210	11/1/56	5	Ohio State	Williamsburg, Va.	Dallas, Tex.	9
32	Thurman, Dennis	CB	5-11	183	4/13/56	6	Southern California	Los Angeles, Calif.	Farmers Branch, Tex.	9
63	Titensor, Glen	C-G	6-4	260	2/21/58	3	Brigham Young	Westminster, Calif.	Dallas, Tex.	4
24	Walls, Everson	CB	6-1	194	12/28/59	3	Grambling	Dallas, Tex.	Dallas, Tex.	9
66	Wells, Norm	T	6-5	261	9/8/57	2	Northwestern	Detroit, Mich.	Richardson, Tex.	0*
11	White, Danny	QB-P	6-2	196	2/9/52	8	Arizona State	Mesa, Ariz.	Wylie, Tex.	9
54	White, Randy	DT	6-4	268	1/15/53	9	Maryland	Wilmington, Del.	Dallas, Tex.	9
15	Wright, Brad	QB	6-2	209	5/15/59	2	New Mexico	Midland, Tex.	Dallas, Tex.	0*
73	Wright, Steve	G-T	6-5	263	4/8/59	3	Northern Iowa	Wayzata, Minn.	Richardson, Tex.	9

* Wells missed '82 season due to injuries; B. Wright active for 9 games, but did not play.

†Option playout; subject to developments.

Traded—Tight end Jay Saldi to Chicago.

Retired—Robert Shaw, 3-year center, on injured reserve in '82.

COACHING STAFF

Head Coach, Tom Landry

Pro Career: Last year's 6-3 regular season record boosted the Cowboys into the playoffs for the sixteenth time in the past 17 years and gave Landry 17 winning seasons in succession. Cowboys became the fourth team in NFL to win a second Super Bowl. They defeated Denver 27-10 in Super Bowl XII on January 15, 1978 at Louisiana Superdome. Dallas has played in four other Super Bowls (V, VI, X, and XIII), winning Game VI 24-3 over Miami. Cowboys' only head coach in their 23-year history, Landry has compiled a 222-129-6 record. Pro defensive back with New York Yanks (AAFC) 1949, New York Giants 1950-55. Player-coach with Giants 1954-55, named all-pro in 1954. Defensive assistant coach with Giants 1956-59 before moving to Dallas as head coach in 1960.

Background: Halfback, University of Texas 1947-48, and played in Longhorns' victories over Alabama in 1948 Sugar Bowl and Georgia in 1949 Orange Bowl.

Personal: Born September 11, 1924 in Mission, Tex. A World War II bomber pilot. Tom and his wife, Alicia, live in Dallas and have three children—Tom Jr., Kitty, and Lisa.

ASSISTANT COACHES

Ermal Allen, special assistant-research and development; born December 25, 1920, Sneedsville, Tenn., lives in Dallas. Quarterback Kentucky 1939-41. Pro back Cleveland Browns (AAFC) 1947. College coach: Kentucky 1948-61. Pro coach: Joined Cowboys in 1962.

Neill Armstrong, research and development; born March 9, 1926, Tishomingo, Okla., lives in Dallas. End Oklahoma State 1943-46. Pro end-defensive back Philadelphia Eagles 1947-51, Winnipeg Blue Bombers (CFL) 1951, 1953-54. College coach: Oklahoma State 1955-61. Pro coach: Houston Oilers 1962-63, Edmonton Eskimos (CFL) 1964-69 (head coach), Minnesota Vikings 1970-77, Chicago Bears 1978-81 (head coach), Cowboys since 1982.

Al Lavan, running backs; born September 13, 1946, Pierce, Fla., lives in Dallas. Defensive back Colorado State 1965-67. Pro defensive back Philadelphia Eagles 1968, Atlanta Falcons 1969-70. College coach: Colorado State 1972, Louisville 1973, Iowa State 1974, Georgia Tech 1977-78, Stanford 1979. Pro coach: Atlanta Falcons 1975-76, Cowboys since 1980.

Alan Lowry, special teams; born November 21, 1950, Irving, Tex., lives in Dallas. Defensive back-quarterback Texas 1970-72. No pro playing experience. College coach: Virginia Tech 1974, Wyoming 1975, Texas 1976-81. Pro coach: Joined Cowboys in 1982.

Jim Myers, assistant head coach-offensive line; born November 12, 1921, Madison, W. Va., lives in Dallas. Guard Tennessee 1941-42, 1946, Duke 1943. No pro playing experience. College coach: Wofford 1947, Vanderbilt 1948, UCLA 1949-56, Iowa State 1957 (head coach), Texas A&M 1958-61 (head coach). Pro coach: Joined Cowboys in 1962.

Dick Nolan, receivers; born March 26, 1932, Pittsburgh, Pa., lives in Dallas. Offensive-defensive back Maryland 1951-53. Pro defensive back New York Giants 1954-57, 1959-61, St. Louis Cardinals 1958, Dallas player-coach 1962. Pro coach: Dallas Cowboys 1963-67, San Francisco 49ers 1968-75 (head coach), New Orleans Saints 1977-80 (head coach), Houston Oilers 1981, rejoined Cowboys in 1982.

Jim Shofner, quarterbacks; born December 18, 1935, Grapevine, Tex., lives in Dallas. Running back Texas Christian 1955-57. Pro defensive back Cleveland Browns 1958-63. College coach: Texas Christian 1964-66, 1974-76 (head coach). Pro coach: San Francisco 49ers 1967-73, 1977, Cleveland Browns 1978-80, Houston Oilers 1981-82, first year with Cowboys.

Gene Stallings, defensive backs; born March 2, 1935, Paris, Tex., lives in Dallas. End Texas A&M 1954-57. No pro playing experience. College coach: Texas A&M 1957, 1965-71 (head coach), Alabama 1958-64. Pro coach: Joined Cowboys in 1972.

Ernie Stautner, defensive coordinator-defensive line; born April 2, 1925, Kham, Bavaria, lives in Dallas. Tackle Boston College 1946-49. Pro defensive tackle Pittsburgh Steelers 1950-63. Pro coach: Pittsburgh Steelers 1963-64, Washington Redskins 1965, Cowboys since 1966.

Jerry Tubbs, linebackers; born January 23, 1935, Breckenridge, Tex., lives in Dallas. Center-linebacker Oklahoma 1954-56. Pro linebacker Chicago Cardinals 1957, San Francisco 49ers 1958-59, Dallas Cowboys 1960-67. Pro coach: Joined Cowboys in 1965.

Bob Ward, conditioning; born July 4, 1933, Huntington Park, Calif., lives in Dallas. Fullback-quarterback Whitworth College 1952-54. Doctorate in physical education, Indiana University. No pro playing experience. College coach: Fullerton, Calif., J.C. (track) 1965-75. Pro coach: Joined Cowboys in 1975.

DALLAS COWBOYS 1983 FIRST-YEAR ROSTER

Name	Pos.	Ht.	Wt.	Birth-date	College	Birthplace	Residence	How Acq.
Botha, Naas	P	5-10	160	2/27/58	Pretoria	Breyton, Transvaal, S.A.	Pretoria, S.A.	FA
Bouier, Lorenzo	RB	6-0	209	2/27/61	Maine	Hartford, Conn.	Hartford, Conn.	D12
Caldwell, Bryan	DE	6-4	248	5/6/60	Arizona State	Oakland, Calif.	Mesa, Ariz.	D3
Eliopulos, Jim (1)	LB	6-3	231	4/18/59	Wyoming	Dearborn, Mich.	Cheyenne, Wyo.	D3 ('82)
Faulkner, Chris	TE	6-4	257	4/13/60	Florida	Tipton, Ind.	Arcadia, Ind.	D4
Gross, Al	CB-S	6-3	190	1/4/61	Arizona	Stockton, Calif.	Stockton, Calif.	D9
Hammond, Ken (1)	G	6-4	270	12/7/59	Vanderbilt	Fort Payne, Ala.	Fort Payne, Ala.	FA
Jeffcoat, Jim	DE	6-5	260	4/1/61	Arizona State	Long Branch, N.J.	Matawan, N.J.	D1
McLean, Scott (1)	LB	6-4	231	12/16/60	Florida State	Clermont, Fla.	Clermont, Fla.	FA
McSwain, Chuck	RB	6-0	190	2/21/61	Clemson	Rutherford, N.C.	Forest City, N.C.	D5
Ricks, Lawrence	RB	5-9	194	6/4/61	Michigan	Barberton, Ohio	Barberton, Ohio	D8
Robinson, Kevin (1)	CB-S	5-11	194	2/19/60	South Carolina State	Union, S.C.	Union, S.C.	FA
Schultz, Chris	T	6-8	259	2/16/60	Arizona	Burlington, Ontario	Burlington, Ontario	D7
Taylor, Dan	T	6-3	258	5/13/59	Idaho State	Olympia, Wash.	Olympia, Wash.	D11
Walter, Mike	LB	6-3	230	11/30/60	Oregon	Salem, Ore.	Eugene, Ore.	D2

Players who report to an NFL team for the first time are designated on rosters as rookies (R). If a player reported to an NFL training camp in a previous year but was not on the active squad for three or more regular season or postseason games, he is listed on the first-year roster and designated by a (1). Thereafter, a player who is on the active squad for three or more regular season or postseason games is credited with an additional year of playing experience.

NOTES

_____

_____

_____

_____

_____

_____

_____

_____

_____

_____

_____

_____

_____

_____

_____

_____

_____

_____

_____

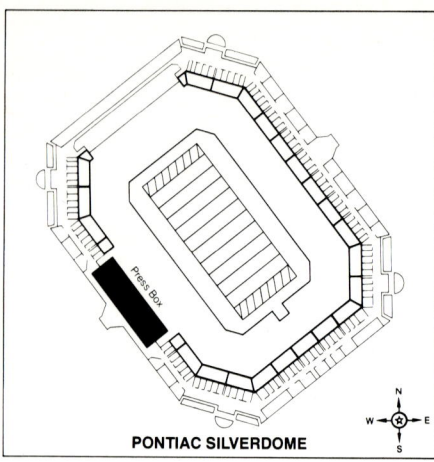

PONTIAC SILVERDOME

Detroit Lions

**National Football Conference
Central Division**

Team Colors: Honolulu Blue and Silver

**Pontiac Silverdome
1200 Featherstone Road — Box 4200
Pontiac, Michigan 48057
Telephone: (313) 335-4131**

Club Officials
President-Owner: William Clay Ford
Executive Vice President-General Manager:
  Russell Thomas
Director of Football Operations-Head Coach:
  Monte Clark
Director of Player Personnel: Tim Rooney
Controller: Charles Schmidt
College Scouts: Jerry Neri (Western Area),
  Joe Bushofsky (Eastern Area), Dick Dierking
  (Central Area)
Director of Public Relations: Don Kremer
Publicity Assistant: Brian Muir
Ticket Manager: Fred Otto
Trainer: Kent Falb
Strength and Conditioning: Gary Wade
Equipment Manager: Dan Jaroshewich
Stadium: Pontiac Silverdome • **Capacity:** 80,638
  1200 Featherstone Road
  Pontiac, Michigan 48057
Playing Surface: AstroTurf
Training Camp: Oakland University
  Rochester, Michigan 48063

1983 SCHEDULE
Preseason
Aug. 5	at Philadelphia	7:30
Aug. 13	at Kansas City	7:30
Aug. 20	**Buffalo**	7:00
Aug. 27	**Cincinnati**	7:00

Regular Season
Sept. 4	at Tampa Bay	1:00
Sept. 11	**Cleveland**	1:00
Sept. 18	**Atlanta**	1:00
Sept. 25	at Minnesota	12:00
Oct. 2	at Los Angeles Rams	1:00
Oct. 9	**Green Bay**	1:00
Oct. 16	**Chicago**	1:00
Oct. 23	at Washington	1:00
Oct. 30	at Chicago	12:00
Nov. 7	**New York Giants** (Monday)	9:00
Nov. 13	at Houston	12:00
Nov. 20	vs. Green Bay at Milwaukee	12:00
Nov. 24	**Pittsburgh** (Thanksgiving)	12:30
Dec. 5	**Minnesota** (Monday)	9:00
Dec. 11	at Cincinnati	1:00
Dec. 18	**Tampa Bay**	4:00

1982 TEAM STATISTICS

	Detroit	Opp.
Total First Downs.	160	162
Rushing.	60	54
Passing.	83	96
Penalty	17	12
Third Down Efficiency.	42/126	50/129
Third Down Percentage	33.3	38.8
Total Net Yards.	2534	2722
Total Offensive Plays	598	591
Avg. Gain per Play.	4.2	4.6
Avg. Gain per Game.	281.6	302.4
Net Yards Rushing.	1022	854
Total Rushing Plays	283	271
Avg. Gain per Rush.	3.6	3.2
Avg. Gain Rushing per Game	113.6	94.9
Net Yards Passing.	1512	1868
Lost Attempting to Pass	30/242	32/230
Gross Yards Passing	1754	2098
Attempts/Completions.	285/136	288/155
Percent Completed	47.7	53.8
Had Intercepted	18	18
Avg. Net Passing per Game	168.0	207.6
Punts/Avg.	48/40.9	46/39.8
Punt Returns/Avg.	26/10.6	26/9.1
Kickoff Returns/Avg.	36/20.8	38/19.9
Interceptions/Avg. Ret.	18/8.6	18/13.8
Penalties/Yards	58/548	74/605
Fumbles/Ball Lost	23/8	21/8
Total Points	181	176
Avg. Points per Game	20.1	19.6
Touchdowns.	19	20
Rushing.	5	6
Passing	12	11
Returns and Recoveries	2	3
Field Goals	16/17	12/21
Conversions	19/19	20/20
Safeties	0	0
Avg. Time of Possession	30:12	29:48

1982 TEAM RECORD

Preseason (2-2)

Detroit		Opponents
16	*Cleveland	17
30	*Los Angeles Raiders	16
27	Cincinnati	23
10	Buffalo	13
83		69

Regular Season (4-5)

Detroit		Opponents	Att.
17	*Chicago	10	71,337
19	Los Angeles Rams	14	59,470
17	Chicago	20	46,783
6	*New York Giants	13	64,348
13	*New York Jets	28	79,361
30	Green Bay	10	51,875
31	*Minnesota	34	73,058
21	Tampa Bay	23	65,997
27	*Green Bay	24	64,377
181		176	576,606

*Home Game

Score by Periods

Detroit	72	31	37	41	—	181
Opponents	24	58	33	61	—	176

Attendance

Home 352,481   Away 224,125   Total 576,606
Single game home record, 80,444 (12-20-81)
Single season home record, 621,353 (1980)

1982 INDIVIDUAL STATISTICS

Rushing

	Att	Yds	Avg	LG	TD
Sims	172	639	3.7	29	4
Bussey	48	136	2.8	10	0
Danielson	23	92	4.0	16	0
King	18	67	3.7	25	0
Hipple	10	57	5.7	20	0
Kane	7	17	2.4	6	0
L. Thompson	2	16	8.0	13	0
Nichols	1	3	3.0	3	0
Rubick	1	1	1.0	1t	1
Scott	1	−6	−6.0	−6	0
Detroit	283	1022	3.6	29	5
Opponents	271	854	3.2	18	6

Field Goal Success

Distance	1-19	20-29	30-39	40-49	50 Over
Made-Att.	0-0	6-6	5-5	5-6	0-0

Passing

	Att	Comp	Pct	Yds	TD	Int	Tkld	Rate
Danielson	197	100	50.8	1343	10	14	19/145	60.3
Hipple	86	36	41.9	411	2	4	11/97	45.0
T. Porter	1	0	0.0	0	0	0	0/0	—
Skladany	1	0	0.0	0	0	0	0/0	—
Detroit	285	136	47.7	1754	12	18	30/242	
Opponents	288	155	53.8	2098	11	18	32/230	

Receiving

	No	Yds	Avg	LG	TD
Sims	34	342	10.1	52	0
Hill	22	252	11.5	27	4
L. Thompson	17	328	19.3	70t	4
Bussey	16	138	8.6	21	0
Scott	13	231	17.8	36	1
T. Porter	9	124	13.8	23	0
King	9	74	8.2	14	1
Nichols	8	146	18.3	48t	2
Norris	3	51	17.0	30	0
Kane	3	25	8.3	12	0
Cobb	1	25	25.0	25	0
Martin	1	18	18.0	18	0
Detroit	136	1754	12.9	70t	12
Opponents	155	2098	13.5	85t	11

Interceptions

	No	Yds	Avg	LG	TD
Watkins	5	22	4.4	20	0
White	3	21	7.0	18	0
Hunter	2	36	18.0	36	0
Cobb	2	12	6.0	12	0
Oldham	1	35	35.0	35t	1
Smith	1	10	10.0	10	0
Gay	1	7	7.0	7	0
Gray	1	5	5.0	5	0
Williams	1	4	4.0	4	0
Hall	1	2	2.0	2	0
Detroit	18	154	8.6	36	1
Opponents	18	248	13.8	97t	1

Punting

	No	Yds	Avg	In 20	LG
Skladany	36	1483	41.2	6	59
James	12	481	40.1	3	50
Detroit	48	1964	40.9	9	59
Opponents	46	1830	39.8	9	53

Punt Returns

	No	FC	Yds	Avg	LG	TD
Martin	26	5	275	10.6	58	0
Detroit	26	5	275	10.6	58	0
Opponents	26	4	237	9.1	35	0

Kickoff Returns

	No	Yds	Avg	LG	TD
Hall	16	426	26.6	96t	1
Martin	16	268	16.8	27	0
King	2	23	11.5	12	0
Kane	1	19	19.0	19	0
L. Lee	1	14	14.0	14	0
Detroit	36	750	20.8	96t	1
Opponents	38	755	19.9	76	0

Scoring

	TD	TD R	TD P	TD Rt	PAT	FG	TP
Murray					16/16	11/12	49
Hill	4	0	4	0			24
Sims	4	4	0	0			24
L. Thompson	4	0	4	0			24
Thomas					3/3	5/5	18
Nichols	2	0	2	0			12
Hall	1	0	0	1			6
King	1	0	1	0			6
Oldham	1	0	0	1			6
Rubick	1	1	0	0			6
Scott	1	0	1	0			6
Detroit	19	5	12	2	19/19	16/17	181
Opponents	20	6	11	3	20/20	12/21	176

Sacks

Baker 8½, Ehrmann 3, English 4½, Gay 5, Green 1, Hunter 1, Oldham 1, Pureifory 7, Smith 1.

FIRST PLAYERS SELECTED
(Since 1941)

Year	Player, College, Position
1941	Jim Thomason, Texas A&M, B
1942	Bob Westfall, Michigan, B
1943	Frank Sinkwich, Georgia, B
1944	Otto Graham, Northwestern, B
1945	Frank Szymanski, Notre Dame, C
1946	Bill Dellastatious, Missouri, B
1947	Glenn Davis, Army, B
1948	Y. A. Tittle, Louisiana State, B
1949	John Rauch, Georgia, B
1950	Leon Hart, Notre Dame, E
1951	Dick Stanfel, San Francisco, G (2)
1952	Yale Lary, Texas A&M, B (3)
1953	Harley Sewell, Texas, G
1954	Dick Chapman, Rice, T
1955	Dave Middleton, Auburn, B
1956	Hopalong Cassady, Ohio State, B
1957	Bill Glass, Baylor, G
1958	Alex Karras, Iowa, T
1959	Nick Pietrosante, Notre Dame, B
1960	John Robinson, Louisiana State, S
1961	Danny LaRose, Missouri, T (2)
1962	John Hadl, Kansas, QB
1963	Daryl Sanders, Ohio State, T
1964	Pete Beathard, Southern California, QB
1965	Tom Nowatzke, Indiana, RB
1966	Nick Eddy, Notre Dame, RB (2)
1967	Mel Farr, UCLA, RB
1968	Greg Landry, Massachusetts, QB
1969	Altie Taylor, Utah State, RB (2)
1970	Steve Owens, Oklahoma, RB
1971	Bob Bell, Cincinnati, DT
1972	Herb Orvis, Colorado, DE
1973	Ernie Price, Texas A&I, DE
1974	Ed O'Neil, Penn State, LB
1975	Lynn Boden, South Dakota State, G
1976	James Hunter, Grambling, DB
1977	Walt Williams, New Mexico State, DB
1978	Luther Bradley, Notre Dame, DB
1979	Keith Dorney, Penn State, T
1980	Billy Sims, Oklahoma, RB
1981	Mark Nichols, San Jose State, WR
1982	Jimmy Williams, Nebraska, LB
1983	James Jones, Florida, RB

LIONS COACHING HISTORY

Portsmouth Spartans 1930-33
(334-317-31)

1930-36	George (Potsy) Clark	53-26-9
1937-38	Earl (Dutch) Clark	14-8-0
1939	Gus Henderson	6-5-0
1940	George (Potsy) Clark	5-5-1
1941-42	Bill Edwards*	4-9-1
1942	John Karcis	0-8-0
1943-47	Charles (Gus) Dorais	20-31-2
1948-50	Alvin (Bo) McMillin	12-24-0
1951-56	Raymond (Buddy) Parker	50-24-2
1957-64	George Wilson	55-45-6
1965-66	Harry Gilmer	10-16-2
1967-72	Joe Schmidt	43-35-7
1973	Don McCafferty	6-7-1
1974-76	Rick Forzano**	15-17-0
1976-77	Tommy Hudspeth	11-13-0
1978-82	Monte Clark	30-44-0

*Resigned after three games in 1942
**Resigned after four games in 1976

DETROIT LIONS 1983 VETERAN ROSTER

No.	Name	Pos.	Ht.	Wt.	Birth-date	NFL Exp.	College	Birthplace	Residence	Games in '82
60	Baker, Al	DE	6-6	260	12/9/56	6	Colorado State	Jacksonville, Fla.	Southfield, Mich.	9
76	Baldischwiler, Karl	T	6-5	260	1/19/56	6	Oklahoma	Okmulgee, Okla.	Oklahoma City, Okla.	9
54	Barnes, Roosevelt	LB	6-2	220	8/3/58	2	Purdue	Ft. Wayne, Ind.	Ft. Wayne, Ind.	9
24	Bussey, Dexter	RB	6-1	210	3/11/52	10	Texas-Arlington	Dallas, Tex.	Birmingham, Mich.	9
31	†Callicutt, Ken	RB	6-0	190	8/20/55	6	Clemson	Chester, S.C.	Milford, Mich.	8
53	Cobb, Garry	LB	6-2	227	3/16/57	5	Southern California	Stamford, Conn.	Rochester, Mich.	6
16	Danielson, Gary	QB	6-2	196	9/10/51	7	Purdue	Detroit, Mich.	Troy, Mich.	8
72	Dieterich, Chris	T	6-3	255	7/27/58	4	North Carolina State	Freeport, N.Y.	Raleigh, N.C.	5
58	Doig, Steve	LB	6-2	240	3/28/60	2	New Hampshire	Melrosa, Mass.	North Reading, Mass.	9
70	Dorney, Keith	T	6-5	260	12/3/57	5	Penn State	Macungie, Pa.	San Juan Capistrano, Calif.	9
61	Elias, Homer	G	6-2	255	5/1/55	6	Tennessee State	Ft. Benning, Ga.	Rochester, Mich.	9
78	English, Doug	DT	6-5	258	8/25/53	7	Texas	Dallas, Tex.	Austin, Tex.	9
	t-Fanning, Mike	DT	6-6	255	2/2/53	9	Notre Dame	Mt. Clemens, Mich.	Inola, Okla.	8
57	Fantetti, Ken	LB	6-2	227	4/7/57	5	Wyoming	Toledo, Ore.	Rochester, Mich.	9
65	Fowler, Amos	C	6-3	253	2/11/56	6	Southern Mississippi	Pensacola, Fla.	Rochester, Mich.	9
79	Gay, William	DE-DT	6-5	255	5/28/55	6	Southern California	San Francisco, Calif.	Rochester, Mich.	9
66	Ginn, Tommie	G	6-3	255	1/25/58	3	Arkansas	Scotia, Calif.	Jacksonville, Tex.	0*
33	Graham, William	CB-S	191	9/27/59		2	Texas	Greenwood, Miss.	Austin, Tex.	7
26	Gray, Hector	CB-S	6-1	190	1/2/57	3	Florida State	Miami, Fla.	Miami, Fla.	8
67	Greco, Don	G	6-3	255	4/1/59	2	Western Illinois	St. Louis, Mo.	St. Louis, Mo.	9
62	Green, Curtis	DE-DT	6-3	252	6/3/57	3	Alabama State	Quincy, Fla.	Quincy, Fla.	7
35	Hall, Alvin	CB-S	5-10	184	8/12/58	3	Miami, Ohio	Dayton, Ohio	Rochester, Mich.	9
51	†Harrell, James	LB	6-1	220	7/19/57	5	Florida	Tampa, Fla.	Tampa, Fla.	9
81	Hill, David	TE	6-2	228	1/1/54	8	Texas A&I	San Antonio, Tex.	Bloomfield Hills, Mich.	9
17	Hipple, Eric	QB	6-2	196	9/16/57	4	Utah State	Lubbock, Tex.	Bloomfield Hills, Mich.	9
28	Hunter, James	CB-S	6-2	195	3/8/54	8	Grambling	Silsbee, Tex.	Southfield, Mich.	7
32	†Kane, Rick	RB	6-0	200	11/12/54	7	San Jose State	Concord, Calif.	Pontiac, Mich.	6
25	†King, Horace	RB	5-11	205	3/5/53	9	Georgia	Athens, Ga.	Rochester, Mich.	9
43	Latimer, Al	CB-S	5-11	177	10/14/57	4	Clemson	Winter Park, Fla.	Lathrup Village, Mich.	4
64	Lee, Larry	G-C	6-2	260	9/10/59	3	UCLA	Dayton, Ohio	Rochester, Mich.	9
14	Machurek, Mike	QB	6-1	205	7/22/60	2	Idaho State	Las Vegas, Nev.	Pocatello, Idaho	0*
83	Martin, Robbie	WR-KR	5-8	177	12/3/58	3	Cal Poly-SLO	Los Angeles, Calif.	Orange, Calif.	9
29	McNorton, Bruce	CB-S	5-11	175	2/28/59	2	Georgetown, Ky.	Daytona Beach, Fla.	Daytona Beach, Fla.	4
63	Moss, Martin	DT	6-4	252	12/16/58	2	UCLA	San Diego, Calif.	Van Nuys, Calif.	5
3	†Murray, Ed	K	5-10	170	8/29/56	4	Tulane	Halifax, Nova Scotia	Drayton Plains, Mich.	7
86	Nichols, Mark	WR	6-2	213	10/29/59	3	San Jose State	Bakersfield, Calif.	Bakersfield, Calif.	7
80	Norris, Ulysses	TE	6-4	232	1/15/57	5	Georgia	Monticello, Ga.	Rochester, Mich.	9
23	†Oldham, Ray	S	5-11	192	2/23/51	11	Middle Tennessee	Chattanooga, Tenn.	Signal Mountain, Tenn.	5
89	Porter, Tracy	WR	6-1	196	6/1/59	3	Louisiana State	Baton Rouge, La.	Baton Rouge, La.	8
75	Pureifory, Dave	DE	6-1	255	7/12/49	12	Eastern Michigan	Pensacola, Fla.	Ypsilanti, Mich.	9
84	Rubick, Rob	TE	6-2	228	9/27/60	2	Grand Valley State	Newberry, Mich.	Walker, Mich.	7
87	Scott, Fred	WR	6-2	190	8/5/52	10	Amherst	Grady, Ark.	Southfield, Mich.	9
20	Sims, Billy	RB	6-0	212	9/18/55	4	Oklahoma	St. Louis, Mo.	Hooks, Tex.	9
1	†Skladany, Tom	P	5-11	195	6/29/55	5	Ohio State	Castle Shannon, Pa.	Birmingham, Mich.	7
50	†Tautolo, Terry	LB	6-2	227	8/30/54	7	UCLA	Corona, Calif.	Long Beach, Calif.	2
39	Thompson, Leonard	WR	5-11	192	7/28/52	9	Oklahoma State	Tucson, Ariz.	Pontiac, Mich.	9
38	Thompson, Vince	RB	6-0	230	2/21/57	2	Villanova	Trenton, N.J.	Levittown, Pa.	0*
55	Turnure, Tom	C	6-4	250	7/9/57	4	Washington	Seattle, Wash.	Seattle, Wash.	9
27	Watkins, Bobby	CB-S	5-10	184	5/31/60	2	Southwest Texas State	Cottonwood, Idaho	Dallas, Tex.	9
59	Williams, Jimmy	LB	6-3	221	11/15/60	2	Nebraska	Washington, D.C.	Rochester, Mich.	6

* Ginn and V. Thompson missed '82 season due to injuries; Machurek active for 5 games with Detroit in '82, but did not play.

†Option playout; subject to developments.

t-Lions traded for Fanning (Los Angeles Rams).

Traded—Guard Russ Bolinger to Los Angeles Rams.

Also played with Lions in '82 — S Bill Cesare (2 games), DT Joe Ehrmann (9), P John James (2), RB Ricky Porter (1), DB Wayne Smith (5), K Bob Thomas (2), LB Stan White (9).

COACHING STAFF

Head Coach, Monte Clark

Pro Career: Starts his sixth season as Lions head coach. Directed Lions to 4-5 mark in 1982. Was head coach of San Francisco 49ers in 1976, guiding them to 8-6 record. Was an assistant under Don Shula in Miami 1970-75 as offensive line coach. Drafted fourth by 49ers in 1959. Played defensive tackle until 1962 when he was traded to Dallas and switched to offensive tackle. Clark was traded to Cleveland and played for the Browns from 1963-69. Career record: 38-50.

Background: Three-year letterman who played offense and defense at Southern California 1956-58, co-captain of the 1958 squad.

Personal: Born January 24, 1937 in Fillmore, Calif. Monte and his wife, Charlotte, live in Bloomfield Township, Mich. and have three children—Bryan, Randy, and Eric.

ASSISTANT COACHES

Don Doll, special assignments; born August 29, 1926, Los Angeles, Calif., lives in Detroit. Defensive back Southern California 1944, 1946-48. Pro defensive back Detroit Lions 1949-52, Washington Redskins 1953, Los Angeles Rams 1954. College coach: Washington 1955, Contra Costa, Calif., J.C. 1956, Southern California 1957-58, Notre Dame 1959-62. Pro coach: Detroit Lions 1963-64, Los Angeles Rams 1965, Washington Redskins 1966-70, Green Bay Packers 1971-73, Baltimore Colts 1974, Miami Dolphins 1975-76, rejoined Lions in 1978.

Fred Hoaglin, offensive line; born January 28, 1944, Alliance, Ohio, lives in Detroit. Center Pittsburgh 1965-67. Pro center Cleveland Browns 1966-72, Baltimore Colts 1973, Houston Oilers 1974-75, Seattle Seahawks 1976. Pro coach: Joined Lions in 1978.

Bill Johnson, offensive backfield; born July 14, 1926, Tyler, Tex., lives in Pontiac, Mich. Center Texas A&M 1944-46. Pro center San Francisco 49ers 1948-55. Pro coach: San Francisco 49ers 1956-67, Cincinnati Bengals 1968-78 (head coach 1976-78), Tampa Bay Buccaneers 1979-82, first year with Lions.

Ed Khayat, defensive line; born September 14, 1935, Moss Point, Miss., lives in Detroit. Lineman Millsaps 1953, Perkinston J.C. 1954, Tulane 1955-56. Pro lineman Washington Redskins 1957, 1962-63, Philadelphia Eagles 1958-61, 1964-65, Boston Patriots 1966. Pro coach: New Orleans Saints 1967-70, Philadelphia Eagles 1971-72 (head coach), Detroit Lions 1973-74, Atlanta Falcons 1975-76, Baltimore Colts 1977-81, rejoined Lions in 1982.

Joe Madden, special teams; born March 5, 1935, Washington, D.C., lives in Pontiac, Mich. Back Maryland 1954-56. No pro playing experience. College coach: Mississippi State 1962, Morehead State 1963, Wake Forest 1964-67, Iowa State 1968-71, Kansas State 1972, Pittsburgh 1973-76, Tennessee 1977-79. Pro coach: Joined Lions in 1980.

Ted Marchibroda, offensive coordinator; born March 15, 1931, Franklin, Pa., lives in Detroit. Quarterback St. Bonaventure 1950-51, Detroit 1953. Pro quarterback Pittsburgh Steelers 1953, 1955-56, Chicago Cardinals 1957. Pro coach: Washington Redskins 1961-65, 1971-73, Los Angeles Rams 1970, Baltimore Colts (head coach) 1975-79, Chicago Bears 1981, Lions since 1982.

Mel Phillips, defensive backfield; born January 6, 1942, Shelby, N.C., lives in Pontiac, Mich. Defensive back North Carolina A&T 1963-65. Pro defensive back San Francisco 49ers 1966-76. Pro coach: Joined Lions in 1980.

Larry Seiple, receivers; born February 14, 1945, Allentown, Pa., lives in Pontiac, Mich. Punter-tight end Kentucky 1964-66. Pro punter Miami Dolphins 1967-77. College coach: Miami 1979. Pro coach: Joined Lions in 1980.

DETROIT LIONS 1983 FIRST-YEAR ROSTER

Name	Pos.	Ht.	Wt.	Birth-date	College	Birthplace	Residence	How Acq.
Baratta, Andy	TE	6-2	226	5/2/60	Miami	Philadelphia, Pa.	Philadelphia, Pa.	FA
Black, Mike	P	6-1	205	1/18/61	Arizona State	Glendale, Calif.	Tempe, Ariz.	D7
Chadwick, Jeff	WR	6-3	180	12/16/60	Grand Valley State	Detroit, Mich.	Dearborn Heights, Mich.	FA
Cofer, Mike	DE	6-5	235	4/7/60	Tennessee	Knoxville, Tenn.	Knoxville, Tenn.	D3
Curley, August	LB	6-3	232	1/24/60	Southern California	Little Rock, Ark.	Los Angeles, Calif.	D4
Darns, Phillip (1)	DE	6-3	245	7/27/59	Mississippi Valley	Tampa, Fla.	Tampa, Fla.	FA
Dunn, Craig	TE	6-4	250	9/23/60	Ohio State	Glen Ridge, N.J.	Montclair, N.J.	FA
Feraday, Dan (1)	QB	6-1	205	6/30/56	Toronto	Toronto, Ont.	Toronto, Ont.	FA
George, Tom	QB	6-0	187	8/17/58	Western Michigan	Mishawaka, Ind.	Kalamazoo, Mich.	FA
Gill, Max	DT	6-2	245	12/14/60	Northern Illinois	Gary, Ind.	Crown Point, Ind.	FA
Hand, Chris	LB	6-2	234	1/9/61	Syracuse	Pompton Plains, N.J.	West Milford, N.J.	FA
Johnson, Demetrious	CB-S	5-11	186	7/21/61	Missouri	St. Louis, Mo.	St. Louis, Mo.	D5
Jones, James	RB	6-3	235	3/21/61	Florida	Pompano Beach, Fla.	Ft. Lauderdale, Fla.	D1
Jones, Stephen	WR	6-0	180	6/8/60	Central Michigan	Flint, Mich.	Flint, Mich.	FA
Lane, Jim	C	6-3	260	9/13/60	Idaho State	Memphis, Tenn.	Memphis, Tenn.	D12
Laube, Dave	G-T	6-3	270	3/3/61	Penn State	Paterson, N.J.	College Park, Pa.	D10
Lee, Edward (1)	WR	5-11	182	12/8/59	South Carolina State	Washington, D.C.	Washington, D.C.	D11('82)
McNatt, Clarence	DE	6-5	237	4/3/60	Detroit	East Elmhurst, N.Y.	Detroit, Mich.	FA
Menas, Tom	G	6-4	265	4/26/60	Kansas State	Highland Park, Mich.	Warren, Mich.	FA
Moore, George	DT	6-0	265	9/23/58	Southern	Mound Bayou, Miss.	Winstonville, Miss.	FA
Mott, Steve	C	6-3	259	3/24/61	Alabama	New Orleans, La.	University, Ala.	D5a
Radeck, Rodger	T	6-6	270	10/27/59	Wayne State	Grand Rapids, Mich.	Rockford, Mich.	FA
Sams, Eric (1)	RB	5-10	200	2/17/59	Wisconsin-Superior	Pittsburgh, Pa.	Pittsburgh, Pa.	FA
Sinclair, Steve	K	5-11	200	8/6/57	West Virginia	Pittsburgh, Pa.	Morgantown, W. Va.	FA
Stapleton, William	CB	5-11	188	1/26/61	Washington	San Francisco, Calif.	Seattle, Wash.	D8
Strenger, Rich	T	6-7	280	3/10/60	Michigan	Port Washington, Wis.	Grafton, Wis.	D2
Tate, Ben	RB	6-0	230	8/29/61	N. Carolina Central	Philadelphia, Pa.	Berlin, Md.	D11
Taylor, Juan (1)	G-T	6-3	270	6/30/60	Lamar	Dallas, Tex.	Dallas, Tex.	FA
Wagoner, Dan (1)	CB-S	5-10	177	12/12/59	Kansas	High Point, N.C.	High Point, N.C.	D9('82)
Washington, Greg	RB	6-0	185	7/7/61	Ferris State	Chicago, Ill.	Lansing, Mich.	FA
Wilkens, Joe	LB	6-1	215	12/2/59	Maryland	Atlantic City, N.J.	Pleasantville, N.J.	FA

Players who report to an NFL team for the first time are designated on rosters as rookies (R). If a player reported to an NFL training camp in a previous year but was not on the active squad for three or more regular season or postseason games, he is listed on the first-year roster and designated by a (1). Thereafter, a player who is on the active squad for three or more regular season or postseason games is credited with an additional year of playing experience.

NOTES

_____
_____
_____
_____
_____
_____
_____
_____
_____
_____
_____
_____
_____
_____
_____
_____

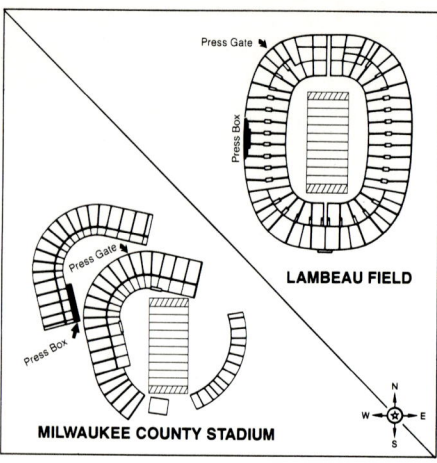

LAMBEAU FIELD

MILWAUKEE COUNTY STADIUM

Green Bay Packers

National Football Conference
Central Division

Team Colors: Dark Green, Gold, and White

1265 Lombardi Avenue
Green Bay, Wisconsin 54303
Telephone: (414) 494-2351

Club Officials
Chairman of the Board: Dominic Olejniczak
President, CEO: Robert Parins
Vice President: Tony Canadeo
Secretary: John Torinus
Treasurer: John S. Stiles
Assistant to the President: Bob Harlan
Assistant to the President: Tom Miller
Green Bay Ticket Director: Mark Wagner
Public Relations Director: Lee Remmel
Director of Player Personnel: Dick Corrick
Director of Pro Personnel: Burt Gustafson
Film Director: Al Treml
Trainer: Domenic Gentile
Equipment Manager: Bob Noel

Stadium: Lambeau Field • **Capacity:** 56,189
1265 Lombardi Avenue
Green Bay, Wisconsin 54303
Milwaukee County Stadium •
Capacity: 55,958
Highway I-94
Milwaukee, Wisconsin 53214

Playing Surfaces: Grass

Training Camp: St. Norbert College
DePere, Wisconsin 54115

1983 SCHEDULE

Preseason
Aug. 6	**Cleveland**	7:00
Aug. 12	at Seattle	7:30
Aug. 20	**Philadelphia**	2:00
Aug. 27	at St. Louis	6:00

Regular Season
Sept. 4	at Houston	12:00
Sept. 11	**Pittsburgh**	12:00
Sept. 18	**Los Angeles Rams** at Milwaukee	12:00
Sept. 26	at New York Giants (Monday)	9:00
Oct. 2	**Tampa Bay**	12:00
Oct. 9	at Detroit	1:00
Oct. 17	**Washington** (Monday)	8:00
Oct. 23	**Minnesota**	12:00
Oct. 30	at Cincinnati	4:00
Nov. 6	**Cleveland** at Milwaukee	12:00
Nov. 13	at Minnesota	12:00
Nov. 20	**Detroit** at Milwaukee	12:00
Nov. 27	at Atlanta	4:00
Dec. 4	**Chicago**	12:00
Dec. 12	at Tampa Bay (Monday)	9:00
Dec. 18	at Chicago	12:00

1982 TEAM STATISTICS

	Green Bay	Opp.
Total First Downs	175	164
Rushing	59	58
Passing	97	96
Penalty	19	10
Third Down Efficiency	50/121	53/138
Third Down Percentage	41.3	38.4
Total Net Yards	2910	2707
Total Offensive Plays	582	622
Avg. Gain per Play	5.0	4.4
Avg. Gain per Game	323.3	300.8
Net Yards Rushing	1081	932
Total Rushing Plays	283	275
Avg. Gain per Rush	3.8	3.4
Avg. Gain Rushing per Game	120.1	103.6
Net Yards Passing	1829	1775
Lost Attempting to Pass	32/239	20/175
Gross Yards Passing	2068	1950
Attempts/Completions	267/143	327/177
Percent Completed	53.6	54.1
Had Intercepted	15	12
Avg. Net Passing per Game	203.2	197.2
Punts/Avg.	42/40.2	46/41.8
Punt Returns/Avg.	26/7.6	27/10.6
Kickoff Returns/Avg.	34/19.5	45/19.4
Interceptions/Avg. Ret.	12/14.5	15/9.7
Penalties/Yards	42/343	72/629
Fumbles/Ball Lost	20/11	26/11
Total Points	226	169
Avg. Points per Game	25.1	18.8
Touchdowns	27	19
Rushing	12	9
Passing	12	9
Returns and Recoveries	3	1
Field Goals	13/18	12/18
Conversions	25/27	17/19
Safeties	0	1
Avg. Time of Possession	29:40	30:20

1982 TEAM RECORD

Preseason (2-2)

Green Bay		Opponents
21	*New York Jets	19
41	*Cincinnati	27
3	Los Angeles Raiders	24
27	New England	41
92		111

Regular Season (5-3-1)

Green Bay		Opponents	Att.
35	*Los Angeles Rams (Mil.)	23	53,694
27	New York Giants	19	68,405
26	*Minnesota (Mil.)	7	44,681
13	New York Jets	15	53,872
33	*Buffalo (Mil.)	21	46,655
10	*Detroit	30	51,875
20	Baltimore (OT)	20	25,920
38	Atlanta	7	50,245
24	Detroit	27	64,377
226		169	459,724

*Home Game   (OT) Overtime

Score by Periods

Green Bay	26	65	64	71	0	—	226
Opponents	59	46	29	35	0	—	169

Attendance

Home 196,905   Away 262,819   Total 459,724
Single game home record, 56,267 (11-28-76; Lambeau Field), 56,258 (9-28-80; Milwaukee County Stadium)
Single season home record, 435,521 (1980)

1982 INDIVIDUAL STATISTICS

Rushing

	Att	Yds	Avg	LG	TD
Ivery	127	453	3.6	32	9
Ellis	62	228	3.7	29	1
Rodgers	46	175	3.8	13	1
Lofton	4	101	25.3	83t	1
Meade	14	42	3.0	19	0
Jensen	9	28	3.1	10	0
Dickey	13	19	1.5	11	0
Huckleby	4	19	4.8	7	0
Jefferson	2	16	8.0	11	0
Stachowicz	2	0	0.0	0	0
Green Bay	283	1081	3.8	83t	12
Opponents	275	932	3.4	36	9

Field Goal Success

Distance	1-19	20-29	30-39	40-49	50 Over
Made-Att.	1-1	4-5	5-5	3-6	0-1

Passing

	Att	Comp	Pct	Yds	TD	Int	Tkld	Rate
Dickey	218	124	56.9	1790	12	14	25/196	75.4
Whitehurst	47	18	38.3	235	0	1	7/43	46.1
Lofton	1	1	100.0	43	0	0	0/0	—
Ivery	1	0	0	0	0	0	0/0	—
Green Bay	267	143	53.6	2068	12	15	32/239	
Opponents	327	177	54.1	1950	9	12	20/175	

Receiving

	No	Yds	Avg	LG	TD
Lofton	35	696	19.9	80t	4
Jefferson	27	452	16.7	50	0
Coffman	23	287	12.5	42	2
Ellis	18	140	7.8	20	0
Ivery	16	186	11.6	62	1
Epps	10	226	22.6	50	2
Rodgers	3	23	7.7	16	0
G. Lewis	3	21	7.0	12	0
Jensen	3	18	6.0	11	1
Meade	3	−5	−1.7	−1	0
Thompson	2	24	12.0	23t	2
Green Bay	143	2068	14.5	80t	12
Opponents	177	1950	11.0	44	9

Interceptions

	No	Yds	Avg	LG	TD
Anderson	3	22	7.3	9	0
Douglass	2	55	27.5	30	0
Harvey	2	32	16.0	17	0
Lee	1	40	40.0	40	0
Gray	1	21	21.0	21	0
Cumby	1	4	4.0	4	0
Hood	1	0	0.0	0	0
Wingo	1	0	0.0	0	0
Green Bay	12	174	14.5	40	0
Opponents	15	146	9.7	36	0

Punting

	No	Yds	Avg	In 20	LG
Stachowicz	42	1687	40.2	7	53
Green Bay	42	1687	40.2	7	53
Opponents	46	1925	41.8	11	55

Punt Returns

	No	FC	Yds	Avg	LG	TD
Epps	20	5	150	7.5	35	0
Gray	6	1	48	8.0	15	0
Green Bay	26	6	198	7.6	35	0
Opponents	27	3	286	10.6	58	0

Kickoff Returns

	No	Yds	Avg	LG	TD
Rodgers	20	436	21.8	76	0
Huckleby	5	89	17.8	26	0
Clark	4	75	18.8	30	0
Meade	2	31	15.5	17	0
Gray	2	29	14.5	25	0
C. Lewis	1	4	4.0	4	0
Green Bay	34	664	19.5	76	0
Opponents	45	875	19.4	96t	1

Scoring

	TD	TD R	TD P	TD Rt	PAT	FG	TP
Stenerud					25/27	13/18	64
Ivery	10	9	1	0			60
Lofton	5	1	4	0			30
Rodgers	3	1	0	2			18
Coffman	2	0	2	0			12
Epps	2	0	2	0			12
Thompson	2	0	2	0			12
Ellis	1	1	0	0			6
Harvey	1	0	0	1			6
Jensen	1	0	1	0			6
Green Bay	27	12	12	3	25/27	13/18	226
Opponents	19	9	9	1	17/19	12/18	169

Sacks

Anderson ½, Butler 2, Douglass 3, Harvey 1, Johnson 5½, Jones 3, C. Merrill 4, Wingo 1.

FIRST PLAYERS SELECTED

Year	Player, College, Position
1936	Russ Letlow, San Francisco, G
1937	Ed Jankowski, Wisconsin, B
1938	Cecil Isbell, Purdue, B
1939	Larry Buhler, Minnesota, B
1940	Hal Van Every, Marquette, B
1941	George Paskvan, Wisconsin, B
1942	Urban Odson, Minnesota, T
1943	Dick Wildung, Minnesota, T
1944	Merv Pregulman, Michigan, G
1945	Walt Schlinkman, Texas Tech, G
1946	Johnny (Strike) Strzykalski, Marquette, B
1947	Ernie Case, UCLA, B
1948	Earl (Jug) Girard, Wisconsin, B
1949	Stan Heath, Nevada, B
1950	Clayton Tonnemaker, Minnesota, C
1951	Bob Gain, Kentucky, T
1952	Babe Parilli, Kentucky, QB
1953	Al Carmichael, Southern California, B
1954	Art Hunter, Notre Dame, T
1955	Tom Bettis, Purdue, G
1956	Jack Losch, Miami, B
1957	Paul Hornung, Notre Dame, B
1958	Dan Currie, Michigan State, C
1959	Randy Duncan, Iowa, B
1960	Tom Moore, Vanderbilt, RB
1961	Herb Adderley, Michigan State, CB
1962	Earl Gros, Louisiana State, RB
1963	Dave Robinson, Penn State, LB
1964	Lloyd Voss, Nebraska, DT
1965	Donny Anderson, Texas Tech, RB
1966	Gale Gillingham, Minnesota, G
1967	Bob Hyland, Boston College, C
1968	Fred Carr, Texas-El Paso, LB
1969	Rich Moore, Villanova, DT
1970	Mike McCoy, Notre Dame, DT
1971	John Brockington, Ohio State, RB
1972	Willie Buchanon, San Diego State, DB
1973	Barry Smith, Florida State, WR
1974	Barty Smith, Richmond, RB
1975	Bill Bain, Southern California, G (2)
1976	Mark Koncar, Colorado, T
1977	Mike Butler, Kansas, DE
1978	James Lofton, Stanford, WR
1979	Eddie Lee Ivery, Georgia Tech, RB
1980	Bruce Clark, Penn State, DE
1981	Rich Campbell, California, QB
1982	Ron Hallstrom, Iowa, G
1983	Tim Lewis, Pittsburgh, DB

PACKERS COACHING HISTORY
(436-328-36)

1921-49	Earl (Curly) Lambeau	216-106-22
1950-53	Gene Ronzani	14-33-1
1954-57	Lisle Blackbourn	17-31-0
1958	Ray (Scooter) McLean	1-10-1
1959-67	Vince Lombardi	98-30-4
1968-70	Phil Bengtson	20-21-1
1971-74	Dan Devine	25-28-4
1975-82	Bart Starr	45-69-3

113

GREEN BAY PACKERS 1983 VETERAN ROSTER

No.	Name	Pos.	Ht.	Wt.	Birth-date	NFL Exp.	College	Birthplace	Residence	Games in '82
59	Anderson, John	LB	6-3	221	2/14/56	6	Michigan	Waukesha, Wis.	Elm Grove, Wis.	9
73	Braggs, Byron	NT	6-4	290	10/10/59	3	Alabama	Los Angeles, Calif.	Montgomery, Ala.	9
93	Brown, Robert	LB	6-2	238	5/21/60	2	Virginia Tech	Edenton, N.C.	Alexandria, Va.	8
19	Campbell, Rich	QB	6-4	224	12/22/58	3	California	Miami, Fla.	Green Bay, Wis.	1
88	Cassidy, Ron	WR	6-0	185	7/23/57	4	Utah State	Ventura, Calif.	Green Bay, Wis.	0*
34	Clark, Allan	RB	5-10	186	6/8/57	4	Northern Arizona	Grand Rapids, Minn.	Attleboro, Mass.	5
82	Coffman, Paul	TE	6-3	218	3/29/56	6	Kansas State	St. Louis, Mo.	Lee's Summit, Mo.	9
52	Cumby, George	LB	6-0	215	7/5/56	4	Oklahoma	Gorman, Tex.	Green Bay, Wis.	9
12	Dickey, Lynn	QB	6-4	220	10/10/49	11	Kansas State	Osawatomie, Kan.	Lenexa, Kan.	9
53	Douglass, Mike	LB	6-0	224	3/15/55	6	San Diego State	St. Louis, Mo.	El Cajon, Calif.	9
31	Ellis, Gerry	RB	5-11	216	11/12/57	4	Missouri	Columbia, Mo.	Columbia, Mo.	9
85	Epps, Phillip	WR	5-10	165	11/11/58	2	Texas Christian	Atlanta, Tex.	Ft. Worth, Tex.	9
79	Fields, Angelo	T	6-6	314	9/14/57	4	Michigan State	Washington, D.C.	Washington, D.C.	0*
57	Gofourth, Derrel	G	6-3	260	3/20/55	7	Oklahoma State	Parsons, Kan.	Stillwater, Okla.	9
24	Gray, Johnnie	S	5-11	185	12/18/53	9	Cal State-Fullerton	Lake Charles, La.	Green Bay, Wis.	9
65	Hallstrom, Ron	G	6-6	286	6/11/59	2	Iowa	Holden, Mass.	Green Bay, Wis.	7
69	Harris, Leotis	G	6-1	267	6/28/55	6	Arkansas	Little Rock, Ark.	Little Rock, Ark.	9
23	Harvey, Maurice	S	5-10	190	1/14/56	5	Ball State	Cincinnati, Ohio	Denver, Colo.	9
38	Hood, Estus	CB-S	5-11	180	11/14/55	6	Illinois State	Hattiesburg, Miss.	Green Bay, Wis.	9
25	Huckleby, Harlan	RB	6-1	199	12/30/57	4	Michigan	Detroit, Mich.	Detroit, Mich.	9
74	Huffman, Tim	T	6-5	277	8/31/59	3	Notre Dame	Canton, Ohio	Green Bay, Wis.	9
40	Ivery, Eddie Lee	RB	6-0	210	7/30/57	4	Georgia Tech	McDuffie, Ga.	Decatur, Ga.	9
83	Jefferson, John	WR	6-1	198	2/3/56	6	Arizona State	Dallas, Tex.	Dallas, Tex.	8
90	Johnson, Ezra	DE	6-4	240	10/2/55	7	Morris Brown	Shreveport, La.	Shreveport, La.	9
21	Jolly, Mike	S	6-3	185	3/19/58	3	Michigan	Detroit, Mich.	Green Bay, Wis.	7
63	Jones, Terry	NT	6-2	259	11/8/56	6	Alabama	Sandersville, Ga.	Tuscaloosa, Ala.	9
64	Kitson, Syd	G	6-4	252	9/27/58	3	Wake Forest	Orange, N.J.	New Providence, N.J.	0*
68	Koch, Greg	T	6-4	265	6/14/55	7	Arkansas	Bethesda, Md.	Green Bay, Wis.	9
60	Laslavic, Jim	LB	6-2	236	10/24/51	10	Penn State	Etna, Pa.	Coronado, Calif.	6
22	Lee, Mark	CB	5-11	187	3/20/58	4	Washington	Hanford, Calif.	Bellevue, Wash.	9
56	Lewis, Cliff	LB	6-1	226	11/9/59	3	Southern Mississippi	Brewton, Ala.	Ft. Walton Beach, Fla.	9
81	Lewis, Gary	TE	6-5	234	12/30/58	3	Texas-Arlington	Mt. Pleasant, Tex.	Arlington, Tex.	9
80	Lofton, James	WR	6-3	187	7/5/56	6	Stanford	Los Angeles, Calif.	Milwaukee, Wis.	9
54	McCarren, Larry	C	6-3	238	11/9/51	11	Illinois	Chicago, Ill.	Green Bay, Wis.	9
29	McCoy, Mike	CB-S	5-11	183	8/16/53	8	Colorado	Memphis, Ark.	Green Bay, Wis.	9
39	Meade, Mike	RB	5-10	228	2/12/60	2	Penn State	Dover, Del.	Dover, Del.	2
78	Merrill, Casey	DE	6-4	255	7/16/57	5	Cal-Davis	Oakland, Calif.	Palm Desert, Calif.	9
62	Merrill, Mark	LB	6-3	234	5/5/55	5	Minnesota	St. Paul, Minn.	New Brighton, Minn.	4
37	Murphy, Mark	S	6-2	199	4/22/58	3	West Liberty State	Canton, Ohio	North Canton, Ohio	9
51	Prather, Guy	LB	6-2	230	3/28/58	3	Grambling	Olney, Md.	Gaithersburg, Md.	9
35	Rodgers, Del	RB	5-10	197	6/22/60	2	Utah	Tacoma, Wash.	Salinas, Calif.	9
58	Rubens, Larry	C	6-1	253	1/25/59	2	Montana State	Spokane, Wash.	Spokane, Wash.	9
55	Scott, Randy	LB	6-1	220	1/31/59	3	Alabama	Atlanta, Ga.	Decatur, Ga.	9
16	Stachowicz, Ray	P	5-11	185	3/6/59	3	Michigan State	Cleveland, Ohio	Broadview Heights, Ohio	9
10	Stenerud, Jan	K	6-2	190	11/26/43	17	Montana State	Fetsund, Norway	Overland Park, Kan.	9
76	Stokes, Tim	T	6-5	252	3/16/50	10	Oregon	Oakland, Calif.	Eugene, Ore.	9
67	Swanke, Karl	T-C	6-6	251	12/29/57	4	Boston College	Elmhurst, Ill.	Green Bay, Wis.	8
75	Turner, Rich	NT	6-2	260	2/14/59	3	Oklahoma	Hugo, Okla.	Norman, Okla.	9
30	Whitaker, Bill	CB-S	6-0	182	11/18/59	3	Missouri	Kansas City, Mo.	Columbia, Mo.	9
17	Whitehurst, David	QB	6-2	204	4/27/55	7	Furman	Baumholder, Germany	Roswell, Ga.	3
50	Wingo, Rich	LB	6-1	230	7/16/56	4	Alabama	Elkhart, Ind.	Green Bay, Wis.	5

* Cassidy and Kitson missed '82 season due to injuries; Fields active for 1 game, but did not play.

†Option playout; subject to developments.

Traded—Tight end John Thompson to Los Angeles Rams.

Retired—Jim Jensen, 6-year running back, 8 games in '82.

Also played with Packers in '82—DE Mike Butler (9 games)

COACHING STAFF

Head Coach, Bart Starr

Pro Career: Starts ninth season as Green Bay head coach following a 5-3-1 record in 1982. Packers quarterback from 1956-71, leading Green Bay to five NFL Championships, 1961-62, 1965-67. Named NFL most valuable player in 1966 and MVP of Super Bowl I and II. Holds the NFL record for most consecutive passes without an interception, 294. Packers assistant coach in charge of quarterbacks in 1972 following his retirement as a player. Career record: 45-69-3.

Background: A high school All-America who became a four-year letter winner at Alabama. Quarterbacked Alabama to victory over Syracuse in 1953 Orange Bowl. Was the second-leading punter in the nation in 1953. Played in Blue-Gray game in 1955.

Personal: Born January 9, 1934 in Montgomery, Ala. Partner in two automobile dealerships in Birmingham, Ala. Bart and his wife, Cherry, live in DePere, Wis., and have two sons — Bart and Bret.

ASSISTANT COACHES

John Brunner, offensive backfield; born September 6, 1937, Perkesie, Pa., lives in Green Bay. Running back East Stroudsburg State 1957-59. No pro playing experience. College coach: Villanova 1967-69, Temple 1970-73, 1976-79, Princeton 1974-75. Pro coach: Detroit Lions 1980-82, first year with Packers.

Lew Carpenter, receivers; born January 12, 1932, Hayti, Mo., lives in Green Bay. Running back-end Arkansas 1950-52. Pro running back-defensive back-end Detroit Lions 1953-55, Cleveland Browns 1957-58, Green Bay Packers 1959-63. Pro coach: Minnesota Vikings 1964-66, Atlanta Falcons 1967-68, Washington Redskins 1969-70, St. Louis Cardinals 1971-72, Houston Oilers 1973-74, Packers since 1975.

Ross Fichtner, defensive backs; born October 26, 1938, McKeesport, Pa., lives in Green Bay. Quarterback Purdue 1957-59. Pro defensive back Cleveland Browns 1960-67, New Orleans Saints 1968. Pro coach: Florida Blazers (WFL) 1974, Chicago Bears 1975-77, Packers since 1980.

Monte Kiffin, linebackers; born February 29, 1940, Lexington, Neb., lives in Green Bay. Defensive end Nebraska 1961-63. Pro defensive end Winnipeg (CFL) 1965-66. College coach: Nebraska 1966-76, Arkansas 1977-79, North Carolina State 1980-82 (head coach). Pro coach: First year with Packers.

Ernie McMillan, offensive line; born February 21, 1938, Chicago Heights, Ill., lives in Green Bay. Tackle Illinois 1958-60. Pro tackle St. Louis Cardinals 1961-74, Green Bay Packers 1975-77. Pro coach: Joined Packers in 1978.

John Meyer, defensive coordinator; born February 20, 1942, Chicago, Ill., lives in Green Bay. Linebacker Notre Dame 1963-64. Pro linebacker St. Louis Cardinals 1965-66, Houston Oilers 1967-68. Pro coach: Houston Oilers 1968, New England Patriots 1969-72, Detroit Lions 1973-74, Packers since 1975.

Bill Meyers, offensive line assistant; born October 8, 1946, Chippewa Falls, Wis., lives in Green Bay. Tackle Stanford 1970-71. No pro playing experience. College coach: California 1972-73, 1977-78, Santa Clara 1974-76, Notre Dame 1979-81. Pro coach: Joined Packers in 1982.

Dick Rehbein, special teams; born November 22, 1955, Green Bay, Wis., lives in Green Bay. Center Ripon 1973-76. No pro playing experience. Pro coach: Joined Packers in 1978.

Bob Schnelker, offensive coordinator; born October 17, 1928, Galion, Ohio, lives in Green Bay. End Bowling Green 1946-50. Pro end Cleveland Browns 1953, New York Giants 1954-60, Minnesota Vikings 1961. Pro coach: Los Angeles Rams 1963-64, Green Bay Packers 1965-71, San Diego Chargers 1972-73, Miami Dolphins 1974, Kansas City Chiefs 1975-77, Detroit Lions 1978-81, rejoined Packers in 1982.

Richard (Doc) Urich, defensive line; born September 10, 1928, Toledo, Ohio, lives in Green Bay. End Miami, Ohio 1948-50. No pro playing experience. College coach: Miami, Ohio 1951-54, Northwestern 1955-63, Notre Dame 1964-65, Buffalo 1966-68, Northern Illinois 1969-70. Pro coach: Buffalo Bills 1971, Denver Broncos 1972-77, Washington Redskins 1978-80, Packers since 1981.

GREEN BAY PACKERS 1983 FIRST-YEAR ROSTER

Name	Pos.	Ht.	Wt.	Birth-date	College	Birthplace	Residence	How Acq.
Bishop, Tom	DE	6-0	233	3/31/61	Ashland College	Mansfield, Ohio	Mansfield, Ohio	FA
Briscoe, Carlton	CB-S	5-11	180	5/29/60	McNeese State	Lafayette, La.	New Iberia, La.	D8
Clark, Jessie	RB	6-0	226	1/3/60	Arkansas	Thebes, Ark.	Crossett, Ark.	D7
Dean, Patrick	NT	6-1	252	4/20/59	Iowa	Bayshore, N.Y.	West Islip, N.Y.	FA
Drechsler, Dave	G	6-3	250	7/18/60	North Carolina	Cleveland, N.C.	Cleveland, N.C.	D2
Ettari, James	NT	6-2	265	1/4/61	Citadel	Brooklyn, N.Y.	Brentwood, N.Y.	FA
Garcia, Eddie (1)	K	5-8	188	4/15/59	Southern Methodist	New Orleans, La.	Dallas, Tex.	D10 ('82)
Ham, Robin	C	6-2	252	7/21/59	West Texas State	Sweetwater, Tex.	Sweetwater, Tex.	D9
Harvey, John	LB	6-2	236	2/17/60	Southern California	Los Angeles, Calif.	Compton, Calif.	D12
Key, Larry	RB	5-9	189	7/12/56	Florida State	Inverness, Fla.	Inverness, Fla.	D10 ('78)
Klinkhammer, Joe	NT	6-4	255	2/26/60	St. Thomas	Northfield, Minn.	Northfield, Minn.	FA
Lewis, Tim	CB-S	5-11	194	12/18/61	Pittsburgh	Perkasie, Pa.	Perkasie, Pa.	D1
Long, Darren	TE	6-3	220	7/12/59	Long Beach State	Exeter, Calif.	Exeter, Calif.	FA
Michuta, Steve	QB	6-3	200	9/3/60	Grand Valley State	Detroit, Mich.	Livonia, Mich.	FA
Miller, Mike	WR	5-11	182	12/29/59	Tennessee	Flint, Mich.	Flint, Mich.	D4
Myatt, Bill	QB	6-3	210	1/4/60	Hayward State	Detroit, Mich.	San Jose, Calif.	FA
Parlavecchio, Chet (1)	LB	6-2	225	2/14/60	Penn State	Newark, N.J.	West Orange, N.J.	D6 ('82)
Pfohl, Larry (1)	G	6-3	270	6/2/58	Miami	Buffalo, N.Y.	Green Bay, Wis.	FA
Phason, Vince (1)	S	5-10	190	2/5/54	Arizona	Oakland, Calif.	Denver, Colo.	FA
Rudzinski, Joe	LB	6-2	230	5/19/61	Notre Dame	Detroit, Mich.	Farmington, Mich.	FA
Sams, Ron	G	6-3	261	4/12/61	Pittsburgh	Bridgeville, Pa.	McDonald, Pa.	D6
Scribner, Bucky	P	6-0	203	7/11/60	Kansas	Lawrence, Kan.	Lawrence, Kan.	D11
Thomas, Bryan	RB	5-9	193	7/8/60	Pittsburgh	Oberlin, Ohio	Oberlin, Ohio	D5
Thomas, Jimmy	CB-S	6-3	190	10/19/60	Indiana	Lakeland, Fla.	Ft. Lauderdale, Fla.	D10a
Williams, Byron	WR	6-1	177	10/31/60	Texas-Arlington	Texarkana, Tex.	Texarkana, Tex.	D10

Players who report to an NFL team for the first time are designated on rosters as rookies (R). If a player reported to an NFL training camp in a previous year but was not on the active squad for three or more regular season or postseason games, he is listed on the first-year roster and designated by à (1). Thereafter, a player who is on the active squad for three or more regular season or postseason games is credited with an additional year of playing experience.

NOTES

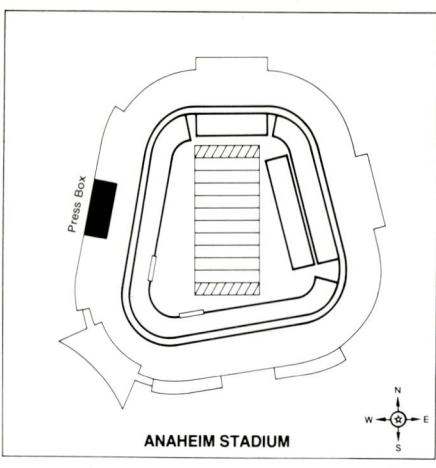

ANAHEIM STADIUM

Los Angeles Rams

**National Football Conference
Western Division**

Team Colors: Royal Blue, Gold, and White

Business Address:
2327 West Lincoln Ave.
Anaheim, California 92801

Ticket Office:
Anaheim Stadium
1900 State College Blvd.
Anaheim, California 92806
Telephone: (714) 535-7267 or (213) 585-5400

Club Officials
President: Georgia Frontiere
Executive Vice President: Ray Nagel
Vice President, Finance: John Shaw
Administrator, Football Operations: Jack Faulkner
Director, Marketing: Les Marshall
Director of Operations: Dick Beam
Director of Player Personnel: John Math
Director of Public Relations: Pete Donovan
Director of Community Relations: Marshall Klein
Trainers: Gary Tuthill, George Menefee
Equipment Manager: Don Hewitt

Stadium: Anaheim Stadium • **Capacity:** 69,007
Anaheim, California 92806

Playing Surface: Grass

Training Camp: California State University
Fullerton, California 92634

1983 SCHEDULE

Preseason
Aug. 6	**San Diego**	7:00
Aug. 15	**Dallas**	7:00
Aug. 20	**New England**	7:00
Aug. 26	at San Diego	7:00

Regular Season
Sept. 4	at New York Giants	1:00
Sept. 11	**New Orleans**	1:00
Sept. 18	vs. Green Bay at Milwaukee	12:00
Sept. 25	at New York Jets	4:00
Oct. 2	**Detroit**	1:00
Oct. 9	at San Francisco	1:00
Oct. 16	**Atlanta**	1:00
Oct. 23	**San Francisco**	1:00
Oct. 30	at Miami	1:00
Nov. 6	**Chicago**	1:00
Nov. 14	at Atlanta (Monday)	9:00
Nov. 20	**Washington**	1:00
Nov. 27	**Buffalo**	1:00
Dec. 4	at Philadelphia	1:00
Dec. 11	**New England**	1:00
Dec. 18	at New Orleans	12:00

1982 TEAM STATISTICS

	L.A. Rams	Opp.
Total First Downs	163	193
Rushing	61	75
Passing	90	107
Penalty	12	11
Third Down Efficiency	43/117	55/126
Third Down Percentage	36.8	43.7
Total Net Yards	3024	3333
Total Offensive Plays	563	606
Avg. Gain per Play	5.4	5.5
Avg. Gain per Game	336.0	370.3
Net Yards Rushing	1025	1202
Total Rushing Plays	251	307
Avg. Gain per Rush	4.1	3.9
Avg. Gain Rushing per Game	113.9	133.6
Net Yards Passing	1999	2131
Lost Attempting to Pass	15/137	18/159
Gross Yards Passing	2136	2290
Attempts/Completions	297/166	281/175
Percent Completed	55.9	62.3
Had Intercepted	14	11
Avg. Net Passing per Game	222.1	236.8
Punts/Avg.	46/42.6	42/38.1
Punt Returns/Avg.	22/11.0	31/12.9
Kickoff Returns/Avg.	45/19.3	36/23.4
Interceptions/Avg. Ret.	11/9.6	14/7.0
Penalties/Yards	63/550	64/531
Fumbles/Ball Lost	23/10	15/7
Total Points	200	250
Avg. Points per Game	22.2	27.8
Touchdowns	25	30
Rushing	13	13
Passing	11	16
Returns and Recoveries	1	1
Field Goals	9/15	14/19
Conversions	23/25	28/30
Safeties	0	0
Avg. Time of Possession	27:52	32:08

1982 TEAM RECORD

Preseason (2-2)

Los Angeles Rams		Opponents
20	*Denver	33
23	Cleveland	26
23	*Seattle	13
20	*San Diego	14
86		86

Regular Season (2-7)

Los Angeles Rams		Opponents	Att.
23	Green Bay (Mil.)	35	53,694
14	*Detroit	19	59,470
17	Atlanta	34	39,686
20	*Kansas City	14	45,793
24	*San Francisco	30	58,574
24	*Denver	27	48,112
31	Los Angeles Raiders	37	56,646
26	*Chicago	34	46,502
21	San Francisco	20	54,256
200		250	462,733

*Home Game

Score by Periods

Los Angeles Rams	68	58	26	48	—	200
Opponents	34	80	41	95	—	250

Attendance

Home 258,451   Away 204,282   Total 462,733
Single game home record, 102,368 (11-10-57; LA Coliseum), 65,154 (12-15-80; Anaheim Stadium)
Single season home record, 519,175 (1973; LA Coliseum), 500,403 (1980; Anaheim Stadium)

1982 INDIVIDUAL STATISTICS

Rushing

	Att	Yds	Avg	LG	TD
Tyler	137	564	4.1	54	9
Guman	69	266	3.9	15	2
J. Thomas	16	80	5.0	11	0
B. Jones	11	73	6.6	17	0
Redden	8	24	3.0	7	0
Cromwell	1	17	17.0	17t	1
Miller	1	5	5.0	5	0
Alexander	1	3	3.0	3	0
Ferragamo	4	3	0.8	2	1
Battle	1	1	1.0	1	0
Waddy	2	−11	−5.5	5	0
L.A. Rams	251	1025	4.1	54	13
Opponents	307	1202	3.9	32	13

Field Goal Success

Distance	1-19	20-29	30-39	40-49	50 Over
Made-Att.	0-0	4-5	5-8	0-0	0-2

Passing

	Att	Comp	Pct	Yds	TD	Int	Tkld	Rate
Ferragamo	209	118	56.5	1609	9	9	7/65	77.7
B. Jones	87	48	55.2	527	2	4	8/72	61.8
Guman	1	0	0.0	0	0	1	0/0	—
L.A. Rams	297	166	55.9	2136	11	14	15/137	
Opponents	281	175	62.3	2290	16	11	18/159	

Receiving

	No	Yds	Avg	LG	TD
Tyler	38	375	9.9	40	4
Guman	31	310	10.0	46	0
Dennard	25	383	15.3	39	2
Barber	18	166	9.2	21	1
Farmer	17	344	20.2	42t	2
Miller	15	346	23.1	85t	1
J. Thomas	8	49	6.1	11	0
D. Hill	7	92	13.1	23	0
Redden	4	16	4.0	11	0
Battle	2	62	31.0	51t	1
Alexander	1	−7	−7.0	−7	0
L.A. Rams	166	2136	12.9	85t	11
Opponents	175	2290	13.1	52	16

Interceptions

	No	Yds	Avg	LG	TD
Perry	3	57	19.0	33	0
Cromwell	3	33	11.0	21	0
P. Thomas	3	0	0.0	0	0
Ekern	1	9	9.0	9	0
Johnson	1	7	7.0	7	0
L.A. Rams	11	106	9.6	33	0
Opponents	14	98	7.0	19	0

Punting

	No	Yds	Avg	In 20	LG
Misko	45	1961	43.6	10	59
L.A. Rams	46	1961	42.6	10	59
Opponents	42	1601	38.1	12	56

Punt Returns

	No	FC	Yds	Avg	LG	TD
Irvin	22	1	242	11.0	63t	1
L.A. Rams	22	1	242	11.0	63t	1
Opponents	31	2	401	12.9	93t	1

Kickoff Returns

	No	Yds	Avg	LG	TD
Redden	22	502	22.8	85	0
Alexander	8	139	17.4	32	0
Guman	8	102	12.8	24	0
Sully	5	84	16.8	24	0
D. Hill	2	42	21.0	24	0
L.A. Rams	45	869	19.3	85	0
Opponents	36	844	23.4	45	0

Scoring

	TD	TD R	TD P	TD Rt	PAT	FG	TP
Tyler	13	9	4	0			78
Lansford					23/24	9/15	50
Dennard	2	0	2	0			12
Farmer	2	0	2	0			12
Guman	2	2	0	0			12
Barber	1	0	1	0			6
Battle	1	0	1	0			6
Cromwell	1	1	0	0			6
Ferragamo	1	1	0	0			6
Irvin	1	0	0	1			6
Miller	1	0	1	0			6
L.A. Rams	25	13	11	1	23/25	9/15	200
Opponents	30	13	16	1	28/30	14/19	250

Sacks

Andrews 3, Doss 4, Fanning 5, Johnson 1, Meisner 1, Ja. Youngblood 4.

FIRST PLAYERS SELECTED

(Since 1941)

Year	Player, College, Position
1941	Rudy Mucha, Washington, C
1942	Jack Wilson, Baylor, B
1943	Mike Holovak, Boston College, B
1944	Tony Butkovich, Illinois, B
1945	Elroy (Crazylegs) Hirsch, Wisconsin, B
1946	Emil Sitko, Notre Dame, B
1947	Herman Wedemeyer, St. Mary's, Cal., B
1948	Tom Keane, West Virginia, B (2)
1949	Bobby Thomason, Virginia Military, B
1950	Ralph Pasquariello, Villanova, B
1951	Bud McFadin, Texas, G
1952	Bill Wade, Vanderbilt, QB
1953	Donn Moomaw, UCLA, C
1954	Ed Beatty, Cincinnati, C
1955	Larry Morris, Georgia Tech, C
1956	Joe Marconi, West Virginia, B
1957	Jon Arnett, Southern California, B
1958	Lou Michaels, Kentucky, T
1959	Dick Bass, Pacific, B
1960	Billy Cannon, Louisiana State, RB
1961	Marlin McKeever, Southern California, E-LB
1962	Roman Gabriel, North Carolina State, QB
1963	Terry Baker, Oregon State, QB
1964	Bill Munson, Utah State, QB
1965	Clancy Williams, Washington State, CB
1966	Tom Mack, Michigan, G
1967	Willie Ellison, Texas Southern, RB (2)
1968	Gary Beban, UCLA, QB (2)
1969	Larry Smith, Florida, RB
1970	Jack Reynolds, Tennessee, LB
1971	Isiah Robertson, Southern, LB
1972	Jim Bertelsen, Texas, RB (2)
1973	Cullen Bryant, Colorado, DB (2)
1974	John Cappelletti, Penn State, RB
1975	Mike Fanning, Notre Dame, DT
1976	Kevin McLain, Colorado State, LB
1977	Bob Brudzinski, Ohio State, LB
1978	Elvis Peacock, Oklahoma, RB
1979	George Andrews, Nebraska, LB
1980	Johnnie Johnson, Texas, DB
1981	Mel Owens, Michigan, LB
1982	Barry Redden, Richmond, RB
1983	Eric Dickerson, Southern Methodist, RB

RAMS COACHING HISTORY

Cleveland 1937-45
(315-262-20)

1937-38	Hugo Bezdek*	1-13-0
1938	Art Lewis	4-4-0
1939-42	Earl (Dutch) Clark	16-26-2
1944	Aldo (Buff) Donelli	4-6-0
1945-46	Adam Walsh	15-5-1
1947	Bob Snyder	6-6-0
1948-49	Clark Shaughnessy	14-8-3
1950-52	Joe Stydahar**	18-9-0
1952-54	Hamp Pool	23-11-2
1955-59	Sid Gillman	28-32-1
1960-62	Bob Waterfield***	9-24-1
1962-65	Harland Svare	14-31-3
1966-70	George Allen	49-19-4
1971-72	Tommy Prothro	14-12-2
1973-77	Chuck Knox	57-20-1
1978-82	Ray Malavasi	43-36-0

*Resigned after three games in 1938
**Resigned after one game in 1952
***Resigned after eight games in 1962

LOS ANGELES RAMS 1983 VETERAN ROSTER

No.	Name	Pos.	Ht.	Wt.	Birth-date	NFL Exp.	College	Birthplace	Residence	Games in '82
35	Alexander, Robert	RB-KR	6-0	185	4/21/58	2	West Virginia	Charleston, W. Va.	Charleston, W. Va.	9
52	Andrews, George	LB	6-3	221	11/28/55	5	Nebraska	Omaha, Neb.	Anaheim, Calif.	9
62	Bain, Bill	G	6-4	285	8/9/52	8	Southern California	Pico Rivera, Calif.	Westminster, Calif.	9
86	†Barber, Mike	TE	6-3	237	6/4/53	7	Louisiana Tech	White Oak, Tex.	Houston, Tex.	9
96	Barnett, Doug	DE-C	6-3	250	4/12/60	2	Azusa Pacific	Montebello, Calif.	West Covina, Calif.	9
81	Battle, Ron	TE	6-3	225	3/27/59	3	North Texas State	Shreveport, La.	Shreveport, La.	9
	t-Bolinger, Russ	G	6-5	260	9/10/54	7	Long Beach State	Wichita, Kan.	Issaquah, Wash.	9
90	Brooks, Larry	DT	6-3	255	6/10/50	12	Va. State-Petersburg	Philadelphia, Pa.	Fountain Valley, Calif.	6
54	Carson, Howard	LB	6-2	230	2/11/57	2	Howard Payne	Hico, Tex.	Grapevine, Tex.	2
50	Collins, Jim	LB	6-2	230	6/11/58	3	Syracuse	Orange, N.J.	Huntington Beach, Calif.	6
42	Collins, Kirk	S	5-11	183	7/18/58	3	Baylor	San Antonio, Tex.	San Antonio, Tex.	9
21	Cromwell, Nolan	S	6-1	200	1/30/55	7	Kansas	Smith Center, Kan.	Anaheim, Calif.	9
70	DeJurnett, Charles	DT	6-4	260	6/17/52	7	San Jose State	Picyun, Miss.	San Diego, Calif.	4
88	Dennard, Preston	WR	6-1	183	11/28/55	6	New Mexico	Cordele, Ga.	Fountain Valley, Calif.	9
71	Doss, Reggie	DE	6-4	263	12/7/56	6	Hampton Institute	Mobile, Ala.	Huntington Beach, Calif.	9
55	Ekern, Carl	LB	6-3	222	5/27/54	7	San Jose State	Richland, Wash.	Fountain Valley, Calif.	3
84	Farmer, George	WR	5-10	175	12/5/58	2	Southern	Los Angeles, Calif.	Los Angeles, Calif.	8
15	Ferragamo, Vince	QB	6-3	212	4/24/54	6	Nebraska	Torrance, Calif.	Irvine, Calif.	7
44	Guman, Mike	RB	6-2	218	4/21/58	4	Penn State	Allentown, Pa.	Tustin, Calif.	9
60	Harrah, Dennis	G	6-5	255	3/9/53	9	Miami	Charleston, W. Va.	Long Beach, Calif.	9
87	Hill, Drew	WR	5-9	170	10/5/56	5	Georgia Tech	Newnan, Ga.	Newnan, Ga.	9
72	Hill, Kent	G	6-5	260	3/7/57	5	Georgia Tech	Americus, Ga.	Americus, Ga.	9
47	Irvin, LeRoy	CB-KR	5-11	184	9/15/57	4	Kansas	Fort Dix, N.J.	Fullerton, Calif.	9
	t-Jeter, Gary	DE	6-4	260	3/24/55	7	Southern California	Weirton, W. Va.	Secaucus, N.J.	4
20	Johnson, Johnnie	S	6-1	183	10/8/56	4	Texas	La Grange, Tex.	Huntington Beach, Calif.	9
24	Jones, A.J.	RB	6-1	202	5/30/59	2	Texas	Youngstown, Ohio	Youngstown, Ohio	6
9	Kemp, Jeff	QB	6-0	201	7/11/59	3	Dartmouth	Santa Ana, Calif.	Fullerton, Calif.	0*
68	Kersten, Wally	T	6-5	270	12/8/59	2	Minnesota	Minneapolis, Minn.	Minneapolis, Minn.	3
4	Lansford, Mike	K	6-0	183	7/20/58	2	Washington	Monterey Park, Calif.	Huntington Beach, Calif.	9
67	Lapka, Myron	DT	6-4	260	5/10/56	3	Southern California	Van Nuys, Calif.	Chatsworth, Calif.	2
59	Lilja, George	C	6-4	250	3/3/58	2	Michigan	Evergreen Park, Ill.	Palos Park, Ill.	9
83	Locklin, Kerry	TE	6-3	217	9/9/59	2	New Mexico State	Las Cruces, N.M.	Rockdale, Tex.	6
69	Meisner, Greg	DE	6-3	253	4/23/59	3	Pittsburgh	New Kensington, Pa.	Huntington Beach, Calif.	6
6	Misko, John	P	6-5	207	10/1/54	2	Oregon State	Highland Park, Mich.	Strathmore, Calif.	9
58	Owens, Mel	LB	6-2	224	12/7/58	3	Michigan	Detroit, Mich.	Balboa, Calif.	7
75	Pankey, Irv	T	6-4	267	12/15/58	4	Penn State	Aberdeen, Md.	Aberdeen, Md.	9
49	Perry, Rod	CB	5-9	185	9/11/53	9	Colorado	Fresno, Calif.	Fresno, Calif.	9
30	Redden, Barry	RB	5-10	205	7/21/60	2	Richmond	Sarasota, Fla.	Warsaw, Ind.	9
57	Reilly, Mike	LB	6-4	217	2/14/59	2	Oklahoma	Miami, Fla.	Miami, Fla.	9
78	Slater, Jackie	T	6-4	271	5/27/54	8	Jackson State	Jackson, Miss.	Anaheim, Calif.	9
56	Smith, Doug	C	6-3	253	11/25/56	6	Bowling Green	Columbus, Ohio	Laguna Hills, Calif.	9
23	Smith, Lucious	CB	5-10	190	1/17/57	4	Cal State-Fullerton	Columbus, Ga.	Anaheim, Calif.	8
37	Sully, Ivory	S	6-0	201	6/20/57	5	Delaware	Salisbury, Md.	Fullerton, Calif.	9
33	Thomas, Jewerl	RB	5-10	228	9/10/57	4	San Jose State	Hanford, Calif.	Anaheim, Calif.	8
27	Thomas, Pat	CB	5-9	190	9/1/54	8	Texas A&M	Plano, Tex.	Plano, Tex.	9
	t-Thompson, John	TE	6-3	226	1/18/57	4	Utah State	Jackson, Miss.	Green Bay, Wis.	9
66	Williams, Eric	LB	6-2	235	6/17/55	7	Southern California	Sacramento, Calif.	Harvester, Mo.	3
85	Youngblood, Jack	DE	6-4	242	1/26/50	13	Florida	Jacksonville, Fla.	Orange, Calif.	9
53	Youngblood, Jim	LB	6-3	231	2/23/50	11	Tennessee Tech	Union, S.C.	Fountain Valley, Calif.	7

* Kemp active for 7 games with Rams in '82, but did not play.

†Option playout; subject to developments.

t-Rams traded for Bolinger (Detroit), Jeter (New York Giants), Thompson (Green Bay).

Traded—Defensive tackle Mike Fanning to Detroit, defensive tackle Cody Jones and running back Wendell Tyler to San Francisco.

Retired—Bert Jones, 10-year quarterback, 4 games in '82.

Also played with Rams in '82—RB Cullen Bryant (1 game), WR Willie Miller (9), WR Billy Waddy (3), T Ron Yary (8).

COACHING STAFF

Head Coach, John Robinson

Pro Career: Became seventeenth head coach in Rams history on February 14, 1983. Arrived with 23 years of coaching experience, including one on the professional level as an assistant with the Oakland Raiders in 1975. No pro playing experience.

Background: Played end for Oregon 1955-58. Began coaching career with his alma mater from 1960-71. Became an assistant at Southern California from 1972-74. Returned as head coach in 1976 before resigning after the 1982 season. Compiled seven-year .819 winning percentage at Southern California with 67 wins, 14 losses, and 2 ties.

Personal: Born July 25, 1935 in Chicago. John and his wife, Barbara, live in Pasadena and have four children—Teresa 23, Lynn 21, David 18, and Christopher 16.

ASSISTANT COACHES

Bob Baker, quarterbacks; born November 28, 1927, Bluffton, Ind., lives in Anaheim. Quarterback Ball State 1947-51. No pro playing experience. College coach: Indiana 1966-72, Illinois 1973, Michigan State 1977-79, Arizona State 1980-82. Pro coach: Calgary (CFL) 1974-76 (1976 head coach), first year with Rams.

Marv Goux, defensive line; born September 8, 1932, Santa Barbara, Calif., lives in Long Beach. Linebacker Southern California 1952, 1954-55. No pro playing experience. College coach: Southern California 1957-82. Pro coach: First year with Rams.

Gil Haskell, special teams; born September 24, 1943, San Francisco, Calif. lives in Diamond Bar. Defensive back San Francisco State 1961, 1963-65. No pro playing experience. College coach: Southern California 1978-82. Pro coach: First year with Rams.

Hudson Houck, offensive line; born January 7, 1943, Los Angeles, Calif., lives in Long Beach. Center Southern California 1962-64. No pro playing experience. College coach: Southern California 1970-72, 1976-82, Stanford 1973-75. Pro coach: First year with Rams.

Jimmy Raye, wide receivers-passing game coordinator; born July 3, 1945, Fayetteville, N.C., lives in Anaheim. Quarterback Michigan State 1965-67. Pro defensive back Philadelphia Eagles 1969. College coach: Michigan State 1971-75, Wyoming 1976. Pro coach: San Francisco 49ers 1977, Detroit Lions 1978-79, Atlanta Falcons 1980-82, first year with Rams.

Steve Shafer, defensive backs; born December 8, 1940, Glendale, Calif., lives in Anaheim. Quarterback-defensive back Utah State 1961-62. Pro defensive back British Columbia (CFL) 1963-67. College coach: San Mateo J.C. 1968-74 (1973-74 head coach), San Diego State 1975-82. Pro coach: First year with Rams.

Fritz Shurmur, inside linebackers; born July 15, 1932, Riverview, Mich., lives in Diamond Bar. Center Albion 1951-53. No pro playing experience. College coach: Albion 1956-61, Wyoming 1962-74 (1971-74 head coach). Pro coach: Detroit Lions 1975-77, New England Patriots 1978-81, Rams since 1982.

Bruce Snyder, running backs-running game coordinator; born March 14, 1940, Santa Monica, Calif., lives in Anaheim. Fullback Oregon 1960-62. No pro playing experience. College coach: Oregon 1966-72, Utah State 1973, Southern California 1974-75, Utah State 1976-82 (head coach). Pro coach: First year with Rams.

Fred Whittingham, outside linebackers; born February 4, 1939, Boston, Mass., lives in Anaheim. Linebacker Brigham Young 1957-58, Cal Poly-SLO 1961-62. Pro linebacker Los Angeles Rams 1964, Philadelphia Eagles 1965-66, 1971, New Orleans Saints 1967-68, Dallas Cowboys 1969-70. College coach: Brigham Young 1973-81. Pro coach: Joined Rams in 1982.

LOS ANGELES RAMS 1983 FIRST-YEAR ROSTER

Name	Pos.	Ht.	Wt.	Birth-date	College	Birthplace	Residence	How Acq.
Anderson, Robin (1)	TE	6-3	240	10/25/57	Brigham Young	Salt Lake City, Utah	Provo, Utah	FA
Bechtold, Bill (1)	C	6-4	250	4/12/60	Oklahoma	Midwest City, Okla.	Midwest City, Okla.	D3 ('82)
Belcher, Jack	C	6-4	258	4/17/61	Boston College	Stoneham, Mass.	Stoneham, Mass.	D9
Burtness, Rich (1)	G	6-5	235	6/25/60	Montana	Anacortes, Wash.	Anacortes, Wash.	FA
Carlos, Ray	T	6-4	250	9/7/59	Cal State-Fullerton	Loma Linda, Calif.	Colton, Calif.	FA
Casper, Clete	QB	6-2	193	10/8/59	Washington State	Issaquah, Wash.	Renton, Wash.	D12
Dickerson, Eric	RB	6-3	218	9/2/60	Southern Methodist	Sealy, Tex.	Sealy, Tex.	D1
Ellard, Henry	WR	5-11	170	7/21/61	Fresno State	Fresno, Calif.	Fresno, Calif.	D2
Ford, Kerry	DE	6-0	221	12/30/60	San Jose State	Los Angeles, Calif.	San Jose, Calif.	FA
Gary, Joe (1)	NT	6-5	255	5/12/59	UCLA	Los Angeles, Calif.	Los Angeles, Calif.	FA
Gomeztrejo, Fred	S	5-11	189	9/21/60	La Verne	La Puente, Calif.	La Verne, Calif.	FA
Grant, Otis	WR	6-3	197	8/13/61	Michigan State	Atlanta, Ga.	Atlanta, Ga.	D5
Haugabrook, Ken	LB	6-3	226	5/8/59	Nevada-Las Vegas	Inglewood, Calif.	Los Angeles, Calif.	FA
Kowalski, Gary	T	6-5	250	7/2/60	Boston College	New Haven, Conn.	Old Saybrook, Conn.	D6
Lazarus, Andrew	RB	5-11	195	1/18/61	Nevada-Las Vegas	Brooklyn, N.Y.	Uniondale, N.Y.	FA
McDonald, James	TE	6-5	218	3/29/61	Southern California	Long Beach, Calif.	Long Beach, Calif.	FA
Nelson, Chuck	K	5-11	175	2/23/60	Washington	Seattle, Wash.	Everett, Wash.	D4
Newsome, Vince	S	6-1	179	1/22/61	Washington	Braintree, England	Seattle, Wash.	D4a
Pryor, David	P	6-3	215	6/18/60	Southern California	Long Beach, Calif.	Marina del Rey, Calif.	FA
Reed, Doug	NT-DE	6-3	250	7/16/60	San Diego State	San Diego, Calif.	San Diego, Calif.	D4
Simmons, Jeff	WR	6-3	195	7/6/60	Southern California	Stockton, Calif.	Los Angeles, Calif.	D7
Shearin, Joe (1)	G	6-4	250	4/16/60	Texas	Dallas, Tex.	Austin, Tex.	D7 ('82)
Speight, Bob (1)	T	6-4	260	11/4/58	Boston University	Terre Haute, Ind.	New Hartford, N.Y.	D9 ('82)
Smith, Gary	WR	6-0	184	12/14/59	Southern Methodist	Houston, Tex.	Houston, Tex.	FA
Smith, Marvin	LB	6-2	225	3/4/57	Cal State-Fullerton	Merced, Calif.	Placentia, Calif.	FA
Sullivan, Tim	LB	6-2	220	7/26/61	Southern California	Bethpage, N.Y.	Long Beach, Calif.	FA
Stoneburner, Ted	RB	5-10	210	7/14/59	Central Connecticut	Hartford, Conn.	Weathersfield, Conn.	FA
Taylor, Lawrence	NT	6-6	270	1/26/59	Nevada-Las Vegas	Warren, Ohio	Warren, Ohio	FA
Tinsley, Scott	QB	6-1	195	11/14/59	Southern California	Oklahoma City, Okla.	Oklahoma City, Okla.	FA
Triplett, Danny	LB	6-4	225	3/15/60	Clemson	Boone, N.C.	Clemson, N.C.	D11
Ward, Terrell	CB	5-9	190	11/17/57	San Diego State	San Francisco, Calif.	San Francisco, Calif.	FA
West, Troy	S	5-10	205	8/26/61	Southern California	Los Angeles, Calif.	Los Angeles, Calif.	D8
Wilcher, Mike	LB	6-3	235	3/20/60	North Carolina	Washington, D.C.	Washington, D.C.	D2a
Williams, Henry	WR	6-0	170	5/16/58	Long Beach State	Blythe, Calif.	Long Beach, Calif.	FA

Players who report to an NFL team for the first time are designated on rosters as rookies (R). If a player reported to an NFL training camp in a previous year but was not on the active squad for three or more regular season or postseason games, he is listed on the first-year roster and designated by a (1). Thereafter, a player who is on the active squad for three or more regular season or postseason games is credited with an additional year of playing experience.

NOTES

_____
_____
_____
_____
_____
_____
_____
_____
_____
_____
_____
_____
_____
_____
_____
_____
_____

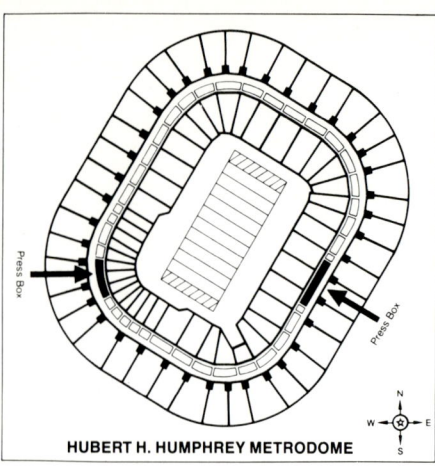

HUBERT H. HUMPHREY METRODOME

Minnesota Vikings

National Football Conference
Central Division

Team Colors: Purple, Gold, and White

9520 Viking Drive
Eden Prairie, Minnesota 55344
Telephone: 612-828-6500

Club Officials
President: Max Winter
Vice President-General Manager: Mike Lynn
Director of Administration: Harley Peterson
Director of Operations: Jeff Diamond
Ticket Manager: Harry Randolph
Director of Football Operations: Jerry Reichow
Director of Player Personnel: Frank Gilliam
Head Scout: Ralph Kohl
Assistant Head Scout: Don Deisch
Scout: John Carson
Director of Public Relations: Merrill Swanson
Assistant Public Relations Director: Kernal Buhler
Public Relations Assistant: Katie Hogan
Trainer: Fred Zamberletti
Equipment Manager: Dennis Ryan

Stadium: Hubert H. Humphrey Metrodome
• **Capacity:** 62,212
500 11th Avenue, So.,
Minneapolis, Minn. 55415

Playing Surface: SuperTurf

Training Camp: Mankato State University
Mankato, Minnesota 56001

1983 SCHEDULE
Preseason

Aug. 6	vs. St. Louis at London, England	TBA
Aug. 13	**Baltimore**	7:30
Aug. 19	at Seattle	7:30
Aug. 26	**Denver**	7:30

Regular Season

Sept. 4	at Cleveland	1:00
Sept. 8	**San Francisco** (Thursday)	7:30
Sept. 18	at Tampa Bay	4:00
Sept. 25	**Detroit**	12:00
Oct. 2	**Dallas**	12:00
Oct. 9	at Chicago	12:00
Oct. 16	**Houston**	12:00
Oct. 23	at Green Bay	12:00
Oct. 30	at St. Louis	12:00
Nov. 6	**Tampa Bay**	12:00
Nov. 13	**Green Bay**	12:00
Nov. 20	at Pittsburgh	1:00
Nov. 27	at New Orleans	12:00
Dec. 5	at Detroit (Monday)	9:00
Dec. 11	**Chicago**	12:00
Dec. 17	**Cincinnati** (Saturday)	3:00

1982 TEAM STATISTICS

	Minnesota	Opp.
Total First Downs..................	167	159
Rushing........................	52	53
Passing........................	107	87
Penalty........................	8	19
Third Down Efficiency..........	43/132	43/127
Third Down Percentage..........	32.6	33.9
Total Net Yards..................	2879	2895
Total Offensive Plays	601	582
Avg. Gain per Play.............	4.8	5.0
Avg. Gain per Game.............	319.9	321.7
Net Yards Rushing..............	912	1020
Total Rushing Plays	245	260
Avg. Gain per Rush.............	3.7	3.9
Avg. Gain Rushing per Game	101.3	113.3
Net Yards Passing..............	1967	1875
Lost Attempting to Pass........	22/138	30/231
Gross Yards Passing............	2105	2106
Attempts/Completions..........	334/187	292/157
Percent Completed.............	56.0	53.8
Had Intercepted...............	12	12
Avg. Net Passing per Game	218.6	208.3
Punts/Avg......................	58/41.1	50/41.9
Punt Returns/Avg..............	24/8.2	30/5.9
Kickoff Returns/Avg............	37/21.2	38/17.4
Interceptions/Avg. Ret.	12/7.6	12/28.1
Penalties/Yards...............	62/496	48/399
Fumbles/Ball Lost.............	12/5	22/9
Total Points..................	187	198
Avg. Points per Game..........	20.8	22.0
Touchdowns...................	23	24
Rushing......................	6	8
Passing......................	15	11
Returns and Recoveries	2	5
Field Goals..................	8/14	11/19
Conversions..................	23/23	21/24
Safeties.....................	1	0
Avg. Time of Possession	30:51	29:09

1982 TEAM RECORD

Preseason (3-2)

Minnesota		Opponents
30	Baltimore	14
17	Atlanta	20
7	*Seattle	3
17	Denver	27
24	*New Orleans	21
95		85

Regular Season (5-4)

Minnesota		Opponents	Att.
17	*Tampa Bay	10	58,440
22	Buffalo	23	77,733
7	Green Bay (Mil.)	26	44,681
35	*Chicago	7	54,724
14	Miami	22	45,721
13	*Baltimore	10	53,981
34	Detroit	31	73,058
14	*New York Jets	42	58,672
31	*Dallas	27	60,007
187		198	527,017

*Home Game

Score by Periods

Minnesota	16	86	27	58	—	187
Opponents	26	54	42	76	—	198

Attendance

Home 285,824   Away 241,193   Total 527,017

Single game home record, 60,740 (10-5-69; U. of Minnesota), 49,784 (4 times, 1972; Metropolitan Stadium), 60,007 (1-3-83; Metrodome)
Single season home record, 367,299 (1980)

1982 INDIVIDUAL STATISTICS

Rushing

	Att	Yds	Avg	LG	TD
Brown	120	515	4.3	30	1
Nelson	44	136	3.1	18	0
Galbreath	39	116	3.0	12	1
Kramer	21	77	3.7	18t	3
Young	16	49	3.1	11	1
Coleman	1	15	15.0	15	0
Dils	1	5	5.0	5	0
Redwine	2	2	1.0	2	0
LeCount	1	−3	−3.0	−3	0
Minnesota	245	912	3.7	30	6
Opponents	260	1020	3.9	99t	8

Field Goal Success

Distance	1-19	20-29	30-39	40-49	50 Over
Made-Att.	0-0	4-5	1-2	3-6	0-1

Passing

	Att	Comp	Pct	Yds	TD	Int	Tkld	Rate
Kramer	308	176	57.1	2037	15	12	21/130	77.3
Dils	26	11	42.3	68	0	0	1/8	49.8
Minnesota	334	187	56.0	2105	15	12	22/138	
Opponents	292	157	53.8	2106	11	12	30/231	

Receiving

	No	Yds	Avg	LG	TD
Brown	31	207	6.7	29	2
S. White	29	503	17.3	65	5
Senser	29	261	9.0	22	1
Rashad	23	233	10.1	21	0
Galbreath	17	153	9.0	32	0
LeCount	14	179	12.8	28	1
McCullum	12	131	10.9	21	0
Nelson	9	100	11.1	22	0
Lewis	8	150	18.8	39t	3
Bruer	8	102	12.8	24	2
Young	4	44	11.0	25	1
Jordan	3	42	14.0	29	0
Minnesota	187	2105	11.3	65	15
Opponents	157	2106	13.4	70t	11

Interceptions

	No	Yds	Avg	LG	TD
Teal	4	15	3.8	13	0
Turner	2	43	21.5	33t	1
Swain	2	20	10.0	16	0
Holloway	1	6	6.0	6	0
Knoff	1	4	4.0	4	0
Studwell	1	3	3.0	3	0
Martin	1	0	0.0	0	0
Minnesota	12	91	7.6	33t	1
Opponents	12	337	28.1	94t	3

Punting

	No	Yds	Avg	In 20	LG
Coleman	58	2384	41.1	7	67
Minnesota	58	2384	41.1	7	67
Opponents	50	2095	41.9	12	59

Punt Returns

	No	FC	Yds	Avg	LG	TD
Payton	22	5	179	8.1	35	0
Bess	2	0	17	8.5	11	0
Hannon	0	1	0	—	0	0
Minnesota	24	6	196	8.2	35	0
Opponents	30	6	176	5.9	26	0

Kickoff Returns

	No	Yds	Avg	LG	TD
Redwine	12	286	23.8	76	0
Payton	12	271	22.6	32	0
Nelson	6	132	22.0	33	0
Nord	3	43	14.3	19	0
Harrell	2	21	10.5	17	0
McDole	1	26	26.0	26	0
Elshire	1	7	7.0	7	0
Minnesota	37	786	21.2	76	0
Opponents	38	663	17.4	30	0

Scoring

	TD	TD R	TD P	TD Rt	PAT	FG	TP
Danmeier					23/23	8/14	47
S. White	5	0	5	0			30
Brown	3	1	2	0			18
Kramer	3	3	0	0			18
Lewis	3	0	3	0			18
Bruer	2	0	2	0			12
Young	2	1	1	0			12
Galbreath	1	1	0	0			6
C. Johnson	1	0	0	1			6
LeCount	1	0	1	0			6
Senser	1	0	1	0			6
Turner	1	0	0	1			6
Team	(Safety)						2
Minnesota	23	6	15	2	23/23	8/14	187
Opponents	24	8	11	5	21/24	11/19	198

Sacks

Bess ½, Blair 1½, Elshire 1, Holloway 2½, C. Johnson 1, Knoff 1, Martin 11½, Mullaney 5, Studwell 3, J. White 3.

FIRST PLAYERS SELECTED

Year	Player, College, Position
1961	Tommy Mason, Tulane, RB
1962	Bill Miller, Miami, WR (3)
1963	Jim Dunaway, Mississippi, T
1964	Carl Eller, Minnesota, DE
1965	Jack Snow, Notre Dame, WR
1966	Jerry Shay, Purdue, DT
1967	Clinton Jones, Michigan State, RB
1968	Ron Yary, Southern California, T
1969	Ed White, California, G (2)
1970	John Ward, Oklahoma State, DT
1971	Leo Hayden, Ohio State, RB
1972	Jeff Siemon, Stanford, LB
1973	Chuck Foreman, Miami, RB
1974	Fred McNeill, UCLA, LB
1975	Mark Mullaney, Colorado State, DE
1976	James White, Oklahoma State, DT
1977	Tommy Kramer, Rice, QB
1978	Randy Holloway, Pittsburgh, DE
1979	Ted Brown, North Carolina State, RB
1980	Doug Martin, Washington, DT
1981	Mardye McDole, Mississippi State, WR (2)
1982	Darrin Nelson, Stanford, RB
1983	Joey Browner, Southern California, DB

VIKINGS COACHING HISTORY
(182-142-9)

1961-66	Norm Van Brocklin	29-51-4
1967-82	Bud Grant	153-91-5

121

MINNESOTA VIKINGS 1983 VETERAN ROSTER

No.	Name	Pos.	Ht.	Wt.	Birth-date	NFL Exp.	College	Birthplace	Residence	Games in '82
21	Bess, Rufus	CB	5-9	185	9/13/56	5	South Carolina State	Hartsville, S.C.	Hartsville, S.C.	8
59	Blair, Matt	LB	6-5	234	9/20/50	10	Iowa State	Honolulu, Ha.	Prior Lake, Minn.	9
62	†Boyd, Brent	G	6-3	260	3/23/57	4	UCLA	La Habra, Calif.	San Diego, Calif.	4
23	Brown, Ted	RB	5-10	210	2/2/57	5	North Carolina State	High Point, N.C.	High Point, N.C.	8
82	†Bruer, Bob	TE	6-5	235	5/22/54	5	Mankato State	Madison, Wis.	Edina, Minn.	8
8	Coleman, Greg	P	6-0	185	9/9/54	7	Florida A&M	Jacksonville, Fla.	Burnsville, Minn.	9
7	Danmeier, Rick	K	6-0	200	4/8/52	6	Sioux Falls	White Bear Lake, Minn.	Burnsville, Minn.	9
12	Dils, Steve	QB	6-1	190	12/8/55	4	Stanford	Vancouver, Wash.	Richfield, Minn.	9
73	Elshire, Neil	DE	6-6	260	3/8/58	3	Oregon	Albany, Ore.	Lake Oswego, Ore.	5
32	Galbreath, Tony	RB	6-0	228	1/29/54	8	Missouri	Fulton, Mo.	Fulton, Mo.	8
61	†Hamilton, Wes	G	6-3	268	4/24/53	8	Tulsa	Texas City, Tex.	Burnsville, Minn.	9
45	Hannon, Tom	S	5-11	190	3/5/55	7	Michigan State	Massillon, Ohio	Reynoldsburg, Ohio	9
36	Harrell, Sam	RB	6-2	225	2/7/57	3	East Carolina	Harrellsville, N.C.	Burnsville, Minn.	1
75	Holloway, Randy	DE	6-5	250	8/26/55	6	Pittsburgh	Sharon, Pa.	Sharon, Pa.	9
51	Hough, Jim	G	6-2	267	8/4/56	6	Utah State	Lynwood, Calif.	Jordan, Minn.	9
24	Howard, Bryan	S	6-0	200	3/6/59	2	Tennessee State	New Orleans, La.	New Orleans, La.	2
56	Huffman, David	C-G	6-6	255	4/4/57	5	Notre Dame	Canton, Ohio	St. Louis Park, Minn.	9
76	Irwin, Tim	T	6-6	275	12/13/58	3	Tennessee	Memphis, Tenn.	Knoxville, Tenn.	9
65	Johnson, Charlie	NT	6-3	265	2/17/52	7	Colorado	West Columbia, Tex.	West Berlin, N.J.	9
52	Johnson, Dennis	LB	6-3	230	6/19/58	4	Southern California	Flint, Mich.	Los Angeles, Calif.	9
53	Johnson, Henry	LB	6-2	235	3/20/58	4	Georgia Tech	Wrens, Ga.	Wrens, Ga.	9
83	Jordan, Steve	TE	6-3	230	1/10/61	2	Brown	Phoenix, Ariz.	Phoenix, Ariz.	9
25	Knoff, Kurt	S	6-2	190	4/6/54	7	Kansas	East Grand Forks, Minn.	Bloomington, Minn.	9
9	Kramer, Tommy	QB	6-2	200	3/7/55	7	Rice	San Antonio, Tex.	Edina, Minn.	9
80	LeCount, Terry	WR	5-10	180	7/9/56	6	Florida	Jacksonville, Fla.	Burnsville, Minn.	9
87	Lewis, Leo	WR	5-8	170	9/17/56	3	Missouri	Columbia, Mo.	Knoxville, Tenn.	9
79	Martin, Doug	DE	6-3	255	5/22/57	4	Washington	Fairfield, Calif.	Bellevue, Wash.	9
84	McCullum, Sam	WR	6-2	190	11/30/52	10	Montana State	McComb, Miss.	Mercer Island, Wash.	6
88	McDole, Mardye	WR	5-11	195	5/1/59	2	Mississippi State	Pensacola, Fla.	Mobile, Ala.	2
54	McNeill, Fred	LB	6-2	230	5/6/52	10	UCLA	Durham, Calif.	Edina, Minn.	9
77	Mullaney, Mark	DE	6-6	245	4/30/53	9	Colorado State	Denver, Colo.	Denver, Colo.	9
20	Nelson, Darrin	RB	5-9	180	1/2/59	2	Stanford	Sacramento, Calif.	Los Angeles, Calif.	7
49	Nord, Keith	S	6-0	195	3/3/57	5	St. Cloud State	Minneapolis, Minn.	Minnetonka, Minn.	9
22	Redwine, Jarvis	RB	5-10	205	5/16/57	3	Nebraska	Los Angeles, Calif.	Inglewood, Calif.	7
78	Riley, Steve	T	6-6	255	11/23/52	10	Southern California	Chula Vista, Calif.	Tustin, Calif.	9
68	Rouse, Curtis	G	6-3	290	7/13/60	2	Tennessee-Chattanooga	Augusta, Ga.	Chattanooga, Tenn.	5
57	Sendlein, Robin	LB	6-3	225	12/1/58	3	Texas	Las Vegas, Nev.	Austin, Tex.	9
81	Senser, Joe	TE	6-4	235	8/18/56	4	West Chester State	Philadelphia, Pa.	Minnetonka, Minn.	9
50	†Siemon, Jeff	LB	6-3	235	6/2/50	12	Stanford	Rochester, Minn.	Edina, Minn.	9
55	Studwell, Scott	LB	6-2	225	8/27/54	7	Illinois	Evansville, Ind.	Lakeville, Minn.	8
29	Swain, John	CB	6-1	195	9/4/59	3	Miami	Miami, Fla.	Miami, Fla.	9
67	†Swilley, Dennis	C	6-3	241	6/28/55	7	Texas A&M	Bossier City, La.	Denton, Tex.	9
66	Tausch, Terry	T	6-5	275	2/5/59	2	Texas	New Braunfels, Tex.	Dallas, Tex.	2
37	Teal, Willie	CB	5-10	195	12/20/57	4	Louisiana State	Texarkana, Tex.	Baton Rouge, La.	9
27	Turner, John	CB	6-0	199	2/22/56	6	Miami	Miami, Fla.	Edina, Minn.	9
72	White, James	NT	6-3	270	10/26/53	8	Oklahoma State	Hot Springs, Ark.	Plymouth, Minn.	9
85	White, Sammy	WR	5-11	190	3/16/54	8	Grambling	Winnsboro, La.	Monroe, La.	7
11	Wilson, Wade	QB	6-3	210	2/1/59	3	East Texas State	Greenville, Tex.	Commerce, Tex.	0*
91	Yakavonis, Ray	NT	6-4	250	1/20/57	3	East Stroudsburg State	Wilkes-Barre, Pa.	Wilkes-Barre, Pa.	2
34	†Young, Rickey	RB	6-2	200	12/7/53	9	Jackson State	Mobile, Ala.	Eden Prairie, Minn.	9

* W. Wilson active for 4 games with Minnesota in '82, but did not play.

†Option playout; subject to developments.

Retired—Eddie Payton, 7-year kick returner, 9 games in '82; Ahmad Rashad, 11-year wide receiver, 7 in '82.

Also played with Vikings in '82—WR Harold Jackson (1 game), CB Walt Williams (1).

COACHING STAFF

Head Coach, Bud Grant

Pro Career: Has guided Minnesota to 11 NFC Central titles in last 15 years (1968-71, 1973-78, 1980) and postseason play 12 of 16 seasons as head coach, including NFL champions in 1969 and NFC champions in 1973, 1974, and 1976. Head coach at Winnipeg of the Canadian Football League for 10 years before joining the Vikings in 1967. Grant's Winnipeg teams won six Western Conference championships and four Grey Cup championships. Played for the Philadelphia Eagles 1951-52 and ranked as the number-two receiver in NFL in 1952. Played 1953-56 with Winnipeg before being named head coach in 1957. NFL record: 153-91-5.

Background: Attended University of Minnesota and was two-time All-Big Ten end. Won four letters in football, two in basketball (forward), and three in baseball (pitcher-outfielder). Played football and basketball at Great Lakes in 1945, first year out of high school. Played 1950-51 with Minneapolis Lakers of the National Basketball Association. Canadian coach of the year in 1965; named Minnesota athlete of the half-century in 1951.

Personal: Born Harry P. Grant on May 20, 1927, Superior, Wis. Bud and his wife, Pat, live in Bloomington, Minn., and have six children—Kathleen, Laurie, Peter, Michael, Bruce, and Dan.

ASSISTANT COACHES

Jerry Burns, offense; born January 24, 1927, Detroit, lives in Eden Prairie, Minn. Quarterback Michigan 1947-50. No pro playing experience. College coach: Hawaii 1951, Whittier 1952, Iowa 1954-65 (head coach 1961-65). Pro coach: Green Bay Packers 1966-67, Vikings since 1968.

Tom Cecchini, defensive line; born September 12, 1944, Detroit, lives in Bloomington, Minn. Linebacker-center Michigan 1963-65. No pro playing experience. College coach: Michigan 1968-69, Xavier 1970-73 (head coach 1972-73), Iowa 1974-75, 1978-79, Tulane 1976-77. Pro coach: Joined Vikings in 1980.

Bob Hollway, defense; born January 29, 1926, Ann Arbor, Mich., lives in Edina, Minn. End Michigan 1947-49. No pro playing experience. College coach: Maine 1951-52, Eastern Michigan 1953, Michigan 1954-66. Pro coach: Minnesota Vikings 1967-70, St. Louis Cardinals 1971-72 (head coach), Detroit Lions 1973-74, San Francisco 49ers 1975, Seattle Seahawks 1976-77, rejoined Vikings in 1978.

Jed Hughes, defensive backs; born November 14, 1947, New York, N.Y. Tight end Gettysburg 1968-70. No pro playing experience. College coach: Stanford 1971-72, Michigan 1973-75, UCLA 1976-81. Pro coach: Joined Vikings in 1982.

Bus Mertes, offensive backs; born October 6, 1923, Chicago, lives in Edina, Minn. Running back Iowa 1939-41. Pro running back Chicago Cardinals 1945, Los Angeles Dons (AAFC) 1946, Baltimore Colts (AAFC) 1947-48, New York Giants 1949-50. College coach: Bradley 1951-52, Kansas State 1953-59, Drake 1960-64. Pro coach: Denver Broncos 1965-66, Vikings since 1967.

John Michels, offensive line; born February 15, 1931, Philadelphia, lives in Bloomington, Minn. Guard Tennessee 1949-52. Pro guard Philadelphia Eagles 1953, 1956, Winnipeg Blue Bombers (CFL) 1957. College coach: Texas A&M 1958. Pro coach: Winnipeg Blue Bombers (CFL) 1959-66, Vikings since 1967.

Floyd Reese, linebackers; born August 8, 1948, Springfield, Mo., lives in Bloomington, Minn. Defensive tackle UCLA 1967-69. No pro playing experience. College coach: UCLA 1970-73, Georgia Tech 1974. Pro coach: Detroit Lions 1975-77, San Francisco 49ers 1978, Vikings since 1979.

Les Steckel, receivers; born July 1, 1946, Whitehall, Pa., lives in Bloomington, Minn. Running back Kansas 1964-67. No pro playing experience. College coach: Colorado 1972-76, Navy 1977. Pro coach: San Francisco 49ers 1978, Vikings since 1979.

MINNESOTA VIKINGS 1983 FIRST-YEAR ROSTER

Name	Pos.	Ht.	Wt.	Birth-date	College	Birthplace	Residence	How Acq.
Achter, Rod	WR	6-1	197	2/14/61	Toledo	Oregon, Ohio	Oregon, Ohio	D9
Ashley, Walker Lee	LB	6-0	234	7/28/60	Penn State	Bayonne, N.J.	Jersey City, N.J.	D3
Brown, Melvin	CB-S	5-11	197	10/25/58	Mississippi	Biloxi, Miss.	University, Miss.	D10
Brown, Norris	TE	6-3	220	7/10/61	Georgia	Laurens, S.C.	Athens, Ga.	D8
Browner, Joey	CB-S	6-2	202	5/15/60	Southern California	Warren, Ohio	Culver City, Calif.	D1
Butcher, Brian	G	6-4	246	9/28/60	Clemson	Knoxville, Tenn.	Clemson, S.C.	D11
Giles, Gene	WR	6-1	180	3/16/59	Minnesota-Duluth	Suffern, N.Y.	Duluth, Minn.	FA
Howard, Mike	WR	6-2	193	2/21/57	Moorhead State	Portsmouth, Va.	Portsmouth, Va.	FA
Jones, Mike	WR	5-11	175	4/14/60	Tennessee State	Chattanooga, Tenn.	Chattanooga, Tenn.	D6
Lee, Carl	CB-S	5-11	176	4/6/61	Marshall	S. Charleston, W. Va.	Huntington, W. Va.	D7
Parmelee, Perry (1)	WR	6-3	190	5/30/60	Santa Clara	Bloomington, Minn.	Menlo Park, Calif.	FA
Patterson, Lamont	WR	5-11	188	6/25/61	Cincinnati	Pittsburgh, Pa.	Cincinnati, Ohio	FA
Stephanos, Bill (1)	T	6-4	262	3/24/57	Boston College	Lynn, Mass.	Lynn, Mass.	D11('81)
Stewart, Mark	LB	6-2	230	10/13/59	Washington	Palo Alto, Calif.	Seattle, Wash.	D5
Storr, Greg	LB	6-2	224	10/16/60	Boston College	Reading, Pa.	Sinking Springs, Pa.	D6
Tate, Walter	C	6-3	244	9/29/60	Tennessee State	Memphis, Tenn.	Memphis, Tenn.	D10a
Turner, Maurice	RB	5-11	203	9/10/60	Utah State	Salt Lake City, Utah	Logan, Utah	D12
Wagner, Vince	K	5-11	175	7/16/59	Northwestern, Minn.	Boseman, Mont.	St. Paul, Minn.	FA
Williams, Elex	CB	5-11	184	8/29/59	Nevada-Las Vegas	Oceanside, Calif.	Oceanside, Calif.	FA

Players who report to an NFL team for the first time are designated on rosters as rookies (R). If a player reported to an NFL training camp in a previous year but was not on the active squad for three or more regular season or postseason games, he is listed on the first-year roster and designated by a (1). Thereafter, a player who is on the active squad for three or more regular season or postseason games is credited with an additional year of playing experience.

NOTES

_____
_____
_____
_____
_____
_____
_____
_____
_____
_____
_____
_____
_____
_____
_____
_____
_____
_____
_____
_____
_____
_____
_____
_____

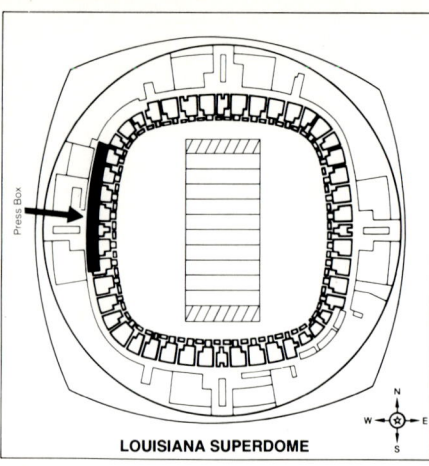

LOUISIANA SUPERDOME

New Orleans Saints

**National Football Conference
Western Division**

Team Colors: Old Gold, Black, and White

944 St. Charles Avenue
New Orleans, Louisiana 70130
Telephone: (504) 525-0792

Club Officials
Owner: John W. Mecom, Jr.
President: Eddie Jones
Vice President-Administration: Fred Williams
Director of Football Operations: Pat Peppler
Head Coach-General Manager: O. A. (Bum) Phillips
Business Manager-Controller: Bob Landry
Director of Public Relations: Greg Suit
Assistant Director of Public Relations:
    Rusty Kasmiersky
Public Relations Assistant: Sylvia Alfortish
Ticket Manager: Bruce Broussard
Marketing Director: Barra Birrcher
Administrative Assistant: Jack Cherry
Trainer: Dean Kleinschmidt
Equipment Manager: Dan Simmons

Stadium: Louisiana Superdome • **Capacity:** 71,330
        1500 Poydras Street
        New Orleans, Louisiana 70112

Playing Surface: AstroTurf

Training Camp: Dodgertown
        Vero Beach, Florida 32960

1983 SCHEDULE

Preseason
July 30	vs. Pittsburgh at Canton, Ohio (HOF)	2:00
Aug. 6	at Tampa Bay	8:00
Aug. 13	at Miami	8:00
Aug. 20	**Houston**	7:00
Aug. 27	**New York Jets**	7:00

Regular Season
Sept. 4	**St. Louis**	12:00
Sept. 11	at Los Angeles Rams	1:00
Sept. 18	**Chicago**	12:00
Sept. 25	at Dallas	12:00
Oct. 2	**Miami**	3:00
Oct. 9	at Atlanta	1:00
Oct. 16	**San Francisco**	12:00
Oct. 23	at Tampa Bay	4:00
Oct. 30	at Buffalo	1:00
Nov. 6	**Atlanta**	12:00
Nov. 13	at San Francisco	1:00
Nov. 21	**New York Jets** (Monday)	8:00
Nov. 27	**Minnesota**	12:00
Dec. 4	at New England	1:00
Dec. 11	at Philadelphia	1:00
Dec. 18	**Los Angeles Rams**	12:00

1982 TEAM STATISTICS

	New Orleans	Opp.
Total First Downs..................	173	151
Rushing.......................	79	58
Passing.......................	76	81
Penalty......................	18	12
Third Down Efficiency...........	48/128	36/103
Third Down Percentage.........	37.5	35.0
Total Net Yards.................	2655	2607
Total Offensive Plays	602	531
Avg. Gain per Play..............	4.4	4.9
Avg. Gain per Game	295.0	289.7
Net Yards Rushing..............	1257	974
Total Rushing Plays	331	255
Avg. Gain per Rush.............	3.8	3.8
Avg. Gain Rushing per Game	139.7	108.2
Net Yards Passing..............	1398	1633
Lost Attempting to Pass.........	23/173	31/231
Gross Yards Passing	1571	1864
Attempts/Completions..........	248/137	245/149
Percent Completed.............	55.2	60.8
Had Intercepted...............	14	9
Avg. Net Passing per Game	155.3	181.4
Punts/Avg......................	46/43.0	51/41.1
Punt Returns/Avg...............	21/6.9	29/8.2
Kickoff Returns/Avg............	26/22.2	20/19.4
Interceptions/Avg. Ret.........	9/12.0	14/5.6
Penalties/Yards...............	63/514	52/459
Fumbles/Ball Lost.............	17/10	23/13
Total Points..................	129	160
Avg. Points per Game...........	14.3	17.8
Touchdowns....................	16	19
Rushing.....................	8	8
Passing.....................	8	11
Returns and Recoveries	0	0
Field Goals..................	6/13	9/12
Conversions..................	15/16	19/19
Safeties.....................	0	0
Avg. Time of Possession	32:06	27:54

1982 TEAM RECORD

Preseason (1-3)

New Orleans		Opponents
20	Houston	22
6	*Kansas City	3
17	*Cleveland	20
21	Minnesota	24
64		69

Regular Season (4-5)

New Orleans		Opponents	Att.
7	*St. Louis	21	58,673
10	Chicago	0	56,600
27	*Kansas City	17	39,341
23	San Francisco	20	51,611
10	*Tampa Bay	13	61,709
0	Atlanta	35	39,535
7	Dallas	21	64,506
10	*Washington	27	48,667
35	*Atlanta	6	47,336
129		160	467,978

*Home Game

Score by Periods

New Orleans	31	27	26	45	—	129
Opponents	14	64	34	48	—	160

Attendance

Home 255,726   Away 212,252   Total 467,978
Single game home record, 84,728 (11-3-68, Tulane Stadium), 70,940 (11-4-79, Louisiana Superdome)
Single season home record, 440,708 (1981)

1982 INDIVIDUAL STATISTICS

Rushing

	Att	Yds	Avg	LG	TD
G. Rogers	122	535	4.4	38	3
Wilson	103	413	4.0	20	3
J. Rogers	60	178	3.0	32	2
Gajan	19	77	4.1	12	0
Merkens	9	30	3.3	19	0
Tyler	10	21	2.1	11	0
Holmes	2	8	4.0	5	0
Thompson	1	2	2.0	2	0
Groth	1	1	1.0	1	0
L. Scott	1	−4	−4.0	−4	0
Stabler	3	−4	−1.3	0	0
New Orleans	331	1257	3.8	38	8
Opponents	255	974	3.8	40	8

Field Goal Success

Distance	1-19	20-29	30-39	40-49	50 Over
Made-Att.	1-1	1-3	1-2	3-6	0-1

Passing

	Att	Comp	Pct	Yds	TD	Int	Tkld	Rate
Stabler	189	117	61.9	1343	6	10	13/106	71.9
Merkens	49	18	36.7	186	1	2	8/49	38.1
Manning	7	1	14.3	3	0	2	2/18	—
Erxleben	2	1	50.0	39	1	0	0/0	—
Holmes	1	0	0.0	0	0	0	0/0	—
N. Orleans	248	137	55.2	1571	8	14	23/173	
Opponents	245	149	60.8	1864	11	9	31/231	

Receiving

	No	Yds	Avg	LG	TD
Groth	30	383	12.8	39	1
Wilson	25	175	7.0	34	2
L. Scott	17	251	14.8	36	0
Brenner	16	171	10.7	25	0
Duckett	12	196	16.3	31	2
Thompson	8	138	17.3	48	1
Hardy	8	67	8.4	31	1
Mauti	4	70	17.5	37	0
Tyler	4	31	7.8	12	0
G. Rogers	4	21	5.3	10	0
J. Rogers	4	17	4.3	6	0
Gajan	3	10	3.3	9	0
Hurley	1	39	39.0	39t	1
Holmes	1	2	2.0	2	0
New Orleans	137	1571	11.5	48	8
Opponents	149	1864	12.5	58t	11

Interceptions

	No	Yds	Avg	LG	TD
Gary	2	25	12.5	19	0
Winston	2	−2	−1.0	0	0
Jackson	1	32	32.0	32	0
Hurley	1	26	26.0	26	0
Paul	1	14	14.0	14	0
Ro. Lewis	1	12	12.0	12	0
Nairne	1	1	1.0	1	0
New Orleans	9	108	12.0	32	0
Opponents	14	79	5.6	35	0

Punting

	No	Yds	Avg	In 20	LG
Erxleben	46	1976	43.0	6	60
New Orleans	46	1976	43.0	6	60
Opponents	51	2094	41.1	11	59

Punt Returns

	No	FC	Yds	Avg	LG	TD
Groth	21	13	144	6.9	18	0
New Orleans	21	13	144	6.9	18	0
Opponents	29	4	239	8.2	19	0

Kickoff Returns

	No	Yds	Avg	LG	TD
Thompson	10	211	21.1	35	0
Wilson	7	192	27.4	75	0
Mauti	5	93	18.6	22	0
Duckett	2	39	19.5	25	0
J. Rogers	1	24	24.0	24	0
Gajan	1	18	18.0	18	0
New Orleans	26	577	22.2	75	0
Opponents	20	388	19.4	30	0

Scoring

	TD	TD R	TD P	TD Rt	PAT	FG	TP
Wilson	5	3	2	0			30
Fritsch					8/9	4/7	20
G. Rogers	3	3	0	0			18
Anderson					6/6	2/5	12
Duckett	2	0	2	0			12
J. Rogers	2	2	0	0			12
Groth	1	0	1	0			6
Hardy	1	0	1	0			6
Hurley	1	0	1	0			6
Thompson	1	0	1	0			6
Erxleben					1/1	0/1	1
New Orleans	16	8	8	0	15/16	6/13	129
Opponents	19	8	11	0	19/19	9/12	160

Sacks

Bordelon 1, B. Clark 5½, Gary 3, Jackson 4½, Kovach 2½, Re. Lewis 3, Moore 4, Nairne 1, Paul 3, Warren 1, Wilks 2, Winston ½.

FIRST PLAYERS SELECTED

Year	Player, College, Position
1967	Les Kelley, Alabama, RB
1968	Kevin Hardy, Notre Dame, DE
1969	John Shinners, Xavier, G
1970	Ken Burrough, Texas Southern, WR
1971	Archie Manning, Mississippi, QB
1972	Royce Smith, Georgia, G
1973	Derland Moore, Oklahoma, DE (2)
1974	Rick Middleton, Ohio State, LB
1975	Larry Burton, Purdue, WR
1976	Chuck Muncie, California, RB
1977	Joe Campbell, Maryland, DE
1978	Wes Chandler, Florida, WR
1979	Russell Erxleben, Texas, P-K
1980	Stan Brock, Colorado, T
1981	George Rogers, South Carolina, RB
1982	Lindsay Scott, Georgia, WR
1983	Steve Korte, Arkansas, G (2)

SAINTS COACHING HISTORY

(63-159-5)

1967-70	Tom Fears*	13-34-2
1970-72	J. D. Roberts	7-25-3
1973-75	John North**	11-23-0
1975	Ernie Hefferle	1-7-0
1976-77	Hank Stram	7-21-0
1978-80	Dick Nolan***	15-29-0
1980	Dick Stanfel	1-3-0
1981-82	O. A. (Bum) Phillips	8-17-0

*Released after seven games in 1970
**Released after six games in 1975
***Released after 12 games in 1980

NEW ORLEANS SAINTS 1983 VETERAN ROSTER

No.	Name	Pos.	Ht.	Wt.	Birth-date	NFL Exp.	College	Birthplace	Residence	Games in '82
7	Andersen, Morten	K	6-2	190	8/19/60	2	Michigan State	Struer, Denmark	Holt, Mich.	8
85	†Brenner, Hoby	TE	6-4	240	6/2/59	3	Southern California	Lynwood, Calif.	San Clemente, Calif.	8
50	†Bordelon, Ken	LB	6-4	226	8/26/54	7	Louisiana State	New Orleans, La.	Kenner, La.	9
67	Brock, Stan	T	6-6	285	6/8/58	4	Colorado	Portland, Ore.	Mandeville, La.	9
75	Clark, Bruce	DE	6-3	250	3/31/58	2	Penn State	New Castle, Pa.	Kenner, La.	9
78	†Clark, Kelvin	G	6-3	265	1/30/56	5	Nebraska	Odessa, Tex.	Kenner, La.	9
83	Duckett, Kenny	WR	6-0	187	10/1/59	2	Wake Forest	Winston-Salem, N.C.	Winston-Salem, N.C.	7
63	Edelman, Brad	G	6-6	255	9/3/60	2	Missouri	Jacksonville, Fla.	Kenner, La.	9
99	Elliott, Tony	NT	6-2	247	4/23/59	2	North Texas State	New York, N.Y.	Metairie, La.	9
14	Erxleben, Russell	P	6-4	219	1/13/57	4	Texas	Seguin, Tex.	Kenner, La.	9
46	†Gajan, Hokie	RB	5-11	211	9/6/59	2	Louisiana State	Baton Rouge, La.	Covington, La.	9
20	†Gary, Russell	S	5-11	195	7/31/59	3	Nebraska	Minneapolis, Minn.	New Orleans, La.	9
33	Gray, Kevin	CB-S	5-11	179	9/11/57	2	Eastern Illinois	Chicago, Ill.	Chicago, Ill.	8
72	Gray, Leon	T	6-3	258	11/15/51	11	Jackson State	Olive Branch, Miss.	Westwood, Mass.	7
86	Groth, Jeff	WR	5-10	172	7/2/57	5	Bowling Green	Mankato, Minn.	Destrehan, La.	9
87	Hardy, Larry	TE	6-3	230	7/9/56	6	Jackson State	Mendenhall, Miss.	Jackson, Miss.	9
62	Hill, John	C	6-2	246	4/16/50	12	Lehigh	East Orange, N.J.	Destrehan, La.	9
45	†Holmes, Jack	RB	6-0	210	6/20/53	6	Texas Southern	Rolling Fork, Miss.	Metairie, La.	5
28	†Hurley, Bill	S	5-11	195	5/16/57	2	Syracuse	Kenmore, N.Y.	Bethel Park, Pa.	9
57	Jackson, Rickey	LB	6-2	230	3/20/58	3	Pittsburgh	Pahokee, Fla.	Metairie, La.	9
52	Kovach, Jim	LB	6-2	225	5/1/56	5	Kentucky	Parma Heights, Ohio	Lexington, Ky.	8
21	Krimm, John	S	6-2	190	5/30/60	2	Notre Dame	Philadelphia, Pa.	Metairie, La.	9
64	Lafary, Dave	T	6-7	275	1/13/55	7	Purdue	Cincinnati, Ohio	Mandeville, La.	9
98	Lewis, Reggie	DE	6-2	248	1/20/54	2	San Diego State	New Orleans, La.	New Orleans, La.	9
29	Lewis, Rodney	CB	5-11	190	4/2/59	2	Nebraska	Minneapolis, Minn.	Lincoln, Neb.	9
84	†Mauti, Rich	WR	6-0	190	5/25/54	6	Penn State	Hollis Place, N.Y.	Mandeville, La.	9
19	Merkens, Guido	QB	6-1	195	8/14/55	6	Sam Houston State	San Antonio, Tex.	Destrehan, La.	9
74	Moore, Derland	NT	6-4	253	10/7/51	11	Oklahoma	Poplar Bluff, Mo.	Covington, La.	9
37	Myers, Tommy	S	6-0	180	10/24/50	11	Syracuse	Cohoes, N.Y.	Kingwood, Tex.	0*
55	†Nairne, Rob	LB	6-4	227	3/24/54	7	Oregon State	Redding, Calif.	Englewood, Colo.	9
66	Oubre, Louis	G	6-4	262	5/15/58	2	Oklahoma	New Orleans, La.	Kenner, La.	9
51	†Paul, Whitney	LB	6-3	220	10/8/55	8	Colorado	Galveston, Tex.	Kansas City, Mo.	9
53	Pelluer, Scott	LB	6-2	215	4/28/59	3	Washington State	Yakima, Wash.	Issaquah, Wash.	6
76	Pietrzak, Jim	C	6-5	260	2/21/53	9	Eastern Michigan	Hamtramck, Mich.	Metairie, La.	9
25	Poe, Johnnie	CB	6-1	185	8/29/59	3	Missouri	St. Louis, Mo.	Kenner, La.	9
58	Redd, Glen	LB	6-1	225	6/17/58	2	Brigham Young	Ogden, Utah	Ogden, Utah	0*
38	Rogers, George	RB	6-2	229	12/8/58	3	South Carolina	Duluth, Ga.	Columbia, S.C.	6
41	Rogers, Jimmy	RB	5-10	190	6/29/55	4	Oklahoma	Earle, Ark.	Kenner, La.	9
80	Scott, Lindsay	WR	6-1	190	12/6/60	2	Georgia	Jesup, Ga.	Kenner, La.	8
54	†Simonini, Ed	LB	6-0	206	2/24/55	8	Texas A&M	Portsmouth, Va.	Owings Mills, Md.	9
79	Slaughter, Chuck	T	6-5	260	11/21/58	3	South Carolina	Conway, S.C.	Kenner, La.	1
16	†Stabler, Ken	QB	6-3	210	12/25/45	14	Alabama	Foley, Ala.	Gulf Shores, Ala.	8
89	Thompson, Aundra	WR	6-1	186	1/2/53	7	East Texas State	Dallas, Tex.	Dallas, Tex.	9
42	†Tyler, Toussaint	RB	6-2	220	3/19/59	3	Washington	Los Angeles, Calif.	San Diego, Calif.	2
73	Warren, Frank	DE	6-4	275	9/14/59	3	Auburn	Birmingham, Ala.	Metairie, La.	9
49	Wattelet, Frank	S	6-0	185	10/25/58	3	Kansas	Paola, Kan.	Joplin, Mo.	9
44	Waymer, Dave	CB	6-1	195	7/1/58	4	Notre Dame	Brooklyn, N.Y.	Los Angeles, Calif.	9
94	Wilks, Jim	DE	6-5	252	3/12/58	3	San Diego State	Los Angeles, Calif.	Altadena, Calif.	8
18	Wilson, Dave	QB	6-3	210	4/27/59	2	Illinois	Anaheim, Calif.	Anaheim, Calif.	0*
30	Wilson, Wayne	RB	6-3	208	9/4/57	5	Shepherd	Montgomery County, Md.	Columbia, Md.	8
56	Winston, Dennis	LB	6-0	228	10/25/55	7	Arkansas	Marianna, Ark.	Fayetteville, Ark.	9

* Myers, Redd, and D. Wilson missed '82 season due to injuries.

†Option playout; subject to developments.

Retired—Toni Fritsch, 11-year kicker, 5 games in '82.

Also played with Saints in '82—TE Don Bass (3 games), G Nat Hudson (4), QB Archie Manning (1), QB Bobby Scott (2).

COACHING STAFF

Head Coach, O.A. (Bum) Phillips

Pro Career: Starts ninth season in the NFL and third with the Saints after signing with New Orleans as head coach on January 22, 1981. He had a career 59-38 record with the Oilers and twice played the AFC bridesmaid role with championship game losses to the Steelers in 1978 and 1979. Joined the Oilers on January 25, 1975 as head coach and general manager after serving as assistant coach with the San Diego Chargers 1967-71 and as defensive coordinator with Oilers in 1974 prior to being named head coach. Career record: 67-55.

Background: Guard at Lamar Junior College 1941, 1946-47, Stephen F. Austin 1948-49. College assistant coach at Texas A&M 1957, Houston 1963-66, Southern Methodist 1971-72, and Oklahoma State 1973. Head coach at Texas-El Paso 1962.

Personal: Born September 29, 1923 in Orange, Tex. Bum and his wife, Helen, live in Destrehan, La., and have six children—Wade, Susan, Cicely, Dee Jean, Andrea, and Kim Ann.

ASSISTANT COACHES

Andy Everest, tight ends; born October 27, 1924, Wichita Falls, Tex., lives in Destrehan, La. Guard Texas-El Paso 1947-50. No pro playing experience. College coach: Foot Hills College 1963-64, U.C.-Santa Barbara 1965-71, Southern Methodist 1972, North Texas State 1973-76. Pro coach: Joined Saints in 1981.

King Hill, offensive coordinator; born November 8, 1936, Freeport, Tex., lives in Ormonv, La. Quarterback Rice, 1954-58. Pro quarterback St. Louis Cardinals 1958-60, 1969, Philadelphia Eagles 1961-67, Minnesota Vikings 1968. Pro coach: Houston Oilers 1972-80, Saints since 1981.

John Levra, offensive backfield; born October 2, 1937, Arkma, Kan., lives in Destrehan, La. Guard-linebacker Pittsburgh (Kan.) State 1963-65. No pro playing experience. College coach: Stephen F. Austin 1971-74, Kansas 1975-78, North Texas State 1979. Pro coach: British Columbia Lions (CFL) 1980, Saints since 1981.

Carl Mauck, offensive line; born July 7, 1947, McLeansboro, Ill., lives in New Orleans. Center Southern Illinois 1965-68. Pro center San Diego Chargers 1969-74, Houston Oilers 1975-80. Pro coach: Joined Saints in 1982.

Lamar McHan, receivers; born December 16, 1932, Lake Village Ark., lives in Metairie, La. Offensive back Arkansas 1951-53. Pro quarterback Chicago Cardinals 1954-58, Green Bay Packers 1959-60, Baltimore Colts 1961-62, San Francisco 49ers 1963. College coach: Northern Arizona 1969-70, Texas-Arlington 1971-73. Pro coach: New Orleans Saints 1974-75, rejoined Saints in 1978.

Russell Paternostro, strength and conditioning; born July 21, 1940, New Orleans, lives in New Orleans. Pro coach: Joined Saints in 1981.

Wade Phillips, defensive coordinator; born June 21, 1947, Orange, Tex., lives in Destrehan, La. Linebacker Houston 1966-69. No pro playing experience. College coach: Oklahoma State 1973-75. Pro coach: Houston Oilers 1976-80, Saints since 1981.

Harold Richardson, special teams; born September 27, 1944, Houston, lives in Destrehan, La. Tight end Southern Methodist 1964-67. No pro playing experience. College coach: Southern Methodist 1971-72, Oklahoma State 1973-76, Texas Christian 1977-78, North Texas State 1979-80. Pro coach: Joined Saints in 1981.

Joe Spencer, quality control; born August 15, 1923, Cleveland County, Okla., lives in Destrehan, La. Tackle Oklahoma State 1942-47. Pro tackle Brooklyn Dodgers (AAFC) 1948, Cleveland Browns 1949, Green Bay Packers 1950-52. College coach: Austin (Tex.) College 1952-60, Kansas 1972-73. Pro coach: Houston Oilers 1961-65, Edmonton Eskimos (CFL) 1966-67, New York Jets 1968-70, St. Louis Cardinals 1971, Chicago Fire (WFL) 1974, Kansas City Chiefs 1975-80, Saints since 1981.

Lance Van Zandt, defensive backfield; born January 19, 1939, Amarillo, Tex., lives in Destrehan, La. Attended Lamar University. College coach: New Mexico Highlands 1966-67, West Texas State 1968-69, Texas A&M 1970-71, Rice 1972, Oklahoma State 1973-74, Nebraska 1976-80. Pro coach: Joined Saints in 1981.

John Paul Young, linebackers; born December 31, 1939, Dallas, Tex., lives in River Ridge, La. Linebacker Texas-El Paso 1959-61. No pro playing experience. College coach: Texas-El Paso 1962-63, Southern Methodist 1967-68, Oklahoma State 1969, Texas A&M 1970-77. Pro coach: Houston Oilers 1978-80, Saints since 1981.

Willie Zapalac, defensive line; born December 11, 1922, Sealy, Tex., lives in Ormonv, La. Fullback Texas A&M 1941-42, 1946. No pro playing experience. College coach: Texas A&M 1953-60, Texas Tech 1961-62, Oklahoma State 1963, Texas 1964-75. Pro coach: St. Louis Cardinals 1976-77, Buffalo Bills 1978-80, Saints since 1981.

NEW ORLEANS SAINTS 1983 FIRST-YEAR ROSTER

Name	Pos.	Ht.	Wt.	Birth-date	College	Birthplace	Residence	How Acq.
Austin, Cliff	RB	6-0	190	3/2/60	Clemson	Atlanta, Ga.	Scottdale, Ga.	D3a
Black, James (1)	DE	6-4	248	11/4/56	South Carolina State	Xenia, Ohio	Gary, Ind.	FA
Close, Calvin (1)	G	6-3	254	11/6/57	Brigham Young	Oxnard, Calif.	Orem, Utah	FA
Dumas, Marvin (1)	WR	5-11	182	2/21/60	Nicholls State	Vacherie, La.	Vacherie, La.	FA
Goodlow, Eugene	WR	6-2	190	12/19/58	Kansas State	St. Louis, Mo.	Rochester, N.Y.	D3a ('82)
Korte, Steve	G	6-2	270	1/15/60	Arkansas	Denver, Colo.	Fayetteville, Ark.	D2
Lewis, Gary	NT	6-3	260	1/14/61	Oklahoma State	Oklahoma City, Okla.	Oklahoma City, Okla.	D4
Lewis, Marvin (1)	RB	6-3	208	1/15/60	Tulane	Texarkana, Tex.	Metairie, La.	D6 ('82)
Martin, Christopher	LB	6-2	232	12/19/60	Auburn	Huntsville, Ala.	Huntsville, Ala.	FA
McKay, Mike	QB	6-2	190	6/28/61	Tulane	Texarkana, Tex.	Metairie, La.	FA
Picolo, John	S	5-11	185	5/7/60	Evangel	New Orleans, La.	Metairie, La.	FA
Tice, John	TE	6-5	242	6/22/60	Maryland	Bayshore, N.Y.	Central Islip, N.Y.	D3
Young, Tyrone	WR	6-6	190	4/29/60	Florida	Ocala, Fla.	Ocala, Fla.	FA

Players who report to an NFL team for the first time are designated on rosters as rookies (R). If a player reported to an NFL training camp in a previous year but was not on the active squad for three or more regular season or postseason games, he is listed on the first-year roster and designated by a (1). Thereafter, a player who is on the active squad for three or more regular season or postseason games is credited with an additional year of playing experience.

NOTES

_____

_____

_____

_____

_____

_____

_____

_____

_____

_____

_____

_____

_____

_____

_____

_____

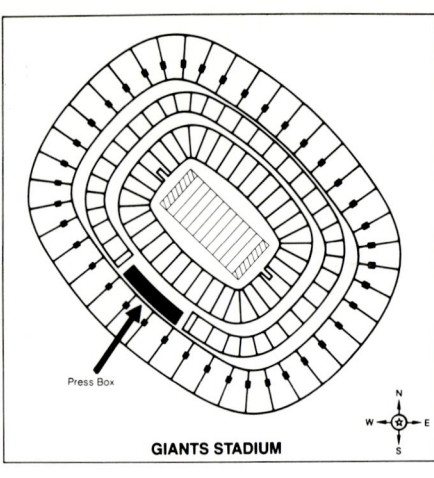

GIANTS STADIUM

New York Giants

**National Football Conference
Eastern Division**

Team Colors: Blue, Red, and White

**Giants Stadium
East Rutherford, New Jersey 07073
Telephone: (201) 935-8111**

Club Officials
President: Wellington T. Mara
Vice President-Treasurer: Timothy J. Mara
Vice President-Secretary: Raymond J. Walsh
Vice President-General Manager: George Young
Assistant General Manager: Terry Bledsoe
Controller: John Pasquali
Director of Player Personnel: Tom Boisture
Director of Pro Personnel: Ernie Adams
Director of Media Services: Ed Croke
Director of Promotions: Tom Power
Director of Special Projects: Victor Del Guercio
Box Office Treasurer: Jim Gleason
Trainer Emeritus: John Dziegiel
Trainers: Dave Barringer, John Johnson
Equipment Manager: Ed Wagner, Jr.

Stadium: Giants Stadium • **Capacity:** 76,891
East Rutherford, N.J. 07073

Playing Surface: AstroTurf

Training Camp: Pace University
Pleasantville, New York 10570

1983 SCHEDULE
Preseason
Aug. 7	**New York Jets**	8:00
Aug. 12	at Pittsburgh	8:00
Aug. 20	**Baltimore**	8:00
Aug. 26	**Miami**	8:00

Regular Season
Sept. 4	**Los Angeles Rams**	1:00
Sept. 11	at Atlanta	1:00
Sept. 18	at Dallas	3:00
Sept. 26	**Green Bay** (Monday)	9:00
Oct. 2	**San Diego**	4:00
Oct. 9	**Philadelphia**	4:00
Oct. 16	at Kansas City	3:00
Oct. 24	at St. Louis (Monday)	8:00
Oct. 30	**Dallas**	1:00
Nov. 7	at Detroit (Monday)	9:00
Nov. 13	**Washington**	4:00
Nov. 20	at Philadelphia	1:00
Nov. 27	at Los Angeles Raiders	1:00
Dec. 4	**St. Louis**	1:00
Dec. 11	**Seattle**	1:00
Dec. 17	at Washington (Saturday)	12:30

1982 TEAM STATISTICS

	New York Giants	Opp.
Total First Downs	153	149
Rushing	47	55
Passing	96	85
Penalty	10	9
Third Down Efficiency	49/123	49/132
Third Down Percentage	39.8	37.1
Total Net Yards	2729	2684
Total Offensive Plays	559	576
Avg. Gain per Play	4.9	4.7
Avg. Gain per Game	303.2	298.2
Net Yards Rushing	842	1118
Total Rushing Plays	244	301
Avg. Gain per Rush	3.5	3.7
Avg. Gain Rushing per Game	93.6	124.2
Net Yards Passing	1887	1566
Lost Attempting to Pass	17/130	31/244
Gross Yards Passing	2017	1810
Attempts/Completions	298/161	244/148
Percent Completed	54.0	60.7
Had Intercepted	9	12
Avg. Net Passing per Game	209.7	174.0
Punts/Avg.	49/42.8	59/41.0
Punt Returns/Avg.	44/8.5	25/8.3
Kickoff Returns/Avg.	39/20.1	34/18.1
Interceptions/Avg. Ret.	12/17.1	9/3.2
Penalties/Yards	47/369	54/417
Fumbles/Ball Lost	19/10	19/6
Total Points	164	160
Avg. Points per Game	18.2	17.8
Touchdowns	18	18
Rushing	7	7
Passing	10	10
Returns and Recoveries	1	1
Field Goals	12/21	12/13
Conversions	18/18	16/18
Safeties	1	0
Avg. Time of Possession	28:41	31:19

1982 TEAM RECORD

Preseason (1-3)

New York Giants		Opponents
14	Baltimore	19
10	*Pittsburgh	13
22	*New York Jets	10
13	Miami (OT)	16
59		58

Regular Season (4-5)

New York Giants		Opponents	Att.
14	*Atlanta	16	74,286
19	*Green Bay	27	68,405
17	*Washington	27	70,766
13	Detroit	6	64,348
17	*Houston	14	71,184
23	*Philadelphia	7	66,053
14	Washington	15	50,030
21	St. Louis	24	39,824
26	Philadelphia	24	55,797
164		160	560,693

*Home Game   (OT) Overtime

Score by Periods

New York Giants	25	51	40	48	—	164
Opponents	31	55	19	55	—	160

Attendance

Home 350,694   Away 209,999   Total 560,693
Single game home record, 76,490 (11-4-79)
Single season home record, 557,530 (1979)

1982 INDIVIDUAL STATISTICS

Rushing

	Att	Yds	Avg	LG	TD
Woolfolk	112	439	3.9	18	2
R. Carpenter	67	204	3.0	23	1
Chatman	22	80	3.6	13	2
Morris	15	48	3.2	7	1
Brunner	19	27	1.4	10	1
Perry	3	14	4.7	15	0
Heater	3	13	4.3	8	0
Eddings	2	12	6.0	16	0
Bright	1	5	5.0	5	0
N.Y. Giants	244	842	3.5	23	7
Opponents	301	1118	3.7	83t	7

Field Goal Success

Distance	1-19	20-29	30-39	40-49	50 Over
Made-Att.	0-0	5-5	5-7	2-8	0-1

Passing

	Att	Comp	Pct	Yds	TD	Int	Tkld	Rate
Brunner	298	161	54.0	2017	10	9	17/130	74.1
N.Y. Giants	298	161	54.0	2017	10	9	17/130	
Opponents	244	148	60.7	1810	10	12	31/244	

Receiving

	No	Yds	Avg	LG	TD
Mullady	27	287	10.6	32	0
Perkins	26	430	16.5	35	2
Gray	25	426	17.0	47	4
Woolfolk	23	224	9.7	40t	2
Mistler	18	191	10.6	24	2
Eddings	14	275	19.6	47	0
Morris	8	34	4.3	13	0
R. Carpenter	7	29	4.1	11	0
Shirk	6	54	9.0	19	0
Bright	2	19	9.5	13	0
Heater	2	15	7.5	12	0
Pittman	1	21	21.0	21	0
Chatman	1	13	13.0	13	0
Perry	1	−1	−1.0	−1	0
N.Y. Giants	161	2017	12.5	47	10
Opponents	148	1810	12.2	57	10

Interceptions

	No	Yds	Avg	LG	TD
Jackson	4	75	18.8	37	0
Kelley	3	27	9.0	14	0
Taylor	1	97	97.0	97t	1
Carson	1	6	6.0	6	0
Currier	1	0	0.0	0	0
Haynes	1	0	0.0	0	0
Reece	1	0	0.0	0	0
N.Y. Giants	12	205	17.1	97t	1
Opponents	9	29	3.2	15	0

Punting

	No	Yds	Avg	In 20	LG
Jennings	49	2096	42.8	16	73
N.Y. Giants	49	2096	42.8	16	73
Opponents	59	2421	41.0	13	59

Punt Returns

	No	FC	Yds	Avg	LG	TD
Bright	37	0	325	8.8	33	0
Pittman	6	3	40	6.7	9	0
Reece	1	0	8	8.0	8	0
N.Y. Giants	44	3	373	8.5	33	0
Opponents	25	4	207	8.3	25	0

Kickoff Returns

	No	Yds	Avg	LG	TD
Woolfolk	20	428	21.4	34	0
Pittman	5	117	23.4	31	0
Heater	5	84	16.8	26	0
Bright	4	72	18.0	20	0
Dennis	3	68	22.7	27	0
McLaughlin	1	14	14.0	14	0
Shaw	1	0	0.0	0	0
N.Y. Giants	39	783	20.1	34	0
Opponents	34	616	18.1	44	0

Scoring

	TD	TD R	TD P	TD Rt	PAT	FG	TP
Danelo					18/18	12/21	54
Gray	4	0	4	0			24
Woolfolk	4	2	2	0			24
Chatman	2	2	0	0			12
Mistler	2	0	2	0			12
Perkins	2	0	2	0			12
Brunner	1	1	0	0			6
R. Carpenter	1	1	0	0			6
Morris	1	1	0	0			6
Taylor	1	0	0	1			6
Team		(Safety)					2
N.Y. Giants	18	7	10	1	18/18	12/21	164
Opponents	18	7	10	1	16/18	12/13	160

Sacks

Burt 1, Carson 3, Currier 2, Hunt 1½, Jackson 1, Marion ½, Martin 6, Neill 2, Sally 1, Tabor 3½, Taylor 7½, Van Pelt 2.

FIRST PLAYERS SELECTED

Year	Player, College, Position
1936	Art Lewis, Ohio U., T
1937	Ed Widseth, Minnesota, T
1938	George Karamatic, Gonzaga, B
1939	Walt Neilson, Arizona, B
1940	Grenville Lansdell, Southern California, B
1941	George Franck, Minnesota, B
1942	Merle Hapes, Mississippi, B
1943	Steve Filipowicz, Fordham, B
1944	Billy Hillenbrand, Indiana, B
1945	Elmer Barbour, Wake Forest, B
1946	George Connor, Notre Dame, T
1947	Vic Schwall, Northwestern, B
1948	Tony Minisi, Pennsylvania, B
1949	Paul Page, Southern Methodist, B
1950	Travis Tidwell, Auburn, B
1951	Kyle Rote, Southern Methodist, B
1952	Frank Gifford, Southern California, B
1953	Bobby Marlow, Alabama, B
1954	Ken Buck, Pacific, C (2)
1955	Joe Heap, Notre Dame, B
1956	Henry Moore, Arkansas, B (2)
1957	Sam DeLuca, South Carolina, T (2)
1958	Phil King, Vanderbilt, B
1959	Lee Grosscup, Utah, B
1960	Lou Cordileone, Clemson, G
1961	Bruce Tarbox, Syracuse, G (2)
1962	Jerry Hillebrand, Colorado, LB
1963	Frank Lasky, Florida, T (2)
1964	Joe Don Looney, Oklahoma, RB
1965	Tucker Frederickson, Auburn, RB
1966	Francis Peay, Missouri, T
1967	Louis Thompson, Alabama, DT (4)
1968	Dick Buzin, Penn State, T (2)
1969	Fred Dryer, San Diego State, DE
1970	Jim Files, Oklahoma, LB
1971	Rocky Thompson, West Texas State, WR
1972	Eldridge Small, Texas A&I, DB
1973	Brad Van Pelt, Michigan State, LB (2)
1974	John Hicks, Ohio State, G
1975	Al Simpson, Colorado State, T (2)
1976	Troy Archer, Colorado, DE
1977	Gary Jeter, Southern California, DT
1978	Gordon King, Stanford, T
1979	Phil Simms, Morehead State, QB
1980	Mark Haynes, Colorado, DB
1981	Lawrence Taylor, North Carolina, LB
1982	Butch Woolfolk, Michigan, RB
1983	Terry Kinard, Clemson, DB

GIANTS COACHING HISTORY
(396-338-31)

1925	Bob Folwell	8-4-0
1926	Joe Alexander	8-4-1
1927-28	Earl Potteiger	15-8-3
1929-30	LeRoy Andrews	26-5-1
1931-53	Steve Owen	154-108-17
1954-60	Jim Lee Howell	54-29-4
1961-68	Allie Sherman	57-54-4
1969-73	Alex Webster	29-40-1
1974-76	Bill Arnsparger*	7-28-0
1976-78	John McVay	14-23-0
1979-82	Ray Perkins	24-35-0

*Released after seven games in 1976

NEW YORK GIANTS 1983 VETERAN ROSTER

No.	Name	Pos.	Ht.	Wt.	Birth-date	NFL Exp.	College	Birthplace	Residence	Games in '82
67	Ard, Billy	G	6-3	250	3/12/59	3	Wake Forest	East Orange, N.J.	Summit, N.J.	9
74	Baldinger, Rich	T	6-4	270	12/31/59	2	Wake Forest	Camp Le Jeune, N.C.	Massapequa, N.Y.	1
60	Benson, Brad	T	6-3	258	11/25/55	6	Penn State	Altoona, Pa.	Duncansville, Pa.	9
45	Bright, Leon	RB	5-9	192	5/19/55	3	Florida State	Merritt Island, Fla.	Rock Ledge, Fla.	8
12	Brunner, Scott	QB	6-5	200	3/24/57	4	Delaware	Sellersville, Pa.	Cranbury, N.J.	9
64	Burt, Jim	NT	6-1	255	6/7/59	3	Miami	Buffalo, N.Y.	Staten Island, N.Y.	4
22	Carpenter, Brian	CB-S	5-10	167	11/27/60	2	Michigan	Flint, Mich.	Ann Arbor, Mich.	4
26	Carpenter, Rob	RB	6-1	230	4/20/55	7	Miami, Ohio	Lancaster, Ohio	Missouri City, Tex.	5
53	Carson, Harry	LB	6-2	235	11/26/53	8	South Carolina State	Florence, S.C.	Ossining, N.Y.	9
31	Chatman, Cliff	RB	6-2	225	3/13/59	2	Central State, Oklahoma	Clinton, Okla.	Lyndhurst, N.J.	6
29	Currier, Bill	S	6-0	202	1/5/55	7	South Carolina	Richmond, Va.	Missouri City, Tex.	9
18	Danelo, Joe	K	5-9	166	9/2/53	9	Washington State	Spokane, Wash.	San Pedro, Calif.	9
46	Dennis, Mike	CB	5-10	190	6/6/58	4	Wyoming	Los Angeles, Calif.	Pasadena, Calif.	9
88	Eddings, Floyd	WR	5-11	177	2/15/58	2	California	Birmingham, Ala.	Pomona, Calif.	4
37	Flowers, Larry	S	6-1	190	4/19/58	3	Texas Tech	Temple, Tex.	Temple, Tex.	6
66	Foote, Chris	C	6-3	250	12/2/56	4	Southern California	Louisville, Ky.	Laguna Hills, Calif.	7
83	Gray, Earnest	WR	6-3	195	3/2/57	5	Memphis State	Greenwood, Miss.	Greenwood, Miss.	9
	Green, Dave	RB	5-10	208	9/7/53	2	Edinboro State	Jacksonville, N.C.	North Olmsted, Ohio	9*
79	Hardison, Dee	DE	6-4	269	5/2/56	6	North Carolina	Jacksonville, N.C.	Clinton, N.C.	5
36	Haynes, Mark	CB	5-11	198	11/6/58	4	Colorado	Kansas City, Kan.	Woodridge, N.J.	9
27	Heater, Larry	RB	5-11	205	1/9/58	3	Arizona	Cincinnati, Ohio	Las Vegas, Nev.	9
61	Hughes, Ernie	C	6-3	265	1/24/55	5	Notre Dame	Boise, Idaho	Mt. Lakes, N.J.	5
57	Hunt, Byron	LB	6-5	230	12/17/58	3	Southern Methodist	Longview, Tex.	Longview, Tex.	9
24	Jackson, Terry	CB	5-11	197	12/9/55	6	San Diego State	Sherman, Tex.	Secaucus, N.J.	8
13	Jennings, Dave	P	6-4	205	6/8/52	10	St. Lawrence	New York, N.Y.	Upper Saddle River, N.J.	9
55	Kelley, Brian	LB	6-3	222	9/1/51	11	California Lutheran	Dallas, Tex.	Upper Saddle River, N.J.	9
72	King, Gordon	T	6-6	275	2/3/56	6	Stanford	Madison, Wis.	Park Ridge, N.J.	9
51	Marion, Frank	LB	6-3	223	3/16/51	7	Florida A&M	Mt. Brook, Fla.	Miami, Fla.	9
75	Martin, George	DE	6-4	245	2/16/53	9	Oregon	Greenville, S.C.	Vacaville, Calif.	9
54	Matthews, Bill	LB	6-2	235	3/12/56	4	South Dakota State	Santa Monica, Calif.	Stoughton, Maine	0*
39	Mayock, Mike	S	6-2	195	8/14/58	2	Boston College	Philadelphia, Pa.	Wynnewood, Pa.	3
76	McGriff, Curtis	DE	6-5	265	5/17/58	4	Alabama	Donaldsville, Ga.	Gordon, Ala.	9
52	McLaughlin, Joe	LB	6-1	235	7/1/57	5	Massachusetts	Springfield, Mass.	Avon, Calif.	8
85	Mistler, John	WR	6-2	186	10/28/58	3	Arizona State	Columbia, Mo.	Cranbury, N.J.	9
20	Morris, Joe	RB	5-7	190	9/15/60	2	Syracuse	Ft. Bragg, N.C.	Ayer, Mass.	5
81	Mullady, Tom	TE	6-3	232	1/30/57	5	Southwestern at Memphis	Dayton, Ohio	Park Ridge, N.J.	9
77	Neill, Bill	NT	6-4	255	3/15/59	3	Pittsburgh	Norristown, Pa.	Pompton Lakes, N.J.	7
86	Perkins, Johnny	WR	6-2	205	4/21/53	7	Abilene Christian	Franklin, Tex.	Granbury, Tex.	8
82	Pittman, Danny	WR	6-2	205	4/3/58	4	Wyoming	Memphis, Tenn.	Pasadena, Calif.	8
28	Reece, Beasley	S	6-1	195	3/18/54	8	North Texas State	Waco, Tex.	Washington Township, N.J.	9
8	Reed, Mark	QB	6-3	195	2/21/59	2	Moorhead	Moorhead, Minn.	Bergenfield, N.J.	0*
17	Rutledge, Jeff	QB	6-1	190	1/22/57	5	Alabama	Birmingham, Ala.	Huntington Beach, Calif.	0*
78	Sally, Jerome	NT	6-3	260	2/24/59	2	Missouri	Chicago, Ill.	Columbia, Mo.	4
44	Shaw, Pete	S	5-10	183	8/25/54	7	Northwestern	Newark, N.J.	La Costa, Calif.	9
87	Shirk, Gary	TE	6-1	220	2/23/50	8	Morehead State	Marysville, Ohio	Mountain Lakes, N.J.	9
69	Simmons, Roy	G	6-3	264	11/8/56	4	Georgia Tech	Savannah, Ga.	Orange, N.J.	0*
11	Simms, Phil	QB	6-3	216	11/3/56	4	Morehead State	Louisville, Ky.	Wyckoff, N.J.	0*
80	Tabor, Phil	DE	6-4	255	11/30/56	5	Oklahoma	Houston, Tex.	Norman, Okla.	9
65	Tautolo, John	G	6-3	260	5/29/59	2	UCLA	Long Beach, Calif.	Bellflower, Calif.	1
56	Taylor, Lawrence	LB	6-3	237	2/4/59	3	North Carolina	Williamsburg, Va.	Upper Saddle River, N.J.	9
68	Turner, J. T.	G	6-3	250	4/17/53	7	Duke	Moultrie, Ga.	Washington Township, N.J.	9
59	Umphrey, Rich	C	6-3	255	12/13/58	2	Colorado	Garden Grove, Calif.	Santa Ana, Calif.	9
10	Van Pelt, Brad	LB	6-5	235	4/5/51	11	Michigan State	Owosso, Mich.	Owosso, Mich.	9
73	Weston, Jeff	T	6-5	280	4/10/56	5	Notre Dame	Jersey City, N.J.	Sparta, N.J.	1
58	Whittington, Mike	LB	6-2	220	8/9/58	4	Notre Dame	Miami, Fla.	Miami, Fla.	9
25	Woolfolk, Butch	RB	6-1	207	3/1/60	2	Michigan	Milwaukee, Wis.	Secaucus, N.J.	9

* Green played 9 games with Cleveland in '82; Matthews and Simms missed entire '82 season due to injuries; Reed active for 7 games with Giants in '82, but did not play; Rutledge active for 9 games, but did not play; Simmons last active with Giants in '81.

Traded—Defensive end Gary Jeter to Los Angeles Rams.

Also played with Giants in '82—LB Mike Curcio (1 game); TE Steve Folsom (2); RB Leon Perry (5).

COACHING STAFF

Head Coach, Bill Parcells

Pro Career: Became twelfth head coach in New York Giants history on December 15, 1982. Parcells begins first campaign as head coach after spending the past two seasons as the Giants' defensive coordinator and linebacker coach. Started pro coaching career in 1980 as linebacker coach with New England.

Background: Linebacker at Wichita State 1961-63. College assistant Hastings (Neb.) 1964, Wichita State 1965, Army 1966-69, Florida State 1970-72, Vanderbilt 1973-74, Texas Tech 1975-77. Air Force 1978 (head coach).

Personal: Born August 22, 1941, Englewood, N.J. Bill and his wife, Judy, live in Upper Saddle River, N.J., and have three daughters—Suzy, Jill, and Dallas.

ASSISTANT COACHES

Bill Belichick, linebackers; born April 16, 1952, Nashville, Tenn., lives in East Rutherford, N.J. Center-tight end Wesleyan 1972-74. No pro playing experience. Pro coach: Baltimore Colts 1975, Detroit Lions 1976-77, Denver Broncos 1978, Giants since 1979.

Tom Bresnahan, offensive line; born January 21, 1935, Springfield, Mass., lives in East Rutherford, N.J. Tackle Holy Cross 1953-55. No pro playing experience. College coach: Williams 1963-67, Columbia 1968-72, Navy 1973-80. Pro coach: Kansas City Chiefs 1981-82, first year with Giants.

Romeo Crennel, special teams; born June 18, 1947, Lynchburg, Va., lives in East Rutherford, N.J., Defensive lineman Western Kentucky 1966-69. No pro playing experience. College coach: Western Kentucky 1970-74, Texas Tech 1975-77, Mississippi 1978-79, Georgia Tech 1980. Pro coach: Joined Giants in 1981.

Ron Erhardt, offensive coordinator; born February 27, 1932, Mandan, N.D., lives in East Rutherford, N.J. College Quarterback Jamestown (N.D.) College 1951-54. No pro playing experience. College coach: North Dakota State 1963-72 (head coach 1966-72). Pro coach: New England Patriots 1973-81 (head coach 1979-81), Giants since 1982.

Len Fontes, defensive backfield; born March 8, 1938, New Bedford, Mass., lives in East Rutherford, N.J. Defensive back Ohio State 1958-59. No pro playing experience. College coach: Eastern Michigan 1968, Dayton 1969-72, Navy 1973-76, Miami 1977-79. Pro coach: Cleveland Browns 1980-82, first year with Giants.

Pat Hodgson, receivers; born January 30, 1944, Columbus, Ga., lives in East Rutherford, N.J. Tight end Georgia 1963-65. Pro tight end Washington Redskins 1966, Minnesota Vikings 1967. College coach: Georgia 1968-70, 1972-77, Florida State 1971, Texas Tech 1978. Pro coach: San Diego Chargers 1978, Giants since 1979.

Lamar Leachman, defensive line; born August 7, 1934, Cartersville, Ga., lives in East Rutherford, N.J. Center-linebacker Tennessee 1952-55. No pro playing experience. College coach: Richmond 1966-67, Georgia Tech 1968-71, Memphis State 1972, South Carolina 1973. Pro coach: New York Stars (WFL) 1974, Toronto Argonauts (CFL) 1975-77, Montreal Alouettes (CFL) 1978-79, Giants since 1980.

Bob Ledbetter, running backs; born September 24, 1934, Tupelo, Miss., lives in East Northport, N.Y. Tackle Mississippi Industrial 1957-59. No pro playing experience. College coach: Southern Illinois 1969-71, Norfolk State 1972-73 (head coach), Grambling 1976. Pro coach: New Orleans Saints 1974-75, New York Jets 1977-82, first year with Giants.

Mike Pope, assistant special teams; born March 15, 1942, Monroe, N.C., lives in River Vale, N.J. Quarterback Lenoir Rhyne 1962-64. No pro playing experience. College coach: Florida State 1970-74, Texas Tech 1975-77, Mississippi 1978-82. Pro coach: First year with Giants.

NEW YORK GIANTS 1983 FIRST-YEAR ROSTER

Name	Pos.	Ht.	Wt.	Birth-date	College	Birthplace	Residence	How Acq.
Allen, Curtis	DE	6-4	250	6/16/60	Drake	Gary, Ind.	Rutherford, N.J.	FA
Belcher, Kevin	G	6-3	255	2/23/61	Texas-El Paso	Detroit, Mich.	Detroit, Mich.	D6
Brockhaus, Jeff (1)	K	6-3	200	4/15/59	Missouri	Ft. Lauderdale, Fla.	St. Louis, Mo.	FA
Brown, Dave	RB	6-1	205	4/4/60	Pacific	Albany, Ga.	Duarte, Calif.	FA
Carney, Cormac	WR	6-0	225	5/6/59	UCLA	Detroit, Mich.	Long Beach, Calif.	FA
Clemens, Joseph	DE	6-4	250	2/17/61	Vanderbilt	Beeville, Tex.	Atlantic Beach, Fla.	FA
De Gruttola, John (1)	RB	5-11	222	3/12/60	Westminster, Pa.	New Castle, Pa.	Elwood City, Pa.	FA
Fagan, Jeff	RB	6-0	225	6/7/61	Alabama	Hollywood, Fla.	Hollywood, Fla.	FA
Fontes, Kevin	WR	5-10	170	7/18/60	Cal State-Sacramento	Sacramento, Calif.	Sacramento, Calif.	FA
Headen, Andy	LB	6-5	230	7/8/60	Clemson	Asheboro, N.C.	Liberty, N.C.	D8
Haji Sheikh, Ali	K	6-0	172	1/11/61	Michigan	Ann Arbor, Mich.	Arlington, Tex.	D9
Ingram, Michael	CB	6-2	194	3/30/60	Southern	Ft. Pierce, Fla.	Ft. Pierce, Fla.	FA
Jenkins, Lee	CB-S	5-11	177	3/2/61	Tennessee	Atlanta, Ga.	Atlanta, Ga.	D11a
Jones, Robbie	LB	6-2	230	12/25/59	Alabama	Demopolis, Ala.	Demopolis, Ala.	D12
Kinard, Terry	S	6-1	190	11/24/59	Clemson	Bit Burge, Germany	Sumter, S.C.	D1
Magwood, Frank	WR	6-0	188	7/7/61	Clemson	Charleston, S.C.	Johns-Island, S.C.	D12a
Marshall, Leonard	DE	6-3	285	10/22/61	Louisiana State	Franklin, La.	Franklin, La.	D2
McConkey, Phil	WR	5-10	165	2/24/57	Navy	Buffalo, N.Y.	Stevensville, Md.	FA
Montz, Mike	RB	6-0	220	3/28/60	Louisiana State	Lutcher, La.	Baton Rouge, La.	FA
Moore, Tim	NT	6-3	280	9/27/60	Southern	New Orleans, La.	New Orleans, La.	FA
Mowatt, Zeke	TE	6-3	238	3/5/61	Florida State	Wauchula, Fla.	Talahassee, Fla.	FA
Nelson, Karl	T	6-6	272	6/14/60	Iowa State	DeKalb, Ill.	DeKalb, Ill.	D3
Patterson, Darrell	LB	6-3	235	12/14/61	Texas Christian	Canonsburg, Pa.	Canonsburg, Pa.	D6a
Pierson, Clenzie	NT	6-7	260	10/21/60	Rice	San Antonio, Tex.	Elmendorf, Tex.	D11
Riddick, Andrew	CB	6-0	180	4/7/61	N. Carolina Central	Plainfield, N.J.	Plainfield, N.J.	FA
Robertson, Alvin	CB	6-0	175	3/11/60	Pittsburg State	Kansas City, Mo.	Pleasanton, Kan.	FA
Rustemeyer, Mike (1)	NT	6-3	265	3/22/60	Rutgers	Hoboken, N.J.	Carteret, N.J.	FA
Scott, Malcolm	TE	6-4	240	7/10/61	Louisiana State	New Orleans, La.	New Orleans, La.	D5
Shoop, Mark	DE	6-6	252	4/8/61	Colorado	Greeley, Colo.	Greeley, Colo.	FA
Short, Daniel	S	6-1	205	2/20/61	Pittsburgh	Aliquippa, Pa.	Aliquippa, Pa.	FA
Teeuws, John	C	6-5	255	3/14/61	Stanford	Indianapolis, Ind.	Indianapolis, Ind.	FA
Tuggle, John	RB	6-1	210	1/13/61	California	Honolulu, Hawaii	San Jose, Calif.	D12b
Versnik, Ron	C	6-0	260	9/23/60	Wisconsin	West Allis, Wis.	West Allis, Wis.	FA
Williams, Jamie	TE	6-5	230	2/25/60	Nebraska	Vero Beach, Fla.	Lincoln, Neb.	D3a
Williams, Perry	CB	6-2	195	5/12/61	North Carolina State	Hamlet, N.C.	Hamlet, N.C.	D7
Wilson, Jackie	WR	6-0	192	10/12/59	Southern Methodist	Kirbyville, Tex.	Kirbyville, Tex.	FA
Wray, Richard	S	6-1	187	4/28/60	Toledo	Rockville Center, N.Y.	Toledo, Ohio	FA
Wrigley, Kurt	WR	5-11	188	2/15/61	William & Mary	Phoenixville, Pa.	Pottstown, Pa.	FA

Players who report to an NFL team for the first time are designated on rosters as rookies (R). If a player reported to an NFL training camp in a previous year but was not on the active squad for three or more regular season or postseason games, he is listed on the first-year roster and designated by a (1). Thereafter, a player who is on the active squad for three or more regular season or postseason games is credited with an additional year of playing experience.

NOTES

_____
_____
_____
_____
_____
_____
_____
_____
_____
_____

Steve Schnall, offensive assistant, administrative assistant; born January 20, 1944, Rockaway Beach, N.Y., lives in Mercerville, N.J. Defensive back Springfield College 1961-65. No pro playing experience. College coach: Widener 1969-70, Lafayette 1971-77, William and Mary 1978, East Carolina 1979, Princeton 1980-82. Pro coach: First year with Giants.

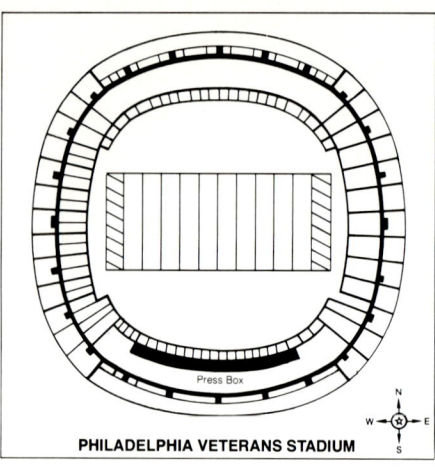

PHILADELPHIA VETERANS STADIUM

Philadelphia Eagles

National Football Conference
Eastern Division

Team Colors: Kelly Green, Silver, and White

Philadelphia Veterans Stadium
Broad Street and Pattison Avenue
Philadelphia, Pennsylvania 19148
Telephone: (215) 463-2500

Club Officials

General Partner: Leonard H. Tose
Vice President-Legal Counsel: Susan Fletcher
Director of Public Relations: Jim Gallagher
Public Relations Assistant: Chick McElrone
Administrative Director: Mimi Box
Sales and Marketing: Bob Caesar
Ticket Manager: Hugh Ortman
Director of Player Personnel: Lynn Stiles
Assistant Director of Player Personnel: Jackie Graves
Talent Scouts: Ken Blair, Jim Katcavage, Phil Neri
Trainer: Otho Davis
Equipment Manager: Rusty Sweeney

Stadium: Philadelphia Veterans Stadium •
Capacity: 72,204
Broad Street and Pattison Avenue
Philadelphia, Pennsylvania 19148

Playing Surface: AstroTurf

Training Camp: West Chester State College
West Chester, Pennsylvania 19380

1983 SCHEDULE

Preseason

Aug. 5	**Detroit**	7:30
Aug. 13	at San Diego	6:00
Aug. 20	at Green Bay	2:00
Aug. 25	**Pittsburgh**	7:30

Regular Season

Sept. 4	at San Francisco	1:00
Sept. 11	**Washington**	1:00
Sept. 18	at Denver	2:00
Sept. 25	**St. Louis**	1:00
Oct. 2	at Atlanta	1:00
Oct. 9	at New York Giants	4:00
Oct. 16	**Dallas**	4:00
Oct. 23	**Chicago**	1:00
Oct. 30	**Baltimore**	1:00
Nov. 6	at Dallas	12:00
Nov. 13	at Chicago	12:00
Nov. 20	**New York Giants**	1:00
Nov. 27	at Washington	1:00
Dec. 4	**Los Angeles Rams**	1:00
Dec. 11	**New Orleans**	1:00
Dec. 18	at St. Louis	12:00

1982 TEAM STATISTICS

	Philadelphia	Opp.
Total First Downs	157	177
Rushing	48	68
Passing	100	100
Penalty	9	9
Third Down Efficiency	33/106	59/132
Third Down Percentage	31.1	44.7
Total Net Yards	2685	2938
Total Offensive Plays	530	614
Avg. Gain per Play	5.1	4.8
Avg. Gain per Game	298.8	326.4
Net Yards Rushing	829	1031
Total Rushing Plays	211	299
Avg. Gain per Rush	3.9	3.4
Avg. Gain Rushing per Game	92.1	114.6
Net Yards Passing	1856	1907
Lost Attempting to Pass	31/244	30/229
Gross Yards Passing	2100	2136
Attempts/Completions	288/168	285/168
Percent Completed	58.3	58.9
Had Intercepted	13	15
Avg. Net Passing per Game	206.2	211.9
Punts/Avg.	44/40.5	38/36.8
Punt Returns/Avg.	22/4.9	31/10.2
Kickoff Returns/Avg.	39/19.7	39/22.7
Interceptions/Avg. Ret.	15/2.8	13/9.1
Penalties/Yards	38/253	45/341
Fumbles/Ball Lost	26/10	20/12
Total Points	191	195
Avg. Points per Game	21.2	21.7
Touchdowns	25	19
Rushing	11	5
Passing	12	14
Returns and Recoveries	2	0
Field Goals	6/9	20/22
Conversions	23/25	19/19
Safeties	0	1
Avg. Time of Possession	26:57	33:03

1982 TEAM RECORD

Preseason (1-3)

Philadelphia		Opponents
7	Tampa Bay	35
14	*New England	7
21	Atlanta	24
24	Pittsburgh	27
66		93

Regular Season (3-6)

Philadelphia		Opponents	Att.
34	*Washington (OT)	37	68,885
24	Cleveland	21	78,830
14	*Cincinnati	18	65,172
9	Washington	13	48,313
20	*St. Louis	23	63,622
7	New York Giants	23	66,053
35	*Houston	14	44,119
24	Dallas	20	46,199
24	*New York Giants	26	55,797
191		195	536,990

*Home Game   (OT) Overtime

Score by Periods

Philadelphia	45	34	36	76	0	—	191
Opponents	36	76	30	50	3	—	195

Attendance

Home 297,595   Away 239,395   Total 536,990
Single game home record, 72,111 (11-1-81)
Single season home record, 557,325 (1980)

1982 INDIVIDUAL STATISTICS

Rushing

	Att	Yds	Avg	LG	TD
Montgomery	114	515	4.5	90t	7
Harrington	56	231	4.1	37	1
Harris	17	39	2.3	14	2
Giammona	11	29	2.6	8	1
Jaworski	10	9	0.9	6	0
Hoover	1	5	5.0	5	0
Campfield	1	2	2.0	2	0
LeMaster	1	−1	−1.0	−1	0
Philadelphia	211	829	3.9	90t	11
Opponents	299	1031	3.4	32t	5

Field Goal Success

Distance	1-19	20-29	30-39	40-49	50 Over
Made-Att.	0-0	1-1	1-1	4-5	0-2

Passing

	Att	Comp	Pct	Yds	TD	Int	Tkld	Rate
Jaworski	286	167	58.4	2076	12	12	31/244	77.5
Pisarcik	1	1	100.0	24	0	0	0/0	—
Giammona	1	0	0.0	0	0	1	0/0	—
Philadelphia	288	168	58.3	2100	12	13	31/244	
Opponents	285	168	58.9	2136	14	15	30/299	

Receiving

	No	Yds	Avg	LG	TD
Carmichael	35	540	15.4	46	4
Smith	34	475	14.0	41t	1
Spagnola	26	313	12.0	57	2
Montgomery	20	258	12.9	42t	2
Campfield	14	141	10.1	24	1
Harrington	13	74	5.7	18	0
Quick	10	156	15.6	49t	1
Giammona	8	67	8.4	16	0
Kab	4	35	8.8	13	1
Harris	3	17	5.7	9	0
Sampleton	1	24	24.0	24	0
Philadelphia	168	2100	12.5	57	12
Opponents	168	2136	12.7	78t	14

Interceptions

	No	Yds	Avg	LG	TD
Edwards	5	3	0.6	3	0
Young	4	0	0.0	0	0
Robinson	3	19	6.3	12	0
Blackmore	1	20	20.0	20t	1
Bunting	1	0	0.0	0	0
Wilson	1	0	0.0	0	0
Philadelphia	15	42	2.8	20t	1
Opponents	13	118	9.1	37	0

Punting

	No	Yds	Avg	In 20	LG
Runager	44	1784	40.5	8	53
Philadelphia	44	1784	40.5	8	53
Opponents	38	1398	36.8	8	55

Punt Returns

	No	FC	Yds	Avg	LG	TD
Henry	20	2	103	5.2	11	0
Sciarra	2	0	5	2.5	5	0
Giammona	0	1	0	—	0	0
Philadelphia	22	3	108	4.9	11	0
Opponents	31	0	316	10.2	33	0

Kickoff Returns

	No	Yds	Avg	LG	TD
Henry	24	541	22.5	44	0
Hoover	7	113	16.1	43	0
Murray	3	42	14.0	16	0
Campfield	2	30	15.0	16	0
Slater	2	30	15.0	16	0
Montgomery	1	12	12.0	12	0
Philadelphia	39	768	19.7	44	0
Opponents	39	885	22.7	58	0

Scoring

	TD	TD R	TD P	TD Rt	PAT	FG	TP
Montgomery	9	7	2	0			54
Franklin					23/25	6/9	41
Carmichael	4	0	4	0			24
Harris	2	2	0	0			12
Spagnola	2	0	2	0			12
Blackmore	1	0	0	1			6
Brown	1	0	0	1			6
Campfield	1	0	1	0			6
Giammona	1	1	0	0			6
Harrington	1	1	0	0			6
Kab	1	0	1	0			6
Quick	1	0	1	0			6
Smith	1	0	1	0			6
Philadelphia	25	11	12	2	23/25	6/9	191
Opponents	19	5	14	0	19/19	20/22	195

Sacks

Brown 4, Bunting 3, Clarke 4½, Hairston 4, Harrison 10½, LeMaster 2, Robinson 1, Wilkes 1.

FIRST PLAYERS SELECTED

Since 1953

Year	Player, College, Position
1953	Al Conway, Army, B (2)
1954	Neil Worden, Notre Dame, B
1955	Dick Bielski, Maryland, B
1956	Bob Pellegrini, Maryland, C
1957	Clarence Peaks, Michigan State, B
1958	Walt Kowalczyk, Michigan State, B
1959	J.D. Smith, Rice, T (2)
1960	Ron Burton, Northwestern, RB
1961	Art Baker, Syracuse, RB
1962	Pete Case, Georgia, G (2)
1963	Ed Budde, Michigan State, G
1964	Bob Brown, Nebraska, T
1965	Ray Rissmiller, Georgia, T (2)
1966	Randy Beisler, Indiana, DE
1967	Harry Jones, Arkansas, RB
1968	Tim Rossovich, Southern California, DE
1969	Leroy Keyes, Purdue, B
1970	Steve Zabel, Oklahoma, TE
1971	Richard Harris, Grambling, DE
1972	John Reaves, Florida, QB
1973	Jerry Sisemore, Texas, T
1974	Mitch Sutton, Kansas, DT (3)
1975	Bill Capraun, Miami, T (7)
1976	Mike Smith, Florida, DE (4)
1977	Skip Sharp, Kansas, DB (5)
1978	Reggie Wilkes, Georgia Tech, LB (3)
1979	Jerry Robinson, UCLA, LB
1980	Roynell Young, Alcorn State, DB
1981	Leonard Mitchell, Houston, DE
1982	Mike Quick, North Carolina State, WR
1983	Michael Haddix, Mississippi State, RB

EAGLES COACHING HISTORY

(272-347-22)

1933-35	Lud Wray	9-21-1
1936-40	Bert Bell	10-44-2
1941-50	Earle (Greasy) Neale*	66-44-5
1951	Alvin (Bo) McMillin**	2-0-0
1951	Wayne Millner	2-8-0
1952-55	Jim Trimble	25-20-3
1956-57	Hugh Devore	7-16-1
1958-60	Lawrence (Buck) Shaw	20-16-1
1961-63	Nick Skorich	15-24-3
1964-68	Joe Kuharich	28-41-1
1969-71	Jerry Williams***	7-22-2
1971-72	Ed Khayat	8-15-2
1973-75	Mike McCormack	16-25-1
1976-82	Dick Vermeil	57-51-0

*Co-coach in Philadelphia-Pittsburgh merger in 1943

**Retired after two games in 1951

***Released after three games in 1971

PHILADELPHIA EAGLES 1983 VETERAN ROSTER

No.	Name	Pos.	Ht.	Wt.	Birth-date	NFL Exp.	College	Birthplace	Residence	Games in '82
96	Armstrong, Harvey	NT	6-2	255	12/29/59	2	Southern Methodist	Houston, Tex.	Houston, Tex.	8
63	Baker, Ron	G	6-4	250	11/19/54	6	Oklahoma State	Emerson, Ind.	Stillwater, Okla.	9
27	Blackmore, Richard	CB	5-10	174	8/14/56	5	Mississippi State	Vicksburg, Miss.	Senatobia, Miss.	4
98	Brown, Gregory	DE	6-5	240	1/5/57	3	Kansas State	Washington, D.C.	Philadelphia, Pa.	9
30	Calhoun, Don	RB	6-0	213	4/29/53	10	Kansas State	Sumner, Okla.	Wichita, Kan.	1
37	Campfield, Billy	RB	6-0	205	8/20/56	6	Kansas	West Point, Ga.	San Antonio, Tex.	6
17	†Carmichael, Harold	WR	6-8	225	9/22/49	13	Southern	Jacksonville, Fla.	Cherry Hill, N.J.	9
71	†Clarke, Ken	NT	6-2	255	8/28/56	6	Syracuse	Savannah, Ga.	Sewell, N.J.	9
57	Curcio, Mike	LB	6-1	237	1/24/57	3	Temple	Hudson, N.Y.	Mays Landing, N.J.	5
25	DeVaughn, Dennis	CB-S	5-10	175	10/28/60	2	Bishop	Los Angeles, Calif.	Dallas, Tex.	4
46	Edwards, Herman	CB	6-0	190	4/27/54	7	San Diego State	Fort Monmouth, N.J.	Seaside, Calif.	9
24	Ellis, Ray	S	6-1	192	4/27/59	3	Ohio State	Canton, Ohio	Canton, Ohio	9
1	Franklin, Tony	K	5-8	182	11/18/56	5	Texas A&M	Big Spring, Tex.	San Antonio, Tex.	9
79	Giddens, Frank	T	6-7	300	1/20/59	3	New Mexico	Lubbock, Tex.	Carlsbad, N.M.	9
58	Griggs, Anthony	LB	6-3	220	2/12/60	2	Ohio State	Lawton, Okla.	Mt. Laurel, N.J.	9
78	Hairston, Carl	DE	6-3	260	12/15/52	8	Maryland-Eastern Shore	Martinsville, Va.	Virginia Beach, Va.	9
35	Harrington, Perry	RB	5-11	210	3/13/58	4	Jackson State	Bentonia, Miss.	Jackson, Miss.	9
68	Harrison, Dennis	DE	6-8	275	7/31/56	6	Vanderbilt	Cleveland, Ohio	Nashville, Tenn.	9
85	Hoover, Melvin	WR	6-0	185	8/21/59	2	Arizona State	Charlotte, N.C.	Charlotte, N.C.	7
7	Jaworski, Ron	QB	6-2	196	3/23/51	10	Youngstown State	Lackawanna, N.Y.	West Berlin, N.J.	9
97	Johnson, Charles	NT	6-1	262	6/29/57	3	Maryland	Baltimore, Md.	Baltimore, Md.	0*
84	Kab, Vyto	TE	6-5	255	12/23/59	2	Penn State	Albany, Ga.	Hawthorne, N.J.	9
73	Kenney, Steve	G	6-4	262	12/26/55	4	Clemson	Wilmington, N.C.	Raleigh, N.C.	9
55	LeMaster, Frank	LB	6-2	238	3/12/52	10	Kentucky	Lexington, Ky.	West Chester, Pa.	9
41	Logan, Randy	S	6-1	195	5/1/51	11	Michigan	Detroit, Mich.	Detroit, Mich.	9
45	Mansfield, Von	CB-S	5-11	185	7/12/60	2	Wisconsin	Anderson, Ind.	Milwaukee, Wis.	7
99	Mitchell, Leonard	DE	6-7	272	10/12/58	3	Houston	Houston, Tex.	Houston, Tex.	9
31	Montgomery, Wilbert	RB	5-10	195	9/16/54	7	Abilene Christian	Greenville, Miss.	West Berlin, N.J.	8
50	†Morriss, Guy	C	6-4	255	5/13/51	11	Texas Christian	Colorado City, Tex.	Sicklerville, N.J.	9
34	Oliver, Hubie	RB	5-10	212	11/12/57	2	Arizona	Elyria, Ohio	Elyria, Ohio	0*
6	Pastorini, Dan	QB	6-2	205	5/26/49	13	Santa Clara	San Francisco, Calif.	Washington Crossing, Pa.	0*
62	Perot, Petey	G	6-2	261	4/18/57	5	Northwestern Louisiana	Natchitoches, La.	Natchitoches, La.	5
9	Pisarcik, Joe	QB	6-4	220	7/2/52	7	New Mexico State	Wilkes-Barre, Pa.	Bradenton, Fla.	1
82	Quick, Mike	WR	6-2	190	5/14/59	2	North Carolina State	Hamlet, N.C.	Hamlet, N.C.	9
56	Robinson, Jerry	LB	6-2	218	12/18/56	5	UCLA	San Francisco, Calif.	West Chester, Pa.	9
4	Runager, Max	P	6-1	189	3/24/56	5	South Carolina	Greenwood, S.C.	West Chester, Pa.	9
87	Sampleton, Lawrence	TE	6-5	233	9/25/59	2	Texas	Waelder, Tex.	Seguin, Tex.	9
21	†Sciarra, John	S	5-11	185	3/2/54	6	UCLA	Los Angeles, Calif.	La Canada-Flintridge, Calif.	8
76	Sisemore, Jerry	T	6-4	265	7/16/51	11	Texas	Olton, Tex.	Leander, Tex.	7
61	Slater, Mark	C	6-2	257	2/1/55	6	Minnesota	Crosby, N.D.	Sicklerville, N.J.	9
81	Smith, Ron	WR	6-1	185	11/20/56	6	San Diego State	Lakeland, Fla.	Anaheim Hills, Calif.	9
88	Spagnola, John	TE	6-4	240	8/1/57	5	Yale	Stroudsburg, Pa.	Bethlehem, Pa.	9
54	Valentine, Zack	LB	6-2	220	5/29/57	5	East Carolina	Edenton, N.C.	Swedesburg, N.J.	8
75	†Walters, Stan	T	6-6	275	5/27/48	12	Syracuse	Rutherford, N.J.	West Chester, Pa.	9
51	Wilkes, Reggie	LB	6-4	230	5/27/56	6	Georgia Tech	Pine Bluff, Ark.	Philadelphia, Pa.	9
22	Wilson, Brenard	S	6-0	175	8/15/55	5	Vanderbilt	Daytona Beach, Fla.	Nashville, Tenn.	8
83	Woodruff, Tony	WR	6-0	175	11/12/58	2	Fresno State	Hazen, Ark.	Fresno, Calif.	2
43	Young, Roynell	CB	6-1	181	12/1/57	4	Alcorn State	New Orleans, La.	New Orleans, La.	9

* Johnson missed '82 season due to injury; Oliver active for 2 games in '82, but did not play; Pastorini active for 7 games in '82, but did not play.

†Option playout; subject to developments.

Also played with Eagles in '82—LB John Bunting (9 games), RB Louie Giammona (9), RB Leroy Harris (7), WR-KR Wally Henry (8), RB Calvin Murray (1).

COACHING STAFF

Head Coach, Marion Campbell

Pro Career: Campbell was named head coach of the Eagles on January 10, 1983 after six seasons as the club's defensive coordinator. Campbell's first association with the Eagles came in 1956 when, as a defensive lineman, he was traded to Philadelphia by San Francisco. He was the 49ers' fourth-round draft choice in 1951 but spent three years in the Army before he joined the 49ers. During his six-year playing career with the Eagles, Campbell played defensive tackle on the Eagles' 1960 NFL Championship team and played in the 1960 and 1961 Pro Bowls. His pro coaching career began in 1962 as an assistant with the Boston Patriots. Two years later he moved into the NFL coaching ranks where he developed outstanding defensive lines at Minnesota (1964-66) and Los Angeles (1967-68). He joined Atlanta in 1969 and was the Falcons' head coach from November of 1974 to October of 1976. His head coaching record was 6-19, including a 4-10 mark in 1975, his only full season as a head coach. He was released by the Falcons after nine games in 1976 and joined the Eagles in 1977.

Background: At the University of Georgia, where he played tackle, he was an All-Southeastern Conference selection three times and the team's most valuable player his senior year.

Personal: Born May 25, 1929 in Chester, S.C., Marion and his wife, June, live in Medford, N.J. and have two children—Scott and Alicia.

ASSISTANT COACHES

John Becker, wide receivers; born February 16, 1943, Alexandria, Va., lives in Philadelphia. Cal State-Northridge 1965. No pro playing experience. College coach: UCLA 1970-71, New Mexico C.C. 1972-73, Los Angeles Valley J.C. 1974-76 (head coach), Oregon 1977-79. Pro coach: Joined Eagles in 1980.

Fred Bruney, assistant head coach-defensive backfield; born December 30, 1931, Martins Ferry, Ohio, lives in Medford, N.J. Back Ohio State 1949-52. Pro defensive back San Francisco 49ers 1953-56, Pittsburgh Steelers 1957, Washington Redskins 1958, Boston Patriots 1960-62. College coach: Ohio State 1959. Pro coach: Boston Patriots 1963, Philadelphia Eagles 1964-68, Atlanta Falcons 1969-76, rejoined Eagles in 1977.

Chuck Clausen, defensive line; born June 23, 1940, Anamosa, Iowa, lives in Mount Laurel, N.J. Defensive lineman New Mexico 1961-63. No pro playing experience. College coach: William & Mary 1969-70, Ohio State 1971-75. Pro coach: Joined Eagles in 1976.

Harry Gamble, administrative assistant; born December 26, 1930, Pitman, N.J., lives in Philadelphia. Offensive lineman Rider College 1948-52. No pro playing experience. College coach: Pennsylvania 1961-65, 1971-80 (head coach), Lafayette 1966-70 (head coach). Pro coach: Joined Eagles in 1981.

Frank Gansz, tight ends-special teams; born November 22, 1938, Altoona, Pa., lives in Philadelphia. Center Navy 1957-59. No pro playing experience. College coach: Air Force 1964-66, Colgate 1968, Navy 1969-72, Oklahoma State 1973, 1975, Army 1974, UCLA 1976-77. Pro coach: San Francisco 49ers 1978, Cincinnati Bengals 1979-80, Kansas City Chiefs 1981-82, first year with Eagles.

George Hill, linebackers; born April 28, 1933, Bay Village, Ohio, lives in Mount Laurel, N.J. Tackle-fullback Denison 1954-57. No pro playing experience. College coach: Findlay 1959, Denison 1960-64, Cornell 1965, Duke 1966-70, Ohio State 1971-78. Pro coach: Joined Eagles in 1979.

Ken Iman, offensive line; born February 8, 1939, St. Louis, Mo., lives in Mount Laurel, N.J. Center-linebacker Southeast Missouri State 1956-59. Pro center Green Bay Packers 1960-63, Los Angeles Rams 1964-74. Pro coach: Joined Eagles in 1976.

Billie Matthews, running backs; born March 15, 1930, Houston, Tex., lives in Philadelphia. Quarterback Southern University 1954-57. No pro playing experience. College coach: Kansas 1970, UCLA 1971-78. Pro coach: San Francisco 49ers 1979-82, first year with Eagles.

PHILADELPHIA EAGLES 1983 FIRST-YEAR ROSTER

Name	Pos.	Ht.	Wt.	Birth-date	College	Birthplace	Residence	How Acq.
Adams, Earnest (1)	LB	6-2	225	3/12/59	Illinois	Ft. Lauderdale, Fla.	Urbana, Ill.	FA
Asmus, Jim	K	6-2	195	12/2/58	Hawaii	Meppal, Holland	Los Angeles, Calif.	FA
Banaciski, Joe	CB-S	6-1	190	3/21/61	Montclair State	Newark, N.J.	South Kiner, N.J.	FA
Birdsey, Don (1)	P	5-11	174	8/16/58	Kansas State	Norwich, Conn.	Houston, Tex.	FA
Brown, Wiley (1)	DE	6-8	225	10/19/60	Louisville	Sylvester, Ga.	Louisville, Ky.	FA
Darby, Byron	DE	6-4	250	6/4/60	Southern California	Los Angeles, Calif.	Inglewood, Calif.	D5
Demeropoulos, Pete	G	6-3	255	3/23/60	Wagner	Brooklyn, N.Y.	Brooklyn, N.Y.	FA
Edgar, Anthony	RB	5-10	190	9/19/59	Hawaii	Los Angeles, Calif.	Compton, Calif.	D7
Everett, Major	RB	5-10	207	1/4/60	Mississippi	Monticello, Miss.	New Hebron, Miss.	FA
Feehery, Gerry	C	6-2	268	3/9/60	Syracuse	Philadelphia, Pa.	Springfield, Pa.	FA
Foules, Elbert	CB-S	5-11	185	7/4/61	Alcorn State	Greenville, Miss.	Greenville, Miss.	FA
Fritzche, Jim (1)	T	6-8	265	10/11/60	Purdue	Berea, Ohio	Wilafayette, Ind.	D8 ('82)
Graham, Pat (1)	NT	6-4	272	4/21/59	California	Palo Alto, Calif.	Sunnyvale, Calif.	FA
Grieve, Curt (1)	WR	6-4	195	8/23/59	Yale	Hammond, Ind.	Pittsburgh, Pa.	D6 ('82)
Haddix, Michael	RB	6-2	225	12/27/61	Mississippi State	Tippah County, Miss.	Walnut, Miss.	D1
Harrell, Ozzie	CB-S	5-11	180	1/4/58	Missouri Southern	Miami, Fla.	Independence, Mo.	FA
Haywood, Rob	G	6-2	257	9/22/61	Princeton	Detroit, Mich.	Detroit, Mich.	FA
Hopkins, Wes	S	6-1	205	9/26/61	Southern Methodist	Birmingham, Ala.	Birmingham, Ala.	D2
Howell, Ken	G	6-3	240	10/26/60	Georgia Tech	Shelby, N.C.	Shelby, N.C.	FA
Jenkins, Ken (1)	RB	5-9	183	5/8/59	Bucknell	Washington, D.C.	Wheaton, Md.	FA
Keeler, K.C.	CB-S	6-0	195	7/26/59	Delaware	Allentown, Pa.	Emmaus, Pa.	FA
Kraynak, Rick	LB	6-1	221	1/20/61	Pittsburgh	Phoenixville, Pa.	Phoenixville, Pa.	D8
Larson, Lee	K	6-1	185	7/1/59	Hawaii	Seoul, Korea	Honolulu, Hawaii	FA
Mangrum, David	QB	6-4	196	10/14/59	Baylor	Harlinger, Tex.	Waco, Tex.	D12
McDonald, Rich	T	6-3	270	12/16/60	Youngstown State	Marion, Ohio	Canton, Ohio	FA
Mini, Vinnie	NT	6-0	265	4/5/61	Temple	Brooklyn, N.Y.	Philadelphia, Pa.	FA
Miraldi, Dean	G	6-5	254	4/8/58	Utah	Culver City, Calif.	Newport Beach, Ca.	D2 ('81)
Mitchell, Harry	RB	6-0	240	3/17/58	Virginia Union	Detroit, Mich.	Richmond, Va.	FA
Natividad, Frank	P	6-2	205	1/11/61	Hawaii	Los Angeles, Calif.	Honolulu, Hawaii	FA
Nizolek, Scott	TE-P	6-2	225	2/23/61	Boston College	Red Bank, N.J.	Branford, Conn.	FA
Oatis, Victor	WR	5-11	178	1/6/59	Northwest Louisiana	Monroe, La.	Winnsboro, La.	D6
Oliver, Ken	WR	6-0	182	8/11/61	Montclair State	Newark, N.J.	Passaic, N.J.	FA
Pelzer, Rich	T	6-6	290	4/20/59	Rhode Island	Brooklyn, N.Y.	Brooklyn, N.Y.	D9
Porter, Rick (1)	RB	5-10	190	1/4/60	Slippery Rock	Baltimore, Md.	Baltimore, Md.	FA
Reeves, Morgan	RB	5-11	190	11/23/58	Michigan State	Columbia, S.C.	Irmo, S.C.	FA
Schultheis, Jon	G-C	6-3	270	7/23/61	Princeton	Elizabeth, N.J.	Keansburg, N.J.	D7a
Schulz, Jody	LB	6-4	235	8/17/60	East Carolina	Easton, Md.	Chester, Md.	D2a
Sebahar, Steve	C	6-4	255	3/4/61	Washington State	Chicago, Ill.	Pleasanton, Calif.	D11
Strauthers, Thomas	DE	6-4	255	4/6/61	Jackson State	Wesson, Miss.	Jackson, Miss.	D10
Sullivan, Brian (1)	K	6-1	175	3/26/59	Santa Clara	Torrance, Calif.	Carlsbad, Calif.	FA
Thomas, Ken	CB-S	5-9	180	9/14/59	Alabama A&M	Birmingham, Ala.	Birmingham, Ala.	FA
Vassar, Brad (1)	LB	6-1	218	4/24/57	Pacific	Sonora, Calif.	Sonora, Calif.	FA
Vura, Gary	QB	6-2	205	10/16/61	Pennsylvania	Cleveland, Ohio	Miami Lakes, Fla.	FA
Wells, Joe	LB	6-2	235	4/26/59	Southern Utah State	Phoenix, Ariz.	Cedar City, Utah	FA
Williams, Michael	RB	6-2	217	7/16/61	Mississippi	Atmore, Ala.	Atmore, Ala.	D4
Williams, Milton (1)	RB	6-1	202	6/18/58	Norwich	New York, N.Y.	Brooklyn, N.Y.	FA
Young, Glen	WR	6-2	205	10/11/60	Mississippi State	Greenwood, Miss.	Greenwood, Miss.	D3

Players who report to an NFL team for the first time are designated on rosters as rookies (R). If a player reported to an NFL training camp in a previous year but was not on the active squad for three or more regular season or postseason games, he is listed on the first-year roster and designated by a (1). Thereafter, a player who is on the active squad for three or more regular season or postseason games is credited with an additional year of playing experience.

NOTES

_____

_____

_____

_____

_____

_____

Jerry Wampfler, offensive line-running game; born August 6, 1932, New Philadelphia, Ohio, lives in Philadelphia. Tackle Miami, Ohio 1951-54. No pro playing experience. College coach: Presbyterian 1955, Miami, Ohio 1963-65, Notre Dame 1966-69, Colorado State 1970-72 (head coach). Pro coach: Philadelphia Eagles 1973-75, Buffalo Bills 1976-77, New York Giants 1978, rejoined Eagles in 1979.

Dick Wood, offensive coordinator; born February 2, 1936, Lanett, Ala., lives in Philadelphia. Quarterback Auburn 1956-59. Pro quarterback Baltimore 1960-61, San Diego 1962, Denver 1962, New York Jets 1963-64, Oakland Raiders 1965, Miami Dolphins 1966. College coach: Georgia 1967-68, Mississippi 1971-73. Pro coach: Oakland Raiders 1969-70, Cleveland Browns 1974, New Orleans Saints 1976-77, Atlanta Falcons 1978-82, first year with Eagles.

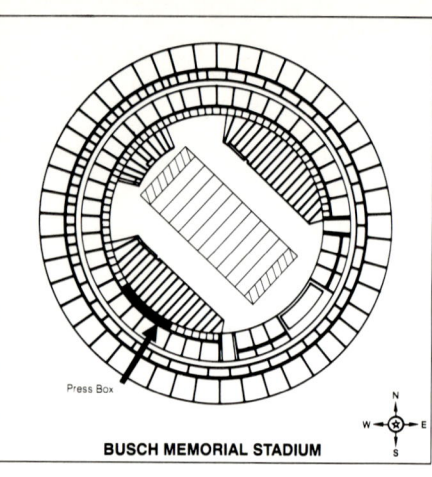

BUSCH MEMORIAL STADIUM

Press Box

St. Louis Cardinals

**National Football Conference
Eastern Division**

Team Colors: Cardinal Red, Black, and
White
**Busch Stadium, Box 888
St. Louis, Missouri 63188
Telephone: (314) 421-0777**

Club Officials

Chairman of the Board, CEO: William V. Bidwill
President: Bing Devine
Director of Pro Personnel: Larry Wilson
Treasurer: Charley Schlegel
Director of Player Personnel: George Boone
Public Relations Director: Susie Mathieu
Media Coordinator: Marty Igel
Director of Community Relations: Adele Harris
Ticket Manager: Steve Walsh
Trainer: John Omohundro
Assistant Trainers: Jim Shearer, Ed Fleming
Equipment Manager: Bill Simmons
Assistant Equipment Manager: Mark Ahlmeier

Stadium: Busch Memorial Stadium •
Capacity: 51,392
200 Stadium Plaza
St. Louis, Missouri 63102
Playing Surface: AstroTurf
Training Camp: Eastern Illinois University
Charleston, Illinois 61920

1983 SCHEDULE

Preseason

Aug. 6	vs. Minnesota at London, England...	TBA
Aug. 13	**Chicago**	6:00
Aug. 20	at Kansas City	7:30
Aug. 27	**Green Bay**	6:00

Regular Season

Sept. 4	at New Orleans	12:00
Sept. 11	**Dallas**	12:00
Sept. 18	**San Francisco**	12:00
Sept. 25	at Philadelphia	1:00
Oct. 2	at Kansas City	3:00
Oct. 9	**Washington**	12:00
Oct. 16	at Tampa Bay	1:00
Oct. 24	**New York Giants** (Monday)	8:00
Oct. 30	**Minnesota**	12:00
Nov. 6	at Washington	4:00
Nov. 13	**Seattle**	12:00
Nov. 20	**San Diego**	12:00
Nov. 24	at Dallas (Thanksgiving)	3:00
Dec. 4	at New York Giants	1:00
Dec. 11	at Los Angeles Raiders	1:00
Dec. 18	**Philadelphia**	12:00

1982 TEAM STATISTICS

	St. Louis	Opp.
Total First Downs	162	163
Rushing	71	58
Passing	81	98
Penalty	10	7
Third Down Efficiency	47/127	52/129
Third Down Percentage	37.0	40.3
Total Net Yards	2542	2848
Total Offensive Plays	579	570
Avg. Gain per Play	4.4	5.0
Avg. Gain per Game	282.4	316.4
Net Yards Rushing	1209	995
Total Rushing Plays	307	256
Avg. Gain per Rush	3.9	3.9
Avg. Gain Rushing per Game	134.3	110.6
Net Yards Passing	1333	1853
Lost Attempting to Pass	32/243	23/182
Gross Yards Passing	1576	2035
Attempts/Completions	240/129	291/174
Percent Completed	53.8	59.8
Had Intercepted	6	6
Avg. Net Passing per Game	148.1	205.9
Punts/Avg.	54/43.8	51/41.2
Punt Returns/Avg.	32/6.0	36/8.0
Kickoff Returns/Avg.	35/20.1	27/20.7
Interceptions/Avg. Ret.	6/8.7	6/6.2
Penalties/Yards	56/528	54/420
Fumbles/Ball Lost	17/10	14/9
Total Points	135	170
Avg. Points per Game	15.0	18.9
Touchdowns	16	21
Rushing	10	5
Passing	6	16
Returns and Recoveries	0	0
Field Goals	8/13	8/18
Conversions	15/16	20/21
Safeties	0	0
Avg. Time of Possession	30:28	29:32

1982 TEAM RECORD

Preseason (1-3)

St. Louis		Opponents
0	Seattle	14
13	San Francisco	16
10	Chicago	3
6	*Kansas City	10
29		43

Regular Season (5-4)

St. Louis		Opponents	Att.
21	New Orleans	7	58,673
7	*Dallas	24	50,705
20	*San Francisco	31	38,064
23	Atlanta	20	33,411
23	Philadelphia	20	63,622
7	*Washington	12	35,308
10	Chicago	7	43,270
24	*New York Giants	21	39,824
0	Washington	28	52,554
135		170	415,431

*Home Game

Score by Periods

St. Louis	31	48	19	37	—	135
Opponents	23	34	37	76	—	170

Attendance

Home 163,901   Away 251,530   Total 415,431
Single game home record, 50,885 (9-2-79)
Single season home record, 384,375 (1981)

1982 INDIVIDUAL STATISTICS

Rushing

	Att	Yds	Avg	LG	TD
Anderson	145	587	4.0	64	3
Morris	84	274	3.3	11	4
Mitchell	39	189	4.8	32t	1
Lomax	28	119	4.3	19	1
Wehrli	1	18	18.0	18t	1
Harrell	4	14	3.5	8	0
Green	6	8	1.3	13	0
St. Louis	307	1209	3.9	64	10
Opponents	256	995	3.9	37	5

Field Goal Success

Distance	1-19	20-29	30-39	40-49	50 Over
Made-Att.	1-1	2-3	3-3	2-6	0-0

Passing

	Att	Comp	Pct	Yds	TD	Int	Tkld	Rate
Lomax	205	109	53.2	1367	5	6	31/234	70.1
Hart	33	19	57.6	199	1	0	0/0	85.2
Harrell	1	1	100.0	10	0	0	0/0	—
Green	1	0	0.0	0	0	0	1/9	—
St. Louis	240	129	53.8	1576	6	6	32/243	
Opponents	291	174	59.8	2035	16	6	23/182	

Receiving

	No	Yds	Avg	LG	TD
Tilley	36	465	12.9	34	2
Green	32	453	14.2	42	3
Anderson	14	106	7.6	19	0
Mitchell	11	149	13.5	30	0
Harrell	11	127	11.5	36	0
Marsh	5	83	16.6	21	0
LaFleur	5	67	13.4	20	1
Shumann	5	58	11.6	23	0
Gray	4	34	8.5	13	0
Morris	4	19	4.8	11	0
Lomax	1	10	10.0	10	0
K. Thompson	1	5	5.0	5	0
St. Louis	129	1576	12.2	42	6
Opponents	174	2035	11.7	55	16

Interceptions

	No	Yds	Avg	LG	TD
Perrin	1	35	35.0	35	0
Griffin	1	8	8.0	8	0
Nelson	1	7	7.0	7	0
Greene	1	2	2.0	2	0
Allen	1	0	0.0	0	0
Dawson	1	0	0.0	0	0
St. Louis	6	52	8.7	35	0
Opponents	6	37	6.2	19	0

Punting

	No	Yds	Avg	In 20	LG
Birdsong	54	2365	43.8	8	65
St. Louis	54	2365	43.8	8	65
Opponents	51	2099	41.2	12	53

Punt Returns

	No	FC	Yds	Avg	LG	TD
Mitchell	27	0	165	6.1	15	0
Green	3	0	20	6.7	11	0
Ferrell	1	0	6	6.0	6	0
Harrell	1	1	1	1.0	1	0
St. Louis	32	1	192	6.0	15	0
Opponents	36	4	288	8.0	38	0

Kickoff Returns

	No	Yds	Avg	LG	TD
Mitchell	16	364	22.8	33	0
Harrell	8	150	18.8	31	0
Ferrell	4	88	22.0	27	0
Love	4	69	17.3	24	0
Morris	1	14	14.0	14	0
Griffin	1	12	12.0	12	0
Ahrens	1	5	5.0	5	0
St. Louis	35	702	20.1	33	0
Opponents	27	558	20.7	44	0

Scoring

	TD	TD R	TD P	TD Rt	PAT	FG	TP
O'Donoghue					15/16	8/13	39
Morris	4	4	0	0			24
Anderson	3	3	0	0			18
Green	3	0	3	0			18
Tilley	2	0	2	0			12
LaFleur	1	0	1	0			6
Lomax	1	1	0	0			6
Mitchell	1	1	0	0			6
Wehrli	1	1	0	0			6
St. Louis	16	10	6	0	15/16	8/13	135
Opponents	21	5	16	0	20/21	8/18	170

Sacks

Brown 3, Dawson 3½, Galloway 2, Greer 7½, Grooms 4½, Junior 1½, Thornton 1.

FIRST PLAYERS SELECTED

Since 1954

Year	Player, College, Position
1954	Lamar McHan, Arkansas, B
1955	Max Boydston, Oklahoma, E
1956	Joe Childress, Auburn, B
1957	Jerry Tubbs, Oklahoma, C
1958	King Hill, Rice, B
1959	Bill Stacy, Mississippi State, B
1960	George Izo, Notre Dame, QB
1961	Ken Rice, Auburn, T
1962	Fate Echols, Northwestern, DT
1963	Jerry Stovall, Louisiana State, S
1964	Ken Kortas, Louisville, DT
1965	Joe Namath, Alabama, QB
1966	Carl McAdams, Oklahoma, LB
1967	Dave Williams, Washington, WR
1968	MacArthur Lane, Utah State, RB
1969	Roger Wehrli, Missouri, DB
1970	Larry Stegent, Texas A&M, RB
1971	Norm Thompson, Utah, CB
1972	Bobby Moore, Oregon, RB-WR
1973	Dave Butz, Purdue, DT
1974	J.V. Cain, Colorado, TE
1975	Tim Gray, Texas A&M, DB
1976	Mike Dawson, Arizona, DT
1977	Steve Pisarkiewicz, Missouri, QB
1978	Steve Little, Arkansas, K
1979	Ottis Anderson, Miami, RB
1980	Curtis Greer, Michigan, DE
1981	E. J. Junior, Alabama, LB
1982	Luis Sharpe, UCLA, T
1983	Leonard Smith, McNeese State, DB

CARDINALS COACHING HISTORY

Chicago 1920-59
(319-420-37)

Year	Coach	Record
1920	Marshall Smith	5-2-1
1921-22	John (Paddy) Driscoll	12-6-3
1923-24	Arnold Horween	13-8-1
1925-26	Norman Barry	16-8-2
1927	Fred Gillies	3-7-1
1928	Guy Chamberlin	1-5-0
1929-30	Ernie Nevers	11-12-3
1931	LeRoy Andrews*	0-2-0
1931	Ernie Nevers	5-2-0
1932	Jack Chevigny	2-6-2
1933-34	Paul Schissler	6-15-1
1935-38	Milan Creighton	16-26-4
1939	Ernie Nevers	1-10-0
1940-42	Jimmy Conzelman	8-22-3
1943-45	Phil Handler**	1-29-0
1946-48	Jimmy Conzelman	27-10-0
1949	Phil Handler-Buddy Parker***	6-5-1
1950-51	Earl (Curly) Lambeau	8-16-0
1952	Joe Kuharich	4-8-0
1953-54	Joe Stydahar	3-20-1
1955-57	Ray Richards	14-21-1
1958-61	Frank (Pop) Ivy	17-31-2
1962-65	Wally Lemm	27-26-3
1966-70	Charley Winner	35-30-5
1971-72	Bob Hollway	8-18-2
1973-77	Don Coryell	42-29-1
1978-79	Bud Wilkinson****	9-20-0
1979	Larry Wilson	2-1-0
1980-82	Jim Hanifan	17-25-0

*Resigned after two games in 1931
**Co-coach with Walt Kiesling of 1944 Card-Pitt team
***Co-coaches
****Released after 13 games in 1979

ST. LOUIS CARDINALS 1983 VETERAN ROSTER

No.	Name	Pos.	Ht.	Wt.	Birth-date	NFL Exp.	College	Birthplace	Residence	Games in '82
58	Ahrens, Dave	LB	6-3	228	12/5/58	3	Wisconsin	Cedar Falls, Iowa	St. Louis, Mo.	9
27	†Allen, Carl	CB	6-0	190	12/21/55	8	Southern Mississippi	Hattiesburg, Miss.	St. Louis, Mo.	9
51	Allerman, Kurt	LB	6-2	222	8/30/55	7	Penn State	Glenridge, N.J.	Ballwin, Mo.	9
32	Anderson, Ottis	RB	6-2	220	1/19/57	5	Miami	West Palm Beach, Fla.	St. Louis, Mo.	8
	t-Audick, Dan	G-T	6-3	253	11/15/54	6	Hawaii	San Bernardino, Calif.	San Diego, Calif.	7
52	Baker, Charlie	LB	6-2	217	9/26/57	4	New Mexico	Mt. Pleasant, Tex.	St. Louis, Mo.	9
46	Bessillieu, Don	CB-S	6-1	200	5/4/56	5	Georgia Tech	Ft. Benning, Ga.	St. Louis, Mo.	3
18	Birdsong, Carl	P	6-0	192	1/1/59	3	Southwest Oklahoma State	Kaufman, Tex.	Amarillo, Tex.	9
71	Bostic, Joe	G	6-3	265	4/20/57	5	Clemson	Greensboro, N.C.	Greensboro, N.C.	8
69	Brown, Rush	DT	6-2	260	6/27/54	4	Ball State	Laurinburg, N.C.	Chesterfield, Mo.	9
64	Clark, Randy	C	6-3	254	7/27/57	4	Northern Illinois	Chicago, Ill.	St. Ann, Mo.	9
60	Cotton, Barney	G	6-5	265	9/30/56	4	Nebraska	Omaha, Neb.	Lincoln, Neb.	0*
73	Dawson, Mike	DT	6-4	270	10/16/53	8	Arizona	Tucson, Ariz.	St. Louis, Mo.	9
72	†Dierdorf, Dan	C	6-3	290	6/29/49	12	Michigan	Canton, Ohio	St. Louis, Mo.	9
31	Ferrell, Earl	RB	6-0	215	3/27/58	2	East Tennessee State	Halifax, Va.	South Boston, Va.	9
65	Galloway, David	DT	6-3	277	2/16/59	2	Florida	Tampa, Fla.	Tampa, Fla.	5
57	Gillen, John	LB	6-3	228	11/5/58	3	Illinois	Arlington Heights, Ill.	St. Louis, Mo.	4
81	Green, Roy	WR	6-0	195	6/30/57	5	Henderson State	Magnolia, Ark.	St. Louis, Mo.	9
75	Greer, Curtis	DE	6-4	252	11/10/57	4	Michigan	Detroit, Mich.	St. Louis, Mo.	9
35	Griffin, Jeff	CB	6-4	185	7/19/58	3	Utah	Carson, Calif.	University City, Mo.	9
78	Grooms, Elois	DE	6-4	250	5/20/53	8	Tennessee Tech	Tomkinsville, Ky.	Mandeville, La.	9
39	Harrell, Willard	RB	5-8	182	9/16/52	9	Pacific	Stockton, Calif.	St. Louis, Mo.	7
17	Hart, Jim	QB	6-1	210	4/29/44	18	Southern Illinois	Evanston, Ill.	St. Louis, Mo.	4
54	Junior, E.J.	LB	6-3	235	12/8/59	3	Alabama	Sallsburg, N.C.	St. Louis, Mo.	9
89	LaFleur, Greg	TE	6-4	236	9/16/58	3	Louisiana State	Lafayette, La.	Velle Platte, La.	9
16	Lisch, Rusty	QB	6-3	213	12/21/56	4	Notre Dame	Belleville, Ill.	Belleville, Ill.	8
15	Lomax, Neil	QB	6-3	215	2/17/59	3	Portland State	Portland, Ore.	West Linn, Ore.	9
40	Love, Randy	RB	6-1	205	9/30/56	5	Houston	Wylie, Tex.	Garland, Tex.	9
80	Marsh, Doug	TE	6-3	240	6/18/58	4	Michigan	Akron, Ohio	St. Louis, Mo.	8
76	Mays, Stafford	DE	6-2	250	3/13/58	4	Washington	Lawrence, Kan.	Tacoma, Wash.	8
87	McGill, Eddie	TE	6-6	225	7/5/60	2	Western Carolina	Asheville, N.C.	Candler, N.C.	9
30	Mitchell, Stump	RB-KR	5-9	188	3/15/59	3	Citadel	St. Mary's, Ga.	St. Louis, Mo.	9
24	Morris, Wayne	RB	6-0	210	5/3/54	8	Southern Methodist	Dallas, Tex.	Dallas, Tex.	9
38	Nelson, Lee	S	5-10	185	1/30/54	8	Florida State	Kissimee, Fla.	Tallahassee, Fla.	8
11	O'Donoghue, Neil	K	6-6	210	6/18/53	7	Auburn	Dublin, Ireland	Indian Rocks, Fla.	8
23	Perrin, Benny	S	6-2	178	10/20/59	2	Alabama	Orange County, Calif.	Decatur, Ala.	9
70	Plunkett, Art	T	6-7	270	3/8/59	3	Nevada-Las Vegas	Chicago, Ill.	Las Vegas, Nev.	9
50	Puki, Craig	LB	6-1	231	1/18/57	4	Tennessee	Seattle, Wash.	Redwood City, Calif.	7
63	Robbins, Tootie	T	6-4	278	6/2/58	2	East Carolina	Windsor, N.C.	St. Louis, Mo.	9
74	Sebro, Bob	G	6-4	255	3/9/59	2	Colorado	Ontario, Calif.	St. Louis, Mo.	0*
53	Shaffer, Craig	LB	6-0	230	3/31/59	2	Indiana State	Terre Haute, Ind.	St. Louis, Mo.	5
67	Sharpe, Luis	T	6-4	260	6/16/60	2	UCLA	Havana, Cuba	Los Angeles, Calif.	9
84	†Shumann, Mike	WR	6-1	185	10/13/55	6	Florida State	Louisville, Ky.	Woodside, Calif.	6
44	Smith, Wayne	CB	6-0	175	5/9/57	4	Purdue	Chicago, Ill.	Chicago, Ill.	6*
21	†Stief, Dave	CB-S	6-3	195	1/29/56	6	Portland State	Portland, Ore.	Homer, Alaska	9
68	Stieve, Terry	G	6-2	265	3/10/54	7	Wisconsin	Baraboo, Wis.	St. Louis, Mo.	9
79	Thornton, Bruce	DT	6-5	263	2/14/58	5	Illinois	Detroit, Mich.	Dallas, Tex.	6
83	Tilley, Pat	WR	5-10	178	2/15/53	8	Louisiana Tech	Marshall, Tex.	Shreveport, La.	9
42	Williams, Herb	CB-S	6-0	200	8/30/58	4	Southern	Baton Rouge, La.	Baton Rouge, La.	7

* Cotton missed '82 season due to injury; Sebro active for 5 games with St. Louis in '82, but did not play; Smith played 5 games with Detroit, 1 with St. Louis in '82.

†Option playout; subject to developments.

t-Cardinals traded for Audick (San Francisco).

Retired—Mel Gray, 12-year wide receiver, 5 games in '82; Roger Wehrli, 14-year cornerback, 8 in '82.

Traded—Guard-tackle George Collins to San Francisco, safety Ken Greene to San Diego.

Also played with Cardinals in '82—CB Tim Collier (4 games), LB Calvin Favron (4), WR Ricky Thompson (3).

COACHING STAFF

Head Coach, Jim Hanifan

Pro Career: Named head coach on January 30, 1980 and posted 5-11 mark in 1980 followed by 7-9 in 1981 and 5-4 in 1982. No stranger to city of St. Louis, where he began his pro coaching career in 1973 as offensive line coach. Served Cardinals in that capacity until 1979 when he left to become assistant head coach of San Diego Chargers. During his first tenure at St. Louis, his offensive lines allowed fewest quarterback sacks in NFL for three straight years (1974-76), including an NFL record low of eight in 1975. Played end for the Toronto Argonauts (CFL) in 1955. Career record: 17-25.

Background: Played end for California 1952-54 and led the nation in receiving as a senior. Began coaching career at Charter Oak High School in Covina, Calif., in 1962. Was a college assistant for 14 years: Yuba, Calif., J.C. 1959-61, Glendale, Calif., J.C. 1964-65, Utah 1966-69, California 1970-71, San Diego State 1972.

Personal: Born September 21, 1933 in Compton, Calif. He and his wife, Mariana, live in St. Louis and have two children — Kathleen and James.

ASSISTANT COACHES

Chuck Banker, special teams-defensive assistant; born March 12, 1941, Prescott Ariz., lives in St. Louis. Linebacker-tight end Pasadena C.C. 1959-60. No pro playing experience. College coach: Glendale, Calif., J.C. 1962-65, Utah 1966-67, 1974-75, Westminster 1968-70, Boise State 1976-79. Pro coach: Joined Cardinals in 1980.

Tom Bettis, defensive coordinator; born March 17, 1933, Chicago, lives in St. Louis. Guard Purdue 1951-54. Pro linebacker Green Bay Packers 1955-61, Pittsburgh Steelers 1962, Chicago Bears 1963. Pro coach: Kansas City Chiefs 1966-77 (head coach for final seven games of 1977), Cardinals since 1978.

Don Brown, strength and conditioning; born February 2, 1951, Butler, Pa., lives in St. Louis. Linebacker Wake Forest 1970-72. No pro playing experience. College coach: Wake Forest 1973, 1975-77. Pro coach: Joined Cardinals in 1978.

Rod Dowhower, offensive coordinator; born April 15, 1943, Ord, Neb., lives in St. Louis. Quarterback San Diego State 1963-64. No pro playing experience. College coach: San Diego State 1968-72, UCLA 1974-75, Boise State 1976, Stanford 1977-79 (head coach 1979). Pro coach: St. Louis Cardinals 1973, Denver Broncos 1980-82, rejoined Cardinals in 1983.

Rudy Feldman, linebackers; born May 18, 1932, San Francisco, lives in St. Louis. Guard UCLA 1950-53. No pro playing experience. College coach: Iowa State 1957, Oklahoma 1963-67, New Mexico 1968-73. Pro coach: San Diego Chargers 1974-77, Cardinals since 1978.

Dick Jamieson, offensive backfield; born November 13, 1937, Streator, Ill., lives in St. Louis. Quarterback Bradley 1955-58. Pro quarterback Baltimore Colts 1959, New York Titans 1960, Houston Oilers 1965. College coach: Bradley 1962-64, Missouri 1972-79. Pro coach: Joined Cardinals in 1980.

Tom Lovat, offensive line; born December 28, 1938, Bingham, Utah, lives in St. Louis. Guard-linebacker Utah 1958-60. No pro playing experience. College coach: Utah 1967, 1972-76 (head coach 1974-76), Idaho State 1968-70, Stanford 1977-79. Pro coach: Saskatchewan Roughriders (CFL) 1971, Green Bay Packers 1980, Cardinals since 1981.

Leon McLaughlin, special assistant; born May 30, 1925, San Diego, Calif., lives in St. Louis. Center-linebacker UCLA 1946-49. Pro center Los Angeles Rams 1951-55. College coach: Washington State 1956, Stanford 1959-65, San Fernando Valley State 1969-70 (head coach). Pro coach: Pittsburgh Steelers 1966-68, Los Angeles Rams 1971-72, Detroit Lions 1973-74, Green Bay Packers 1975-76, New England Patriots 1977, Cardinals since 1978.

ST. LOUIS CARDINALS 1983 FIRST-YEAR ROSTER

Name	Pos.	Ht.	Wt.	Birth-date	College	Birthplace	Residence	How Acq.
Bedford, Vance (1)	CB	5-11	170	8/20/58	Texas	Houston, Tex.	Houston, Tex.	D5 ('82)
Bird, Steve	WR	5-11	171	10/20/60	Eastern Kentucky	Indianapolis, Ind.	Corbin, Ky.	D5
Blair, Ken (1)	WR	6-0	195	5/9/58	Missouri	Oklahoma City, Okla.	Oklahoma City, Okla.	FA
Boliaux, Guy (1)	LB	6-1	214	9/21/59	Wisconsin	Chicago, Ill.	Des Plaines, Ill.	FA
Bolton, David (1)	WR	6-3	190	8/28/60	Washington, Mo.	St. Louis, Mo.	St. Louis, Mo.	FA
Brown, Otis	RB	5-11	200	2/3/60	Jackson State	Monroe, La.	Bastrop, La.	D9
Burgess, Fernanza	QB	6-1	210	3/6/60	Morris Brown	Miami, Fla.	Miami, Fla.	FA
Butler, Anson	RB	6-0	212	10/1/59	Georgetown, Ky.	Frankfort, Germany	Radcliffe, Ky.	FA
Cox, Todd	K	5-11	178	4/4/60	Dubuque	Davenport, Iowa	DeWitt, Iowa	FA
Dailey, Darnell (1)	LB	6-3	223	9/8/59	Maryland	Baltimore, Md.	Silver Springs, Md.	D9 ('82)
Dardar, Ramsey	DT	6-2	264	10/3/59	Louisiana State	Cecelia, La.	Breaux Bridge, La.	D3
Duda, Mark	DT	6-3	263	2/4/61	Maryland	Wilkes Barre, Pa.	Plymouth, Pa.	D4
Falcinelli, Alex	K	5-11	175	1/1/61	Rutgers	Miami, Fla.	New Brunswick, N.J.	FA
Harris, Bob	S	6-2	205	11/11/60	Auburn	Everett, Wash.	Decatur, Ga.	D8
Jett, DeWayne (1)	WR	6-2	195	2/24/58	Hawaii	Minneapolis, Minn.	Northridge, Calif.	FA
Johannes, Michael	P	6-3	192	5/13/61	Indiana State	Sheboygan, Wis.	Ft. Wayne, Ind.	FA
Kehr, Rick (1)	T	6-4	265	6/18/59	Carthage	Phoenixville, Pa.	Stream Wood, Ill.	FA
Lane, James	LB	6-3	225	5/13/60	Alabama State	Montgomery, Ala.	Montgomery, Ala.	D12
Mack, Cedrick	CB	6-0	190	9/14/60	Baylor	Freeport, Tex.	Freeport, Tex.	D2
Ross, Walter	RB	5-11	190	12/23/60	Northern Colorado	Aberdeen, S.D.	Aberdeen, S.D.	FA
Sample, Ted (1)	RB	5-11	224	8/22/58	East Texas State	Miami, Okla.	Garland, Tex.	FA
Schmitt, George	CB	5-11	193	3/6/61	Delaware	Bryn Mawr, Pa.	Broomall, Pa.	D6
Scott, Carlos	C	6-4	300	7/2/60	Texas-El Paso	Hempstead, Tex.	El Paso, Tex.	D7
Smith, Eric	WR	6-4	190	7/1/60	Georgetown, D.C.	Bethesda, Md.	Potomac, Md.	FA
Smith, Leonard	CB	5-11	190	9/2/60	McNeese State	New Orleans, La.	Lake Charles, La.	D1
Thompson, Ken (1)	WR	6-2	170	12/6/58	Utah State	Snyder, Tex.	Snyder, Tex.	FA
Washington, Lionel	WR	6-0	184	10/21/60	Tulane	New Orleans, La.	Lutcher, La.	D4a
Williams, Aaron	WR	6-0	170	7/27/60	Washington	Stuttgart, Germany	Tacoma, Wash.	D11

Players who report to an NFL team for the first time are designated on rosters as rookies (R). If a player reported to an NFL training camp in a previous year but was not on the active squad for three or more regular season or postseason games, he is listed on the first-year roster and designated by a (1). Thereafter, a player who is on the active squad for three or more regular season or postseason games is credited with an additional year of playing experience.

NOTES

_____
_____
_____
_____
_____
_____
_____
_____
_____
_____
_____

Floyd Peters, assistant head coach-defensive line; born May 21, 1936, Council Bluffs, Iowa, lives in St. Louis. Defensive tackle San Francisco State 1954-57. Pro defensive tackle Baltimore Colts 1958, Cleveland Browns 1959-62, Detroit Lions 1963, Philadelphia Eagles 1964-69, Washington Redskins 1970. Pro coach: Washington Redskins 1970, New York Giants 1974-75, San Francisco 49ers 1976-77, Detroit Lions 1978-81, Cardinals since 1982.

Emmitt Thomas, receivers; born June 4, 1943, Angleton, Tex., lives in St. Louis. Quarterback-wide receiver Bishop College 1963-65. Pro defensive back Kansas City Chiefs 1966-78. College coach: Central Missouri State 1979-80. Pro coach: Joined Cardinals in 1981.

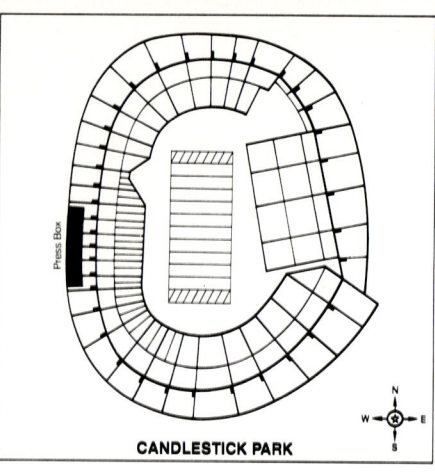

CANDLESTICK PARK

San Francisco 49ers

**National Football Conference
Western Division**

Team Colors: Forty Niners Gold
and Scarlet

**711 Nevada Street
Redwood City, California 94061
Telephone (415) 365-3420**

Club Officials
Owner, Chairman of the Board: Edward J. DeBartolo, Jr.
President, Head Coach: Bill Walsh
General Manager: John McVay
Director of Marketing and Community Affairs:
  Ken Flower
Director of Pro Scouting: Alan Webb
Director of College Scouting: Tony Razzano
Director of Public Relations: Hal Lundgren
Publicity Director: Jerry Walker
Business Manager: Keith Simon
Ticket Manager: Ken Dargel
Trainer: Lindsy McLean
Assistant Trainer: John Miller
Equipment Manager: Chico Norton
Equipment Assistant: Bronco Hinek

Stadium: Candlestick Park • **Capacity:** 61,185
  San Francisco, California 94124
Playing Surface: Grass
Training Camp: Sierra Community College
  Rocklin, California 95677

1983 SCHEDULE
Preseason
Aug. 6	at Los Angeles Raiders	6:00
Aug. 14	**New England**	1:00
Aug. 20	at San Diego	6:00
Aug. 27	**Seattle**	2:00

Regular Season
Sept. 4	**Philadelphia**	1:00
Sept. 8	at Minnesota (Thursday)	7:30
Sept. 18	at St. Louis	12:00
Sept. 25	**Atlanta**	1:00
Oct. 2	at New England	1:00
Oct. 9	**Los Angeles Rams**	1:00
Oct. 16	at New Orleans	12:00
Oct. 23	at Los Angeles Rams	1:00
Oct. 30	**New York Jets**	1:00
Nov. 6	**Miami**	1:00
Nov. 13	**New Orleans**	1:00
Nov. 20	at Atlanta	4:00
Nov. 27	at Chicago	12:00
Dec. 4	**Tampa Bay**	1:00
Dec. 11	at Buffalo	1:00
Dec. 19	**Dallas** (Monday)	6:00

1982 TEAM STATISTICS

	San Francisco	Opp.
Total First Downs	183	170
Rushing	49	71
Passing	121	88
Penalty	13	11
Third Down Efficiency	47/120	38/120
Third Down Percentage	39.2	31.7
Total Net Yards	3242	3035
Total Offensive Plays	587	596
Avg. Gain per Play	5.5	5.1
Avg. Gain per Game	360.2	337.2
Net Yards Rushing	740	1199
Total Rushing Plays	219	303
Avg. Gain per Rush	3.4	4.0
Avg. Gain Rushing per Game	82.2	133.2
Net Yards Passing	2502	1836
Lost Attempting to Pass	20/166	15/113
Gross Yards Passing	2668	1949
Attempts/Completions	348/215	278/158
Percent Completed	61.8	56.8
Had Intercepted	11	9
Avg. Net Passing per Game	278.0	204.0
Punts/Avg.	45/37.2	50/42.7
Punt Returns/Avg.	30/11.1	20/11.2
Kickoff Returns/Avg.	36/20.6	40/21.4
Interceptions/Avg. Ret.	9/16.7	11/11.8
Penalties/Yards	45/451	58/542
Fumbles/Ball Lost	17/10	14/4
Total Points	209	206
Avg. Points per Game	23.2	22.9
Touchdowns	25	24
Rushing	6	9
Passing	17	14
Returns and Recoveries	2	1
Field Goals	12/17	13/19
Conversions	23/25	23/24
Safeties	0	0
Avg. Time of Possession	28:31	31:29

1982 TEAM RECORD

Preseason (2-2)

San Francisco		Opponents
14	*Los Angeles Raiders	17
16	*St. Louis	13
9	San Diego	23
17	Seattle	13
56		66

Regular Season (3-6)

San Francisco		Opponents	Att.
17	*Los Angeles Raiders	23	59,748
21	Denver	24	73,899
31	St. Louis	20	38,064
20	*New Orleans	23	51,611
30	Los Angeles Rams	24	58,574
37	*San Diego	41	55,988
7	*Atlanta	17	53,234
26	Kansas City	13	24,319
20	*Los Angeles Rams	21	54,256
209		206	469,693

*Home Game

Score by Periods

San Francisco	37	81	23	68	—	209
Opponents	44	64	37	61	—	206

Attendance

Home 274,837 Away 194,856 Total 469,693
Single game home record, 61,214 (4 times, 1972)
Single season home record, 442,067 (1972)

1982 INDIVIDUAL STATISTICS

Rushing

	Att	Yds	Avg	LG	TD
Moore	85	281	3.3	19	4
Ring	48	183	3.8	11	1
Montana	30	118	3.9	21	1
Cooper	24	77	3.2	9	0
V. Williams	20	68	3.4	12	0
Easley	5	11	2.2	5	0
Lawrence	5	7	1.4	4	0
Nehemiah	1	−1	−1.0	−1	0
Solomon	1	−4	−4.0	−4	0
San Francisco	219	740	3.4	21	6
Opponents	303	1199	4.0	54	9

Field Goal Success

Distance	1-19	20-29	30-39	40-49	50 Over
Made-Att.	0-0	1-3	5-6	6-7	0-1

Passing

	Att	Comp	Pct	Yds	TD	Int	Tkld	Rate
Montana	346	213	61.6	2613	17	11	20/166	87.9
Francis	1	1	100.0	45	0	0	0/0	
Benjamin	1	1	100.0	10	0	0	0/0	—
S. Francisco	348	215	61.8	2668	17	11	20/166	
Opponents	278	158	56.8	1949	14	9	15/113	

Receiving

	No	Yds	Avg	LG	TD
D. Clark	60	913	15.2	51	5
Moore	37	405	10.9	55	4
Francis	23	278	12.1	26	2
Young	22	189	8.6	30	0
Solomon	19	323	17.0	46t	3
Cooper	19	153	8.1	20	1
Ring	13	94	7.2	15	0
Nehemiah	8	161	20.1	55	1
Wilson	6	80	13.3	27	1
V. Williams	4	33	8.3	13	0
Ramson	2	27	13.5	21	0
Lawrence	2	12	6.0	6	0
San Francisco	215	2668	12.4	55	17
Opponents	158	1949	12.3	46	14

Interceptions

	No	Yds	Avg	LG	TD
Hicks	3	5	1.7	3	0
Lott	2	95	47.5	83t	1
Wright	1	31	31.0	31	0
Horn	1	19	19.0	19	0
Harper	1	0	0.0	0	0
Reynolds	1	0	0.0	0	0
San Francisco	9	150	16.7	83t	1
Opponents	11	130	11.8	32	0

Punting

	No	Yds	Avg	In 20	LG
Miller	44	1676	38.1	11	80
San Francisco	45	1676	37.2	11	80
Opponents	50	2134	42.7	10	58

Punt Returns

	No	FC	Yds	Avg	LG	TD
Solomon	13	1	122	9.4	27	0
Hicks	10	1	54	5.4	13	0
McLemore	7	0	156	22.3	93t	1
Ring	0	1	0		0	0
San Francisco	30	3	332	11.1	93t	1
Opponents	20	4	224	11.2	67t	1

Kickoff Returns

	No	Yds	Avg	LG	TD
McLemore	16	353	22.1	45	0
Lawrence	9	190	21.1	30	0
Ring	6	145	24.2	41	0
Ramson	2	20	10.0	13	0
Ferrari	2	19	9.5	11	0
Moore	1	15	15.0	15	0
San Francisco	36	742	20.6	45	0
Opponents	40	857	21.4	55	0

Scoring

	TD	TD R	TD P	TD Rt	PAT	FG	TP
Wersching					23/25	12/17	59
Moore	8	4	4	0			48
D. Clark	5	0	5	0			30
Solomon	3	0	3	0			18
Francis	2	0	2	0			12
Cooper	1	0	1	0			6
Lott	1	0	0	1			6
McLemore	1	0	0	1			6
Montana	1	1	0	0			6
Nehemiah	1	0	1	0			6
Ring	1	1	0	0			6
Wilson	1	0	1	0			6
S. Francisco	25	6	17	2	23/25	12/17	209
Opponents	24	9	14	1	23/24	13/19	206

Sacks

Board ½, Dean 3½, Harty 2½, Kugler 2, McColl ½, Pillers 3, Stover 2, Turner 1.

FIRST PLAYERS SELECTED

Year	Player, College, Position
1950	Leo Nomellini, Minnesota, T
1951	Y. A. Tittle, Louisiana State, B
1952	Hugh McElhenny, Washington, B
1953	Harry Babcock, Georgia, E
1954	Bernie Faloney, Maryland, B
1955	Dickie Moegle, Rice, B
1956	Earl Morrall, Michigan State, B
1957	John Brodie, Stanford, B
1958	Jim Pace, Michigan, B
1959	Dave Baker, Oklahoma, B
1960	Monty Stickles, Notre Dame, E
1961	Jimmy Johnson, UCLA, CB
1962	Lance Alworth, Arkansas, WR
1963	Kermit Alexander, UCLA, CB
1964	Dave Parks, Texas Tech, WR
1965	Ken Willard, North Carolina, RB
1966	Stan Hindman, Mississippi, DE
1967	Steve Spurrier, Florida, QB
1968	Forrest Blue, Auburn, C
1969	Ted Kwalick, Penn State, TE
1970	Cedrick Hardman, North Texas State, DE
1971	Tim Anderson, Ohio State, DB
1972	Terry Beasley, Auburn, WR
1973	Mike Holmes, Texas Southern, DB
1974	Wilbur Jackson, Alabama, RB
1975	Jimmy Webb, Mississippi State, DT
1976	Randy Cross, UCLA, C (2)
1977	Elmo Boyd, Eastern Kentucky, WR (3)
1978	Ken MacAfee, Notre Dame, TE
1979	James Owens, UCLA, WR (2)
1980	Earl Cooper, Rice, RB
1981	Ronnie Lott, Southern California, DB
1982	Bubba Paris, Michigan, T (2)
1983	Roger Craig, Nebraska, RB (2)

49ERS COACHING HISTORY
(207-233-12)

1950-54	Lawrence (Buck) Shaw	33-25-2
1955	Norman (Red) Strader	4-8-0
1956-58	Frankie Albert	19-17-1
1959-63	Howard (Red) Hickey*	27-27-1
1963-67	Jack Christiansen	26-38-3
1968-75	Dick Nolan	56-56-5
1976	Monte Clark	8-6-0
1977	Ken Meyer	5-9-0
1978	Pete McCulley**	1-8-0
1978	Fred O'Connor	1-6-0
1979-82	Bill Walsh	27-33-0

*Resigned after three games in 1963
**Released after nine games in 1978

SAN FRANCISCO 49ERS 1983 VETERAN ROSTER

No.	Name	Pos.	Ht.	Wt.	Birth-date	NFL Exp.	College	Birthplace	Residence	Games in '82
68	Ayers, John	G	6-5	265	4/14/53	7	West Texas State	Carrizo Springs, Tex.	Canyon, Tex.	8
63	†Beeson, Terry	LB	6-3	233	9/19/55	7	Kansas	Coffeyville, Kan.	Seattle, Wash.	5
7	Benjamin, Guy	QB	6-3	210	6/27/55	6	Stanford	Hollywood, Calif.	Montara, Calif.	2
76	Board, Dwaine	DE	6-5	250	11/29/56	4	North Carolina A&T	Union Hall, Va.	Foster City, Calif.	1
	†Bungarda, Ken	T	6-6	270	1/25/57	2	Missouri	Hartford, Conn.	Redwood City, Calif.	0*
57	Bunz, Dan	LB	6-4	225	10/7/55	5	Long Beach State	Roseville, Calif.	Loomis, Calif.	1
60	Choma, John	G-C	6-6	261	2/9/55	3	Virginia	Cleveland, Ohio	Burlingame, Calif.	7
15	Clark, Bryan	QB	6-2	196	7/27/60	2	Michigan State	Redwood City, Calif.	Bloomfield Hills, Mich.	0*
87	Clark, Dwight	WR	6-4	210	1/8/57	5	Clemson	Kinston, N.C.	Redwood Shores, Calif.	9
90	Clark, Mike	DE	6-4	250	3/30/59	3	Florida	Dothan, Ala.	Graceville, Fla.	6
47	†Collier, Tim	CB	6-0	176	5/31/54	8	East Texas State	Dallas, Tex.	St. Louis, Mo.	5*
	t-Collins, George	G-T	6-2	270	12/9/55	6	Georgia	Macon, Ga.	Athens, Ga.	
49	Cooper, Earl	RB	6-2	227	9/17/57	4	Rice	Lexington, Tex.	Houston, Tex.	9
51	Cross, Randy	G	6-3	265	4/25/54	8	UCLA	New York, N.Y.	Redwood City, Calif.	8
74	Dean, Fred	DE	6-2	236	2/24/52	9	Louisiana Tech	Arcadia, La.	Foster City, Calif.	9
62	Downing, Walt	C-G	6-3	270	6/11/56	6	Michigan	Coatesville, Pa.	Mountain View, Calif.	9
	Evans, Chuck	LB	6-3	235	12/19/56	3	Stanford	West Covina, Calif.	Los Gatos, Calif.	0*
71	Fahnhorst, Keith	T	6-6	273	2/6/52	10	Minnesota	St. Cloud, Minn.	St. Paul, Minn.	9
	Favron, Calvin	LB	6-1	227	7/3/57	5	Southeastern Louisiana	New Orleans, La.	White Castle, La.	4*
54	Ferrari, Ron	LB	6-0	212	7/30/59	2	Illinois	Springfield, Ill.	Moweaqua, Ill.	9
81	Francis, Russ	TE	6-6	242	4/3/53	8	Oregon	Seattle, Wash.	Honolulu, Ha.	9
24	Gervais, Rick	S	5-11	190	11/4/59	3	Stanford	Bend, Ore.	Redwood City, Calif.	9
59	Harper, Willie	LB	6-2	215	7/30/50	10	Nebraska	Toledo, Ohio	Belmont, Calif.	5
75	Harty, John	DT	6-4	263	12/17/58	3	Iowa	Sioux City, Iowa	Sioux City, Iowa	9
22	Hicks, Dwight	S	6-1	189	4/5/56	5	Michigan	Mt. Holly, N.J.	Palo Alto, Calif.	9
55	Horn, Bob	LB	6-4	230	2/6/54	8	Oregon State	Salem, Ore.	San Diego, Calif.	9
	t-Jones, Cody	DT	6-5	255	5/3/51	9	San Jose State	San Francisco, Calif.	Huntington Beach, Calif.	9
50	Judie, Ed	LB	6-2	231	7/6/59	2	Northern Arizona	Tyler, Tex.	Belmont, Calif.	7
66	Kennedy, Allan	T	6-7	275	1/8/58	2	Washington State	Vancouver, Canada	San Mateo, Calif.	0*
67	Kugler, Pete	DT-DE	6-4	255	8/9/59	3	Penn State	Cherry Hill, N.J.	Cherry Hill, N.J.	7
20	Lawrence, Amos	RB	5-10	179	1/9/58	3	North Carolina	Norfolk, Va.	Durham, N.C.	8
52	Leopold, Bobby	LB	6-1	215	10/18/57	4	Notre Dame	Port Arthur, Tex.	Mountain View, Calif.	6
42	Lott, Ronnie	CB	6-0	199	5/8/59	3	Southern California	Albuquerque, N.M.	Santa Clara, Calif.	9
78	Mason, Lindsey	T	6-5	275	8/1/55	5	Kansas	Baltimore, Md.	Oakland, Calif.	9
53	†McColl, Milt	LB	6-6	220	8/28/59	3	Stanford	Oak Park, Ill.	Menlo Park, Calif.	9
43	McLemore, Dana	KR-CB	5-10	183	7/1/60	2	Hawaii	Los Angeles, Calif.	Milpitas, Calif.	8
3	Miller, Jim	P	5-11	183	7/5/57	4	Mississippi	Ripley, Miss.	Ripley, Miss.	9
16	Montana, Joe	QB	6-2	200	6/11/56	5	Notre Dame	Monongahela, Pa.	Woodside, Calif.	9
25	Moore, Jeff	RB	6-0	196	8/20/56	4	Jackson State	Kosciusko, Miss.	Kosciusko, Miss.	9
83	Nehemiah, Renaldo	WR	6-1	177	3/24/59	2	Maryland	Newark, N.J.	Gaithersburg, Md.	8
	Perry, Leon	RB	5-11	230	8/14/57	4	Mississippi	Centerville, Miss.	Jackson, Miss.	4*
65	Pillers, Lawrence	DT-DE	6-4	250	11/4/52	8	Alcorn A&M	Hazelhurst, Miss.	San Mateo, Calif.	9
56	Quillan, Fred	C	6-5	266	1/27/56	6	Oregon	West Palm Beach, Fla.	San Mateo, Calif.	9
80	Ramson, Eason	TE	6-2	234	4/30/56	5	Washington State	Sacramento, Calif.	Foster City, Calif.	9
64	Reynolds, Jack	LB	6-1	232	11/22/47	14	Tennessee	Cincinnati, Ohio	San Salvadore, Bahamas	9
30	Ring, Bill	RB	5-10	215	12/13/56	3	Brigham Young	Des Moines, Iowa	San Mateo, Calif.	8
88	Solomon, Freddie	WR	5-11	185	1/11/53	9	Tampa	Sumter, N.C.	Temple Terrace, Fla.	9
72	Stover, Jeff	DE	6-5	275	5/22/58	2	Oregon	Corning, Calif.	Chico, Calif.	9
79	Stuckey, Jim	DE	6-4	251	6/21/58	4	Clemson	Cayce, S.C.	Clemson, S.C.	9
28	Thomas, Lynn	CB	5-11	181	7/9/59	3	Pittsburgh	Pascagoula, Miss.	Pascagoula, Miss.	9
58	Turner, Keena	LB	6-2	219	10/22/58	4	Purdue	Chicago, Ill.	San Carlos, Calif.	9
	t-Tyler, Wendell	RB	5-10	198	5/20/55	6	UCLA	Shreveport, La.	West Covina, Calif.	9
14	†Wersching, Ray	K	5-11	210	8/21/50	11	California	Mondsee, Austria	Leucadia, Calif.	9
45	Williams, Newton	RB	5-10	204	5/10/59	2	Arizona State	Charlotte, N.C.	Tempe, Ariz.	6
40	Williams, Vince	RB	6-0	231	10/24/59	2	Oregon	Tacoma, Wash.	Redwood City, Calif.	2
27	Williamson, Carlton	S	6-0	204	6/12/58	3	Pittsburgh	Atlanta, Ga.	Atlanta, Ga.	8
85	Wilson, Mike	WR	6-3	210	12/19/58	3	Washington State	Los Angeles, Calif.	Carson, Calif.	6
21	Wright, Eric	CB	6-1	180	4/18/59	3	Missouri	St. Louis, Mo.	San Carlos, Calif.	7
86	†Young, Charle	TE	6-4	234	2/5/51	11	Southern California	Fresno, Calif.	Belmont, Calif.	9

* Bungarda last active with San Francisco in '80; B. Clark active for 7 games with San Francisco, but did not play; Collier played 3 games with St. Louis, 2 with San Francisco in '82; Evans last active with New Orleans in '81; Favron played 4 games with St. Louis in '82; Kennedy last active with San Francisco in '81; Perry played 4 games with New York Giants in '82.

†Option playout; subject to developments.

t-49ers traded for Collins (St. Louis), Jones (Los Angeles Rams), Tyler (Los Angeles Rams).

Traded—Guard-tackle Dan Audick to St. Louis.

Also played with 49ers in '82—RB Walt Easley (2 games), RB Ricky Patton (1), LB Eric Scoggins (3), DB Tim Washington (1).

COACHING STAFF

Head Coach, Bill Walsh

Pro Career: Begins fifth season as an NFL head coach. Directed 49ers to NFC championship in 1981 and Super Bowl XVI victory over Cincinnati, 26-21. Started pro coaching career in 1966 as offensive backfield coach for the Oakland Raiders. He then spent eight seasons (1967-75) in Cincinnati, where he was responsible for coaching the Bengals' quarterbacks and receivers. His tenure in Cincinnati was followed by a season with the San Diego Chargers as offensive coordinator. While at Cincinnati he tutored Ken Anderson, who became the first NFL quarterback to lead the league in passing two straight seasons. At San Diego, he helped develop the talents of quarterback Dan Fouts. No pro playing experience. Career record: 27-33.

Background: End at San Jose State in 1953-54. Started college coaching career at California, where he served under Marv Levy from 1960-62. In 1963, he joined John Ralston's Stanford staff and worked with the defensive backfield for three seasons. Returned to Stanford as head coach in 1977 and directed Cardinals to a two-year record of 17-7, including wins in the Sun and Bluebonnet Bowls. Received his master's degree in history from San Jose State in 1959.

Personal: Born November 30, 1931, in Los Angeles. He and his wife, Geri, live in Menlo Park and have three children—Steve, Craig, and Elizabeth.

ASSISTANT COACHES

Jerry Attaway, conditioning; born January 3, 1946, Susanville, Calif., lives in San Carlos. Defensive back Yuba J.C. 1964-65, Cal-Davis 1967. No pro playing experience. College coach: Cal-Davis 1970-71, Idaho 1972-74, Utah State 1975-77, Southern California 1978-82. Pro coach: First year with 49ers.

Paul Hackett, quarterbacks-receivers; born July 5, 1947, Burlington, Vt., lives in Redwood City. Quarterback Cal-Davis 1965-68. No pro playing experience. College coach: Cal-Davis 1970-71, California 1972-75, Southern California 1976-80. Pro coach: Cleveland Browns 1981-82, first year with 49ers.

Norb Hecker, linebackers; born May 26, 1927, Berea, Ohio, lives in San Francisco. End Baldwin-Wallace 1947-50. Pro end-defensive back Los Angeles Rams 1951-53, Toronto Argonauts (CFL) 1954, Washington Redskins 1955-57. College coach: Stanford 1972-78. Pro coach: Hamilton Tiger-Cats (CFL) 1958, Green Bay Packers 1959-65, Atlanta Falcons 1966-68 (head coach), New York Giants 1969-71, 49ers since 1979.

Sherman Lewis, running backs, born June 29, 1942, Louisville, Ky., lives in Redwood City. Running back Michigan State 1961-63. Pro running back Toronto (CFL) 1964-65, New York Jets 1966. College coach: Michigan State 1969-82. Pro coach: First year with 49ers.

Bobb McKittrick, offensive line; born December 29, 1935, Baker, Ore., lives in San Mateo. Guard Oregon State 1955-57. No pro playing experience. College coach: Oregon State 1961-64, UCLA 1965-70. Pro coach: Los Angeles Rams 1971-72, San Diego Chargers 1974-78, 49ers since 1979.

Bill McPherson, defensive line; born October 24, 1931, Santa Clara, Calif., lives in San Jose. Tackle Santa Clara 1950-52. No pro playing experience. College coach: Santa Clara 1963-74, UCLA 1975-77. Pro coach: Philadelphia Eagles 1978, 49ers since 1979.

Ray Rhodes, defensive backfield; born October 20, 1950, Mexia, Tex., lives in Fremont. Running back-receiver Texas Christian 1969-70, Tulsa 1972-73. Pro defensive back New York Giants 1974-79, San Francisco 49ers 1980. Pro coach: Joined 49ers in 1981.

George Siefert, defensive coordinator; born January 22, 1940, San Francisco, Calif., lives in Sunnyvale. Linebacker Utah 1960-62. No pro playing experience. College coach: Westminster 1965 (head coach), Iowa 1966, Oregon 1967-71, Stanford 1972-74, 1977-79, Cornell 1975-76 (head coach). Pro coach: Joined 49ers in 1980.

Fred von Appen, special teams; born March 22, 1942, Eugene Ore., lives in Cupertino. Lineman Linfield College 1960-63. No pro playing experience. College coach: Linfield 1967-68, Arkansas 1969-70, Virginia Tech 1971, Oregon 1972-76, Stanford 1977-78, 1982, Arkansas 1981. Pro coach: Green Bay Packers 1979-80, first year with 49ers.

SAN FRANCISCO 49ERS 1983 FIRST-YEAR ROSTER

Name	Pos.	Ht.	Wt.	Birth-date	College	Birthplace	Residence	How Acq.
Barbee, Mike	DE	6-3	237	12/10/59	UCLA	Sacramento, Calif.	Los Angeles, Calif.	FA
Belluomini, Paul (1)	C	6-0	220	3/31/57	Cal-Davis	Oakland, Calif.	Davis, Calif.	FA
Carion, Curt (1)	P	5-11	180	8/11/59	West Virginia	New Kensington, Pa.	New Kensington, Pa.	FA
Castellanos, Rudy (1)	QB	6-2	215	11/29/55	San Diego State	Burlingame, Calif.	San Bruno, Calif.	FA
Chapman, Robbie	S	6-1	197	11/7/58	San Diego State	Riverside, Calif.	San Diego, Calif.	FA
Coffman, Ricky (1)	WR	6-0	195	11/5/58	UCLA	Youkuskia, Japan	Long Beach, Calif.	FA
Collie, Scott	WR	6-1	191	4/21/60	Brigham Young	Concordia, Kan.	Mission Viejo, Calif.	FA
Corsinotti, Dave (1)	NT	6-3	270	9/8/59	Southern California	San Francisco, Calif.	San Francisco, Calif.	FA
Craig, Roger	RB	6-1	222	7/10/60	Nebraska	Davenport, Iowa	Davenport, Iowa	D2
Curry, Pat (1)	DE	6-5	250	9/23/60	Montana	Billings, Mont.	Billings, Mont.	FA
Daum, Charles (1)	T	6-6	249	11/3/59	Cal Poly-SLO	Kenosha, Wis.	Oceanside, Calif.	FA
Drake, Don (1)	DE	6-3	253	9/20/59	Cal Poly-Pomona	Omaha, Neb.	Covina, Calif.	FA
Durden, Mike	CB	6-0	185	5/4/59	UCLA	Los Angeles, Calif.	Los Angeles, Calif.	FA
Ellison, Riki Gray	LB	6-2	220	8/15/60	Southern California	Christchurch, N.Z.	Tucson, Ariz.	D5
Foster, Greg (1)	RB	6-2	215	2/15/59	Illinois	St. Louis, Mo.	Urbana, Ill.	FA
Griffin, Ike	DE-NT	6-4	262	2/28/60	Michigan State	Gary, Ind.	Gary, Ind.	FA
Harmon, Kirk (1)	LB	6-2	227	10/22/58	Pacific	Burbank, Calif.	Burbank, Calif.	FA
Harris, Larry (1)	WR	6-2	195	5/8/59	Stanford	Kansas City, Kan.	Milpitas, Calif.	FA
Harris, Steve (1)	CB	6-2	202	8/6/58	North Alabama	Walker County, Ala.	Cordova, Ala.	FA
Hill, Dan	TE	6-3	224	1/9/60	Nebraska	Falls City, Neb.	Falls City, Neb.	FA
Holmoe, Tom	CB-S	6-2	180	3/7/60	Brigham Young	Los Angeles, Calif.	La Crescenta, Calif.	D4
Hubble, Robert (1)	DE	6-7	242	9/20/58	Rice	Kerrville, Tex.	Houston, Tex.	FA
Joiner, Jim (1)	WR	6-2	195	6/25/59	Miami	Detroit, Mich.	Detroit, Mich.	FA
Jones, Arrington (1)	RB	6-0	230	2/16/59	Winston-Salem	Richmond, Va.	Richmond, Va.	FA
Kelley, Ken	LB	6-2	225	6/20/60	Penn State	Darby, Pa.	Stratford, N.J.	FA
Kirkpatrick, Ron	DE	6-5	242	2/1/61	Utah	Escondido, Calif.	San Diego, Calif.	FA
Knudsen, Chris (1)	G	6-4	260	11/26/59	Arizona	Inglewood, Calif.	Bothell, Wash.	FA
Lahay, Bruce (1)	P-K	6-0	215	2/24/59	Arkansas	St. Louis, Mo.	Fayetteville, Ark.	FA
Larry, Admiral (1)	CB	5-11	190	9/1/58	Nevada-Las Vegas	New Orleans, La.	Omaha, Neb.	FA
Lawson, Lonnie	CB	6-0	185	12/13/61	Utah	Fort Worth, Tex.	Fort Worth, Tex.	FA
Lopes, Merv (1)	WR	6-0	175	6/16/59	Hawaii	Honolulu, Hawaii	Honolulu, Hawaii	FA
Macaulay, John (1)	C	6-3	254	4/27/59	Stanford	San Diego, Calif.	Portola Valley, Calif.	FA
Merrell, Jeff	NT	6-4	264	1/14/61	Nebraska	Huntsville, Ala.	Lincoln, Neb.	D10
Monroe, Carl	RB-KR	5-8	166	2/20/60	Utah	Pittsburgh, Pa.	San Jose, Calif.	FA
Montgomery, Blanchard	LB	6-2	236	2/17/61	UCLA	Los Angeles, Calif.	Los Angeles, Calif.	D3
Morrison, Tim (1)	G	6-3	260	12/10/58	Georgia	Boaz, Ala.	Athens, Ga.	FA
Moten, Gary	LB	6-1	210	4/3/61	Southern Methodist	Galveston, Tex.	Clute, Tex.	D7
Mularkey, Mike	TE	6-4	245	11/19/61	Florida	Miami, Fla.	Lauderdale By Sea, Fla.	D9
Naber, Ken (1)	P-K	6-3	180	2/24/59	Stanford	Cincinnati, Ohio	Cincinnati, Ohio	FA
Nanney, Lee	T	6-4	260	6/14/60	Clemson	Greenville, S.C.	Moore, S.C.	FA
Otterson, Phil	WR	6-2	197	4/1/59	Santa Clara	Novato, Calif.	San Jose, Calif.	FA
Saipale, Toa	RB	6-2	216	1/27/60	UCLA	Los Angeles, Calif.	Los Angeles, Calif.	FA
Sapolu, Jesse	G	6-4	260	3/10/61	Hawaii	Laie, Western Samoa	Honolulu, Hawaii	D11
Sykes, Greg (1)	NT-DE	6-5	268	10/30/58	Washington State	Los Angeles, Calif.	Los Angeles, Calif.	FA
Vogel, Ron	TE	6-3	220	4/20/61	Oregon State	San Diego, Calif.	Corvallis, Ore.	FA
Wellman, Mike (1)	G-C	6-4	265	7/15/56	Kansas	Newton, Kan.	Lawrence, Kan.	FA
Whiteside, Mike (1)	WR	6-0	177	10/29/58	Fresno State	Los Angeles, Calif.	San Mateo, Calif.	FA
Williams, James (1)	NT-DE	6-6	265	12/31/57	North Carolina A&T	Abbeville, S.C.	Calhoun Falls, S.C.	FA
Wimmer, Gary	LB	6-1	225	3/9/61	Stanford	Pocatello, Idaho	Stanford, Calif.	FA
Wong, Darryl	QB	6-2	190	7/23/60	Dartmouth	San Francisco, Calif.	San Francisco, Calif.	FA
Worthy, Fred	TE	6-5	235	5/25/59	Clemson	Summerville, S.C.	Summerville, S.C.	FA
Wring, Alfred (1)	NT	6-3	275	11/4/57	Johnson C. Smith	Delray Beach, Fla.	Delray Beach, Fla.	FA

Players who report to an NFL team for the first time are designated on rosters as rookies (R). If a player reported to an NFL training camp in a previous year but was not on the active squad for three or more regular season or postseason games, he is listed on the first-year roster and designated by a (1). Thereafter, a player who is on the active squad for three or more regular season or postseason games is credited with an additional year of playing experience.

NOTES

_____

_____

_____

_____

_____

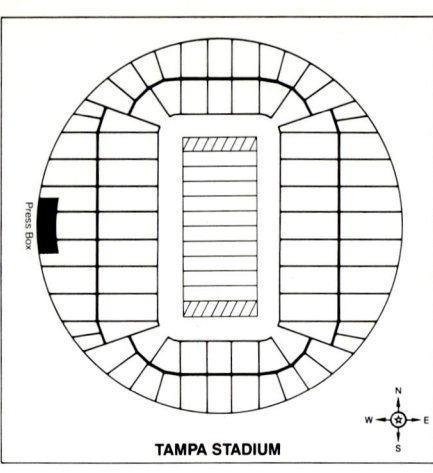

TAMPA STADIUM

Tampa Bay Buccaneers

**National Football Conference
Central Division**

Team Colors: Florida Orange, White, and
Red

**One Buccaneer Place
Tampa, Florida 33607
Telephone: (813) 870-2700**

Club Officials
Owner: Hugh F. Culverhouse
President: Hugh F. Culverhouse
Vice President: Joy Culverhouse
Vice President-Head Coach: John H. McKay
Secretary/Treasurer: Ward Holland
Director of Administration: Herbert M. Gold
Assistant to the President: Phil Krueger
Director of Player Personnel: Ken Herock
Director of Public Relations and Promotions: Bob Best
Assistant Director of Public Relations: Rick Odioso
Assistant Director of Promotions: Jim Rowe
Director of Ticket Operations: John Sheffield
Assistant Director of Ticket Operations: Terry Wooten
College Personnel: Craig Fertig, Bill Groman,
   George Saimes
Controller: Ed Easom
Trainer: Tom Oxley
Assistant Trainer: Scott Anderson
Equipment Manager: Frank Pupello

Stadium: Tampa Stadium • **Capacity:** 72,812
         North Dale Mabry
         Tampa, Florida 33607

Playing Surface: Grass

Training Camp: One Buccaneer Place
         Tampa, Florida 33607

1983 SCHEDULE
Preseason
Aug. 6	**New Orleans**	8:00
Aug. 13	at Houston	8:00
Aug. 20	**Atlanta**	8:00
Aug. 26	**New England**	8:00

Regular Season
Sept. 4	**Detroit**	1:00
Sept. 11	at Chicago	12:00
Sept. 18	**Minnesota**	4:00
Sept. 25	**Cincinnati**	1:00
Oct. 2	at Green Bay	12:00
Oct. 9	at Dallas	3:00
Oct. 16	**St. Louis**	1:00
Oct. 23	**New Orleans**	4:00
Oct. 30	at Pittsburgh	1:00
Nov. 6	at Minnesota	12:00
Nov. 13	at Cleveland	1:00
Nov. 20	**Chicago**	1:00
Nov. 27	**Houston**	1:00
Dec. 4	at San Francisco	1:00
Dec. 12	**Green Bay** (Monday)	9:00
Dec. 18	at Detroit	4:00

1982 TEAM STATISTICS

	Tampa Bay	Opp.
Total First Downs..................	163	160
Rushing.......................	52	72
Passing.......................	105	76
Penalty......................	6	12
Third Down Efficiency..........	48/127	47/122
Third Down Percentage.........	37.8	38.5
Total Net Yards..................	2895	2442
Total Offensive Plays...........	587	564
Avg. Gain per Play.............	4.9	4.3
Avg. Gain per Game............	321.7	271.3
Net Yards Rushing...............	952	1058
Total Rushing Plays	268	285
Avg. Gain per Rush.............	3.6	3.7
Avg. Gain Rushing per Game.....	105.8	117.6
Net Yards Passing...............	1943	1384
Lost Attempting to Pass........	11/128	25/224
Gross Yards Passing	2071	1608
Attempts/Completions..........	308/164	254/145
Percent Completed.............	53.2	57.1
Had Intercepted................	11	11
Avg. Net Passing per Game	215.9	153.8
Punts/Avg......................	40/40.5	42/43.4
Punt Returns/Avg...............	25/5.7	23/8.3
Kickoff Returns/Avg.............	33/16.6	40/21.8
Interceptions/Avg. Ret..........	11/12.6	11/10.4
Penalties/Yards................	38/297	38/325
Fumbles/Ball Lost..............	28/12	15/10
Total Points...................	158	178
Avg. Points per Game...........	17.6	19.8
Touchdowns....................	15	21
Rushing....................	6	9
Passing....................	9	10
Returns and Recoveries	0	2
Field Goals....................	18/23	12/17
Conversions...................	14/15	16/21
Safeties......................	0	0
Avg. Time of Possession	29:35	30:25

1982 TEAM RECORD

Preseason (3-1)

Tampa Bay		Opponents
35	*Philadelphia	7
28	*Washington	13
6	Houston	21
34	*Atlanta	0
103		41

Regular Season (5-4)

Tampa Bay		Opponents	Att.
10	Minnesota	17	58,440
13	*Washington	21	66,824
9	Dallas	14	49,578
23	*Miami	17	65,854
13	New Orleans	10	61,709
17	New York Jets	32	28,147
24	*Buffalo	23	62,510
23	*Detroit	21	65,997
26	*Chicago (OT)	23	68,112
158		178	527,171

*Home Game   (OT) Overtime

Score by Periods

Tampa Bay	9	40	51	55	3	—	158
Opponents	46	53	43	36	0	—	178

Attendance

Home 329,297   Away 197,874   Total 527,171
Single game home record, 71,733 (10-4-81)
Single season home record, 545,980 (1979)

1982 INDIVIDUAL STATISTICS

Rushing

	Att	Yds	Avg	LG	TD
Wilder	83	324	3.9	47	3
Owens	76	238	3.1	14	1
Carver	70	229	3.3	13t	1
Williams	35	158	4.5	14	2
Morton	2	3	1.5	2	0
Giles	1	1	1.0	1	0
House	1	−1	−1.0	−1	0
Tampa Bay	268	952	3.6	47	6
Opponents	285	1058	3.7	25	9

Field Goal Success

Distance	1-19	20-29	30-39	40-49	50 Over
Made-Att.	0-0	10-11	5-6	1-3	2-3

Passing

	Att	Comp	Pct	Yds	TD	Int	Tkld	Rate
Williams	307	164	53.4	2071	9	11	11/128	69.4
Golsteyn	1	0	0.0	0	0	0	0/0	—
Tampa Bay	308	164	53.2	2071	9	11	11/128	
Opponents	254	145	57.1	1608	10	11	25/224	

Receiving

	No	Yds	Avg	LG	TD
Wilder	53	466	8.8	32	1
Giles	28	499	17.8	48	3
House	28	438	15.6	62t	2
T. Bell	15	203	13.5	25	0
Jones	14	205	14.6	26	1
Carter	10	140	14.0	27	0
Owens	8	42	5.3	12	1
Carver	4	46	11.5	24	1
Obradovich	2	22	11.0	15	0
J. Bell	1	5	5.0	5	0
Morton	1	5	5.0	5	0
Tampa Bay	164	2071	12.6	62t	9
Opponents	145	1608	11.1	49	10

Interceptions

	No	Yds	Avg	LG	TD
Colzie	3	64	21.3	51	0
Brown	3	31	10.3	24	0
Washington	3	13	4.3	13	0
Green	1	31	31.0	31	0
Thomas	1	0	0.0	0	0
Tampa Bay	11	139	12.6	51	0
Opponents	11	114	10.4	39t	1

Punting

	No	Yds	Avg	In 20	LG
Swider	39	1620	41.5	6	59
Tampa Bay	40	1620	40.5	6	59
Opponents	42	1824	43.4	9	59

Punt Returns

	No	FC	Yds	Avg	LG	TD
T. Bell	9	1	62	6.9	14	0
Holt	16	0	81	5.1	22	0
Tampa Bay	25	1	143	5.7	22	0
Opponents	23	4	192	8.3	22	0

Kickoff Returns

	No	Yds	Avg	LG	TD
Morton	21	361	17.2	26	0
Carver	3	62	20.7	25	0
Owens	3	52	17.3	27	0
Smith	3	47	15.7	24	0
Yarno	1	14	14.0	14	0
Obradovich	1	12	12.0	12	0
Davis	1	0	0.0	0	0
Tampa Bay	33	548	16.6	27	0
Opponents	40	870	21.8	50	0

Scoring

	TD	TD R	TD P	TD Rt	PAT	FG	TP
Capece					14/14	18/23	68
Wilder	4	3	1	0			24
Giles	3	0	3	0			18
Carver	2	1	1	0			12
House	2	0	2	0			12
Williams	2	2	0	0			12
Jones	1	0	1	0			6
Owens	1	0	1	0			6
Tampa Bay	15	6	9	0	14/15	18/23	158
Opponents	21	9	10	2	16/21	12/17	178

Sacks

Brantley 2, Colzie 2, Green 2⅓, Hawkins 2⅓, Logan 4⅚, Reese 1, Selmon 4, Stalls 6½.

FIRST PLAYERS SELECTED

Year	Player, College, Position
1976	Lee Roy Selmon, Oklahoma, DT
1977	Ricky Bell, Southern California, RB
1978	Doug Williams, Grambling, QB
1979	Greg Roberts, Oklahoma, G (2)
1980	Ray Snell, Wisconsin, G
1981	Hugh Green, Pittsburgh, LB
1982	Sean Farrell, Penn State, G
1983	Randy Grimes, Baylor, C (2)

BUCCANEERS COACHING HISTORY

(37-67-1)

1976-82	John McKay	37-67-1

TAMPA BAY BUCCANEERS 1983 VETERAN ROSTER

No.	Name	Pos.	Ht.	Wt.	Birth-date	NFL Exp.	College	Birthplace	Residence	Games in '82
30	Barrett, Dave	RB	6-0	230	9/9/59	2	Houston	Corpus Christi, Tex.	Tampa, Fla.	7
82	Bell, Jerry	TE	6-5	230	3/7/59	2	Arizona State	Derby, Conn.	Tampa, Fla.	9
83	Bell, Theo	WR	6-0	190	12/21/53	7	Arizona	Bakersfield, Calif.	Tampa, Fla.	9
52	Brantley, Scot	LB	6-1	230	2/24/58	4	Florida	Chester, S.C.	Lutz, Fla.	9
34	Brown, Cedric	S	6-2	200	5/6/54	7	Kent State	Columbus, Ohio	Tampa, Fla.	9
78	Cannon, John	DE	6-5	250	7/30/60	2	William & Mary	Long Branch, N.J.	Holmdel, N.J.	9
3	Capece, Bill	K	5-7	170	4/1/59	3	Florida State	Miami, Fla.	Tallahassee, Fla.	9
87	Carter, Gerald	WR	6-1	190	6/19/57	4	Texas A&M	Bryan, Tex.	Bryan, Tex.	9
28	Carver, Melvin	RB	5-11	215	7/14/59	2	Nevada-Las Vegas	Pensacola, Fla.	Tampa, Fla.	9
20	Colzie, Neal	S	6-2	200	2/28/53	9	Ohio State	Fitzgerald, Ga.	Tampa, Fla.	9
33	†Cotney, Mark	S	6-0	200	6/25/52	8	Cameron State	Altus, Okla.	Tampa, Fla.	9
71	Crowder, Randy	NT	6-3	255	7/30/52	6	Penn State	Farrell, Pa.	Tampa, Fla.	0*
58	Davis, Jeff	LB	6-0	225	1/26/60	2	Clemson	Greensboro, N.C.	Greensboro, N.C.	9
27	Dykes, Donald	CB	5-11	185	8/24/55	4	Southeast Louisiana	Independence, La.	Hammond, La.	1*
62	Farrell, Sean	G	6-3	260	5/25/60	2	Penn State	Southampton, N.Y.	Clearwater, Fla.	9
88	Giles, Jimmie	TE	6-3	245	11/8/54	7	Alcorn State	Greenville, Miss.	Tampa, Fla.	9
11	Golsteyn, Jerry	QB	6-4	200	8/6/54	5	Northern Illinois	West Allis, Wis.	Chula Vista, Fla.	1
53	Green, Hugh	LB	6-2	225	7/27/59	3	Pittsburgh	Natchez, Miss.	Tampa, Fla.	9
73	†Hannah, Charley	T	6-6	265	7/26/55	7	Alabama	Albertville, Ala.	Albertville, Ala.	7
59	Hawkins, Andy	LB	6-2	230	3/31/58	4	Texas A&I	Bay City, Tex.	Bay City, Tex.	9
21	Holt, John	CB-S	5-11	180	5/14/59	3	West Texas State	Lawton, Okla.	Tampa, Fla.	9
89	House, Kevin	WR	6-1	180	12/20/57	4	Southern Illinois	St. Louis, Mo.	Tampa, Fla.	9
56	Johnson, Cecil	LB	6-2	235	8/19/55	7	Pittsburgh	Miami, Fla.	Tampa, Fla.	9
84	Jones, Gordon	WR	6-0	190	7/25/57	5	Pittsburgh	Buffalo, N.Y.	Tampa, Fla.	9
57	Leonard, Jim	C-G	6-3	260	10/19/57	4	Santa Clara	Santa Cruz, Calif.	Clearwater, Fla.	9
76	Logan, David	NT	6-2	255	10/25/56	7	Pittsburgh	Pittsburgh, Pa.	Pittsburgh, Pa.	9
45	Middleton, Terdell	RB	6-0	205	4/8/55	7	Memphis State	Memphis, Tenn.	Tampa, Fla.	2
24	Morris, Thomas	CB-S	5-11	175	4/2/60	2	Michigan State	Anniston, Ala.	Tampa, Fla.	8
1	Morton, Michael	KR-RB	5-8	180	2/6/60	2	Nevada-Las Vegas	Birmingham, Ala.	Inglewood, Calif.	9
35	Moser, Rick	RB	6-0	210	12/18/56	6	Rhode Island	White Plains, N.Y.	Thousand Oaks, Calif.	7*
86	†Obradovich, Jim	TE	6-2	225	4/2/53	9	Southern California	Los Angeles, Calif.	Hermosa Beach, Calif.	9
44	†O'Steen, Dwayne	CB	6-1	195	12/20/54	6	San Jose State	Los Angeles, Calif.	Los Angeles, Calif.	3*
26	Owens, James	RB	5-11	195	7/5/55	5	UCLA	Sacramento, Calif.	Tampa, Fla.	8
15	Quinn, Jeff	QB	6-3	205	2/16/58	4	Nebraska	Ord, Neb.	Lincoln, Neb.	0*
75	†Reavis, Dave	T	6-5	265	6/19/50	9	Arkansas	Nashville, Tenn.	Tampa, Fla.	7
66	Reese, Booker	DE	6-6	260	9/20/59	2	Bethune-Cookman	Jacksonville, Fla.	Jacksonville, Fla.	7
61	Roberts, Greg	G	6-3	265	11/19/56	5	Oklahoma	Nacogdoches, Tex.	Tampa, Fla.	7
74	Sanders, Gene	T	6-3	270	11/10/56	5	Texas A&M	New Orleans, La.	Tampa, Fla.	4
63	Selmon, Lee Roy	DE	6-3	250	10/20/54	8	Oklahoma	Eufaula, Okla.	Tampa, Fla.	9
22	†Smith, Johnny Ray	CB	5-9	180	9/7/57	2	Lamar	Crockett, Tex.	Cleveland, Tex.	9
72	Snell, Ray	G-T	6-4	265	2/24/58	4	Wisconsin	Baltimore, Md.	Tampa, Fla.	7
65	Stalls, Dave	DE	6-5	250	9/19/55	7	Northern Colorado	Madison, Wis.	Wheat Ridge, Colo.	9
9	†Swider, Larry	P	6-2	195	2/1/55	5	Pittsburgh	Limestone, Maine	Hazelwood, Mo.	9
41	Thomas, Norris	CB	6-0	185	5/3/54	7	Southern Mississippi	Inverness, Miss.	Gulfport, Miss.	9
	t-Thompson, Jack	QB	6-3	217	5/18/56	5	Washington State	American Samoa	Seattle, Wash.	1
81	Tyler, Andre	WR	6-0	180	7/17/59	2	Stanford	Tucson, Ariz.	Long Beach, Calif.	0*
40	†Washington, Mike	CB	6-2	200	7/1/53	8	Alabama	Montgomery, Ala.	Montgomery, Ala.	8
90	†White, Brad	NT	6-2	250	10/18/58	3	Tennessee	Rexburg, Idaho	Idaho Falls, Idaho	9
32	Wilder, James	RB	6-3	225	5/12/58	3	Missouri	Sikeston, Mo.	Tampa, Fla.	9
12	†Williams, Doug	QB	6-4	220	8/9/55	6	Grambling	Zachary, La.	Tampa, Fla.	9
50	Wilson, Steve	C	6-4	265	5/19/54	8	Georgia	Fort Sill, Okla.	Tampa, Fla.	8
54	Wood, Richard	LB	6-2	230	5/31/53	9	Southern California	Elizabeth, N.J.	Tampa, Fla.	9
68	Yarno, George	G	6-2	260	8/12/57	5	Washington State	Spokane, Wash.	Spokane, Wash.	9

* Crowder missed '82 season due to injury; Dykes played 1 game with San Diego in '82; Moser played 6 games with Pittsburgh, 1 game with Tampa Bay in '82; O'Steen played 3 games with Baltimore, 1 postseason game with Tampa Bay in '82; Quinn active for 1 game with Pittsburgh, 4 games with Tampa Bay in '82, but did not play; Tyler active for 7 games with Tampa Bay in '82, but did not play.

†Option playout; subject to developments.

t-Buccaneers traded for Thompson (Cincinnati).

Also played with Buccaneers in '82—K Brian Clark (1 game), DE Robert Cobb (3), LB Dana Nafziger (8).

COACHING STAFF

Head Coach, John McKay

Pro Career: Starts eighth season as Buccaneers head coach. Led Tampa Bay to division championship in 1981. In 1979, guided Tampa Bay to NFC Central title and first playoff berth. Under his direction, Buccaneers became the second expansion team to qualify for the playoffs in one of its first four seasons and the first expansion team to win 10 games in one of its first four seasons. Drafted by the New York Yankees (AAFC) in 1950 but turned down pro playing career. Career record: 37-67-1.

Background: Defensive back Purdue 1946, transferred to Oregon and played both ways 1947-49. Holds Oregon records for most touchdowns rushing in a game and highest career average per carry. Assistant coach at Oregon 1950-58 and Southern California 1959. Head coach at Southern California 1960-75. Directed Southern California teams to four national championships and nine Bowl appearances (Rose 8, Liberty 1). Southern California coaching record: 127-40-8.

Personal: Born July 5, 1923, Everettsville, West Virginia. John and his wife, Corky, live in Tampa and have four children — Michele, John Jr., Richard, and Terri.

ASSISTANT COACHES

Boyd Dowler, quarterbacks; born October 18, 1937, Rock Springs, Wyo., lives in Tampa. Quarterback Colorado 1955-58. Pro wide receiver Green Bay Packers 1959-69, Washington Redskins 1971. Pro coach: Los Angeles Rams 1970, Washington Redskins 1971-72, Philadelphia Eagles 1973-75, Cincinnati Bengals 1976-79, Buccaneers since 1980.

Frank Emanuel, special teams; born December 4, 1942, Clio, S.C., lives in Tampa. Linebacker Tennessee 1963-1965. Pro linebacker Miami Dolphins 1966-69, New Orleans Saints 1970. College coach: Memphis State 1972-73, Wichita State 1974, Vanderbilt 1975-76, Louisville 1977-78, Tennessee 1979-81. Pro coach: Joined Buccaneers in 1982.

Wayne Fontes, defensive coordinator-defensive backs; born February 17, 1940, New Bedford, Mass., lives in Tampa. Defensive back Michigan State 1959-62. Pro defensive back New York Titans (AFL) 1963-64. College coach: Dayton 1968, Iowa 1969-71, Southern California 1972-75. Pro coach: Joined Buccaneers in 1976.

Abe Gibron, defensive line; born September 22, 1925, Michigan City, Ind., lives in Tampa. Guard Purdue 1945-47. Pro guard Buffalo Bills (AAFC) 1949, Cleveland Browns 1950-55, Philadelphia Eagles 1956-57, Chicago Bears 1958-59. Pro coach: Washington Redskins 1960-64, Chicago Bears 1965-74 (head coach 1972-74), Chicago Wind (WFL) 1975 (head coach), Buccaneers since 1976.

Jim Gruden, running backs; born January 28, 1937, Cleveland, Ohio, lives in Tampa. Quarterback Heidelberg 1956-57. No pro playing experience. College coach: Heidelberg 1966-68, Dayton 1969-72, Indiana 1973-77, Notre Dame 1978-80. Pro coach: Joined Buccaneers in 1982.

Kim Helton, offensive line, born July 28, 1948, Pensacola, Fla., lives in Tampa. Center Florida 1967-69. No pro playing experience. College coach: Florida 1972-78, Miami 1979-82. Pro coach: First year with Buccaneers.

Chip Myers, wide receivers, born July 9, 1945, Panama City, Fla., lives in Tampa. Receiver Northwest Oklahoma 1964-66. Pro receiver San Francisco 49ers 1967, Cincinnati Bengals 1969-76. College coach: Illinois 1980-82. Pro coach: First year with Buccaneers.

Howard Tippett, linebackers; born September 23, 1938, Tallassee, Ala., lives in Tampa. Quarterback-safety East Tennessee State 1955-57. No pro playing experience. College coach: Tulane 1963-65, West Virginia 1966, 1971, Houston 1967-70, Mississippi State 1972-73, 1979, Washington State 1976, Oregon 1977-78, UCLA 1980. Pro coach: Jacksonville Sharks (WFL) 1974-75, Buccaneers since 1981.

TAMPA BAY BUCCANEERS 1983 FIRST-YEAR ROSTER

Name	Pos.	Ht.	Wt.	Birth-date	College	Birthplace	Residence	How Acq.
Arbubakrr, Hasson	DE	6-4	250	12/9/60	Texas Tech	Newark, N.J.	Newark, N.J.	D9
Atkins, Kal (1)	DE	6-4	240	7/3/60	Illinois	Orlando, Fla.	Tampa, Fla.	D8
Barousse, Mark	WR	5-9	175	1/28/60	McNeese State	Lake Charles, La.	Lafayette, La.	FA
Branton, Gene	WR	6-4	210	11/23/62	Texas Southern	Tampa, Fla.	Tampa, Fla.	D6
Castille, Jeremiah	CB-S	5-10	180	1/15/61	Alabama	Columbus, Ga.	Phenix City, Ala.	D3
Chickillo, Tony	NT	6-3	260	9/8/60	Miami	Miami, Fla.	Miami, Fla.	D5
Coles, Joel	RB	6-0	220	2/7/60	Penn State	Pittsburgh, Pa.	Pittsburgh, Pa.	FA
Durham, Darius	WR	6-2	195	5/27/61	San Diego State	Long Beach, Calif.	Garden Grove, Calif.	D10
Ferraro, Joe (1)	DE	6-4	255	5/23/60	Boston College	New Haven, Conn.	Killingsworth, Conn.	FA
Garcia, Frank (1)	P	6-1	190	6/5/57	Arizona	Tucson, Ariz.	Tucson, Ariz.	FA
Girgash, Paul	LB	6-1	200	2/10/61	Michigan	Lakewood, Ohio	Lakewood, Ohio	FA
Grimes, Randy	T-G	6-4	280	7/20/60	Baylor	Tyler, Tex.	Waco, Tex.	D2
Harmon, Greg	LB	6-3	230	11/14/59	Houston	El Campo, Tex.	El Campo, Tex.	FA
Harris, Herbert	WR	6-1	190	5/4/61	Lamar	Houston, Tex.	Houston, Tex.	FA
Hewko, Bob	QB	6-3	195	6/8/60	Florida	Abington, Pa.	North Palm Beach, Fla.	FA
Higginbotham, John	NT	6-2	265	4/26/59	NE Oklahoma State	Hugo, Okla.	Hugo, Okla.	D12
Jeffers, Lemont (1)	LB	6-3	220	4/15/60	Tennessee	Hampton, Va.	Hampton, Va.	FA
Kaplan, Ken	T	6-5	270	1/12/60	New Hampshire	Boston, Mass.	Brockton, Mass.	D6
Kim, Peter	K	5-8	165	4/11/59	Alabama	Seoul, South Korea	Honolulu, Hawaii	FA
LaBeaux, Sandy (1)	CB-S	6-3	205	8/22/61	Cal State-Hayward	San Antonio, Tex.	San Ramon, Calif.	FA
Ledbetter, Welden	RB	6-0	215	10/23/60	Oklahoma	St. Louis, Mo.	St. Louis, Mo.	D7
Samuelson, John	LB	6-2	220	6/26/60	Azusa Pacific	Covina, Calif.	Covina, Calif.	D8
Thomas, Kelly	T	6-6	270	9/9/60	Southern California	Lynwood, Calif.	La Mirada, Calif.	D4
Wampler, Chris	DE	6-2	250	10/12/61	Tennessee	Loudon, Tenn.	Lenoir City, Tenn.	FA
Witte, Mark	TE	6-3	230	12/3/59	North Texas State	Corpus Christi, Tex.	San Marcos, Tex.	D11

Players who report to an NFL team for the first time are designated on rosters as rookies (R). If a player reported to an NFL training camp in a previous year but was not on the active squad for three or more regular season or postseason games, he is listed on the first-year roster and designated by a (1). Thereafter, a player who is on the active squad for three or more regular season or postseason games is credited with an additional year of playing experience.

NOTES

_____
_____
_____
_____
_____
_____
_____
_____
_____
_____
_____
_____
_____
_____
_____
_____
_____
_____
_____
_____
_____
_____
_____

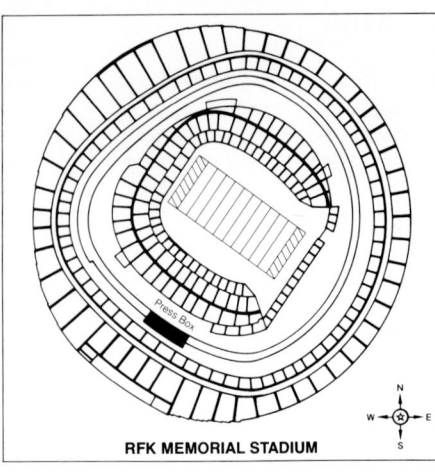

RFK MEMORIAL STADIUM

Washington Redskins

National Football Conference
Eastern Division

Team Colors: Burgundy and Gold

Redskin Park,
P.O. Box 17247
Dulles International Airport,
Washington, D.C. 20041
Telephone: (703) 471-9100

Club Officials

Chairman of the Board-Chief Operating Executive:
  Jack Kent Cooke
President: Edward Bennett Williams
Executive Vice President: John Kent Cooke
Senior Vice President: Gerard T. Gabrys
Board of Directors: Jack Kent Cooke, John Kent
  Cooke, Lawrence Lucchino, W. Jarvis Moody,
  Robert A. Schulman, William A. Shea,
  Edward Bennett Williams
General Manager: Bobby Beathard
Assistant General Managers: Bobby Mitchell,
  Charles Casserly
Director of Player Personnel: Mike Allman
Director of Pro Scouting: Kirk Mee
Director of College Scouting: Dick Daniels
Director of Public Relations: Charles M. Taylor
Assistant Public Relations Directors: Bill Keenist,
  Ronn Levine
Ticket Manager: George X. Christophel
Head Trainer: Lamar (Bubba) Tyer
Assistant Trainers: Joe Kuczo, Keoki Kamau
Equipment Manager: Jay Brunetti
Director of Photography: Nate Fine

Stadium: Robert F. Kennedy Stadium •
  Capacity: 55,045
  East Capitol Street
  Washington, D.C. 20003
Playing Surface: Grass (PAT)
Training Camp: Dickinson College
  Carlisle, Pennsylvania 17013

1983 SCHEDULE

Preseason

Aug. 6	at Atlanta	8:00
Aug. 12	**Cincinnati**	7:30
Aug. 19	**Miami**	8:00
Aug. 27	at Buffalo	6:00

Regular Season

Sept. 5	**Dallas** (Monday)	9:00
Sept. 11	at Philadelphia	1:00
Sept. 18	**Kansas City**	1:00
Sept. 25	at Seattle	1:00
Oct. 2	**Los Angeles Raiders**	1:00
Oct. 9	at St. Louis	12:00
Oct. 17	at Green Bay (Monday)	8:00
Oct. 23	**Detroit**	1:00
Oct. 31	at San Diego (Monday)	6:00
Nov. 6	**St. Louis**	4:00
Nov. 13	at New York Giants	4:00
Nov. 20	at Los Angeles Rams	1:00
Nov. 27	**Philadelphia**	1:00
Dec. 4	**Atlanta**	1:00
Dec. 11	at Dallas	3:00
Dec. 17	**New York Giants** (Saturday)	12:30

1982 TEAM STATISTICS

	Washington	Opp.
Total First Downs	165	151
Rushing	66	47
Passing	87	93
Penalty	12	11
Third Down Efficiency	55/133	40/115
Third Down Percentage	41.4	34.8
Total Net Yards	2985	2560
Total Offensive Plays	598	554
Avg. Gain per Play	5.0	4.6
Avg. Gain per Game	331.7	284.4
Net Yards Rushing	1140	946
Total Rushing Plays	315	247
Avg. Gain per Rush	3.6	3.8
Avg. Gain Rushing per Game	126.7	105.1
Net Yards Passing	1845	1614
Lost Attempting to Pass	30/223	32/256
Gross Yards Passing	2068	1870
Attempts/Completions	253/162	275/146
Percent Completed	64.0	53.1
Had Intercepted	9	11
Avg. Net Passing per Game	205.0	179.3
Punts/Avg.	52/37.3	56/40.1
Punt Returns/Avg.	38/7.8	30/3.5
Kickoff Returns/Avg.	30/21.6	42/17.3
Interceptions/Avg. Ret.	11/7.7	9/7.6
Penalties/Yards	46/404	52/419
Fumbles/Ball Lost	15/7	23/13
Total Points	190	128
Avg. Points per Game	21.1	14.2
Touchdowns	19	16
Rushing	5	8
Passing	13	8
Returns and Recoveries	1	0
Field Goals	20/21	6/9
Conversions	16/19	14/16
Safeties	0	0
Avg. Time of Possession	32:18	27:42

1982 TEAM RECORD

Preseason (0-4)

Washington		Opponents
7	Miami	24
13	Tampa Bay	28
14	*Buffalo	20
21	Cincinnati	28
55		100

Regular Season (8-1)

Washington		Opponents	Att.
37	Philadelphia (OT)	34	68,885
21	Tampa Bay	13	66,824
27	New York Giants	17	70,766
13	*Philadelphia	9	48,313
10	*Dallas	24	54,633
12	St. Louis	7	35,308
15	*New York Giants	14	50,030
27	New Orleans	10	48,667
28	*St. Louis	0	52,554
190		128	495,980

*Home Game   (OT) Overtime

Score by Periods

Washington	36	67	22	62	3	—	190
Opponents	17	33	43	35	0	—	128

Attendance

Home 205,530   Away 290,450   Total 495,980
Single game home record, 55,045 (9-8-80, 9-6-81)
Single season home record, 427,651 (1979)

1982 INDIVIDUAL STATISTICS

Rushing

	Att	Yds	Avg	LG	TD
Riggins	177	553	3.1	19	3
Washington	44	190	4.3	40	1
Harmon	38	168	4.4	20	1
Theismann	31	150	4.8	16	0
Wonsley	11	36	3.3	7	0
Monk	7	21	3.0	14	0
Walker	2	11	5.5	6	0
Jackson	4	6	1.5	2	0
Giaquinto	1	5	5.0	5	0
Washington	315	1140	3.6	40	5
Opponents	247	946	3.8	64	8

Field Goal Success

Distance	1-19	20-29	30-39	40-49	50 Over
Made-Att.	1-1	6-6	8-8	5-6	0-0

Passing

	Att	Comp	Pct	Yds	TD	Int	Tkld	Rate
Theismann	252	161	63.9	2033	13	9	30/223	91.3
Washington	1	1	100.0	35	0	0	0/0	—
Washington	253	162	64.0	2068	13	9	30/223	
Opponents	275	146	53.1	1870	8	11	32/256	

Receiving

	No	Yds	Avg	LG	TD
Monk	35	447	12.8	43	1
Brown	32	690	21.6	78t	8
Warren	27	310	11.5	29	0
Washington	19	134	7.1	17	1
Walker	12	92	7.7	25t	1
Harmon	11	86	7.8	28	0
Riggins	10	50	5.0	11	0
Seay	6	154	25.7	37	0
M. Williams	3	14	4.7	6	0
Giaquinto	2	65	32.5	36	0
Didier	2	10	5.0	8	1
Jackson	1	9	9.0	9	0
Garrett	1	6	6.0	6	0
Wonsley	1	1	1.0	1t	1
Washington	162	2068	12.8	78t	13
Opponents	146	1870	12.8	62t	8

Interceptions

	No	Yds	Avg	LG	TD
V. Dean	3	62	20.7	26	0
White	3	4	1.3	4	0
Murphy	2	0	0.0	0	0
Peters	1	14	14.0	14	0
McDaniel	1	7	7.0	7	0
Manley	1	-2	-2.0	-2	0
Washington	11	85	7.7	26	0
Opponents	9	68	7.6	15	0

Punting

	No	Yds	Avg	In 20	LG
Hayes	51	1937	38.0	10	58
Washington	52	1937	37.3	10	58
Opponents	56	2247	40.1	5	58

Punt Returns

	No	FC	Yds	Avg	LG	TD
Nelms	32	0	252	7.9	28	0
Giaquinto	5	2	34	6.8	12	0
G. Williams	1	0	9	9.0	9	0
Washington	38	2	295	7.8	28	0
Opponents	30	3	106	3.5	11	0

Kickoff Returns

	No	Yds	Avg	LG	TD
Nelms	23	557	24.2	58	0
Garrett	2	35	17.5	18	0
Giaquinto	1	21	21.0	21	0
Wonsley	1	14	14.0	14	0
Harmon	1	13	13.0	13	0
Anderson	1	7	7.0	7	0
G. Williams	1	2	2.0	2	0
Washington	30	649	21.6	58	0
Opponents	42	726	17.3	33	0

Scoring

	TD	TD R	TD P	TD Rt	PAT	FG	TP
Moseley					16/19	20/21	76
Brown	8	0	8	0			48
Riggins	3	3	0	0			18
Washington	2	1	1	0			12
Didier	1	0	1	0			6
Harmon	1	1	0	0			6
Jordan	1	0	0	1			6
Monk	1	0	1	0			6
Walker	1	0	1	0			6
Wonsley	1	0	1	0			6
Washington	19	5	13	1	16/19	20/21	190
Opponents	16	8	8	0	14/16	6/9	128

Sacks

Brooks 1, Butz 4½, Grant 2½, Kaufman 1½, Kubin ½, Liebenstein 1, Manley 6½, McGee 6½, Mendenhall 1, Milot 3, Murphy 1, Olkewicz 3.

FIRST PLAYERS SELECTED
(Since 1947)

Year	Player, College, Position
1947	Cal Rossi, UCLA, B
1948	Harry Gilmer, Alabama, B
1949	Rob Goode, Texas A&M, B
1950	George Thomas, Oklahoma, B
1951	Leon Heath, Oklahoma, B
1952	Larry Isbell, Baylor, B
1953	Jack Scarbath, Maryland, B
1954	Steve Meilinger, Kentucky, E
1955	Ralph Guglielmi, Notre Dame, B
1956	Ed Vereb, Maryland, B
1957	Don Bosseler, Miami, B
1958	M. Sommer, George Washington, B (2)
1959	Don Allard, Boston College, B
1960	Richie Lucas, Penn State, QB
1961	Norman Snead, Wake Forest, QB
1962	Ernie Davis, Syracuse, RB
1963	Pat Richter, Wisconsin, TE
1964	Charley Taylor, Arizona State, RB-WR
1965	Bob Breitenstein, Tulsa, T (2)
1966	Charlie Gogolak, Princeton, K
1967	Ray McDonald, Idaho, RB
1968	Jim Smith, Oregon, DB
1969	Eugene Epps, Texas-El Paso, DB (2)
1970	Bill Brundige, Colorado, DT (2)
1971	Cotton Speyrer, Texas, WR (2)
1972	Moses Denson, Maryland State, RB (8)
1973	Charles Cantrell, Lamar, G (5)
1974	Jon Keyworth, Colorado, TE (6)
1975	Mike Thomas, Nevada-Las Vegas, RB (6)
1976	Mike Hughes, Baylor, G (5)
1977	Duncan McColl, Stanford, DE (4)
1978	Tony Green, Florida, RB (6)
1979	Don Warren, San Diego State, TE (4)
1980	Art Monk, Syracuse, WR
1981	Mark May, Pittsburgh, T
1982	Vernon Dean, San Diego State, DB (2)
1983	Darrell Green, Texas A&I, DB

REDSKINS COACHING HISTORY

Boston 1932-36
(326-309-26)

1932	Lud Wray	4-4-2
1933-34	William (Lone Star) Dietz	11-11-2
1935	Eddie Casey	2-8-1
1936-42	Ray Flaherty*	56-23-3
1943	Arthur (Dutch) Bergman	7-4-1
1944-45	Dudley DeGroot	14-6-1
1946-48	Glen (Turk) Edwards	16-18-1
1949	John (Billick) Whelchel**	2-4-1
1949-51	Herman Ball***	5-15-0
1951	Dick Todd	5-4-0
1952-53	Earl (Curly) Lambeau	10-13-1
1954-58	Joe Kuharich	26-32-2
1959-60	Mike Nixon	4-18-2
1961-65	Bill McPeak	21-46-3
1966-68	Otto Graham	17-22-3
1969	Vince Lombardi	7-5-2
1970	Bill Austin	6-8-0
1971-77	George Allen	69-35-1
1978-80	Jack Pardee	24-24-0
1981-82	Joe Gibbs	20-9-0

*Retired to enter Navy
**Released after seven games in 1949
***Released after three games in 1951

WASHINGTON REDSKINS 1983 VETERAN ROSTER

No.	Name	Pos.	Ht.	Wt.	Birth-date	NFL Exp.	College	Birthplace	Residence	Games in '82
53	Bostic, Jeff	C	6-2	245	9/18/59	4	Clemson	Greensboro, N.C.	Reston, Va.	9
69	Brooks, Perry	DT	6-3	265	12/4/54	6	Southern	Bogalousa, La.	Reston, Va.	5
87	Brown, Charlie	WR	5-10	179	10/29/58	2	South Carolina State	John's Island, S.C.	Sterling, Va.	9
65	Butz, Dave	DT	6-7	295	6/23/50	10	Purdue	Lafayette, Ala.	Belleville, Ill.	9
82	†Caster, Rich	TE	6-5	230	11/16/48	13	Jackson State	Mobile, Ala.	Westbury, N.Y.	1
35	Claitt, Rickey	RB	5-10	206	4/12/57	3	Bethune-Cookman	Sylvester, Ga.	Cassleberry, Fla.	0*
51	Coleman, Monte	LB	6-2	235	11/4/57	5	Central Arkansas	Pine Bluff, Ark.	Herndon, Va.	8
	Crissy, Cris	WR	5-11	195	2/3/59	2	Princeton	Penn Yan, N.Y.	Arlington, Va.	0*
54	†Cronan, Peter	LB	6-2	238	1/13/55	6	Boston College	Bourue, Mass.	Watertown, Mass.	7
32	Dean, Vernon	CB-S	5-11	178	5/5/59	2	San Diego State	Los Angeles, Calif.	Los Angeles, Calif.	9
86	†Didier, Clint	TE	6-5	240	4/4/59	2	Portland State	Pasco, Wash.	Eltopia, Wash.	8
89	Garrett, Alvin	WR	5-7	178	10/1/56	4	Angelo State	Mineral Wells, Tex.	Arlington, Va.	9
30	Giaquinto, Nick	RB	5-11	204	4/4/55	4	Connecticut	Bridgeport, Conn.	Stratford, Conn.	7
77	†Grant, Darryl	DT	6-1	265	11/22/59	3	Rice	San Antonio, Tex.	San Antonio, Tex.	9
68	Grimm, Russ	G	6-3	273	5/2/59	3	Pittsburgh	Scottsdale, Pa.	Oakton, Va.	9
38	Harmon, Clarence	RB	5-11	209	11/30/55	7	Mississippi State	Kosciusko, Miss.	Herndon, Va.	9
5	Hayes, Jeff	P	5-11	175	8/19/59	2	North Carolina	Elkin, N.C.	Alexandria, Va.	9
8	Holly, Bob	QB	6-2	205	6/1/60	2	Princeton	Clifton, N.J.	Alexandria, Va.	0*
40	†Jackson, Wilbur	RB	6-1	219	11/19/51	9	Alabama	Ozark, Ala.	Ozark, Ala.	1
66	†Jacoby, Joe	T	6-7	295	7/6/59	3	Louisville	Louisville, Ky.	Vienna, Va.	9
22	Jordan, Curtis	CB-S	6-2	205	1/25/54	7	Texas Tech	Lubbock, Tex.	Lubbock, Tex.	9
55	Kaufman, Mel	LB	6-2	218	2/24/58	3	Cal Poly-SLO	Los Angeles, Calif.	Los Angeles, Calif.	9
50	Kubin, Larry	LB	6-2	234	2/26/59	2	Penn State	Union, N.J.	Reston, Va.	9
62	Laster, Donald	T	6-5	285	12/13/58	2	Tennessee State	Albany, Ga.	Albany, Ga.	8
79	†Liebenstein, Todd	DE	6-6	245	1/9/60	2	Nevada-Las Vegas	Las Vegas, Nev.	Salem, Ore.	9
56	Lowry, Quentin	LB	6-2	225	11/11/57	3	Youngstown State	Shaker Heights, Ohio	Reston, Va.	9
72	Manley, Dexter	DE	6-3	253	2/7/59	3	Oklahoma State	Houston, Tex.	Reston, Va.	9
73	May, Mark	G	6-6	288	11/2/59	3	Pittsburgh	Oneonta, N.Y.	Oakton, Va.	9
46	McDaniel, LeCharls	CB	5-9	169	10/15/58	3	Cal Poly-SLO	Ft. Bragg, N.C.	Salinas, Calif.	9
78	McGee, Tony	DE	6-4	250	1/18/49	13	Bishop	Battle Creek, Mich.	Norton, Mass.	9
76	Mendenhall, Mat	DE	6-6	255	5/14/57	3	Brigham Young	Salt Lake City, Utah	Alpine, Utah	9
57	Milot, Rich	LB	6-4	237	5/28/57	5	Penn State	Coraopolis, Pa.	Herndon, Va.	9
81	Monk, Art	WR	6-3	209	12/5/57	4	Syracuse	White Plains, N.Y.	Arlington, Va.	9
3	Moseley, Mark	K	6-0	205	3/12/48	12	Stephen F. Austin	Laneville, Tex.	Haymarket, Va.	9
29	†Murphy, Mark	S	6-4	210	7/13/55	7	Colgate	Fulton, N.Y.	Sterling, Va.	9
21	Nelms, Mike	S-KR	6-1	185	4/8/55	4	Baylor	Ft. Worth, Tex.	Herndon, Va.	9
79	†Ogrin, Pat	DT	6-5	265	2/10/58	2	Wyoming	Ft. Worth, Tex.	Butte, Mont.	3
52	Olkewicz, Neal	LB	6-0	227	1/30/57	5	Maryland	Phoenixville, Pa.	Herndon, Va.	9
17	Owen, Tom	QB	6-1	194	9/1/52	10	Wichita State	Shreveport, La.	Wichita, Kan.	0*
23	Peters, Tony	S	6-1	190	4/28/53	9	Oklahoma	Oklahoma City, Okla.	Chantilly, Va.	9
44	Riggins, John	RB	6-2	235	8/4/49	12	Kansas	Seneca, Kan.	Lawrence, Kan.	8
80	Seay, Virgil	WR	5-8	175	1/1/58	3	Troy State	Moultrie, Ga.	Moultrie, Ga.	8
74	Starke, George	T	6-5	260	7/18/48	11	Columbia	New York, N.Y.	Washington, D.C.	9
7	Theismann, Joe	QB	6-0	195	9/9/49	10	Notre Dame	New Brunswick, N.J.	Vienna, Va.	9
88	Walker, Rick	TE	6-4	235	5/28/55	7	UCLA	Santa Ana, Calif.	Alexandria, Va.	9
85	Warren, Don	TE	6-4	242	5/5/56	5	San Diego State	Bellingham, Wash.	Huntington Beach, Calif.	9
25	Washington, Joe	RB	5-10	179	9/24/53	8	Oklahoma	Crockett, Tex.	Reisterstown, Md.	7
45	†White, Jeris	CB	5-10	188	9/3/52	10	Hawaii	Ft. Worth, Tex.	Sarasota, Fla.	9
34	†Williams, Clarence	RB	5-10	185	1/25/55	6	South Carolina	Oakley, S.C.	San Diego, Calif.	0*
47	Williams, Greg	CB-S	5-11	185	8/1/59	2	Mississippi State	Greenville, Miss.	Alexandria, Va.	9
84	Williams, Mike	TE	6-4	245	8/27/59	2	Alabama A&M	Lafayette, Ala.	Reston, Va.	6
39	Wonsley, Otis	RB	5-10	214	8/13/57	3	Alcorn State	Pascagoula, Miss.	Moss Point, Miss.	9

* Claitt, Crissy missed '82 season due to injuries; Holly active with Washington for 9 games in '82, but did not play; Owen active for 7 games, but did not play; C. Williams active for 1 game, but did not play.

†Option playout; subject to developments.

Retired—Joe Lavender, 10-year cornerback, 7 games in '82.

Also played with Redskins in '82—G Fred Dean (5 games), K Dan Miller (1); T Garry Puetz (2).

COACHING STAFF

Head Coach, Joe Gibbs

Pro Career: Enters third year as Redskins coach. Led Redskins to an 8-1 record last season and 27-17 win over Miami in Super Bowl XVII. Named head coach on January 13, 1981 after spending eight years as an NFL assistant coach and nine years on the college level. Came to Redskins from the San Diego Chargers where he was offensive coordinator in 1979 and 1980. Prior to that, he was offensive coordinator for the Tampa Bay Buccaneers in 1978 and offensive backfield coach for the St. Louis Cardinals from 1973-77. While he was with San Diego, the Chargers won the AFC West title and led the NFL in passing two straight years. No pro playing experience. Career record: 20-9.

Background: Played tight end, linebacker, and guard under Don Coryell at San Diego State in 1961 and 1962 after spending two years at Cerritos (Calif.) J.C. (1959-60). Started his college coaching career at San Diego State (1964-66) followed by stints at Florida State (1967-68), Southern California (1969-70), and Arkansas (1971-72).

Personal: Born November 25, 1940, in Mocksville, N.C. Graduated from Santa Fe Springs, California, high school. Two-time national racquetball champion and ranked second in the over-35 category in 1978. He and his wife, Pat, live in Washington, D.C. and have two sons—J.D. and Coy.

ASSISTANT COACHES

Don Breaux, offensive backs; born August 3, 1940, Jennings, La., lives in Washington, D.C. Quarterback McNeese State 1959-61. Pro quarterback Denver Broncos 1963, San Diego Chargers 1964-65. College coach: Florida State 1966-67, Arkansas 1968-71, 1977-80, Florida 1973-74, Texas 1975-76. Pro coach: Joined Redskins in 1981.

Joe Bugel, assistant head coach-offensive; born March 10, 1940, Pittsburgh, Pa., lives in Washington, D.C. Guard Western Kentucky 1960-62. No pro playing experience. College coach: Western Kentucky 1964-68, Navy 1969-72, Iowa State 1973, Ohio State 1974. Pro coach: Detroit Lions 1975-76, Houston Oilers 1977-80, Redskins since 1981.

Bill Hickman, administrative assistant; born June 21, 1923, Baltimore, Md., lives in Washington, D.C. Halfback Virginia 1946-48. No pro playing experience. College coach: Virginia 1949, Duke 1950, North Carolina State 1951, Vanderbilt 1953, North Carolina 1966-72. Pro coach: Washington Redskins 1973-77, Los Angeles Rams 1978-80, rejoined Redskins in 1981.

Larry Peccatiello, linebackers; born December 21, 1935, Newark, N.J., lives in Washington, D.C. Receiver William & Mary 1955-58. No pro playing experience. College coach: William & Mary 1961-68, Navy 1969-70, Rice 1971. Pro coach: Houston Oilers 1972-75, Seattle Seahawks 1976-80, Redskins since 1981.

Richie Petitbon, assistant head coach-defense; born April 18, 1938, New Orleans, lives in Washington, D.C. Back Tulane 1955-58. Pro defensive back Chicago Bears 1959-67, Los Angeles Rams 1969-70, Washington Redskins 1971-73. Pro coach: Houston Oilers 1974-77, Redskins since 1978.

Jerry Rhome, quarterbacks; born March 6, 1942, Dallas, Tex., lives in Washington, D.C. Quarterback Southern Methodist 1960-61, Tulsa 1963-64. Pro quarterback Dallas Cowboys 1965-68, Cleveland Browns 1969, Houston Oilers 1970, Los Angeles Rams 1971-72. College coach: Tulsa 1973-75. Pro coach: Seattle Seahawks 1976-82, first year with Redskins.

Dan Riley, conditioning; born October 19, 1949, Syracuse, N.Y., lives in Chantilly, Va. No college or pro playing experience. College coach: Army 1973-76, Penn State 1977-81. Pro coach: Joined Redskins in 1982.

Wayne Sevier, special teams; born July 3, 1941, San Diego, lives in Washington, D.C. Quarterback Chaffey, Calif., J.C. 1960, San Diego State 1961-62. No pro playing experience. College coach: California Western 1968-69. Pro coach: St. Louis Cardinals 1974-75, Atlanta Falcons 1976, San Diego Chargers 1979-80, Redskins since 1981.

Warren Simmons, tight ends; born February 25, 1942, Poughkeepsie, N.Y., lives in Washington, D.C. Center San Diego State 1963-65. No pro playing experience. College coach: Cal State-Fullerton 1972-75, Cerritos, Calif., J.C. 1976-80. Pro coach: Joined Redskins in 1981.

Charley Taylor, wide receivers; born September 28, 1942, Grand Prairie, Tex., lives in Reston, Va. Running back Arizona State 1962-64. Pro wide receiver Washington Redskins 1964-76. Pro coach: Joined Redskins in 1982.

LaVern Torgeson, defensive line; born February 28, 1929, LaCrosse, Wash., lives in Washington, D.C. Center-linebacker Washington State 1948-50. Pro linebacker Detroit Lions 1951-54, Washington Redskins 1955-58. Pro coach: Washington Redskins 1959-61, 1971-77, Pittsburgh Steelers 1962-68, Los Angeles Rams 1969-70, 1978-80, rejoined Redskins in 1981.

WASHINGTON REDSKINS 1983 FIRST-YEAR ROSTER

Name	Pos.	Ht.	Wt.	Birth-date	College	Birthplace	Residence	How Acq.
Anderson, Stuart (1)	LB	6-1	247	12/25/59	Virginia	Mathews, Va.	Charlottesville, Va.	FA
Anthony, Jesse	CB	6-2	190	7/26/60	Knoxville	Macon, Ga.	Macon, Ga.	FA
Armstead, Charles	CB	5-9	170	6/2/61	Illinois	San Fernando, Calif.	San Fernando, Calif.	FA
Arnold, Ray	WR	6-0	186	1/13/60	Cal State-Hayward	Baltimore, Md.	Poway, Calif.	FA
Bequette, Jay	C	6-1	270	6/7/61	Arkansas	Lawrence, Kan.	Crystal City, Mo.	FA
Booker, Steve	LB	6-1	210	9/30/60	Cal Poly-SLO	Huntington Pk., Calif.	Los Angeles, Calif.	FA
Boyd, John	WR	6-0	200	12/11/60	Indiana	New Castle, Ind.	New Castle, Ind.	FA
Brown, Harold	WR	6-2	200	6/6/60	Iowa State	Ravenna, Ohio	Kent, Ohio	FA
Coffey, Ken (1)	CB-S	6-0	190	7/11/60	S.W. Texas State	Rantoul, Ill.	Reston, Va.	D9 ('82)
Deery, Tom (1)	S	6-1	200	2/4/60	Widener	Blackwood, Pa.	West Coastville, Pa.	FA
Evans, Reggie (1)	WR	5-11	201	1/5/59	Richmond	Newport News, Va.	Newport News, Va.	FA
Gandy, Geff	LB	6-1	228	5/1/60	Baylor	Dallas, Tex.	San Antonio, Tex.	D10
Gilbert, Marcus	RB	5-10	195	12/22/60	Texas Christian	Dallas, Tex.	Dallas, Tex.	D9
Green, Darrell	CB-KR	5-8	170	2/15/60	Texas A&I	Houston, Tex.	Houston, Tex	D1
Hallstrom, Todd	T	6-6	265	4/1/60	Minnesota	Mora, Minn.	Mora, Minn.	D8
Hayes, Jay (1)	DE	6-6	250	3/3/60	Idaho	Pittsburgh, Pa.	Bridgeville, Pa.	FA
Heflin, Van (1)	TE	6-3	240	4/4/59	Vanderbilt	Atlanta, Ga.	Nashville, Tenn.	FA
Hines, Joe	LB	6-0	225	2/14/60	Texas Christian	Newark, N.J.	Fort Worth, Tex.	FA
Hoggard, Dee Dee	CB	6-0	185	5/20/61	North Carolina State	Ahoskie, N.C.	Raleigh, N.C.	FA
Jones, Greg	RB	5-11	190	7/1/60	Alcorn State	Milwaukee, Wis.	Lorman, Miss.	FA
Jones, Keith (1)	T	6-5	285	8/13/57	West Virginia	Charleston, W. Va.	Charleston, W. Va.	FA
Kellin, Kevin	DT	6-5	260	11/16/59	Minnesota	Hampton, Iowa	Grand Rapids, Minn.	FA
Laufenberg, Babe	QB	6-2	195	12/5/59	Indiana	Burbank, Calif.	Canoga Park, Calif.	D6a
Mann, Charles	DE	6-6	250	4/12/61	Nevada-Reno	Sacramento, Calif.	Sacramento, Calif.	D3
Miller, Shawn	DE	6-4	250	3/14/61	Utah State	Ogden, Utah	Logan, Utah	FA
Newton, Nathan	G	6-2	275	12/20/61	Florida A&M	Orlando, Fla.	Orlando, Fla	FA
Nyce, Jeff	C	6-2	250	12/13/60	North Carolina State	Lansdale, Pa.	Cary, N.C.	FA
O'Neil, Brian	S	6-3	190	11/12/61	Alfred	Buffalo, N.Y.	Geneseo, N.Y.	FA
Orgas, Fred	LB	6-4	225	7/28/60	Minnesota	Minneapolis, Minn.	Minneapolis, Minn.	FA
Riggins, Charles (1)	DE	6-3	245	11/9/60	Bethune-Cookman	Sanford, Fla.	Sanford, Fla.	FA
Schachtner, John (1)	LB	6-3	220	4/9/59	Northern Arizona	Glendale, Calif.	Herndon, Va.	D7 ('82)
Smigelsky, Dave (1)	P	5-11	180	7/3/59	Virginia Tech	Perth Amboy, N.J.	Clinton, N.J.	FA
Smith, Darryl	CB	6-0	195	7/8/60	Virginia	Hampton, Va.	Newport News, Va.	FA
Thompson, George (1)	TE	6-2	225	3/12/59	Albany State	St. Petersburg, Fla.	St. Petersburg, Fla.	FA
Toney, Gerald	TE	6-2	220	7/15/61	Citadel	Darlington, S.C.	Darlington, S.C.	FA
Vines, Vic	S	6-0	190	12/28/60	Baylor	Odessa, Tex.	Odessa, Tex.	FA
Williams, Richard	RB	6-0	205	9/13/60	Memphis State	Eustis, Fla.	Eustis, Fla.	D2
Winckler, Bob	G	6-3	290	4/16/61	Wisconsin	West Bend, Wis.	Madison, Wis.	D6

Players who report to an NFL team for the first time are designated on rosters as rookies (R). If a player reported to an NFL training camp in a previous year but was not on the active squad for three or more regular season or postseason games, he is listed on the first-year roster and designated by a (1). Thereafter, a player who is on the active squad for three or more regular season or postseason games is credited with an additional year of playing experience.

NOTES

_____
_____
_____
_____
_____
_____
_____
_____
_____
_____

1983 NFL Roster of Officials

Art McNally, Supervisor of Officials
Jack Reader, Assistant Supervisor of Officials
Nick Skorich, Assistant Supervisor of Officials
Stu Kirkpatrick, Officiating Assistant
Mark Burns, Officiating Assistant

No.	Name	Position	College	No.	Name	Position	College
115	Ancich, Hendi	Umpire	Harbor College	68	Leimbach, John	Umpire	Missouri
112	Austin, Gerald	Side Judge	Western Carolina	18	Lewis, Bob	Field Judge	No College
22	Baetz, Paul	Back Judge	Heidelberg	21	Liske, Pete	Back Judge	Penn State
14	Barth, Gene	Referee	St. Louis	49	Look, Dean	Side Judge	Michigan State
59	Beeks, Bob	Line Judge	Lincoln	90	Mace, Gil	Side Judge	Westminster
17	Bergman, Jerry	Head Linesman	Duquesne	82	Mallette, Pat	Field Judge	Nebraska
110	Botchan, Ron	Umpire	Occidental	26	Marion, Ed	Head Linesman	Pennsylvania
101	Boylston, Bob	Umpire	Alabama	94	Marshall, Vern	Line Judge	Linfield
43	Cashion, Red	Referee	Texas A&M	116	McCallum, Chuck	Field Judge	Michigan State
16	Cathcart, Royal	Side Judge	UC Santa Barbara	48	McCarter, Gordon	Referee	Western Reserve
24	Clymer, Roy	Back Judge	New Mexico State	95	McElwee, Bob	Referee	Navy
27	Conway, Al	Umpire	Army	41	McKenzie, Dick	Line Judge	Ashland
61	Creed, Dick	Side Judge	Louisville	108	McLaughlin, Bob	Head Linesman	Xavier
78	Demmas, Art	Umpire	Vanderbilt	76	Merrifield, Ed	Field Judge	Missouri
45	DeSouza, Ron	Line Judge	Morgan State	35	Miles, Leo	Head Linesman	Virginia State
74	Dodez, Ray	Head Linesman	Wooster	117	Montgomery, Ben	Line Judge	Morehouse
31	Dolack, Dick	Field Judge	Ferris State	88	Moss, Dave	Umpire	Dartmouth
6	Dooley, Tom	Referee	VMI	55	Musser, Charley	Field Judge	North Carolina State
102	Douglas, Merrill	Side Judge	Utah	10	Myers, Tom	Umpire	San Jose State
5	Douglas, Ray	Back Judge	Baltimore	83	O'Brien, Bill	Field Judge	Indiana
12	Dreith, Ben	Referee	Colorado State	51	Orem, Dale	Line Judge	Louisville
87	Ferguson, Dick	Side Judge	West Virginia	77	Orr, Don	Field Judge	Vanderbilt
39	Fette, Jack	Line Judge	No College	64	Parry, Dave	Side Judge	Wabash
57	Fiffick, Ed	Umpire	Marquette	44	Peters, Walt	Line Judge	Indiana State, Pa.
111	Frantz, Earnie	Head Linesman	No College	92	Poole, Jim	Back Judge	San Diego State
71	Frederic, Bob	Referee	Colorado	58	Quinby, Bill	Side Judge	Iowa State
62	Gandy, Duwayne	Side Judge	Tulsa	53	Reynolds, Bill	Line Judge	West Chester State
50	Gereb, Neil	Umpire	California	80	Rice, Bob	Side Judge	Denison
72	Gierke, Terry	Head Linesman	Portland State	98	Rosser, Jimmy	Back Judge	Auburn
15	Glass, Bama	Line Judge	Colorado	29	Sanders, J. W.	Back Judge	Southern Illinois
85	Glover, Frank	Head Linesman	Morris Brown	56	Shannon, Carver	Line Judge	Southern Illinois
4	Gosier, Wilson	Line Judge	Fort Valley State	70	Seeman, Jerry	Referee	Winona State
34	Graf, Fritz	Field Judge	Western Reserve	109	Semon, Sid	Head Linesman	Southern California
23	Grier, Johnny	Field Judge	D.C. Teachers	7	Silva, Fred	Referee	San Jose State
63	Hagerty, Ligouri	Head Linesman	Syracuse	20	Sinkovitz, Frank	Umpire	Duke
40	Haggerty, Pat	Referee	Colorado State	3	Smith, Boyce	Line Judge	Vanderbilt
96	Hakes, Don	Field Judge	Bradley	119	Spitler, Ron	Field Judge	Panhandle State
104	Hamer, Dale	Head Linesman	California State, Pa.	91	Stanley, Bill	Field Judge	Redlands
42	Hamilton, Dave	Umpire	Utah	38	Swanson, Bill	Back Judge	Lake Forest
105	Hantak, Dick	Back Judge	S.E. Missouri	37	Toler, Burl	Head Linesman	San Francisco
66	Hawk, Dave	Side Judge	Southern Methodist	52	Tompkins, Ben	Back Judge	Texas
46	Heberling, Chuck	Referee	Washington & Jefferson	32	Tunney, Jim	Referee	Occidental
19	Hensley, Tommy	Umpire	Tennessee	93	Vaughan, Jack	Field Judge	Mississippi State
54	Johnson, Jack	Line Judge	Pacific Lutheran	36	Veteri, Tony	Head Linesman	No College
114	Johnson, Tom	Head Linesman	Miami, Ohio	79	Ward, Ed	Side Judge	Southern Methodist
97	Jones, Nathan	Side Judge	Lewis & Clark	28	Wedge, Don	Back Judge	Ohio Wesleyan
60	Jorgensen, Dick	Referee	Wisconsin	89	Wells, Gordon	Umpire	Occidental
106	Jury, Al	Back Judge	San Bernardino Valley	30	Wilford, Dan	Line Judge	Mississippi
107	Kearney, Jim	Back Judge	Pennsylvania	99	Williams, Banks	Back Judge	Houston
67	Keck, John	Umpire	Cornell College	8	Williams, Dale	Head Linesman	Cal State-Northridge
25	Kelleher, Tom	Back Judge	Holy Cross	84	Wortman, Bob	Field Judge	Findlay
73	Knight, Pat	Back Judge	Southern Methodist	11	Wyant, Fred	Referee	West Virginia
65	Kragseth, Norm	Head Linesman	Northwestern				
120	Lane, Gary	Side Judge	Missouri				

152

Numerical Roster

No.	Referees
6	Tom Dooley
7	Fred Silva
9	Jerry Markbreit
11	Fred Wyant
12	Ben Dreith
14	Gene Barth
32	Jim Tunney
40	Pat Haggerty
43	Red Cashion
46	Chuck Heberling
48	Gordon McCarter
60	Dick Jorgensen
70	Jerry Seeman
71	Bob Frederic
95	Bob McElwee

No.	Umpires
10	Tom Myers
19	Tommy Hensley
20	Frank Sinkovitz
27	Al Conway
42	Dave Hamilton
50	Neil Gereb
57	Ed Fiffick
67	John Keck
68	John Leimbach
78	Art Demmas
88	Dave Moss
89	Gordon Wells
101	Bob Boylston
110	Ron Botchan
115	Hendi Ancich

No.	Head Linesmen
8	Dale Williams
17	Jerry Bergman
26	Ed Marion
35	Leo Miles
36	Tony Veteri
37	Burl Toler
63	Ligouri Hagerty
65	Norm Kragseth
72	Terry Gierke
74	Ray Dodez
85	Dale Hamer
104	Dale Hamer
108	Bob McLaughlin
109	Sid Semon
111	Earnie Frantz
114	Tom Johnson

No.	Line Judges
3	Boyce Smith
4	Wilson Gosier
15	Bama Glass
30	Dan Wilford
39	Jack Fette
41	Dick McKenzie
44	Walt Peters
45	Ron DeSouza
51	Dale Orem
53	Bill Reynolds
54	Jack Johnson
56	Carver Shannon
59	Bob Beeks
94	Vern Marshall
117	Ben Montgomery

No.	Back Judges
5	Ray Douglas
21	Pete Liske
22	Paul Baetz
24	Roy Clymer
25	Tom Kelleher
28	Don Wedge
29	J. W. Sanders
38	Bill Swanson
52	Ben Tompkins
73	Pat Knight
92	Jim Poole
98	Jimmy Rosser
99	Banks Williams
105	Dick Hantak
106	Al Jury
107	Jim Kearney

No.	Side Judges
16	Royal Cathcart
49	Dean Look
58	Bill Quinby
61	Richard Creed
62	Duwayne Gandy
64	Dave Parry
66	Dave Hawk
79	Ed Ward
80	Bob Rice
87	Dick Ferguson
90	Gil Mace
97	Nate Jones
102	Merrill Douglas
112	Gerald Austin
120	Gary Lane

No.	Field Judges
18	Bob Lewis
23	Johnny Grier
31	Dick Dolack
34	Fritz Graf
55	Charley Musser
76	Ed Merrifield
77	Don Orr
82	Pat Mallette
83	Bill O'Brien
84	Bob Wortman
91	Bill Stanley
93	Jack Vaughan
96	Don Hakes
116	Chuck McCallum
119	Ron Spitler

1983 Officials at a Glance

Referees

Gene Barth, No. **14,** St. Louis, president, oil company, 13th year.
Red Cashion, No. **43,** Texas A&M, chairman of the board, insurance company, 12th year.
Tom Dooley, No. **6,** VMI, general contractor, 6th year.
Ben Dreith, No. **12,** Colorado State, teacher-counselor, 24th year.
Bob Frederic, No. **71,** Colorado, president, printing and lithography company, 16th year.
Pat Haggerty, No. **40,** Colorado State, teacher and coach, 19th year.
Chuck Heberling, No. **46,** Washington & Jefferson, executive administrator, state high school athletic program, 19th year.
Dick Jorgensen, No. **60,** Wisconsin, president, commercial bank, 16th year.
Jerry Markbreit, No. **9,** Illinois, national sales manager, 8th year.
Gordon McCarter, No. **48,** Western Reserve, industrial sales, 17th year.
Bob McElwee, No. **95,** U.S. Naval Academy, owner, construction company, 8th year.
Jerry Seeman, No. **70,** Winona State, assistant superintendent, 9th year.
Fred Silva, No. **7,** San Jose State, vice-president, director of chain store sales, 17th year.
Jim Tunney, No. **32,** Occidental, president of motivation company and professional speaker, 24th year.
Fred Wyant, No. **11,** West Virginia, executive insurance sales director, former NFL player, 18th year.

Umpires

Hendi Ancich, No. **115,** Harbor, longshoreman, 2nd year.
Ron Botchan, No. **110,** Occidental, college professor, former AFL player, 4th year.
Bob Boylston, No. **101,** Alabama, manufacturers representative, 6th year.
Al Conway, No. **27,** Army, national director, industrial sales, 15th year.
Art Demmas, No. **78,** Vanderbilt, investments and financial planning, insurance company, 16th year.
Ed Fiffick, No. **57,** Marquette, podiatric physician, 5th year.
Neil Gereb, No. **50,** California, supervisor, aircraft company, 3rd year.
Dave Hamilton, No. **42,** Utah, hospital administrator, 9th year.
Tommy Hensley, No. **19,** Tennessee, owner, land development & management company, 17th year.
John Keck, No. **67,** Cornell, petroleum distributor, 12th year.
John Leimbach, No. **68,** Missouri, school teacher, 3rd year.
Dave Moss, No. **88,** Dartmouth, insurance, 4th year.
Tom Myers, No. **10,** San Jose State, vice-president, retail sales corporation, 5th year.
Frank Sinkovitz, No. **20,** Duke, president, marketing company, former NFL player, 26th year.
Gordon Wells, No. **89,** Occidental, college professor, physical education, 12th year.

Head Linesmen

Jerry Bergman, No. **17,** Duquesne, administrative assistant, 18th year.
Ray Dodez, No. **74,** Wooster, communications consultant, 16th year.
Ernie Frantz, No. **111,** vice-president and manager, land title company, 3rd year.
Terry Gierke, No. **72,** Portland State, real estate broker, 3rd year.
Frank Glover, No. **85,** Morris Brown, assistant area superintendent, 12th year.
Ligouri Hagerty, No. **63,** Syracuse, manager, sporting goods company, 8th year.
Dale Hamer, No. **104,** California State-Pa., senior planning specialist, 6th year.
Tom Johnson, No. **114,** Miami-Ohio, teacher and coach, 2nd year.
Norm Kragseth, No. **65,** Northwestern, chairman of physical education department, 10th year.
Ed Marion, No. **26,** Pennsylvania, vice-president, pension marketing, insurance company, 24th year.
Bob McLaughlin, No. **108,** Xavier, president, art sign company, 6th year.
Leo Miles, No. **35,** Virginia State, university athletic director, former NFL player, 15th year.
Sid Semon, No. **109,** Southern California, chairman of physical education department, 6th year.
Burl Toler, No. **37,** University of San Francisco, director of certificated services, 19th year.
Tony Veteri, No. **36,** sales manager, consumer products, 23rd year.
Dale Williams, No. **8,** Cal State-Northridge, coordinator of athletic officials, 4th year.

Line Judges

Bob Beeks, No. **59,** Lincoln, law enforcement officer, 16th year.
Ron DeSouza, No. **45,** Morgan State, vice-president, student affairs, 4th year.
Jack Fette, No. **39,** district sales manager, sporting goods company, 19th year.
Bama Glass, No. **15,** Colorado, owner, consumer products, 5th year.
Wilson Gosier, No. **4,** Fort Valley State, assistant director, professional practices commission, 4th year.
Jack Johnson, No. **54,** Pacific Lutheran, fund raising consultant, 8th year.
Vern Marshall, No. **94,** Linfield College, counseling coordinator, 8th year.
Dick McKenzie, No. **41,** Ashland, vice-president, insurance agency, 6th year.
Ben Montgomery, No. **117,** Morehouse, assistant principal, 2nd year.
Dale Orem, No. **51,** Louisville, owner, sporting goods company, 4th year.
Walt Peters, No. **44,** Indiana State, insurance broker, 16th year.
Bill Reynolds, No. **53,** West Chester State, teacher and athletic director, 9th year.
Carver Shannon, No. **56,** Southern Illinois, executive, aircraft corporation, former NFL player, 1st year.
Boyce Smith, No. **3,** Vanderbilt, president and general manager, steel company, 3rd year.
Dan Wilford, No. **30,** Mississippi, hospital executive, 1st year.

Back Judges

Paul Baetz, No. **22,** Heidelberg, financial consultant, 6th year.
Roy Clymer, No. **24,** New Mexico State, area manager, gas company, 4th year.
Ray Douglas, No. **5,** Baltimore, distribution manager, 16th year.
Dick Hantak, No. **105,** Southeast Missouri, high school department chairman, 6th year.
Al Jury, No. **106,** San Bernardino Valley, state traffic officer, 6th year.
Jim Kearney, No. **107,** Pennsylvania, account manager, 6th year.
Tom Kelleher, No. **25,** Holy Cross, president, marketing company, 24th year.
Pat Knight, No. **73,** Southern Methodist, president, lumber company, former NFL player, 11th year.
Pete Liske, No. **21,** Penn State, general manager, manufacturing and sales company, former NFL Player, 1st year.
Jim Poole, No. **92,** San Diego State, physical education professor, 9th year.
Jimmy Rosser, No. **98,** Auburn, personnel director, 7th year.
J.W. Sanders, No. **29,** Southern Illinois, physical education professor, 4th year.
Bill Swanson, No. **38,** Lake Forest, real estate appraiser, 20th year.
Ben Tompkins, No. **52,** Texas, attorney, 13th year.
Don Wedge, No. **28,** Ohio Wesleyan, marketing executive, 12th year.
Banks Willliams, No. **99,** Houston, vice-president-sales, concrete company, 6th year.

Side Judges

Gerald Austin, No. **112,** Western Carolina, high school principal, 2nd year.
Royal Cathcart, No. **16,** UC-Santa Barbara, broker and managing partner, former NFL player, 13th year.
Richard Creed, No. **61,** Louisville, real estate management, 6th year.
Merrill Douglas, No. **102,** Utah, deputy sheriff, former NFL player, 3rd year.
Dick Ferguson, No. **87,** West Virginia, commissioner of officials, 10th year.
Duwayne Gandy, No. **62,** Tulsa, sales-public relations, oil field wireline service, 3rd year.
Dave Hawk, No. **66,** Southern Methodist, co-owner, warehousing company, 12th year.
Nate Jones, No. **97,** Lewis and Clark, high school principal, 7th year.
Gary Lane, No. **120,** Missouri, director of marketing, former NFL player, 2nd year.
Dean Look, No. **49,** Michigan State, director of marketing & sales, former AFL player, 12th year.
Gil Mace, No. **90,** Westminster, national accounts manager, 10th year.
Dave Parry, No. **64,** Wabash, high school athletic director, 9th year.
Bill Quinby, No. **58,** Iowa State, director, personnel services, 6th year.
Bob Rice, No. **80,** Denison, physical education department chairman, 15th year.
Ed Ward, No. **79,** Southern Methodist, attorney, 6th year.

Field Judges

Dick Dolack, No. **31,** Ferris State, pharmacist, 18th year.
Fritz Graf, No. **34,** Western Reserve, area manager, medical and hospital equipment company, 24th year.
Johnny Grier, No. **23,** D.C. Teachers, planning engineer, telephone company, 3rd year.
Don Hakes, No. **96,** Bradley, high school dean of students, 7th year.
Bob Lewis, No. **18,** supervisor, air force base, 8th year.
Pat Mallette, No. **83,** Nebraska, real estate broker, 15th year.
Chuck McCallum, No. **116,** Michigan State, executive director, physicians foundation, 2nd year.
Ed Merrifield, No. **76,** Missouri, sales manager, heavy equipment, 9th year.
Charley Musser, No. **55,** North Carolina State, vice-president and general manager, refining company, 12th year.
Bill O'Brien, No. **82,** Indiana, university department chairman-professor, 17th year.
Don Orr, No. **77,** Vanderbilt, president, machine company, 13th year.
Ron Spitler, No. **119,** Panhandle State, transportation director, 2nd year.
Bill Stanley, No. **91,** Redlands, college athletic director, 10th year.
Jack Vaughan, No. **93,** Mississippi State, real estate broker, 8th year.
Bob Wortman, No. **84,** Findlay, owner, insurance company, 18th year.

Official Signals

1

TOUCHDOWN, FIELD GOAL, or SUCCESSFUL TRY
Both arms extended above head.

2

SAFETY
Palms together above head.

3

FIRST DOWN
Arms pointed toward defensive team's goal.

4

DEAD BALL or NEUTRAL ZONE ESTABLISHED
One arm above head with an open hand.
With fist closed: **Fourth Down.**

5

BALL ILLEGALLY TOUCHED, KICKED, OR BATTED
Fingertips tap both shoulders.

6

TIME OUT
Hands crisscrossed above head.
Same signal followed by placing one hand on top of cap: **Referee's Time Out.**
Same signal followed by arm swung at side: **Touchback.**

7

NO TIME OUT or TIME IN WITH WHISTLE
Full arm circled to simulate moving clock.

8

DELAY OF GAME or EXCESS TIME OUT
Folded arms.

9

FALSE START, ILLEGAL SHIFT, ILLEGAL PROCEDURE, ILLEGAL FORMATION, or KICKOFF OR SAFETY KICK OUT OF BOUNDS
Forearms rotated over and over in front of body.

10

PERSONAL FOUL
One wrist striking the other above head.
Same signal followed by swinging leg: **Running Into or Roughing Kicker.**
Same signal followed by raised arm swinging forward: **Running Into or Roughing Passer.**
Same signal followed by hand striking back of calf: **Clipping.**

11

HOLDING
Grasping one wrist, the fist clenched, in front of chest.

12

ILLEGAL USE OF HANDS, ARMS, OR BODY
Grasping one wrist, the hand open and facing forward, in front of chest.

13

PENALTY REFUSED, INCOMPLETE PASS, PLAY OVER or MISSED GOAL
Hands shifted in horizontal plane.

14

PASS JUGGLED INBOUNDS AND CAUGHT OUT OF BOUNDS
Hands up and down in front of chest (following incomplete pass signal).

15

ILLEGAL FORWARD PASS
One hand waved behind back followed by loss of down signal.

16

INTENTIONAL GROUNDING OF PASS
Parallel arms waved in a diagonal plane across

17

INTERFERENCE WITH FORWARD PASS or FAIR CATCH
Hands open
and extended forward from
shoulders with hands vertical.

18

INVALID FAIR CATCH SIGNAL
One hand waved above head.

19

INELIGIBLE RECEIVER or INELIGIBLE MEMBER OF KICKING TEAM DOWNFIELD
Right hand touching top of cap.

20

ILLEGAL CONTACT
One open hand extended forward.

21

OFFSIDE or ENCROACHING
Hands on hips.

22

ILLEGAL MOTION AT SNAP
Horizontal arc with one hand.

23

LOSS OF DOWN
Both hands held behind head.

24

CRAWLING, INTERLOCKING INTERFERENCE, PUSHING, or HELPING RUNNER
Pushing movement of hands
to front with arms downward.

25

**TOUCHING A FORWARD
PASS OR SCRIMMAGE KICK**
Diagonal motion of
one hand across another.

26

**UNSPORTSMANLIKE
CONDUCT (Non-contact fouls)**
Arms outstretched, palms down.
(Same signal means continuous
action fouls are disregarded.)

27

**ILLEGAL CUT or
BLOCKING BELOW
THE WAIST**
Hand striking front of knee.

28

ILLEGAL CRACKBACK
Strike of an open right hand
against the right mid thigh.

29

PLAYER DISQUALIFIED
Ejection signal.

30

TRIPPING
Repeated action of right foot
in back of left heel.

NFL Digest of Rules

This Digest of Rules of the National Football League has been prepared to aid players, fans, and members of the press, radio, and television media in their understanding of the game.

It is not meant to be a substitute for the official rule book. In any case of conflict between these explanations and the official rules, the rules always have precedence.

In order to make it easier to coordinate the information in this digest the topics discussed generally follow the order of the rule book.

Officials' Jurisdictions, Positions, and Duties

Referee—General oversight and control of game. Gives signals for all fouls and is final authority for rule interpretations. Takes a position in backfield 10 to 12 yards behind line of scrimmage, favors right side (if quarterback is right-handed passer). Determines legality of snap, observes deep back(s) for legal motion. On running play, observes quarterback during and after handoff, remains with him until action has cleared away, then proceeds downfield, checking on runner and contact behind him. When runner is downed, Referee determines forward progress from wing official and if necessary, adjusts final position of ball.

On pass plays, drops back as quarterback begins to fade back, picks up legality of blocks by near linemen. Changes to complete concentration on quarterback as defenders approach. Primarily responsible to rule on possible roughing action on passer and if ball becomes loose, rules whether ball is free on a fumble or dead on an incomplete pass.

During kicking situations, Referee has primary responsibility to rule on kicker's actions and whether or not any subsequent contact by a defender is legal.

Umpire—Primary responsibility to rule on players' equipment, as well as their conduct and actions on scrimmage line. Lines up approximately four to five yards downfield, varying position from in front of weakside tackle to strongside guard. Looks for possible false start by offensive linemen. Observes legality of contact by both offensive linemen while blocking and by defensive players while they attempt to ward off blockers. Is prepared to call rule infractions if they occur on offense or defense. Moves forward to line of scrimmage when pass play develops in order to insure that interior linemen do not move illegally downfield. If offensive linemen indicate screen pass is to be attempted, Umpire shifts his attention toward screen side, picks up potential receiver in order to insure that he will legally be permitted to run his pattern and continues to rule on action of blockers. Umpire is to assist in ruling on incomplete or trapped passes when ball is thrown overhead or short.

Head Linesman—Primarily responsible for ruling on offside, encroachment, and actions pertaining to scrimmage line prior to or at snap. Keys on closest setback on his side of the field. On pass plays, Linesman is responsible to clear this receiver approximately seven yards downfield as he moves to a point five yards beyond the line. Linesman's secondary responsibility is to rule on any illegal action taken by defenders on any delay receiver moving downfield. Has full responsibility for ruling on sideline plays on his side, e.g., pass receiver or runner in or out of bounds. Together with Referee, Linesman is responsible for keeping track of number of downs and is in charge of mechanics of his chain crew in connection with its duties.

Linesman must be prepared to assist in determining forward progress by a runner on play directed toward middle or into his side zone. He, in turn, is to signal Referee or Umpire what forward point ball has reached. Linesman is also responsible to rule on legality of action involving any receiver who approaches his side zone. He is to call pass interference when the infraction occurs and is to rule on legality of blockers and defenders on plays involving ball carriers, whether it is entirely a running play, a combination pass and run, or a play involving a kick.

Line Judge—Straddles line of scrimmage on side of field opposite Linesman. Keeps time of game as a backup for clock operator. Along with Linesman is responsible for offside, encroachment, and actions pertaining to scrimmage line prior to or at snap. Line Judge keys on closest setback on his side of field. Line Judge is to observe his receiver until he moves at least seven yards downfield, Judge then moves toward backfield side, being especially alert to rule on any back in motion and on flight of ball when pass is made (he must rule whether forward or backward). Line Judge has primary responsibility to rule whether or not passer is behind or beyond line of scrimmage when pass is made. He also assists in observing actions by blockers and defenders who are on his side of field. After pass is thrown, Line Judge directs attention toward activities that occur in back of Umpire. During punting situations, Line Judge remains at line of scrimmage to be sure that only the end men move downfield until kick has been made. He also rules whether or not the kick crossed line and then observes action by members of the kicking team who are moving downfield to cover the kick.

Back Judge—Operates on same side of field as Line Judge, 17 yards deep. Keys on wide receiver on his side. Concentrates on path of end or back, observing legality of his potential block(s) or of actions taken against him. Is prepared to rule from deep position on holding or illegal use of hands by end or back or on defensive infractions committed by player guarding him. Has primary responsibility to make decisions involving sideline on his side of field, e.g., pass receiver or runner in or out of bounds.

Back Judge makes decisions involving catching, recovery, or illegal touching of a loose ball beyond line of scrimmage; rules on plays involving pass receiver, including legality of catch or pass interference; assists in covering actions of runner, including blocks by teammates and that of defenders; calls clipping on punt returns; and, together with Field Judge, rules whether or not field goal attempts are successful.

Side Judge—Operates on same side of field as Linesman, 17 yards deep. Keys on wide receiver on his side. Concentrates on path of end or back, observing legality of his potential block(s) or of actions taken against him. Is prepared to rule from deep position on holding or illegal use of hands by end or back or on defensive infractions committed by player guarding him. Has primary responsibility to make decisions involving sideline on his side of field, e.g., pass receiver or runner in or out of bounds.

Side Judge makes decisions involving catching, recovery, or illegal touching of a loose ball beyond line of scrimmage; rules on plays involving pass receiver, including legality of catch or pass interference; assists in covering actions of runner, including blocks by teammates and that of defenders; and calls clipping on punt returns.

Field Judge—Takes a position 25 yards downfield. In general, favors the tight end's side of field. Keys on tight end, concentrates on his path and observes legality of tight end's potential block(s) or of actions taken against him. Is prepared to rule from deep position on holding or illegal use of hands by end or back or on defensive infractions committed by player guarding him.

Field Judge times interval between plays on 30-second clock plus intermission between two periods of each half; makes decisions involving catching, recovery, or illegal touching of a loose ball beyond line of scrimmage; is responsible to rule on plays involving end line, calls pass interference, fair catch infractions, and clipping on kick returns; and, together with Back Judge, rules whether or not field goals and conversions are successful.

Definitions

1. **Chucking:** Warding off an opponent who is in front of a defender by contacting him with a quick extension of arm or arms, followed by the return of arm(s) to a flexed position, thereby breaking the original contact.
2. **Clipping:** Throwing the body across the back of an opponent's leg or hitting him from the back while moving up from behind unless the opponent is a runner or the action is in close line play.
3. **Close Line Play:** The area between the positions normally occupied by the offensive tackles, extending three yards on each side of the line of scrimmage.
4. **Crackback:** Eligible receivers who take or move to a position more than two yards outside the tackle may not block an opponent below the waist if they then move back inside to block.
5. **Dead Ball:** Ball not in play.
6. **Double Foul:** A foul by each team during the same down.
7. **Down:** The period of action that starts when the ball is put in play and ends when it is dead.
8. **Encroachment:** When a player is in the neutral zone at the time of the snap or makes contact with an opponent before the ball is snapped.
9. **Fair Catch:** An unhindered catch of a kick by a member of the receiving team who must raise one arm a full length above his head while the kick is in flight.
10. **Foul:** Any violation of a playing rule.
11. **Free Kick:** A kickoff, kick after a safety, or kick after a fair catch. It may be a placekick, dropkick, or punt, except a punt may not be used on a kickoff.
12. **Fumble:** The loss of possession of the ball.
13. **Impetus:** The action of a player that gives momentum to the ball.

14. **Live Ball:** A ball legally free kicked or snapped. It continues in play until the down ends.
15. **Loose Ball:** A live ball not in possession of any player.
16. **Muff:** The touching of a loose ball by a player in an unsuccessful attempt to obtain possession.
17. **Neutral Zone:** The space the length of a ball between the two scrimmage lines. The offensive team and defensive team must remain behind their end of the ball.
    Exception: The offensive player who snaps the ball.
18. **Offside:** A player is offside when any part of his body is beyond his scrimmage or free kick line when the ball is snapped.
19. **Own Goal:** The goal a team is guarding.
20. **Pocket Area:** Applies from a point two yards outside of either offensive tackle and includes the tight end if he drops off the line of scrimmage to pass protect. Pocket extends longitudinally behind the line back to offensive team's own end line.
21. **Possession:** When a player controls the ball throughout the act of clearly touching both feet, or any other part of his body other than his hand(s), to the ground inbounds.
22. **Punt:** A kick made when a player drops the ball and kicks it while it is in flight.
23. **Safety:** The situation in which the ball is dead on or behind a team's own goal if the impetus comes from a player on that team. Two points are scored for the opposing team.
24. **Shift:** The movement of two or more offensive players at the same time before the snap.
25. **Striking:** The act of swinging, clubbing, or propelling the arm or forearm in contacting an opponent.
26. **Sudden Death:** The continuation of a tied game into sudden death overtime in which the team scoring first (by safety, field goal, or touchdown) wins.
27. **Touchback:** When a ball is dead on or behind a team's own goal line, provided the impetus came from an opponent and provided it is not a touchdown or a missed field goal.
28. **Touchdown:** When any part of the ball, legally in possession of a player inbounds, is on, above, or over the opponent's goal line, provided it is not a touchback.
29. **Unsportsmanlike Conduct:** Any act contrary to the generally understood principles of sportsmanship.

Summary of Penalties
Automatic First Down
1. Awarded to offensive team on all defensive fouls with these exceptions:
    (a) Offside.
    (b) Encroachment.
    (c) Delay of game.
    (d) Illegal substitution.
    (e) Excessive time out(s).
    (f) Incidental grasp of face mask.
Loss of Down (No yardage)
1. Second forward pass behind the line.
2. Forward pass strikes ground, goal post, or crossbar.
3. Forward pass goes out of bounds.
4. Forward pass is first touched by eligible receiver who has gone out of bounds and returned.
5. Forward pass touches or is caught by an ineligible receiver on or behind line.
6. Forward pass thrown from behind line of scrimmage after ball once crossed the line.
Five Yards
1. Crawling.
2. Defensive holding or illegal use of hands (automatic first down).
3. Delay of game.
4. Encroachment.
5. Too many time outs.
6. False start.
7. Illegal formation.
8. Illegal shift.
9. Illegal motion.
10. Illegal substitution.
11. Kickoff out of bounds between goal lines and not touched.
12. Invalid fair catch signal.
13. More than 11 players on the field at snap for either team.
14. Less than seven men on offensive line at snap.

15. Offside.
16. Failure to pause one second after shift or huddle.
17. Running into kicker (automatic first down).
18. More than one man in motion at snap.
19. Grasping face mask of opponent.
20. Player out of bounds at snap.
21. Ineligible member(s) of kicking team going beyond line of scrimmage before ball is kicked.
22. Illegal return.
23. Failure to report change of eligibility.
10 Yards
1. Offensive pass interference.
2. Ineligible player downfield during passing down.
3. Holding, illegal use of hands, arms or body by offense.
4. Tripping by a member of either team.
5. Helping the runner.
6. Illegal batting or punching a loose ball.
7. Deliberately kicking a loose ball.
15 Yards
1. Clipping below the waist.
2. Fair catch interference.
3. Illegal crackback block by offense.
4. Piling on (automatic first down).
5. Roughing the kicker (automatic first down).
6. Roughing the passer (automatic first down).
7. Twisting, turning, or pulling an opponent by the face mask.
8. Unnecessary roughness.
9. Unsportsmanlike conduct.
10. Delay of game at start of either half.
11. Illegal blocking below the waist.
12. A tackler using his helmet to butt, spear, or ram an opponent.
13. Any player who uses the top of his helmet unnecessarily.
Five Yards and Loss of Down
1. Forward pass thrown from beyond line of scrimmage.
10 Yards and Loss of Down
1. Intentional grounding of forward pass (safety if passer is in own end zone). If foul occurs more than 10 yards behind line, play results in loss of down at spot of foul.
15 Yards and Loss of Coin Toss Option
1. Team's late arrival on the field prior to scheduled kickoff.
15 Yards (and disqualification if flagrant)
1. Striking opponent with fist.
2. Kicking or kneeing opponent.
3. Striking opponent on head or neck with forearm, elbow, or hands whether or not the initial contact is made below the neck area.
4. Roughing kicker.
5. Roughing passer.
6. Malicious unnecessary roughness.
7. Unsportsmanlike conduct.
8. Palpably unfair act. (Distance penalty determined by the Referee after consultation with other officials.)
15 Yards and Automatic Disqualification
1. Using a helmet that is not worn as a weapon.
Suspension From Game
1. Illegal equipment. (Player may return after one down when legally equipped.)
Touchdown
1. When Referee determines a palpably unfair act deprived a team of a touchdown. (Example: Player comes off bench and tackles runner apparently en route to touchdown.)

Field
1. Sidelines and end lines are out of bounds. The goal line is actually in the end zone. A player with the ball in his possession scores when the ball is on, above, or over the goal line.
2. The field is rimmed by a white border, a minimum six feet wide, along the sidelines. All of this is out of bounds.
3. The hashmarks (inbound lines) are 70 feet, 9 inches from each sideline.
4. Goal posts must be single-standard type, offset from the end line and painted bright gold. The goal posts must be 18 feet, 6 inches wide and the top face of the crossbar must be 10 feet above the ground. Vertical posts extend at least 30 feet above the crossbar. A ribbon 4 inches by 42 inches long is to be attached to the top of each post. The actual goal is the plane extending indefinitely above the crossbar and between the outer edges of the posts.

5. The field is 360 feet long and 160 feet wide. The end zones are 30 feet deep. The line used in try-for-point plays is two yards out from the goal line.
6. Chain crew members and ball boys must be uniformly identifiable.
7. All clubs must use standardized sideline markers. Pylons must be used for goal line and end line markings.
8. End zone markings and club identification at 50 yard line must be approved by the Commissioner to avoid any confusion as to delineation of goal lines, sidelines, and end lines.

Ball

1. The home club must have 24 balls available for testing by the Referee one hour before game time. In case of bad weather, a playable ball is to be substituted on request of the offensive team captain.

Coin Toss

1. The toss of coin will take place within three minutes of kickoff in center of field. The toss will be called by the visiting captain. The winner may choose one of two privileges and the loser gets the other:
   (a) Receive or kick
   (b) Goal his team will defend
2. Immediately prior to the start of the second half, the captains of both teams must inform the officials of their respective choices. The loser of the original coin toss gets first choice.

Timing

1. The stadium clock is official. In case it stops or is operating incorrectly, the Line Judge takes over the official timing on the field.
2. Each period is 15 minutes. The intermission between the periods is two minutes. Halftime is 15 minutes, unless otherwise specified.
3. On charged team time outs, the Field Judge starts watch and blows whistle after 1 minute 30 seconds. However, Referee may allow two minutes for injured player and three minutes for equipment repair.
4. Each team is allowed three time outs each half.
5. Offensive team has 30 seconds to put the ball in play. The time is displayed on two 30-second clocks, which are visible to the players, officials, and fans. Field Judge is to call a delay of game penalty (five yards) when the time limit is exceeded. In case 30-second clocks are not operating, Field Judge takes over the official timing on the field.
6. Clock will start running when ball is snapped following all changes of team possession.

Sudden Death

1. The sudden death system of determining the winner shall prevail when score is tied at the end of the regulation playing time of all NFL games. The team scoring first during overtime play shall be the winner and the game automatically ends upon any score (by safety, field goal, or touchdown) or when a score is awarded by Referee for a palpably unfair act.
2. At the end of regulation time the Referee will immediately toss coin at center of field in accordance with rules pertaining to the usual pregame toss. The captain of the visiting team will call the toss.
3. Following a three-minute intermission after the end of the regulation game, play will be continued in 15-minute periods or until there is a score. There is a two-minute intermission between subsequent periods. The teams change goals at the start of each period. Each team has three time outs and general provisions for play in the last two-minutes of a half shall prevail. Disqualified players are not allowed to return.
   Exception: In preseason and regular season games there shall be a maximum of 15 minutes of sudden death with two time outs instead of three. General provisions for play in the last two minutes of a half will be in force.

Timing in Final Two Minutes of Each Half

1. On kickoff, clock does not start until the ball has been legally touched by player of either team in the field of play. (In all other cases, clock starts with kickoff.)
2. A team cannot "buy" an excess time out for a penalty. However, a fourth time out is allowed without penalty for an injured player, who must be removed immediately. A fifth time out or more is allowed for an injury and a five-yard penalty is assessed if the clock was running. Additionally, if the clock was running and the score is tied or the team in possession is losing, the ball cannot be put in play for at least 10 seconds on the fourth or more time out. The half or game can end while those 10 seconds are run off on the clock.
3. If the defensive team is behind in the score and commits a foul when it has no time outs left in the final 30 seconds of either half, the offensive team can decline the penalty for the foul and have the time on the clock expire.

Try-for-Point

1. After a touchdown, the scoring team is allowed a try-for-point during one scrimmage down. The ball may be spotted anywhere between the inbounds lines, two or more yards from the goal line. The successful conversion counts one point, whether by run, kick, or pass.
2. The defensive team never can score on a try-for-point. As soon as defense gets possession, or kick is blocked, ball is dead.
3. Any distance penalty for fouls committed by the defense that prevent the try from being attempted can be enforced on the succeeding kickoff. Any foul committed on a successful try will result in a distance penalty being assessed on the ensuing kickoff.

Players-Substitutions

1. Each team is permitted 11 men on the field at the snap.
2. Unlimited substitution is permitted. However, players may enter the field only when the ball is dead. Players who have been substituted for are not permitted to linger on the field. Such lingering will be interpreted as unsportsmanlike conduct.
3. Players leaving the game must be out of bounds on their own side, clearing the field between the end lines, before a snap or free kick. If player crosses end line leaving field, it is delay of game (five-yard penalty).

Kickoff

1. The kickoff shall be from the kicking team's 35 yard line at the start of each half and after a field goal and try-for-point. A kickoff is one type of free kick.
2. Either a one-, two-, or three-inch tee may be used (no tee permitted for field goal or try-for-point plays). The ball is put in play by a placekick or dropkick.
3. If kickoff clears the opponent's goal posts it is not a field goal.
4. A kickoff is illegal unless it travels 10 yards OR is touched by the receiving team. Once the ball is touched by the receiving team it is a free ball. Receivers may recover and advance. Kicking team may recover but NOT advance UNLESS receiver had possession and lost the ball.
5. When a kickoff goes out of bounds between the goal lines without being touched by the receiving team, it must be kicked again. There is a five-yard penalty for a short kick or an out-of-bounds kick.
6. When a kickoff goes out of bounds between the goal lines and is touched last by receiving team, it is receiver's ball at out-of-bounds spot.

Free Kick

1. In addition to a kickoff, the other free kicks are a kick after a safety and a kick after a fair catch. In both cases, a dropkick, placekick, or punt may be used (a punt may not be used on a kickoff.)
2. On free kick after a fair catch, captain of receiving team has the option to put ball in play by punt, dropkick, or placekick without a tee, or by snap. If the placekick or dropkick goes between the uprights a field goal is scored.
3. On a free kick after a safety, the team scored upon puts ball in play by a punt, dropkick, or placekick without tee. No score can be made on a free kick following a safety, even if a series of penalties place team in position. (A field goal can be scored only on a play from scrimmage or a free kick after a fair catch.)

Field Goal

1. All field goals attempted and missed from scrimmage line beyond the 20 yard line will result in the defensive team taking possession of the ball at the scrimmage line. On any field goal attempted and missed from scrimmage line inside the 20 yard line, ball will revert to defensive team at the 20 yard line.

Safety

1. The important factor in a safety is impetus. Two points are scored for the opposing team when the ball is dead on or behind a team's own goal line if the impetus came from a player on that team.

Examples of Safety:

(a) Blocked punt goes out of kicking team's end zone. Impetus was provided by punting team. The block only changes direction of ball, not impetus.
(b) Ball carrier retreats from field of play into his own end zone and is downed. Ball carrier provides impetus.
(c) Offensive team commits a foul and spot of enforcement is behind its own goal line.
(d) Player on receiving team muffs punt and, trying to get ball, forces or illegally kicks it into end zone where he or a teammate recovers. He has given new impetus to the ball.

Examples of Non-safety:

(a) Player intercepts a pass inside his own 5 yard line and his momentum carries him into his own end zone. Ball is put in play at spot of interception.

(b) Player intercepts a pass in his own end zone and is downed. Impetus came from passing team, not from defense. (Touchback)

(c) Player passes from behind his own goal line. Opponent bats down ball in end zone. (Incomplete pass)

Measuring

1. The forward point of the ball is used when measuring.

Position of Players at Snap

1. Offensive team must have at least seven players on line.
2. Offensive players, not on line, must be at least one yard back at snap. (**Exception:** player who takes snap.)
3. No interior lineman may move after taking or simulating a three-point stance.
4. No player of either team may invade neutral zone before snap.
5. No player of offensive team may charge or move, after assuming set position, in such manner as to lead defense to believe snap has started.
6. If a player changes his eligibility, the Referee must alert the defensive captain after player has reported to him.
7. All players of offensive team must be stationary at snap, except one back who may be in motion parallel to scrimmage line or backward (not forward).
8. After a shift or huddle all players on offensive team must come to an absolute stop for at least one second with no movement of hands, feet, head, or swaying of body.
9. Linemen may lock legs only with the snapper.
10. Quarterbacks can be called for a false start penalty (five yards) if their actions are judged to be an obvious attempt to draw an opponent offside.

Use of Hands, Arms, and Body

1. No player on offense may assist a runner except by blocking for him. There shall be no interlocking interference.
2. A runner may ward off opponents with his hands and arms but no other player on offense may use hands or arms to obstruct an opponent by grasping with hands, pushing, or encircling any part of his body during a block.
3. Pass blocking is the obstruction of an opponent by use of that part of the body above the knees. During a legal block, hands (open or closed) must be inside the blocker's elbows and can be thrust forward to contact an opponent as long as the contact is inside the frame. Hands cannot be thrust forward above the frame to contact an opponent on the neck, face, or head. (**Note:** The frame is defined as that part of the opponent's body below the neck that is presented to the blocker.) Blocker cannot use his hands or arms to push from behind, hang onto, or encircle an opponent in a manner that restricts his movements as the play develops. By use of up and down action of arm(s), the blocker is permitted to ward off the opponent's attempt to grasp his jersey or arm(s) and prevent legal contact to the head.
4. A defensive player may not tackle or hold an opponent other than a runner. Otherwise, he may use his hands, arms, or body only:
   (a) To defend or protect himself against an obstructing opponent.
   Exception: An eligible receiver is considered to be an obstructing opponent ONLY to a point five yards beyond the line of scrimmage unless the player who receives the snap clearly demonstrates no further intention to pass the ball. Within this five-yard zone, a defensive player may make contact with an eligible receiver that may be maintained as long as it is continuous and unbroken. The defensive player cannot use his hands or arms to push from behind, hang onto, or encircle an eligible receiver in a manner that restricts movement as the play develops. Beyond this five-yard limitation, a defender may use his hands or arms ONLY to defend or protect himself against impending contact caused by a receiver. In such reaction, the defender may not contact a receiver who attempts to take a path to evade him.
   (b) To push or pull opponent out of the way on line of scrimmage.
   (c) In actual attempt to get at or tackle runner.
   (d) To push or pull opponent out of the way in a legal attempt to recover a loose ball.
   (e) During a legal block on an opponent who is not an eligible pass receiver.

(f) When legally blocking an eligible pass receiver above the waist.
   Exception: Eligible receivers lined up within two yards of the tackle, whether on or immediately behind the line, may be blocked below the waist at or behind the line of scrimmage. NO eligible receiver may be blocked below the waist after he goes beyond the line.
   Note: Once the quarterback hands off or pitches the ball to a back, or if the quarterback leaves the pocket area, the restrictions on the defensive team relative to the offensive receivers will end, provided the ball is not in the air.

5. A defensive player must not contact an opponent above the shoulders with the palm of his hand except to ward him off on the line. This exception is permitted only if it is not a repeated act against the same opponent during any one contact. In all other cases the palms may be used on head, neck, or face only to ward off or push an opponent in legal attempt to get at the ball.

6. Any offensive player who pretends to possess the ball or to whom a teammate pretends to give the ball may be tackled provided he is crossing his scrimmage line between the ends of a normal tight offensive line.

7. An offensive player who lines up more than two yards outside his own tackle or a player who, at the snap, is in a backfield position and subsequently takes a position more than two yards outside a tackle may not clip an opponent anywhere nor may he contact an opponent below the waist if the blocker is moving toward the ball and if contact is made within an area five yards on either side of the line.

8. A player of either team may block at any time provided it is not pass interference, fair catch interference, or unnecessary roughness.

9. A player may not bat or punch:
   (a) A loose ball (in field of play) toward his opponent's goal line or in any direction in either end zone.
   (b) A ball in player possession or attempt to get possession.
   (c) A pass in flight forward toward opponent's goal line.
   Exception: A forward or backward pass may be batted in any direction at any time by the defense.

10. No player may deliberately kick any ball except as a punt, dropkick, or placekick.

Forward Pass

1. A forward pass may be touched or caught by any eligible receiver. All members of the defensive team are eligible. Eligible receivers on the offensive team are players on either end of line (other than center, guard, or tackle) or players at least one yard behind the line at the snap. A T-formation quarterback is not eligible to receive a forward pass during a play from scrimmage.
   Exception: T-formation quarterback becomes eligible if pass is previously touched by an eligible receiver.

2. An offensive team may make only one forward pass during each play from scrimmage (Loss of down).

3. The passer must be behind his line of scrimmage (Loss of down and five yards, enforced from the spot of pass).

4. Any eligible offensive player may catch a forward pass. If a pass is touched by one offensive player and touched or caught by a second eligible offensive player, pass completion is legal. Further, all offensive players become eligible once a pass is touched by an eligible receiver or any defensive player.

5. The rules concerning a forward pass and ineligible receivers:
   (a) If ball is touched accidentally by an ineligible receiver on or behind his line: loss of down.
   (b) If ineligible receiver is illegally downfield: loss of 10 yards.
   (c) If touched or caught (intentionally or accidentally) by ineligible receiver beyond the line: loss of 10 yards.
   (d) If ineligible receiver is illegally downfield: loss of 10 yards.

6. If a forward pass is caught simultaneously by eligible players on opposing teams, possession goes to passing team.

7. Any forward pass becomes incomplete and ball is dead if:
   (a) Pass hits the ground or goes out of bounds.
   (b) Hits the goal post or the cross bar of either team.
   (c) Is caught by offensive player after touching ineligible receiver.
   (d) An illegal pass is caught by the passer.

8. A forward pass is complete when a receiver clearly touches the ground with both feet inbounds while in possession of the ball. If a receiver is carried out of bounds by an opponent while in possession in the air, pass is complete at the out-of-bounds spot.

9. If an eligible receiver goes out of bounds accidentally or is forced out by a defender and returns to catch a pass, the play is regarded as a pass caught out of bounds. (Loss of down, no yardage.)

10. On a fourth down pass—when the offensive team is inside the opposition's 20 yard line—an incomplete pass results in a loss of down at the line of scrimmage.

11. If a personal foul is committed by the defense prior to the completion of a pass, the penalty is 15 yards from the spot where ball becomes dead.

12. If a personal foul is committed by the offense prior to the completion of a pass, the penalty is 15 yards from the previous line of scrimmage.

Intentional Grounding of Forward Pass

1. Intentional grounding of a forward pass is a foul: loss of down and 10 yards from previous spot if passer is in the field of play or loss of down at the spot of the foul if it occurs more than 10 yards behind the line or safety if passer is in his own end zone when ball is released.

2. It is considered intentional grounding of a forward pass when the ball strikes the ground after the passer throws, tosses, or lobs the ball to prevent a loss of yards by his team.

Protection of Passer

1. By interpretation, a pass begins when the passer—with possession of ball—starts to bring his hand forward. If ball strikes ground after this action has begun, play is ruled an incomplete pass. If passer loses control of ball prior to his bringing his hand forward, play is ruled a fumble.

2. No defensive player may run into a passer of a legal forward pass after the ball has left his hand (15 yards). The Referee must determine whether opponent had a reasonable chance to stop his momentum during an attempt to block the pass or tackle the passer while he still had the ball.

3. Officials are to blow the play dead as soon as the quarterback is clearly in the grasp of any tackler.

Pass Interference

1. There shall be no interference with a forward pass thrown from behind the line. The restriction for the passing team starts with the snap. The restriction on the defensive team starts when the ball leaves the passer's hand. Both restrictions end when the ball is touched by anyone.

2. The penalty for defensive pass interference is an automatic first down at the spot of the foul. If interference is in the end zone, it is first down for the offense on the defense's 1 yard line. If previous spot was inside the defense's 1 yard line, penalty is half the distance to the goal line.

3. The penalty for offensive pass interference is 10 yards from the previous spot.

4. It is interference when a player's movement beyond the passing team's line materially hinders the progress of an eligible opponent in his attempt to reach a pass.

   Exception: Such incidental movement or contact when two or more eligible players make a simultaneous and bona fide attempt to catch or bat the ball is permitted. "Simultaneous and bona fide" means the contact of an eligible receiver and a defensive player when each is playing the ball and contact is unavoidable and incidental to the act of trying to catch or bat the ball.

5. It must be remembered that defensive players have as much right to the path of the ball as eligible receivers. Any bodily contact, however severe, is not interference if a player is making a bona fide and simultaneous attempt to catch or bat the ball.

Backward Pass

1. Any pass not a forward pass is regarded as a backward pass or lateral. A pass parallel to the line is a backward pass. A runner may pass backward at any time. Any player on either team may catch the pass or recover the ball after it touches the ground.

2. A backward pass that strikes the ground can be recovered and advanced by offensive team.

3. A backward pass that strikes the ground can be recovered but cannot be advanced by the defensive team.

4. A backward pass caught in the air can be advanced by the defensive team.

Fumble

1. The distinction between a fumble and a muff should be kept in mind in considering rules about fumbles. A fumble is the loss of possession of the ball. A muff is the touching of a loose ball by a player in an unsuccessful attempt to obtain possession.

2. A fumble may be advanced by any player on either team regardless of whether recovered before or after ball hits the ground.

3. If an offensive player fumbles anywhere on the field during a fourth down play, or if a player fumbles on any down after the two-minute warning in a half, only the fumbling player is permitted to recover and/or advance the ball. If recovered by any other offensive player, the ball is dead at the spot of the fumble unless it is recovered behind the spot of the fumble. In that case, ball is dead at spot of recovery. Any defensive player may recover and/or advance any fumble.

   Exception: The fourth-down fumble does not apply if a player touches, but does not possess, a direct snap from center, i.e., a snap in flight as opposed to a hand-to-hand exchange.

Kicks From Scrimmage

1. Any punt or missed field goal that touches a goal post is dead.

2. During a kick from scrimmage, only the end men, as eligible receivers on the line of scrimmage at the time of the snap, are permitted to go beyond the line before the ball is kicked.

   Exception: An eligible receiver who, at the snap, is aligned or in motion behind the line and more than one yard outside the end man on his side of the line, clearly making him the outside receiver, REPLACES that end man as the player eligible to go downfield after the snap. All other members of the kicking team must remain at the line of scrimmage until the ball has been kicked.

3. Any punt that is blocked and does not cross the line of scrimmage can be recovered and advanced by either team. However, if offensive team recovers it must make the yardage necessary for its first down to retain possession if punt was on fourth down.

4. The kicking team may never advance its own kick even though legal recovery is made beyond the line of scrimmage. Possession only.

5. A member of the receiving team may not run or rough a kicker who kicks from behind his line unless contact is:
   (a) Incidental to and after he had touched ball in flight.
   (b) Caused by kicker's own motions.
   (c) Occurs during a quick kick, or a kick made after a run, or after kicker recovers a loose ball. Ball is loose when kicker muffs snap or snap hits ground.
   (d) Defender is blocked into kicker.
   The penalty for running into the kicker is 5 yards and an automatic first down. For roughing the kicker: 15 yards and disqualification if flagrant.

6. If a member of the kicking team attempting to down the ball on or inside opponent's 5 yard line carries the ball into the end zone, it is a touchback.

7. Fouls during a punt are enforced from the previous spot (line of scrimmage).

   Exception: Illegal touching, illegal fair catch, invalid fair catch signal, and fouls by the receiving team during loose ball after ball is kicked.

8. While the ball is in the air or rolling on the ground following a punt or field goal attempt and receiving team commits a foul before gaining possession, receiving team will retain possession and will be penalized for its foul.

9. It will be illegal for a defensive player to jump or stand on any player, or be picked up by a teammate or to use a hand or hands on a teammate to gain additional height in an attempt to block a kick (Penalty 15 yards, unsportsmanlike conduct).

10. A punted ball remains a kicked ball until it is declared dead or in possession of either team.

11. Any member of the punting team may down the ball anywhere in the field of play. However, it is illegal touching (Official's time out and receiver's ball at spot of illegal touching). This foul does not offset any foul by receivers during the down.

12. Defensive team may advance all kicks from scrimmage (including unsuccessful field goal) whether or not ball crosses defensive team's goal line. Rules pertaining to kicks from scrimmage apply until defensive team gains possession.

Fair Catch

1. The member of the receiving team must raise one arm full length above his head while kick is in flight. (Failure to give proper sign: receivers' ball five yards behind spot of signal.)

2. No opponent may interfere with the fair catcher, the ball, or his path to the ball. Penalty: 15 yards from spot of foul and fair catch is awarded.

3. A player who signals for a fair catch is not required to catch the ball. However, if a player signals for a fair catch, he may not block or initiate contact with any player on the kicking team until the ball touches a player. Penalty: snap 15 yards behind spot of foul.

4. If ball hits ground or is touched by member of kicking team in flight, fair catch signal is off and all rules for a kicked ball apply.
5. Any advance by a fair catch receiver is delay of game. No specific distance is specified for "undue advance" as ball is dead at spot of catch. If player comes to a reasonable stop, no penalty. For violation, five yards.
6. If time expires while ball is in play and a fair catch is awarded, receiving team may choose to extend the period with one free kick down. However, placekicker may not use tee.

Foul on Last Play of Half or Game

1. On a foul by defense on last play of half or game, the down is replayed if penalty is accepted.
2. On a foul by the offense on last play of half or game, the down is not replayed and the play in which the foul is committed is nullified.
   Exception: Fair catch interference, foul following change of possession, illegal touching. No score by offense counts.
3. On double foul on last play of half or game, down is replayed.

Spot of Enforcement of Foul

1. There are four basic spots at which a penalty for a foul is enforced:
   (a) Spot of foul: The spot where the foul is committed.
   (b) Previous spot: The spot where the ball was put in play.
   (c) Spot of snap, pass, fumble, return kick, or free kick: The spot where the act connected with the foul occurred.
   (d) Succeeding spot: The spot where the ball next would be put in play if no distance penalty were to be enforced.
      Exception: If foul occurs after a touchdown and before the whistle for a try-for-point, succeeding spot is spot of next kickoff.
2. All fouls committed by offensive team behind the line of scrimmage and in the field of play shall be penalized from the previous spot.
3. When spot of enforcement for fouls involving defensive holding or illegal use of hands by the defense is behind the line of scrimmage, any penalty yardage to be assessed on that play shall be measured from the line if the foul occurred beyond the line.

Double Foul

1. If there is a double foul during a down in which there is a change of possession, the team last gaining possession may keep the ball unless its foul was committed prior to the change of possession.
2. If double foul occurs after a change of possession, the defensive team retains the ball at the spot of its foul or dead ball spot.
3. If one of the fouls of a double foul involves disqualification, that player must be removed, but no penalty yardage is to be assessed.
4. If the kickers foul during a punt before possession changes and the receivers foul after possession changes, penalties will be offset and the down is replayed.

Penalty Enforced on Following Kickoff

1. When a team scores by touchdown, field goal, extra point, or safety and either team commits a personal foul, unsportsmanlike conduct, or obvious unfair act during the down, the penalty will be assessed on the following kickoff.

Guide for Statisticians

The chief statistician is selected by the individual club, subject to the Commissioner's approval. It is recommended that he have a minimum of two assistants plus a play-by-play typist. He shall have the responsibility to make decisions involving judgment, i.e., yardage on all plays, etc., and shall communicate such decisions to the press box via a loudspeaker system. He is to provide the news media with a halftime summary score sheet and at the conclusion of the game with a final summary score sheet. These pre-printed forms are to be provided by the home club, which is responsible for the duplicating of all copy and distribution in the press box.

In addition, the chief statistician shall prepare an official score blank provided by the league and, within an hour after the game, phone the league statisticians with the necessary information. This official score blank should then be mailed with two copies of the play-by-play to the statisticians. The chief statistician shall audit the statistics from the play-by-play and notify the league statisticians of any areas of disagreement between the play-by-play and the official score blank; such notification shall occur within 24 hours after completion of the game.

Games Played

A player is credited with a game played when he participated in at least one play, even if the only play in which he is involved is nullified by penalty, or even if no playing time is consumed.

Credit a player with a game started when he participates in Team A's first offensive play, or Team B's first offensive play. For purposes of this rule, the following plays are *not* regarded as offensive plays:
   1. A kickoff
   2. An extra point attempt
   3. A punt or a field goal attempt from behind the line of scrimmage
   4. A free kick following a safety

A play nullifed by penalty shall be regarded as a play for purposes of this rule.

Example I: A player on Team A returns the opening kickoff to Team B's 2 yard line. On first down, Team A uses a double-tight end offense; the second tight end is used in place of a wide receiver, who is the usual starter. On first-and-goal, Team A is penalized for holding. On first-and-goal from the 12, the wide receiver replaces the second tight end in the lineup. *Scoring:* Credit the tight end with a game started; no game started for the wide receiver.

Determining the Yard Line

If any point of the football rests on or above any yard stripe, future action is to be computed from that yard line. However, if all of the football has been advanced beyond any yard stripe, future action is computed from the first yard line in advance of the football.

The principle is to be followed on all spotting situations, regardless of down, with the following exceptions:
   1. In certain situations (any down but first) where there is less than a yard to gain for a first down, it may be necessary to spot the ball back one yard to conform with the principle that there must always be, for statistical purposes, at least one yard remaining to be gained for a first down.
   2. When, on first down, the ball rests just outside a defensive team's 10 yard line, it will be necessary to designate the scrimmage line as the 11 inasmuch as it would be possible for the offensive team to advance for a first down without scoring a touchdown.
   3. See field goal section for determining yard line of attempts.

First Downs

Statistics are to be compiled on all first downs made via rushing, passing, and penalties.

First downs are compiled only from plays originating from the line of scrimmage and a first down shall be credited to each scoring play resulting from rushes or forward passes, regardless of the distance covered.

If a fumble occurs on a scrimmage play and the resultant *fumble return* or *loose ball* yardage provides the yardage necessary for a first down or a touchdown, the first down shall be credited to the category initiating the action. (For a passing category to be initiated, a pass must be thrown.) A first down is never scored if the team loses possession of the ball on the play, even if the required distance is achieved.

On broken plays where there is a fumble and subsequent recovery, and advance results in a first down or a touchdown, it shall be considered a first down rushing. Similarly, if following a blocked punt or field goal attempt, a player on the kicking team recovers and runs for a first down or a touchdown, credit a *first down rushing,* even though any yardage gained is treated as miscellaneous yardage.

Example 1. Passer attempting to pass fumbles. Teammate recovers and advances to first down. This is a *first down rushing,* but yardage is *fumble yardage.* (See Fumble Section, paragraph 8, and Passing Plays, paragraph 12.)

Ordinarily, there can be only one first down on a play. However, if a team advances by scrimmage action enough yardage for a first down and then a penalty that would ordinarily produce a first down (i.e., any *automatic first down* penalty or *15-yard penalty*) is assessed against the defense from the spot at which the scrimmage play concludes, two first downs (one by the scrimmage category initiating the action and one by penalty) shall be credited.

On the last play of the second or fourth quarter, or of an overtime period, if, in the scorer's judgment, offensive team advances the ball to a first down, credit should be given whether or not the officials so signify.

Third Down Efficiency

A third down attempt is credited whenever the offensive team is credited with either a rushing attempt, a pass, or a sack on its third down play. A third down conversion is credited whenever the offensive team is credited with either a first down rushing or a first down passing on its third down play.

EXCEPTION: Do not credit a third down attempt when the offensive team commits a foul (and the penalty is accepted by the defense), the spot of enforcement is in advance of the line of scrimmage, and the down remains the same.

Example I: Third-and-2 at midfield. Running back gains three yards but defense is offside. Offense elects to take a penalty; first-and-10 at the 45. *Scoring:* No entry is made in the third down efficiency category, since the first down was awarded by penalty.

Example II: Third-and-2 at midfield. Running back gains three yards, and defensive team is charged with facemask foul (not flagrant), moving the ball to the 42. *Scoring:* Two first downs are awarded (one rushing, one by penalty); credit a third down attempt and conversion, since the offense had made a first down without regard to the penalty.

Example III: Third-and-10 at midfield, offensive team ahead with 30 seconds remaining in the game. Quarterback falls to the ground after taking the snap, making no effort to gain yardage. *Scoring:* One third down attempt.

Example IV: Third-and-20 at offensive team's 1 yard line. Quarterback punts from behind the line of scrimmage. *Scoring:* No third down attempt.

Example V: Third-and-10 at midfield. Running back gains six yards, but a teammate is guilty of a personal foul, three yards in advance of the line of scrimmage. *Scoring:* Running back gets one rush for three yards, and his team is charged with a 15-yard penalty. No third down attempt is scored, since the spot of enforcement of the foul is ahead of the line of scrimmage. The next play is third-and-22 at the offensive team's 38.

Example VI: Third-and-10 at midfield. Quarterback scrambles one yard beyond the line, then throws a forward pass caught by a teammate. *Scoring:* Quarterback gets one rush for one yard, his team gets a five-yard penalty, and a third down attempt is scored, since the down changes. Next play is fourth-and-14 at the offensive team's 46.

Time of Possession

Time of possession is computed from the first play initiated by a team from the line of scrimmage until it scores, loses possession, or until the half or the game ends. When a change of possession (punt, fumble, interception, blocked kick) occurs during a play, consider the original team in possession until the play ends.

EXCEPTION: On a kickoff or on a free kick following a safety, all time consumed is credited to the team that first gains possession of the kick. (If neither team gains possession and the kick goes out of bounds, all time consumed is credited to the receiving team.)

Example I: Kickoff with 8:00 to play in the first quarter bounces off receiving team player and is recovered by kicking team with 7:50 to play. *Scoring:* Ten seconds of possession time is credited to kicking team, since it was the team that first *gained possession* of the kickoff.

Example II: Second-and-goal at the 1 yard line. Quarterback fumbles snap, defensive player recovers and runs the length of the field for a touchdown. Play consumes 25 seconds. *Scoring:* Original offensive team (the team that lost the fumble) is credited with 25 seconds of possession time.

Measuring a Scoring Drive

Scoring drive yardage is measured from the initial line of scrimmage to the goal line, in the event of a touchdown, or from the initial line of scrim-

mage to the last line of scrimmage for field goals, not the spot from which the kick is attempted. Penalty plays (where the down remains the same but the ball changes position) are not included in the total number of plays in a scoring drive. No scoring drive should exceed the total number of yards from the initial line to the goal line or to the last line of scrimmage for field goals.

Penalty Plays

Plays in which penalties are involved are scored as follows:

1. If the play is nullified in its entirety, and the penalty is to be assessed from the line of scrimmage, the penalty reflects the entire yardage. An example of this is a play nullified by offside, delay of game, offensive fouls at or behind the line of scrimmage, etc.

2. If a penalty occurs within the framework of a play and there is both yardage gained as well as penalty yardage assessed, the play is scored as follows in order to account for change in ball position:

Credit the offensive player(s) with yardage gained to the point of the infraction, and charge the offending team with the yardage specified by the infraction. This principle shall also apply in the case of a penalty occurring during a punting play (while the ball is in the air); if the penalty is assessed from the point of infraction, no return will be credited to receiving team. Offending (punting) team will be credited with downed punt and charged with penalty yardage specified.

Example I: Running back rushes for 25 yards, but a teammate is called for clipping 20 yards in advance of the line of scrimmage. *Scoring:* Running back gets one rushing attempt for 20 yards (to point of infraction). His team is penalized 15 yards. This accounts for forward movement of the ball of net 5 yards.

Example II: Quarterback completes pass for 17 yards to tight end and clipping occurs 15 yards in advance of line of scrimmage. *Scoring:* Quarterback is credited with one pass attempt, one pass completion for 15 yards. Tight end gets one pass reception for 15 yards. Team is charged with 15-yard penalty from point of infraction.

Example III: Running back gains 7 yards rushing, but offensive clipping occurs 5 yards in advance of line of scrimmage. Credit runner with 5 yards rushing (to point of infraction), team with 15-yard penalty from point of infraction even though play results in a 10-yard net loss from scrimmage.

Example IV: With ball at midfield, quarterback is tackled attempting to pass at his own 40, where the defensive team commits a facemask foul (*not* flagrant). Ball is moved back to midfield, according to rule, and offensive team is awarded a first down. *Scoring:* A sack for a ten-yard loss. Then, defensive team is charged with one penalty for ten yards. Credit the offensive team with a first down by penalty.

If the overall movement of the ball on a first down play is to a point beyond that needed for a first down, score a first down on the play. (Such action on a second, third, or fourth down play would be reflected by officials awarding a first down.)

Caution: Do not be confused by the fact that the down does not change in above circumstances unless the net yardage of play and penalty exceeds that needed for a first down.

3. When the spot of enforcement of a foul is at or behind the spot of possession on an interception, punt return, kickoff return, recovered fumble or miscellaneous yardage play, the player is credited with one return for no yards. Penalty yardage shall commence from the spot of enforcement.

Example: Player receives a punt on his own 40 and returns to his 48. His teammate is called for clipping at his 35. The 15-yard penalty is enforced from there, and the ball is moved to the 20. *Scoring:* Credit the returner with one return for no yards; his team is penalized 15 yards.

4. The receiving team commits an infraction while a punt is in the air and the yardage is enforced from the point of the infraction. *Scoring:* If the ball is handled, one punt return for no yards or a fair catch, as the case may be. If the infraction occurs in front of the returner, the punt should be measured to the point at which the punt ends.

5. A pass interference call is wholly a penalty play and first downs are credited accordingly.

6. When an offensive foul occurs on the last play of a half *and the offensive team gains yardage on the play,* the play is *nullifed* in its entirety. Charge the team with one penalty for *no yards.*

EXCEPTION: When the foul is in advance of the line of scrimmage, and the normal spot of enforcement would be beyond the line of scrimmage, credit yards gained to the spot of the foul. Charge the team with one penalty for *no yards.* Also, if on the last play of a half, the defensive team scores on a play during which the offensive team commits a foul, the play stands and the score counts, because the penalty is declined.

Example I: Second-and-4 at offensive team's 20 yard line. On last play of half, player runs for 6 yards, but a teammate is offside. *Scoring:* The play is nullified (no rushing attempt). Charge one penalty for *no yards.*

Example II: Second-and-4 at offensive team's 20 yard line. On last play of half, player runs for 30 yards, but a teammate is called for clipping at his own 45 yard line. *Scoring:* Since this foul occurred downfield within the framework of the play, player receives one rush for 25 yards (to point of foul) and his team gets a first down rushing. Charge the team with one penalty for *no yards.*

Example III: Second-and-4 at offensive team's 20 yard line. On last play of a half, a pass is incomplete. Offensive team is called for holding behind the line of scrimmage. *Scoring:* Since the offensive team did not gain yardage, charge the passer with one attempt. Do *not* charge a penalty.

Example IV: Second-and-4 at offensive team's 20 yard line. On last play of a half, quarterback is sacked for a loss of 12 yards; a teammate is called for holding behind the line of scrimmage. *Scoring:* Since the offensive team did not gain yardage, score one sack for 12 yards. Do *not* charge a penalty.

Example V: Second-and-4 at offensive team's 20 yard line. On last play of a half, quarterback's pass is intercepted at the 50. The ball is returned to the 30, but a teammate of the interceptor is called for clipping at the 40. Meanwhile, the original offensive team was guilty of illegal motion at the snap. *Scoring:* The offensive team did not gain yardage, so the play stands; score an interception, and credit the interceptor with 10 return yards (to the spot of the foul). Charge *his* team with one penalty for *no yards.*

Example VI: Second-and-4 at offensive team's 20 yard line. On last play of a half, offensive team is guilty of illegal motion at the snap. Running back gains two yards and fumbles; defensive player recovers at the 22 and returns to the 10. *Scoring:* Since offensive team's runner gained yardage on the play, this play is nullified in its entirety. Charge the offensive team with one penalty for *no yards.*

Example VII: Second-and-4 at offensive team's 20 yard line. On last play of a half, offensive team is guilty of illegal motion at the snap. Running back fumbles at 22, but ball bounces back to the 18, where anyone recovers and is tackled. *Scoring:* Running back gets one rush for minus two yards. Do *not* charge a penalty.

7. Penalty yardage may be assessed on an extra point attempt.

Example I: Defensive team is offside as an extra point attempt is good. The penalty is assessed on the subsequent kickoff. *Scoring:* One penalty for 5 yards.

Example II: Offensive team is offside as an extra point attempt is good. Ball is moved back from the 2 to the 7 yard line for the next attempt. *Scoring:* One penalty for 5 yards.

Example III: Defensive team is offside as an extra point attempt is missed. The offensive team elects:

(a) to rekick, with the ball remaining at the 2 yard line. *Scoring:* Defensive team is charged with one penalty, no yards.

(b) to rekick, with the ball moved to the 1 yard line. *Scoring:* Defensive team is charged with one penalty for 1 yard.

Rushing

All plays from scrimmage are rushing plays unless:

1. There is a kick from behind the line of scrimmage; or

2. There is a pass from behind the line of scrimmage; or

3. A player makes an apparent attempt to pass at any time before he or a teammate is tackled, steps out of bounds or fumbles behind or at the line of scrimmage.

There is no separate category for "yards lost" rushing, and the yardage for both individual and team is determined by deducting the minus figures from the plus figures to arrive at *net yards gained.* For example, a player gains 5 yards on one attempt and minus 2 on another. His totals would be 2 rushing attempts and a net gain of 3 yards.

A run from a fake punt or field goal formation is considered a rushing attempt.

On a rushing play, the last player to handle a pitchout, backward pass, handoff, or reverse is charged with a rushing attempt, and is responsible for any yardage gained or lost from scrimmage, *provided* that he receives the ball at or behind the line of scrimmage. If a player receives a pitchout, backward pass, handoff, or reverse beyond the line of scrimmage, credit the player responsible with yardage gained to the point of the second player's possession.

Example I: First-and-10 on opponent's 20 yard line. Player runs to the 18, then pitches back to a teammate on the 22, where the teammate is downed. *Scoring:* Second player gets one rush, minus 2 yards.

Example II: First-and-10 on opponent's 20 yard line. Player runs to the 15, then pitches back to a teammate on the 18; teammate runs to the 8. *Scoring:* First player gets one rush, 2 yards; second player gets 10 yards rushing (*no* rushing attempt); credit a first down rushing.

Example III: First-and-10 on opponent's 20 yard line. Player runs to the 15, pitches back to a teammate on the 18, where he is downed. *Scoring:* First player gets one rush, 2 yards.

Example IV: First-and-10 on opponent's 20 yard line. Quarterback hands ball to runner, who is about to be tackled at 25 when he laterals or hands ball to a teammate on the 26, where the teammate is downed. *Scoring:* Last player handling ball gets one rush, minus 6 yards.

Example V: First-and-10 on opponent's 20 yard line. Player runs to the 3, then laterals to a teammate on the 5, where the teammate is downed. *Scoring:* First player gets one rush, 15 yards; credit a first down rushing.

Example VI: First-and 10 on opponent's 20 yard line. Player runs to the 3, then laterals to a teammate on the 5; teammate runs for a touchdown. *Scoring:* First player gets one rush, 15 yards; second player gets 5 yards and touchdown rushing (*no* rushing attempt); credit a first down rushing.

For fumbles on rushing plays see Fumbles section.

Passing

The passing category includes both the forward pass and the forward pass reception. (In this section, the word "pass" shall indicate "forward pass" unless otherwise noted.)

Passing yardage is computed from the line of scrimmage and includes the length of the pass plus the running yardage gained or lost by the receiver after the completion.

If a forward pass is completed behind the line of scrimmage and the receiver is downed, credit the passer with an attempt and completion and the minus yardage.

A forward pass ruled complete due to interference is not considered an attempt or a completion. It is a penalty play (yardage and first down).

Charge a player with a pass attempt when he:

1. Throws a completed pass;

2. Throws an intercepted pass;

3. Throws an incomplete pass, including when:

A. The pass strikes the ground or goes out of bounds;

B. The pass accidentally touches an ineligible offensive player on or behind the line of scrimmage;

C. The pass is the second forward pass from behind the line of scrimmage and it is caught by an offensive player; when this occurs, no completion or yardage is credited for the original (completed) pass;

D. The pass is caught by an ineligible offensive player on or behind the line of scrimmage;

E. The pass is thrown from behind the line of scrimmage, after having been carried or passed backward from a spot behind the line;

F. The pass is touched by an eligible offensive player returning from out of bounds.

Do *not* charge a pass attempt when the acceptance of a penalty nullifies the play in its entirety (e.g., roughing the passer on an incomplete pass), if the penalty is for a continuing action foul.

At times, a penalty will be enforced *in addition* to the loss of down, which is the result of an incompletion. In these cases, charge a pass attempt as well as any penalty yardage that is enforced. *Examples:* Intentional grounding, ineligible receiver touches a pass beyond the line of scrimmage, etc.

When a player throws a forward pass from beyond the line of scrimmage, and the penalty is accepted, do *not* charge the passer with a pass attempt. Credit him with yards gained (in the category initiating the action) to the point of the pass; penalty yardage will commence from that spot.

Example I: Second-and-10 at own 30 yard line. Quarterback, back to pass, runs beyond line and throws forward pass at 34. *Scoring:* One rush for 4 yards; one penalty for 5 yards.

Example II: Second-and-10 at own 30 yard line. Pass is completed to 50, where the receiver, attempting to lateral, throws a forward pass. *Scoring:* One completion for 20 yards; one penalty for 5 yards. Credit a first down passing.

When the defense declines a penalty for a forward pass thrown in advance of the line of scrimmage, the scoring shall reflect the actual ball movement during the play.

Example III: Second-and-10 at own 30 yard line. Pass is completed to 50, where the receiver, attempting to lateral, throws a forward pass that is intercepted at opponent's 49 and returned for a touchdown. *Scoring:* One completion (reception) for 20 yards. Player receiving the original pass also gets one pass (intercepted). (Defense declines the penalty in order to score the touchdown.)

The same rules apply when a forward pass not from scrimmage is thrown (e.g., on a punt return): No pass attempt is charged, unless the ball is intercepted. Penalty yardage is assessed from the spot of the foul.

In passing statistics there is a category called "sacks and yards lost attempting to pass." It shall be determined by the following rules:

1. When the quarterback or a teammate, makes an apparent attempt to pass at any time before he or a teammate is tackled, steps out of bounds, or fumbles behind or at the line of scrimmage, the play is scored as a sack and any yards lost attempting to pass. (Should he advance the ball across the line of scrimmage, it is a rushing play.)

2. When the quarterback is tackled or, after *gaining possession* of the snap, he fumbles or falls down, while retreating to his normal passing position, it shall be scored as a sack and yards lost attempting to pass, even though he may not have assumed a passing position.

Example I: Second-and-1 at own 20 yard line. Quarterback, back to pass, fumbles the ball while standing in the pocket, without any defensive contact. He recovers at the 13. *Scoring:* One sack and 7 yards lost, a fumble, and an own recovery.

Example II: Second-and-1 at own 20 yard line. Quarterback takes snap, then while retreating to pass, fumbles. Ball rolls to 10, and then is batted back to the 5, where a player recovers and is downed. *Scoring:* Charge one sack and 10 yards lost (to point of first batting). The other 5 yards are the result of a loose ball. (See Fumbles, 6. E. (b).)

Example III: Third-and-25 at own 40 yard line. Quarterback fumbles snap on what appears to be a definite passing down. He recovers at the 35. *Scoring:* An aborted play; quarterback gets one rush for no yards, a fumble, an own recovery, and minus 5 (fumble yardage) yards.

3. When a quarterback rolls out, or a player other than the quarterback handles the ball on an option play, or takes the snap in a "shotgun" formation, and makes an *apparent attempt* to pass before being tackled or stepping out of bounds behind or at the line of scrimmage, it shall be scored as a sack and any yards lost attempting to pass. If the player makes no *apparent attempt* to pass, the play shall be considered a rushing play.

4. The individual passer shall not be charged with an attempted forward pass, or yardage lost, when the play is scored as a sack. However, the yardage lost on such plays MUST be deducted from his team's gross passing yardage to reflect *net yards gained passing.*

For fumbles on passing plays see Fumbles section.

Sacks

Credit a sack to the appropriate defensive player whenever a sack is scored against the offensive team, subject to the following principles:

1. When the player making an apparent attempt to pass is tackled or downed at or behind the line of scrimmage, credit a sack to the defensive player who tackled or downed the potential passer.

EXCEPTION: If the potential passer fumbles *before contact by the defense,* no sack is credited to any *individual* defensive player.

2. When the player making an apparent attempt to pass steps out of bounds at or behind the line of scrimmage in order to avoid imminent contact with a defensive player, credit that defensive player with a sack. If the potential passer steps out of bounds *without* the pressure of such imminent contact, no sack is credited to any *individual* defensive player.

When one defensive player is *primarily* responsible for a sack, as defined by the foregoing principles, he shall receive credit for a sack. When two or more defensive players are adjudged by the official scorer to be equally responsible for a sack, credit for the sack shall be divided equally between or among the responsible defensive players.

Example I: Second-and-10 at midfield. In retreating to pass, quarterback fumbles the ball without having been touched by a defender, and recovers at his own 40, where he is downed by the defensive tackle. *Scoring:* A sack for 10 yards, but no individual defensive player is credited with the sack.

Example II: Second-and-10 at midfield. Quarterback, trying to pass, eludes defensive tackle's rush and, at his own 40, runs upfield toward sidelines. At his own 47, pursued by the defensive tackle, he goes out of bounds before he can be hit by a linebacker, who is charging toward the quarterback from his downfield position, and who was about to stop the

quarterback's advance, should he have remained in-bounds. *Scoring:* A sack for three yards; credit the sack to the linebacker, for it was because of imminent contact with *him* that the quarterback elected to run out of bounds. (The pursuing defensive tackle has already been eluded by the quarterback.)

Lateral Passes

Lateral passes subsequent to the originating play are considered as part of the play from which they originate. The receiver of a lateral is given credit for the yardage he gains from the point of the lateral *BUT* he is not given an attempt, return, or reception on the play. (See Exceptions listed under Kickoff Returns.) For example, a forward pass is completed and the receiver advances 40 yards, then laterals to a teammate who advances the ball an additional 20 yards. This is considered a 60-yard pass play. The first receiver is credited with the reception and 40 yards gained; his teammate, although not credited with a reception, would appear in the pass receiving section with 20 yards gained, annotated with an asterisk (*Lateral). If a touchdown is scored as a result of such a play, the player who scores shall be credited with a touchdown via receiving. In any case the original play determines in what category the touchdown was made.

When the receiver of a backward pass, or lateral, is beyond the line of scrimmage, it is *his* position that determines the yardage gained by each of the individuals involved. The player who throws the pass is credited with yards gained only to the point at which the pass is caught or (if muffed) is recovered, provided this point is behind the spot of the pass.

Example: Second-and-20 on own 20 yard line. Player catches a forward pass at his own 40, then throws a backward pass to teammate on the 38. The teammate then:

(a) is downed at the 38. *Scoring:* First player gets one reception for 18 yards.

(b) runs to the 45. *Scoring:* First player gets one reception for 18 yards; second player gets 7 yards in pass receiving category, but is not credited with a reception. Credit a first down passing.

(c) muffs the ball and an opponent recovers on the 33. *Scoring:* First player gets one reception for 13 yards and a fumble. Opponent gets a fumble recovery.

Interceptions

Interception yardage is computed from the point where the impetus of the act of interception ends and the intercepting player begins forward or backward movement on his own. This *includes* the end zone area of the intercepting player, except that a player making an interception in his own end zone shall not be credited with any return yardage if the ball becomes dead behind his own goal line.

Example I: Player intercepts the ball five yards deep in his end zone, and returns to his 7 yard line. *Scoring:* 12-yard return.

Example II: Player intercepts the ball five yards deep in his end zone, starts to run, but stops one yard short of the goal line, where he downs the ball or is tackled for a touchback. *Scoring:* One interception for no yards; the ball never left the end zone.

Punts

All punts from behind or on the line of scrimmage shall be measured from the line of scrimmage to the point at which the impetus of the punt ends, or the ball goes out of bounds, or is downed. If a punt goes into the end zone, measure its length to the goal line, unless the ball is fielded and returned out of the end zone by the receiving team (in such a case, measure the punt to the spot of possession in the end zone by the receiver). All punts from beyond the line of scrimmage, and all punts following an exchange of possession ("return kicks") shall be measured from the spot of the kick to the point at which the impetus of the punt ends, or the ball goes out of bounds or is downed.

EXCEPTION: If a punt is touched (but not possessed) by the receiving team and is recovered by the kicking team in the end zone, measure the punt to the point at which the ball is spotted on the field of play (either the spot of the touch or the 1 yard line).

The impetus of a punt continues until the receiving team is in possession or the kickers legally recover, unless:

(a) the ball is batted or kicked by the kicking team (measure the punt to the spot of the bat or kick); or

(b) the receiving team has touched the ball, causing the ball to change direction and bounce toward the kickers' goal line; measure the punt to the spot of the touch.

Example I: A punt from the 50 touches a receiver on the 10, and is recovered by the kickers in the end zone. *Scoring:* A 40-yard punt; kickers' ball, first-and-10 at the 10.

Example II: A punt from the 50 is rolling slowly on the 10 when a kicking team player running downfield accidentally knocks the ball into the end zone for a touchback. *Scoring:* A 40-yard punt.

Example III: A punt from the 50 is muffed by a receiver on the 10. The ball bounces upfield where it is recovered by anyone at the 18. *Scoring:* A 40-yard punt (to the spot of the first touch by receivers).

Example IV: A punt from the 50 goes into the end zone (three yards deep), where a receiving team player fields it and returns to the 7. *Scoring:* A 53-yard punt and a 10-yard return.

A blocked punt is scored *only* when the punted ball fails to go beyond the line of scrimmage. A "partially blocked" punt that travels beyond the line of scrimmage is *not* a blocked punt. A blocked punt is charged as a punt to the team, but not to the individual punter.

Do not charge a player with a punt unless he actually punts the ball. Note that if the center snap is *satisfactory* and the punter does not fumble, but is tackled before he punts or while attempting to run, the play is a rushing play. If the play develops as action off a fake punt play, score the play as a rush, pass, or tackled attempting to pass consistent with the basic scoring rules on scrimmage plays.

Credit a player with an inside-20 when his punt is not returned to the receivers' 20 yard line or beyond. A touchback is *not* an inside-20. When there is a penalty during the return, the point at which the return ends statistically is the determining spot for crediting an inside-20.

If, following a punt or punt return, the ball is positioned between the receivers' 19 and 20 yard lines, *no inside 20 is scored* if the ball is statistically determined to be on the 20 yard line.

Example V: A punt from the 50 is caught on the 15 and returned to the 30. Receivers commit a clipping foul at the 30, and the ball is moved back to the 15. *Scoring:* A 35-yard punt, 15-yard return, and a 15-yard penalty. Do not credit an inside-20, since the return took the ball to the 30. First-and-10 at the 15.

Example VI: Fourth-and-seven at midfield. Punter receives snap, runs toward the line of scrimmage and beyond to opponents' 45, where he punts to opponents' 10, out of bounds. *Scoring:* One rush for five yards, one punt for 35 yards, and an inside-20.

To compile the net punting average of each punter, divide the total number of punts (including blocked punts not charged against him individually) into his gross punting yardage minus touchbacks (delete 20 yards per touchback) and minus return yardage. *Example:* Player punts 59 times for 2,536 gross yards, a 43.0 average. Two additional punts are blocked, for which he is not charged. Of his 59 punts, 11 result in touchbacks and 29 are returned for 179 yards. To compute his Punting Game effectiveness, divide 61 punts into net yardage of 2,137 (2,536 minus 220 for touchbacks minus 179 return yardage). His team's Punting Game effectiveness when he is punting is 35.3.

Blocked Kicks

When a punt or a field goal attempt is blocked and recovered by the offensive team behind the line of scrimmage any running advance is treated as miscellaneous yardage. In the rare case when the offensive player attempts a forward pass after a blocked kick, include it as a passing attempt and any completion as passing yardage. However, if the player is tackled behind the line of scrimmage *do not* treat this as yards lost attempting to pass. In the latter case merely note the player recovered a blocked kick. NOTE: Regardless of any subsequent action the original blocked punt or field goal must be recorded.

Punt Returns

A punt return is credited to the first player on the receiving team who gains possession of the punt.

EXCEPTION: If, prior to the receiving team gaining possession of the punt, the ball is muffed or touched by a receiver *who is trying to gain possession,* then the punt return is credited to the player who first muffed or touched the ball. (Note that this exception does *not apply* if the ball touches a player who was *not* trying to gain possession.)

If the punt is legally recovered by the kicking team before any receiving team player gains possession, then charge a punt return to the first player on the receiving team who touched (or was touched by) the ball, whether or not he was trying to gain possession.

Example I: Punt from the 50. Receiver tries to catch the ball on the 20, but it bounces off (or through) his hands and is recovered by a teammate on the 12. *Scoring:* A 38-yard punt (the impetus of the punt continued to

the 12 yard line). The punt return is credited to the player who muffed the ball at the 20; he also gets a fumble, and the recovering player is credited with an own recovery.

Example II: Punt from the 50. Ball is touched by a receiver on the 20 (whether or not he was trying to gain possession), and kicking team player recovers at the 15. *Scoring:* A 35-yard punt (the impetus of the punt continued to the 15 yard line). The punt return is credited to the player who touched (or was touched by) the ball at the 20; he also gets a fumble, and the appropriate player on the kicking team is credited with an opponents' recovery.

Example III: Punt from the 50. Ball bounces at the 25, and after taking an unusual bounce, strikes the leg of a receiver who is trying to avoid the ball. The ball rolls to the 20, where it is recovered by another receiving-team player. *Scoring:* A 30-yard punt (the impetus of the punt continued to the 20 yard line). The punt return is credited to the player who recovered (and first possessed) the ball, since the prior touching was *not* by a player who was trying to gain possession.

Do not charge a punt return to a player who:
(1) signals for, and makes a fair catch; or
(2) signals for a fair catch, but is fouled before having the opportunity to make the catch.

In both of the above circumstances, credit a fair catch. Do *not* credit a fair catch if the player muffs the ball following a fair catch signal, regardless of who recovers the ball. Credit the player with a punt return and fumble; the appropriate player is credited with a fumble recovery.

The distance of a punt return shall be measured from the point at which the impetus of the punt ends and the receiver is able to initiate forward progress.

Example IV: A player takes a punt on his own 30, runs back 10 yards to his own 20, then forward to the 35. The punt return is measured as five yards.

Example V: A player takes a punt on his own 30 but retreats 3 yards to the 27 because the impetus of the punt requires him to move backward. He then advances back to the 30. The punt is recorded to the 27, and the punt return is measured as 3 yards.

Example VI: A player catches the ball on his own 30, runs back 20 yards and is tackled on his own 10. The punt return is recorded as minus 20 yards, and the punt is recorded ONLY to the 30 yard line.

Return by the defensive player of a blocked punt is not considered a punt return. The player and the yardage gained shall be noted on the back of the official score blank under "remarks."

On the score blank the total punts for the team should equal the total punt returns, plus the fair catches, plus the punts out of bounds, plus the punt touchbacks, plus punts downed, and punts blocked. Official scorers should always reconcile these figures on the score blank.

For fumbles on punt returns see Fumbles section.

Kickoff Returns

A kickoff return is credited to the first player on the receiving team who gains possession of the kickoff except:
(1) if the player who fields the kickoff makes no effort to advance an apparent onside kick, and if the first touching of the ball is within 15 yards of the spot of the kick, *no kickoff return is credited.*
(2) when the receiver of the kickoff *makes no advance of* the ball, but instead laterals or hands off to a teammate. If there is no fumble during the exchange (meaning if the ball does *not* touch the ground), the second player is given credit for any return and the yardage is computed from the point at which he gains possession.
(3) when the receiver of the kickoff gains less than 10 yards before he laterals or hands off to a teammate and that teammate gains more yardage than the original handler of the kickoff. In such a case, the second player receives credit for a kickoff return and yardage; the first player gets no return but does get return yards (not more than nine).
(4) if, prior to the receiving team gaining possession of the kickoff, the ball is muffed or touched by a receiver *who is trying to gain possession,* and the first player who gains possession makes no effort to advance the ball, then the kickoff return and a fumble are credited to the player who first muffed or touched the ball.
(5) if the receiving team downs the ball in the end zone for a touchback, even if there is touching by players on either team on the field of play.
Note that a kickoff return is credited on any kickoff that is first touched by the receivers more than 15 yards from the spot of the kick, except if the receiver downs the ball in the end zone for a touchback. When no player on the receiving team gains possession of a kickoff, do not credit a kickoff

return unless the ball goes out of bounds or is recovered by the kicking team *after* touching (or having been touched by) a receiving team player, *and* the first such touching is more than 15 yards from the spot of the kick. In such a case, credit a kickoff return and a fumble to the player on the receiving team who touched (or was touched by) the ball.

The distance of a kickoff shall be measured from the point at which the impetus of the kickoff ends and the receiver *gains possession and is able to initiate forward progress.* This includes the *end zone area.* For example, a player takes the kickoff on the 10, runs back to the 5 and then advances to the 20. He is credited with a 10-yard return. Another example: A player takes the kickoff on the 10, but retreats to the 7 because the impetus of the kickoff requires him to do so. He then advances to the 20. He is credited with a 13-yard return. A third example: A player takes the ball on the 10, but runs back to the 5, where he is tackled. He is credited with one kickoff return for MINUS 5 yards.

Example I: A player receives a kickoff on the 20, makes no attempt to advance but laterals to a teammate on the 15, who then advances to the 17. The first player is not credited with a kickoff return, but his teammate is credited with one return for 2 yards.

Example II: A player receives the kickoff on the 20, makes no attempt to advance, but laterals to a teammate on the 15. The teammate then retreats and is tackled on the 12. The first player is not credited with a return, but the teammate is credited with one return for MINUS 3 yards.

Example III: A player receives the kickoff on the 20 and then runs laterally across the field and hands off to a teammate on the 18. The teammate returns to the 25 and is credited with one return for 7 yards.

Example IV: A player receives the kickoff on the 20, *then advances to the 22* before lateralling to a teammate on the 15. The teammate advances to the 30. The first player is credited with no return for 2 yards and the second player one return for 8 yards.

Example V: A player receives the kickoff on the 20, *then advances to the 22* before lateralling to a teammate on the 15. The teammate is tackled on the 17. The first player is credited with one kickoff return for MINUS 3 yards and second player is not credited with a return or yardage.

Example VI: A player receives a kickoff on the 20, *then advances to the 22* before handing off to a teammate. The teammate then runs to the 30. In this instance, the first player is credited with no return for 2 yards and the second player one return for 8 yards.

Example VII: A player receives a kickoff on the 20, *then advances to the 22* before handing off to a teammate, who then retreats and is tackled on the 19. The first player is credited with one kickoff return for no yards and the second player with no kickoff return with MINUS 1 yard.

If the lateral is a bad pass or the handoff is fumbled, then the first player is credited with one return for no yardage and the remainder of the play is treated as a fumble. For this and other fumbles on kickoff returns, see Fumbles section.

The general provisions for scoring a fair catch, which appear in the Punt Returns section, also apply to kickoff returns.

Free Kicks

Free kicks shall be scored as kickoffs in all instances, regardless of whether they are punted or made from placement. The receiver gets credit for a kickoff return in all cases.

EXCEPTION: When a free kick is called for (following a fair catch of a punt) to attempt a field goal, the kicker shall be charged with a field goal attempt. Any yardage on a runback by an opposing player shall be credited as miscellaneous yardage, as with any other field goal attempt.

Fumbles

Definitions of Fumbles and Recoveries

1. A fumble is an act that results in an individual's loss of possession of the ball or his failure to handle a ball which has been properly centered or handed to him. *EXCEPTIONS:* No fumble shall be charged (a) on an attempted point-after-touchdown, or (b) on a momentary bobble of the ball at the point of reception if in the scorer's judgement the bobble had no effect on the continuing action, provided that the ball has not touched the ground or another player. A fumble is also charged in certain instances in which a player *muffs* a ball punted to him. See Punt Returns section.

2. If a fumbled ball (a) goes out of bounds and remains in possession of the team fumbling, or (b) goes over the end line for a touchback or safety, score the play as a fumble and also note it as "fumble out of bounds" under the fumbles section.

3. "Own recovery" designates a fumble recovered by any member of the team committing the fumble. "Opponent's recovery" designates a fumble recovered by any member of the team *not* committing the fumble. Note that there must be a "recovery" for every fumble charged except for fumbles that go out of bounds. "Fumbles lost" refers to all fumbles which result in opponent's recoveries, or which are fumbled through the end zone for touchbacks. (Note: A fumble through a team's *own* end zone for a safety is *not* a fumble lost.)

4. When a fumbled ball is touched by several players, only the player who lost possession originally shall be charged with a fumble and only the player who ultimately gains possession shall be credited with a recovery. There can be more than one fumble and more than one recovery on a single play only if possession is clearly established following the original fumble.

5. When a bobbled ball is recovered out of the air by a teammate or an opponent, it shall be scored as a fumble and a recovery. *EXCEPTION:* If a receiver juggles a pass without establishing possession and a teammate or an opponent gains possession in the air, it shall be scored as a completed pass or interception as the case may be.

Principles of Scoring Yardage on Fumble Plays

6. Any yardage gained or lost on a rushing play in which a fumble occurs—except on Aborted Plays described in Number 7—shall be recorded as follows:

A. When a player recovers his own fumble, credit him with net yardage gained or lost on the play in the category initiating the action. (Charge him with a fumble and credit him with "own recovery.")

B. When a teammate recovers:
(a) Behind (or on) the line of scrimmage, charge the player who fumbled with all yardage lost, if any, to the point of recovery or the new line of scrimmage, whichever is less.
(b) Beyond the line of scrimmage, credit the player who fumbled with yardage gained to the point of his advance or the point of recovery, whichever is less.

C. When an opponent recovers:
(a) Behind (or on) the line of scrimmage, charge the player who fumbled with yardage lost, if any, to the point of recovery.
(b) Beyond the line of scrimmage, credit the player who fumbled with yardage gained to the point of his advance or the point of recovery, whichever is less.

D. A teammate or opponent who recovers shall be credited with fumble yardage for any gain or loss from the point of recovery. If a teammate recovers *behind* the line of scrimmage and advances the ball, fumble yardage commences from the line of scrimmage. The theory is that the player who fumbled shall benefit from any advance a teammate may make behind the line of scrimmage. (Note that no minus yardage can be charged unless a teammate or opponent causes the minus yardage by running or throwing the ball after gaining possession of it.)

E. (a) When a fumbled ball rolls free and is recovered beyond the point of the fumble (by either a teammate or an opponent), any yardage between the spot of the fumble and the spot of recovery is loose ball yardage.
(b) When a fumbled ball is touched, legally batted, or kicked by any player (including the player who fumbled), and the spot of this action is behind the spot of the fumble, charge the player who fumbles with yardage lost to the spot of the first such touch, bat, or kick; the rest of the yardage is loose ball yardage. If an opponent eventually gains possession, his fumble yardage shall be credited from the spot at which he gains possession. If a teammate gains possession, his fumble yardage shall commence at the spot of the fumble or the spot of possession (whichever is nearer the opponents' goal line).

Scoring of Fumble Plays

ABORTED PLAYS

7. An *aborted play* is a play from scrimmage which falls into one of the following categories:

A. the ball is *clearly* centered improperly, meaning that the ball does not reach the intended receiver of the snap within the frame of his body or arm-span;
B. the intended ball-handler fumbles the snap from center;
C. a player hands off or laterals improperly, behind the line of scrimmage;
D. a backward pass (including a handoff) behind the line of scrimmage is mishandled, resulting in the ball touching the ground or being caught in flight by another player.

In each of these cases, charge a rush for no yards. In A. and B., the rush is charged to the player who receives, or intended to receive, the snap from center. In C. and D., the rush is charged to the player who hands off or laterals improperly, or who throws a backward pass which is muffed.

EXCEPTION: If the player charged with the rush recovers the loose ball and advances beyond the line of scrimmage, credit any advance as rushing yardage.

When the ball is clearly centered improperly, charge the center with a fumble and any yards lost as fumble yardage. On any other aborted play, the player charged with the rush is also charged with a fumble and any yards lost as fumble yardage.

If a teammate recovers behind the line of scrimmage and advances beyond the line, credit that player with fumble yardage equal to the distance between the old and new lines of scrimmage.

If an opponent recovers behind the line of scrimmage, charge fumble yardage to the offensive player to the point of recovery *only*.

If a player from either team (other than the player charged with the rush) makes the initial recovery beyond the line of scrimmage, the ball movement to the point of recovery shall be treated as loose ball yardage. If the player charged with the rush makes such a recovery, credit him with rushing yardage equal to the gain on the play.

Example I: Second-and-10 at own 20 yard line. Quarterback fumbles the snap, and the teammate recovers at the 15, where he is downed. *Scoring:* Quarterback gets one rush for no yards, a fumble, and minus 5 yards as fumble yardage. Teammate gets an own recovery.

Example II: Same play as above, except that the teammate advances to:

A. the 18 yard line. *Scoring:* Quarterback gets one rush for no yards, a fumble and minus 2 yards as fumble yardage. Teammate gets an own recovery.

B. the 30 yard line. *Scoring:* Quarterback gets one rush for no yards and a fumble. Teammate gets an own recovery, 10 yards (fumble yardage) and team is credited with a first down *rushing*.

Example III: Second-and-10 at own 20 yard line. Quarterback fumbles the snap, then recovers and advances to the 24. *Scoring:* Quarterback gets one rush for 4 yards, a fumble, and an own recovery.

Example IV: Fourth-and-10 at own 20 yard line. Punter intends to receive snap, but it is clearly centered improperly. Then:

A. Punter recovers at the 5 where he is downed. *Scoring:* Center gets a fumble and minus 15 as fumble yardage. Punter gets one rush for no yards and an own recovery.

B. Punter recovers at the 5 and runs to the 22. *Scoring:* Center gets a fumble. Punter gets an own recovery, and a rush for 2 yards.

C. Blocking back recovers at the 5, where he is downed or the ball is declared dead. *Scoring:* Center gets a fumble and minus 15 as fumble yardage. Punter gets a rush for no yards. Blocking back gets an own recovery.

D. Blocking back recovers at the 5, runs to the 35. *Scoring:* Center gets a fumble. Punter gets one rush for no yards. Blocking back gets an own recovery, 15 yards (fumble yardage), and team is credited with a first down *rushing*.

Example V: Second-and-10 at own 20 yard line. Quarterback takes snap, turns to hand off to running back, and the exchange is mis-handled. The ball bounces free and is recovered by anyone at the 12. *Scoring:* Quarterback gets one rush for no yards, a fumble, and minus 8 as fumble yardage. Credit the recovery to the appropriate player.

Example VI: Second-and-10 at own 20 yard line. Quarterback receives snap and tosses a backward pass (pitchout or lateral). The pass is satisfactory, but the ball bounces off the running back's hands and is recovered by an opponent at the 11. *Scoring:* Quarterback gets one rush for no yards and a fumble for minus 9 (fumble yardage). Credit the player recovering the ball with an opponents' recovery.

Example VII: Second-and-10 at own 20 yard line. Same play as Example VI, except that when the running back muffs the ball, it bounces forward, and an offensive tackle recovers on the 25 and runs to the 35. *Scoring:* Quarterback gets one rush for no yards and a fumble. Tackle gets an own recovery and 10 yards (fumble yardage). Credit a first down *rushing*.

Example VIII: Second-and-10 at own 20 yard line. Quarterback hands off to running back; running back's handoff to wide receiver is mis-handled. The ball is recovered at the 12. *Scoring:* Running back gets one rush for no yards and a fumble for minus 8 (fumble yardage).

RUSHING PLAYS

8. When a player recovers his own fumble:

Example I: With ball on opponent's 30, running back rushes to 20, where he is tackled and fumbles. He recovers on the 25 and advances to the 21. *Scoring:* Running back is credited with one rush for 9 yards and is charged with a fumble.

Example II: With ball on opponent's 30, running back rushes to the 29, where he is tackled and fumbles. He falls on his own fumble at the 31. *Scoring:* Running back is credited with one rush for minus 1 yard and is charged with a fumble.

9. When a teammate recovers:

Example I: With ball on opponent's 30, running back rushes to the 20, where he is tackled and fumbles. A teammate recovers the ball on the 25. *Scoring:* Running back is credited with one rush for 5 yards and is charged with a fumble.

Example II: With ball on opponent's 30, running back rushes to the 20, where he is tackled and fumbles. A teammate recovers the ball on the 15. *Scoring:* Running back is credited with one rush for 10 yards and is charged with a fumble. Teammate is credited with no yardage.

Example III: With ball on opponent's 30, running back rushes to the 28, where he is tackled and fumbles. A teammate recovers at the 31 — a net loss of 1 yard. *Scoring:* Running back is credited with one rush for minus 1 yard and is charged with a fumble.

Example IV: With ball on opponent's 30, running back is tackled 2 yards behind the line of scrimmage and fumbles. A teammate recovers the ball at the 34 — a net loss of 4 yards. *Scoring:* Running back is charged with one rushing attempt for minus 4 yards and a fumble.

Example V: With ball on opponent's 30, running back is tackled 4 yards behind line of scrimmage and fumbles. A teammate recovers the ball at the 34 and advances it to the 29 — a net gain of 1 yard on the play. *Scoring:* Running back is charged with one rushing attempt for no gain and with a fumble. Teammate is credited with plus 1 yard of fumble yardage.

Example VI: With ball on opponent's 30, running back is tackled four yards behind the line of scrimmage and fumbles. A teammate recovers the ball at the 34 and advances it to the 32 — a net loss of 2 yards on the play. *Scoring:* Running back is charged with one rushing attempt for minus 2 yards and also with a fumble.

Example VII: In the same circumstances as Example VI, the teammate recovers the ball at the 36 and, while retreating in an attempt to elude tacklers, is tackled at the 40 — a net loss of 10 yards on the play. *Scoring:* Running back is charged with one rushing attempt for minus 6 yards and a fumble. Teammate is charged with minus 4 fumble yards because he caused the additional loss.

10. When an opponent recovers:

Example I: With ball on opponent's 30, running back rushes to 28, where he is tackled and fumbles. Opponent recovers the ball on the 25. *Scoring:* Running back is credited with one rush for 2 yards and is charged with a fumble.

Example II: With ball on opponent's 30, running back rushes to 28, where he is tackled and fumbles. Opponent recovers the ball on the 32. *Scoring:* Running back is charged with one rush for minus 2 yards and also with a fumble.

Example III: With ball on opponent's 30, running back rushes to 28, where he is tackled and fumbles. Opponent recovers the ball at the 25 and returns it the 32 before being tackled. *Scoring:* Running back is credited with one rush for 2 yards and is charged with a fumble; opponent is credited with 7 yards of fumble yardage.

Example IV: With ball on opponent's 30, running back is tackled at the 32 and fumbles. Opponent recovers the ball at the 28. *Scoring:* Running back is charged with one rush for no yards and also with a fumble.

Example V: With ball on opponent's 30, running back rushes to the 25, where he is tackled and fumbles. An opponent picks up the ball at the 28 and runs it back and fumbles at the 30, where the ball is recovered. *Scoring:* Regardless of which team recovers the second fumble, credit the original ball carrier with one rush for 5 yards and also with a fumble; credit the opponent who recovered the first fumble with plus 5 yards of fumble yardage and also charge him with a fumble.

PASSING PLAYS

11. When a passer fumbles while attempting to pass, charge him with "tackled" and a fumble and with all yardage lost to the point of recovery as yards lost attempting to pass.

EXCEPTION 1: If a teammate or an opponent legally bats, or kicks, or deflects a ball the yardage lost is to the point of the first touch. (See Rule 6 par. b.)

EXCEPTION 2: If the point of recovery is in advance of the original line of scrimmage or if the player recovering the fumble advances the ball beyond the line of scrimmage, charge the passer with "tackled" for no yards and also with a fumble, and credit the player who advanced the ball with fumble yardage equal to the distance between the old and the new lines of scrimmage.

Example I: With ball on opponent's 30, quarterback goes back to pass and is hit by defense at 38, fumbles and ball bounces backward to 41, where he, a teammate, or an opponent recovers. *Scoring:* Charge quarterback with "tackled," 11 yards lost attempting to pass, and a fumble.

Example II: In the same circumstances as Example I, the ball is recovered at the 35, 3 yards in advance of the spot where the fumble occurred. *Scoring:* Charge quarterback with "tackled," 5 yards lost attempting to pass, and a fumble.

Example III: In the same circumstances as Example I, the quarterback or a teammate recovers and advances the ball to the opponent's 28. *Scoring:* Charge quarterback with "tackled," no yards lost attempting to pass, and a fumble; credit player recovering with 2 yards of fumble yardage.

Example IV: In the same circumstances as Example I, the ball bounces backward to the 41 where it is deflected by an opponent and eventually recovered by the quarterback himself on the 50 yard line. *Scoring:* Charge the quarterback with a "sack" and 11 yards lost attempting to pass plus a fumble and an own recovery. The additional 9 yards lost are the result of a loose ball.

Example V: In the same circumstances as Example I, the ball bounces backward to 41, where an opponent picks it up and runs to midfield before being tackled. *Scoring:* Charge quarterback with "tackled," 11 yards lost attempting to pass and a fumble; credit opponent recovering with 9 yards of fumble yardage.

RECEPTIONS, INTERCEPTIONS, AND RETURNS

12. When a player fumbles after catching or intercepting a pass or on a punt return or kickoff return, he shall be credited with a gain or loss to (a) his original point of advance or (b) the point of fumble recovery, whichever is less. *EXCEPTION:* If the player recovers his own fumble, all yardage gained or lost shall be credited in the category initiating the action.

Example I: A receiver, after catching a pass, is 40 yards in advance of the line of scrimmage when he fumbles. He, a teammate, or an opponent recovers the ball 37 yards in advance of the line of scrimmage. *Scoring:* Play is listed as a 37-yard pass.

Example II: In the same situation as Example I, the receiver recovers his own fumble and advances to a point 45 yards in advance of the line of scrimmage before being tackled. *Scoring:* Play is listed as a 45-yard pass.

Example III: In the same situation as Example I, a teammate recovers and advances the ball to a point 45 yards in advance of the line of scrimmage before being tackled. *Scoring:* Play is listed as a 40-yard pass; teammate who recovered is credited with 5 yards of fumble yardage.

Example IV: Kick return man receives a punt on his own 10, and returns to his 35, where he fumbles. The ball bounces forward to the 40, where he recovers his own fumble. *Scoring:* Kick returner is credited with a punt return of 30 yards.

Example V: In the same situation as Example IV, the ball is recovered at the 40 by a teammate or an opponent. *Scoring:* Kick returner is credited with a punt return of 25 yards; the remaining yardage is treated as being the result of a loose ball.

Example VI: In the same situation as Example IV, the ball bounces back to the 30, where the kick returner, a teammate, or an opponent recovers. *Scoring:* Kick returner is credited with a punt return of 20 yards.

Example VII: Kick return man receives a punt on his own 20, retreats trying to elude a tackler and is tackled at the 17, where he fumbles. The ball bounces back to the 15, where it is recovered. *Scoring:* Kick returner is charged with a punt return of minus 5 yards, regardless of who recovers.

Touchdowns

There are three types of touchdowns—rushing, passing, and returns. The only touchdowns considered touchdowns passing are those that result from a completed forward pass from a teammate. On the score blank all touchdowns should be noted in their respective categories according to the manner made (rushing, passing, punt returns, fumbles recovered, etc.).

Extra Points

Players attempting conversions shall not be charged with an extra point missed when a bad pass from center, or a muff by the ball holder, pre-

vents an opportunity to kick. However, attempts at conversions that are blocked shall be scored as extra points missed. (*EXCEPTION:* If, in the judgment of the official scorer, an error in the center snap or placement of the ball by the holder is the direct cause of a blocked attempt, the kicker shall not be charged with an attempt. The same exception may be applied to field goal attempts.) No fumble should be charged on an attempted conversion.

Note: No rushing attempt, or pass attempt, or completion, shall be credited on an extra point attempt.

Field Goals

Field goals shall be measured from the spot of the kick. Spot of an attempt is dictated by the same principle as used in determining the line of scrimmage.

Example: If any point of the football when kicked rests on or above any yard stripe, credit distance from that yard stripe. If all of the ball rests between yards stripes, credit distance from the yard line nearest the intended goal.

Kicker is not charged with a field goal attempt if he does not actually kick. If player holding the ball juggles it long enough to prevent kicker from making an attempt, charge ball holder with a rush and yardage lost as fumble yardage, plus a fumble and his own fumble recovered. (Also see the exception paragraph in Extra Points section regarding blocked field goals.)

SPECIAL NOTE—If the center snap is *satisfactory* and the holder does *not fumble* the snap or mis-handle the placement of the ball, but is instead smothered at the spot or tackled after he attempts to run, charge the holder with a rush and any yards lost as rushing yardage.

If the play develops as action off a fake field goal attempt, charge the holder with a rush, or pass or "tackled" consistent with the basic scoring rules on scrimmage plays.

All yardage gained by a player in returning an unsuccessful field goal attempt should be noted on the back of the score blank under "remarks."

For blocked field goal attempts, see Blocked Kicks section.

Safeties

Credit a player with a safety when:

    A. He downs an opponent behind the opponent's goal line;
    B. He causes an opponent to step out of bounds behind the opponent's goal line;
    C. He blocks a kick or deflects a backward pass and the ball goes out of the end zone behind the opponent's goal line.

Example I: Fourth-and-10 at own 4 yard line. Defensive tackle blocks a punt. The ball is recovered in the end zone by the punter, and cornerback downs the punter there. *Scoring:* Credit the cornerback with a safety.

Example II: Fourth-and-10 at own 4 yard line. Offensive team decides to allow a safety rather than to kick on fourth down. Punter lingers near end line, consuming time until defensive tackle chases him out of bounds. *Scoring:* Credit defensive tackle with a safety.

Unless a safety falls into one of the categories listed above, no credit shall be given to any individual.

Qualifications for Individual Leaders

Rushing: Most net yards gained (minimum 100 carries to qualify for highest average gain).

Passing: Minimum average of 12 passes attempted per each team's game to qualify. Standings are based on percent of completions, percent of touchdown passes per attempt, percent of pass attempts intercepted, and average gain per attempted pass. Passers are rated against a standard in each of the four categories and the passer with the most rating points is the leader.

Pass Receptions: Most receptions (minimum 32 to qualify for highest average gain).

Pass Interceptions: Most interceptions.

Scoring: Most total points scored.

Punting: Longest average distance per punt (minimum average of 2½ punts per each of team's games, 40 for season). Blocked punts are not charged to individual punter.

Punt Returns: Average per return (minimum average of one return per each of team's games).

Kickoff Returns: Average per return (minimum average of one return per each of team's games.)

1983 Schedule and Note Calendar

All times P.M. local daylight.
Nationally televised games in parentheses. CBS and NBC television
doubleheader games in the regular season to be announced.

Preseason/First Week

Saturday, July 30	Pittsburgh ___ vs. New Orleans ___ at Canton, Ohio	(ABC) 2:00
Thursday, August 4	Baltimore ___ at Houston ___	7:00
Friday, August 5	Detroit ___ at Philadelphia ___	7:30
	Seattle ___ at Denver ___	7:00
Saturday, August 6	Buffalo ___ at Chicago ___	6:00
	Cleveland ___ at Green Bay ___	7:00
	Kansas City ___ at Cincinnati ___	7:00
	Miami ___ at Dallas ___	8:00
	Minnesota ___ vs. St. Louis ___ at London, England	TBA
	New Orleans ___ at Tampa Bay ___	8:30
	Pittsburgh ___ vs. New England ___ at Knoxville	7:30
	San Diego ___ at Los Angeles Rams ___	7:30
	San Francisco ___ at Los Angeles Raiders ___	6:00
	Washington ___ at Atlanta ___	8:00
Sunday, August 7	New York Jets ___ at New York Giants ___	8:00

Preseason/Second Week

Friday, August 12	Cincinnati ___ at Washington ___	7:30
	Green Bay ___ at Seattle ___	7:30
	New York Giants ___ at Pittsburgh ___	(ABC) 8:00
Saturday, August 13	Atlanta ___ at Denver ___	7:00
	Baltimore ___ at Minnesota ___	7:30
	Chicago ___ at St. Louis ___	6:00
	Cleveland ___ at Buffalo ___	6:00
	Detroit ___ at Kansas City ___	7:30
	Los Angeles Raiders ___ vs. New York Jets ___ at Giants Stadium	8:00
	New Orleans ___ at Miami ___	8:00
	Philadelphia ___ at San Diego ___	6:00
	Tampa Bay ___ at Houston ___	8:00
Sunday, August 14	New England ___ at San Francisco ___	(NBC) 1:00
Monday, August 15	Dallas ___ at Los Angeles Rams ___	7:00

Preseason/Third Week

Thursday, August 18	New York Jets ___ at Cincinnati ___	(CBS) 9:00
Friday, August 19	Miami ___ at Washington ___	(ABC) 8:00
	Minnesota ___ at Seattle ___	7:30
Saturday, August 20	Atlanta ___ at Tampa Bay ___	8:00
	Baltimore ___ at New York Giants ___	8:00
	Buffalo ___ at Detroit ___	7:00
	Chicago ___ at Los Angeles Raiders ___	8:00
	Cleveland ___ at Denver ___	7:00
	Houston ___ at New Orleans ___	7:00
	New England ___ at Los Angeles Rams ___	7:00
	Philadelphia ___ at Green Bay ___	(CBS) 2:00
	Pittsburgh ___ at Dallas ___	(NBC) 8:00
	St. Louis ___ at Kansas City ___	7:30
	San Francisco ___ at San Diego ___	6:00

Preseason/Fourth Week

Thursday, August 25	Pittsburgh ___ at Philadelphia ___	7:30
Friday, August 26	Baltimore ___ at Atlanta ___	8:00
	Denver ___ at Minnesota ___	7:30
	Los Angeles Raiders ___ at Cleveland ___	(NBC) 8:00
	Los Angeles Rams ___ at San Diego ___	7:00
	Miami ___ at New York Giants ___	8:00
	New England ___ at Tampa Bay ___	8:00
Saturday, August 27	Cincinnati ___ at Detroit ___	7:00
	Green Bay ___ at St. Louis ___	6:00
	Houston ___ at Dallas ___	(CBS) 8:00
	Kansas City ___ at Chicago ___	6:00
	New York Jets ___ at New Orleans ___	7:00
	Seattle ___ at San Francisco ___	2:00
	Washington ___ at Buffalo ___	6:00

First Week

Sunday, September 4 **(NBC-TV doubleheader)**	Atlanta ___ at Chicago ___	12:00
	Baltimore ___ at New England ___	1:00
	Denver ___ at Pittsburgh ___	1:00
	Detroit ___ at Tampa Bay ___	1:00
	Green Bay ___ at Houston ___	12:00
	Los Angeles Raiders ___ at Cincinnati ___	1:00
	Los Angeles Rams ___ at New York Giants ___	1:00
	Miami ___ at Buffalo ___	1:00
	Minnesota ___ at Cleveland ___	1:00
	New York Jets ___ at San Diego ___	1:00
	Philadelphia ___ at San Francisco ___	1:00
	St. Louis ___ at New Orleans ___	12:00
	Seattle ___ at Kansas City ___	3:00
Monday, September 5	Dallas ___ at Washington ___	(ABC) 9:00

Second Week

Thursday, September 8	San Francisco ___ at Minnesota ___	(ABC) 7:30
Sunday, September 11 **(NBC-TV doubleheader)**	Buffalo ___ at Cincinnati ___	1:00
	Cleveland ___ at Detroit ___	1:00
	Dallas ___ at St. Louis ___	12:00
	Denver ___ at Baltimore ___	4:00
	Houston ___ at Los Angeles Raiders ___	1:00
	New England ___ at Miami ___	4:00
	New Orleans ___ at Los Angeles Rams ___	1:00
	New York Giants ___ at Atlanta ___	1:00
	Pittsburgh ___ at Green Bay ___	12:00
	Seattle ___ at New York Jets ___	4:00
	Tampa Bay ___ at Chicago ___	12:00
	Washington ___ at Philadelphia ___	1:00
Monday, September 12	San Diego ___ at Kansas City ___	(ABC) 8:00

Third Week

Thursday, September 15	Cincinnati ___ at Cleveland ___	(ABC) 8:30
Sunday, September 18 **(CBS-TV doubleheader)**	Atlanta ___ at Detroit ___	1:00
	Baltimore ___ at Buffalo ___	1:00
	Chicago ___ at New Orleans ___	12:00
	Kansas City ___ at Washington ___	1:00
	Los Angeles Rams ___ vs. Green Bay ___ at Milwaukee	12:00
	Minnesota ___ at Tampa Bay ___	4:00
	New York Giants ___ at Dallas ___	3:00
	New York Jets ___ at New England ___	1:00
	Philadelphia ___ at Denver ___	2:00
	Pittsburgh ___ at Houston ___	12:00
	San Diego ___ at Seattle ___	1:00
	San Francisco ___ at St. Louis ___	12:00
Monday, September 19	Miami ___ at Los Angeles Raiders ___	(ABC) 6:00

Fourth Week

Sunday, September 25
(CBS-TV doubleheader)

Atlanta ___ at San Francisco ___	1:00
Chicago ___ at Baltimore ___	2:00
Cincinnati ___ at Tampa Bay ___	1:00
Cleveland ___ at San Diego ___	1:00
Detroit ___ at Minnesota ___	12:00
Houston ___ at Buffalo ___	1:00
Kansas City ___ at Miami ___	1:00
Los Angeles Raiders ___ at Denver ___	2:00
Los Angeles Rams ___ at New York Jets ___	4:00
New England ___ at Pittsburgh ___	1:00
New Orleans ___ at Dallas ___	12:00
St. Louis ___ at Philadelphia ___	1:00
Washington ___ at Seattle ___	1:00

Monday, September 26 Green Bay ___ at New York Giants ___   (ABC) 9:00

Fifth Week

Sunday, October 2
(NBC-TV doubleheader)

Baltimore ___ at Cincinnati ___	1:00
Dallas ___ at Minnesota ___	12:00
Denver ___ at Chicago ___	12:00
Detroit ___ at Los Angeles Rams ___	1:00
Houston ___ at Pittsburgh ___	1:00
Los Angeles Raiders ___ at Washington ___	1:00
Miami ___ at New Orleans ___	3:00
Philadelphia ___ at Atlanta ___	1:00
St. Louis ___ at Kansas City ___	3:00
San Diego ___ at New York Giants ___	4:00
San Francisco ___ at New England ___	1:00
Seattle ___ at Cleveland ___	1:00
Tampa Bay ___ at Green Bay ___	12:00

Monday, October 3 New York Jets ___ at Buffalo ___   (ABC) 9:00

Sixth Week

Sunday, October 9
(CBS-TV doubleheader)

Buffalo ___ at Miami ___	1:00
Denver ___ at Houston ___	12:00
Green Bay ___ at Detroit ___	1:00
Kansas City ___ at Los Angeles Raiders ___	1:00
Los Angeles Rams ___ at San Francisco ___	1:00
Minnesota ___ at Chicago ___	12:00
New England ___ at Baltimore ___	2:00
New Orleans ___ at Atlanta ___	1:00
New York Jets ___ at Cleveland ___	1:00
Philadelphia ___ at New York Giants ___	4:00
Seattle ___ at San Diego ___	1:00
Tampa Bay ___ at Dallas ___	3:00
Washington ___ at St. Louis ___	12:00

Monday, October 10 Pittsburgh ___ at Cincinnati ___   (ABC) 9:00

Seventh Week

Sunday, October 16
(CBS-TV doubleheader)

Atlanta ___ at Los Angeles Rams ___	1:00
Buffalo ___ at Baltimore ___	2:00
Chicago ___ at Detroit ___	1:00
Cincinnati ___ at Denver ___	2:00
Cleveland ___ at Pittsburgh ___	1:00
Dallas ___ at Philadelphia ___	4:00
Houston ___ at Minnesota ___	12:00
Los Angeles Raiders ___ at Seattle ___	1:00
Miami ___ at New York Jets ___	1:00
New York Giants ___ at Kansas City ___	3:00
St. Louis ___ at Tampa Bay ___	1:00
San Diego ___ at New England ___	1:00
San Francisco ___ at New Orleans ___	12:00

Monday, October 17 Washington ___ at Green Bay ___   (ABC) 8:00

Eighth Week

Sunday, October 23	Atlanta ____ at New York Jets ____		1:00
(NBC-TV doubleheader)	Chicago ____ at Philadelphia ____		1:00
	Cleveland ____ at Cincinnati ____		1:00
	Detroit ____ at Washington ____		1:00
	Kansas City ____ at Houston ____		12:00
	Los Angeles Raiders ____ at Dallas ____		(ABC) 8:00
	Miami ____ at Baltimore ____		2:00
	Minnesota ____ at Green Bay ____		12:00
	New England ____ at Buffalo ____		1:00
	New Orleans ____ at Tampa Bay ____		4:00
	Pittsburgh ____ at Seattle ____		1:00
	San Diego ____ at Denver ____		2:00
	San Francisco ____ at Los Angeles Rams ____		1:00
Monday, October 24	New York Giants ____ at St. Louis ____		(ABC) 8:00

Ninth Week

Sunday, October 30	Baltimore ____ at Philadelphia ____		1:00
(CBS-TV doubleheader)	Dallas ____ at New York Giants ____		1:00
	Detroit ____ at Chicago ____		12:00
	Green Bay ____ at Cincinnati ____		4:00
	Houston ____ at Cleveland ____		1:00
	Kansas City ____ at Denver ____		2:00
	Los Angeles Rams ____ at Miami ____		1:00
	Minnesota ____ at St. Louis ____		12:00
	New England ____ at Atlanta ____		1:00
	New Orleans ____ at Buffalo ____		1:00
	New York Jets ____ at San Francisco ____		1:00
	Seattle ____ at Los Angeles Raiders ____		1:00
	Tampa Bay ____ at Pittsburgh ____		1:00
Monday, October 31	Washington ____ at San Diego ____		(ABC) 6:00

Tenth Week

Sunday, November 6	Atlanta ____ at New Orleans ____		12:00
(NBC-TV doubleheader)	Baltimore ____ at New York Jets ____		4:00
	Buffalo ____ at New England ____		1:00
	Chicago ____ at Los Angeles Rams ____		1:00
	Cincinnati ____ at Houston ____		12:00
	Cleveland ____ vs. Green Bay ____ at Milwaukee		12:00
	Denver ____ at Seattle ____		1:00
	Los Angeles Raiders ____ at Kansas City ____		12:00
	Miami ____ at San Francisco ____		1:00
	Philadelphia ____ at Dallas ____		12:00
	St. Louis ____ at Washington ____		4:00
	San Diego ____ at Pittsburgh ____		1:00
	Tampa Bay ____ at Minnesota ____		12:00
Monday, November 7	New York Giants ____ at Detroit ____		(ABC) 9:00

Eleventh Week

Sunday, November 13	Buffalo ____ at New York Jets ____		1:00
(CBS-TV doubleheader)	Cincinnati ____ at Kansas City ____		12:00
	Dallas ____ at San Diego ____		1:00
	Denver ____ at Los Angeles Raiders ____		1:00
	Detroit ____ at Houston ____		12:00
	Green Bay ____ at Minnesota ____		12:00
	Miami ____ at New England ____		1:00
	New Orleans ____ at San Francisco ____		1:00
	Philadelphia ____ at Chicago ____		12:00
	Pittsburgh ____ at Baltimore ____		2:00
	Seattle ____ at St. Louis ____		12:00
	Tampa Bay ____ at Cleveland ____		1:00
	Washington ____ at New York Giants ____		4:00
Monday, November 14	Los Angeles Rams ____ at Atlanta ____		(ABC) 9:00

Twelfth Week

Sunday, November 20	Baltimore ___ at Miami ___	1:00
(NBC-TV doubleheader)	Chicago ___ at Tampa Bay ___	1:00
	Cleveland ___ at New England ___	1:00
	Detroit ___ vs. Green Bay ___ at Milwaukee	12:00
	Houston ___ at Cincinnati ___	1:00
	Kansas City ___ at Dallas ___	3:00
	Los Angeles Raiders ___ at Buffalo ___	1:00
	Minnesota ___ at Pittsburgh ___	1:00
	New York Giants ___ at Philadelphia ___	1:00
	San Diego ___ at St. Louis ___	12:00
	San Francisco ___ at Atlanta ___	4:00
	Seattle ___ at Denver ___	2:00
	Washington ___ at Los Angeles Rams ___	1:00
Monday, November 21	New York Jets ___ at New Orleans ___	(ABC) 8:00

Thirteenth Week

Thursday, November 24	Pittsburgh ___ at Detroit ___	(NBC) 12:30
(Thanksgiving Day)	St. Louis ___ at Dallas ___	(CBS) 3:00
Sunday, November 27	Baltimore ___ at Cleveland ___	1:00
(CBS-TV doubleheader)	Buffalo ___ at Los Angeles Rams ___	1:00
	Denver ___ at San Diego ___	1:00
	Green Bay ___ at Atlanta ___	4:00
	Houston ___ at Tampa Bay ___	1:00
	Kansas City ___ at Seattle ___	1:00
	Minnesota ___ at New Orleans ___	12:00
	New England ___ at New York Jets ___	1:00
	New York Giants ___ at Los Angeles Raiders ___	1:00
	Philadelphia ___ at Washington ___	1:00
	San Francisco ___ at Chicago ___	12:00
Monday, November 28	Cincinnati ___ at Miami ___	(ABC) 9:00

Fourteenth Week

Thursday, December 1	Los Angeles Raiders ___ at San Diego ___	(ABC) 6:00
Sunday, December 4	Atlanta ___ at Washington ___	1:00
(NBC-TV doubleheader)	Buffalo ___ at Kansas City ___	12:00
	Chicago ___ at Green Bay ___	12:00
	Cincinnati ___ at Pittsburgh ___	1:00
	Cleveland ___ at Denver ___	2:00
	Dallas ___ at Seattle ___	1:00
	Los Angeles Rams ___ at Philadelphia ___	1:00
	Miami ___ at Houston ___	12:00
	New Orleans ___ at New England ___	1:00
	New York Jets ___ at Baltimore ___	4:00
	St. Louis ___ at New York Giants ___	1:00
	Tampa Bay ___ at San Francisco ___	1:00
Monday, December 5	Minnesota ___ at Detroit ___	(ABC) 9:00

Fifteenth Week

Saturday, December 10	Atlanta ___ at Miami ___	(CBS) 4:00
	Pittsburgh ___ at New York Jets ___	(NBC) 12:30
Sunday, December 11	Baltimore ___ at Denver ___	2:00
(CBS-TV doubleheader)	Chicago ___ at Minnesota ___	12:00
	Cleveland ___ at Houston ___	12:00
	Detroit ___ at Cincinnati ___	1:00
	Kansas City ___ at San Diego ___	1:00
	New England ___ at Los Angeles Rams ___	1:00
	New Orleans ___ at Philadelphia ___	1:00
	St. Louis ___ at Los Angeles Raiders ___	1:00
	San Francisco ___ at Buffalo ___	1:00
	Seattle ___ at New York Giants ___	1:00
	Washington ___ at Dallas ___	3:00
Monday, December 12	Green Bay ___ at Tampa Bay ___	(ABC) 9:00

Sixteenth Week

Friday, December 16	New York Jets ___ at Miami ___	(ABC)	9:00
Saturday, December 17	Cincinnati ___ at Minnesota ___	(NBC)	3:00
	New York Giants ___ at Washington ___	(CBS)	12:30
Sunday, December 18	Buffalo ___ at Atlanta ___		1:00
(NBC-TV doubleheader)	Denver ___ at Kansas City ___		12:00
	Green Bay ___ at Chicago ___		12:00
	Houston ___ at Baltimore ___		2:00
	Los Angeles Rams ___ at New Orleans ___		12:00
	New England ___ at Seattle ___		1:00
	Philadelphia ___ at St. Louis ___		12:00
	Pittsburgh ___ at Cleveland ___		1:00
	San Diego ___ at Los Angeles Raiders ___		1:00
	Tampa Bay ___ at Detroit ___		4:00
Monday, December 19	Dallas ___ at San Francisco ___	(ABC)	6:00

First Round Playoff Games

Saturday, December 24, 1983 — American Football Conference

_____ at _____ (NBC)

Monday, December 26, 1983 — National Football Conference

_____ at _____ (CBS)

Site Priorities

Two wild card teams (fourth- and fifth-best records) from each conference will enter the first round of the playoffs. The wild cards from the same conference will play each other. Home clubs will be the clubs with the best won-lost-tied percentage in the regular season. If tied in record, the tie will be broken by the tie-breaking procedure already in effect.

Divisional Playoff Games

Saturday, December 31, 1983 — American Football Conference

_____ at _____ (NBC)

National Football Conference

_____ at _____ (CBS)

Sunday, January 1, 1984 — American Football Conference

_____ at _____ (NBC)

National Football Conference

_____ at _____ (CBS)

Site Priorities

In each conference, the two division winners with the highest won-lost-tied percentage during the regular season will be the home teams. The division winner with the best percentage will be host to the wild card winner from the first round playoff, and the division winner with the second best percentage will be host to the third division winner, unless the wild card team is from the same division as the winner with the highest percentage. In that case, the division winner with the best percentage will be host to the third division winner and the second highest division winner will be host to the wild card.

Conference Championship Games, Super Bowl XVIII, and AFC-NFC Pro Bowl

Sunday, January 8, 1984 — American Football Conference Championship Game

_____ at _____ (NBC)

National Football Conference Championship Game

_____ at _____ (CBS)

Sunday, January 22, 1984 — Super Bowl XVIII at Tampa Stadium, Tampa, Florida

_____ vs. _____ (CBS)

Sunday, January 29, 1984 — AFC-NFC Pro Bowl at Honolulu, Hawaii

AFC _____ vs. NFC _____ (ABC)

Site Priorities for Championship Games

The home teams will be the surviving divisional playoff winners with the best won-lost-tied percentage during the regular season. The wild card team will never be the home team, in either the divisional playoffs or the championship games. Any ties in won-lost-tied percentage will be broken by the tie-breaking procedures already in effect.